Routledge Handbook of Trends and Issues in Global Tourism Supply and Demand

This Handbook provides a comprehensive overview of trends and issues in the global supply and demand on tourism.

With contributions from 70 authors, this Handbook showcases a diverse range of perspectives with insights from around the globe. It reviews the interactions among trends and issues, and it emphasises the importance of tracking and interpreting these on a global scale. The book is organised into three parts, with Part I focusing on supply-side trends, including transport, attractions, culture, heritage tourism, technology, policies, and destination management. Part II critically reviews the external factor trends, including the impact of terrorism, multi-crisis destinations, Generation Z's important contributions to the sector, the regulation of sharing economy platforms and nature tourism in the future. Part III focuses on market-led trends such as bleisure, glamping, VFR travel, transformational tourism and new trends in wellness tourism following the post-COVID era. The book also provides predictions for the upcoming decades.

This Handbook will be a vital tool for researchers, students, and practitioners in the tourism and hospitality sector to further develop their knowledge and expertise in the field. It examines business and policy implications, offering guidance for developing sustainable competitive advantage.

Alastair M. Morrison is a Research Professor at the University of Greenwich in London, UK, and formerly an Associate Dean and Distinguished Professor Emeritus at Purdue University, USA, specialising in the area of tourism and hospitality marketing in the School of Hospitality and Tourism Management. Professor Morrison is ranked in the top 2% of scientists in the world based on the science-wide author database developed by Elsevier and Stanford University since 2019. He has published several books and around 350 academic articles and conference proceedings, as well as over 50 research monographs related to marketing and tourism. He is the co-Editor-in-Chief of the *International Journal of Tourism Cities* and a Fellow of the International Academy for the Study of Tourism. Professor Morrison has served as the President of the International Tourism Studies Association (ITSA), Chairman of the Travel & Tourism Research Association (TTRA) – Canada Chapter, Board member of the CenStates TTRA Chapter, Vice President of the International Society of Travel and Tourism Educators (ISTTE), and Chairman of Association of Travel Marketing Executives (ATME).

Dimitrios Buhalis is Director of the eTourism Lab and Deputy Director of the International Centre for Tourism and Hospitality Research at Bournemouth University Business School, UK. He is a Strategic Management and Marketing expert with specialisation in Information Communication Technology applications in the Tourism Travel, Hospitality and Leisure industries. He is the Editor in Chief of *Tourism Review* and the Editor in Chief of the *Encyclopedia of Tourism Management and Marketing*. Professor Buhalis has written and co-edited more than 25 books and 300 scientific articles and is recognised as a Highly Cited Researcher by Clarivate™ with more than 61000 citations and h-index 105 on Google Scholar. He is ranked in the top 2% of scientists in the world based on the science-wide author database developed by Elsevier and Stanford University since 2019. Dimitrios is a past President of the International Federation for Information Technologies in Travel and Tourism (IFITT) and a past Vice President of the International Academy for the Study of Tourism.

Routledge Handbook of Trends and Issues in Global Tourism Supply and Demand

Edited by Alastair M. Morrison and
Dimitrios Buhalis

LONDON AND NEW YORK

Designed cover image: unsplash.com / Massimiliano Donghi

First published 2024
by Routledge
4 Park Square, Milton Park, Abingdon, Oxon OX14 4RN

and by Routledge
605 Third Avenue, New York, NY 10158

Routledge is an imprint of the Taylor & Francis Group, an informa business

© 2024 selection and editorial matter, Alastair M. Morrison and Dimitrios Buhalis; individual chapters, the contributors

The right of Alastair M. Morrison and Dimitrios Buhalis to be identified as the authors of the editorial material, and of the authors for their individual chapters, has been asserted in accordance with sections 77 and 78 of the Copyright, Designs and Patents Act 1988.

All rights reserved. No part of this book may be reprinted or reproduced or utilised in any form or by any electronic, mechanical, or other means, now known or hereafter invented, including photocopying and recording, or in any information storage or retrieval system, without permission in writing from the publishers.

Trademark notice: Product or corporate names may be trademarks or registered trademarks, and are used only for identification and explanation without intent to infringe.

British Library Cataloguing-in-Publication Data
A catalogue record for this book is available from the British Library

ISBN: 978-1-032-19773-9 (hbk)
ISBN: 978-1-032-19774-6 (pbk)
ISBN: 978-1-003-26079-0 (ebk)

DOI: 10.4324/9781003260790

Typeset in Times New Roman
by SPi Technologies India Pvt Ltd (Straive)

To Sheng Hua, Andy, and Alick
To Maria and Stella

Contents

List of Figures	xi
List of Tables	xiv
List of Contributors	xvi
Introduction ALASTAIR M. MORRISON AND DIMITRIOS BUHALIS	1

PART I
Supply-side trends — 5

1.1 Transportation — 7

1 High-speed rail growth — 9
FRANCESCA PAGLIARA, JUAN CARLOS MARTÍN, CONCEPCIÓN ROMÁN AND BARTOSZ BURSA

2 New aircraft and airports — 22
EVANGELOS KILIPIRIS AND ANDREAS PAPATHEODOROU

3 Cruise lines: Market growth and diversification — 34
MICHAEL CLANCY

4 Cruises: Environmental impacts and policy — 45
TIMOTHY MACNEILL

1.2 Attractions, culture, and heritage tourism — 57

5 A scenario planning approach to safety in visitor attractions — 61
AARON THAM

6 Wine tourism: Current trends and future prospects — 71
HAIYAN SONG AND WEIXI (EDITH) YUAN

7 Culinary tourism: Dualistic erosion and the enhancement of food cultures — 84
SOPHIA LINGHAM, LOUISE MANNING AND DAMIAN MAYE

8 The Homestays concept in the Indian tourism and hospitality industry 103
SUNEEL KUMAR, MARCO VALERI AND VARINDER KUMAR

9 Cultural heritage tourism and ethical trends 117
ELENI MAVRAGANI AND SOFIA AVRAMIDOU

10 Challenges and opportunities in cultural tourism: Insights from Canada 127
LOUIS-ETIENNE DUBOIS, SHAWN NEWMAN AND FRÉDÉRIC DIMANCHE

11 Edutainment interpretation trends in dark tourism 138
BRIANNA WYATT

12 Modelling heritage justice for under-represented communities 148
DEEPAK CHHABRA

13 Creative tourism trends 163
DIOGO MOLEIRO AND LÍGIA RIBEIRO

1.3 Technology 177

14 Intermediation, disintermediation and reintermediation: Tourism distribution in the electronic age 179
PETER O'CONNOR

15 Technology trends and trip planning 189
KIM-IENG LOI AND JOSE WENG CHOU WONG

16 Digital-free tourism: The state of the art and future research directions 199
WENJIE CAI AND BRAD MCKENNA

17 The metaverse as a new travel marketing platform 209
MIN JUNG KIM AND DAE-YOUNG KIM

18 Challenges and opportunities for the incorporation of robots in hotels 221
CRAIG WEBSTER AND STANISLAV IVANOV

1.4 Policies and issues 233

19 Urbanisation: Trends and issues in world tourism cities 235
CRISTINA MAXIM

20 Overtourism: Trends, issues, impacts and implications 246
RICHARD W. BUTLER AND RACHEL DODDS

21 Issues and policies that have an impact on future trends in global tourism 256
DAVID L. EDGELL, SR.

22 Tourism policies for the next normal: Trends and issues from global case studies 271
VANESSA G. B. GOWREESUNKAR, SHEM WAMBUGU MAINGI AND CHRIS COOPER

1.5 Destination management 287

23 Tourist Behavioural Intention Trends 289
PEDRO VAZ SERRA AND CLÁUDIA SEABRA

24 Professional destination management trends and issues 301
ALASTAIR M. MORRISON

PART II
External factor trends 317

25 Terrorism threat and its influence on leisure and travel behaviours of Millennials 321
CLÁUDIA SEABRA

26 Multi-crisis destinations (MCDs): Towards a future research agenda 338
SOFIA LACHHAB, ALASTAIR M. MORRISON, TINA ŠEGOTA, AND J. ANDRES COCA-STEFANIAK

27 Understanding Gen Z as a future workforce in the hospitality and tourism industry 352
ANGIE YEONSOOK IM AND DAE-YOUNG KIM

28 Forced displacement: The 'refugee crisis' and its impact on global tourism 363
SHIMA B. AFSHAN, CHERYL COCKBURN-WOOTTEN AND ALISON J. MCINTOSH

29 Leading social change through prison fine dining as a new form of global tourism 373
MARIA GEBBELS, ALISON J. MCINTOSH AND TRACY HARKISON

30 Sharing economy legislation: Regulating peer-to-peer tourism platforms such as Airbnb and Uber 383
DANIEL GUTTENTAG

31 Re-imagining tourism in a world of declining nature 394
DAVID NEWSOME

PART III
Market-led trends 407

32 Bleisure trends: Combining business and leisure travel 411
GOKCE OZDEMIR AND DUYGU CELEBI

33 "Glamping": Camping in its "green" and luxurious version 421
SPYRIDOULA DIMITRA SOUKI

34 VFR travel: Opportunities, trends, and issues 433
ELISA ZENTVELD

35 Transformational tourism: A visionary approach to sustainable tourism? 443
G. L. W. ROSHINI N. NANDASENA, ALASTAIR M. MORRISON, WENJIE CAI AND J. ANDRES COCA-STEFANIAK

36 Sport tourism in times of the VUCA world 459
EKATERINA GLEBOVA, FATEME ZARE, ROBERT BOOK, MICHEL DESBORDES AND GABOR GECZI

37 German holiday travel demand trends 469
DIRK SCHMÜCKER, ANNE KÖCHLING, AND MARTIN LOHMANN

38 New trends in wellness tourism: Restoration and regeneration 480
MELANIE KAY SMITH

39 Accelerated trends in tourism marketing and tourist behaviour 497
METIN KOZAK

40 Re-enacting dark histories 509
BRIANNA WYATT

Index *520*

Figures

0.1	Editors, themes, and objectives of book	2
0.2	Classification scheme for trends and issues	3
1.1	Visual abstract: High-speed rail growth	18
2.1	Comparison of non-seat as part of total revenues 2013–2021	24
2.2	Comparison of aeronautical, non-operating and non-aeronautical revenues	28
3.1	Cruise ship at dock in the Bahamas	35
4.1	Jevons' Paradox – as efficiency increases, so do emissions	52
5.1	Scenario-planning framework for safety in visitor attractions	66
5.2	Future-focussed safety in visitor attractions model employing scenario planning techniques	67
6.1	Wine tourism development	73
6.2	Framework of wine tourism supply and demand	76
6.3	Visual abstract – Wine tourism: Current trends and future prospects	81
7.1	Innovative food artwork at Erimitis Restaurant, Paxos, Corfu	88
7.2	Food memories: Picnic featuring traditional mainland Greek foods	91
7.3	Padron peppers enjoyed during the Camino de Santiago – food putting an area 'on the map'	92
8.1	Process of collecting data and information	105
8.2	General outline of the procedure of how to start a homestay business	109
8.3	Conceptual model of long term relationship	110
8.4	Challenges in homestay business	111
9.1	Relationships in cultural heritage tourism	118
9.2	Outcomes of cultural heritage tourism	120
10.1	Shaw Festival	130
10.2	Woodland Cultural Center	131
10.3	Cultural tourism: A Canadian perspective	135
11.1	Dark visitor attraction interpretation	139
11.2	Edutainment scale	140
12.1	Heritage justice paradigm	159
13.1	The themes of the creative tourism research	164
13.2	Opportunities and challenges of future research on creative tourism	171
14.1	Overview of primary hotel distribution channels	183

15.1	Comparison of different periods of trip planning	196
16.1	Digital detox cabin	204
17.1	Classification of Metaverse	211
17.2	Hangang Park in Zepeto	215
17.3	Virtual influencers	217
18.1	Pepper robot	223
18.2	A room-service delivery robot	223
19.1	Key stakeholders in a destination and their roles in sustainable tourism	239
19.2	Visual abstract – Urbanisation: Trends and issues in World Tourism Cities	243
20.1	Elements leading to overtourism	247
21.1	Vaccinations were part of the global strategy to stimulate travel and tourism	259
22.1	Future tourism policy pillars	276
23.1	Saudi Arabia is a Middle Eastern destination that plans to attract more tourists	295
24.1	Roles of destination management	305
26.1	Steps in developing the multi-crisis destination index (MCDI)	341
26.2	Indexes of international tourist arrivals, 1995–2019	342
26.3	Egypt events timeline, 2004–2018	343
26.4	The adaptive cycle or "Holling Loop"	346
27.1	Gen Z are digital natives	357
27.2	The process of human resource management for Gen Z	358
28.1	International key sites of displacement globally since the 1950s	364
28.2	Word frequency used in research about refugees in the tourism literature	366
29.1	Clink restaurant at HMP Cardiff	376
30.1	Uber does not own the vehicles that are used	385
31.1	The numbat is an endangered small marsupial with only two naturally occurring remnant populations in southwestern Australia	398
32.1	Bleisure offerings of destinations	415
33.1	Glamping in yurts in Sweden	424
33.2	Visual abstract glamping	431
34.1	VFR travel definitional model	437
35.1	Artistic rendering of transformational tourism conceptual model	444
35.2	Volunteers working alongside local teachers to deliver basic and interactive English lessons at pre-schools in the Hikkaduwa area of Sri Lanka	450
35.3	Depiction of tourism experiences and quotes about travel in Sri Lanka	451
35.4	Future trends and research directions for transformational tourism	452
36.1	Sport tourism in 2022: Trends, problems, solutions, predictions for future	465
36.2	Future of sport tourism in the VUCA world	466
37.1	Trend estimation for the future: Schematic illustration of the approach	470

37.2 Key figures for the demand for holiday trips of five days and longer
     in the German market   473
38.1 The five Rs of wellness tourism   492
40.1 Hale Farm & Village Civil War re-enactment   510
40.2 Zero Latency VR experience   515
40.3 A timeline of re-enacting dark histories   516

Tables

3.1	Global cruise ship arrivals, 2000–2021	36
4.1	Cruising environmental impact types	47
6.1	Key studies in wine tourism on from a supply and demand perspective	75
17.1	Dimensions of Metaverse	213
18.1	Trends and issues with regards to the switchover to robot labour	227
19.1	Key roles played by new technologies in city destinations	241
21.1	Ten important current and future world tourism issues	257
24.1	Historical timeline of major events and publications in destination management	302
24.2	Academic publishing on destination management and destination marketing	303
24.3	Recent trends for destination management	304
24.4	Competencies for professional destination management	307
24.5	Roles and initiatives of stakeholders with DMOs and destination management	311
24.6	Potential contributions of DMOs to SDGs	312
25.1	Risk perceptions when travelling	325
25.2	Feelings of (un)safety travelling in Europe vs outside Europe	325
25.3	Interest about terrorism in media	326
25.4	Feelings about terrorism threat	327
25.5	Terrorism threat in tourism and leisure activities	327
25.6	Factorial analysis of feelings of (un)safety travelling in Europe	328
25.7	Factorial analysis of feelings of (un)safety travelling outside Europe	329
25.8	Factorial analysis of interest about terrorism in media	329
25.9	Factorial analysis of feelings about terrorism threat	330
25.10	Correlations between risk perception types and the dimensions of feelings of (un)safety and interest about terrorism information in media	332
25.11	Correlations between feelings of (un)safety travelling in and outside Europe and the dimensions of feelings about terrorism threat and interest about terrorism information in the media	333
26.1	Potential indicator indexes by type of crisis	340
26.2	Global Peace Index ratings for 2021	344
26.3	The five most negatively ranked countries for safety and security and ongoing conflicts	344
26.4	Recommended stakeholder actions and initiatives	349
27.1	Comparisons of generations	353

28.1	Major sources of refugees since 2000	364
29.1	Prison categories	376
29.2	Benefits of employing Clink graduates	378
30.1	Key stakeholders in the regulation of Airbnb and Uber, and their primary interests	387
31.1	Understanding the tourism-nature relationship and a vision for the future	401
31.2	Behavioural codes and practices designed to promote appropriate individual and community responsibility and relevant action plans and policies pertaining to the future of tourism and the natural environment	402
34.1	Relationship between VFR typologies for domestic travel by Australians in 2021	435
34.2	Relationship between VFR typologies for domestic travel by Australians in 2008–2009	436
35.1	Participant information	447
35.2	Recommended stakeholder actions and initiatives	454
35.3	SDGs and potential contributions of transformational tourism	455
37.1	Structure of holiday tourism demand in Germany in 2019 and 2020, and expected structure for 2030	474
38.1	Types of wellness tourism	485
38.2	Examples of types of retreats and their purported benefits	488
39.1	Major trends in tourism marketing	498

Contributors

Shima B. Afshan is a Ph.D. candidate in Tourism Management at the Waikato Management School, *Te Whare Wānanga o Waikato*, The University of Waikato, Hamilton, New Zealand. For her Ph.D., she is trying to understand the experiences of people with refugee background in tourism. Shima is interested in issues relating to justice in tourism, inclusive tourism, and inclusive research.

Sofia Avramidou is a Political Scientist with a Master's degree in Tourism Business Administration at Hellenic Open University in Greece. She is a Business Consultant to local government organisations, specialising in human resource management and cultural event planning. Mrs Avramidou has participated at international scientific conferences and has written a book chapter about cultural heritage tourism and directed authenticity. Her research interests focus on heritage tourism, international relations and cultural diplomacy.

Robert Book is an Associate Professor in the Department of Sports, Physical Education, and Outdoor Studies at the University of South-Eastern Norway. His research spans across the fields of sport psychology and sociology, is highly critical, and has investigated athletic talent development environments within underserved and disadvantaged communities. He serves on the executive committee at the International Society of Qualitative Research in Sport, Exercise and Health, is on the editorial board of Frontiers in Sport and Active Living, and has numerous publications in journals such as the Psychology of Sport and Exercise, *Qualitative Research in Sport, Exercise, and Health*, and the *Journal of Sport and Exercise Psychology*.

Bartosz Bursa works as a Senior Scientist in the Unit of Intelligent Transport Systems at the University of Innsbruck, Austria where he obtained his Ph.D. in 2020. He is also a visiting scholar at Auburn University, Alabama, USA. Prior to that, he worked as a consultant and transportation expert in the UK, Germany and Poland. He was involved in transport planning and traffic engineering projects of all sizes and levels of complexity. His research area focuses on data collection and modeling of decision-making behaviour in tourism and leisure travel. He is interested in models of tourists' and visitors' transport mode choice for long-distance travel and mobility within destinations. He has authored articles in leading transportation journals.

Richard W. Butler is Emeritus Professor of Tourism in the Strathclyde Business School in Glasgow, U.K., and is based in northern Canada. He was trained as a geographer at Nottingham University (BA) and the University of Glasgow (Ph.D.). He taught at the University of Western Ontario (1967–97), University of Surrey (1997–2005), and

Strathclyde University (2005–2012). He was a founding member of the International Academy for the Study of Tourism, and served two terms as President. He has supervised over 100 Masters and Doctoral students and published 25 books on tourism. In 2016 he was awarded the Ulysses Prize for "outstanding creation and dissemination of knowledge".

Wenjie Cai is an Associate Professor in Tourism and the Associate Head of Research and Knowledge Exchange at the School of Management and Marketing, University of Greenwich, London, UK. Wenjie received his Ph.D. in Tourism from the University of Surrey, UK. He is an experienced qualitative researcher. His research interests include digital wellbeing, social inclusion, knowledge creation, technology use, and consumer behaviour. Wenjie aims to advocate digital wellbeing and support marginalised and disadvantaged groups through his research.

Duygu Celebi is a full-time Lecturer in the Department of Gastronomy and Culinary Arts at Yasar University, Turkey. She holds Bachelor's and Master's degrees in Tourism Management and a Ph.D. in Business Administration. Her research interests include tourism marketing, destination marketing, social media marketing, special interest tourism, gastronomy, and also social entrepreneurship in the gastronomy field.

Deepak Chhabra teaches in the School of Community Resources and Development at Arizona State University, Phoenix (USA). She also holds the position of Senior Sustainability Scientist. Her research interests include authenticity and authentication of heritage; social/economic viability of tourism; and wellbeing through alternate healing/preventive therapeutic settings and programs.

Michael Clancy is Professor of Politics and Head of the Department of Politics, Economics, and International Studies at the University of Hartford, Connecticut, USA. He specialises in various aspects of the political economy of global tourism. He is the author of two books, and the editor of a third. He has contributed multiple journal articles and book chapters on tourism and national development, cruise tourism, slow tourism, sex tourism, tourism and nation-branding, overtourism, short-term holiday rentals, and tourism ethics. His current work involves post-COVID tourism policy and sustainability.

J. Andres Coca-Stefaniak is a Professor and Associate Head (Research & Knowledge Exchange), School of Business, Operations and Strategy at the University of Greenwich, London, U.K. Previously he was Head of Research, International Partnerships and Thought Leadership at the Association of Town and City Management. He is co-editor of the *Routledge Handbook of Tourism Cities* (2020), Co-Editor-in-Chief of the *International Journal of Tourism Cities*, and a member of the editorial board of several academic journals in tourism, hospitality and urban management. He has managed international research projects with a combined cumulative budget of US$18 million and delivered expert evidence to policy makers in the U.K. and the European Commission.

Cheryl Cockburn-Wootten is the Director of Teaching & Learning for the School of Management & Marketing, at the Waikato Management School, *Te Whare Wānanga o Waikato*, The University of Waikato, Hamilton, New Zealand. Her work critically analyses the communicative aspects of managing the act of organising and nurturing relationships with communities for change. Research interests and teaching fall within critical communication, with a focus on tourism, critical hospitality, equity, dignity, accessibility, and stakeholders.

Chris Cooper is at the School of Events, Tourism and Hospitality Management Leeds Beckett University in the U.K. Chris has more than forty years' experience in tourism and has worked as a researcher and teacher in every region of the world. Chris works with international agencies, including the United Nations World Tourism Organization (UNWTO), the European Union, the International Labour Organization, the OECD, the Inter-American Development Bank and ASEAN. He held the Chair of the UNWTO's Education Council from 2005 to 2007 and was awarded the United Nations Ulysses Medal for contributions to tourism education and policy in 2009. Chris was Co-Founder of Progress in Tourism, Hospitality and Recreation Research and the *International Journal of Tourism Research* and is now the Co-Editor of *Current Issues in Tourism*. He is a member of the editorial board for leading tourism, hospitality and leisure journals and has authored a number of leading text and research books in tourism, including *Essentials of Tourism* for Sage. He is the co-series editor of the influential Channel View book series 'Aspects of Tourism'.

Michel Desbordes is at the Université Paris-Saclay, France. He is a specialist in sports marketing with a research focus on the management of sports events, sports sponsorship and marketing applied to football. He has published 34 books and 58 academic articles in the *International Journal of Sports Marketing and Sponsorship*; *European Sport Management Quarterly*; and the *International Journal of Sport Management and Marketing*, amongst others. From January 2009 to 2019, he was the Editor of the *International Journal of Sports Marketing and Sponsorship*.

Frédéric Dimanche is the Director of Ted Rogers School of Hospitality and Tourism Management at Toronto Metropolitan University in Canada. He obtained his Ph.D. from the University of Oregon (USA). He then worked as a Professor in the School of Hotel Restaurant and Tourism Administration at the University of New Orleans. After over 15 years in the USA, where he also worked as Research Director of The Olinger Group, a full service marketing research firm, he joined SKEMA Business School in 2001 to create and develop on the French Riviera the Center for Tourism Management and award-winning Master programs in tourism, event, and hospitality management before joining Ryerson University in 2015. (Ryerson University was renamed Toronto Metropolitan University in 2022.) He has published numerous tourism-related research articles and has co-authored one book (in French) on hospitality management and another one on tourism in Russia. Frederic is a past President of the Travel and Tourism Research Association Europe and a member of the International Academy for the Study of Tourism.

Rachel Dodds is a Professor at the Ted Rogers School of Hospitality and Tourism Management as well as past Director of the Hospitality and Tourism Research Institute at the Toronto Metropolitan University in Canada. She is passionate about change and making tourism more sustainable. Her research focuses on sustainable tourism, overtourism, policy and development, and consumer behaviour. She has written a number of academic books as well as books for government and the mainstream consumer. She has lived and worked in four continents and travelled to over 85 countries.

Louis-Etienne Dubois is an Associate Professor of Creative Industries Management at Toronto Metropolitan University's School of Creative Industries, in Canada. He is also Associate researcher at MINES ParisTech's Centre for Scientific Management. He holds a Ph.D. from HEC Montréal and from MINES ParisTech. His research activities aim at developing a better understanding of production and innovation processes in cultural and creative organisations.

David L. Edgell, Sr. was a former Professor of Trade, Tourism, and Economic Development at East Carolina University and The George Washington University in the USA. He specialised in "managing sustainable tourism" and "tourism policy and planning". His post-graduate work included econometrics (MIT), Executive Leadership (Harvard), and Social Sciences (University of Michigan). He served as the Acting U.S. Under Secretary of Commerce for Travel and Tourism, as the first Commission of Tourism in the U.S. Virgin Islands and as Senior Vice President for Strategic Marketing at MMGY Global. He has written a dozen books and over 100 articles on trade, tourism, and economic development. Globally, he received many awards and honors. He was the recipient of the Department of Commerce's highest medal awards: Bronze, Silver, and Gold and Mexico's prestigious Miguel Aleman's Silver Medal for international tourism leadership.

Maria Gebbels is a Senior Lecturer in Hospitality Management at the Greenwich Business School, University of Greenwich, in London, U.K. Her main research focuses on gender issues and career development in hospitality, professionalism, in-prison fine dining, hospitality in adventure tourism, and critical hospitality as a lens to understand social relations.

Gabor Geczi is the Director of the Institute of Economy and Social Sciences at the Hungarian University of Sports Sciences in Budapest, Hungary and Head of the Department of Sports Management. He is a specialist in coaching, mentoring, management, strategic thinking, sports science coaching, development organisational culture, organisational management, training and development. He has published 36 academic articles in English and Hungarian, and is currently undertaking project work in Hungary.

Ekaterina Glebova is pursuing her academic interests in research at an intersection of sports and technological transformation at the University Paris Saclay in France. She has over ten years of international experience in marketing, consultancy and business development. She has published numerous book chapters and articles in peer-reviewed journals (e.g. *Journal of Sport Management and Marketing*, *Frontiers in Psychology, Physical Culture and Sport: Studies and Research*). Ekaterina holds a few visiting faculty positions, including at the Hungarian University of Sports Science and the EDHEC Business School in Nice.

Vanessa G. B. Gowreesunkar is an Associate Professor at the Anant National University in India. Previously, she was Head of Department for Hospitality and Tourism at the University of Africa Toru Orua, Nigeria. With over a decade of experience in teaching, training and research, Vanessa has brought her contributions in a number of international universities/institutions. She is an editorial board member of several scientific journals, and has a number of publications in Scopus-Indexed journals. She serves as Deputy Chair for the Tourism, Infrastructure and Energy cluster at the African Union Economic and Social Council. She is the National Coordinator for the Women

Advancement for Economic and Leadership Empowerment (WAELE). She is also a member of the IUCN Tourism and Protected Areas Specialist Group.

Daniel Guttentag is an Assistant Professor in Hospitality and Tourism Management in the School of Business at the College of Charleston, South Carolina, USA. He serves as Director of the University's Office of Tourism Analysis. He holds a Ph.D. in Recreation and Leisure Studies and a Master's degree in Tourism Policy and Planning, from the University of Waterloo (Canada). He publishes regularly on topics related to tourism technology, with a particular focus on Airbnb and virtual reality tourism.

Tracy Harkison is an Associate Professor and Hospitality Undergraduate Programme Leader at the School of Hospitality and Tourism in Auckland University of Technology – *Te Wananga Aronui o Tamaki Makaurau*. Her research focuses on the luxury accommodation experience, co-creation, hospitality for good, and hospitality education.

Angie Yeonsook Im is a Ph.D. candidate in Hospitality Management at the University of Missouri, in the United States. She received a master's degree in Business Administration from the University of British Columbia, Vancouver, Canada. Her research interests include consumer behaviour, sustainable destination management, organisational behaviour, leadership, and hospitality education.

Stanislav Ivanov is a Professor and Vice Rector (Research) at Varna University of Management, Bulgaria, and Director of Zangador Research Institute. He is the Editor-in-chief of the *European Journal of Tourism Research* and *ROBONOMICS: The Journal of the Automated Economy*. He serves on the Editorial Boards of over 30 other journals. His research interests include robonomics, robots and automation technologies, and revenue management. Prof. Ivanov's publications have appeared in different academic journals – *Annals of Tourism Research*, *Tourism Management*, *Tourism Management Perspectives*, *Tourism Economics*, *Technology in Society* and other journals.

Evangelos Kilipiris is Ph.D. Student at the University of Aegean focusing on Tourism and Aviation. He is a researcher at ETEM (Laboratory for Tourism Research and Studies) of the University of the Aegean. He holds Master Degrees on Tourism Management (International Hellenic University, Greece) and Air Transport Management (University of Surrey, U.K.), while he has participated in numerous research projects regarding Tourism and Air Transport subjects. He is an Adjunct Professor at the International Hellenic University and a member of the Hellenic Aviation Society.

Dae-Young Kim is a Professor of Hospitality Management at the University of Missouri, USA. His research expertise includes consumer behaviour, destination marketing, information technology, meetings, cognitive psychology in hospitality and tourism management. He received his Ph.D. (2006) and M.S. degree (2002) in the Department of Hospitality and Tourism Management at Purdue University. He has published more than 150 peer-reviewed journal articles and conference proceedings.

Min Jung Kim is a Ph.D. candidate in Hospitality Management at the University of Missouri in the United States. She received a master's degree in Tourism and Hospitality Administration from Hanyang University, Seoul, South Korea. Her research interests include landmark marketing, social media marketing, and destination management.

Anne Köchling is a researcher at the German Institute for Tourism Research at the West Coast University of Applied Sciences, FH Westküste in Germany. She holds degrees in

International Business Studies and Tourism Management as well as a Ph.D. in Business Psychology and has several years of practical experience in destination marketing and management. During the last 13 years, she was in charge of numerous research projects and has published several scientific articles in tourism journals and books. Her research interests are in destination marketing and management, tourist experiences and tourist behaviour.

Metin Kozak is with Kadir Has University, Turkey. He holds a Ph.D. degree from Sheffield Hallam University, U.K. As a visiting scholar, Metin was affiliated with the University of Namur, Hong Kong Polytechnic University, and Bournemouth University. He serves as an editorial board member and ad hoc reviewer of many journals. He is elected as the Fellow of the International Academy for the Study of Tourism, and Tourist Research Centre. He has been invited as a guest lecturer/speaker to conduct seminars/lectures worldwide. He has also had an extensive experience in the creation and organisation of 50+ conferences. His research interests entail marketing and consumer behaviour.

Suneel Kumar is Associate Professor in Department of Commerce in Shaheed Bhagat Singh College, University of Delhi, India. He received his Ph.D. in Tourism Marketing and Tourists Behaviour from Himachal Pradesh University Shimla, Himachal Pradesh, in India. He is working on a Major Research Project as a Co-Principal Investigator which has been awarded by ICSSR, Ministry of Education, Government of India entitled "Eco-Tourism: A Panacea for Sustainable Development in Himachal Pradesh". His current research interests lie in Tourism and Hospitality Management, Rural Tourism, Sustainability and Green Practices and Destination Branding.

Varinder Kumar is doing his Ph.D. at the Faculty of Management Studies, University of Delhi in India. Along with his Ph.D., he also works as an assistant professor at Shaheed Bhagat Singh Evening College. His current research interests lie in tourism and hospitality management, community-based tourism, smart tourism, sustainability, and social media marketing.

Sofia Lachhab is a Ph.D. candidate at the Greenwich Business School, University of Greenwich, London, U.K. She holds a master's degree in International Tourism and Hospitality Management from Bedfordshire University, U.K. Sofia previously enjoyed a career in the hotel and entertainment industry, working with Hilton Hotels and Walt Disney World. Her research interests are in tourism crisis management and resilience. She is a member of the U.K. Institute of Hospitality, U.K. Council for Hospitality Management Education (CHME) and a Peer Reviewer at the *International Journal of Tourism*.

Sophia Lingham is a Ph.D. researcher at the Royal Agricultural University, U.K. Her research focuses on the socio-economic aspects of food networks and food SMEs. She concentrates on horizontal linkages between food and drink SMEs within alternative food networks, and their role in facilitating people to revalue food by promoting the non-financial values of food. She holds a Masters in Sustainable Agriculture and Food Security (with Distinction) from the RAU and a First Class Bachelor of Laws Degree from the Open University.

Martin Lohmann is a Consumer Psychologist who has specialised in Tourism Research since the 1980s. Martin teaches at the MCI in Innsbruck (Austria), in the CAS Tourism and

Digitalization at the University of Bern (Switzerland) and in the Master in Sustainable Tourism and Hospitality Management (STHM) program at CBS in Copenhagen (Denmark). Until 2022, he was director of the NIT, Institute for Tourism Research in Northern Europe, in Kiel, and Professor of Business Psychology at Leuphana University Lüneburg in Germany. In numerous research projects and publications, Martin investigated the demand perspective in tourism, also with respect to, e.g., sustainable travel. He is scientific advisor for the German consumer travel survey "Reiseanalyse".

Kim-Ieng Loi is the Vice-President of the Macao Institute for Tourism Studies (IFTM) in Macao SAR, China. She graduated with Ph.D. in Tourism from the James Cook University in Australia under the supervision of Professor Philip Pearce and Dr. Laurie Murphy. Her research areas surround tourist behaviours, destination planning and marketing and tourism product development. She publishes regularly in international conferences and academic journals. In her 20 years of work in the academia, she has conducted various tourism researches, quality assurance projects and coordinated regular programme review and revision activities. Dr. Loi also sits in multiple public and private associations and committees related to tourism education and talent development.

Damian Maye is Professor in Agri-Food Studies at the Countryside and Community Research Institute, University of Gloucestershire. His research covers various aspects of agri-food studies, rural geography and geographies of food, with a particular focus on agri-food sustainability and governance. This includes work on alternative food networks, sustainable food chains, biosecurity and farming practices. He recently co-authored a major new book on Geographies of Food. He is Associate Editor of Journal of Rural Studies; Frontiers in Veterinary Science (Veterinary Humanities and Social Sciences); AGER – Journal of Depopulation and Rural Development Studies; and Chair of the RGS-IBG Food Geographies Research Group.

Alison J. McIntosh is Professor of Tourism and Hospitality at the Auckland University of Technology, New Zealand. As a critical scholar, her main research interests are in social justice, inclusion, accessibility and sustainability through tourism and hospitality. Her research work focuses on notions of hospitality as advocacy and welcome to improve the lives of our most vulnerable populations. A central theme of her research is that experiential, qualitative and social justice analyses reveal subjective, emotional, spiritual and neglected aspects of tourism experiences. Her research prioritises otherwise unheard voices, personal dimensions, distinct types of tourism encounters, and tourism in marginalised contexts.

Timothy MacNeill is Director of Sustainability Studies and Senior Teaching Professor in Political Science at Ontario Tech University in Canada. He is an expert in economic, social, and environmental impacts of development projects and alternatives to development that are authored by communities, Indigenous peoples, civil society groups, and governments. Dr. MacNeill holds interdisciplinary Bachelors, Masters, and Doctoral degrees that focus on economic, cultural, and political theory in global context. He is the author of two books: One on Indigenous alternatives to development, and the other on the integration of culture into economic theory. His numerous academic articles apply a decoloniality perspective on community/environmental impact studies, Green Basic Income proposals, community-led social economy projects, Indigenous economics, and resistance to coloniality.

Brad McKenna is an Associate Professor in Information Systems at the University of East Anglia, U.K. Brad received his Ph.D. in Information Systems from the University of Auckland, New Zealand. Brad's research interests can be characterised as an examination of the relationships between information technology and people. Brad has always been interested in how and why people use technology, and how technological configurations impact the people that use them. He has been able to explore this with multiple research interest areas such as virtual worlds, social media, systems analysis, mobile services, and user requirements.

Shem Wambugu Maingi is a Lecturer and Researcher in Tourism Management at the Department of Hospitality and Tourism Management at Kenyatta University in Kenya. Dr Shem Maingi has widely published in Scopus-indexed journals and books internationally. He is an expert member of the African Union Economic, Social and Cultural Council (AU-ECOSOCC). He is also an expert member of the International Scientific Committee on Cultural Tourism of ICOMOS (ICTC).

Louise Manning is Professor of Sustainable Agri-food Systems at the Lincoln Institute for Agri-food Technology, University of Lincoln, U.K. She is a Fellow of the Institute of Food Science and Technology, and Associate Editor of the *British Food Journal*. Louise has authored and co-edited more than 150 scientific articles, book chapters, books and policy papers. She speaks frequently at conferences and on the media on food policy and food supply topics. She has an h-index of 33 on Google Scholar.

Juan Carlos Martín is a Full Professor of the Applied Economic Analysis Department at the University of Las Palmas de Gran Canaria in Spain. He has more than 25 years of professional experience in the field of transport economics in the areas of urban transport, air transport and its regulation. He is an active member of the Research Institute (TIDES) "Tourism and Sustainable Economic Development" and has participated in European Union (EU) projects and also worked for other international top-level institutions, such as the World Bank and the Ministry of Public Works in Spain. He is the European Regional Editor of *Transportation Journal* and the Vice-President of Nectar. He is a co-author of four books and monographs, more than 100 peer-reviewed papers and book chapters in the field of tourism and transport economics. He has taught transport and tourism courses in Belgium, the U.K., Portugal, Ecuador, Bolivia, Spain and Morocco.

Eleni Mavragani is Assistant Professor in Marketing Management, at the University of Macedonia Business School in Greece and Adjunct Lecturer and Course Leader at the Hellenic Open University in Greece. She has published several articles in academic journals, books and scientific conferences. She has taught courses in marketing and tourism in several universities and she has also been involved in Greek and European financed projects about tourism and culture. Her research interests include tourism marketing, cultural and museum marketing.

Cristina Maxim is a Senior Lecturer in Tourism at the University of West London in the U.K. She is the co-author of *World Tourism Cities: A systematic approach to urban tourism*, published by Routledge, and an Associate Editor for the *International Journal of Tourism Cities*. Cristina regularly publishes articles in peer-reviewed academic journals and presents at recognised international conferences. She is currently working on several research projects that look at world tourism cities, sustainable tourism, destination management, and local government.

Diogo Moleiro is resident Teacher and Coordinator of the Tourism course at Espinho Professional School (ESPE), Espinho, Portugal and non-resident Teacher at Porto, Portugal. He is also a Ph.D. student in Tourism at the University of Aveiro. He has some articles published on the themes of perceptions and attitudes of residents and tourists in urban tourism context, tourism marketing, tourism networks, tourism experience and creative tourism. He also published an entry about gentrification in the *Encyclopedia of Tourism Management and Marketing*.

G. L. W. Roshini N. Nandasena is a Ph.D. researcher at the University of Greenwich, currently working as a postgraduate teaching assistant. She is a member of the Faculty of Business Tourism & Marketing Research Centre (University of Greenwich) and a reviewer for the International Journal of Tourism Cities (IJTC). She has always been fascinated with travelling as its open window allowed her to see the world. It helped her choose my research project in Transformational Tourism, specifically to explore the nature of tourist transformation through memorable travel experiences.

Shawn Newman is a consultant, educator, and cultural producer based in Toronto, Canada. Formerly the Executive Director of Public Access and Managing Editor of *PUBLIC: Art | Culture | Ideas*, he frequently advises on local, provincial, and national initiatives, including recent work with the Canada Council for the Arts, CC UNESCO, and more. He is also the Research & Impact Manager at the Toronto Arts Council and Foundation, and holds a Ph.D. in Cultural Studies from Queen's University.

David Newsome works in Environment and Conservation at Murdoch University in Perth, Western Australia. His research focuses on nature-based tourism with a particular emphasis on the environmental impacts of recreation and tourism, the sustainability of tourism in national parks and nature reserves, the evaluation of the quality of ecotourism operations, sustainable trail management, geological tourism, and wildlife tourism. David is a member of the IUCN World Commission on Protected Areas. His publications include some 160 journal articles, book chapters and reports and the widely cited academic texts *Natural Area Tourism: Ecology, Impacts and Management* and *Wildlife Tourism*.

Peter O'Connor is Professor of Strategic Management at the University of South Australia. His primary research and teaching interests focus on the effect of digital on business, particularly on retailing and marketing. Peter has published in leading academic journals, including the *Journal of Marketing*, the *Harvard Business Review*, the *Journal of Retailing and Consumer Services, Tourism Management*, the *Cornell Quarterly* and the *International Journal of Hospitality Management*, amongst others. Prior to joining UniSA, Peter founded the Chair in Digital Disruption at ESSEC Business School in France, where he held a variety of other academic roles.

Gokce Ozdemir holds an associate professorship in Marketing at Yasar University's Department of Tourism Management in Turkey. She graduated from Dokuz Eylul University with an MA and a Ph.D. in tourism management. She has concentrated her writing and research on issues related to tourism marketing, destination marketing, event management, and the sharing economy in the travel industry.

Francesca Pagliara is Associate Professor in Transport Engineering at the Department of Civil, Architectural and Environmental Engineering of the University of Naples Federico II in Italy. She has been visiting Professor at several European and non-European Universities. She is author of academic books and more than 100 papers. She participated in several research projects. Her main fields of research are the wider socio-economic impacts of high-speed rail systems, the analysis and quantification of the impact of the transportation system on the tourism market, public engagement in the transportation decision-making process, transit-oriented development policies and integrated land-use/transport models.

Andreas Papatheodorou is Professor in Industrial and Spatial Economics with Emphasis on Tourism at the Department of Tourism Economics and Management, University of the Aegean, Greece, where he also directs the MSc Programme in Strategic Management of Tourism Destinations and Hospitality Enterprises. An Oxford University MPhil (Economics) and DPhil (Economic Geography) holder, he has published extensively in the areas of air transport and tourism and been involved in a large number of research and consulting projects. He is the Editor-in-Chief of the *Journal of Air Transport Studies* and an Associate Editor of *Annals of Tourism Research*. Andreas is the President of the Hellenic Aviation Society and participates in the Panel of Experts of the United Nations World Tourism Organization (UNWTO).

Lígia Ribeiro is a non-resident Assistant Professor at Escola Superior de Educação de Coimbra (ESEC) in Coimbra, Portugal. She is also a professor at Escola de Hotelaria e Turismo do Porto, in Porto, Portugal and a resident trainer at the Global Distribution System (GDS) Galileo. She is a specialist in travel agencies, tour operators and aviation and is currently attending the last year of her Ph.D. at the University of Aveiro, Portugal.

Concepción Román is Professor at the Applied Economic Analysis Department of the University of Las Palmas de Gran Canaria, Spain. She is the director of the Research Unit "Tourism and Transport" at the University Institute of Tourism and Economic Sustainable Development (Tides). She has more than 25 years of professional experience in the field of transport economics in the areas of tourism and demand transport modelling, air transport and its regulation. She participated as an expert and consultant in some projects of the European Union (EU) and other international top-level institutions. She is co-author of 15 books and monographs, more than 80 peer-reviewed papers and book chapters since 1993 in the field of tourism and transport economics. She has taught transport and tourism courses in Belgium, Portugal, Ecuador, Bolivia, Spain and Morocco.

Dirk Schmücker is the Scientific Director of NIT, the Institute for Tourism Research in Northern Europe, based in Germany. He received his Ph.D. in Economics and Social Sciences from Lüneburg University and has been working in consumer research in tourism since 1995. His research interests are in consumer research, impact research and trend research in tourism.

Cláudia Seabra is a Professor in the Faculty of Arts and Humanities at the University of Coimbra, Portugal. She coordinates the Ph.D. in Tourism, Heritage, and Territory. She earned a Ph.D. in Tourism and a Post-Ph.D. in Economic and Social Geography. She is affiliated with the CEGOT – Geography and Spatial Planning Research Centre; and collaborates with CISeD – Research Centre in Digital Services. Risk in tourism and safety and tourism are her research interests. She has published in the *Journal of Business Research*, *Tourism Management*, the *Annals of Tourism Research*, the *International Journal of Tourism Cities*, the *European Journal of Marketing*, the *Journal of Marketing Management*, *ANATOLIA*, the *Journal of Hospitality and Tourism Technology*, among others.

Tina Šegota is a Senior Lecturer at the Faculty of Business at the University of Greenwich in London, U.K. She is also an Associate Professor in Tourism at the Faculty of Tourism at the University of Maribor, Slovenia. She is a multi-award-winning academic with research and teaching experience in marketing and tourism worldwide. Her current research interests include destination advertising and marketing, tourism seasonality, tourism and quality of life, place branding and place attachment, and children in tourism destinations.

Melanie Kay Smith (Ph.D.) is an Associate Professor, Researcher and Consultant whose work focuses on urban planning, cultural tourism, wellness tourism experiences and the relationship between tourism and wellbeing. She is Programme Leader for BSc and MSc Tourism Management at Budapest Metropolitan University in Hungary. She has lectured in the UK, Hungary, Estonia, Germany, Austria and Switzerland as well as being an invited Keynote speaker in many countries worldwide. She was Chair of ATLAS (Association for Tourism and Leisure Education) for seven years and has undertaken consultancy work for UNWTO and ETC as well as regional and national projects on cultural and health tourism. She is the author or editor of several books as well as more than 100 journal articles and book chapters. Her most recent research focuses on wellness tourism, the impacts of 'overtourism' in cultural cities and urban green spaces.

Haiyan Song is Mr. and Mrs. Chan Chak Fu Professor in International Tourism in the School of Hotel and Tourism Management and Deputy Dean Research at The Hong Kong Polytechnic University, Hong Kong SAR, China. His research interests are in the areas of tourism demand analysis, service quality management, tourism supply chain management and wine economics. He has published widely in such journals as *Annals of Tourism Research*, *Tourism Management* and the *Journal of Travel Research*. Professor Song is Editor-in Chief of the *Journal of China Tourism Research* and Associate Editor of *Annals of Tourism Research*.

Spyridoula Dimitra Souki works at the University of Ioannina in Greece. She is a graduate of International & European Studies from Pantion University in Greece and Translation and Interpreting (Strasbourg University, France) and holds a Master's degree on Tourism Business Administration from the Hellenic Open University in Greece. She worked for ten years at the Labor Inspectorate (as an Inspector) and for ten more years as a Labor advisor, as an auditor of National and European Grants Programs (NSRF) and as an auditor of the Insurance Department. She has researched in adult education, and vocational training concerning tourism, marketing, and communication. She has published articles in international journals and lectured at international scientific conferences.

Aaron Tham is the Subject Component Lead in Tourism, Leisure and Events Management at the University of the Sunshine Coast, Australia. He is an active researcher with primary interests in the area of emerging technologies and event legacies. Aaron is a Senior Fellow of the Higher Education Academy and is the Immediate Past Vice President and Conference Chair of the Travel and Tourism Research Association Asia Pacific Chapter. Aaron currently sits on the Committee for Brisbane Taskforce for the 2032 Brisbane Olympics Legacies, and also serves as the Managing Editor for the International Journal of Hospitality and Tourism Administration.

Marco Valeri is a Senior Lecturer in Organizational Behaviour, Faculty of Economics, Niccolò Cusano University, Rome in Italy and a Senior Lecturer in NCIUL – London. He is Visiting Professor at the Faculty of Social Sciences and Leisure Management, School of Hospitality, Tourism and Events, Taylor's University, Subang Jaya 47500 (Malaysia). His research areas include competitive advantage, sustainability and green practices, strategy implementation, knowledge management, family business and tourism hotel/lodging management, crisis management, destination marketing, information technology and developing countries, and network analysis. He serves on the Editorial Boards of several academic journals covering tourism and hospitality management. He is also a member of several editorial boards of international tourism journals, and a reviewer and editor of several handbooks on entrepreneurship, tourism and hospitality management.

Pedro Vaz Serra is a Ph.D. Candidate in Tourism, Heritage, and Territory, and a Researcher at CEGOT – Geography and Spatial Planning Research Centre, at the University of Coimbra, Portugal. He has a Master's degree in Social Intervention, Innovation, and Entrepreneurship and a degree in Economics from the University of Coimbra, Portugal. He holds a postgraduate degree in Strategic Management and Value Creation from Católica Lisbon School of Business & Economics, and is in Senior Management Programme at AESE – Business School Lisbon, in collaboration with IESE – Business School of the University of Navarra, Madrid Campus, Spain. He performed local, regional, and national functions in the financial and business sectors, and he has participated, as a speaker, in many congresses.

Craig Webster is an Associate Professor in the Department of Applied Business Studies at Ball State University, USA. His research interests include automation in hospitality and tourism, robonomics, the political economy of tourism, and event management. Dr. Webster's research has appeared in many different journals, including *Annals of Tourism Research*, *Tourism Management*, *Event Management*, *Tourism Economics*, *Technology in Society* and *Tourism Geographies*, and many others. He is the co-editor of two books, *Future Tourism: Political, Social and Economic Challenges* and *Robots, Artificial Intelligence and Service Automation in Travel, Tourism and Hospitality*.

Jose Weng Chou Wong is an Associate Professor and Programme Director in the Faculty of Hospitality and Tourism Management at Macao University of Science and Technology, Macao SAR, China. His research interests include memorable tourism experience, value co-creation, and hospitality management. His work has appeared in the *Journal of Travel Research*, the *Journal of Sustainable Tourism*, the *International Journal of Hospitality Management*, the *International Journal of Contemporary Hospitality Management*, *Current Issues in Tourism*, the *Journal of Hospitality* and *Tourism Management*, among others. He is an editorial board member for the *Journal of Hospitality and Tourism Research*, the *Journal of Vacation Marketing*, and the *Journal of Hospitality and Tourism Insights*.

Brianna Wyatt is a Senior Lecturer and the Subject Coordinator for the postgraduate programs in Hospitality, Tourism, and Events for the Oxford Brookes Business School at Oxford Brookes University, UK. She specializes in dark tourism with emphasis in interpretation and experience design. Her publications explore the use of edutainment interpretation in lighter dark visitor attractions. She also has industry experience working in heritage and dark visitor attractions and museums, as well as with the World Heritage Centre, and sits on the Editorial Board of the *World Leisure Journal*.

Weixi (Edith) Yuan is a Research Assistant in the School of Hotel and Tourism Management at The Hong Kong Polytechnic University, Hong Kong SAR, China. Her research interests include wine tourism marketing, information communication technology in marketing, multisensory marketing of wine, wine consumer behaviour and tourist behaviour.

Fateme Zare is a Ph.D. student at the Hungarian University of Sports Sciences in Budapest, Hungary. She has published a number of articles on political and social issues in elite sport, the effects of COVID-19 on sport management, and tourism. It is her goal to complete a dissertation on the expected outcomes of elite sport policies in various countries. She is also an active member of the Budapest Association for International Sports (BAIS). Her work included coordinating a project about the inclusion of hair impaired youth in sports.

Elisa Zentveld is a Professor of Social Justice at Federation University Australia. She was previously the Chair of the Academic Board and an Associate Professor of Tourism and Management at Federation University. She has published over 60 papers, co-edited three books, and written the only book discussing the relationship between family violence and tourism (*Control, Abuse, Bullying, and Family Violence in Tourism Industries*). Elisa is a TEQSA panel expert with 14 awards that recognise her outstanding contribution to research and education. Elisa is recognised as the world's leading expert in Visiting Friends and Relatives (VFR) travel.

Introduction

Alastair M. Morrison and Dimitrios Buhalis

Rationale for Handbook

The main aim of the ***Routledge Handbook of Trends and Issues in Global Tourism*** is to provide a comprehensive and considered text on trends and issues within tourism worldwide. The following quote expresses the difficulties that exist in finding systematic and credible information on trends and issues:

> Pinpointing trends and issues in international tourism is challenging in itself as there are no books or comprehensive documentation sources for these data. The proverbial 'searching for a needle in a haystack' is a good metaphor for anyone trying to gather this information in order to look ahead. Also, the changes impacting tourism are so dynamic and often unpredictable that searching for trends and issues can be an endless and certainly is an ongoing task.
>
> (Morrison, 2021, p. 219)

This situation was exacerbated by the COVID-19 pandemic that began in early 2020 and whose effects continued through to 2022 and 2023. In fact, a concoction of trends and issues were already in play when the global public health crisis arrived; however, scholars were tending to treat these separately without duly considering their interrelationships and combined effects. Thus, the main reason for writing the *Routledge Handbook on Trends and Issues in Global Tourism* was to raise this theme from a peripheral and *ad hoc* topic to a mainstream subject in tourism and hospitality education and research, and in so doing address a gap in the market of related books.

Handbook volumes

There are two volumes of the Handbook – the *Routledge Handbook on Trends and Issues in Global Tourism* and the *Routledge Handbook of Trends and Issues in Sustainability, Planning and Development, Management, and Technology*. The first volume covers major trends and issues in global tourism; the second reviews trends and issues in four thematic areas of tourism. There are 78 chapters in total, contributed by 147 authors from more than 30 countries (Figure 0.1).

Editors: Alastair M. Morrison and Dimitrios Buhalis

Routledge Handbook of Trends and Issues in Global Tourism, publication in 2023

- The main themes and objectives of the Handbook are to:
- 1. Highlight the importance of tracking and interpreting global trends and issues in tourism.
- 2. Propose clear definitions and a systematic classification scheme for trends and issues.
- 3. Identify and describe the major trends and issues affecting tourism.
- 4. Review the interactions among trends and issues, and the results of their combined impacts.
- 5. Delineate theoretical and practical approaches for tracking and interpreting trends and issues.
- 6. Provide a comprehensive academic and practitioner reference source on trends and issues in global tourism.

Figure 0.1 Editors, themes, and objectives of book.
Photo courtesy of Unsplash.com, Katerina Kerdi.

Introduction 3

Themes and objectives

The main themes and objectives of the Handbook are to:

1. Highlight the importance of tracking and interpreting global trends and issues in tourism
2. Propose clear definitions and a systematic classification scheme for trends and issues
3. Identify and describe the major trends and issues affecting tourism
4. Review the interactions among trends and issues, and the results of their combined impacts
5. Delineate theoretical and practical approaches for tracking and interpreting trends and issues
6. Provide a comprehensive academic and practitioner reference source on trends and issues in global tourism.

Structure

There is no single book on the market that comprehensively deals with global trends and issues in tourism, and that is the main differentiator for the *Routledge Handbook of Trends and Issues in Global Tourism*. Notwithstanding this, the book uses a systematic classification of trends and issues that is not found elsewhere, while having a set of contributing authors from among the leading tourism scholars in the world and thereby solidifying its credibility and authority.

The innovative Handbook structure is based on the proposed classification scheme (Figure 0.2). This avoids the "laundry list" approaches by acknowledging the fundamental sources of trends and issues. The Handbook accepts that not all tourism markets are the same and that they need separate attention with respect to trends and issues. Therefore, the contents reflect major trip purpose market segments including leisure/pleasure, business/MICE, and VFR (visiting friends and relatives), while also recognising differences among domestic, outbound, and inbound markets. It is acknowledged that the

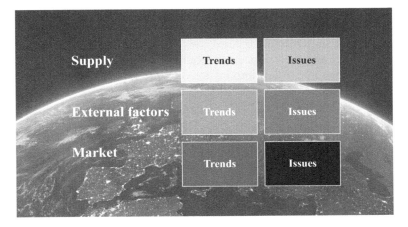

Figure 0.2 Classification scheme for trends and issues.
Photo courtesy of Microsoft 365.

supply sub-sectors of tourism are diverse and tend to be dissimilarly influenced by specific trends and issues, and these differences are reflected in the text as are variations by geographic regions.

The basic structure of the contents of the two volumes is as follows:

Routledge Handbook of Trends and Issues in Global Tourism

Part I: Supply-side trends

- Transportation
- Attractions, culture, and heritage tourism
- Technology
- Policies and issues
- Destination management

Part II: External factor trends
Part III: Market-led trends

Routledge Handbook of Trends and Issues in Sustainability, Planning and Development, Management, and Technology

- Sustainability
- Planning and development
- Management
- Technology

Emphasis areas

The contributing authors were asked to focus on certain emphasis areas. These included:

- Major trends and issues in the topic field up to 2021–2022, including the work of key contributors
- Stakeholders and their interest and involvement with the topic field
- Predictions for 2032, 2042 and 2052
- Opportunities and challenges with these trends and/or issues – Who wins and who loses?
- Do they contribute to SDGs? If so, how?
- Catalysts of change and their impacts for tourism destinations and stakeholders
- Stakeholder, business and policy implications – Who needs to do what, and when?

Reference

Morrison, A. M. (2021). Reflections on trends and issues in global tourism. In P. U. C. Dieke, B. King, and R. Sharpley (eds.). *Tourism in development: Reflective essays*, pp. 218–232. Wallingford, UK: CABI Publishing.

Part I
Supply-side trends

1.1
Supply-side trends
Transportation

High-speed rail growth is the topic of the first chapter, by **Francesca Pagliara, Juan Carlos Martín, Concepción Román**, and **Bartosz Bursa**. High-speed rail (HSR) has been increasing its popularity among passengers and has become the dominant rail passenger transport mode chosen in recent years. At the same time, the rapid growth of HSR has also brought tremendous opportunities for regional development. Chapter 1 identifies the main current trends in HSR as: The positive effects are limited to large cities, metro areas and regions with already well-developed tourism markets; the positive effects are mainly observable over the short term in "younger" networks (e.g., China and Italy); the positive effects are not sustained over the longer term as they fade with time as observed in "older" networks (e.g., France and Japan); there is the need to improve HSR lines connecting protected areas in order to support sustainable tourism; and there is a great deal of uncertainty regarding whether or not HSR could substantially contribute to tourism development in other countries, in particular the U.S.

Evangelos Kilipiris and **Andreas Papatheodorou** write on *New aircraft and airports* in Chapter 2. The highly competitive industry environment constantly pushes airlines and airports to implement new and innovative strategies in order to secure their financial viability. Increasing passenger flows, new trends in travel habits, the rise of competition among industry companies, and the implementation of sustainability policies have been only some of the challenges which the industry has to face. Furthermore, the COVID-19 health pandemic swiftly changed the perception of travel and aviation has been the most affected sector among many others related to tourism. Health protocols, vaccination policies and country restrictions formed a dynamic environment in which airlines were forced to operate and survive. The aviation industry is trying to maintain its crucial role by adapting itself into an environment which is characterised by uncertainty at different levels.

Cruise lines: Market growth and diversification is covered by **Michael Clancy** in the third chapter. Cruise ship tourism constitutes one of the fastest-growing segments of the global tourism industry. Chapter 3 documents important trends and issues facing the industry in the 21st century. These include concentration of ownership within the global cruise ship industry, increasing segmentation of demand, and the geographic shift of the centre of cruising from North America/Caribbean and Europe to Asia and, in particular, China. While there are many challenges facing the future cruise industry, two stand out: the balance of positive and negative impacts on ports of call, and the global environmental impact of cruising. In both areas, the industry has faced growing pushback.

Timothy MacNeill explores *Cruises: Environmental impacts and policies* in Chapter 4. As the reality of human impact on the natural environment has become widely acknowledged,

8 *Supply-side trends*

debate has turned to policies required to mitigate and adapt to these impacts. Since cruise tourism is a notably environmentally damaging human practice, the industry provides an informative and important case through which these debates can be investigated. This chapter aims to contribute to the understanding of theoretical, social, and practical implications of cruise tourism into the future. Key to this is to question if the industry can become sustainable through self or externally imposed regulation, or if its growth should be discouraged altogether. This chapter addresses these issues by offering a description of the historical growth of the industry and future trajectories, then provides a summary of its environmental impacts, and finally discusses technological and policy proposals for impact mitigation.

1 High-speed rail growth

Francesca Pagliara, Juan Carlos Martín, Concepción Román and Bartosz Bursa

Introduction

Continuous innovation of transportation technology and the constant construction of High-speed rail (HSR) have jointly triggered the "second railway age". Over the past decade, a remarkable growth of the HSR network in China has been registered, changing the spatial structure of the cities across the whole transportation network. According to China's Ministry of Transport, the total length of China's HSR network reached 35,000 km at the end of 2019, accounting for approximately 70% of the global total. With respect to the total traffic on the Chinese HSR, it has increased substantially with an annual growth rate of 16.8%, reaching 680.5 billion passenger-km in 2018 (Yin et al., 2019). Nonetheless, the central government of China is continuing to expand its HSR network and aims to cover almost 80% of cities. HSR has been increasing its popularity among passengers and has become the dominant rail passenger transport mode chosen in recent years. Simultaneously, the rapid growth of HSR has also brought tremendous opportunities for regional development.

It is evident that the development of tourism is closely related to the improvement in transportation accessibility (Guirao and Campa, 2015; Campa et al., 2016). Thus, the tourism sector can benefit from the expansion of the HSR network, which, in turn, improves the transport accessibility of the cities served (Ravazzoli et al., 2017). An extensive body of literature documents the effects of HSR in many contexts from different perspectives, such as the demand and the spatial structure. At the same time, rail tourism has also been coined for particular iconic trains such as the Orient Express, which are characterised by special train operators that make use of rail tracks owned and managed by other infrastructure companies. These types of tourist products are not the focus of the chapter.

The paper by Bonnafous (1987) can be considered seminal in the analysis of the possible effects of the French TGV connecting Paris with Lyon on the tourism market. Indeed, he pointed out that "since it involves travel, it is not surprising that tourism should be the first to show the effects of the introduction of high-speed trains" (p. 135). Moreover, he stated that hotel business was characterised by two different effects. Firstly, a decrease in the number of overnight stays as more day-return journeys were carried out by high-speed trains; secondly, the development of tourist packages travelling by TGV. The inauguration of the HSR line linking Barcelona and Perpignan significantly increased the daily trips in the market of Barcelona (Masson and Petiot, 2009). Similarly, Cuenca and Toledo experienced an increase in the tourism industry due to HSR (Varela and Martínez, 2016). Ureña et al. (2009) declared that large intermediate cities served by HSR, such as Lille, Zaragoza and Cordoba, benefited from a growth in urban and business tourism. Surveys in France showed

DOI: 10.4324/9781003260790-4

that HSR increased the attraction of Disneyland Paris (Delaplace et al., 2016) and allowed visitors to re-visit Paris and Madrid (Delaplace et al., 2014b; Pagliara et al., 2014; Pagliara et al., 2015). Although previous studies have mainly identified positive economic effects of HSR on tourism, there are also studies that did not find such evidence. For instance, Albalate and Fageda (2016) showed that HSR development is not always positively associated with tourism.

The approaches present in the literature to model the impact of HSR on tourism vary considerably. Generalized Estimating Equations (GEEs) are usually chosen, assuming that the relations are constant across all zones of the study area, i.e. the associations are spatially stationary (Pagliara et al., 2017). The limited ability of this technique to take spatial effects into account can be overcome through the specification of spatial regression models. In general, the commonly used spatial models are: The Geographically Weighted Poisson Regression (GWPR); the Spatial Autoregressive Regression (SAR) model; and the Conditional Autoregressive Regression (CAR) model. One of the main advantages of the GWPR model lies in the graphical support it provides for the representation of the impacts of the selected variables on the different zones of the area under study (Pagliara and Mauriello, 2020). More recently, Chen et al. (2022) use a fuzzy-set qualitative comparative analysis on a sample of 153 Chinese cities to analyse the main drivers of the city's tourism arrivals and revenues. To that aim, the authors use transport connectivity of traditional rail, air travel and high-speed rail, jointly with other supply factors that include city size, economic development and the endowment of tourism resources.

Major trends and issues

These methodological advancements allowed researchers to investigate the wider impacts of HSR developments with a so far unprecedented level of detail, leading to an abundance of studies searching for correlations between HSR and an increase in tourism demand. A particularly strong focus has been laid on the consequences for regional tourism economies, resulting from the undeniable accessibility gains offered by HSR. Here, substantial differences have been discovered between different geographical areas of the world.

The dynamic expansion of the Chinese HSR network has led to a generally positive impact on the tourism industry, including the increase in overnights, revenue (Li and Chen, 2019) and the number of international arrivals (Chen and Haynes, 2015). The after-effects are unevenly distributed, however, with less-developed and peripheral regions experiencing better accessibility (Li et al., 2020; Yin et al., 2019) and more arrivals, but no necessarily revenue benefits as opposed to central cities and metropolitan areas (Gao et al., 2019). These asymmetric effects of HSR growth (Wang et al., 2012) and the competition between the agglomeration and dispersion effects in China (Wang et al., 2018; Zhou et al., 2023) are slowly being recognised. Similarly to the observations from China, Japan and Taiwan city tourism have benefited from the HSR connections (Cheng, 2010; Kurihara and Wu, 2016; Sun and Lin, 2018).

The results of corresponding European studies are more ambiguous, and – given the significantly slower rate of HSR network growth than in Asia – the observed effects are, as yet, far less visible (Campa et al., 2016; Gutiérrez et al., 2020). In fact, they are often dependent on the city size (Blanquart and Koning, 2017) and existing tourism potential (Delaplace et al., 2014a; Masson and Petiot, 2009). Unlike in China (Yin et al., 2019), the registered positive effects of HSR developments on tourism growth are limited to larger cities and central regions (see Albalate and Fageda, 2016; Guirao and Campa, 2016; or

Albalate et al., 2017) for evidence from Spain, Pagliara et al. (2017) or Cascetta et al. (2020) for Italy, and Bazin et al. (2013) for France), whereas these benefits are not being observed in the hinterland (Albalate et al., 2021). Furthermore, in Europe as well as in China, the positive effects of HSR on tourism demand tend to fade over time (Albalate and Fageda, 2016; Liu and Shi, 2019).

The often-inconclusive and mixed findings from various parts of the world with respect to HSR impact on various sectors of economy (Campos and Rus, 2009; Givoni, 2006), including the tourism industry (Blanquart and Koning, 2017) should be of certain concern for HSR planning in the U.S. (Albalate and Bel, 2012), where not only is there no real HSR network, but the conventional passenger rail service is also in need of improvement (Levinson, 2012). Amtrak's Acela service, which operates in the Northeast Corridor between Washington, D.C. and Boston, is the only rail service in the U.S. to qualify as an HSR (Scales, 2016) (albeit only on a fraction of the 460-mile length of line). The Acela line owes its undoubted economic success to the segment of passengers travelling for business purposes (Chen, 2010). However, its significance for tourism has not yet been precisely assessed. The 380-mile-long section of a long-awaited California High-Speed Rail stretching from San Francisco and Sacramento to Los Angeles and San Diego is currently under construction. Although this, as well as other planned sections (such as the Appalachian corridor), are forecasted to have a positive impact on accessibility, the effects are likely to be unequally distributed (Chandra and Vadali, 2014; Murakami and Cervero, 2017) and the overall economic case is often brought into question (Button, 2012). So far, there are no credible ex-ante estimates regarding HSR impact on the tourism industry along these lines. The expectations, however, are high.

Similar to the case of the U.S., other large countries, such as India, Brazil and Australia, are also considering investing in HSR. In the Australian case, Hensher et al. (2014) have scrutinised a proposed project linking Sydney and Melbourne and have identified potentially substantial social accessibility benefits of HSR for non-work-related activities (leisure, tourism, visiting friends, etc.), in particular among residents of non-metropolitan areas.

Recent research and reports recognise massive public use and (over)tourism as one of the main environmental pressures and impacts on protected areas, internationally (Carballo et al., 2019; Wall, 2020) and nationally (Gómez-Limón and García, 2014; Gühnemann et al., 2021). Factors related to the impact of tourism on ecosystems can include: transport mode used for long-distance trips to the destination and for mobility on site (Bursa et al., 2022), the types of visitors, the duration of the visit, the season and the time of the day when activities take place, and also the spatial distribution of visitors. Sustainable mobility plans are therefore necessary. Mobility plans incorporate legal instruments and measures for the spatial planning and management of transport services and infrastructure. These plans should be developed in collaboration with regional mobility agencies to organise collective and public transport services, offering alternatives to the use of private vehicles. Likewise, traffic congestion and greenhouse gas emissions should be avoided, establishing use limitations, ordering traffic and implementing monitoring and prevention systems through digital tools and reservation programs for high-capacity infrastructures (e.g. trains, cable cars or buses) (EcoUnion, 2021). Where this is possible, HSR can be a good solution to serve these protected areas and national parks. One example can be found in the Partenio regional park in the Campania region in the south of Italy, where the new HS/HC line connecting Naples with Bari (works in progress) will have a station, that in Cancello, serving this protected area.

The current trends of HSR on tourism can be systematised in the following way:

- The positive effects are, in general, limited to large cities, metro areas and regions with already well-developed tourism markets.
- The positive effects are mainly short-term observable in "younger" networks (e.g., China and Italy).
- The positive effects are not sustainable in the long term as they fade with time as observed in "older" networks (e.g., France and Japan).
- To improve HSR lines connecting protected areas in order to support sustainable tourism.
- Given the contradictory evidence extracted from various regions of the world, there is a great deal of uncertainty regarding to whether HSR could substantially contribute to tourism development in other countries, in particular the U.S.

Stakeholder interests and involvement

The most commonly identified impacts of HSR refer mainly to changes in mobility patterns, the effects on the economy and urban transformation (Feliu, 2012). Hence, HSR links favour local development and also represent an opportunity for smaller cities to promote tourism products where the role played by local stakeholders is important. While HSR was originally conceived as an alternative to air transportation to link the largest urban areas in the country, medium-sized cities along the corridor have benefited from these significant reductions in travel time, making local services more accessible, particularly tourism attractions (Ureña et al., 2009).

In this context, the successful promotion of tourism depends to a large extent on the organisational capacity of social actors to create strategies focused on exploiting the advantages of the HSR network for the city in question. Thus, the leading stakeholders may include institutional departments such as the city council as well as province and regional administration; private companies closely related to tourism activities such as tour operators, travel agencies, hotels, managers of other tourist accommodations like vacation houses, restaurants and bars, and other companies benefiting from tourist activity such as transport companies, taxis, and commerce in general. In fact, the list of local stakeholders resembles quite closely the complex integrated product represented by the "six As": Access (i.e., the accessibility to a location); attractions (i.e., the local attractive factors); accommodation (i.e., hotel structures); amenities (i.e., the tourist services); assemblage (i.e., the activity of tour operators); and ancillary services (i.e., agencies offering services like tours and local institutes and supporting organisations) (Della Corte et al., 2010).

Feliu (2012) examined the local development associated with HSR building in three medium-sized cities in different countries of Europe, namely Lleida (Spain), Avignon (France) and Novara (Italy). The experience of Lleida serves as a demonstration effect of the impact of the HSR on a boost to tourism by promoting active tourism activities in the Pyrenean region. The involvement of stakeholders can be either formal or informal, participating in the strategic plans of urban development at different levels. The development of tourist packages using HSR has been shown to be fruitful on some occasions in which tour operators have carefully listened to the tourist preferences. Other emblematic projects were developed during the phase of HSR construction, including convention centres, shopping malls, offices, theatres and residential areas. In this case, tourism can be boosted by different events such as fairs, conferences, congresses, research and development meetings and educational courses. These new products would have been impossible without the HSR link.

The network of local stakeholders might be formed by a number of stakeholders with different ambitions and objectives for tour package development. On the one hand, it is the tourist destination management organisation (DMO), the entity that could lead the network of stakeholders involved, particularly because the tour package needs to be developed around a HSR station located within a particular destination, and it is the DMO that has the relevant powers for tour package development. The vision and proficiency of DMO officials will be crucial to develop successful tour packages. DMOs might have different territorial jurisdictions that depend on the tourism laws in different countries. The difference at the territorial level is usually the cause of a somewhat conflictive relationship as it is possible that different jurisdictions are not in the hands of the same political party. Thus, some stakeholders might distrust others as they might have a different vision for the territory.

This section ends with some insights that can be used by stakeholder experts involved in tour package development. Feliu (2012) argued that for those experts who want the work to be more beneficial for the territory, more efficient, and long-lasting while it meets the functional aims at a local, regional, or national level, they need to give importance to elements such as local complexity, endogenous resources, a search for dialogue, the mobilisation of stakeholders and good management of conflicts. Especially, he found that if conflicts are the result of a lack of dialogue or a desire to impose a solution, supra-local stakeholders should understand and favour reaching an agreement because the entire success of the tour package is at stake, a process that is mainly administered on a local scale and by local stakeholders.

Future trends

The absence of a strong economic case in tourism in favor of HSR can be compensated by a range of other benefits, such as the environment-friendly characteristics of HSR compared to other modes and by the potential to substitute emission-intensive air transport, especially on short-haul routes. These are the emerging research topics with respect to HSR that will presumably dominate the field in the near future, considering the acceleration in climate change that the world wants to prevent. In this case, it will be interesting to analyse whether the domestic tourism facilitated by road and air can be either partly or fully substituted by HSR. In fact, it is well known that tourists' motivations to visit a city can be affected by the existence of HSR.

The previous sections highlight important information about the existing relationship between HSR and tourism growth and find, in particular, that the relationship is highly affected by the analysed countries as well as the previous existing tourism markets. However, as far as the authors are aware, in the current literature there is a lack of studies exploring tourists' behaviour changes with respect to the introduction of tour packages, which take into account different levels of integration between the main stakeholders involved, namely HSR, hotels and attractions. The two first sections, which reviewed the existing studies on HSR and tourism growth, also highlighted that there is a need to study tourists' reactions with respect to integrated HSR tour packages as an alternative to more conventional tourist products, since this issue remains unexplored. Furthermore, it is surprising that no previous study has analysed tourists' preferences with respect to a possible tour package, including HSR as the transport mode. Therefore, there is still an ample room to study the relationship between HSR and tourism growth, applying discrete choice analysis using stated preference data.

Jou and Chen (2020) found that HSR services can foster tourism demand and proposed two main recommendations: (1) in terms of HSR operations, more intense related promotions and marketing campaigns should be developed involving the HSR companies, hotel associations, destination marketing officers and other stakeholders interested in local developments such as special events associated to festivals, carnival, sports, and religious festivities; and (2) the interior or exterior of some particular trains could be painted in order to promote special events aimed at enhancing tourism growth associated with HSR. In this sense, it is extremely important to analyse tourist preferences and willingness to pay (WTP) for these types of services, focusing mainly on the level of integration between HSR, hotels and some important attractions, as well as the ease of buying these new products. It is expected that the adoption rates of the new tourism products could be affected by some socio-demographic variables that need to be considered. For example, people who are younger, have had more years of education and are more technologically competent, and who live or stay near HSR stations, are more likely to buy these new products in comparison with the counterpart segment formed by older and less technological competent citizens who either live or stay in suburban areas.

Pattanaro (2020) reviewed the most relevant literature on rail tourism, principally highlighting the link between rail tourism and sustainability. The author also analysed the implemented tools and initiatives of three national train operating companies, in France, Switzerland and Italy, respectively. Three different information sources are analysed by the author for each of the companies included in the study: (1) the corporate sustainability strategy; (2) the business-to-consumer (B2C) website; and (3) the digital or printed promotional material provided to potential or actual passengers. The emphasis is then changed towards attracting responsible tourists in order to understand the main actions and initiatives that need to be addressed by HSR operators in the strategy of attracting more tourists. Thus, responsible or green tourists could be defined as those who are willing to change previous mobility habits with more eco-friendly options. Thus, it is interesting that the three corporate sustainability strategies made an explicit reference to the Paris Agreement on Climate Change and the UN 2030 Agenda for Sustainable Development with its 17 Sustainable Development Goals. The carbon emissions of a particular trip are compared with those of other transport modes such as private car and plane. Thus, the estimated figures of emission savings are reported in the digital and printed version of the train tickets in Italy. The author also found that multi-operators and multi-experience tour packages have been developed by the companies, including hotels, car rentals or sharing systems, luggage shipping, museums and guided tours.

As mentioned, it seems that HSR operators have not fully exploited the concept of green tourism in order to identify the needs of the tourists and the evolution of this market segment. Pattanaro (2020) advised the companies to establish an online survey in order to get more information about tourist profiles. In addition, rail tourism needs to be further studied in order to deepen the knowledge about: (1) the way in which the concept of responsible tourists could be targeted; (2) what kind of potential networking and partnership activities with specialised tour operators could be developed; and (3) which type of measures and indicators could be used to monitor the performance of responsible HSR-tourism initiatives.

Opportunities and challenges with these trends and issues

An integrated approach between transportation systems facilitating intermodality, such as rail and air services, should represent an important topic to be discussed in terms of the Sustainable Development Goals it can foster. It is considered a valid solution to the several transport problems that modern societies face (e.g., rising levels of accidents, emissions, and noise from transport) and plays an important role by enabling better mobility for travellers (Pagliara et al., 2021).

Intermodality at airports can involve a combination of: (1) accessibility to airports: local services between the airport and the neighbouring city (e.g., via train); (2) complementary feeder services between the airport and the different parts of the surrounding region (mainly provided by buses, conventional trains, and more recently HSTs); (3) competing services between major city centres of neighbouring regions; and (4) alternative services that fully replace airline feeder services to airports (in general, for those services of less than three hours' train ride).

Partial or full substitution for air can be considered successful on short- or medium-haul journeys of up to three hours provided by a high speed train (e.g., between Brussels and Paris). In this case, the train link can also be used to complement air travel, which can be used for the return journey or even at the beginning or end of an intercontinental flight, thus requiring that rail and air schedules, fares, and other transport facilities are carefully coordinated (www.atag.org).

D'Alfonso et al. (2016) built a duopoly model to evaluate the environmental effects of HSR–air transport competition, capturing the effects of induced demand, schedule frequency and HSR speed. They demonstrated that the net environmental impact could be negative since there was a trade-off between the substitution effect – the number of passengers using the HSR who had been shifted from air transport – and the traffic generation effect – the additional demand that was generated by the HSR.

Indeed, for the case of the London–Paris market, served by HSR, they showed that the introduction of HSR was detrimental to local air pollution (LAP), while it was beneficial to greenhouse-gas (GHG) emissions. HSR entry increased neither LAP nor GHG emissions when the ratio between HSR and air transport emissions was relatively low. LAP pollutants include hydrocarbons (HC), carbon monoxide (CO), oxides of nitrogen (NOx), sulphur dioxide (SO2), and particulates (PM). The impact on climate change is mainly due to GHG emissions such as carbon dioxide (CO_2) (Seinfeld and Pandis, 2012). In general, HSR operations are not considered to contribute significantly to climate change due to lower emission rates of CO_2.

Since the magnitude of the environmental friendliness of HSR compared to air transport hinges on the mix of energy sources used to generate the electricity (which is heavily constrained by the country in which HSR operates), regulators should assess the implications of HSR entry considering the energy policy and mitigation strategies available to transport modes.

Catalysts, stakeholders, business and policy implications

HSR has been proven to be a catalyst for tourism (Bonnafous, 1987) as the new transport mode reduced the average travel time between the main cities of countries that have developed such networks. HSR stations can also play a determinant role in boosting tourism for some cities, as the quality of the HSR network depends also on the accessibility to HSR stations. In this sense, tourism can be benefitted from the reduction of the inter-city travel time, but the benefits can be offset if HSR stations are not well connected to city centres or tourist attractions by public transport. In addition, it is well known that HSR fosters the possibility of visiting nearby cities in the same day so some tourists become visitors (Campa et al., 2016), and it is the value of the tourist attractions of a city, in the form of landscape, gastronomy, architectural, historical and cultural heritage, and special events and festivals, which becomes fundamental for increasing the length of the stay in the cities.

As previously stated, HSR companies need to recognise the potential of tourism development to attract visitors, so they will be the main stakeholder to develop an adequate strategy in the tour-package formation with other important stakeholders. The development of tour packages using HSR as a transport mode can also be a DMO manager initiative. Some of the best practices can be seen in China, where, for example, an online travel agency (OTA), China Discovery, has developed eight different tour packages which have HSR as the main transport mode: (1) 6 Days Amazing Harbin Snow Ice Tour from Beijing by High Speed Train; (2) 9 Days Guilin Guizhou Minority Culture and Landscape Exploration by High Speed Train; (3) 14 Days Wild China Tours from Shanghai to Yunnan on Expresses; (4) 12 Days China Xiapu Mudflats Xiamen Tulou Coastal Tour by Bullet Train; (5) 15 Days Classic Ancient China Silk Road Tour with Bullet Train Experience; (6) 6 Days Xiamen Fujian Tulou & Yellow Mountain Amusing Tour; (7) 11 Days Essence of China Culture Tour by High Speed Trains; and (8) 4 Days Sanya Relaxing Holiday with Circular-island High Speed Train Experience. It is interesting to observe that, in the case of some of the tour packages, travel by HSR is seen as the most exciting part of the trip. It can be said that the interest in travel by train overcomes the need for a transport mode to an experiential form in the trip itself. It is a sort of recovery of the nostalgia for the China's Orient Express (Prideaux, 1999).

HSR has brought a renewed interest in rail as a form of boosting tourism, and it is time for the railways to regain the old glory obtained 150 years ago when Thomas Cook, the father of the modern tourism industry, used rail to carry the first organised tour from Leicester to Loughborough on 5 July 1841. Cook was principally moved by an interest on broadening the mind and improving the soul of the travellers instead of making money. The first tour package has evolved dramatically with respect to objectives, stakeholders involved, business plans, organisational procedures, and policy implications. Independent of the evolution, the revitalisation of HSR is the most important implication of such developments. The authors think that HSR tourism is still underexploited in most of the countries and China can be seen as an exception that can be further analysed. It is perhaps true that some organisational procedures can be better addressed by the peculiarities of the Chinese political regime, and that some different territorial jurisdictions make such developments more difficult in other parts of the world.

Conclusions

The "second railway age" started with the introduction and development of HSR that has fostered a revitalisation in the tourism industry for some intermediate cities connected to the new transport network. Bonnafous (1987) was the first to analyse the effects of HSR on tourism in the Paris–Lyon corridor and found a dual effect into the increasing number of visitors and the decreasing length of stay. Most of the studies have found a positive impact of HSR on tourism. However, the effects are not always present, depending also on several factors that are not intrinsically related to the transport system itself. Nevertheless, the future of transport and tourism can exploit all the existing synergies thanks to the advancement of technology (Duval, 2020).

The recent Chinese HSR development has gained academic attention, and numerous studies have found the previously mentioned positive effects of HSR on tourism, in which some central cities and metropolitan areas have become the most acknowledged winners. However, the findings in other regions of the world, especially in Europe, are not so conclusive. This inconclusiveness and mixed findings are the source of significant concerns for the development of HSR in other parts of the world such as in the U.S., India, Brazil and Australia. Four trends have been found in this chapter: (1) the positive effects are mainly observed in cities and metro areas that have already well-developed tourism markets; (2) the positive effects are mainly short-term observable in "younger" networks (e.g., China and Italy); (3) the positive effects are not sustainable in the long term and fade away with time; and (4) the contradictory evidence extracted from various regions of the world triggered the existing uncertainty regarding the development of new HSR networks in other parts of the world.

The synergies between HSR and tourism promotion depends, in large part, on the organisational capacity of different stakeholders that could be involved in developing attractive tour packages. The stakeholders list should contain the Della Corte et al. (2010) "six As", namely access (i.e., the accessibility to a location); attractions (i.e., the local attractive factors); accommodation (i.e., hotel structures); amenities (i.e., the tourist services); assemblage (i.e., the activity of tour operators) and ancillary services (i.e., agencies, offering services like tours and local institutes and supporting organisations). Tour packages can only succeed if tourist preferences are analysed and studied by highly competent DMO officials, who are the main catalysts of these new products. Organisational risks are usually the cause of a bad tour package design, and, among these, different territorial jurisdictions, which depend on the tourism laws in different countries, are cited as one of the main causes (Feliu, 2012). The author concluded that stakeholders need to pay attention to elements such as local complexity, endogenous resources, search for dialogue, mobilisation, and good management of conflicts in order to develop successful tour packages.

Jou and Chen (2020) found that the synergies between HSR and tourism might be better exploited with: (1) tour package development with marketing and promotion; and (2) special events developed in some cities could be promoted with interior or exterior paintings in some trains. Pattanaro (2020) found that ecotourism or green tourists are concepts that are not well developed in the synergies between HSR and tourism, and recommended HSR operators to analyse tourist preferences with an online survey that deals with: (1) the way in which the concept of responsible tourists could be targeted; (2) what kind of the potential networking and partnership activities with specialised tour operators could be developed; and (3) which type of measures and indicators could be used to monitor the performance of responsible HSR-tourism initiatives.

In this sense, green tourism promoted by tour packages developed with HSR as the main transport mode for inter-city mobility can also be fostered by the intermodal platforms that can be developed in the main airport gateways at a national level between air transport and HSR (Pagliara et al., 2021). Some of the best tour packages development has been found in China, where it seems that HSR is recapturing some of the old glory obtained by the iconic Orient Express. Tour package development is highly affected by factors such as objectives, stakeholder involvement, business plans, organisational procedures and political engagement. The potential synergies can be developed at its maximum if professional leaders adequately handle some existing barriers.

A visual abstract of this chapter is provided in Figure 1.1.

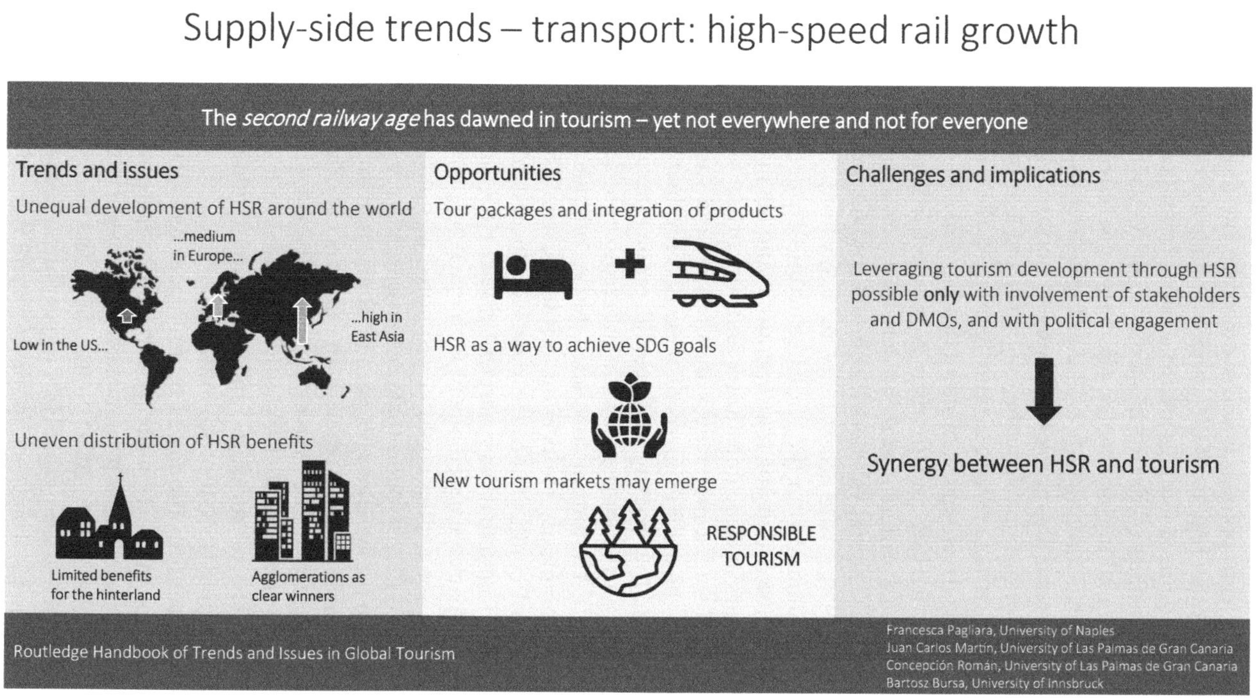

Figure 1.1 Visual abstract: High-speed rail growth.

References

Albalate, D. and Bel, G. (2012) High-speed rail: Lessons for policy makers from experiences abroad. *Public Administration Review*, 72, 336–349.

Albalate, D., Campos, J. and Jiménez, J.L. (2017) Tourism and high speed rail in Spain: Does the AVE increase local visitors? *Annals of Tourism Research*, 65, 71–82.

Albalate, D., Campos, J. and Jiménez, J.L. (2021) High-speed rail and tourism in spanish low-density areas: Not always a solution, *The Impact of Tourist Activities on Low-Density Territories: Evaluation Frameworks, Lessons, and Policy Recommendations* eds R.P. Marques, A.I. Melo, M.M. Natário and R. Biscaia, pp. 183–202. Cham: Springer International Publishing.

Albalate, D. and Fageda, X. (2016) High speed rail and tourism: Empirical evidence from Spain. *Transportation Research Part A: Policy and Practice*, 85, 174–185.

Bazin, S., Beckerich, C. and Delaplace, M. (2013) Desserte TGV et villes petites et moyennes. Une illustration par le cas du tourisme à Arras, Auray, Charleville-Mézières et Saverne. *Les Cahiers scientifiques du transport*, 63, 33–61.

Blanquart, C. and Koning, M. (2017) The local economic impacts of high-speed railways: Theories and facts. *European Transport Research Review*, 9, 12. https://doi.org/10.1007/s12544-017-0233-0

Bonnafous, A. (1987) The regional impact of the TGV. *Transportation*, 14, 127–137.

Bursa, B., Mailer, M., Axhausen, K.W. (2022) Intra-destination travel behavior of alpine tourists: A literature review on choice determinants and the survey work. *Transportation*. doi:10.1007/s11116-022-10267-y

Button, K. (2012) Is there any economic justification for high-speed railways in the United States? *Journal of Transport Geography*, 22, 300–302.

Campa, J.L., López-Lambas, M.E. and Guirao, B. (2016). High speed rail effects on tourism: Spanish empirical evidence derived from China's modelling experience. *Journal of Transport Geography*, 57, 44–54.

Campos, J. and de Rus, G. (2009) Some stylized facts about high-speed rail: A review of HSR experiences around the world. *Transport Policy*, 16, 19–28.

Carballo, R.R., León, C.J. and Carballo, M.M. (2019) Fighting overtourism in Lanzarote (Spain). *Worldwide Hospitality and Tourism Themes*, 11(5), 506–515.

Cascetta, E., Cartenì, A., Henke, I. and Pagliara, F. (2020) Economic growth, transport accessibility and regional equity impacts of high-speed railways in Italy: Ten years ex post evaluation and future perspectives. *Transportation Research Part A: Policy and Practice*, 139, 412–428.

Chandra, S. and Vadali, S. (2014) Evaluating accessibility impacts of the proposed America 2050 high-speed rail corridor for the Appalachian Region. *Journal of Transport Geography*, 37, 28–46.

Chen, J., Li, M. and Xie, C. (2022) Transportation connectivity strategies and regional tourism economy – empirical analysis of 153 cities in China. *Tourism Review*, 77(1), 113–128.

Chen, Z. (2010) Who Rides the High Speed Rail in the United States: The Acela Express Case Study, *Proceedings of the ASME Joint Rail Conference 2010: Presented at [the] ASME 2010 Joint Rail Conference, April 27-29, 2010, Urbana, Illinois, USA / sponsored by the [Rail] Transportation Division, ASME*, pp. 357–365. New York, NY: American Society of Mechanical Engineers.

Chen, Z. and Haynes, K.E. (2015) Impact of high-speed rail on international tourism demand in China. *Applied Economics Letters*, 22, 57–60.

Cheng, Y.-H. (2010) High-speed rail in Taiwan: New experience and issues for future development. *Transport Policy*, 17, 51–63.

D'Alfonso, T., Jiang, C. and Bracaglia, V. (2016). Air transport and high-speed rail competition: Environmental implications and mitigation strategies. *Transportation Research Part A: Policy and Practice*, 92, 261–276.

Delaplace, M., Bazin, S., Pagliara, F. and Sposaro, A. (2014a). *High Speed Rail System and the Tourism Market: Between Accessibility, Image and Coordination Tool.* ERSA conference papers.

Delaplace, M., Pagliara, F. and La Pietra, A. (2016). Does high-speed rail affect destination choice for tourism purpose? Disneyland Paris and Futuroscope case studies. *Belgeo*, 3, 1–23.

Delaplace, M., Pagliara, F., Perrin, J. and Mermet, S. (2014b) Can High Speed Rail foster the choice of destination for tourism purpose? *Procedia Social and Behavioral Sciences*, *111*, 166–175.

Della Corte, V., Piras, A. and Zamparelli, G. (2010) Brand and image: The strategic factors in destination marketing. *International Journal of Leisure and Tourism Marketing*, *1*(4), 358–377.

Duval, D.T. (2020). Transport and tourism: A perspective article. *Tourism Review*, *75*(1), 91–94.

EcoUnion (2021) Managing (over)tourism in natural protected areas: Learnings from national parks in Spain and Europe. Report available at https://www.ecounion.eu/portfolio/natur/

Feliu, J. (2012) High-speed rail in European medium-sized cities: Stakeholders and urban development. *Journal of Urban Planning and Development*, *138*(4), 293–302.

Gao, Y., Su, W. and Wang, K. (2019) Does high-speed rail boost tourism growth? New evidence from China. *Tourism Management*, *72*, 220–231.

Givoni, M. (2006) Development and impact of the modern high-speed train: A review. *Transport Reviews*, *26*, 593–611.

Gómez-Limón, García y García, Ventura (2014) Capacidad de acogida de uso público en los Espacios Naturales Protegidos. *Cuadernos de la Red de Parques Nacionales*, *3*, 84. Acceso desde https://www.miteco.gob.es/es/ceneam/recursos/materiales/acogida-uso-publico.aspx

Gühnemann, A., Kurzweil, A., Mailer, M. (2021) Tourism mobility and climate change – A review of the situation in Austria. *Journal of Outdoor Recreation and Tourism 34*, 100382.

Guirao, B. and Campa, J.L. (2015). The effects of tourism on HSR: Spanish empirical evidence derived from a multi-criteria corridor selection methodology. *Journal of Transport Geography*, *47*, 37–46.

Guirao, B. and Campa, J.L. (2016) Should implications for tourism influence the planning stage of a new HSR network? The experience of Spain. *The Open Transportation Journal*, *10*, 22–34.

Gutiérrez, A., Miravet, D., Saladié, Ò. and Clavé, S.A. (2020) High-speed rail, tourists' destination choice and length of stay: A survival model analysis. *Tourism Economics*, *26*, 578–597.

Hensher, D.A., Ellison, R.B. and Mulley, C. (2014) Assessing the employment agglomeration and social accessibility impacts of high speed rail in Eastern Australia. *Transportation*, *41*, 463–493.

Jou, R.C. and Chen, K.H. (2020). The Relationship between High Speed Rail and Tourism. *Sustainability*, *12*(12), 5103.

Kurihara, T. and Wu, L. (2016) The impact of high speed rail on tourism development: A case study of Japan. *The Open Transportation Journal*, *10*, 35–44.

Levinson, D.M. (2012) Accessibility impacts of high-speed rail. *Journal of Transport Geography*, *22*, 288–291.

Li, L., Lu, L., Xu, Y. and Sun, X. (2020) Influence of high-speed rail on tourist flow network in typical tourist cities: An empirical study based on the Hefei–Fuzhou high-speed rail in China. *Asia Pacific Journal of Tourism Research*, *25*, 1215–1231.

Li, M. and Chen, J. (2019) High-speed rail network in China: The contribution of fast trains to regional tourism and economic development. *Tourism Review*, *75*, 414–432.

Liu, Y. and Shi, J. (2019) How inter-city high-speed rail influences tourism arrivals: Evidence from social media check-in data. *Current Issues in Tourism*, *22*, 1025–1042.

Masson, S. and Petiot, R. (2009) Can the high speed rail reinforce tourism attractiveness? The case of the high speed rail between Perpignan (France) and Barcelona (Spain). *Technovation*, *29*(9), 611–617

Murakami, J. and Cervero, R. (2017). High-speed rail and economic development: business agglomerations and policy implications. In Blas Luis Pérez Henríquez and Elizabeth Deakin, Eds., *High-speed rail and sustainability*. London: Routledge.

Pagliara, F., Delaplace, M. and Vassallo, J.M. (2014). High-Speed trains and tourists: What is the link? Evidence from the French and Spanish capitals. *WIT Transactions and the Built Environment*, *138*, 17–27.

Pagliara, F., Delaplace, M. and Vassallo, J.M. (2015). High-speed rail systems and tourists' destination choice: The case studies of Paris and Madrid. *International Journal of Sustainable Development & Planning*, *3*, 395–405.

Pagliara, F., Martín, J.C. and Román, C. (2021) Airport network planning and its integration with the HSR system. In: Vickerman, Roger (eds.) *International Encyclopedia of Transportation. Vol. 5*, pp. 222–228. Oxford, UK: Elsevier Ltd.

Pagliara, F. and Mauriello, F. (2020) Modelling the impact of high speed rail on tourists with geographically weighted poisson regression. *Transportation Research Part A: Policy and Practice*, *132*, 780–790.

Pagliara, F., Mauriello, F. and Garofalo, A. (2017). Exploring the interdependences between High Speed Rail systems and tourism: Some evidence from Italy, *Transportation Research Part A: Policy and Practice*, *106*, 300–308.

Pattanaro, G. (2020) Getting responsible travellers on board. *WIT Transactions on Ecology and the Environment*, *248*, 117–126.

Prideaux, B. (1999) Tracks to tourism: Queensland rail joins the tourist industry. *International Journal of Tourism Research*, *1*(2), 73–86.

Ravazzoli, E., Streifeneder, T. and Cavallaro, F. (2017) The effects of the planned high-speed rail system on travel times and spatial development in the European Alps. *Mountain Research and Development*, *37*(1), 131–140.

Seinfeld, J.H. and Pandis, S.N., (2012) *Atmospheric Chemistry and Physics: From Air Pollution to Climate Change*. John Wiley & Sons Ltd., Hoboken, NJ.

Sun, Y.-Y. and Lin, Z.-W. (2018). Move fast, travel slow: The influence of high-speed rail on tourism in Taiwan. *Journal of Sustainable Tourism*, *26*(3), 433–450.

Ureña, J.M., Menerault, P. and Garmendia, M. (2009) The high-speed rail challenge for big intermediate cities: A national, regional and local perspective. *Cities*, *26*, 266–279.

Varela, V.C. and Martínez, J.N. (2016). High-speed railway and tourism: Is there an impact on intermediate cities? Evidence from two case studies in Castilla-La Mancha (Spain). *Journal of Urban & Regional Analysis*, *8*(2):133–158.

Wall, G. (2020) From carrying capacity to overtourism: A perspective article. *Tourism Review*, *75*(1), 212–215.

Wang, D.-G., Niu, Y. and Qian, J. (2018). Evolution and optimization of China's urban tourism spatial structure: A high speed rail perspective. *Tourism Management*, *64*, 218–232.

Wang, X., Huang, S., Zou, T. and Yan, H. (2012). Effects of the high speed rail network on China's regional tourism development. *Tourism Management Perspectives*, *1*, 34–38.

Yin, P., Pagliara, F. and Wilson, A. (2019) How does high-speed rail affect tourism? A case study of the capital region of China. *Sustainability*, *11*(2), 472.

Zhou, X., Chen, S. and Zhang, H. (2023). Travel on the road: does China's high-speed rail promote local tourism? *Environmental Science and Pollution Research*, *30*, 501–514.

2 New aircraft and airports

Evangelos Kilipiris and Andreas Papatheodorou

Introduction

The aviation industry is one of the main pillars of the tourism sector. The estimated revenue of the industry is more than US$220 billion (Statista, 2021) while at the same time airlines, airports and other aviation stakeholders provide 65.5 million jobs worldwide (ATAG, 2022). However, the highly competitive industry environment constantly pushes airlines and airports to implement new and innovative strategies in order to secure their financial viability. Increasing passenger flows, new trends in travel habits, the rise of competition among industry companies and the implementation of sustainability policies have been only some of the challenges which the industry has to face. Moreover, the COVID-19 health pandemic swiftly changed the perception of travel and aviation has been the most affected sector among many others related to tourism (Rahman et al., 2021). Health protocols, vaccination policies and country restrictions formed a dynamic environment in which airlines were forced to operate and survive. The aviation industry is trying to maintain its crucial role by adapting itself into an environment which is characterised by uncertainty at different levels.

Moreover, social, business and technological advancements shaped radical changes among the traditional air transport industry. Disruption of business travel, the rise of new airline business models, the introduction of new aircraft types, and new ways of travel and customer-oriented strategies pushed the industry to introduce new products and services. Airlines were confronted with the constant rise of competition, as well as fuel price increases, which led them to launch new business models; explore new revenue streams; and create modernised as well as efficient aircraft. COVID-19 forced airlines to implement new health safety protocols for their passengers and crew and implement strategies to provide the optimal onboard passenger experience. Moreover, the commitment of the industry for a more sustainable and greener future has added another layer of challenges for airlines (Karaman et al., 2018).

At the same time, airports are trying to confront the global pandemic by prioritising initiatives towards passenger health and safety. To avoid crowded terminals, airports implement strategies which will provide optimal passenger flows while at the same time ensuring the enhancement of customer experience. Moreover, airports enter in the digital era by introducing a variety of technologies (Zaharia & Pietreanu, 2018). Vaccination visas, digital passports, contactless technologies, robotics and data management systems constitute some of the integrated technologies gradually introduced in airport operations. The financial viability of airports also has a crucial role in the formulation of strategic planning. Airport aeronautical and non-aeronautical charges, slot allocation rules and revenue management tactics relate to their revenue streams. Moreover, sustainability is also a high priority issue for the airport industry.

The urgency for new and innovative strategies is now greater than ever in the aviation sector. The constant challenges force airlines and airports to grow and follow new paths which will ensure their future viability.

Airlines and safety measures for COVID-19

COVID-19 has undisputedly become a major issue for the airlines through introducing new challenges to the industry. Health protocols, vaccination policies, country travel restrictions and variants of COVID-19 developed a dynamically changing environment in which airlines had to adapt and make critical decisions in a short period of time.

The protection of passengers and crew has been an absolute priority for the airlines. At first, airlines installed new, High Efficiency Particulate Air (HEPA) filters to provide maximum air cleaning. In addition, almost every airline in the world required the use of face masks by passengers and crew members onboard. This measure was immediately introduced by airlines, after the COVID-19 breakout, for flights of any duration. Nonetheless, as vaccination levels increased worldwide, such measures gradually became optional for passengers and crew. Moreover, COVID-19 initiated the development and introduction of contemporary disinfection techniques by using UV light robots. This also helped airlines minimise ground times and optimise their turnaround timeframes. To address this matter, airlines applied strategies such as reduced onboard catering services, parking spots closer to terminals, several seating allocation tactics as well as different boarding and disembarkation procedures. Moreover, airlines requested from ground handling services companies to increase, even double, the number of their cleaning staff to reduce ground and turnaround times.

The passenger experience

The global health pandemic was responsible for the dawn of a new era regarding the way people wish to travel. Significant changes in mindset and behaviour have forced airlines and airports to introduce innovative ways to enhance the experience of their customers, on the ground and in the air. In any case, it is very important for the industry not solely to focus on the issues caused by the COVID-19 health crisis. As global air travel had constantly increased in recent decades, airlines developed new and innovative policies to provide unique onboard experiences for their passengers. Flights became an important part of passengers' entire trip experiences, thus airlines invested greatly on this matter.

The strong competition within the industry significantly decreased passenger yields over the years (IATA, 2022); as a result, airlines were forced to implement new revenue-generation strategies. In terms of new revenue streams, airlines introduced numerous ancillary revenue policies to generate more profits. Non-seat-related revenue strategies have rapidly been embraced by most airlines and now account for a major share of their total revenues (Figure 2.1).

Frequent flyer loyalty programs (FFP) have rapidly become a critical strategy for airlines to generate more profit by providing their customers several perks. For several airlines, Frequent Flyer Programs account for more than 50% of their total ancillary revenues; in the case of GOL, a Brazilian low-fare airline, this accounts for 90% of its ancillary profits (Ideaworks, 2022). Moreover, as the tourism industry continued to grow, airlines positioned

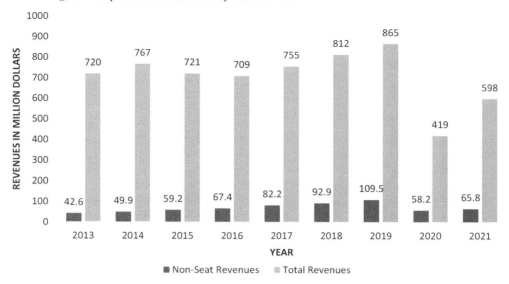

Figure 2.1 Comparison of non-seat as part of total revenues 2013–2021.
Sources: IATA (2022); Ideaworks (2022).

themselves strategically in the tourism market by collaborating with several other tourism stakeholders such as car rentals and hotel chains. Passengers have been able to book their flights as well as other tourism products regarding their destination. Taking into consideration the complexity of organising a trip, airlines took advantage of their website's traffic to offer numerous options to their customers, all in one website. Such non-flight-related ancillary strategies promptly connected with airline FFPs (Ideaworks, 2022).

The evolution of modern travel demanded the provision of better and customised services from airlines. To address the vast variety of customer needs, the industry introduced a wide range of dynamic packaging strategies. Such strategies are closely connected to flight-related ancillary revenue streams. Widely implemented by low fare airlines (LFAs), these dynamic packaging techniques include payments for products closely related to the air fare. Under such systems, airlines offer a basic air fare and charge passengers for any additional services such as baggage fees, in-flight entertainment, meals/beverages, priority boarding, seat assignment, extra legroom or lounge access (Warnock-Smith et al., 2017). Furthermore, to maximise any possible revenue, airlines also offer bundles which include a mixture of product options for their passengers.

The cabin is rapidly becoming a valued product in all types of aircraft, especially those operating on long-haul routes (Hugon-Duprat & O'Connell, 2015). The emergence of the long-haul low-fare model, as well as the introduction of ultra-long-haul flights, forced traditional airlines to enhance passenger experience at any level. Meanwhile, several studies highlight the willingness of passengers to pay more money for enhanced passenger experience (Balcombe et al., 2009). Price-sensitive business passengers, as well as comfort-minded leisure passengers, are eager to pay extra for their comfort during the flight (Claussen and O'Higgins, 2010), a fact that enabled airlines to invest more on the wide installation of premium economy seats. Airlines positioned premium economy class between economy and business class in terms of airfare, onboard services, comfort. Mostly embraced by international travellers (Jeon & Lee, 2020), the premium economy proved to be a successful strategy for airlines due to the value-for-money feeling it provides. Moreover, Kuo and Jou (2017) argued that travellers are willing to pay more for an upgrade to premium economy class, even for a short-haul flight. In terms of airline economics, the establishment of premium economy class fills the considerable price gap between economy and business class by providing an alternative for airlines to attract a greater market share.

COVID-19 has deeply affected the air transport industry and set new standards for the airlines. The new norms require from airlines and passengers to follow health safety guidelines and measures, a fact that rapidly made airlines to modify their onboard products and services. Passenger experience ushers in a new era and differs dramatically from what passengers were familiar with. The use of masks during flights has been one of the measures rapidly adopted by the industry. Interacting with the passengers has always been a major part of the experience in the cabin (KPMG, 2020). Especially in the premium cabins, where customised services are a main part of the experience, the lack of personalisation has downgraded the offering. In terms of onboard catering services, the pandemic has formed a new dynamic environment by introducing protocols which elevated catering standards in terms of safety, cleaning and sanitising (Inflight Catering Market, 2022). The introduction of such tactics deeply affected the onboard catering processes, and thus also the passenger experience. To address the issue, airlines formed tier-based complimentary onboard services schemes by providing the optimal food experience to high- and low-value customers.

The uncertainty, as well as the change of onboard services, created a difficult environment for airlines. To restore passenger confidence and optimal passenger experience, the airline industry needs to enact several strategies built on seven main pillars, i.e., integrity, resolution, expectations, empathy, personalisation, time, and effort (KPMG, 2020). Moreover, COVID-19 forced airlines to upgrade the onboard passenger experience by investing in digitalisation and connectivity. WiFi connectivity in every class of service, the installation of IFE systems (In-Flight Entertainment), contactless technology and tailor-made services linked to passengers' social media represent some examples of strategies applied to enhance the passenger experience. The pandemic forced airlines to accept and take advantage of digital solutions and transform their products at every level. Digitalisation of the industry is a breakthrough and passenger experience can be highly affected by such strategies. Airlines have already integrated numerous digital approaches into their action plans and now is the turn for airports to embrace similar blueprints.

Environmental sustainability and the new aircraft era

As already discussed, the constant advance of technology is closely related to the future development of the air transport sector. Simultaneously, the evolution of travel standards, the constant surge of fuel prices, the establishment of new airline business models as well as industry's commitment to carbon footprint reduction, pushed aircraft manufacturers to make substantial investments in the introduction of new and more efficient types of aircraft. The airline industry accounts for 2% of global carbon emissions (ATAG, 2022) and major strategies have been implemented for the industry to reach its goal of net zero-carbon footprint by 2050 (IATA, 2022). In the last 30 years, the airline industry achieved to reduce its carbon emissions by 53% (Airbus, 2022); however, only 13% of total passenger traffic is serviced by new-generation aircraft. Aircraft manufacturers agree on the fact that the industry has, more than ever before, embraced the concept of sustainability which justifies the extensive decision for fleet modernisation. This is closely connected to reduced fuel consumption (IATA, 2022) as more efficient engines have been introduced into the market. Aircraft engine manufacturers constantly seek to develop new technologies for more efficient engine options for jet and turboprop aircraft (Kellner, 2021).

However, the relatively lower fuel consumption and emissions have not been the only alternative which the industry relies on for a more sustainable future. IATA (2021) identified that sustainable aviation fuels (SAF) will be the main driver for the airline industry's effort to reduce emissions even by 80%. Most recently, Airbus introduced its prototype hydrogen-powered aircraft, which projected encouraging results. In addition, significant funds have been invested on the development of all-electric passenger aircraft with companies already presenting their prototypes (Korn, 2022).

At the same time, more efficient engines installed in smaller aircraft provide the opportunity for airlines to greatly expand their network. Thus, numerous airlines, such as TAP Portugal and JetBlue, started to operate transatlantic or transcontinental flights using smaller, more economical, single-aisle aircraft. It is estimated that more than 75% of future aircraft demand will be for small aircraft (Airbus, 2022). Due to the efficiency and range advantages, such aircraft can benefit airlines which use the hub-and-spoke model while they can also expand their regional network of services.

Moreover, the introduction of more efficient aircraft initiated the establishment of new airline business models as well as new routes. The viability of the long-haul low fare airlines, such as the Singapore-based Scoot, relies on the economics of such single-aisle aircraft which provide wide range and low fuel consumption. Under these circumstances, long-haul low-fare airlines can implement their fare strategies and serve long-distance destinations at the same time. Direct flights from Sydney to London with Qantas and Singapore to New York with Singapore Airlines are examples of the emergence of a new era on long-haul travel. In addition, Bauer et al. (2020) argue that ultra-long-haul business model emerged through the pandemic as passengers were concerned about using connecting airports. The appearance of ultra-long-haul travels introduced not only more efficient but also faster aircraft. Supersonic passenger travel may prove financially viable in the future with airlines like United Airlines to commit to this effort (Fox, 2021).

Finally, the use of unmanned aerial vehicles (UAVs) for urban mobility and cargo operations presents disruptive results for the industry. Mostly introduced by cargo companies, UAVs have been presented as the future of delivery operations, although they are still at an initial stage. Moreover, passenger-grade autonomous aerial vehicles have significant development potential; however, commercial introduction at a wide scale may prove rather difficult any time soon (Konopka, 2022). In essence, new technology trends have been witnessed in the industry while the adoption of new contemporary strategies by aircraft manufacturers reveal major future opportunities for airlines. Moreover, the new greener aircraft types and engines justify the airlines' commitment towards the industry's development of sustainable goals. At the same time, more aviation stakeholders, such as airports, invest towards the same principles.

The digital age of airports

The airport sector continuously experiences rapid and disruptive changes. The strong bargaining position of many airlines, as well as competition from rival airports, creates ar range of business challenges. In addition, customer expectations are constantly surging due to rapid advancements in mobile and digital technologies (Amadeus, 2018). To meet these challenges, airports introduce and implement several strategies which will ensure their digital transformation. The Airports Council International (ACI, 2021) underlines the importance of airports' digital transformation and points out the urgency for a holistic integration across all airport segments.

Digital transformation is mostly focused on the evolution of the passenger experience. By adapting new technologies, airports are able to offer optimal services for their customers. Automation technologies are becoming widely installed in airports to achieve less crowded terminals and to retain a smooth passenger flow. Common examples of automation processes include the self-check kiosks as well as the customs control equipment instruments, which provide the fundamentals for stable passenger flows and avoidance of crowded terminals. Most recently, automation processes have been installed on baggage handling systems (Shen et al., 2020) through the use of automated guided vehicles (AGVs) and RFID technology. The adoption of similar strategies is closely connected to the "Airport 4.0" strategy which many airports have included into their business plans (International Airport Review, 2022). This strategy embraces the implementation of digital solutions for optimal airport management while at the same time providing passengers with useful information (Halpern et al., 2021).

In particular, Airport 4.0 promotes the extensive use of the latest digital technologies regarding augmented reality, biometric access control, artificial intelligence, virtual or robotic assistants inside the terminals and 'non-stop' passage through security and customs screening (Frost & Sullivan, 2018). The application of such technologies provides opportunities for airport managers to introduce contemporary solutions for an optimal passenger experience. In terms of operations, airport managers can monitor passenger flows, manage autonomous vehicles, provide aircraft guidance via virtual control towers, use drones to inspect the airfield and, most importantly, maintain continuous interaction with the traveller.

Social media have been used extensively by airlines to attract a greater audience, provide information, interact with passengers or even as revenue streams. The importance of social media has also been promptly recognised by airports. According to CAPA (2013), airports launched several social media strategies to reduce their operational costs and increase opportunities for the commercialisation of non-aeronautical profits and higher engagement with passengers. The COVID-19 crisis created a fruitful environment for airports to optimise their use of social media strategies. It is widely accepted by airport managers that social media represent a useful tool for airports to face serious challenges (Simplifying, 2019). Loyalty establishment, creation of a brand name, crisis management situations and enhancement of customer services are among the advantages which are provided by social media.

Moreover, this unlimited flow of information through social media created the phenomenon of social media big data (Stieglitz et al., 2018), which provide essential information about user profiles and habits. Airports can formulate customised products for their passengers and directly promote specific services by using essential information connected to their customers' social media profiles. In addition, the use of big data provides the opportunity for airports to develop and execute their strategic plans more accurately. The massive availability of data should be an opportunity for airports to connect with their customers at a personal level while at the same time those data can provide numerous opportunities for airports to introduce new revenue streams.

Airport aeronautical and non-aeronautical revenue streams

The constant pressure for airports to become financially self-sufficient and to pursue profit maximisation through their aeronautical, as well as their non-aeronautical, revenue streams (Zhang & Zhang, 1997) has forced them to establish a variety of revenue strategies. The COVID-19 pandemic strongly impacted the airport industry and, after years of consistent and robust growth in global passenger traffic, world airports are now on the same level as 25 years ago (ACI, 2022a). In addition, the strong competition between airports, as well as the development of many regional airports, has formed an extremely difficult environment for financial viability. Hence, revenue maximisation has been essential for airports.

Aeronautical revenues count for 55% of industry revenues (ACI, 2019) and airports are heavily dependent on them (Figure 2.2). Airport charges, one of airports' aeronautical streams of profit, have been a major challenge for the industry. In many countries, charges imposed by the largest airports are regulated while medium or small-scale airports are free to pursue their own pricing strategy (Conti et al., 2019). This way of separating airports has become an issue as airports lose their advantage of negotiation while the balance of power tilts towards airlines as they have the option of choosing. The COVID-19 pandemic has deeply affected the airport industry as it lost 50% of its revenues while fixed costs remain a major challenge for airports. Moreover, a specific regulatory framework has been introduced to achieve a more efficient aviation ecosystem (ACI, 2021).

Slot management has been significantly discussed as a major issue at airports. In previous years, the surge of passenger volumes, in combination with the limited airport capacity, created an imbalance which led to exceptional terminal congestion as well as flight delays (Madas & Zografos, 2010). Moreover, airport slots were highly regulated and restrictions were applied due to the passenger volume. Airports addressed this issue by introducing demand management measures in the form of slot allocation; however, the global scenery changed dramatically during the pandemic. The industry witnessed a rapid decrease of

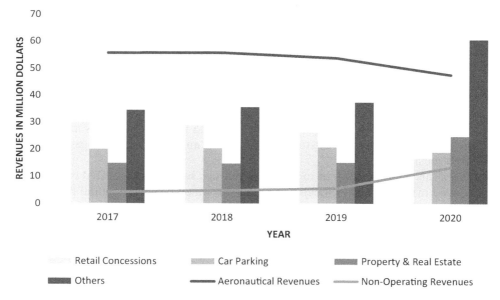

Figure 2.2 Comparison of aeronautical, non-operating and non-aeronautical revenues.
Source: ACI, 2022; WSP, 2021.

international passenger traffic while at the same time domestic traffic was less affected. Governments lifted restrictions on airport slot usage, especially in hub airports, to speed up the airport traffic recovery process (Hou, Wang & Yang, 2021). At the same time, in Europe and the US the relocation of airport slots, from major to regional airports, is an alternative that is widely considered. Thus, both airports can benefit in terms of fast traffic recovery.

Moreover, airports are also heavily dependent on their non-aeronautical revenue streams. Figure 2.2 presents a clear overview of the significance of non-aeronautical revenues for the financial viability of the airport industry. Retail concessions, car parking and real estate represent the major share of the non-aeronautical revenue sources for airports and even during the pandemic they produced significant profits (ACI, 2022b). However, the travel standards have changed dramatically due to COVID-19 restrictions while at the same time passengers developed a social distancing lifestyle. Thus, in the future, airports will be forced to optimise their non-aeronautical profits by introducing new strategies in terms of airport space management. The concept of revenue management application in airports has been an issue of discussion (Papayiannis et al., 2018; Klein et al., 2020), with applications mostly for airport car parking. Moreover, similar applications can be applied into lounges, duty-free shops as well as restaurants.

As an emerging trend, many cities around the world recognising the convenient location of their airports, as well as their opportunities to attract more commercial activities, have initiated major developments around them (Kidokoro & Zhang, 2022). The term airport-city describes the extended development of non-aeronautical-related facilities around an airport. Airport-cities accommodate a wide variety of facilities and businesses such as hotels, logistics centres, tax-free zones (Abu Dhabi Airport, Manchester Airport), academies and learning centres (Gulf Centre for Aviation Studies at Abu Dhabi Airport), and health as well as major convention centres (Hong Kong International Airport, Stockholm Arlanda).

Airport sustainability practices

Sustainability is a long-term endeavour to which airports have committed at a major level (ICAO, 2022). Following airlines' example, the airport industry constantly seeks to introduce, and finally implement, strategies towards a more sustainable future of operations. The application of sustainability strategies can deeply affect airports on a multidimensional scale. Master planning procedures, operations and maintenance can prove potential challenges for managers when sustainability tactics are adopted (Monsalud et al., 2015). However, the complexity of a system such as an airport requires encompassing a variety of strategies on different levels.

The reduction of carbon emissions has been the main target of the industry towards sustainability. Through the Airport Carbon Accreditation Programme, the industry set specific targets which include actions regarding environmental airport charges, stakeholders' strong involvement and monitoring as well as specific measures towards mitigation of the environmental impacts of airports (EASA, 2021). Vehicle fleet, airport infrastructure, environmental management systems, airport surface access as well as energy solutions represent strategic areas for concentration and action.

Conclusions

The air transport sector has been one of the most competitive industries. In this constantly changing environment, airlines and airports, aim to implement contemporary strategies which will ensure their future financial viability. COVID-19 has been a major challenge for the industry by creating a dynamically changing scenery.

From the airlines' perspective, introducing safety measures to prevent any spread of the virus was crucial. New disinfection technologies, protective measures and vaccination policies were only a few of the strategies adopted by airlines. In addition, the continuous competition, as well as new travel models, forced airlines to invest greatly in passenger experience strategies and new revenue streams. The introduction of new products and onboard services initiates a new era for passengers' experience in the cabin while the heavily implemented ancillary revenue strategies ensure revenue maximisation for the airline. Airlines are at the forefront of discussion regarding sustainability issues within the industry. The reduction of carbon emissions put the pressure on aircraft manufacturers which they introduced new-generation aircraft, from an efficiency and a technological point of view. Simultaneously, the presentation of operative aircraft using hydrogen, plans for electric aircraft and the extensive use of UAVs reflect industry's commitment to a more sustainable future. At last, the reinstating of supersonic commercial flights shapes a contemporary new business environment.

Airports have been a major pillar of the aviation industry and equally affected by the global health pandemic. To address the new normal, airports adopted and introduced a holistic digital profile. The digital transformation of an airport greatly impacts its operational and commercial sector. Robotics, artificial intelligence, and automated systems are some of the new technologies embraced by the airports to address baggage handling, customs, and passenger flow issues. Furthermore, the enhancement of passenger experience rapidly became a matter of significance for airports. As airport customers evolve into digital travellers and extensively use their social media, airports leveraged from their use and established strategies towards passenger experience, data management and revenue generation. However, the airports' financial viability has been at the centre of discussion, due to the pandemic. New regulations on airport charges, as well as slot allocation strategies, were introduced by the industry regulators to secure their economic future. Moreover, the airport industry implemented several sustainability strategies to reduce its carbon footprint and invest on a greener future.

The aviation industry represents a major part of the global supply and tourism chain. The crucial position of air transportation initiated major breakthroughs with great impact at every operational level among most of the industries. The influential role of aviation should be carefully considered by all stakeholders and collocate with the promotion of new technologies, strategies and ideas for the future.

References

ACI (2019) *ACI Economics Report affirms the importance of non-aeronautical revenues for airports' financial sustainability – ACI World*. ACI World. (2019). Retrieved 1 June 2022, from https://aci.aero/2019/03/28/aci-economics-report-affirms-the-importance-of-non-aeronautical-revenues-for-airports-financial-sustainability/

ACI. (2022a). *A glimpse into airports' financial activities during the first year of the pandemic – ACI Insights. ACI Insights.* Retrieved 1 February 2022, from https://blog.aci.aero/a-first-in-depth-look-into-airports-financial-activities-during-the-first-year-of-the-pandemic/#:~:text=In%202020%2C%20aeronautical%20revenue%20continued,of%20the%20total%20(down%206

ACI. (2022b). *Non-aeronautical revenues: Diversify and grow*. Airport World. Retrieved 1 June 2022, from https://airport-world.com/non-aeronautical-revenues-diversify-and-grow/#:~:text=Meanwhile%2C%20with%20greater%20immunity%20from,a%2019.1%25%20share%20in%202020

Airbus Global Market Forecast 2021–2040. Airbus.com. (2022). Retrieved 1 June 2022, from https://www.airbus.com/sites/g/files/jlcbta136/files/2021-11/Airbus-Global-Market-Forecast-2021-2040.pdf

Airline Industry Statistics Confirm 2020 Was Worst Year on Record. Iata.org. (2021). Retrieved 1 June 2022, from https://www.iata.org/en/pressroom/pr/2021-08-03-01/

Airport Charges: Challenging the Conventional Wisdom – ACI Insights. ACI Insights. (2021). Retrieved 1 July 2022, from https://blog.aci.aero/airport-charges-challenging-the-conventional-wisdom

Airport digital transformation. Amadeus.com. (2018). Retrieved 1 June 2022, from https://amadeus.com/documents/en/airports/research-report/airports-digital-transformation.pdf

Airports | European Aviation Environmental Report. Easa.europa.eu. (2022). Retrieved 1 June 2022, from https://www.easa.europa.eu/eaer/climate-change/airports

Airports save over 170,000 tonnes of CO2 emissions. Aviationbenefits.org. (2022). Retrieved 1 June 2022, from https://aviationbenefits.org/case-studies/airports-save-over-170-000-tonnes-of-co2-emissions

ATAG. (2022). *Sustainable Development Goals and Aviation*. Aviationbenefits.org. Retrieved 1 February 2022, from https://aviationbenefits.org/un-sustainable-development-goals/sustainable-development-goals-and-aviation/

Atag.org. (2020). *Facts & figures*. Retrieved 1 June 2022, from https://www.atag.org/facts-figures.html.

Atag.org. (2022). *Facts & figures*. Retrieved 1 June 2022, from https://www.atag.org/facts-figures.html

Aviation: Benefits Beyond Borders 2020. Aviationbenefits.org. (2020). Retrieved 1 July 2022, from https://aviationbenefits.org/downloads/aviation-benefits-beyond-borders-2020

Balcombe, K., Fraser, I., & Harris, L. (2009). Consumer willingness to pay for in-flight service and comfort levels: A choice experiment. *Journal Of Air Transport Management*, *15*(5), 221–226. https://doi.org/10.1016/j.jairtraman.2008.12.005

Bauer, L., Bloch, D., & Merkert, R. (2020). Ultra-Long-Haul: An emerging business model accelerated by COVID-19. *Journal of Air Transport Management*, *89*, 101901. https://doi.org/10.1016/j.jairtraman.2020.101901

CAPA – Centre for Aviation. (2013). *CAPA-SITA Report: Indian air passengers ready to embrace self-service, mobile and social media*. Retrieved 1 June 2022, from https://centreforaviation.com/analysis/reports/capa-sita-report-indian-air-passengers-ready-to-embrace-self-service-mobile-technologies-and-socia-130824

Claussen, J., & O'Higgins, E. (2010). Competing on value: Perspectives on business class aviation. *Journal of Air Transport Management*, *16*(4), 202–208. https://doi.org/10.1016/j.jairtraman.2010.01.005

Conti, M., Ferrara, A., & Ferraresi, M. (2019). Did the EU Airport Charges Directive lead to lower aeronautical charges? Empirical evidence from a diff-in-diff research design. *Economics of Transportation*, *17*, 24–39. https://doi.org/10.1016/j.ecotra.2018.12.001

European Union Aviation Safety Agency (EASA). (2021). Aviation environmental impacts, https://www.easa.europa.eu/eco/eaer/topics/aviation-environmental-impacts

Fox, C. (2021). United plans supersonic passenger flights by 2029. *BBC News*. Retrieved 1 June 2022, from https://www.bbc.com/news/technology-57361193

Frost, & Sullivan. (2018). *Digital Transformation Of Airport Airside Operations Airports Invest In Digitalisation Of Airside Operations To Achieve Operational Efficiencies And Reduce Impact Of Disruptions*. Adbsafegate.com. Retrieved 1 June 2022, from https://adbsafegate.com/media/9744/digital-transformation-of-airport-airside-operations-white-paper.pdf

Halpern, N., Mwesiumo, D., Suau-Sanchez, P., Budd, T., & Bråthen, S. (2021). Segmentation of passenger preferences for using digital technologies at airports. *Journal of Air Transport Management*, *91*(102005), 113. https://doi.org/10.1016/j.jairtraman.2020.102005

Hou, M., Wang, K., & Yang, H. (2021). Hub airport slot Re-allocation and subsidy policy to speed up air traffic recovery amid COVID-19 pandemic – case on the Chinese airline market. *Journal of Air Transport Management*, *93*, 102047. https://doi.org/10.1016/j.jairtraman.2021.102047

Hugon-Duprat, C., & O'Connell, J. (2015). The rationale for implementing a premium economy class in the long haul markets – Evidence from the transatlantic market. *Journal of Air Transport Management, 47*, 11–19. https://doi.org/10.1016/j.jairtraman.2015.03.005

IATA. (2021). *2050: Net-zero carbon emissions*. Airlines.iata.org. Retrieved 1 June 2022, from https://airlines.iata.org/analysis/2050-net-zero-carbon-emissions#:~:text=At%20the%2077th%20IATA%20Annual,sustainably%20is%20not%20an%20option

IATA. (2022). *Re-fleeting helps reduce CO2 emissions*. Iata.org. Retrieved 1 June 2022, from https://www.iata.org/en/iata-repository/publications/economic-reports/re-fleeting-helps-reduce-co2-emissions

ICAO. (2022). *Airport Carbon Accreditation – Empowering Airports to Reduce Their Emissions*. Icao.int. Retrieved 1 June 2022, from https://www.icao.int/environmental-protection/Documents/EnvironmentalReports/2019/ENVReport2019_pg168-170.pdf

Ideaworks. (2022). *The 2021 Car Trawler Yearbook of Ancillary Revenue*. Ideaworkscompany.com. Retrieved 1 June 2022, from https://ideaworkscompany.com/wp-content/uploads/2021/09/2021-Ancillary-Revenue-Yearbook.pdf

Industry Statistics Fact Sheet. IATA. (2020). Retrieved 1 June 2022, from https://www.iata.org/en/iata-repository/publications/economic-reports/airline-industry-economic-performance-june-2020-data-tables/

Inflight Catering Market. (2022). *Inflight Catering Market – Growth, Trends, COVID-19 Impact, and Forecasts (2022–2027)*. Researchandmarkets.com. Retrieved 1 June 2022, from https://www.researchandmarkets.com/reports/4756858/inflight-catering-market-growth-trends-COVID

International Airport Review. (2022). *Digitalisation, sustainability and resilience: The keys to recovery*. internationalairportreview.com. Retrieved 1 June 2022, from https://www.internationalairportreview.com/article/157864/digitalisation-sustainability-resilience-recovery/

Jeon, M., & Lee, J. (2020). Estimation of willingness-to-pay for premium economy class by type of service. *Journal of Air Transport Management, 84*, 101788. doi: 10.1016/j.jairtraman.2020.101788

Karaman, A.S., Kilic, M. and Uyar, A. (2018). Sustainability reporting in the aviation industry: worldwide evidence. *Sustainability Accounting, Management and Policy Journal, 9*(4), 362–391. https://doi.org/10.1108/SAMPJ-12-2017-0150

Kellner, T. (2021). *The Future Of Flight: Engine-Maker Unveils New Technology Development Program To Cut CO_2 Emissions By 20% | GE News*. Ge.com. Retrieved 1 June 2022, from https://www.ge.com/news/reports/the-future-of-flight-engine-maker-unveils-new-technology-development-program-to-cut-co2

Kidokoro, Y., & Zhang, A. (2022). Airport cities and social welfare. *Transportation Research Part B: Methodological, 158*, 187–209. https://doi.org/10.1016/j.trb.2021.12.010

Klein, R., Koch, S., Steinhardt, C., & Strauss, A. (2020). A review of revenue management: Recent generalizations and advances in industry applications. *European Journal of Operational Research, 284*(2), 397–412. https://doi.org/10.1016/j.ejor.2019.06.034

Konopka, B. (2022). *Europe's first 'passenger drone' takes to the skies*. Thefirstnews.com. Retrieved 1 June 2022, from https://www.thefirstnews.com/article/is-it-a-bird-is-it-a-plane-no-its-a-jetson-one-europes-first-passenger-drone-takes-to-the-skies-27156

Korn, J. (2022). Alice, the first all-electric passenger airplane, takes flight. *CNN Business*, https://www.cnn.com/2022/09/27/tech/eviation-alice-first-flight/index.html

KPMG. (2020). *Customer experience in the new reality*. KPMG ASSETS. Retrieved 1 May 2022, from https://assets.kpmg/content/dam/kpmg/campaigns/global-cee-project/pdf/customer-experience-in-new-reality-airlines-sector-v2.pdf

Kuo, C., & Jou, R. (2017). Willingness to pay for airlines' premium economy class: The perspective of passengers. *Journal of Air Transport Management, 59*, 134–142. https://doi.org/10.1016/j.jairtraman.2016.12.005

Losses Reduce but Challenges Continue – Cumulative $201 Billion Losses for 2020–2022. Iata.org. (2022). Retrieved 1 June 2022, from https://www.iata.org/en/pressroom/2021-releases/2021-10-04-01/

Lovell, T. (2022). Swiss startup trials UV light cleaning robots to make air travel safer. MobiHealthNews. Retrieved 20 February 2022 from: https://www.mobihealthnews.com/news/emea/swiss-startup-trials-uv-light-cleaning-robots-make-air-travel-safer

de Lucas, M. (2018). *Digital maturity matters in a competitive airport landscape, Amadeus*, https://amadeus.com/en/insights/blog/digital-maturity-airport-landscape

Madas, M., & Zografos, K. (2010). Airport slot allocation: A time for change?. *Transport Policy*, *17*(4), 274–285. https://doi.org/10.1016/j.tranpol.2010.02.002

Monsalud, A., Ho, D., & Rakas, J. (2015). Greenhouse gas emissions mitigation strategies within the airport sustainability evaluation process. *Sustainable Cities and Society*, *14*, 414–424. https://doi.org/10.1016/j.scs.2014.08.003

O'Connell, J., & Williams, G. (2011). *Air Transport in the 21st Century* (1st ed.). London: Routledge.

Papayiannis, A., Johnson, P., Yumashev, D., & Duck, P. (2018). Revenue management of airport car parks in continuous time. *IMA Journal of Management Mathematics*, *30*(1), 1–35. https://doi.org/10.1093/imaman/dpy015

Rahman, M., Gazi, M., Bhuiyan, M., & Rahaman, M. (2021). Effect of COVID-19 pandemic on tourist travel risk and management perceptions. *PLOS ONE*, *16*(9), e0256486. https://doi.org/10.1371/journal.pone.0256486

Schultz, M., Evler, J., Asadi, E., Preis, H., Fricke, H., & Wu, C. (2020). Future aircraft turnaround operations considering post-pandemic requirements. *Journal of Air Transport Management*, *89*, 101886. https://doi.org/10.1016/j.jairtraman.2020.101886

Shen, K., Li, C., Xu, D., Wu, W., & Wan, H. (2020). Sensor-network-based navigation of delivery robot for baggage handling in international airport. *International Journal of Advanced Robotic Systems*, *17*(4), 172988142094473. https://doi.org/10.1177/1729881420944734

Simplifying. (2019). *Airlines' Priorities & Budget Forecast For Social Media 2019 – Simplifying*. Simplifying. Retrieved 1 June 2022, from http://simpliflying.com/2018/airline-social-media-outlook-2019.

Statista. (2021). *Worldwide revenue with passengers in air traffic 2005–2022 | Statista*. Retrieved 1 June 2022, from https://www.statista.com/statistics/263042/worldwide-revenue-with-passengers-in-air-traffic/

Stieglitz, S., Mirbabaie, M., Ross, B., & Neuberger, C. (2018). Social media analytics – Challenges in topic discovery, data collection, and data preparation. *International Journal of Information Management*, *39*, 156–168. https://doi.org/10.1016/j.y2017.12.002

Teixeira, F.P., Higa, F.M., Jakabi, R.M., & Ribeiro, R.M. (2020). COVID 19 Impact on Aircraft Ground Time at Congonhas Airport (CGH). Retrieved from https://commons.erau.edu/brazil-graduate-works/13

The impact of COVID-19 on the airport business – and the path to recovery – ACI World. ACI World. (2022). Retrieved 1 July 2022, from https://aci.aero/2022/02/24/the-impact-of-COVID-19-on-the-airport-business-and-the-path-to-recovery-4/

Warnock-Smith, D., O'Connell, J., & Maleki, M. (2017). An analysis of ongoing trends in airline ancillary revenues. *Journal of Air Transport Management*, *64*, 42–54. https://doi.org/10.1016/j.jairtraman.2017.06.023

Wiegmann, A., & Miller, J. (2021). *Swiss robots use UV light to zap viruses aboard passenger planes*. REUTERS. Retrieved 1 June 2022, from https://www.reuters.com/article/us-health-coronavirus-swiss-robot-idUSKBN2BO4OX

WSP. (2021). *Fuelling Airport Recovery Via Non-Aeronautical Revenue*. WSPglobal. Retrieved 1 May 2022, from https://www.wsp.com/en-SA/insights/fuelling-airport-recovery-via-non-aeronautical-revenue

Zaharia, S., & Pietreanu, C. (2018). Challenges in airport digital transformation. *Transportation Research Procedia*, *35*, 90–99. https://doi.org/10.1016/j.trpro.2018.12.016

Zhang, A., & Zhang, Y. (1997). Concession revenue and optimal airport pricing. *Transportation Research Part E: Logistics And Transportation Review*, *33*(4), 287–296. https://doi.org/10.1016/s1366-5545(97)00029-x

3 Cruise lines
Market growth and diversification

Michael Clancy

Introduction

Cruise ship tourism constitutes one of the fastest-growing segments of global tourism. Worth some $35.8 billion in 2018, it has doubled in size each decade since 1990 (Kizielewicz, 2019; MacNeill & Wozniak, 2018). In 2019, the last full year prior to the COVID-19 pandemic, the industry recorded some 29.5 million passengers (Cruise Market Watch, 2022b), and, according to the leading industry body, the Cruise Line Industry Association (CLIA) generated some 1.8 million jobs and $154 million in economic activity directly and indirectly (CLIA, 2021). The rapid growth, uneven spread, and changing market structure of the cruise industry warrant further attention. This chapter will focus on the evolution of the activity since its modern foundation, chronicling growth and spatial concentration. It also documents the changing geographic and market segmentation of the industry. It discusses the social and economic impact of cruise tourism, as well as environmental issues, before finally looking to the future of the industry.

Overview: Cruise industry growth and diversification

As Figure 3.1 demonstrates, cruise ship tourism has grown rapidly in recent decades, with passenger growth averaging 6.6% compounded annually between 1990 and 2019 (Cruise Market Watch, 2022b). Modern cruising is roughly a half century old, tracing its origins to the 1970s in the Mediterranean (Pallis & Vaggelas, 2019). In 1970, just a half million cruise passengers set sail, but the centre of global cruising quickly shifted to the North American/Caribbean market, and that market has predominated ever since (Figure 3.1). In 1990, 3.7 million cruise passengers disembarked, and by the year 2000, some 90% of 7.2 million cruise passengers originated from North America (Table 3.1). Most sailed to the Caribbean.

Today passenger origins and itineraries are steadily diversifying. At first, this was the result of growth of the Mediterranean and European sending markets. In 2019 Europe accounted for just under 26% of global cruises customers (25.9%) while North America accounted for 52% (CLIA, 2021). In 2017 the Mediterranean and Europe combined made up 27.1% of the global deployment of cruise ships while the Caribbean's share fell to 35.4% (Honey, 2019). Rather than competing, however, these two markets are best understood as complementary, with the Caribbean experiencing its peak season in the winter while the Mediterranean services most of its customers in the summer. Cruise companies redeploy many ships seasonally to take advantage of this and maximise revenues per ship. Broken down by country, the U.S. remains the largest cruise passenger market. In 2017 it accounted for 11.9 million passengers, well in front of second-ranked

Figure 3.1 Cruise ship at dock in the Bahamas.
Photo: Courtesy, Unsplash.com.

China, with 2.4 million. Germany was next at 2.19 million, followed by the U.K. (1.93 million), Australia (1.34 million), Canada (0.92 million), and Italy (0.77 million) (FCAA, 2019).

From the 1970s to the 1990s cruise passengers tended to be older and middle class, but today passengers are much more diverse, with a growing proportion coming from Gen X, Millennials and Gen Z, solo travelers, and women. This segmentation results, in large part, from changes in marketing by large cruise firms. It also reflects two seemingly counter-trends: growing segmentation in the product at the same time there is growing concentration of market share among industry firms. Today the global cruise industry is dominated by the *Big Three* firms: Carnival Corporation and plc, Royal Caribbean Cruises Ltd. (RCCL), and Norwegian Cruise Lines Holdings (NCLH). Together they operate multiple brands that control roughly 75% of global passenger capacity. Carnival, the world's largest cruise ship operator, operated 98 ships under nine separate brands in 2021 (down from more than 100 ships and 10 lines pre-pandemic), carrying 43% of all passengers. RCCL operated 64 ships under four wholly owned brands plus two more lines where it holds 50% share, and its market share of passengers was 23%. Norwegian Cruises had 9.5% of the global passenger market on its three brands and 28 ships. A fourth firm, MSC Cruises, based in Europe, is the largest privately owned cruise ship firm in the world. In 2021 it captured 10.2% of the passenger market (Cruise Market Watch, 2022a). A fifth player, Genting Hong Kong Ltd., is another sizeable publicly traded firm, operating ten ships through three

Table 3.1 Global cruise ship arrivals, 2000–2021 (millions of passengers carried)

Year	Passengers (millions)	Index
2000	7.2	100.0
2001	7.5	104.2
2002	8.6	119.4
2003	9.5	131.9
2004	10.5	145.8
2005	11.1	154.2
2006	12.0	166.7
2007	14.6	202.8
2008	15.8	219.4
2009	17.2	238.9
2010	18.4	255.6
2011	19.3	268.1
2012	20.3	281.9
2013	21.0	291.7
2014	21.6	300.0
2015	22.6	313.9
2016	24.2	336.1
2017	25.2	350.0
2018	26.5	368.1
2019	27.5	381.9
2020	7.1	98.6
2021	13.9	193.1

Source: Cruise Market Watch (2022b).

separate lines carrying roughly 2.6% of global passengers in 2021. As the discussion below details, the COVID pandemic has severely destabilised the industry, but, as of February 2022, there were some 64 global brands in operation, with a total of 230 ships and 420,711 berths (Cruise Industry News, 2022). This compares to 307 ships with some 524,000 berths in operation in 2017 (Peručić, 2019).

While the structure of cruise industry ownership is characterised by high ownership concentration, the proliferation of cruise lines is indicative of increased segmentation of the cruise product. Today, there are four main classifications of cruise holidays: budget (4.9% of passenger capacity in 2018), contemporary (69.3%), premium (21.1%), and luxury (1.9%). The ships themselves are designed and built to reflect these classes. The remainder is made up by niche categories. Contemporary cruises target mass tourists and tend to offer standard packaging, shorter duration (seven days or less), lower passenger spending, and a lower crew-to-guest ratio (UNWTO, 2016). This segment has driven the trend of building larger and larger ships. In the late 1990s, the largest ships were roughly 80,000 gross tonnage (GT) and could accommodate 2,000 guests. By 2017 there were some 72 ships in service that were more than 100,000 GT, including 16 that were over 150,000 GT (Peručić, 2019). Today's largest megaships total more than 200,000 GT and can accommodate well over 5,000 passengers. Royal Caribbean International's Oasis class ships, first introduced in 2009, are the largest. In January 2022 RCI took delivery of *Wonder of the Seas*, its fifth Oasis class ship and, at nearly 237,000GT, the largest ship in the world. Passenger capacity on *Wonder of the Seas* comes in at just under 5,700, along with 2,300 crew (RCCL, 2021;

Schuler, 2022). Genting Hong Kong's Dream Cruises *Global Dream* ship is, at the time of this writing, some 75% complete. Though smaller in gross tonnage than the Oasis class ships, the *Global Dream* is slated to accommodate nearly 10,000 passengers at full capacity.

The emphasis on ever-bigger ships addresses the largest segment of the industry, contemporary, where firms seek economies of scale. In addition, it is made possible by the growing concentration of the industry. While the shift towards larger ships has been an important trend for the past two or three decades, growing market segmentation has led lines to also place more orders for smaller specialty ships. In the past decade the fastest-growing segment, in terms of guest capacity, has been premium (Cruise Industry News, 2019). In early 2019, just prior to the onset of the COVID pandemic, the eight-year order book for new ships totalled 125 ocean ships. While 21 were for ships larger than 150,000 GT, including nine over 200,000 GT, 32 orders were for specialty expedition ships and eight more were for small coastal ships (Cruise Industry News, Cruise Ship Orderbook, reported in Peručić, 2019).

Issues

A comprehensive summary of the issues and controversies associated with the cruise industry is beyond the scope of this chapter due to space limitations. These include controversies associated with Flags of Convenience (FoC), which often limit legal, financial and regulatory control of ships (Chin, 2016; Honey, 2019), as well as related issues associated with labor on cruise ships (Chin, 2016; Terry, 2011; War on Want, 2002). Instead, it will focus on the economic and social impact of cruises at the destination as well as environmental issues associated with the industry.

Economic and social impact

The economic model followed by the modern cruise industry is that of enclave tourism. The ship itself – with its ever-growing sets of amenities – constitutes the primary destination. For many consumers, a major attraction of cruise tourism over other forms of tourism is the seemingly all-inclusive price. While onboard, however, passengers occupy what Weaver (2005) refers to as "spaces of containment," and are often subject to monopoly pricing (Vogel, 2012; Weaver, 2005). As a result, as much as 20–35% of cruise ship revenues come from ancillary services, which include onboard spending through shopping, casinos, activities, upgrades, and add-on experiences, along with cruise line-sponsored shore excursions. This economic model also has important ramifications for ports of call. To be sure, this varies widely, with European ports in larger cities drawing higher per passenger spending. Overall, however, earnings from cruise ship tourism in destinations tends to be low, is narrowly distributed, and is subject to significant leakage (UNWTO, 2016).

In their meta-analysis of several impact studies, Chen et al. (2019) argue that overall port spending, including that not just from passengers but also crew and supplies, is significant. Comparative and micro-studies, however, are less positive. For example, in Belize, one study found that cruise ship passengers accounted for 75% of international visitors but only 25% of revenues and 10% of employment (CESD, 2006, reported in Klein, 2011; Russell, 2005, reported in UNWTO, 2016). Similarly, Brida and Zapata (2010) found that cruise tourists to Costa Rica spent less than other tourists to the country, and the total spent by cruise tourists was the equivalent of just 2% of what land tourists in the country spent. In neighbouring Honduras, a study by MacNeill and Wozniak (2018) found that the arrival of cruise ships to one new locale beginning in 2014 had little positive developmental impact in the area based on various measures.

In part, these limitations on material benefits accruing to the destination have been the result of conscious strategies undertaken by cruise lines to capture shore revenues for themselves. Cruise lines sell shore excursions with local firms, but frequently charge those approved or recommended firms as much as 50% of more of the excursion cost (Klein, 2011). Similar arrangements go for being listed as "preferred vendors" onshore. In many destinations, cruise lines continue to internalise more shore operations, from building private cruise terminals, including related amenities such as shops, beaches and attractions, to even setting up their own private islands, enclosed and insulated from the larger destination ports themselves (Pallis & Vaggelas, 2019; Rodrigue & Notteboom, 2013). In such cases, passengers move from one enclave on the ship to another on these islands. Finally, the growth of cruise tourists to individual destinations have been found to lead to a decrease in higher-spending, land-based tourists (UNWTO, 2016).

A related issue associated with cruise tourism has been termed "people pollution" (UNWTO, 2016). This refers to the sudden infiltration of large numbers of cruise tourists who overwhelm local streets on port calls, thereby contributing to a deteriorating quality of life for residents. In some places, this forms part of the larger phenomenon of overtourism and has led to anti-cruise ship protests and activism (Klein & Sitter, 2016). In Venice, local political movements recently targeted cruise ships and especially megaships that brought larger flows of tourists to the old centre city (Pallis & Vaggelas, 2019; Vianello, 2017). In another case, the city of Dubrovnik, Croatia created a "Respect the City" program in 2017 in response to overtourism and a year later limited the number of cruise ship arrivals to two per day and a maximum of 4,000 cruise ship passengers per day (CLIA, 2021). In Key West, Florida, voters successfully passed three referenda in 2020 that severely limited the number and size of cruise ship arrivals to the city, as well as curtailing passenger numbers. The next year, after heavy lobbying by cruise ship interests and their allies at the state level, the Florida State Legislature passed legislation that was signed by the Governor to overturn those local restrictions (Morin, 2021).

Environmental impact

The myriad of environmental issues raised by the cruise industry is beyond the scope of this chapter, but, as Klein (2011) argues, three stand out: wastewater, solid waste, and air emissions. These are all especially relevant to the United Nations Sustainable Development Goals, in particular SDG Number 14: Life Below Water (Pakbeen, 2018). The largest cruise ships are akin to small cities and produce large amounts of wastewater. This includes black water (sewage) and grey water (from faucets, showers and the like). According to one estimate, an average seven-day cruise generates one million tons of grey water, 210,000 liters of sewage, and 25,000 liters of oil-contaminated water (Špolijarić, 2020). For decades, this waste was simply dumped into the sea, including, at times, areas close to shore. Beginning in the early 2000s the industry began moving to advanced wastewater treatment systems (AWTS). This shift came largely in response to more stringent regional regulations. As late as 2008, however, only one of Carnival Cruise Lines 22 ships was equipped with AWTS and just over half of Royal Caribbean's had the systems (Klein, 2011). AWTS systems still produce a high volume of sewage sludge, and much of the grey water remains untreated. Both continue to be routinely dumped into international waters. Individual ships and lines have continued to be found in violation of discharge regulations near shore. Finally, much of the non-sewage and non-grey water garbage generated on ships is incinerated. This can include toxic chemicals. The result is air pollution and ash that is commonly dumped into ocean waters (Moscovici, 2017).

Despite lax regulations dealing with disposal of sewage, grey water and garbage, cruise companies continue to run afoul of the law. Honey and Bray (2019) report that between 2003 and 2013 four cruise lines were fined between $200,000 and $2 million for illegal dumping of oil, fuel, untreated wastewater, garbage and bilge water. In 2016, Princess Cruise Lines agreed to pay a $40 million fine as part of a plea bargain in U.S. Federal Court admitting it illegally dumped oil contaminated waste into the sea and then tried to cover it up. The fine, the result of a guilty plea to felony charges, was the largest ever imposed for intentional vessel pollution and included probation for the parent company, Carnival. Less than three years later, in 2019, Carnival was fined an additional $20 million for violating that probation through further violations, mainly involving improper and illegal disposal of solid waste (Mervosh, 2019). The 2021 Cruise Ship Report Card, the most recent annual evaluation by the environmental organisation Friends of the Earth, gave 18 leading cruise lines grades of C, D, and F regarding sewage treatment (Friends of the Earth, 2022).

Air emissions from running cruise ships have also become increasingly controversial. Global shipping as a whole contributed an estimated 3.1% of all global CO_2 emissions in 2012 (UNWTO, 2016). Although cruise ships make up a miniscule percentage of that total, their practices have come under greater scrutiny as global climate change has become more acute. By some measures, CO_2 emissions from the global cruise ship fleet have grown significantly since 2016 (Špolijarić, 2020) due to the continued expansion of the industry. Fuel tends to be the single-largest operating expense (UNWTO, 2016). Traditionally, ships run on inexpensive heavy fuel oil (HFO), among the dirtiest fuels available. The fuel emits high amounts of CO_2 sulphur oxide, dust, heavy metals and other pollutants, which, among other things, produce dangerously poor air quality on the ships themselves. One study found that passengers walking on the top deck of a modern cruise ship experience air quality roughly equivalent to that during rush hour in Beijing (Kennedy, 2019). Ships also typically burn fuel while at port (hotelling), resulting in significant air pollution to the port and surrounding area (Honey & Bray, 2019; Moscovici, 2017; Murena et al., 2018; Perdiguero & Sanz, 2020; Pesce et al., 2018).

Many destinations have started regulating cruise ship emissions in port. The European Community set in place very low limits of sulphur (0.1%) for ships burning fuel in port beginning in 2010. Shortly after this, the International Convention for the Prevention of Pollution from Ships (MARPOL), legislation put forward by the International Maritime Organization (IMO), set similar limits in place in sensitive Sulphur Dioxide Emissions Control Areas (Baltic Sea, North Sea, English Channel), as did the North America Emission Control Area (IMO, 2008; Klein, 2011; Murena et al., 2018). At the global level, MARPOL set into action a gradually decreased limit for ship emissions of sulphur dioxide, starting at 4.5% content but falling to a cap of 0.5% in 2020. Regulation of other pollutants, such as nitrogen oxide, have also been put into place by the IMO, with progressive reductions beginning in 2000 and culminating in what is known as Tier III, which went into effect in some emission control areas (ECAs) and would later expand into others.

Cruise industry response to these regulations has been varied. One early strategy was to burn slightly less dirty diesel fuel rather than HFO while in port. A second has been to eliminate burning fuel onboard while in port and instead connect to the local power grid. Both require ship retrofitting and practices have varied widely. In Alaska, the city of Juneau began connecting the local power grid to cruise ships back in 2001, but the port of Miami, the single-largest home port of cruise ships globally, only signed such an agreement with six major lines in early 2021 (Parkinson, 2021). Connecting to local power can also put excessive pressure on local power grids. Many destinations cannot meet that demand or require expensive expansion and upgrades of facilities. In its 2021 annual report, CLIA (2021) identifies just 14 ports worldwide where arriving ships can plug into the local grid. Cruise companies have also invested in emissions mitigations systems, oftentimes referred to as "scrubbers." They use sea water to capture many of the airborne pollutants, but most are open-loop systems that release the resulting washwater into the sea. One recent report estimated that cargo and cruise ships together release more than ten billion metric tonnes of that polluted water into the ocean each year, and that cruise ships dump much of that near ports (Osipova et al., 2021). The scrubbers have been a favoured choice of the industry in recent years because they are less expensive than buying cleaner fuel, but have been criticised as an "environmental dodge" (Laville, 2018).

Several cruise lines have trumpeted plans to build new ships with alternative fuels to meet growing environmental concerns and regulation. Two lines from Royal Caribbean recently announced the building of new ships that will run on liquid natural gas (LNG). Carnival also has at least four LNG-powered ships in service in 2020 and several more in the building or planning stage. It also used dual-fuel engines on two AIDA ships starting in 2015, burning LNG fuel while in port on those ships. MSC Cruises is scheduled to take delivery of its first LNG-powered ship, MSC *World Europa*, in 2022 and has five such ships on order by 2026. Disney and AIDA have announced they will only order LNG-power ships in the future (Pallis & Vaggelas, 2019). While LNG produces fewer pollutants than HFO, it contains very high levels of a powerful greenhouse gas, methane, which, depending on the specific engine in question, can actually lead to higher greenhouse gas emissions than bunker fuel (Gallucci, 2020; Savvides, 2019). Some in industry see LNG as a transition fuel, and research on alternatives such as hydrogen, ammonia, methanol, biogas from dead fish, and wind for propulsion continues (Ullrich, 2021).

Cruise lines have used their response to tightening air and water regulations to launch larger public sustainability campaigns in recent years (Pakbeen, 2018). RCCL partnered with the World Wildlife Fund (WWF) in 2016 on a highly publicised broad sustainability campaign. It included sustainably certified shore excursions, seafood sourcing, protection of endangered species, reduction in greenhouse gas emissions, and other measures. It also included a $5 million philanthropic contribution (Royal Caribbean & WWF, 2018). Similarly, CLIA regularly touts the industry's commitment to responsible tourism, including emphasis of many of the initiatives and responses noted above, along with newer ones such as eliminating straws and introducing on-ship composting (CLIA, 2021). Royal Caribbean boasts that one of its newest and largest ships, *Symphony of the Seas*, is a zero-landfill ship. As the cruise industry continues to grow, however, its overall contribution to global climate change, ocean, and port pollution – as well as transparency surrounding these issues (Papathanassis, 2020) – is likely to draw additional scrutiny.

Conclusion

Few industries were hit harder by the global COVID pandemic than tourism, and the cruise tourism sub-sector suffered even more. Carnival recorded losses of more than $10 billion in 2020, and other cruise companies were also deep in the red after cruising came to a complete halt for more than a year (Aspin, 2021). Similarly, RCCL reported eight consecutive quarterly losses as of early 2022 (Levin & Bloomberg, 2022). Meanwhile Genting Hong Kong went into liquidation in early 2022. The company was the most vertically integrated of the large cruise firms, owning German cruise ship builder MV Werfden, along with ten ships on three lines. Although anticipated by previous occasional norovirus outbreaks on individual ships, the pandemic has highlighted larger health issues aboard cruise ships. Small cabins, windows that do not open, the cramped living spaces for crew, and relatively small and crowded public spaces all make cruise ships ripe for the spread of viruses. To the extent that COVID may signal a "new normal" of the global spread of disease in the future, designers of ships will need to take additional measures to protect passengers and their industry.

Post-pandemic three trends seem most likely: Further concentration among the *Big Three* firms, accelerated segmentation within the most mature markets, and a longer-term shift toward Asia. Ownership concentration peaked in roughly 2017 and since then new start-ups and the shedding of ships and lines by the large firms have temporarily reduced the dominance of the *Big Three*. The pandemic-induced recession put huge financial pressure on all firms, and Carnival, RCCL and NCLH appear best poised to weather it. Smaller players that are part of larger diversified firms – Disney Cruises and Virgin Cruises, for example – are also likely to emerge well-positioned. If other small and specialty cruise firms emerge weakened by the pandemic, expect further consolidation. The *Big Three* are also well positioned to meet segmented demand in mature markets. As the discussion above demonstrates, the cruising demographics continue to change, as does their desired cruise experience. The growth of ultra-luxury, adventure, and expeditionary sectors will further segment the industry.

Finally, the industry has been looking at Asia and in particular China for some time. Cruise tourism in the region has grown from less than 1% of the global market in 2004 to 15% in 2018 (Pallis & Vaggelas, 2019). Once negligible, the China market now ranks second in the world (FCAA, 2019). Over the past decade China has upgraded cruise ports near major population centers and plans new ports in at least 15 cities by 2030 (Ke, 2016). By one estimate, demand there is growing by 20% annually and could reach 30 million annually by 2030 (Ke, 2016). Cruise companies have responded by delivering dedicated new ships to the region. Carnival also created a joint venture with the China State Shipbuilding Corporation (CSSC) in 2018. The new company bought two existing ships from Carnival's Costa line and committed to building two new ships in China, the first one to be delivered in 2023 (Carnival, 2018). Other global firms have also entered the China market either alone or through joint ventures as have a few domestic firms (Ke, 2016; Minter, 2021). Going forward, China will likely replace the U.S. as the centre for global cruising within 10–20 years.

The pandemic has been extremely costly and disruptive to the cruise industry. Over the medium and long-term future, however, a return to previous growth levels appears likely, especially with what is likely to be booming growth in Asia. Many of the controversies associated with the industry, from labour practices to negative impacts on destinations, and cruise ships' environmental footprint are likely to remain and even intensify. Indeed, the biggest future threats to the industry are the ones noted above: the balance between negative and positive impacts of cruise tourism on destinations, and the environmental impact of the industry. Cruise lines have made much noise in the past few years about both, in particular the latter. Addressing each in a serious manner, however, will be expensive and constitutes a significant challenge to the existing cruise industry business model.

References

Aspin, M. (2021, January 11). Carnival lost $10.2 billion last year – But says it can survive 2021 without cruises. *Fortune*. https://fortune.com/2021/01/11/carnival-cruises-COVID-19-losses-q4-earnings/

Brida, J. G., & Zapata, S. (2010). Economic impacts of cruise tourism: The case of Costa Rica. *Anatolia*, *21*(2), 322–338. https://doi.org/10.1080/13032917.2010.9687106

Carnival. (2018). *Carnival Corporation Launches Cruise Joint Venture in China | Carnival Corporation & plc*. Carnival Corporation & plc. https://www.carnivalcorp.com/news-releases/news-release-details/carnival-corporation-launches-cruise-joint-venture-china-0/

CESD. (2006). *Cruise tourism in Belize: Perceptions of economic, social and environmental impact*. Centre for Ecotourism and Sustainable Development.

Chen, J. M., Petrick, J. F., Papathanassis, A., & Li, X. (2019). A meta-analysis of the direct economic impacts of cruise tourism on port communities. *Tourism Management Perspectives*, *31*, 209–218. https://doi.org/10.1016/j.tmp.2019.05.005

Chin, C. B. N. (2016). *Cruising in the Global Economy: Profits, Pleasure and Work at Sea*. London: Routledge.

CLIA. (2021). *State Of The Cruise Industry Outlook 2021* (p. 30). Cruise Line Industry Association. https://cruising.org:443/en/news-and-research/research/2020/december/state-of-the-cruise-industry-outlook-2021

Cruise Industry News. (2019). *Cruise Industry News Annual Report, 2019* (No. 32; p. 400). Cruise Industry News.

Cruise Industry News. (2022). *Cruise Ships in Service, February 2022* (No. 8; p. 52). Cruise Industry News. www.CruiseIndustryNews.com

Cruise Market Watch. (2022a). *2021 Worldwide Cruise Line Market Share*. Cruise Market Watch. https://cruisemarketwatch.com/market-share/

Cruise Market Watch. (2022b). *Growth of the Ocean Cruise Line Industry*. Cruise Market Watch. https://cruisemarketwatch.com/growth/

FCAA. (2019). *2019 Cruise Industry Overview* (p. 40). FCAA.

Friends of the Earth. (2022). *2021 Cruise Ship Report Card*. Friends of the Earth. https://foe.org/cruise-report-card/

Gallucci, M. (2020, February 5). Do cruise companies' green claims hold water? *Grist*. https://grist.org/energy/do-cruise-companies-green-claims-hold-water/

Honey, M. (2019). *Cruise Tourism in the Caribbean: Selling Sunshine*. Routledge.

Honey, M., & Bray, S. (2019). Environmental "Footprint" of the Cruise Industry. In *Cruise Ship Tourism in the Caribbean: Selling Sunshine*. Routledge.

IMO. (2008). *Annex VI: Amendments to the Annex of the Protocol of 1997 to Amend the International Convention for the Prevention of Pollution From Ships, 1973, as modified by the Protocol of 1978 relating thereto (Revised MARPOL Annex VI): Annex 13 (Resolution MEPC.176(58))*. IMO. https://www.imo.org/en/OurWork/Environment/Pages/Air-Pollution.aspx

Ke, X. (2016). China's cruise industry: Progress, challenges and outlook. *Maritime Affairs: Journal of the National Maritime Foundation of India*, *12*, 38–45.

Kennedy, R. D. (2019). *An investigation of air pollution on the decks of 4 cruise ships* (p. 19) [A Report for Stand.earth]. https://www.stand.earth/latest/protect-arctic/carnivals-cruise-pollution/investigation-air-quality-carnival-corp-cruise

Kizielewicz, J. (2019). Prospects of development of the cruise ship tourism market – the case study of the Baltic Sea region. *Prace Naukowe Uniwersytetu Ekonomicznego We Wrocławiu*, vol. *63*, no. 7, 244–255.

Klein, R. A. (2011). Responsible Cruise Tourism: Issues of Cruise Tourism and Sustainability. *Journal of Hospitality and Tourism Management*, *18*(1), 107–116. https://doi.org/10.1375/jhtm.18.1.107

Klein, R. A., & Sitter, K. C. (2016). Troubled Seas: The Politics of Activism Related to the Cruise Industry. *Tourism in Marine Environments*, *11*(2–3), 146–158. https://doi.org/10.3727/154427315X14513374773526

Laville, S. (2018, October 29). Thousands of ships could dump pollutants at sea to avoid dirty fuel ban. *The Guardian*. https://www.theguardian.com/environment/2018/oct/29/thousands-of-ships-could-dump-pollutants-at-sea-to-avoid-dirty-fuel-ban

Levin, J., & Bloomberg (2022, February 4). Royal Caribbean posts another loss as Omicron hurts cruise bookings. *Fortune*. https://fortune.com/2022/02/04/royal-caribbean-fourth-quarter-loss-omicron-cruise-bookings/

MacNeill, T., & Wozniak, D. (2018). The economic, social, and environmental impacts of cruise tourism. *Tourism Management*, *66*, 387–404. https://doi.org/10.1016/j.tourman.2017.11.002

Mervosh, S. (2019, June 4). Carnival cruises to pay $20 million in pollution and cover-up case. *The New York Times*. https://www.nytimes.com/2019/06/04/business/carnival-cruise-pollution.html

Minter, A. (2021, October 14). China's cruise industry is finally set to sail. *Bloomberg.Com*. https://www.bloomberg.com/opinion/articles/2021-10-14/china-s-cruise-industry-is-finally-set-to-sail

Morin, R. (2021, March 27). Rough waters in Key West as city, cruise industry and state lawmakers tangle over its future. *Washington Post*. https://www.washingtonpost.com/national/rough-waters-in-key-west-as-city-cruise-industry-and-state-lawmakers-tangle-over-its-future/2021/03/26/6fedba3e-8ca3-11eb-a6bd-0eb91c03305a_story.html

Moscovici, D. (2017). Environmental impacts of cruise ships on Island Nations. *Peace Review*, *29*(3), 366–373. https://doi.org/10.1080/10402659.2017.1344580

Murena, F., Mocerino, L., Quaranta, F., & Toscano, D. (2018). Impact on air quality of cruise ship emissions in Naples, Italy. *Atmospheric Environment*, *187*, 70–83.

Osipova, L., Georgeff, E., & Comer, B. (2021). *Global scrubber washwater discharges under IMO's 2020 fuel sulphur limit* (p. 32). International Council on Clean Transportation. https://theicct.org/publication/global-scrubber-washwater-discharges-under-imos-2020-fuel-sulfur-limit/

Pakbeen, H. (2018). Comparative Study of Leading Cruise Lines' Sustainability Practices and Environmental Stewardship in Contribution to SDGs' Sea and Water Conservation Goal. *European Journal of Sustainable Development*, *7*(3), 507–516. https://doi.org/10.14207/ejsd.2018.v7n3p507

Pallis, A. A., & Vaggelas, G. K. (2019). The changing geography of cruise shipping. In *Waterborne Transport Geographies*. Edward Elgar Publishing.

Papathanassis, A. (2020). Current issues in cruise tourism: Deconstructing the 6th International Cruise Conference. *Current Issues in Tourism*, *23*(14), 1711–1717. https://doi.org/10.1080/13683500.2019.1654984

Parkinson, B. (2021, February 19). Six Cruise Lines Sign Deal To Bring Shore Power To Port Miami. *Cruise Radio – Daily Updates On The Cruise Industry*. https://cruiseradio.net/six-cruise-lines-sign-deal-to-bring-shore-power-to-portmiami/

Perdiguero, J., & Sanz, A. (2020). Cruise activity and pollution: The case of Barcelona. *Transportation Research Part D: Transport and Environment*, *78*, 102181. https://doi.org/10.1016/j.trd.2019.11.010

Peručić, D. (2019). *Analysis of the World Cruise Industry*. *5:1*, 89–99. https://www.proquest.com/openview/07dfcc8d862a577102aba7e611d97625/1.pdf?pq-origsite=gscholar&cbl=2049763

Pesce, M., Terzi, S., Al-Jawasreh, R. I. M., Bommarito, C., Calgaro, L., Fogarin, S., Russo, E., Marcomini, A., & Linkov, I. (2018). Selecting sustainable alternatives for cruise ships in Venice using multi-criteria decision analysis. *Science of the Total Environment*, *642*, 668–678. https://doi.org/10.1016/j.scitotenv.2018.05.372

RCCL. (2021). *Royal Caribbean Group Annual Report 2021*. RCCL.

Rodrigue, J.-P., & Notteboom, T. (2013). The geography of cruises: Itineraries, not destinations. *Applied Geography*, *38*, 31–42. https://doi.org/10.1016/j.apgeog.2012.11.011

Royal Caribbean & WWF. (2018). *2018 Partnership Report*.

Russell, D. M. (2005). *Belize Tourism Policy*. Belize Tourism Board.

Savvides, N. (2019, December 13). LNG could raise GHG emissions says SINTEF. *Seatrade Maritime*. https://www.seatrade-maritime.com/bunkering/lng-could-raise-ghg-emissions-says-sintef

Schuler, M. (2022, January 28). *Royal Caribbean takes delivery of new world's largest cruise ship: Wonder of the seas*. GCaptain. https://gcaptain.com/royal-caribbean-takes-delivery-worlds-largest-cruise-ship/

Špoljarić, T. (2020). The negative impact of the cruising industry on the environment. *Journal of Maritime & Transportation Sciences*, *59*(1), 85–94. https://doi.org/10.18048/2020.59.05.

Terry, W. C. (2011). Geographic limits to global labor market flexibility: The human resources paradox of the cruise industry. *Geoforum*, *42*(6), 660–670. https://doi.org/10.1016/j.geoforum.2011.06.006

Ullrich, A. (2021, December 21). Fuelling the future of the cruise industry with sustainable choices. *CruiseandFerry.Net*. https://www.cruiseandferry.net/articles/fuelling-the-future-of-the-cruise-industry-with-sustainable-choices-1

UNWTO. (2016). *Sustainable Cruise Tourism Development Strategies – Tackling the Challenges in Itinerary Design in South-East Asia*. World Tourism Organization (UNWTO). https://doi.org/10.18111/9789284417292

Vianello, M. (2017). The No Grandi Navi Campaign: Protests against cruise tourism in Venice. In *Protest and Resistance in the Tourist City*,. Routledge.

Vogel, M. (2012). Pricing and revenue management for cruises. In *The Business and Management of Ocean Cruises* (pp. 131–144). CAB International.

War on Want. (2002). *Sweatships* (p. 19). https://waronwant.org/resources/sweatships

Weaver, A. (2005). Spaces of Containment and Revenue Capture: 'Super-Sized' Cruise Ships as Mobile Tourism Enclaves. *Tourism Geographies*, *7*(2), 165–184.

4 Cruises

Environmental impacts and policy

Timothy MacNeill

Introduction

As the reality of human impact on the natural environment has become increasingly widely acknowledged, debate has turned to policies required to mitigate and adapt to these impacts. Since cruise tourism is a notably environmentally damaging human practice, the industry provides an informative and important case through which these debates can be investigated. This chapter aims to contribute to the understanding of theoretical, social, and practical implications of cruise tourism into the future. Key to this is to question if the industry can become sustainable through self- or externally imposed regulation, or if its growth should be dissuaded altogether. This chapter addresses these issues by offering a description of the historical growth of the industry and future trajectories, then providing a summary of its environmental impacts, and by discussing technological and policy proposals for impact mitigation.

History, structure, and stakeholders

Cruise tourism has its roots as a limited elite-based leisure activity in the 1930s (Cerchiello & Vera-Rebollo, 2019). In the 1960s and 1970s, the industry experienced modest growth, but its size has increased roughly twice as fast as all other tourism sectors from the 1980s onward (Kester, 2002). Although the industry experienced a major pause in 2020 due to the COVID-19 pandemic, it is showing signs of returning to this growth path. Projections are for the US$150 billion global industry to increase passenger usage and income by an average of 10% a year for the foreseeable future (Data Intelligence, 2021). Although cruise tourism exhibits unique economic realities, many environmental impacts and technological realities are shared with the larger US$10.5 billion global shipping industry of which it is a part (Talley, 2003).

Because the industry is complex, global, and involves various economic, environmental, and political impacts, multiple stakeholders with varying interests in the activity can be identified. Most broadly, present and future human and non-human populations of the world are stakeholders regarding environmental concerns – especially related to climate change and global biodiversity loss. More direct stakeholders are the cruise ship companies and their investors. Since the industry involves substantial fixed costs, and thus economies of scale, it tends toward oligopoly (Bull, 2013). The four largest cruise lines account for 87% of the global industry, with the top two representing 72%. Specifically, Royal Caribbean, with its nine brands, accounts for 47% of the industry, followed by Carnival's three brands and 26%, Norwegian's three brands and 9.5%, and finally MSC's 7%. Because of their status

DOI: 10.4324/9781003260790-7

as publicly traded corporations, the interest of cruise ship companies is ultimately limited to generating profits for shareholders. This is done within constraints imposed by government environmental regulation.

Consumers/passengers are another major stakeholder group. Their interests focus on services received per dollar spent and that their health is not adversely affected by a cruise. Evidence of cruise ship consumer preferences for the environment is contradictory. Some studies do not indicate that environmental sustainability is an important spending consideration for passengers (Adams et al., 2017) while others suggest there is a demand for ecotourism-type port excursions (Thurau et al., 2015). When considering ports, passengers prefer unique physical characteristics (hot springs, beaches, climate), cultural experiences (dance, food, music), and high-quality infrastructure (sanitation, cleanliness, restaurants, safety) (Brida et al., 2013).

Cruise destination ports and their surrounding communities and environments are another major stakeholder in the industry. Ports are selected by cruise ship companies based on the preferences of passengers and additionally quality, cost, and suitability, of port infrastructure for ships. Since the market to establish ports is oligopsonistic (featuring few cruise ship companies as 'buyers'), there can be intense competition that incentivises localities to invest private and public money in port infrastructure and destination activities while competing to offer lower port fees. This 'race to the bottom' regarding port costs to cruise lines and passengers can also produce a pressure for ports to reduce environmental regulations and worker compensation (Papachristou et al., 2020). There is a hierarchy of power in ports as well, with more established destinations able to attract cruise ships much more easily than smaller, non-traditional, destinations (Marti, 1991). In the latter case, competition can increase economic marginalisation of local communities, inspire the avoidance of environmental regulations, and exacerbate existing political corruption. The interests of local ports include employment generation, economic development, and environmental protection. However, amidst inequities, inter-port competition, and political corruption, local ports can simply be seen as a means by which local elites and international investors might increase their economic standing at the cost of local peoples' livelihoods and environmental health (MacNeill, 2017).

Many environmental problems are considered in an anthropocentric way – meaning that environmental impacts are only problems if they impact human health or economic possibilities currently or in the future (MacNeill, 2020b). This is a very Western way of viewing the world, its actors, and its stakeholders. Many Indigenous populations, however, utilise nature-centric, relational, ontologies that presume the natural world to have an interest of its own. This is not a trivial observation. Nations with substantial cruise tourism industries, such as Ecuador, have entrenched the rights of nature in their natural constitutions according to the cosmologies of their Indigenous populations. Others, such as Peru, Guatemala, Mexico, Canada, and Honduras, have significant Indigenous populations, many of which live near cruise ship ports that use their culture to attract visitors (MacNeill, 2020a, 2020b). Using Indigenous culture to attract tourists while degrading the natural environment is often considered cultural expropriation in the interest of narrow economic interests of non-Indigenous investors. Understanding the environment and Indigenous populations as stakeholders in their own right helps us to view this clearly. It also helps us to transcend a narrow Western-centric view that may be overly focussed on efficiency and even the outright domination/control of nature as environmental and industrial policy solutions.

The existence of these varying stakeholders complicates the cost–benefit analysis of cruise tourism dramatically. Cruise ship companies and their shareholders privilege profits, while their passengers value their own health, experiences, and lower prices for services on- and off-ship. Local ports and their populations value economic development, security, and environmental protection. The global community values healthy ecosystems and stable climates, while the disturbance of nature at all could be thought of as damaging in its own right. The sustainable development approach to evaluating development (encapsulated in the UN Sustainable Development Goals) promises that technologies and efficiencies can be nurtured to allow economic growth and ecological health (UN, 2015). De-growth perspectives (which align broadly to Indigenous ideas of environmental protection) reject that economic growth can be environmentally sustainable (Hickel & Kallis, 2020). Tensions between these two schools of thought must be considered when evaluating environmental considerations of cruise tourism.

Environmental impacts

Cruise tourism impacts the natural environment in numerous ways. Carić (2012) suggests that the most important impacts come from the materials that leave ships. These include waste, gases, nutrients, bacteria, viruses, biocides, hydrocarbons, invasive species, noise, and light. These materials produce many negative environment-related effects, such as climate change, respiratory disease, epidemics, viral/bacterial contamination, acidification, contamination with eco-toxic metals, eutrophication, smog, biodiversity loss, fragmentation/deterioration/loss of ecosystems, collisions, and disorientation of biodiversity via sound and light pollution. Johnson (2002) argues that a life-cycle analysis of impacts should be used. This adds infrastructure-based impacts, such as pollution, habitat destruction, and environmental disruption from ship/port construction and dismantlement. It also includes the increased imposition of sewage and solid waste from cruise passengers that disembark at a port of call.

Augmenting Johnson's (2002) categorisation, Table 4.1 shows four interrelated types of environmental impact from cruise ships. First, operational impacts include direct and indirect air and water pollution through emission from the ship, as well as impacts of energy/fuel use. Second, infrastructure impacts include damage from the building and destruction of ports and ships. Third, destination use impacts, include the effects of extra solid waste and sewage, sound, light, and cultural pollution on the destination port and surrounding ecosystem. Fourth, waste impacts include disposal of oils, garbage, sewage, plastics and hazardous substances from the ship itself.

Table 4.1 Cruising environmental impact types

Operational impacts	Port-use impacts
Local air pollution at ports	Sanitation
Greenhouse gas emissions	Water use
Water pollution from bilge/ballast	Waste
Anti-fouling toxicity	
Noise and light pollution	
Infrastructure impacts	**Waste impacts**
Ship construction	Inorganic waste
Ship destruction	Organic waste
Port construction	Hazardous waste

Most research attention has focussed on operational impacts, and most specifically pollution and greenhouse gas emissions. Regarding local port pollution from ships, the biggest culprits are NO_x, SO_2, and $PM_{2.5}$. Nitric Oxide (NO_x) contributes to smog, acid rain, fine-particle pollution, and ground-level ozone. Sulphur dioxide (SO_2) is poisonous and causes many pulmonary problems in humans. Fine particulate matter ($PM_{2.5}$) has human health, climate, and ecosystem impacts. Combined health impacts of these emissions have been calculated at US$6 per passenger (Maragkogianni & Papaefthimiou, 2015). Concerning SO_x, the two largest cruise ship companies, Carnival Corporation and Royal Caribbean Cruises, produce two and ten times the emissions of all European cars, respectively (Abbasov et al., 2019). Furthermore, air pollution on the ship deck itself has been noted for its potential negative impact of passenger health (Lloret et al., 2021).

Understanding greenhouse gas emissions from cruise ships requires a comparative perspective. The average European's yearly carbon footprint is 6.7 tonnes of CO_2 (Eurostat, 2021), and the maximum allowable level required to avert dangerous climate change is about two billion per person per year (De Pryck, 2021). The average cruise ship passenger emits nearly half of their yearly maximum allowable amount on just a single one-week cruise (Griffith, 2021). A large cruise ship can have a carbon footprint greater than 12,000 cars, and passengers on a seven-day Antarctic cruise can produce as much CO_2 as the average European produces in an entire year (Lloret et al., 2021). Cruising is one of the most damaging human activities when comparing GHG to economic contribution. For example, the carbon intensity (as metric tonnes per millions of dollars) of the European Union economy is 91, for the Carnival cruise company, it is 256 (Griffith, 2021). Cruise ships are powered by heavy fuel oil, which is considered the dirtiest fossil fuel. These ships also incorporate multiple waste-producing leisure activities that require large amounts of energy and do not exist with cargo shipping. Many of these wastes are incinerated – creating air pollution of various kinds (Brida & Zapata, 2010).

Water pollution is also a serious operational impact. Contaminated water from toilets, or "blackwater", and water from bathing/cleaning ("greywater") are emitted from ships with varying amounts of treatment. These wastewaters threaten ecology and increase potential for harmful algal blooming. Micropollutants can also be contained in this water – including pharmaceuticals and pathogens (Lloret et al., 2021). Since many cruise ships do not sufficiently clean these wastewaters, effluents often contain levels of harmful materials in excess of most minimum safety standards. Regarding sewage treatment, all 18 cruise ship companies surveyed by Friends of the Earth received a mark of "C" or lower on a scale of "F" to "A" (FOE, 2020).

The discharge of bilge water and ballast water is also a major environmental concern. Hydrocarbons are contained in such waters, even when they have been treated for removal. Globally, hydrocarbons emitted by the shipping industry through bilge water are three times that from reported oil spills and/or collisions (Lloret et al., 2021). In addition to hydrocarbons, bilge and ballast waters can contain microplastics, microbes, and invasive species. Through ballast and bilge water, onboard 'hitch-hiking' and through attachment to the hull, invasive species and pathogens have been transported through the world. These have been shown to negatively impact local ecosystems and even be involved in species extinction (Abdulla & Linden, 2008).

Anti-fouling agents are applied to the outside hull of nearly all ocean-going ships. These are biocidal metal-based compounds designed to prevent sea life, such as algae and barnacles, from growing. Some have found this to be one of the most serious environmental threats emanating from cruise ships (Carić et al., 2016). These agents are toxic to non-target organisms.

They inhibit photosynthesis and Krebs cycle enzymes, increasing stress associated with oxidation, reducing reproductive abilities of local organisms, and contributing to antibiotic-resistant bacterial strains. High levels of such materials have thus been associated with lowering biodiversity, representing a major concern especially in marine protected areas – many of which are frequently visited by cruise ships (Lloret et al., 2021).

Additional operational environmental impacts associated with cruise ships relate to noise pollution, animal impacts, and marine accidents. Noise pollution in shipping zones has been found to be high. This is especially important for cruise ships, whose routes tend to cross into marine protected zones with high levels of biodiversity. This can disorient fish and mammal species, resulting in behaviour and habitat use modification that impact species reproduction and reduce important ecological services performed by some species (Lloret et al., 2021). It can also lead to increased animal impacts with ships. The same can be said for light pollution, which can especially disorient migrating birds and interfere with migrations of zooplankton and cephalopods (Longcore & Rich 2004). In addition, ships can impact reef habitats, undermining biodiversity. The sediments drawn up by the movement of large ships can disrupt local reefs and river inlet ecosystems (Lloret et al., 2021).

Infrastructure creation and destruction also carries large environmental impacts. There have been no explicit research published on cruise ship building, but impacts related to general shipbuilding can be high. Just the production of steel hulls has been associated with abiotic depletions, acidification, eutrophication, climate change, ozone depletion, biological toxicity, and photochemical oxidation (Önal et al., 2021). The dismantling of ships at the end of their lifecycle can release heavy metals such as lead, cadmium, chromium, and mercury as well as toxic substances like PCBs, asbestos, and oil into the air, aquatic, and terrestrial environment. These impacts are more pronounced with cruise ships compared with other shipping, because they use a wide variety of materials in their construction to serve multiple leisure purposes (Lloret et al., 2021).

The construction of ports can be damaging as well. Dredging can harm seafloors, reefs, and river/ocean water exchange flows, while construction can be carbon intensive (Johnson, 2002). Local environmental damage can be made worse in smaller ports by a 'race-to-the-bottom' dynamic, where environmental regulations, community control, and taxation capacity are reduced in competition to attract cruise ships. This can be worse in cases of weak or corrupt states, resulting in fisheries damage, biodiversity loss, local flooding, and lack of investment in infrastructure to accommodate the impacts generated by cruise ship passengers at port (MacNeill & Wozniak, 2018).

Port-use impacts refer to the water, sanitation infrastructure, and solid waste removal needs of passengers when at port. All of these things tend to be public goods funded by municipalities through tax receipts. Taxes are collected on a per-passenger basis by municipal authorities, as an income tax on corporate profits, or via value added taxation on the purchases of tourists in port. Remote ports, often in more environmentally sensitive areas, do not have the relative drawing power to demand high port taxes. Thus, the per-head port tax in the Honduran port of Trujillo, for example, is US$1 while the port of Miami charges over $12, and Bermuda has a head tax of about $65 (Brida & Zapata, 2010). Since food and lodging are provided by the cruise ship, per passenger spending of cruise tourists is at least 30% less than that of land tourists. Finally, cruise ships tend to fly 'flags of convenience' – naming their home country as one with significant income tax advantages. Thus, low corporate income taxes are paid, and they tend to be paid to tax haven jurisdictions instead of ports that operate infrastructure to accommodate cruise ships and passengers (Brida & Zapata, 2010).

All of these elements lower tax receipts usable for infrastructure in ports, and this can have dramatic social, economic, and environmental implications. Without sufficient income from tourist spending and taxation, ports have difficulty generating economic spillovers/multipliers and cannot properly process the sewage and waste generated by cruise ship passengers. The only study that directly measured the results of these dynamics was carried out in the remote Honduran port of Trujillo (MacNeill & Wozniak, 2018). The research found that local residents were less able to provide necessities for their families three years after the opening of the Trujillo cruise port, when compared with the previous situation. Garbage from cruise passengers overloaded landfills or just remained on the beach, contributing to an informal dump, in front of a local village. Additional sewage generated by visitors flowed freely into the Caribbean Ocean. Water resources were also over-utilised by cruise passengers in the drought-prone region, contributing to increased water service disruptions to local people. In addition, ecological restrictions had been weakened in the area in order to attract private investment for the cruise port. As a result, the building of the port-initiated flooding, which displaced hundreds of people and impacted local biodiversity. These injuries, combined with anger over the forced demolition of an Indigenous village to make way for the port's construction, led to substantial Indigenous-led social movement activity against the cruise ship port – eventually contributing to its closure in 2019 after only five years of operation (MacNeill, 2020b). Trujillo, Honduras, is not an isolated case. A cost–benefit analysis of a Croatian port found total environmental costs to be seven times larger than the economic benefit (Carić, 2012).

Since cruise vessels are floating all-inclusive resorts, they generate more waste than most ships do. Although they represent less than 1% of the entire shipping industry, cruisers produce approximately 25% of the waste from the sector (Lloret et al., 2021). Cruise passengers have been found to generate 50% more waste than average while on cruise, than they do at home (Véronneau & Roy, 2009). Organic wastes may be dumped overboard in international waters, or incinerated, thus increasing air pollution emitted. It is difficult to monitor cruise ships while at sea, but it is suspected that they contribute to the introduction of hazardous substances such as dioxins, macro waste, and micro plastics into the marine environment (Lloret et al., 2021).

Abatement and regulation possibilities

The environmental impacts of cruise tourism have not gone unnoticed by industry, social movements, or governing bodies. Many of these actors have pushed for the increased regulation (or self-regulation) of impacts. An important initial problem, however, is reporting and monitoring. There is no independent and verifiable system of monitoring all environmental impacts of the cruising industry. Most impacts and moves toward abatement are reported by the cruise ship companies themselves in a non-transparent way (Johnson, 2002). This leaves even the data around emissions and abatement to be suspect.

Nonetheless, industry leaders have begun reporting environmental information publicly, with some publishing yearly sustainability reports (International Marine Organization, 2022). Advanced wastewater treatment systems have been developed and have begun to be used by larger cruisers. Many are in the process of halting the use of single-use plastics. Exhaust gas cleaning systems are being integrated in newer ships or retrofitted on older ones. New less-toxic hull coatings have been developed. Liners have switched to LED lighting and have begun seeking efficiencies by using heat recovery systems that take advantage of heat generation of engines for ship heating.

Many of these moves have been implemented in accordance with national and international regulations (Lloret et al., 2021). Notable among these conventions are the MARIPOL International Convention on the Prevention of Pollution from Ships, the International Convention on the Control of Harmful Anti-Fouling Systems on Ships, the International Convention for the Control and Management of Ships' Ballast Water and Sediments, the Convention on Migratory Species, and the Paris Agreement on Climate Change. Such conventions rely on states to implement recommendations. Not only have governments been slow to generate legislation and enforce law, but they also do not hold force in international waters, leaving cruise tourism largely unregulated. This may contribute to the failing marks that continue to be given to cruise ship companies by non-governmental monitoring groups (FOE, 2020).

Aside from difficulties with monitoring and the muted effect of international conventions, environmental abatement is impeded by ship lifespans, economic and political power imbalances, and industry growth imperatives. Most cruise liners are built with a 30-year intended lifespan. Unless retrofitting is possible, this means more efficient liners are very slow to be brought into active use. The sunk costs implicated in each cruise ship assures that they will not be removed from use until their workable lifespan is complete. This makes implementation of newer, more efficient technologies very slow. There are interesting technologies currently in the design phase, such as the EOSEAS Green Cruise Ship Concept, which uses efficiencies and wind-assisted propulsion to reduce power consumption and CO_2 emissions by an estimated 50% (EOSEAS, 2022). Such concepts are only currently in design phase however.

Given the oligopolistic industry structure, cruise corporations are beholden primarily to shareholders and their overwhelming goal is to create profits. This has resulted in practices such as using tax havens as home ports and resulted in a race-to-the bottom regarding environmental regulation and taxes/fees to fund environmentally sound sewage and solid waste treatment systems at ports. Local populations and environments are often the victims of this disproportionate power of cruise companies to choose their ports according to limited economic criteria. Unless significant and binding international regulation, including competition, environmental, and minimal tax laws are created, this dynamic can be expected to continue – especially in the weak states that are commonly cruise ship destinations.

Publicly listed cruise ship corporations have an additional economic imperative beside profit – long-term growth. This can create increased environmental impacts despite efficiencies in energy use, better ship design, and cleaner modes of operation. The case of greenhouse gas emissions is illustrative of this. The cruise industry has made efforts toward greenhouse gas abatement. For example, the two largest cruise ship companies have managed to reduce the intensity of their emissions per passenger by about 13% since 2013. As Figure 4.1 shows, despite this, total emissions for those companies increased by over 10% during that time (Griffith, 2021). This is entirely the result of industry expansion. Paradoxically, such expansions are often the result of increased energy efficiencies in industries.

This last point is related to a phenomenon called the Jevons' Paradox. The effect was first studied in 1865 by economist William Stanley Jevons as he noted that innovations in coal use efficiency actually resulted in the use of more coal as opposed to less.

Efficiency gains reduce costs relative to output. Since companies tend toward equating the revenues of each additional unit sold with its cost, reduced costs per unit spur the industry to increase output by expanding fleet sizes. This suggest that energy efficiencies realised through technological innovation will result in an expansion of output with increased environmental impacts (Alcott, 2005). Considering the data in Figure 4.1, this is currently occurring in the cruise sector.

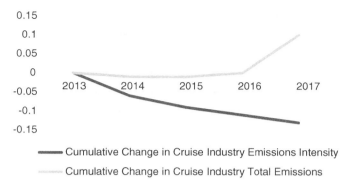

Figure 4.1 Jevons' Paradox – as efficiency increases, so do emissions

Despite the fact that technologically devised efficiencies take a long time to design and implement, the largest cruise ship companies have committed to net zero emissions by 2050 and a 40% reduction by 2030. An obvious problem here is that these reductions are based on a per-passenger rate, and thus do not account to potential additional impacts from efficiency-generated industry expansion. A more immediate issue is that cruise companies are purchasing carbon offsets in order to achieve short-term net emissions reductions, instead of upgrading efficiency. Evidence suggests, however, that 75% to 85% of such credits do not provide real CO_2 reductions. Furthermore, additional non-climate-related environmental impacts of offsets are not quantified, often leading to perverse environmentally damaging effects (Kollmuss et al., 2015; Cames et al., 2016).

A medium-term solution to greenhouse gas emissions that is being pursued by cruise ship companies is to search for ways for ships to burn cleaner fuels. This would allow companies to avoid costly construction of new ships. This is the mode currently endorsed by the Cruise Lines International Association. Unfortunately, the main fuel candidates – biofuels, fuel cells, and liquified natural gas – are not able to achieve net zero without the use of carbon offsets (Smith et al., 2021). They also fall victim to Jevons' paradox.

Summary and conclusion

Cruise tourism has been the fastest-growing tourism sector for the past few decades and is projected to grow equally fast into the future. Although there is no comprehensive lifecycle total of environmental impacts of cruising, there is ample evidence that it is a disproportionately harmful activity. There are various impacts associated with daily operations, provision of infrastructure, port-use impacts, and on-ship waste generation. Waste impacts and local air/water pollution problems are proving the easiest to remedy through relatively easily deployable efficiency systems and technologies on ships.

Environmentally sustainable production of near-zero impact ships may be possible by 2050, but this estimation relies on the development of technologies and manufacturing techniques that have not yet been prototyped. Furthermore, several studies have found that the adoption of new, cleaner, ships by 2050 is not sufficient if the industry wishes to restrict damage to a level sufficient to meet international, scientifically established, goals regarding climate change. In realisation of this, the industry is attempting to implement nearer-term carbon reduction plans that use efficiencies, alternative fuels, and offsets to reduce emissions. Unfortunately, offsets have been found to be largely ineffective in reducing actual carbon emissions. To make this more difficult, research has found that operational efficiencies and carbon offsets actually tend to increase absolute industry environmental impacts over time by spurring industry expansion. This phenomenon is observable in cruise industry data over the past decade. Additional environmental problems are generated by the oligopolistic structure of the cruise ship industry and the regulative environmental race-to-the bottom that this structure inspires as port areas reduce taxation and protections as they compete for contracts with a few large industry players.

The case of cruise ships exposes some notable tensions in the concept of sustainable development, and the United Nations Sustainable Development Goals (SDGs) in particular. The SDGs set a framework to reduce elements like poverty, hunger, and environmental degradation while promoting overall economic growth. This frame ultimately relies on efficiencies and technological change to reduce environmental impacts. As we see with the cruise industry, however, these technologically induced efficiencies, if even possible, tend to generate economic expansion and increase overall environmental burdens. Solutions do exist, however. First, industry oligopolistic power could be reduced through the establishment of enforceable global environmental protections and minimum standard port-fees, along with the implementation of competition laws. Next, a globally enforceable cap on total industry greenhouse gas emissions could be instituted, thus preventing efficiency-induced growth that increases impacts. Similar caps and monitoring could be applied to the full menu of other environmental impacts discussed above. This may inspire smaller-scale, environmentally tenable – much higher-priced – niche cruising to replace the current mass-transportation, oligopolistic model. This would require that existing international conventions be accorded more legal/regulatory power than they currently have, but it does not require that they change their scientifically established guidelines. Given the problems with relying on technology alone to reduce environmental impacts, these measures offer a more realistic and potentially effective path to sustainability than do approaches based on often-conflicting sustainable development goals.

References

Abdulla, A., & Linden, O. (2008). *Maritime traffic effects on biodiversity in the Mediterranean Sea: Review of impacts, priority areas and mitigation measures.* Malaga: IUCN Centre for Mediterranean Cooperation.

Abbasov, F., Earl, T., Jeanne, N., Hemmings, B., Gilliam, L., & Calvo Ambel, C. (2019). *One Corporation to Pollute Them All: Luxury cruise air emissions in Europe.* www.transportenvironment.org.

Adams, S. A., Font, X., & Stanford, D. (2017). All aboard the corporate socially and environmentally responsible cruise ship: A conjoint analysis of consumer choices. *Worldwide Hospitality and Tourism Themes*, 9(1), 31–43.

Alcott, B. (2005). Jevons' Paradox. *Ecological Economics*, 54(1), 9–21.

Brida, J. G., Pulina, M., Riaño, E., & Aguirre, S. Z. (2013). Cruise passengers in a homeport: A market analysis. *Tourism Geographies*, 15(1), 68–87.

Brida, J. G., & Zapata, S. (2010). Cruise tourism: Economic, socio-cultural and environmental impacts. *International Journal of Leisure and Tourism Marketing*, 1(3), 205–226.

Bull, A. O. (2013). Cruise tourism. In *Handbook of tourism economics: Analysis, new applications and case studies*. Singapore: World Scientific.

Cames, M., Harthan, R. O., Füssler, J., Lazarus, M., Lee, C. M., Erickson, P., & Spalding-Fecher, R. (2016). *How additional is the clean development mechanism?* Berlin: Öko Institute.

Carić, H. (2012). Cruise tourism environmental risks. In *Cruise tourism and society* (pp. 47–67). Berlin: Springer.

Carić, H., Klobučar, G., & Štambuk, A. (2016). Ecotoxicological risk assessment of antifouling emissions in a cruise ship port. *Journal of Cleaner Production*, 121, 159–168.

Cerchiello, G., & Vera-Rebollo, J. F. (2019). From elitist to popular tourism: Leisure cruises to Spain during the first third of the twentieth century (1900–1936). *Journal of Tourism History*, 11(2), 144–166.

Data Intelligence. (2021). *Cruise Tourism Market*. https://www.dataintelligence.com/research-report/cruise-tourism-market

De Pryck, K. (2021). Intergovernmental expert consensus in the making: The case of the summary for policy makers of the IPCC 2014 Synthesis Report. *Global Environmental Politics*, 21(1), 108–129.

EOSEAS. (2022). *Green Cruise Ship Concept*. https://www.stirlingdesign.fr/presses/conferences/stirling_design_green_ship_copenhagen.pdf

Eurostat. (2021). *Greenhouse Gas Emission Statistics – Carbon Footprints*. https://ec.europa.eu/eurostat/statistics-explained/index.php?title=Main_Page

FOE. (2020). Cruise Ship Report Card – Friends of the Earth [WWW Document]. https://foe.org/cruise-report-card/.

Griffith University. (2021). Global Sustainable Tourism Dashboard. https://www.tourismdashboard.org/explore-the-data/cruise-ship/

Hickel, J., & Kallis, G. (2020). Is green growth possible? *New Political Economy*, 25(4), 469–486.

International Marine Organization [IMO]. (2022). Initial IMO Greenhouse Gas Strategy. https://www.imo.org/en/MediaCentre/HotTopics/Pages/Reducing-greenhouse-gas-emissions-from-ships.aspx

Johnson, D. (2002). Environmentally sustainable cruise tourism: A reality check. *Marine Policy*, 26(4), 261–270.

Kester, J.G.C. (2002). Cruise tourism. *Tourism Economics*, 9(3), 337–350.

Kollmuss, A., Schneider, L., & Zhezherin, V. (2015). *Has joint implementation reduced GHG emissions? lessons learned for the design of carbon market mechanisms*. Stockholm: Environment Institute.

Lloret, J., Carreño, A., Carić, H., San, J., & Fleming, L. E. (2021). Environmental and human health impacts of cruise tourism: A review. *Marine Pollution Bulletin*, 173, 112979.

Longcore, T., & Rich, C. (2004). Ecological light pollution. *Frontiers in Ecology and the Environment*, 2(4), 191–198.

MacNeill, T. (2017). Development as Imperialism: Power and the perpetuation of poverty in afro-Indigenous communities of coastal Honduras. *Humanity & Society*, 41(2), 209–239.

MacNeill, T. (2020a). Indigenous food sovereignty in a captured state: the Garifuna in Honduras. *Third World Quarterly*, 41(9), 1537–1555.

MacNeill, T. (2020b). *Indigenous cultures and Sustainable development in Latin America* (p. 253). New York: Palgrave Macmillan/Springer Nature.

MacNeill, T., & Wozniak, D. (2018). The economic, social, and environmental impacts of cruise tourism. *Tourism Management*, 66, 387–404.

Maragkogianni, A., & Papaefthimiou, S. (2015). Evaluating the social cost of cruise ships air emissions in major ports of Greece. *Transportation Research Part D: Transport and Environment*, 36, 10–17.

Marti, B. E. (1991). Cruise ship market segmentation: a 'non-traditional' port case study. *Maritime Policy & Management*, 18(2), 93–103.

Önal, M., Neşer, G., & Gürsel, K. T. (2021). Environmental impacts of steel ship hulls building and recycling by life cycle assessment (LCA). *Ships and Offshore Structures*, 16(10), 1061–1066.

Papachristou, A. A., Pallis, A. A., & Vaggelas, G. K. (2020). Cruise home-port selection criteria. *Research in Transportation Business & Management*, 100584.

Talley, W. K. (2003). Environmental impacts of shipping. In *Handbook of Transport and the Environment*. Emerald Group Publishing Limited.

Smith, T., Domagoj, B., Fahnestock, J., Galbraith, C., Velandia Perico, C., Rojon, I., & Shaw, A. (2021). *A Strategy for the Transition to Zero-Emission Shipping*. London: UMAS.

Thurau, B., Seekamp, E., Carver, A. D. and Lee, J. G. (2015). Should cruise ports market ecotourism? A comparative analysis of passenger spending expectations within the Panama Canal Watershed. *International Journal of Tourism Research*, *17*(1), 45–53.

United Nations. (2015). *Sustainable Development Goals*. https://www.un.org/sustainabledevelopment/development-agenda/

Véronneau, S., & Roy, J. (2009). Global service supply chains: An empirical study of current practices and challenges of a cruise line corporation. *Tourism Management*, 30(1), 128–139.

1.2
Supply-side trends
Attractions, culture, and heritage tourism

Aaron Tham provides Chapter 5 on *A scenario planning approach to safety in visitor attractions*. Safety is a pivotal factor to any visitor attraction as it seeks to deliver a secure environment for all its stakeholders to engage with its range of activities. However, literature surrounding safety in visitor attractions remains largely implicit, or fragmented. This chapter unpacks the use of scenario planning as an approach to safety in visitor attractions, prompted by the growing tide of unpredictable and non-linear crises and disasters that have confronted the industry over the past decade. The aim of this chapter is therefore to spark future theoretical and managerial reflections on how to identify a range of scenarios that perhaps raise (un)safe practices in visitor attractions, and the mechanisms to address and mitigate unnecessary incidents of death, injury, or reputational risk to organisations. In turn, a safe attraction also enjoys a positive product and service quality perception among its visitor clientele.

Wine tourism: Current trends and future prospects is the topic of Chapter 6 by **Haiyan Song and Weixi (Edith) Yuan**. This chapter discusses the development of global wine tourism from the perspectives of wine producers, distributors, and consumers. It also explores wine tourism trends through the lens of supply and demand. Wine tourism destinations that depend on exporting wine and attracting international tourists have suffered severely during the ongoing COVID-19 pandemic. Given a lack of research on wine tourism supply and demand, particularly in the wake of COVID-19, this chapter explores this topic and provides insights into stakeholder performance during the wine tourism development process, with a focus on China. It analyses trends of consumer demand and explore the integration of regional wine brands and local wine tourism resources. Furthermore, it discusses e-commerce and digital platform development and promotion, to provide suggestions for the development of wine tourism in emerging economies. The chapter explores current and future challenges for the sector, including COVID-19 and post-pandemic recovery, to illustrate the need to integrate regional resources and invest in local tourism infrastructure, which are often lacking. Suggestions for the future wine tourism development up to 2042 are provided.

Sophia Lingham and Louise Manning contribute Chapter 7 on *Culinary tourism: Dualistic erosion and enhancement of food cultures*. The role of local gastronomy and cultural foods is arguably as important to the modern tourist industry as it is to its historic local foundations. This chapter delves into the world of culinary tourism and compares and contrasts certain aspects between Mediterranean countries and the U.K. from consumer and producer perspectives, and with reference to the Sustainable Development Goals (SDGs). Multiple stakeholders are considered, along with recent food trends in the form of

DOI: 10.4324/9781003260790-8

cultural goods, the increasingly nebulous term of 'identity', food memories, and new developing forms of economy. Looking to the future, predictions and opportunities such as agritourism and social equality are analysed, providing context to this chapter's snapshot of the current foodscape.

Chapter 8 is on *Homestays concept in Indian tourism and hospitality industry* by **Suneel Kumar, Marco Valeri**, and **Varinder Kumar**. Homestays have grown in popularity in the post-COVID period, as social distance, sanitation, hygiene, and privacy have surfaced as major issues for tourists. Over the last few years, international tourists and locals have increasingly preferred intimate hotels to traditional hotels in quest of their unique local travel experiences. Furthermore, the relaxed adaptability, and the value for money provided by a homestay, particularly when travelling in a large group, are factors fuelling the growth of this industry. This chapter explores the potential of homestays in a Himalayan state (Himachal Pradesh and Uttarakhand) and looks for initiatives and patterns related to this scheme.

Eleni Mavragani and **Sofia Avramidou** are the authors of Chapter 9 on *Cultural heritage tourism and ethical trends*. The chapter approaches cultural heritage and describes a series of ethical issues concerning the management and marketing of monuments that arise in times of war and peace. It explores ethical issues and trends regarding intercultural monuments, selective memory management and examines the politicisation of heritage and the polarity between cultural nationalism and cultural internationalism. The challenge of the chapter is to investigate the concept of cultural heritage tourism in the light of the interactions between tourism and heritage, the actions taken by international organisations for the management of heritage, and the ethical issues and trends also concerning the management of UNESCO monuments. The contribution of the chapter lies in the fact that it investigates two social phenomena, tourism, and cultural heritage, that overcome the problematic theories of conflict and become allies under the roof of the ethical management of monuments.

Challenges in developing cultural tourism: Insights from Canada is the title of Chapter 10, written by **Louis-Etienne Dubois, Frédéric Dimanche**, and **Shawn Newman**. Cultural tourism has garnered significant attention, in the field and in academia, over the last few decades. The COVID-19 pandemic, which abruptly closed international borders and cultural venues, further highlighted the economic importance of cultural tourism for communities around the world. Based on the case of Ontario, Canada, this chapter explores ongoing challenges, as well as trends related to cultural tourism. It identifies the lack of institutional coordination and support, as well as social justice considerations, as issues requiring immediate attention for this sector to continue developing. The chapter also suggests how demographic and technological changes, in addition to a renewed appreciation of the arts, are bound to further complexify and grow cultural tourism offerings. Implications for stakeholders are offered in closing.

Brianna Wyatt contributes Chapter 11 on *Edutainment experiences in dark tourism: Re-enacting dark heritage*. Dark tourism has become a major contributor to the wider tourism industry. While traditionally its visitor experiences have relied on static, non-personal interpretation methods, technological advances and changes in demand have triggered a rising trend of edutainment interpretation which blurs the boundaries of entertainment and education to create simulated and engaging moments of history. These experiences have long been criticised within the academic community as frivolous amusements that trivialise history. However, considering the growing public preference for edutainment experiences it is necessary that this topic be brought to the forefront of research. This chapter discusses the use and growing trend of edutainment interpretation within dark tourism practice. Finally, it sets out predictions of future trends based on current edutainment practices and visitor observations within the context of dark tourism.

Modelling heritage justice for under-represented communities is the topic of Chapter 12 by **Deepak Chhabra**. From the standpoint of sustainable heritage tourism, it has become critical to scrutinise the intersection between authenticity, heritage justice and wellbeing. The authenticity discourse has become increasingly relevant in the heritage justice deliberations, particularly in the context of under-represented communities. This chapter contextualises a heritage justice paradigm that strives to strengthen the traditional foundations of under-represented communities by safeguarding their cultural authenticity and nurturing their hedonic and eudaimonic wellbeing. Barriers and enablers of heritage justice are identified and a heritage justice model is proposed. This line of inquiry has been sparsely explored in documented literature.

Diogo Moleiro and **Lígia Ribeiro** write about ***Creative tourism trends*** in Chapter 13. A growing body of literature on creative tourism has emerged since the term was first introduced about two decades ago as a way to refer to a type of tourism that offers visitors the opportunity to apply their creative potential through active participation in learning experiences characteristic of the destination where they take place. This growing awareness that visitors are increasingly seeking to play an active role during their travels by participating in local socio-cultural experiences is a direct consequence of their desire to experience the culture of others. As such, it has become evident that around the world there is exponential growth in experiential travel aimed at this niche of visitors, as it involves more experiential encounters and greater learning opportunities for the visitor. This chapter analyses trends in creative tourism. Its analysis is based on its impacts, players, main catalysts, opportunities, challenges, implications, and future forecasts. Since the growth of academic studies as well as the increase in practical efforts on the ground to promote creative tourism are current evidence and it is seen as a niche capable of enhancing sustainable tourism.

5 A scenario planning approach to safety in visitor attractions

Aaron Tham

Introduction

Safety is of paramount importance to the attractions industry, especially as a key feature of the tourism sector that brings in large-scale visitor numbers and employs numerous staff across its operations (Postma, 2014). Due to the concentration of individuals to a single site each day, attractions have an added level of risk resulting from any threats to safety for all its stakeholders (e.g., staff, visitors and contractors). As such, attractions have to pay particular attention to safety, evidenced by rising costs of insurance confronting the industry through a combination of health risks, natural disasters and terrorism, among others (Heikell, 2022).

This chapter unpacks the use of scenario planning as an approach to safety in visitor attractions, prompted by the growing tide of unpredictable and non-linear crises and disasters that have confronted the industry over the past decade. The aim of this chapter is therefore to spark future theoretical and managerial reflections on how to identify a range of scenarios that perhaps raise (un)safe practices in visitor attractions, and the mechanisms to address and mitigate unnecessary incidents of death, injury, or reputational risk to organisations. In turn, a safe attraction also enjoys a positive product and service quality perception among its visitor clientele (Zou & Meng, 2020). Favourable word of mouth, and online reviews in the current marketplace, can lead to loyal and repeat visitors that become a competitive advantage for the favouring of one visitor attraction over another (Nowacki, 2009). For this reason, paying attention to safety is pivotal to the success of any visitor attraction.

Definition and scope of visitor attractions

Visitor attractions are often defined as places of interest (Middleton, 1989). As such, attractions are markers displaying the unique attributes of a place (Leask & Fyall, 2006). While there is consensus that attractions help shape the destination image of a location, some scholars have also expressed that attractions embody various dimensions from natural (e.g., parks and reserves), to man-made environments, such as casinos, events and cultural precincts (Weidenfeld, Butler, & Williams, 2010). As such, various types of attractions have been identified in tourism literature. For instance, Swarbrooke (2002) classified visitor attractions into four groups – natural attractions (beach, mountains), events (e.g., sporting activities, festivals, World Expos), manufactured attractions (theme parks, museums), and unintentional manufactured attractions (churches, castles, memorials). Kusen (2010) provided a further differentiation of attraction types, with 16 classifications as follows:

1. Attractions for attractions
2. Climate
3. Cultural and religious institutions
4. Famous persons and historical events
5. Fauna
6. Flora
7. Geological features
8. Natural spas/sanitariums
9. Protected cultural heritage
10. Protected natural heritage
11. Special events/happenings
12. Sport and recreation facilities
13. The culture of life and work
14. Tourism para-attractions
15. Tourism paths, trails and roads
16. Water

Evidently, the vast array of attractions on offer is an attempt by any destination to devise strategies that cater to different market segments (Jurowski & Olsen, 1995). As such, it is likely that all destinations continually reinvent themselves through developing attractions in order to appeal to visitor needs and wants. This has led Peters and Weiermair (2000) to conclude that a hypercompetitive environment exists to ensure that attractions remain appealing to the evolving tastes of visitors. Then, as more visitors engage with the different attractions, these locations are no longer merely considered to be places of interest but are expected to be corporate citizens to deliver safe and secure premises for enjoyment (Lawton, 2005). Stakeholders, too, would be very interested in witnessing how attractions comply with safety regulations to determine whether they would continue engaging with the provider when safety incidents threaten its usual operations (Milman, Okumus, & Dickson, 2010). For example, when a natural disaster occurs, visitors want to see how the attraction responds before determining whether it is safe to return to it (Dennien & Lynch, 2020).

In this aspect, Leiper's (1990) model of attractions epitomises how visitors select where to go in order to fulfil their travel needs. Specifically, he argued that visitors do not necessarily gravitate to any single attraction, but are instead lured to its ability to satisfy specific experiences. This model has engineered other studies to validate attraction systems. For instance, Richards (2002) ascertained that the model applies to the context of cultural tourism, where visitors seeking to acquire knowledge about foreign places are clearly attracted to destinations that are very different to the home environment. The activity-based model of destination choice developed by Moscardo, Morrison, Pearce, Lang, and O'Leary (1996) also asserts that destination choice is derived from a match between activity types undertaken at specific attractions. All the same, participation in visitor attractions is evaluated based on a range of heuristics, including perceived safety.

Safety and its role in visitor attractions

Visitor attractions have had a long-standing relationship with safety because of organisational compliance to national and local laws at the point of inception. Management must deal with a repertoire of safety checks to ensure that the visitor experience is one that can be conducted in a manner that allows for the thrills and enjoyment without compromising security. Issues that need to be addressed include policies for food safety and hygiene, managing unruly guest behaviour, terrorism, electrical fires, other natural disasters, as well as health pandemics such as SARS, MERS and the ongoing COVID-19 outbreak. The challenge of addressing safety in visitor attractions is that such issues are often unpredictable and therefore result in reactive rather than proactive actions among operators (Leask, 2016). Unlike products that can be pre-tested, visitor attractions are mostly purchased sight unseen and only encountered during the host–guest exchange when the service is performed (Britton, 1991). Moreover, each of the aforementioned types of attractions warrants a personalised approach to managing safety and risks, as they differ in size and complexity. For instance, the evaluation of risks for a high-ropes adventure tourism course would vary significantly to an art gallery and its required disaster assessments. Nonetheless, the notion of safety is closely interwoven with the discussion of crises and disasters and hence these concepts will be subsequently reviewed.

Crises and disasters, at a broad level, refer to issues or incidents that threaten a business and its daily operations. In a tourism context, Faulkner (2001) differentiated crises and disasters based on whether these issues were organisation-induced (e.g., gas explosion) or externally-induced (e.g., earthquake). Regardless of who is culpable for inducing the perceived threats to personal harm and safety, it is acknowledged that such crises and disasters often disrupt the operations of visitor attractions unless operators, and customers, feel it is safe to visit again. The World Travel & Tourism Council (2021) estimated that it takes, on average, between ten months and four years for a destination, and its tourism attractions to recover from a crisis or disaster, contingent on its severity and perceived threats to safety.

Amidst this backdrop, there is consensus that the management of crises and disasters goes through three main stages: pre-crisis, in-crisis, and post-crisis (Ritchie, 2004). Each of these stages then warrants its own response and communication strategies as organisations take the necessary steps to localise the threats to safety, disseminate information in a timely manner, and resolve issues that arise not limited to treatment of injuries, legal compensations, or asset repairs. Whilst these strategies appear consistent across the globe, successful efforts at crisis or disaster management remain elusive. For instance, the Dreamworld theme park Australian incident, which led to four deaths in 2016, took almost four years to complete its legal investigations and led to the organisation being fined US$2.5 million over safety breaches (Huxley, 2020). Likewise, the 2018 volcanic eruption in the tourist attraction White Island (Whakaari) in New Zealand is being handled by the courts as more than 13 different organisations are being investigated for safety breaches that claimed the lives of 21 tourists (Taylor, 2020). Similar incidents are likely to have occurred elsewhere and reiterate the growing expectations of stakeholders for visitor attractions to deal with safety and ensure appropriate communication and recovery marketing messages are in place (Scott, Laws, & Prideaux, 2006). Yet it is argued that no two crises or disasters are identical, and so management of safety in visitor attractions requires a contextual approach. In addition, visitor attractions are likely to be exposed to a wider range of crises and disasters into the future. Then, as visitor attractions reopen to cater to guests keen to engage since the onset of the COVID-19 pandemic, safety incidents continue to surface and require responses from operators (see, for instance, Read, 2022; Vera, 2022). This therefore triggers the need to invoke scenario planning techniques to help organisations prepare for safety planning and design as they operate visitor attractions of the future.

Scenario planning and implications for visitor attractions

Scenario planning is a future-focussed technique that allows organisations an opportunity to make contingencies to answer the what if questions posed by uncertain outcomes (Oliver & Parrett, 2018). It has been employed in the business fraternity for over three decades and seeks to empower managers to be more proactive whilst operating in a volatile, uncertain, complex and ambiguous (VUCA) world (Coates, 2000). Indeed, for a tourism sector like visitor attractions, operations have become less predictable due to the range of issues that could compromise safety, not limited to deviant behaviour (either by employee or customer), as well as other externalities (equipment malfunction, natural disasters). For this reason, scenario planning calls for organisations to be demonstrate greater dexterity in dealing with possible futures (Schoemaker, 2020).

Despite its merits, scholars also caution against the pitfalls of scenario planning if the specific circumstances/contexts are not clearly articulated (Amer, Daim, & Jetter, 2013). Importantly, the various scenarios that emerge should be those that are highly probable and informed by a range of wider external environmental triggers, e.g., technology advances (Varum & Melo, 2010). These factors, in turn, lead to organisational decision-making that should inform best practices for strategic futures (Keough & Shanahan, 2008). As such, some studies have advocated for a rigorous approach to undertake scenario planning. For instance, Moriarty (2012) conceptualised scenario planning into a model comprising of three stages – present operating environment, possible future operating environments, and possible future states of affairs. In contrast, Duinker and Greig (2007) adopted a deductive approach featuring seven steps:

1. Definition of the topic/problem and focus of scenario planning
2. Identification and review of key factors or external environment influences
3. Identification of critical uncertainties
4. Definition of scenario logics
5. Creation of scenarios
6. Assessment of business implications as well as to other stakeholders
7. Proposal of actions and policy outcomes

Then, by extension, scenario planning should be adopted towards visitor attractions given the unpredictable nature of (un)safe incidents. In fact, scenario-based training has already been introduced to crisis management in a human resource context, using case studies of disasters such as Hurricane Katrina and September 11 (Moats, Chermack, & Dooley, 2008). Next, scenario planning will be applied to visitor attractions and how safety cold be better managed in the future.

The first step is to examine the future operating landscapes of visitor attractions in the coming decade, or, better still, extrapolating to 2052. Arguably one of the main trends shaping future visitor attractions is the greater adoption of technology as a facilitator of the experience (Jackson, 2019). In the first decade to 2032, attractions would likely feature virtual/augmented reality (VR/AR), smartphone apps, gamification, simulations, and visualisations to enhance memorability, authenticity, and hedonic outcomes (Shen, Sotiriadis, & Zhang, 2020). Related to safety, these technological features could also lead to an increase in health side-effects e.g., giddiness, as well as accidents where users clash with others due to a lack of awareness of their surroundings. For these reasons, visitor attractions should incorporate training and induction programmes for staff and subsequently users to adequately prepare them for the use of such technologies to alleviate safety concerns during the service encounters. At present, there are likely to be training manuals for employees, though guest preparation is often reduced to just a single session prior to use, usually just lasting a few minutes. In future, visitors could perhaps be provided with a safety video and instructions via email or the app, at the point of booking, or as a follow-up reminder before the visit date. All the same, this development is tied in with Sustainable Development Goal 9, which targets industry, innovation and infrastructure as a vehicle to drive greener futures for the attraction sector.

A second trend that has emerged is greater calls for visitor attractions to cater towards people with varying levels of abilities. The growth and attention towards accessible tourism extends to visitor attractions because of the increasing number of people with temporal or permanent disabilities, who display a greater propensity to spend and stay longer at a destination (Gillovic & McIntosh, 2020). This raises significant considerations for visitor attractions from a safety perspective, as infrastructure and services need to be retrofitted for designed to be fit for purpose (Cloquet, Palomino, Shaw, Stephen, & Taylor, 2018). Tourism futures catering to accessibility may require a longer time frame to deliver, so it is more likely that scenarios featuring inclusive attraction design principles can realistically be delivered in 2042, factoring in some of the following questions from an operational perspective:

- Can the river cruise cater to persons in wheelchairs?
- Will the cable car have audio cues for those that are visually impaired?
- To what extent will rock climbing be safe enough for individuals that have mobility impairment?

Then, human resources will need to also be trained to deliver inclusive and accessible attractions to ensure that all visitors can enjoy their experiences in a safe and secure manner (Somnuxpong & Wiwatwongwana, 2020). After all, catering to people with different abilities will require a range of policies and procedures to remove barriers for participation, such as operating an accessible bungee-jumping activity. These developments are relevant to Sustainable Development Goal 10 on reducing inequalities, so that people with varying levels of abilities can participate in 'tourism for all'.

The third major global trend affecting the future of visitor attractions is the shift from organisational-centric forms of delivery to socially co-created authentic experiences, such as festivals and events (Richards, King, & Yeung, 2020). In this vein, the decentralisation of festivals and events as attractions are an attempt to reduce the seasonality effect confronting destinations, by featuring a range of activities to entice and spread out visitor numbers over a year. Such events also enable a destination to create its unique destination image and brand, such as that of Burning Man and Coachella. However, the spike in number of festivals and events can also prompt safety concerns, because not all event organisers or attendees may be versed in terms of risk and crisis management (Markwell & Tomsen, 2010). Incidents of food poisoning, terrorism, equipment fires, drug- and alcohol-induced violence continue to surface at festivals and events around the world. These issues can cast negative perceptions of some festivals and events as dangerous attractions, resulting in a loss of existing or potential markets (Scott & Scott, 2020). Such developments are likely to manifest ubiquitously in 2052, where numerous destinations can afford to invest and have reliable big data resources to facilitate this real-time decision-making. This can then serve as a key tool for Sustainable Development Goal 11 on sustainable cities and communities.

Issues such as overtourism, inefficiencies lost due to traffic congestion, for example, can be addressed in a coherent and integrated manner.

A fourth and generally under-investigated safety concern relates to cybersecurity of visitor attractions considering recent malware and breaches that have exposed copious amounts of data related to user privacy and financial details. Like many other sectors of the tourism industry, visitor attractions increasingly transact on electronic commerce platforms and mobile payment options such as Google Pay or Apple Pay in a contactless environment to facilitate efficient booking arrangements. However, these mechanisms are not entirely free from phishing and other cybersecurity threats, which when compromised result in operator and visitors being exposed to frauds and compromised financial access (Chen & Fiscus, 2018). This necessitates visitor attractions to undertake two-factor authentication that may appear as an inconvenience to customers but provide an additional layer of security and peace of mind when paying for attraction tickets or packages. Another alternative to overcome cybersecurity threats is to facilitate payment options using cryptocurrencies, which are conducted on the back of blockchains. Such mechanisms increase the level of financial safety as each stakeholder on the transaction has to 'approve' the payment in order to proceed (Luo & Zhou, 2021). This reiterates the importance of Sustainable Development Goal 17 (Partnership for the Goals), and how different stakeholder groups need to come together to realise the desired safety goals for attraction providers in this area of cybersecurity. This prompts attraction providers to work with blockchain platforms and customers to ensure that there is a safe and secure way to conduct transactions and will likely see greater adoption over the coming decades.

In summary, these four scenarios precipitate visitor attractions to consider how best to mitigate safety breaches across a range of different consumer touchpoints. From the point of service design to the end of the service encounter, there are numerous fail points that could derail safety outcomes to any visitor attraction. The above-mentioned scenarios provide a useful vantage point upon which various stakeholder groups to the visitor attraction industry need to adopt targeted strategies or policies to ensure safety compliance and recovery in the future.

A scenario planning framework for safety in visitor attractions

Findings derived from the four scenarios discussed previously has led to the development of a scenario planning framework for safety in visitor attractions (Figure 5.1).

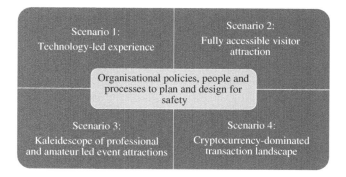

Figure 5.1 Scenario-planning framework for safety in visitor attractions.

Following these scenarios in Figure 5.1, visitor attractions will also need to identify monitoring indicators to ascertain the presence, performance, and proficiency of their safety standards to combat the threats posed by any future likely crises or disasters that compromise their daily operations, as argued by Konno, Nonaka, and Ogilvy (2014). Examples of some of these safety indicators include:

- Frequency of safety breaches/incidents per year
- Length of safety breach and response time to contain the risk
- Severity of risk (e.g., death, permanent disability, financial losses, lawsuits)
- Periodic safety training and induction for staff (and corresponding completion rates/results)
- Guest perception of visitor attraction in terms of safety performance (pre-, during, and post-visit)
- Awards and safety standards attained (such as ISO 18001 or 45001)
- Mock safety breach/incidents and evaluation of staff performance
- Regular forums with other tourism or business sector leaders to keep abreast of latest developments in safety, e.g., reduction in drowning, and smart technologies to monitor such risks, especially in times where surf patrol is unavailable, or not operating

Evidently, the scenario planning approach to safety in visitor attractions is not intended to be a merely prescriptive tool. Rather, it provides a timely introspection of the complex and unpredictable nature of crises and disasters that can impede on safe operations across the visitor attraction industry. As such, scenario planning offers an important starting point to consider likely future operating landscapes, and the iterative approaches needed to prepare business strategies and models to deal with the likely scenarios. This then ensures that visitor attractions possess a competitive advantage to manage safety and deliver a responsible, timely and consolidated visitor experience moving into the future.

This chapter provides fresh insights to deal with safety in visitor attractions by adopting a futures perspective. This will obviously be contingent on what risks are posed to the diversity of attractions, and the length and severity of the crisis/disaster presented. Therefore, by integrating existing literature on safety in visitor attractions by other scholars (e.g., Erfurt, 2022; Gstaettner, Lee, Weiler, & Rodger, 2019), the following future-focussed attraction safety management model in Figure 5.2 is proposed.

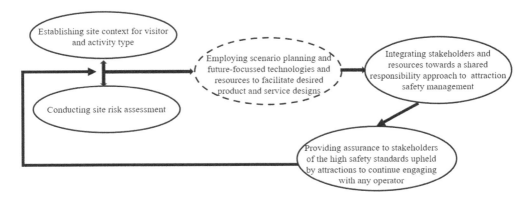

Figure 5.2 Future-focussed safety in visitor attractions model employing scenario planning techniques.

At a managerial and operational level, this chapter provides tangible and actionable recommendations as a call for action. Whilst each attraction operator will likely have safety manuals and protocols as part of their duty of care, the unpredictability and increasing frequency of crises and disasters precipitates quick and real-time information underpinned by reviews of scenario plans. Therefore, future strategic initiatives for attraction owners and operators should also evolve as we approach the next few decades. Pertinently, visitor safety must now also consider physical and virtual threats (e.g., cyberattacks) and offer a tiered and collaborative response. Some of these tools featuring big data are already in place and provide a mechanism towards a tiered response to safety. For instance, assets and equipment can track visitor numbers and so warn operators when optimal capacity is reached. Likewise, monitoring and assurance can take place with multilingual capability to warn stakeholders of impending threats to safety, e.g., natural disasters such as bushfires. Other implications for safety management in visitor attractions can also consider how training and leadership within corporate cultures evolve to manage intergenerational workforce featuring Millennials, Generation Z and subsequent generations (Generation Alpha and Beta).

References

Amer, M., Daim, T. U., & Jetter, A. (2013). A review of scenario planning. *Futures*, *46*(Feb), 23–40.

Britton, S. (1991). Tourism, capital, and place: Towards a critical geography of tourism. *Environment and Planning D: Society and Space*, *9*(4), 451–478.

Chen, H. S., & Fiscus, J. (2018). The inhospitable vulnerability: A need for cybersecurity risk assessment in the hospitality industry. *Journal of Hospitality and Tourism Technology*, *9*(2), 223–234.

Cloquet, I., Palomino, M., Shaw, G., Stephen, G., & Taylor, T. (2018). Disability, social inclusion and the marketing of tourist attractions. *Journal of Sustainable Tourism*, *26*(2), 221–237.

Coates, J. (2000). Scenario planning. *Technological Forecasting and Social Change*, *65*(1), 115–123.

Dennien, M., & Lynch, L. (2020, August 13). Binna Burra to reopen for visitors after fire devastation. *Brisbane Times*. https://www.brisbanetimes.com.au/national/queensland/binna-burra-to-reopen-for-visitors-one-year-after-fire-devastation-20200813-p55la0.html

Duinker, P. N., & Greig, L. A. (2007). Scenario analysis in environmental impact assessment: Improving explorations of the future. *Environmental Impact Assessment Review*, *27*(3), 206–219.

Erfurt, P. (2022). Volcano tourism and visitor safety: Still playing with fire? A 10-year update. *Geoheritage*, *14*(Article number 56).

Faulkner, B. (2001). Towards a framework for tourism disaster management. *Tourism Management*, *22*(2), 135–147.

Gillovic, B., & McIntosh, A. (2020). Accessibility and inclusive tourism development: Current state and future agenda. *Sustainability*, *12*(22), 9722.

Gstaettner, A. M., Lee, D., Weiler, B., & Rodger, K. (2019). Visitor safety in recreational protected areas: Exploring responsibility-sharing from a management perspective. *Tourism Management*, *75*(Dec.), 370–380.

Heikell, L. (2022, June 13). Iconic Wellington attractions feeling the pinch as insurance costs soar. *Newshub*. https://www.newshub.co.nz/home/money/2022/06/iconic-wellington-attractions-feeling-the-pinch-as-insurance-costs-soar.html

Huxley, J. (2020, September 28). Dreamworld operator Ardent Leisure fined $3.6m for Thunder River Rapids Ride deaths. *ABC News*. https://www.abc.net.au/news/2020-09-28/qld-dreamworld-ardent-leisure-court-thunder-river-rapids-ride/12709338

Jackson, V. (2019, January 16). *Why augmented reality is the future for visitor attractions*. https://medium.com/mighty-missions/why-augmented-reality-is-the-future-for-visitor-attractions-2c37a756f331

Jurowski, C., & Olsen, M. D. (1995). Scanning the environment of tourism attractions: A content analysis approach. *Journal of Travel & Tourism Marketing*, *4*(1), 71–96.

Keough, S. M., & Shanahan, K. J. (2008). Scenario planning: Toward a more complete model for practice. *Advances in Developing Human Resources*, *10*(2), 166–178.

Konno, N., Nonaka, I., & Ogilvy, J. (2014). Scenario planning: The basics. *World Futures*, *70*(1), 28–43.

Kusen, E. (2010). A system of tourism attractions. *Tourism*, *58*(4), 409–424.

Lawton, L. J. (2005). Resident perceptions of tourist attractions on the Gold Coast of Australia. *Journal of Travel Research*, *44*(2), 188–200.

Leask, A. (2016). Visitor attraction management: A critical review of research 2009–2014. *Tourism Management*, *57*(Dec), 334–361.

Leask, A., & Fyall, A. (2006). Researching the management of visitor attractions: International comparative study issues. *Tourism Recreation Research*, *31*(2), 23–32.

Leiper, N. (1990). Tourist attraction systems. *Annals of Tourism Research*, *17*(3), 367–384.

Luo, L., & Zhou, J. (2021). BlockTour: A blockchain-based smart tourism platform. *Computer Communications*, *175*, 186–192.

Markwell, K., & Tomsen, S. (2010). Safety and hostility at special events: Lessons from Australian gay and lesbian festivals. *Event Management*, *14*(3), 225–238.

Middleton, V. T. C. (1989). Marketing implications for attractions. *Tourism Management*, *10*(3), 229–232.

Milman, A., Okumus, F., & Dickson, D. (2010). The contribution of theme parks and attractions to the social and economic sustainability of destinations. *Worldwide Hospitality and Tourism Themes*, *2*(3), 338–345.

Moats, J. B., Chermack, T. J., & Dooley, L. M. (2008). Using scenarios to develop crisis managers: Applications of scenario planning and scenario-based training. *Advances in Developing Human Resources*, *10*(3), 397–424.

Moriarty, J. P. (2012). Theorising scenario analysis to improve future perspective planning in tourism. *Journal of Sustainable Tourism*, *20*(6), 779–800.

Moscardo, G., Morrison, A. M., Pearce, P. L., Lang, C., & O'Leary, J. (1996). Understanding vacation destination choice through travel motivations and activities. *Journal of Vacation Marketing*, *2*(2), 109–122.

Nowacki, M. M. (2009). Quality of visitor attractions, satisfaction, benefits and behavioural intentions of visitors: Verification of a model. *International Journal of Tourism Research*, *11*(3), 297–309.

Oliver, J. J., & Parrett, E. (2018). Managing future uncertainty: Reevaluating the role of scenario planning. *Business Horizons*, *61*(2), 339–352.

Peters, M., & Weiermair, K. (2000). Tourist attractions and attracted tourists. *Journal of Tourism Studies*, *11*(1), 22–29.

Postma, A. (2014). The future of visitor attractions in the Netherlands. *Tourism Recreation Research*, *39*(3), 437–452.

Read, C. (2022, April 5). Boy rushed to hospital after falling from Movie World ride. *Brisbane Times*. https://www.brisbanetimes.com.au/national/queensland/boy-falls-from-movie-world-ride-suffers-head-injuries-20220405-p5ab1b.html#:~:text=A%2012%2Dyear%2Dold%20boy,Oxenford%20about%201pm%20on%20Tuesday.

Richards, G. (2002). Tourism attraction systems – Exploring cultural behavior. *Annals of Tourism Research*, *29*(4), 1048–1064.

Richards, G., King, B., & Yeung, E. (2020). Experiencing culture in attractions, events and tour settings. *Tourism Management*, *79*(Aug), 104104.

Ritchie, B. W. (2004). Chaos, crises and disasters: A strategic approach to crisis management in the tourism industry. *Tourism Management*, *25*(6), 669–683.

Schoemaker, P. J. H. (2020). How historical analysis can enrich scenario planning. *Futures & Foresight Science*, *2*(3–4), e35.

Scott, I., & Scott, R. J. (2020). Pill testing at music festivals: Is it evidence-based harm reduction? *Internal Medicine Journal*, *50*(4), 395–402.

Scott, N., Laws, E., & Prideaux, B. (2006). Tourism crises and marketing recovery strategies. *Journal of Travel & Tourism Marketing*, *23*(2–4), 1–13.

Shen, S., Sotiriadis, M., & Zhang, Y. (2020). The influence of smart technologies on customer journey in tourist attractions within the smart tourism management framework. *Sustainability*, *12*(10), 4157.

Somnuxpong, S., & Wiwatwongwana, R. (2020). The ability to support accessible tourism in Chiang Mai, Thailand. *African Journal of Hospitality, Tourism and Leisure*, *9*(1), article 69.

Swarbrooke, J. (2002). *The development and management of visitor attractions*. London: Prentice Hall.

Taylor, P. (2020, November 30). *White Island volcano: New Zealand authorities charge 13 parties over disaster*. The Guardian. https://www.theguardian.com/world/2020/nov/30/white-island-volcano-new-zealand-authorities-charge-13-parties-over-disaster

Varum, C. A., & Melo, C. (2010). Directions in scenario planning literature – A review of the past decades. *Futures*, *42*(4), 355–369.

Vera, A. (2022, April 19). *A boy fell from a free-fall ride in Florida. An investigation is underway, but who regulates these parks?* CNN. https://edition.cnn.com/2022/04/02/us/florida-park-amusement-experts-regulation/index.html

Weidenfeld, A., Butler, R. W., & Williams, A. M. (2010). Clustering and compatibility between tourism attractions. *International Journal of Tourism Research*, *12*(1), 1–16.

World Travel & Tourism Council. (2021, February 25). *Crisis readiness*. https://wttc.org/Portals/0/Documents/Reports/2019/Crisis%20Preparedness%20Management%20Recovery-Crisis%20Readiness-Nov%202019.pdf?ver=2021-02-25-182725-567

Zou, Y., & Meng, F. (2020). Chinese tourists' sense of safety: Perceptions of expected and experienced destination safety. *Current Issues in Tourism*, *23*(15), 1886–1899.

6 Wine tourism

Current trends and future prospects

Haiyan Song and Weixi (Edith) Yuan

Introduction

Wine tourism has received increasing attention because of booming wine consumption and domestic tourism product development over the last two decades. Increased wine consumption, positive wine tourism experiences, and social media promotion have driven the growth of wine tourism globally (Duan et al., 2018; Gu et al., 2018; Qiu et al., 2013). The United Nations World Tourism Organization (UNWTO) describes tourism as an economic, social, and cultural asset (UNWTO, 2008). Wine tourism is thus a unique regional product that links the economic, social, and cultural aspects of the tourism, wine, and hospitality industries.

The wine tourism industry contributes to regional development and is becoming a mainstream driver of tourism development (UNWTO, 2021). Despite the challenges of the COVID-19 pandemic and the poor seasonal conditions that preceded the pandemic, some wine regions' domestic tourism industries have recovered quickly. For example, China organised the first wine festival since the onset of the pandemic in the region of Ningxia in September 2021. Such positive developments warrant a review of the wine tourism phenomenon and its future growth from the perspective of tourism supply and demand before and after the onset of the COVID-19 pandemic.

The pandemic has caused worldwide health and social damage since the end of 2019, and the effects are expected to continue (McKinsey, 2021). These adverse effects also extended to the global wine tourism industry. According to a 2020 global report, 53% of the wineries lost more than 50% of their income, and 47% of wineries saw a decrease of over 90% in international visitors; overall, the reported revenues were much lower than that of 2019 (WineTourism.com, 2020).

With vaccination campaigns and societal reopening expected to drive recovery, the 5th UNWTO International Conference on Wine Tourism on 8–10 September 2021 considered how wine tourism could benefit rural development (UNWTO, 2021). The conference concluded that wine businesses should stimulate recovery by focusing on domestic travel. This was consistent with the 2021 McKinsey report, which showed that demand for domestic travel was approaching pre-pandemic levels. International travel restrictions remain the primary explanation for the dramatic decrease in international visitors (UNWTO, 2021).

Wine tourism integrates the economic models of wine production and regional tourism. Tourism is a critical sector in advanced economics, and wineries' income often increases by approximately 20% when they offer tourism services (WineTourism.com, 2020). Furthermore, wine tourism and domestic tourism development drive wine industry and destination development. Given strong confidence in domestic and local tourism forecasting (McKinsey, 2021), many studies have shown that domestic tourism will drive the post-pandemic recovery of the tourism industry and improve regional economic resilience (Moya Calderón et al., 2021; OECD, 2020; UNWTO, 2021). The predictions of Zhang et al. (2021) suggested that the markets of Macao, Mainland China, and Taiwan might recover more quickly than other source markets. This was consistent with the 2021 McKinsey report indicating that Chinese travellers' confidence had recovered quickly, which would drive rapid domestic travel market recovery. Tourists participating in domestic leisure trips in 2020 increased from 54% in May to 73% in August compared with the same period in 2019 (McKinsey, 2020) with the domestic tourism market expected to maintain this rate of growth. Wine consumption in emerging economies, including China, are also expected to support an increasingly stable market over the next five years (Liu & Song, 2021). China is consistently the world's largest e-commerce market for alcoholic beverages, with a value two to three times higher than the second-largest market, the U.S. (McKinsey, 2020). The Chinese wine market thus retains considerable potential to develop wine products and services, with the rising demand and rapid recovery of wine consumption and the optimistic demand forecasts for the domestic tourism market in developing economies.

China's wine tourism industry is an example of how low confidence in local wine and emerging wine regions can inhibit wine tourism development, as well as industry stakeholders who lack guidance for navigating this new marketplace. Although wine tourism has attracted increased consumer attention, it remains an emerging market that has not yet gained widespread acceptance. Given a lack of research on wine tourism supply and demand, particularly in the wake of COVID-19, this chapter explores this topic and provides insights into stakeholder performance during the wine tourism development process, with a focus on China. We also analyse trends of consumer demand and explore the integration of regional wine brands and local wine tourism resources. Furthermore, we discuss e-commerce and digital platform development and promotion, to provide suggestions for the development of wine tourism in emerging economies. We explore current and future challenges for the sector, including COVID-19 and post-pandemic recovery, to illustrate the need to integrate regional resources and invest in local tourism infrastructure, which are often lacking. In addition, our plan is to update this review periodically in the future to ensure that policy interventions meet the needs of customers and tourism businesses and that appropriate interventions are implemented at each stage of the recovery. Future research should further facilitate sustainable wine tourism development through the creation of a wine tourism ecosystem. Ultimately, this review aims to document wine tourism supply and demand interactions, bolster regional wine tourism brands, and enhance the wine tourism industry globally.

International wine tourism

Wine tourism has become a globally competitive market over the last 25 years (Carlsen, 2004), bringing considerable economic benefits to destinations. Wine tourism connects to the wine region, local products, and tourists' demand for authentic experiences. The UNWTO predicted that demand for wine tourism would increase as consumers seek domestic tourism experiences in the post-pandemic era (UNWTO, 2021). This section thus provides a systematic overview of supply and demand, support for tourism experiences, regional development, tourism trends, and innovations, to explore the new orientation of wine tourism. We also summarise the results of current conference reports and recent academic studies to evaluate the further development of the wine tourism industry.

Wine tourism development and trends

According to the literature, development integrates consumer demand for wine tourism and the available supply from the industry (Winemakers' Federation of Australia, 1998; Brown & Getz, 2006; Hall et al., 1997; Sigala & Haller, 2019). The complex and widely used definition of wine tourism was established between 1997 and 2021 (Figure 6.1). More recent consumer research has focused on the sustainable development of the wine tourism ecosystem.

Hall and Macionis proposed the first widely recognised wine tourism market definition (1997, p. 6) as 'Visitation to vineyards, wineries, wine festivals and wine events for which grape wine tasting and experiencing the attributes of a grape wine region are the prime motivating factors for visitors'. (Brown and Getz (2006) developed a marketing perspective emphasising consumer behaviour to promote wine-related attractions and imagery. However, new technology such as social media has altered marketing in the wine tourism industry. Thach and Cogan-Marie (2018) conducted the first study exploring social media and digital marketing development in wine tourism in the Burgundy region of France. From the perspective of suppliers, their study concluded that wineries in Burgundy should improve their digital marketing strategies to attract more tourists and create a more positive brand perception (Thach & Cogan-Marie, 2018; Canovi & Pucciarelli, 2019). Many recent studies have focused on sustainability in wine tourism (Santos et al., 2021). Wine tourism development mentioned in these studies conforms highly to the Sustainable Development Goals (SDGs) adopted by the United Nations in 2015 to ensure that all people enjoy peace and prosperity by 2030 (United Nations, 2019). The framework for understanding and creating knowledge in wine tourism integrates inputs (wine tourists, wine suppliers, wine destinations), co-creation processes (social practices), and outputs (wine tourism experiences) to evaluate impacts on individual actors and the overall wine tourism ecosystem. Santos et al. (2021) concluded that wine tourism is generally offered alongside rural, ecological, cultural, and adventure tourism and that digital and hybrid wine events are innovations in the wine tourism ecosystem.

Based on this literature review, we identified the factors explaining the development of wine tourism from the perspective of supply and demand. By examining supply and demand, this study explored wine tourism from the perspectives of experience, regional tourism development, trends, and innovation.

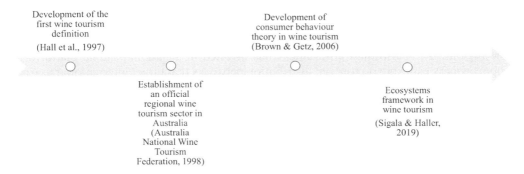

Figure 6.1 Wine tourism development.

Source: Developed by the authors.

Wine tourism supply and demand

The first framework for wine tourism research was derived from supply-led and demand-driven perspectives (Carlsen, 2004). Building synergy amongst wine tourism supply and demand chains can multiply economic effects, offer more appealing tourism, and generate social sustainability. Sigala and Robinson (2019) summarised the studies on sustainable practice in wine tourism from the perspective of supply and demand. The supply factors included competitiveness, innovation, and regional development; the demand factors were awareness and recognition (Sigala & Robinson, 2019). We collected key studies from the available literature on wine tourism from this perspective and summarised the primary factors supporting future wine tourism development (Table 6.1). We also developed a framework, based on previous studies, for the factors that determine wine tourism supply and demand shown in Table 6.1.

The three main factors driving and shaping wine tourist demand are experience, current trends, and tourism consumption (Sigala & Robinson, 2019, p. 6). On the demand side, the quality of the experience predicts the loyalty to, and satisfaction with, wine tourism destinations, and structural modelling has demonstrated the importance of aesthetic experience in predicting positive memories and destination loyalty in the wine tourism context (Quadri-Felitti & Fiore, 2013). Major current trends have involved consumers attaching more importance to health and wine quality and wanting educational experiences (Sigala & Robinson, 2019). Educational wine tourism experiences have also been shown to predict satisfaction and the creation of memories (Quadri-Felitti & Fiore, 2013). Market research conducted by the Hong Kong Trade Development Council (HKTDC) in 2020 showed that consumers in mainland China are increasingly knowledgeable about wine: 25% of the respondents said they had intermediate or advanced knowledge, and 41% said they drank wine once or more each week (HKTDC, 2021). Consequently, wine production quality, authentic experiences, and sustainable development have received frequent mention in the recent wine tourism market.

On the supply side, wine tourism is delivered by a collection of disparate businesses (Quadri-Felitti, 2015), thus necessitating the identification of stakeholders in the wine region (McGregor & Robinson, 2019). Stakeholder theory divides tourism into government, communities, tourism suppliers, and tourists. From a supply perspective, the government is essential for domestic wine tourism development, as it can provide assistance with logistical or bureaucratic problems such as landscape preservation and infrastructure maintenance, understand locals, and support the marketing of wineries through cooperation between organisations (Quadri-Felitti, 2015). For example, the Chinese government has promoted the integrated development of high-quality wine and culture tourism resources to accelerate the construction of wine tourism destinations in the main Chinese wine regions. The Australian government has invested in a national online platform to support winery exposure on tourism distribution networks that target international tourists (Fountain et al., 2020).

The winery is the primary factor in wine tourism. Visits to a winery generate brand loyalty, sales, and positive word of mouth for the winery and wine region (Fountain et al., 2020). The tourism activities offered by wineries can increase consumer exposure, improve brand awareness and loyalty, and build positive relationships through wine festivals, educational opportunities, and regional tours. Wineries can increase their exposure through websites, as even small wineries can offer descriptions of their wines and provide online distribution services and virtual tours. The attractiveness and authenticity of the winescape through online

Table 6.1 Key studies in wine tourism on from a supply and demand perspective

Research Focus	Author	Factors mentioned in the study	Main conclusion	Further development
Demand analysis	Brown and Getz (2006); Johnson and Bruwer (2007)	1. Regional resource collaboration 2. Promoting the regional brand 3. Authentic experience of the wine region 4. High-yield wine production 5. Government support	• Cultural tourism production benefits long-term tourism. • High-quality wine enhances consumer confidence. • Additional wine information enhances brand loyalty. • Stakeholder collaboration is necessary for sustainable tourism development.	• Wine should be further integrated into lifestyle and influence travel preferences. • Wine clubs should become vehicles for building awareness of wine tourism.
Supply analysis	Quadri-Felitti (2015); Duan et al. (2018); Canovi and Pucciarelli (2019)	1. Authenticity. 2. Unique characteristics of the wine region brand. 3. Social media information. 4. Sustainability and health products.	• Tourists require clear information on wine tourism. • Wineries should utilise the potential of social media. • Positive experiences on package tours offered by the local government can be synergised with the winery and local agency. • Authentic experience shows more important for the tourists.	• The wine region should enhance educational entertainment; escapist experiences will increase wine region loyalty. • Local stakeholders should seek to cooperate. • Rural sectors should be included on social media platforms.

Source: Information collected by the authors.

platforms can play a critical role in generating and driving wine tourism demand. For this reason, the number of wine websites in Australia doubled in 1999 (Hall et al., 2004). The inclusion of wine distributors, travel agencies, and other intermediary businesses also benefits regional tourism development and improves the local tourism industry.

Wine tourism development enhances regional tourism, wine consumption, tourism agency income, and wine tourism experiences; however, research has shown that wine tourism development is limited by poor collaboration governance and lacks pooled resources. It has also demonstrated that wine tourism companies lack the collective capacity to engage other suppliers within the wine tourism ecosystems (Johnson & Bruwer, 2007; Duan et al., 2018). Academic studies and practical research in this field are limited (Quadri-Felitti, 2015). Therefore, stakeholder management must be improved, and an academic strategy for wine tourism must be developed that integrates the supply and demand sides of the industry (Figure 6.2). The UNWTO's wine tourism development conference review of research for 2020–2021 indicated two trends and three essential directions. The trends include connecting tourists to regional territories and growing demand for authentic experiences; the essential directions are innovation, partnership, and coordination.

Moreover, the trend of sustainable wine tourism is a critical part of the tourism industry's bid to achieve the UN's SDGs by 2030, especially the 17 SDGs included in the following goals: Goal 8: Decent work and economic growth; Goal 9: Industry, innovation, and infrastructure; and Goal 17: Partnership for achieving the goals. The proposed SDGs could be achieved through wine and tourism in a region, thus improving wine tourism development in the future.

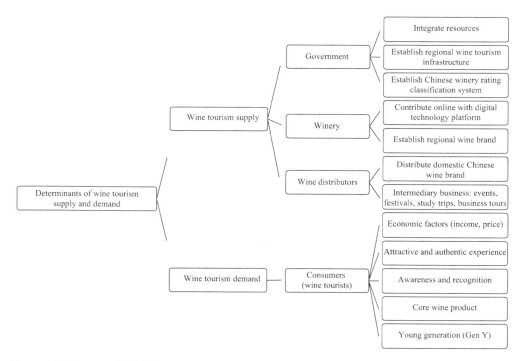

Figure 6.2 Framework of wine tourism supply and demand.
Source: Developed by the authors.

In summary, supply and demand factors and current trends combined with SDGs have informed the future development of the wine tourism market:

- Technological innovation in wine tourism: Qiu et al. (2013) and Canovi and Pucciarelli (2019) concluded that wineries should adopt an official website and social media presence to promote activities, wine education, and products. The wine tourism industry should also develop virtual experiences and digital and hybrid wine events (Santos et al., 2021; Sigala & Haller, 2019; UNWTO, 2021). This factor contributes to Goal 9 of SDGs.
- Integration of regional wine tourism resources: Goal 17 – government support and effective stakeholder communication promote rural development. The local community should also contribute to the exposure of the regional wine brand and local resource integration (Alonso & Liu, 2010). Establishing a regional wine tourism brand is an important strategy (Qiu et al., 2013).
- Development of authentic experiences: Authentic experiences are in increasing demand and can boost the image of wine regions. This factor also supports the domestic economic recovery and encourages local farmers to seek employment. This is a particularly important issue for countries with travel restrictions and those recovering from the COVID-19 pandemic (UNWTO, 2021). This factor contributes to Goal 8 of SDGs.
- Establishment of sustainable wine tourism products: Wine consumers and tourists desire healthy products and sustainable wine production, so such products must be integrated into wine tourism development (Santos et al., 2021).

Wine tourism in China

Domestic and international wine tourism has now been established in China for more than ten years (Qiu et al., 2013), leading casual tourists and wine enthusiasts to participate in regional wine tourism. For example, the most prominent wine-producing company, Changyu Winery, established the first wine tourism attraction in China in 2006, with services such as catering and accommodation. In 2021, the Global Wine Tourism Organization (GWTO) honoured China's Ningxia wine region as the 'World Wine Tourism Destination'. However, few wineries provide tourism services in China (Duan et al., 2018). This section presents research conducted to define the wine tourism supply market based on the earlier supply and demand analysis.

Wine tourism phenomena in China

Gu et al. (2018) claimed that Chinese wine tourists are inexperienced at selecting wine, but some reports have stated that wine consumption behaviour in China is changing (Liu & Murphy, 2017; HKTDC, 2018, 2021; Liu & Song, 2021). People are more likely to explore aspects such as the culture and historical background of a given wine product rather than relying solely on its price or origin to judge its quality (Liu & Murphy, 2017). The HKTDC (2018) also found that drinking wine has become part of Chinese people's lifestyle and therefore more integrated into their everyday routines. Recent studies have shown that Chinese wine consumers are increasingly knowledgeable about wine due to the actions of educational organisations, public events, wine tastings, and wine festivals (HKTDC, 2021; Liu & Song, 2021) such as the Hong Kong Wine and Dine Festival, Vinexpo Shanghai, and the Shenzhen International Wine and Spirits Fair. Consumers' curiosity can be aroused through the stories behind the products; thus, the recent growth of wine consumption and the current lack of wine tourism suppliers in China have prompted the growth of the wine tourism industry.

Several trends in China's wine market changed between 2019 and 2021. For example, the International Organization of Vine and Wine (OIV) reported that China was ranked as the highest wine-consuming country in Asia (OIV, 2021). Furthermore, the government has invested financially and politically in wine tourism development while ensuring high-quality and improved winery facilities to produce high-quality wine products. Despite the expansion of the domestic wine market, the consumption of imported wine still exceeds that of Chinese wine, accounting for approximately 60% of the market share by volume (IWSC, 2021). This may be attributed to the lack of confidence in the quality of domestic wine, the lack of domestic brand awareness, and a lack of stakeholder cooperation in wine production (Duan et al., 2018; Quadri-Felitti, 2015). In addition, imported wines often have zero import tariffs, which increases their competitiveness. To address these problems, this review examined the profile of wine tourists (Gu et al., 2018), wine tourism experiences (Fountain et al., 2020; Duan et al., 2018), marketing strategies (Qiu et al., 2013), and travel behaviour (Fountain et al., 2020). These perspectives revealed the supply and demand factors and experience, marketing promotion, and consumer behaviour regarding wine tourism in China. Based on prior research, this section develops detailed and practical targets for supply and demand in the Chinese wine tourism market to establish a clear path to wine tourism development.

Gu et al. (2018) showed that wine tourists generally wish to try excellent wine, while Chinese wine tourists prefer more attractions at destinations, so package tours should include more activities and events centred around wine.

Like the global wine tourism industry, Chinese wineries should integrate more services. Those concerned with the supply side should focus on the key factors of government, wineries, travel agencies, and wine distributors (Duan et al., 2018; Gu et al., 2018). Chinese wine tourism development is strongly affected by the government. For example, local governments could boost wine tourism through tax reductions for wine-related industries (Duan et al., 2018). In addition, provincial governments could offer a tax amnesty for personal capital investment in local wine tourism and fund universities for local wine tourism research. Qiu et al. (2013) stated that establishing global brands and slogans could enhance confidence in, and knowledge of, domestic wine products such as the 'Shandong Peninsula' and 'Helan Mountain'. Finally, Qiu et al. (2013) stated the importance of technological innovation in wine tourism.

Case study of a Chinese wine region: Ningxia

Tourism resources in Ningxia are relatively abundant, with good quality and a clear set of advantages in natural and man-made heritages, infrastructure, and marketing resources (Wang et al., 2018). Moreover, government support and effective stakeholder communication promote rural development in Ningxia. Because of their unique climate and geography, the eastern foothills of the Helan Mountains in Ningxia are known as 'the Bordeaux of China' and are one of the country's three main geographical attractions. Presently, this region has 184 wineries and a unique rural landscape and social culture that cater to the pursuit of a slow lifestyle and the desire for modern ecotourism experiences (Wang et al., 2018).

Given the profile of the Ningxia wine region and the overall current outlook in research and news regarding the wine tourism market in China, we adopted the SWOT (strengths, weaknesses, opportunities, and threats) model for this section of the chapter, to define the main challenges, trends, and opportunities for wine tourism in the region and provide practical suggestions for its development.

The strengths of China's wine tourism marketing strategy include, but are not limited to: 1) high-quality wine products to increase their popularity in the global market, 2) wine regions with unique climate and geography, 3) government support for the wine tourism industry, 4) continued participation in competitions, fairs, and events, and 5) concern for the country's position as a premium producer. Its weaknesses include: 1) limitations due to COVID-19 pandemic restrictions, 2) lack of local infrastructure in Chinese wine regions, 3) lack of tourism resources in wine regions, 4) limited integration in wine regions, and 5) low brand awareness. However, opportunities in wine tourism include: 1) innovation in digital market development distribution channels, 2) the size of the potential market for wine consumption and domestic travel, 3) consumer willingness to pay a premium for high-quality wine products, 4) consumers' emphasis on the health benefits of wine, 5) wine consumption as a lifestyle, and 6) China's rapid recovery from the COVID-19 pandemic. Finally, threats include: 1) low-level wine knowledge for the average consumer, 2) low confidence in domestic wine, and 3) the influence of changing pandemic conditions on future development.

Conclusions

Wine tourism is a rapidly developing industry that deserves further research, particularly regarding the inevitable changes related to COVID-19 and post-pandemic development. For example, the pandemic has reinforced the importance of sustainability and health factors in the minds of consumers. The main objectives of this chapter were to explicate the supply and demand components of wine tourism development and provide insight into the behaviour of stakeholders and tourists during the development process, particularly in the emerging market of China. The chapter defined several goals for wine tourism: 1) promote regional tourism development, 2) enhance wine tourism experiences, and 3) improve wine tourism income. However, several challenges remain to be solved.

From a supply perspective, the main findings indicated that regional wine tourism lacks cooperation between government, wineries and wine distributors with respect to the utilisation of local resources. However, joint promotion and cooperation between the government, wineries, and wine distributors can lead to positive results for the wine region and for domestic tourism. The findings also indicated the limitations of collaboration in wine regions, consistent for the global and Chinese markets.

From a demand perspective, wine tourists have started pursuing authentic experiences in wine regions. Importantly, our findings showed that e-commerce and social media greatly enhanced exposure to wineries. Stakeholders should therefore develop social media to attract the attention of wine tourists and increase the availability of wine and tourism information.

Wine tourism in China remains in the early stages of development and currently lacks an active tourism market. Opportunities for the growth of the wine industry and domestic tourism are excellent, particularly given support from the government and demand from wine tourists. Wine and wine tourism can make substantial contributions to regional economies (Hall et al., 2004) and redefine the images of destinations. Regions should thus aim to promote wine tourism by increasing wine consumption and brand awareness. Furthermore, analysis of wine tourism from a supply and demand perspective facilitates the development of a concrete strategy and encourages cooperation among stakeholders while meeting the desires of wine tourists by educating consumers, promoting wine tourism experiences, contributing to local wine brand establishment, and advertising regional wine products.

Furthermore, we found that the social benefits of the wine industry were remarkable. The development of the wine industry employs local farmers, achieving the UN's SDG Goal 8 with sustainable economic growth and decent employment for all. The wine industry has greatly boosted local economies and employment. Sustainable and health-oriented wine products attract the attention of wine consumers, especially Chinese wine consumers. Therefore, organic and green practices in viticulture, cultivation, and production offer wine tourism a bright future.

According to the published studies and our own research on wine tourism in various parts of the world, including China, future trends (2022–2052) could be summarised as follows.

The government:

- Further enhancing cooperation in wine regions: collaboration between the government, wineries, and wine distributors will encourage regional wine tourism development and regional wine brand establishment.

Marketing and promotion:

- Changing wine distribution channels: wine distributors will adopt more e-commerce and utilise social media as the leading distribution channels for wine and tourism products.
- Domestic wine production and consumption: these will be dominant in the wine trade due to anti-globalisation and protectionism.
- Sustainable and healthy wine tourism products: wine labelling emphasising the importance of green and health products will be a long-term trend.

Wine tourists:

- Wine tourism demand will continue to grow. Consumers desire authenticity and eco-development in wine regions. Therefore, the integration of education and business will emerge as an important part of the wine tourism portfolio in all wine regions of the world.
- Wine consumption behaviour will evolve, with consumers emphasising more the health benefits and sustainability of wine products.

Figure 6.3 provides a visual abstract of this chapter.

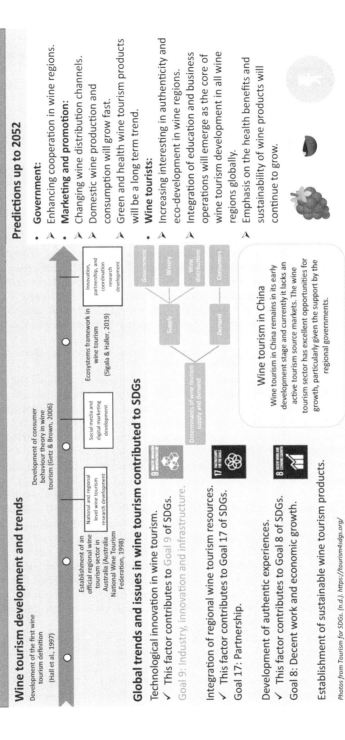

Figure 6.3 Wine tourism visual abstract.

References

Alonso, A., & Liu, Y. (2010). Wine tourism development in emerging Western Australian regions. *International Journal of Contemporary Hospitality Management*, 22(2), 245–262.

Brown, G., & Getz, D. (2006). Critical success factors for wine tourism regions: A demand analysis. *Tourism Management*, 27(1), 146–158.

Canovi, M., & Pucciarelli, F. (2019). Social media marketing in wine tourism: Winery owners' perceptions. *Journal of Travel & Tourism Marketing*, 36(6), 653–664.

Carlsen, J. (2004). A review of global wine tourism research. *Journal of Wine Research*, 15(1), 5–13.

Duan, B., Arcodia, C., Ma, E., & Hsiao, A. (2018). Understanding wine tourism in China using an integrated product-level and experience economy framework. *Asia Pacific Journal of Tourism Research*, 23(10), 949–960.

Fountain, J., Yuan, J. J., Zhai, B., Bauman, M. J., Williams, H. A., & Gu, Q. (2020). Wine tourism development in China. In Huang, S., & Chen, G. (Eds.), *Handbook on tourism and China* (pp. 187–201). Cheltenham, UK: Edward Elgar Publishing.

Gu, Q., Qiu, H., King, B. E. M., & Huang, S. (2018). Wine tourism involvement: A segmentation of Chinese tourists. *Journal of Travel & Tourism Marketing*, 35(5), 633–648.

Hall, C. M., & Macionis, N. (1997). Wine tourism and network development in Australia and New Zealand: Review, establishment and prospects. *International Journal of Wine Marketing*, 9(2), 5–31.

Hall, C. M., Sharples, E., Cambourne, B., & Macionis, N. (2004). *Wine tourism around the world: Development, management and markets*. Oxford, UK: Butterworth-Heinemann. (2004).

HKTDC. (2018). *China's wine market consumer preferences (1): Wine category, drinking occasion and price*. [Online]. Retrieved 9 October 2020, from https://hkmb.hktdc.com/en/1X0AD6OU/hktdc-research/China%E2%80%99s-Wine-Market-Consumer-Preferences-1-Wine-Category-Drinking-Occasion-and-Price

HKTDC. (2021). *Wine industry in Hong Kong*. [Online]. Retrieved 28 October 2021, from https://research.hktdc.com/en/article/MzEzOTc5OTQ3

IWSC. (2021). *IWSC market insight: The Chinese wine market*. [Online]. Retrieved 19 December 2021, from https://www.iwsc.net/news/wine/iwsc-insight-the-chinese-wine-market

Johnson, R., & Bruwer, J. (2007). Regional brand image and perceived wine quality: The consumer perspective. *International Journal of Wine Business Research*, 19(4), 276–297.

Liu, A., & Song, H. (2021). Analysis and forecasts of the demand for imported wine in China. *Cornell Hospitality Quarterly*, 62(3), 371–385.

Liu, F., & Murphy, J. (2017). A qualitative study of Chinese wine consumption and purchasing. *International Journal of Wine Business Research*, 19(2), 98–113.

McGregor, A., & Robinson, R. N. S. (2019). Wine industry and wine tourism industry collaboration: A typology and analysis. In Sigala, M., & Robinson, R. N. S. (Eds.) *Wine tourism destination management and marketing* (pp. 381–397). London, UK: Palgrave Macmillan.

McKinsey. (2020). *What can other countries learn from China's travel recovery path?* [Online]. Retrieved 15 October 2021, from https://www.mckinsey.com/industries/travel-logistics-and-infrastructure/our-insights/what-can-other-countries-learn-from-chinas-travel-recovery-path

McKinsey. (2021). *China's uneven travel recovery: Long road to international travel furthers domestic opportunities*. Retrieved 19 October 2021, from https://www.mckinsey.com/industries/travel-logistics-and-infrastructure/our-insights/chinas-uneven-travel-recovery-long-road-to-international-travel-furthers-domestic-opportunities

Moya Calderón, M., Chavarría Esquivel, K., Arrieta García, M. M., & Lozano, C. B. (2021). Tourist behaviour and dynamics of domestic tourism in times of COVID-19. *Current Issues in Tourism*, 1–5.

OECD. (2020). *Tourism policy responses to the coronavirus (COVID-19)*. [Online]. Retrieved 18 October 2020, from https://www.oecd.org/coronavirus/policy-responses/tourism-policy-responses-to-the-coronavirus-COVID-19-6466aa20/

OIV. (2021). *State of the world vitivinicultural sector in 2020*. Retrieved 20 October 2021, from https://www.oiv.int/public/medias/7909/oiv-state-of-the-world-vitivinicultural-sector-in-2020.pdf.

Qiu, H. Z., Yuan, J. J., Ye, B. H., & Hung, K. (2013). Wine tourism phenomena in China: An emerging market. *International Journal of Contemporary Hospitality Management*, 25(7), 1115–1134.

Quadri-Felitti, D. L. (2015). A supply-side stakeholder analysis of rural wine tourism development: The case of Lake Erie's southern shore. *International Journal of Social Ecology and Sustainable Development*, 6(2), 74–89.

Quadri-Felitti, D. L., & Fiore, A. M. (2013). Destination loyalty: Effects of wine tourists' experiences, memories, and satisfaction on intentions. *Tourism and Hospitality Research*, 13(1), 47–62.

Santos, V., Ramos, P., Sousa, B., & Valeri, M. (2021). Towards a framework for the global wine tourism system. *Journal of Organizational Change Management*. DOI: 10.1108/JOCM-11-2020-0362

Sigala, M., & Haller, C. (2019). The impact of social media on the behavior of wine tourists: A typology of power sources. In Sigala, M., & Robinson, R. N. S. (Eds.). *Management and marketing of wine tourism business* (pp. 139–154). London, UK: Palgrave Macmillan.

Sigala, M., & Robinson, R. N. S. (2019). Introduction: Wine destination management and marketing – Critical success factors. In Sigala, M., & Robinson, R. N. S. (Eds.). *Wine tourism destination management and marketing* (pp. 1–8). London, UK: Palgrave Macmillan.

Thach, L., & Cogan-Marie, L. (2018). Wine tourism in Burgundy, France: An analysis of marketing practices. *Tourism Review International*, 22(1), 81–95.

United Nations (2019). *Sustainable development goals*. [Online]. Retrieved on 6 May 2022, from http://www.undp.org/content/undp/en/home/sustainable-development-goals.html

UNWTO. (2008). *Glossary of tourism terms*. [Online]. Retrieved 26 April 2022, from https://www.unwto.org/glossary-tourism-terms

UNWTO. (2021). *Innovation and partnerships to make wine tourism driver rural development*. [Online]. Retrieved 15 October 2021, from https://www.unwto.org/news/innovation-and-partnerships-to-make-wine-tourism-driver-rural-development

Wang, L., Liu, J. M., & Wang, L. E. (2018). Tourism resource assessment and spatial analysis of wine tourism development: A case study of the eastern foothills of China's Helan Mountains. *Journal of Mountain Science*, 15(3), 645–656.

Winemakers' Federation of Australia. (1998). *National Wine Tourism Strategy*. Adelaide, Australia: Winemakers' Federation of Australia.

WineTourism.com. (2020). *5th UNWTO Global Conference on Wine Tourism*. [Online]. Retrieved 19 October 2021, from https://www.winetourism.com/5th-unwto-global-conference-on-wine-tourism/

Zhang, H., Song, H., Wen, L., & Liu, C. (2021). Forecasting tourism recovery amid COVID-19. *Annals of Tourism Research*, 87(C). https://doi.org/10.1016/j.annals.2021.103149.

7 Culinary tourism
Dualistic erosion and the enhancement of food cultures

Sophia Lingham, Louise Manning and Damian Maye

Introduction

Gastronomy is a central part of the tourism experience (DEFRA, 2017), the local foods concerned being a type of cultural asset (Choe & Kim, 2019, p. 254). Culinary tourism has been defined as eating, tasting, buying and appreciating local food products, where opportunities for memorable food and drink experiences are important components of visiting an area (Hall & Gössling, 2016; Ottenbacher & Harrington, 2011; Smith & Xiao, 2008). Culinary tourism "significantly emphasizes a relationship between the insider and outsider created via food as culture" (Ellis et al., 2018, p. 253), with associated culinary culture, local knowledge, and the placing of emphasis on the special 'flavour of not just of a dish, but of a locality' (Horng & Tsai, 2010, p. 75). Ellis et al. conceptualised the five prongs of food tourism which are just as relevant for culinary tourism: motivation (of consumers), culture (of consumers and of the host culture), authenticity, management and marketing, and destination orientation (heritage and image of destination), which we will consider in this chapter. The scope of culinary tourism includes wine and beer/ales tourism, gourmet tourism and gastronomic tourism, and the economies associated with artisan food (Lingham et al., 2022). One example is the development of the Michelin-starred restaurant sector into a cultural industry. Indeed, "tourists can access culinary experiences through local and unique restaurants, breweries, wineries, culinary events, farmers' markets and agri-tourism" (Björk & Kauppinen-Räisänen, 2014a; Lane, 2010; Testa et al., 2019; Wolf, 2014). Gastronomic and wine tourism promotes and brands destinations "'through maintaining and preserving local traditions and diversities, and harnessing and rewarding authenticity" (UNWTO, 2019).

This chapter delves into the world of culinary tourism and compares and contrasts certain aspects between Mediterranean countries and the U.K. for consumers and producers. The chapter will consider firstly catalysts for culinary tourism and improvement, the relevant stakeholders, and then analyse current and future trends and issues, specifically relating to cultural goods, identity, food memories, and new forms of economy in relation to the erosive and enhancive capabilities of culinary tourism. It will briefly reflect on the SDGs 3, 5, 8, 9 and 12 among others within this.

Catalysts for culinary tourism

Cultural distance refers to the extent of difference between tourists' home cultures and the culture of the destination being visited (McKercher & Chow, 2001). McKercher and Chow posit that the greater the cultural distance, the greater the tourists' interests in participating in cultural tourism activities, such as culinary tourism. Ergo, the catalyst for the tourist is the desire to experience something they could not experience in their normal routine. In this desire for experience, gastronomy/food is one of the elements that conveys a sense of authenticity to tourist destinations providing connections with traditions and ways of living of the past (Cafiero et al., 2019). Importance is given to the specificity of experience that cannot be easily transferred or replicated elsewhere, the idea of terroir. Thus, for host areas, capitalising on this desire for an authentic experience becomes a catalyst for them to nurture culinary tourism and local food businesses.

These local foods can create niche markets, part of an artisanal economy, providing pull factors for the promotion of tourism (Horng & Tsai, 2012; Okumus et al., 2007; Sanchez-Cañizares & Castillo-Canalejo, 2015). For instance, Sanchez-Cañizares and Castillo-Canalejo (2015) found in their research in Spain and Slovenia that tourists were willing to pay 10–40% more for a traditional meal over other types of food or drink. Globally, there are moves to promote gastronomy as a catalyst for tourism in places not currently known for their food identity, such as Slovenia and Turkey (Okumus et al., 2007; Ottenbacher & Harrington, 2011; Sanchez-Cañizares & Castillo-Canalejo, 2015), possibly by using local food traditions or creating new ones with foods produced from local ingredients. Maintaining and expanding traditional practices plays to the appreciation of cultural difference and the desire to experience it.

New technologies are another catalyst making more local means of culinary tourism greatly accessible. For instance, the online platforms EatWith and The Travelling Spoon allow locals and tourists alike to experience home-cooked cultural food in an informal home setting, linking into ideas of conviviality and social connection. Indeed, technology is a catalyst for many types of culinary tourism, not just for marketing purposes, but also the development and improvement of the destination/experience itself. For instance, Italian wine routes were established by Law No. 268/1999 and for tourism through Article No. 87 of the Consolidated Law on Vines and Wine No. 238/2016, yet too many stakeholders and a lack of organisation hampers their potential. Festa et al. (2020) suggest that by increasing the use of technologies (even as basic as website management and app use), wine routes and producers will improve the organising of their own wine events, and this will lead to better and stronger collaboration between the producers, the multiple actors running the routes, and tourism operators. These basic suggestions could mean having one independent body responsible for the wine routes to manage relationships between stakeholders and territories more effectively and to support producers appropriately. Indeed, improving outreach via government tourism websites can draw attention to local or traditional food cultures, placing importance on website currency, provision of information about culture and etiquette surrounding local foods, and creating a good story around the food. However, if the marketers lack the right knowledge or experience of the food, the possibility of creating a strong image or brand will be reduced (Horng & Tsai, 2010).

Media and previous experiences, especially the degree of satisfaction, influence culinary tourism through peoples' expectations of a food or experience (McKercher & Chow, 2001). This can be extended beyond the tourism sphere to all consumers, whereby the expectation of a given food or experience is affected by previous experiences or media and as a result affecting the level of food satisfaction. Perceptions of locally produced food may be that it will have more flavour and the food may be rejected if it does not. Tourist satisfaction occurs when a "gastronomic destination fulfils consumers' performance criteria" (Esitti & Buluk, 2018, p. 423). Understanding these criteria, therefore, is fundamental for destinations and marketers, who can influence or promote these criteria via branding, media or selling a story. Creating stories is an important opportunity, as if food tourists know what to expect from a certain culture, they may subconsciously align these criteria with these expectations, making it easier for destinations to fulfil them in practice.

Stakeholder interests and involvement

The stakeholders involved in the culinary tourism industry are numerous. Roy et al. (2017) list restaurants, chefs, wholesale distributors, local farmers and/or farmers' market vendors as examples, but local residents, cooperative members, small business owners, local government/council, also qualify. This section concentrates on some of these stakeholders to provide context. Businesses promoting local food, artisan food, and culinary tourism have been proposed as drivers of tourism (Collinson, 2018; Smith & Xiao, 2008; Testa et al., 2019), providing not only an authentic cultural experience for tourists whilst at the destination, but potentially post-visit, when they become distant consumers (Fonte, 2010). This viewpoint supports forms of innovative entrepreneurship (Metaxas & Karagiannis, 2016), which generally requires low investment whilst also achieving high return on investment, with regional foods strengthening an area's place on the map as a tourist destination (Figure 7.3) and also rejuvenating culinary traditions which, but for the tourist market, may have been lost in history due to lack of local participation or awareness. For example, Trikalinos is a Greek innovator that has updated the traditional fish roe product to an internationally renowned gastronomic health product, using food as a tool to rebrand a location or geographic area and create a sense of social community. Indeed, Metaxas and Karagiannis (2016) studied how local food and culture could be used to create economic prosperity in countries like Greece which struggle economically and to put a "degraded commercial suburb (Keramikos) onto the 'culinary map of Athens'" (Metaxas & Karagiannis, 2016, p. 15), rebranding it into a fashionable, desirable area via restaurant 'Funky Gourmet'. The stakeholders involved in this project included the restaurant founders, their staff, the producers from whom they obtain their ingredients, the local council, the owners of the building (if rented), tourists, and to some extent the locals and new businesses it has attracted to the area. Food tourism thus is a mechanism for socio-cultural preservation, enhancement and development, via these entrepreneurial stakeholders. Collinson (2018, p. 32) states:

> Food tourists have become an important consumer category in their own right, with an acknowledged higher spending power in comparison to other types of tourists.

Thus, depending on the region and the outcomes sought, tourists as stakeholders through food tourism support local economies and help preserve cultural landscape and heritage (Santucci, 2013; Testa et al., 2019). However, it is hard to quantify how many tourists travel exclusively to pursue food interests. Much research has been done to calculate this, but as Mckercher et al. (2008) highlight many of these methods are flawed or take a narrow view.

These are examples of the culture economy approach to rural development as an attempt to "revalorise place through its cultural identity" (Ray, 1998, p. 3). As Ray highlights, globalisation or Europeanisation and localisation influence each other dynamically here. Stakeholders perceive local food as an approach concerned with production in the local area, with networks of people working together to create new forms of production or new sets of resources to improve the prosperity of the local area, but also with exogenous factors in mind. Stakeholders are discussed further in relation to opportunities and challenges of the food tourism industry.

Major trends and issues up to 2021

Cultural goods

Extending the context of culinary tourism is the development of artisanal or local products as cultural goods. This has two aspects. The first aspect relates to the product's relationship with its *location*. It promotes products traditionally eaten by locals, but which have not yet become mainstream or are enjoying a resurgence, like seaweed in Western Ireland (Collinson, 2018), transforming them into cultural goods (Bourdieu, 1986), increasing their importance for the local population and further afield. For instance, the Falmouth Oyster Festival simultaneously promotes sustainable gastronomy, the preservation of local foods and culinary knowledge, whilst enhancing culinary tourism, transforming the oysters into a cultural good. There is great potential to use this growing demand to support food networks which may be unable to survive with solely a local customer base. Culinary tourism can therefore maintain or even re-create the social value of local food, "enable(ing) the continuity of local foods, reinterpreted in the light of urban consumption" (Privitera et al., 2018). Indeed, this ability is well documented (Collinson, 2018; Everett & Aitchison, 2008; Maffesoli, 1996; Ray, 1998; Winterhalter, 2019), and is apparent in urban and rural areas e.g., the Gastronomic Ape Piaggo food truck selling reinterpreted Italian staple food on Rome's streets, or London's urban Borough Market which has transformed from a traditional staple market into a hub for cultural foods.

The second aspect relates to the relationship between the product/food experience and the tourist. The premise of cultural capital theory, developed in the 1980s, is that by consuming local food at a destination, tourists can obtain knowledge, experience and develop an appreciation of a local culture (Choe & Kim, 2019), thereby accruing cultural capital (Chang et al., 2011). According to Bourdieu's (1984) theory, cultural capital generally refers to the knowledge and experience people acquire through the course of their lives that enables them to succeed more than someone with less cultural capital. Although, for Bourdieu, if the acquisition or experience of cultural goods/experiences is dictated by socio-economic factors, these cultural goods also translate as symbols of class distinction. Indeed, if such products are classed as artisan, they may be unobtainable to the locals in the area they are produced, and, for many tourists, thereby segregating the territory of cultural goods only to the more affluent. However, multiple examples disprove this, with the development of gastro-markets which provide good food at low prices, such as London's Borough Market where apples are 40p each whilst a small rock oyster costs 70p, and traditional markets across the country such as Kirkgate market where three sea bream can be bought for £10 (Borough Market Online, 2022; Brennan, 2018; Myers, 2021; Winterhalter, 2019, p.131).

However, the possibility of travel to experience different cultures and food traditions in situ may be open to few people. Indeed, it may be a self-perpetuating prophecy, where those less educated in the importance of other cultures, partly due to not being exposed to them, are less open to experiencing such radically different ways of being and eating. Is there still evidence of this continuing in modern day? The answer is affirmative. For instance, in many Greek islands, tourists' food expectations fuel an inauthentic tourist experience which mimics a tourist's normal diet. The island of Corfu is a good example. Due to the dichotomy of affluence its tourists possess, there are many tavernas which provide British and American foods, televise U.K. football, and serve mainly beer found in the U.K. In other areas of Corfu, there are high-end, expensive tavernas serving innovative cuisine made from local foods, and gentrifying/updating more traditional dishes, stretching almost to

88 *Sophia Lingham et al.*

artwork. There are also a few tavernas offering local traditional Corfiot dishes, with Greek wines, in a more rustic setting. Therefore, despite an area being famous for its local cuisine, with many tourists visiting to sample it, there are an apposite number of tourists who visit purely for the sun and sea, and not the local food. Thus, the act of travelling itself does not lead to cultural capital acquisition per se and local food does not always become a cultural good. What is it that makes these tourists unwilling/unable to sample local foods and traditional culture? This is difficult to answer. In contrast, there are many tourist areas in Northern England, home to many different culinary cultures and identities, so tourists, even within their own country, can be exposed to an alternative culinary experience, popular with locals and tourists, such as Stella's Kitchen in Eyam, the Peak District (Kisob, 2021, 2022).

More recently, Mapes (2020) drew attention to 'elite authenticity'. Although her research only concentrated on one artisan cured meat producer in Switzerland, thereby lacking the power of generalisation, she argues that artisanal producers were enhancing class inequality, under the guise of being socially virtuous. This provides new fuel to Bourdieu's theory of social inequality via cultural capital. Indeed, de Jong and Varley (2017) posited similarly that food tourism policy unfairly ignores, marginalises and even discourages promotion of lower-class foods, such as the Scottish deep-fried Mars bar, even if there is tourist desire for it. This links to the first aspect relating to cultural goods, but, instead of supporting a local food, elite authenticity tries to eradicate it, potentially either limiting the promotion of unhealthy products, or to disassociate Scotland from such unhealthy products, but possibly also to disassociate the location with globalised brands like Mars and instead concentrate

Figure 7.1 Innovative food artwork at Erimitis Restaurant, Paxos, Corfu.

on promoting more local foods. These first two arguments are not particularly strong, however, with many other traditional Scottish delicacies not being promoted from the health perspective (e.g., whisky), and with many countries exhibiting healthy and unhealthy cuisine examples as part of their heritage cuisine. Maybe the demonisation of localised global foods like the deep-fried Mars bar are more class-focused, and their non-promotion is an attempt to draw attention away from the levels of social inequality experienced in Scotland. Perhaps more 'middle-classed' products drive more sense of identification from food tourists and provide greater local revenue because they are sold at higher prices. As such, the continuation and promotion of cultural goods within an area may become dependent on current socio-political influences which tourism may not overcome. However, the sharing of such cuisines, culinary heritage and ideas through an artisan business can instead bring people together, tourists and locals, as seen in Stella's Kitchen and Yorkshire Dama Cheese, new cuisines attracting much interest (Kisob, 2022; Razan, 2020). Evidently, these examples show culinary tourism as providing an opportunity for elitism and cultural marginalisation, and contrastingly for cross-cultural integration and equity in a local community (and via tourists when they return home).

To counter this idea that such food tourism creates gentrification, Ray's (1998) work on cultural economies argues more favourably in the direction of such cultural products and experiences as a way of redevelopment and appreciation of an area by its residents and tourists; when locals realise tourists wish to experience their local culture, they become more proud of it and more willing to showcase traditions and provide this knowledge. Again, this links back to the relationship between the product and its location (the first aspect), by valuing foods or ways of consumption which are in danger of being lost; it may even provide means of rebranding an area. Ray's theory is discussed more fully in the next section.

Identity

Identity may relate to the identity of the tourist area and community, and also to the tourists, either individually or as a group. From an individual/tourist identity perspective, food is a social marker (Finkelstein, 2014, p. 5) which extends from domestic to tourist settings. Food fashions (Bersanetti, 2018; Harrington, 2008; Mapes, 2020), such as vegetarianism, veganism, local food, organic, see many followers base their decisions on real health-related or fully-researched scientific environmental and nutritional understanding and reasoning, whilst others merely follow the latest fad the media or their social circle are drawing attention to, without a fully researched scientific understanding as an individual. Although, it has been argued that doctors are becoming more important in changing consumer food behaviours than marketing (Bersanetti, 2018). Whatever the impetus, food is becoming a way of expressing one's identity (Bersanetti, 2018; Finkelstein, 2014), and it is interesting to ponder whether food provides the ability for someone to express their identity (and indeed change identity depending on which social groups they wish to be associated with (Berger, 2008)), or whether food fads reduce identity where choices change depending on current trends or social desirables. This impacts tourism, as food tourists, in line with Bourdieu's theory, differentiate themselves from their home country, seeking an experience to enhance/develop or support their identity. Others may seek food/gastronomic experiences which sit within their current ideals.

As Germann Molz (2016) describes, food consumption through tourist experiences allows tourists to enhance and stray from their cultural norms. For instance, many food tourists may visit Mediterranean countries to sample the 'healthy' Mediterranean Diet, but actually find that whilst many olive-oil-based dishes are healthy, there are many national traditional dishes which are deep-fried, contain vast amounts of sweetener, cream and pastry. As such, tourists may instead learn that 'healthy diets' focus more on balance, environment and conviviality than they do on healthy foods. It would be interesting to determine how tourists' food identity at home changes when they are on holiday/away from home. Some tourists might find it difficult to express their food identity whilst on holiday, where traditional dishes do not naturally fulfil their more routine culinary requirements. This could prove a barrier for locations who lack understanding of recent food trends or wish to keep their gastronomy traditional and authentic.

From a tourist destination perspective, retaining regional identity, conservation of traditional heritage, skills and ways of life, are all desirable within regions, especially ones with strong community spirit. An association between these factors and food tourism was found in Cornwall, U.K. (Everett & Aitchison, 2008). Interestingly though, in seeking out cultures different to their own, some tourists, especially Western tourists (Sanchez-Cañizares & Castillo-Canalejo, 2015), may be deterred by unfamiliar local foods in other countries. Tourists may impose cultural similarity by dictating the foods they will eat as part of a cultural experience, challenging the authenticity of the food they consume. Lash and Urry (1994) distinguished between authenticity seekers who look for truly authentic experiences different to normal, and allegoric game players who accept the experience constructed for them. McKercher and Chow (2001) posit, using the typology of Wang (1999) on existential authenticity, that despite tourist experiences not being strictly locally traditional, the fact that their experiences are intrinsically authentic, creates a sense of being, that captures its own innate authenticity. As these may be inter- or intra-personal, the potential for local food to create neo-authentic experiences may relate to the local traditional culture, a developing tourist culture with roots in tradition, or an entirely new concept of culture whether based on people or just the food experience. Perhaps to be truly authentic, the tourist experience needs not only to be based on local traditions, but also to meet local needs with the local area having cultural control and the resulting economic activity (Ray, 1998). If this is not the case, it could be argued such approaches are merely neo-colonialism.

Messors in Italy provides an example of the former, creating opportunities for visitors to appreciate the connections between humans, cultural traditions, and the landscape that can still be tasted in the food (Messors, 2021), focusing on integrity and celebrating cultural identity. This approach manages to "dignify these traditions" (Kilburn & Nicole, 2018) whilst operating within EU food safety regulations which many authentic, historic food production methods would not satisfy. Some academics, however, posit that such culinary tourism is unlikely to enhance local food cultures long-term, instead being merely a fad which will dissipate with time. McKercher et al. (2008) suggest food tourism can co-align with ecotourism, cultural and heritage tourism of special interest which to date have had minimal effect, although some examples exist e.g., The Pig hotel chain in the U.K. (Ketter, 2020; The Pig, 2022) and destination identities promoting sustainable socio-cultural tourism for all may become more popular in the future (Ferrer-Roca et al., 2020; NECSTouR, 2019).

Food memories

The food experiences that culinary tourism provides mean consumption may not be the primary aim, instead the focus is on the cultural experience (Privitera et al., 2018), seeing

Figure 7.2 Food memories: Picnic featuring traditional mainland Greek foods.

or even keeping the product as a keepsake, and creating a food memory (Collinson, 2018) (thereby expanding food culture beyond country borders) (Figure 7.2). Food memories and the need for specific marketing to prolong these lived experiences and create destination branding are important too (Björk and Kauppinen-Räisänen (2014b). This creates two paradoxes, firstly between food in the globalised world and the desire for convergence of food and products (Pavlidis & Markantonatou, 2020), compared with individual food experiences located in a place or context with a given story. The second paradox is between modern technology-saturated consumer society focused on pecuniary value, and the traditional/cultural experiences sought by culinary tourists which extend beyond financial value. Tangible food quality and intangible experiential factors are not necessarily correlated i.e., someone may not enjoy a particular food, but instead may enjoy the overall experience, and the former does not necessarily reduce the latter (McKercher & Chow, 2001).

New forms of economy

With an increase in food tourists seeking traditional foods and experiences, culinary tourism is a trend which could benefit the tourism sector. Street food, food trucks, and gastromarkets are all examples of new food trends, creating a new food language (Winterhalter, 2019), and placing an emphasis on more convivial food culture, or at least food being consumed in more communal areas, providing an opportunity to socialise (Taheri et al., 2021). This supports the popularity of tourist destinations which exhibit this style of eating, such

92 *Sophia Lingham et al.*

as areas of the Mediterranean, and the development of a tourist economy rooted in social connection: a socialised or familiar economy. A familiar economy might thus be initialising which goes beyond the social economy, i.e., economic activities place people ahead of profit, are democratically and autonomously managed, and focus on the primacy of people and work in the distribution of revenues (Defourny & Develtere, 1999), towards a focus on community, connection, cooperation, and socialisation. From a tourism perspective, this creates an opportunity for culinary tourists to become part of a familiar economy rather than merely witness it, where businesses have specific responsibility to influence how culinary tourism impacts local food culture, especially whether it is enhanced or eroded.

The gastronomic experiences tourists gain are derived from their patronage of eating establishments, and these businesses are crucial in linking local producers with consumers (Sanchez-Cañizares & Castillo-Canalejo, 2015), providing an authentic cultural experience through developing an artisanal economy, whereby selective use of technology is paired with tradition. Usually, artisan entrepreneurs are microbusinesses or small or medium-sized enterprises (SMEs) focused on smaller markets, product authenticity, and searching "for social innovation through novel cooperation models" (Darnhofer & Strauss, 2015, p. i). Here, profit is secondary to cooperation and continuation of heritage, creating culinary tourism which enhances the local food economy.

Herein, the culinary economy borders on circular, more holistic economies. For instance, nearly half the culinary tourists in Italy are Italian (43%), and Italy has had significant growth in internal culinary tourism in recent years (Ferrari & Gilli, 2015; Testa et al., 2019).

Figure 7.3 Padron peppers enjoyed during the Camino de Santiago – food putting an area on the map.

In contrast, the U.K. ranks fifth in a survey as an attractive country for food and drink, behind Mediterranean countries (Italy, France, Spain) and the U.S. (DEFRA, 2017). Being rooted in the national psyche in some countries, culinary tourism can maintain and enhance food culture and a culinary economy and having local support may reduce the erosive influence of international tourists, where catering to their needs is less important. As hospitality and the food industry are well-respected industries in much of the Mediterranean, with many restaurants and tavernas being passed down through generations of the same family, this influences the social importance of food and the success of a culinary economy. Nurturing belief in either culinary culture or culinary business in the local community reduces the impact of tourism as an eroding force, redefining the food culture of the location.

Culture was depicted as "the web of significance which man himself has spun" (Geertz, 1973). The promotion of culture, food culture and traditions within it, is a popular form of local conservation and rebranding. As such, it can form its own culture economy, still relevant today as a means to "revalorise place through its cultural identity" (Ray, 1998, p. 3) in pursuit of rural development. Ray argued that it originates from a combination of changes within consumer capitalism towards postmodernism, an impact from the trajectory of EU rural development policy (which support local/rural culture and development and simultaneously continues the Single Market), and regionalism expressing social cultures. However, the Greek economic bailout, with the EU requirements to stamp out some long-standing traditions in line with EU working regulations, may suggest that homogenisation will always take priority (Clifton et al., 2018; Sutton, 2016). This creates two competing goals: requiring tourist locations to be attractive to outside investment and global tourism, and also seeking to capture a desire for local identity, termed neotribalism (Maffesoli, 1996). Balancing these without eroding local food cultures is challenging when outside investors do not value existing food cultures. As such, the culture economy, with the culinary sub-economy represents a wider oxymoron which the "heterogenisation of complexity of space and everyday life" (Lash & Urry, 1994, p. 3) fails to provide. In fact, different tourist types form a dichotomy between those who reject abstract, commercialised, blanket forms of tourism, and those who seek and feel comfort in it, thus fuelling its existence.

Forms of cultural economy include what Ray termed ethno/cultural tourism, i.e., selling the culture and history of an area by marketing something with the identity of the place, as well as local crafts and food culture. Interestingly, he highlights the necessity of selling itself to itself (1998, p. 7), to encourage local cooperatives, drive self-confidence and wider confidence in the local culture or environment, allowing locals to develop loyalty and socio-cultural-environmental vibrancy to promote to tourists and outside investment, helping more locals stay in the area rather than emigrate for work, reinstating pride in local identity (Cole, 2006; Treephan et al., 2019). As a result, tourism may indirectly lead local communities to appreciate their own cultures more, knowing that others are interested in discovering and experiencing them. In this sense, and using the Sustainable Development Goals as a lens, SDG 8 is fulfilled by providing decent sustainable work and economic growth opportunities, which, in turn, aids SDG 3 of good health and wellbeing, including mental wellbeing. Thus, the potential to enhance local food cultures and local economies is great: not only do tourists directly bring money into an area, but they also give locals reason to stay and become entrepreneurial, deriving economic benefit and creating a positive-feedback mechanism, as the more local businesses there are, the more the tourists will want to experience them.

Culinary tourism within a cultural economy also creates a post-visit market for specific products for which intellectual property (IP) can be applied, thereby creating internationally marketable traditional identity for food products. The ironic paradox here, however, is that in order for these local initiatives to sustainably thrive, and for SDG 9 for resilient infrastructure and sustainable innovation (United Nations, 2015) to be supported, the global and regional capitalist structure must be employed. As Ray points out, however bottom-up these approaches may appear to be, they still require the enabling mechanism of extra-local forces (p. 8). Paradoxically, these extra-local forces, i.e., tourists, currency exchange, and entrepreneurship, are the very foundations of the revitalisation of the small/local cultures and villages, that the homogenisation drivers of global capitalism tend to erode. Perhaps tourism can support a new model of capitalism, and the interaction of economic, physical, natural, social and human capital, focused on local needs, enabling enrichment and enhancement of local culture. Food-related cultural tourism creates social and economic pathways to maintaining traditional farming methods and environmental awareness creating an interplay between the monetary economy, the familiar economy, the culture economy and its subset, the culinary economy.

Trends, issues, opportunities, and predictions for the future

Many trends, issues and challenges arise from food tourism pivoting from the positive, authentic experience through to (in)authentic experiences via in-situ food consumption, food loss and waste, sustainability issues, reduced wellbeing, lack of good practice in culinary and gastronomy tourism, the lack of protection of Indigenous cuisines (Horng & Tsai, 2012; Okumus et al., 2007; Taheri et al., 2021), and an inequality of access and engagement promoted by the wealth divide. The key trends are considered here.

There is a growing trend to strengthen the relationship between agriculture and tourism, see Vourdoubas' (2020) research in Crete and Martindale's (2021) research in China where Beijing's Xiedau Green Resort started out as a small community-supported agriculture (CSA) in the 1990s and developed into an agri-tourism hub, as a 180-hectare enterprise-based recreational agriculture park (Martindale, 2021; Thornton, 2018; Yang et al., 2016). This focus on the expanding middle class, also widening consumer interest in agriculture offering producers a sustainable means of diversifying and continuing traditional practices, creates opportunities for integrated and sustainable urban–rural development (Yang et al., 2010). Herein, the potential for enhancing food culture and providing opportunities for long-term preservation of traditions is clear, albeit the model lacks inclusivity with a focus on the affluent, reinforcing the wealth divide failing to promote inclusive growth and reduce inequalities (SDG 10).

A great challenge is phantom demand, i.e., the 'apparent demand identified in market research that does not translate into real market opportunities' (McKercher et al. 2008, p. 138), insinuating that novelty is not promoted but instead is subsumed into an existing generic mix. Therefore, marketing and the culinary experience offered must be more convincingly promoted to the right new market. There are examples, such as Messors in Italy, which seem to buck the trend and take immersive, sustainable tourism to the next level, tapping into a new foodie ecotourism. However, whether ecotourism is sustainable is worthy of further critique. Promoting an area through its specific territorial food products can be based on consumption or general promotion of a certain quality of life (Ray, 1998). The interest in the Mediterranean Diet, focusing on local, seasonal, and fresh food, cooked simply with little processing and consumed with others, taps into an emotional pull of rediscovery of a perceived simpler, more wholesome, rooted, and healthier way of life. The advent of the COVID-19 pandemic has led many individuals to re-evaluate their priorities and so rediscovery through tourism may gain interest rather than being a phantom demand or short-lived fad. This is something the next decade will prove either way.

Tourism gives women a different purpose where lack of education can otherwise be limiting (Anthopoulou & Koutsou, 2014). Empirical knowledge and expertise, rather than training, that is transmitted from generation to generation, orally, means women can engage in rural tourism working in teams or cooperatively (Koutsou et al., 2009). This is a growing trend throughout many tourist areas in Greece, such as the Women's Agrotourist Cooperative of Zagora in Pelion or the Women's Cooperative in Ikaria. This contrasts with younger, better educated and more confident women who choose private forms of enterprise. This empowerment of women through culinary tourism, via education or intergenerational learning, goes some way to achieving a more gender equal society in local and rural areas of countries such as Greece, directly linking to the fifth SDG of gender equality. There are many areas, though, where tourism is limited either due to minimal marketing, lack of English speakers, or perhaps even a desire to preserve their way of life. Generally, empowerment is hindered by three factors: firstly, the influence of younger entrepreneurial women may not reach more rural areas; secondly, national and international tourism is non-existent in remote areas; and thirdly, many remote rural areas experience youth emigration to cities like Athens, reducing the possibility of handing down knowledge to future generations.

Culinary tourism has the potential to reduce culinary xenophobia and racism; foreign foods may be feared when migrants open new ethnic restaurants (Anderson et al., 2021) and when tourists visit a new area. Experiencing these cultural foods with the people whose identity they are part of, may promote positive intercultural relations (Anderson et al., 2021) at the tourist destination and when returning home. A home-building multiculturalism approach to culinary tourism (Anderson et al., 2021; Hage, 1997), whereby the preparation and consumption of a dish is shared by providers and tourists, is a new possibility for culinary tourism, where the emphasis is on relationship building. As 'it is not so much the food itself that is an object of cultural experience but rather it is the subject's experience with the food that takes it to a higher level of significant meaning' (Germann Molz, 2016; Long, 2004; Stowe & Johnston, 2012, p. 465). The EatWith experiences are certainly a testament to this and a model which is becoming a popularised way of eating out, perhaps even to rival restaurants 20–30 years hence. This inclusive cross-cultural integration rejects the notion that culinary tourism is a form of neo-colonialism (Anderson et al., 2021; Stowe & Johnston, 2012) instead, moving past acceptance to understanding and celebration.

Multiple stakeholders with competing agendas are a challenge, e.g., despite Italy being the largest wine producer globally, there is much scope to improve their wine tourism sector. Terroir is central to the wine industry (Festa et al., 2020; Santini, 2019), underpinning brand identity and reputation. Multiple stakeholders hinder wine tourism, with governance and management of wine routes being hampered by contested responsibilities in public/private collaboration, rendering many inoperable and lacking identity (Bregoli et al., 2016). There is opportunity to simplify with an independent body to improve outreach and sustainability of wine route tourism. However, collaboration involving public bodies is likely to take some time, so it may be the mid-2030s when this opportunity is fully grasped.

Ellis et al. (2018) suggest that food/culinary tourism is a form of cultural anthropology via the interactions of tourists with place through the medium of food (p. 261). Being a cultural experience, they highlight that authenticity relating to locality is paramount, showcasing its heritage, not a new authenticity made for tourists. To gain the most from food tourism, especially in rural locations which could be inundated with tourists disrupting their activities, specific and appropriate management is required for the commercialisation of food heritage, supply and production. Increasing tourist numbers must be managed efficiently, to avoid overtourism (Ferrer-Roca et al., 2020). Additionally, local communities must strongly resist multinationals and external investors wishing to develop their cultures. Ensuring sustainable production and consumption patterns by 2030 (SDG 12) requires local collaboration, cooperation and support. Strong collaboration and links between stakeholders, small businesses and local government are also needed (Ellis et al., 2018) and this may link to SDG 17, focusing on partnerships.

Some local tourist boards may have a propensity to discourage culturally lower-class or more unhealthy foods (de Jong & Varley, 2017; Fox & Smith, 2011). With a variety of healthy and unhealthy products being promoted and widely available in the Mediterranean, diversity helps create a wider, inclusive appreciation for all food cultures. For instance, the consumption of fried Japanese dumplings and tempura is classed almost as healthy, and Greek spanakopita is a normal part of the diet. In order to attract middle-class tourists with spending power, future emphasis may be placed on healthier food products, or arguably on innovative/different reincarnations of heritage products.

Education is a necessary part of sustainable food tourism, to engage, appreciate, experience and preserve different cultures and local traditions. Arguably, in a world concentrating on reducing personal environmental footprints, encouraging food tourism is difficult. In recent years, food has been the catalyst for new ways of travel, with companies like Intrepid creating a Vegan Real Adventures travel plan, putting food, albeit not necessarily cultural food, at the heart of sustainable tourism. Additionally, Michelin, in 2020 created a green star for restaurants at the forefront of sustainable gastronomy, paving the way for a new food tourism focus. Many regions at immediate risk from climate change need recognition, understanding, support and solidarity and food tourism could provide a means for doing so. Word of mouth, or of social media, is a route particularly significant in marketing food destinations, especially as photos of food are the second most popular posts after selfies on Instagram (Amato et al., 2017). As media and social media attention appears influential in gaining swift policy decisions or at least great public support (Mavrodieva et al., 2019), their ability to promote sustainable tourism and food cultures in danger of disappearing could be vital; it is a mechanism by which change can be realised within the decade rather than merely on a longer-term trajectory.

Major contributions of this chapter

This chapter has provided an overview of culinary tourism in the context of the culture economy and, more specifically, the culinary economy. The examples provided have also been linked to their role in delivering the SDGs. The examples of culinary tourism show the potential to either erode or enhance the local food economy, especially if it is focused on monetary rather than culture-based outcomes. The type of culinary tourism developed depends on the tourists of interest, the strength and confidence of the local community, how dependent they are on outside investment, and whether this investment promotes local food and traditions, or a more stylised food culture. Reimagined economies such as familiar economy (coined here), artisan economy, and culinary economy highlight the emphasis on connection and relationships within culinary tourism based either on monetary transactions or alternatively on non-financial values and experiences.

Commoditisation can support local food culture development and conservation through tourism, but local autonomy is essential.

In delivering the SDGs, cultural tourism needs to address equality of access and experience, and inclusive growth through sustainable business models and equal access to opportunity irrespective of gender or status. The familiar economy encompasses cultural and economic aspects and the business models employed – the focus on entrepreneurial behaviour and innovation – are worthy of further study. The work of Bourdieu and Ray are both relevant, with examples of their theories seen as enacted in cultural tourism, especially where tourists travel in order to reinforce their own social status and their innate capacity to be educated. This may create a respect for the food culture of the destination or purely serve as a tick-box exercise (been there/done that). However, creating desirable or alternative food experiences, whether based in traditional culture or in emergent food culture, means that food businesses in a location can capitalise on this market and create local resilient, economic growth.

A key question emerging from this chapter for future study is whether some tourists, no matter how exposed they are to traditional cultures and authenticity, will continue to desire a home from home food experience, but in warmer climes? This may lead to a cultural shift in more traditional foods in these locations where the focus is on experience rather than authenticity. Cultural shift to meet the demands of tourists recreates notions of authenticity and culinary culture, even tending towards monoculturalism. Culinary tourism focusing on identity, identity of place and self and their sustainable alignment requires greater consideration as these multiple aspects need to be captured in each place-based offering.

References

Amato, G., Bolettieri, P., De Lira, V. M., Muntean, C. I., Perego, R., & Renso, C. (2017). Social media image recognition for food trend analysis. *SIGIR 2017 – Proceedings of the 40th International ACM SIGIR Conference on Research and Development in Information Retrieval*, 1333–1336. https://doi.org/10.1145/3077136.3084142

Anderson, L., Benbow, H. M., & Manzin, G. (2021). Europe on a Plate: Food, Identity and Cultural Diversity in Contemporary Europe. *Australian and New Zealand Journal of European Studies*, 8(1). https://doi.org/10.30722/ANZJES.VOL8.ISS1.15155

Anthopoulou, T., & Koutsou, S. (2014). Local agri-food products of women's cooperatives – The 'feminine side' of quality (Greece). In Rytkoenen (Ed.), *Food and Rurality in Europe: Economy, Environment and Institutions in Contemporary rural Europe* (pp. 159–180). Stockholm: Elanders Tryckeri AB. https://www.diva-portal.org/smash/get/y2:710865/FULLTEXT01.pdf#page=167

Berger, J. (2008). Identity Signalling, Social Influence, and Social Contagion. In M. Prinstein & K. Dodge (Eds.), *Understanding peer influence in children and adolescents* (pp. 181–202). Guildford: The Guildford Press. https://books.google.co.uk/books?id=n2Cr7GC0QX4C&pg=PR13&dq=food+fashions+and+identity&lr=&source=gbs_selected_pages&cad=3#v=onepage&q=food fashions and identity&f=false

Bersanetti, F. (2018). Food is the new Fashion. *Micro & Macro Marketing*, 1, 155–168. https://doi.org/10.1431/89489

Björk, P., & Kauppinen-Räisänen, H. (2014a). Culinary-gastronomic tourism – a search for local food experiences. *Nutrition & Food Science*, 44(4), 294–309. https://doi.org/10.1108/NFS-12-2013-0142

Björk, P., & Kauppinen-Räisänen, H. (2014b). Exploring the multi-dimensionality of travellers' culinary-gastronomic experiences. *Current Issues in Tourism*, 19(12), 1260–1280. https://doi.org/10.1080/13683500.2013.868412

Borough Market Online. (2022). *Shop Fruit & Veg from Borough Market – Good Sixty*. Goodsixty. Co.Uk. https://www.goodsixty.co.uk/shop/in-borough-market/4396-fruit-veg

Bourdieu, P. (1984). *Distinction: A Social Critique of the Judgement of Taste – Pierre Bourdieu – Google Books* (R. Nice (ed.); Illustrated, reprint). Cambridge, MA: Harvard University Press. https://books.google.co.uk/books?id=nVaS6gS9Jz4C&lr&source=gbs_book_other_versions

Bourdieu, P. (1986). The Forms of Capital. In J. G. Richardson (Ed.), *Handbook of Theory and Research for the Sociology of Education* (pp. 241–258). San Francisco: Greenwood Press.

Bregoli, I., Hingley, M., Del Chiappa, G., & Sodano, V. (2016). Challenges in Italian wine routes: managing stakeholder networks. *Qualitative Market Research*, 19(2), 204–224. https://doi.org/10.1108/QMR-02-2016-0008/FULL/XML

Brennan, A. (2018, September 12). London Bridge and Borough Market cheap eats: Best food under £10 | London Evening Standard | Evening Standard. *Evening Standard.* https://www.standard.co.uk/reveller/restaurants/london-bridge-and-borough-market-cheap-eats-best-restaurants-food-and-meals-under-ps10-a3933996.html

Cafiero, C., Palladino, M., Marcianò, C., & Romeo, G. (2019). Traditional agri-food products as a leverage to motivate tourists: A meta-analysis of tourism-information websites. *Journal of Place Management and Development*, 13(2), 195–214. https://doi.org/10.1108/JPMD-05-2019-0032

Chang, R. C. Y., Kivela, J., & Mak, A. H. N. (2011). Attributes that influence the evaluation of travel dining experience: When East meets West. *Tourism Management*, 32(2), 307–316. https://doi.org/10.1016/J.TOURMAN.2010.02.009

Choe, J. Y., & Kim, S. S. (2019). Development and validation of a multidimensional tourist's local food consumption value (TLFCV) scale. *International Journal of Hospitality Management*, 77, 245–259.

Clifton, J., Diaz-Fuentes, D., & Gomez, A. L. (2018, November 15). *Ideology (not economics) explains why the Troika treated Ireland less harshly than Greece.* London School of Economics Blog. https://blogs.lse.ac.uk/europpblog/2018/11/15/ideology-not-economics-explains-why-the-troika-treated-ireland-less-harshly-than-greece/

Cole, S. (2006). Cultural tourism, community participation and empowerment. In *Cultural Tourism in a Changing World: Politics, Participation and (Re)Presentation* (pp. 87–103). Bristol, UK: Channel View Publications. https://doi.org/10.21832/9781845410452-008/MACHINEREADABLECITATION/RIS

Collinson, P. (2018). Consuming Traditions: Artisan Food and Food Tourism in Western Ireland. In A. F. X. Medina & J. Tresserras (Eds.), *Food, Gastronomy and Tourism Social and Cultural Perspectives* (pp. 31–48). Universidad de Guadalajara.

Darnhofer, I., & Strauss, A. (2015). *Rethink: Rethinking the links between farm modernization, rural development and resilience in a world of increasing demands and finite resources: Organic farming and resilience case study report.* http://citeseerx.ist.psu.edu/viewdoc/download?doi=10.1.1.705.7470&rep=rep1&type=pdf

de Jong, A., & Varley, P. (2017). Food tourism policy: Deconstructing boundaries of taste and class. *Tourism Management*, 60, 212–222. https://doi.org/10.1016/J.TOURMAN.2016.12.009

Defourny, J., & Develtere, P. (1999). The Social Economy: The Worldwide Making of a Third Sector. In J. Defourny, P. Develtere, & B. Fonteneau (Eds.), *L'economie sociale au Nord et au Sud* (pp. 3–31). Centre D'Economie Sociale, Universite De Liege. https://www.researchgate.net/publication/240335888_The_Social_Economy_The_Worldwide_Making_of_a_Third_Sector

DEFRA. (2017). *Food is Great.* https://www.visitbritain.org/sites/default/files/vb-corporate/Documents-Library/documents/food_drink_research_summary_12.07.17_v4.pdf

Ellis, A., Park, E., Kim, S., & Yeoman, I. (2018). What is food tourism? *Tourism Management*, 68, 250–263. https://doi.org/10.1016/j.tourman.2018.03.025

Esitti, B., & Buluk, B. (2018). Sustainable Gastronomy Tourism and Tourist Satisfaction. In Bülent Cercis Tanritanir & Sevilay Özer (Eds.), *Academic Research in Social, Human And Administrative Sciences-II* (1st ed., pp. 419–438). Cankaya, Ankara, Turkey: Gece Kitapligi. www.gecekitapligi.com

Everett, S., & Aitchison, C. (2008). The role of food tourism in sustaining regional identity: A case study of Cornwall, South West England. *Journal of Sustainable Tourism*, 16(2), 150–167. https://doi.org/10.2167/jost696.0

Ferrari, S., & Gilli, M. (2015). Authenticity and experience in sustainable food tourism. In P. Sloan, W. Legrand, C. Hindley, A. Justenlund, & A. Justenlund (Eds.), *The Routledge Handbook of Sustainable Food and Gastronomy* (1st ed., Issue 19617, pp. 347–357). Routledge. https://doi.org/10.4324/9780203795699-44

Ferrer-Roca, N., Weston, R., Guia, J., Mihalic, T., Blasco, D., Prats, L., Lawler, M., & Jarratt, D. (2020). Back to the future: challenges of European tourism of tomorrow. *Journal of Tourism Futures*, 7(2), 184–191. https://doi.org/10.1108/JTF-10-2019-0114/FULL/PDF

Festa, G., Shams, S. M. R., Metallo, G., & Cuomo, M. T. (2020). Opportunities and challenges in the contribution of wine routes to wine tourism in Italy – A stakeholders' perspective of development. *Tourism Management Perspectives*, 33, 100585. https://doi.org/10.1016/J.TMP.2019.100585

Finkelstein, J. (2014). Fashionable Food. In J. Finklestein (Ed.), *Fashioning Appetite: Restaurants and the Making of Modern Identity* (pp. 1–36). I.B. New York: Tauris. https://books.google.co.uk/books?hl=en&lr=&id=0GGJDwAAQBAJ&oi=fnd&pg=PP1&dq=food+fashions+and+identity&ots=buz5SUHqhI&sig=9Z634d-kk4F-SdgnHMlx_4mJS_c#v=onepage&q=food fashions and identity&f=false

Fonte, M. (2010). Introduction: Food Relocalisation and Knowledge Dynamics for Sustainability in Rural Areas. In M. Fonte & A. Papadopoulos (Eds.), *Naming Food After Places: Food Relocalisation and Knowledge Dynamics in Rural Development* (pp. 1–38). London: Routledge. https://www.book2look.com/embed/9781317090762

Fox, R., & Smith, G. (2011). Sinner Ladies and the gospel of good taste: geographies of food, class and care. *Health & Place*, 17(2), 403–412. https://doi.org/10.1016/J.HEALTHPLACE.2010.07.006

Geertz, C. (1973). *The interpretation of cultures*. Basic Books.

Germann Molz, J. (2016). Eating Difference: The Cosmopolitan Mobilities of Culinary Tourism. *Space and Culture*, 10(1), 77–93. https://doi.org/10.1177/1206331206296383

Hage, G. (1997). At Home in the Entrails of the West: Multiculturalism Ethnic Food and Migrant Home-Building. In H. Grace, G. Hage, L. Johnson, J. Langsworth, & M. Symonds (Eds.), *Home/World: Community, identity and marginality in Sydney's West* (pp. 99–153). London: Pluto Press. https://www.academia.edu/12916012/At_Home_in_the_Entrails_of_the_West_Multiculturalism_Ethnic_Food_and_Migrant_Home_Building

Hall, M., & Gössling, S. (2016). *Food Tourism and Regional Development: Networks, products and trajectories* (M. Hall & S. Gössling (eds.); 1st ed.). Routledge. https://www.routledge.com/Food-Tourism-and-Regional-Development-Networks-products-and-trajectories/Hall-Gossling/p/book/9781138592414

Harrington, R. J. (2008). Defining Gastronomic Identity. *Journal of Culinary Science & Technology*, 4(2–3), 129–152. https://doi.org/10.1300/J385V04N02_10

Horng, J.-S., & Tsai, C.-T. (2010). Government websites for promoting East Asian culinary tourism: A cross-national analysis. *Tourism Management*, 31, 74–85. https://doi.org/10.1016/j.tourman.2009.01.009

Horng, J.-S., & Tsai, C.-T. (Simon). (2012). Culinary tourism strategic development: an Asia-Pacific perspective. *International Journal of Tourism Research*, 14(1), 40–55. https://doi.org/10.1002/JTR.834

Ketter, E. (2020). Millennial travel: tourism micro-trends of European Generation Y. *Journal of Tourism Futures*, 7(2), 192–196. https://doi.org/10.1108/JTF-10-2019-0106/FULL/PDF

Kilburn, N., & Nicole. (2018). Culinary tourism, the newest crop in Southern Italy's farms and pastures. *Anthropology of Food*, 13. https://doi.org/10.4000/AOF.8384

Kisob, S. (2021, November 4). *BBC iPlayer – The Hairy Bikers Go North – Series 1: 7. The Peak District*. BBC. https://www.bbc.co.uk/iplayer/episode/m001187b/the-hairy-bikers-go-north-series-1-7-the-peak-district

Kisob, S. (2022). *African Caribbean Food Peak District | Hope Valley | Stella's Kitchen*. Stella's Kitchen. https://www.stellas-kitchen.co.uk/

Koutsou, S., Notta, O., Samathrakis, V., & Partalidou, M. (2009). Women's Entrepreneurship and Rural Tourism in Greece: Private Enterprises and Cooperatives. *South European Society and Politics*, 14(2), 191–209. https://doi.org/10.1080/13608740903037968

Lane, C. (2010). Michelin-Starred Restaurant Sector as a Cultural Industry: A Cross-National Comparison of Restaurants in the UK and Germany. *Food, Culture and Society*, *13*(4), 493–519. https://agris.fao.org/agris-search/search.do?recordID=US201400143854#

Lash, S., & Urry, J. (1994). *Economies of signs and space*. London: SAGE.

Lingham, S., Hill, I., & Manning, L. (2022). Artisan Food Production: What Makes Food "Artisan"? In L.-P. Dana, V. Ramadani, R. Palalic, & A. Salamzadeh (Eds.), *Artisan and Handicraft Entrepreneurs* (1st ed., pp. 101–117). Cham, Switzerland: Springer International Publishing. https://doi.org/10.1007/978-3-030-82303-0

Long, L. (2004). Culinary Tourism: A Folkloric Perspective on Eating and Otherness. In L. Long (Ed.), *Culinary Tourism* (pp. 20–50). The University Press of Kentucky Louisville. https://www.kentuckypress.com/9780813122922/culinary-tourism/

Maffesoli, M. (1996). *The time of the tribes*. London: SAGE.

Mapes, G. (2020). Marketing elite authenticity: Tradition and terroir in artisanal food discourse. *Discourse, Context & Media*, *34*, 100328. https://doi.org/10.1016/J.DCM.2019.100328

Martindale, L. (2021). From Land Consolidation and Food Safety to Taobao Villages and Alternative Food Networks: Four Components of China's Dynamic Agri-Rural Innovation System. In *Journal of Rural Studies* (Vol. 82, pp. 404–416). Elsevier Ltd. https://doi.org/10.1016/j.jrurstud.2021.01.012

Mavrodieva, A. V., Rachman, O. K., Harahap, V. B., & Shaw, R. (2019). Role of Social Media as a Soft Power Tool in Raising Public Awareness and Engagement in Addressing Climate Change. *Climate*, *7*(10), 122. https://doi.org/10.3390/CLI7100122

McKercher, B., & Chow, S-M. B. (2001). Cultural distance and participation in cultural tourism. *Pacific Tourism Review*, *5*(1), 23–32. https://www.ingentaconnect.com/contentone/cog/ptr/2001/00000005/f0020001/art00005

McKercher, B., Okumus, F., & Okumus, B. (2008). Food Tourism as a Viable Market Segment: It's all about you cook the numbers! *Journal of Travel & Tourism Marketing*, *25*(2), 137–148.

Messors. (2021). *Immersive art, history and food culture experiences in Italy*. Messors.Com. https://messors.com/about-art-food-culture-italy/

Metaxas, T., & Karagiannis, D. (2016). Culinary tourism in greece: can the past define the future? Dimensions of innovation, entrepreneurship and regional development. *Journal of Developmental Entrepreneurship*, *21*(3). https://doi.org/10.1142/S1084946716500187

Myers, S. (2021, October 21). *BBC iPlayer – The Hairy Bikers Go North – Series 1: 5. West Yorkshire*. BBC. https://www.bbc.co.uk/iplayer/episode/m0010tmx/the-hairy-bikers-go-north-series-1-5-west-yorkshire

NECSTouR. (2019). *NECSTouR Roadmap 2019-2021: The 5 "S" of the Tourism of Tomorrow | necstour*. Necstour roadmap 2019-2021: the 5 "s" of the tourism of tomorrow. https://necstour.eu/publications/necstour-roadmap-2019-2021-5-s-tourism-tomorrow

Okumus, B., Okumus, F., & McKercher, B. (2007). Incorporating local and international cuisines in the marketing of tourism destinations: The cases of Hong Kong and Turkey. *Tourism Management*, *28*(1), 253–261. https://doi.org/10.1016/J.TOURMAN.2005.12.020

Ottenbacher, M. C., & Harrington, R. J. (2011). A Case Study of a Culinary Tourism Campaign in Germany: Implications for Strategy Making and Successful Implementation. *Journal of Hospitality & Tourism Research*, *37*(1), 3–28. https://doi.org/10.1177/1096348011413593

Pavlidis, G., & Markantonatou, S. (2020). Gastronomic tourism in Greece and beyond: A thorough review. In *International Journal of Gastronomy and Food Science* (Vol. 21, p. 100229). AZTI-Tecnalia. https://doi.org/10.1016/j.ijgfs.2020.100229

Privitera, D., Nedelcu, A., & Nicula, V. (2018). Gastronomic and food tourism as an economic local resource: case studies from romania and italy. *GeoJournal of Tourism and Geosites*, *21*(1), 143–157. http://gtg.webhost.uoradea.ro/

Ray, C. (1998). Culture, intellectual property and territorial rural development. *Sociologia Ruralis*, *38*(1), 3–20. https://doi.org/10.1111/1467-9523.00060

Razan, A. (2020). *Home – Yorkshire Dama Cheese*. Yorkshire Dama Cheese. https://yorkshiredamacheese.co.uk/

Roy, H., Hall, C. M., & W. Ballantine, P. (2017). Trust in local food networks: The role of trust among tourism stakeholders and their impacts in purchasing decisions. *Journal of Destination Marketing & Management*, 6(4), 309–317. https://doi.org/10.1016/J.JDMM.2017.07.002

Sanchez-Cañizares, S., & Castillo-Canalejo, A. M. (2015). A comparative study of tourist attitudes towards culinary tourism in Spain and Slovenia. *British Food Journal*, 117(9), 2387–2411. https://doi.org/10.1108/BFJ-01-2015-0008

Santini, C. (2019). The Business of Wine Tourism: Evolution and Challenges. *Management and Marketing of Wine Tourism Business: Theory, Practice, and Cases*, 261–276. https://doi.org/10.1007/978-3-319-75462-8_13

Santucci, F. M. (2013). Agritourism for Rural Development in Italy, Evolution, Situation and Perspectives. *British Journal of Economics Management & Trade*, 3(3), 186–200. https://www.researchgate.net/publication/272758807_Agritourism_for_Rural_Development_in_Italy_Evolution_Situation_and_Perspectives

Smith, S. L. J., & Xiao, H. (2008). Culinary Tourism Supply Chains: A Preliminary Examination. *Journal of Travel Research*, 46, 289–299. https://doi.org/10.1177/0047287506303981

Stowe, L., & Johnston, D. (2012). Throw your napkin on the floor: Authenticity, culinary tourism, and a pedagogy of the senses. *Australian Journal of Adult Learning*, 52(3).

Sutton, D. (2016). "Let Them Eat Stuffed Peppers": An Argument of Images on the Role of Food in Understanding Neoliberal Austerity in Greece. *Gastronomica*, 16(4), 8–17. https://doi.org/10.1525/GFC.2016.16.4.8

Taheri, B., Gannon, M., & Fletcher, J. (2021). Contemporary issues and future trends in food tourism Editor-in-Chief. *International Journal of Tourism Research*, 23(2), 147–149.

Testa, R., Galati, A., Schifiani, G., Di Trapani, A. M., & Migliore, G. (2019). Culinary Tourism Experiences in Agri-Tourism Destination and Sustainable Consumption- Understanding Italian Tourists' Motivations. *Sustainability*, 11(4588).

The Pig. (2022). *About THE PIG hotels and restaurants – THE PIG*. About Us. https://www.thepighotel.com/about-us/

Thornton, A. (2018). *Space and Food in the City: Cultivating Social Justice and Urban Governance*. Cham, Switzerland: Springer. https://books.google.co.uk/books?id=uXZZDwAAQBAJ&lr=&source=gbs_navlinks_s

Treephan, P., Visuthismajarn, P., & Isaramalai, S.-A. (2019). A Model of Participatory Community-Based Ecotourism and Mangrove Forest Conservation in Ban Hua Thang, Thailand. *African Journal of Hospitality, Tourism and Leisure*, 8(5). http//:www.ajhtl.comID:https://orcid.org/0000-0002-7779-2136ID:https://orcid.org/0000-0001-5614-5952

United Nations. (2015). *THE 17 GOALS | Sustainable Development*. The 17 Goals. https://sdgs.un.org/goals

UNWTO. (2019, May 13). *Guidelines for the Development of Gastronomy Tourism*. Gastronomy and Wine Tourism; World Tourism Organization (UNWTO). https://doi.org/10.18111/9789284420957

Vourdoubas, J. (2020). *The Nexus Between Agriculture and Tourism in the Island of Crete, Greece zero co2-interreg europe project view project The Nexus Between Agriculture and Tourism in the Island of Crete, Greece*. 8(2). https://doi.org/10.5296/jas.v8i2.16602

Wang, N. (1999). Rethinking authenticity in tourism experience. *Annals of Tourism Research*, 26(2), 349–370. https://doi.org/10.1016/S0160-7383(98)00103-0

Winterhalter, C. (2019). Recent Gastro-Trends: Food Surfing on the Streets. *Engaging with Fashion*, 119–146. https://doi.org/10.1163/9789004382435_009

Wolf, E. (2014). *Have Fork Will Travel: A Practical Handbook for Food & Drink Tourism Professionals* (J. Bussell, C. Campbell, K. McAree, & W. Lange-Faria (eds.)). CreateSpace Independent Publishing Platform. https://www.amazon.co.uk/Have-Fork-Will-Travel-Professionals/dp/1490533990

Yang, Z., Cai, J., & Sliuzas, R. (2010). Agro-tourism enterprises as a form of multi-functional urban agriculture for peri-urban development in China. *Habitat International*, *34*(4), 374–385. https://doi.org/10.1016/j.habitatint.2009.11.002

Yang, Z., Hao, P., Liu, W., & Cai, J. (2016). Peri-urban agricultural development in Beijing: Varied forms, innovative practices and policy implications. *Habitat International*, *56*, 222–234. https://doi.org/10.1016/j.habitatint.2016.06.004

8 The homestays concept in the Indian tourism and hospitality industry

Suneel Kumar, Marco Valeri and Varinder Kumar

Introduction

The tourism sector has had an enormous impact on the global economy. Large and growing economies, as well as developed economies, all have a considerable reliance on the tourist sector. Tourism is a significant source of revenue and employment for nations that attract increasing numbers of tourists and has also had a considerable influence on the world's major economies. In order to accommodate the demand for visitor lodging, various homestay facilities have sprouted up. There seems to be no finer opportunity to learn about native customs and culture than to engage themselves in that as much as possible. Living like a local allows tourists to fully engage themselves in the tradition that is so well known across the world without ever leaving home. The biggest rational reason to pick a homestay over a hotel is obviously is the cost factor, sometimes it is up to 50% cheaper, and it does not include hidden expenses or a plethora of charges. Meals are mainly provided and guest hosts can recommend affordable places in the vicinity. Furthermore, homestays are gradually becoming a profitable business option for property owners with additional rooms to host visitors. It is a lucrative and low-investment business opportunity for any smart businessperson. The increasing popularity of homestays, which is projected to be a $15 billion worldwide sector, has created considerable potential in India (Sapam, 2019). For example, MakeMyTrip's homestay listings account for roughly 5–7% of overall income, which the company intends to increase over the next year. India is one of the top three growing countries in the world for Airbnb, the major player in the homestay business (Sapam, 2019).

Literature review

Over the years, there seems to be a significant increase in study linked to the homestay model, as several authorities have adopted homestays to boost their rural local tourism industry (Ristiawan & Tiberghien, 2021). Homestay refers to renting lodging at someone's home away of his or her region, permitting the tourist to explore a different culture and lifestyle, distinct traditions, or even dialect (Basak, Bose, Roy, Chowdhury, & Sarkar, 2021). The homestay sector is a subset of the larger tourist and hospitality sector, being focused on special traits such as quality, heterogeneity, and separateness. Indeed, the homestay theme is one that promotes a feeling of connection. Homestays are a high-intensity host and guest engagement space with four long-term community-based tourism (CBT) goals: ecological (Velan Kunjuraman & Hussin, 2017), social, culture and local livelihood security (W. B. Lama & Sattar, 2002). A homestay service is often run by people who own residences in rural locations, wherein travellers may spend their holiday experiencing the local cultural way of life in a native community. Homestays offer low-cost lodging facilities to travellers with numerous opportunities to engage with the host family and learn and experience their style of living. Furthermore, the eating experience is usually engaging, as visitors are invited into a loving family atmosphere. Cultural homestays (Escolar-Jimenez, 2020), homestays on farms (Pasanchay & Schott, 2021), heritage homestays (Rasoolimanesh, Dahalan, & Jaafar, 2016), agro homestays (Paul & Patil, 2022), leisure homestays, cottage homestays (Janjua, Krishnapillai, & Rahman, 2021), and more versions of the rural homestay idea exist (Long, Liu, Zhang, Yu, & Jiang, 2018). In the literature, other titles for homestays include home-based enterprises (Habeeb, Arya, & Ahmad, 2021), business home enterprises (Phunnarong, 2021), and commercial homes (Ly, Leung, & Fong, 2022).

Homestays have increased in number as a means of preserving culture, the natural environment, and encouraging the rural tourist industry. Furthermore, the homestay is a type of community-based tourism that contributes significantly to the development of rural and agricultural community members (Agarwal, 2022). The homestay not only perks the host and guest, but also the middlemen and the tourist attraction. Whenever the local community directly benefits from tourist activities, it is more inspired to maintain the location's natural climate and conditions. Furthermore, homestays have the capacity to generate extra revenue for the local inhabitants, who may be struggling with constrained sources of income, relatively few employment options, and the daily struggles of remote locations (Bhuiyan, Siwar, & Ismail, 2013; Ismail, Hanafiah, Aminuddin, & Mustafa, 2016). Homestays also contribute to the preservation of local society and cultural values. They help to preserve the community way of life, belief systems, and traditions for coming generations (M. Lama, 2013; Samsudin & Maliki, 2015). Communities take pride in spotlighting their culture to travellers, and the homestay becomes a tool for the promotion of native culture and customs to the outside universe (Promburom, 2022).

Nonetheless, despite numerous advantages, the development of homestays faces a number of challenges. Sood, Lynch, and Anastasiadou (2017) focused on the Kullu region of the Indian Himalayas and discussed several socio-cultural barriers to the growth of homestays in the area. Caste systems, traditional social belief systems, and increased female workload are all disadvantages, as is the conflict of harvest time and tourist arrival period.

Community members are sometimes concerned about development because they fear changes in household roles, loss of cultural values (Dong, 2020; Escolar-Jimenez, 2020), language barriers (Velan Kunjuraman & Hussin, 2017; Kunjuraman, Hussin, & Yasir, 2015), less younger generation participation (Mohamed & Aminudin, 2016), a lack of skills and self-belief (Chipumuro & Lynette, 2011; Leung, Tuan Phong, Fong, & Zhang, 2021), and safety issues (Danthanarayana, Amarawansha, & Gamage, 2021; Saraithong & Chancharoenchai, 2011). The usage of a residential area for a homestay operators indicates a compromise between welcoming family or friends and creating a professional setting akin to a hotel or equivalent accommodation idea (Agyeiwaah, 2019). Homestays are an excellent choice for less developed nations to earn income for native communities, while they provide a one-of-a-kind adventure for travellers (Kayat, 2011). For the homeowner, it provides a revenue source as well as a means of developing what may be long-lasting connections with visitors (Kontogeorgopoulos, Churyen, & Duangsaeng, 2015). Homestays, in a round-about way, allow locals to participate in the tourist sector. According to a study by Rai, Ansari, Ganguly, Giri, & Rai (2021), homestays aid in the survival of real local culture. Homestays cater to tourists who want personalised service, real cultures, and community interactions (Rai et al., 2021).

The Indian government acknowledges that India has enormous tourist potential and it is actively working to expand the many types of tourism accessible. As a result, the government has strengthened its tourist expenditure, increased spending on travel and tourism infrastructure facilities, and advocated 100% foreign direct investment in the field. This is a 'first-of-its-kind' chapter that derives knowledge about homestay-related schemes and motivation drivers and challenges faced by operators in the Himalayan region in India. This research is the first research in itself uncovering details and will lay the groundwork for future researchers.

Objectives of the chapter

- To study the trends and initiatives related to homestay businesses in the Himalayan region (Himachal Pradesh and Uttarkhand) of India
- To examine the drivers of motivation and challenges for the hosts in homestay businesses in the Himalayan region of India

Research methodology

This chapter's research is based on primary and secondary data. To collect the primary data, the authors conducted a short unstructured interview, in which we asked questions of homestay operators. The questions were mostly related to homestay businesses and the problems related to them. We asked a total of ten questions to the homestay operators, out of which we found the answers of six relevant and we have included a short summary of their answers in this chapter. The first question was related to their cultural impact. The second question was about the use of items used in the homestay and the third question was about their time management schedule. Fourth question was related to language problems and the rest of the questions were related to the participation of the younger generation in this business and security concerns. To collect secondary data, we first visited the Government of India website (data.gov.in). With the help of website (gov.data.in) we gained access to the Ministry of Tourism GoI, from where we obtained literature about the schemes and policies related to tourism, which we have also discussed in our chapter. After that, some literature was also collected from the official website of the Himachal and Uttarkhand government. We also collected literature from Google Scholar (research papers, book chapters), blogs and news articles (Figure 8.1).

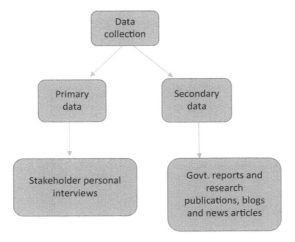

Figure 8.1 Process of collecting data and information.

Overview of Incredible India Bed & Breakfast (IIB&B)/Homestay Scheme

To promote tourism, the Indian government has allowed international tourists visiting Incredible India to stay with a local family, experience its customs, and enjoy the country's realistic gastronomy (Geary, 2013). The Ministry of Tourism has integrated international media campaigns covering Europe, the U.S. and Canada, Australia, the Far East, and the Asia Pacific region under the Incredible India publicity campaign, which features India as a 'must-see' desired location. This campaign is based on generic and niche areas in order to turn India into a year-round destination. In addition, special focus has been put on marketing India as a MICE destination. "Generic India," "Come to India – Walk with the Buddha," "The Indian Himalayas," and "Indian Monsoon" are the specific motifs (Dash & Sharma, 2021; Kerrigan, Shivanandan, & Hede, 2012). The campaign's objective is to attract foreign visitors by aligning India as a one-of-a-kind destination, as the land of five senses, a journey of the soul and mind.

Hotels, as well as other forms of ancillary accommodations, are an important aspect of a tourist's visit to a location, and the services offered by them can make the trip more exciting and unforgettable. The Ministry of Tourism, Government of India (GOI) has classified fully functional bed & breakfast, also known as homestay facilities, as "Incredible India Bed & Breakfast/Homestay Establishments" with the objective of bringing tourists comfortable homestay establishments with standardised world-class services, and to supplement the availability of accommodation in tourist attractions. The core idea behind these efforts is to create a clean and cheap environment for domestic and international tourists, as well as offering the possibility for domestic and international tourists to stay with a local community to learn about Indian and regional cultures, customs, and gastronomy. Incredible India Bed & Breakfast/ Homestay amenities are divided into two categories: silver and gold. These amenities will be divided according to the fees received for the categorisation of IIB&B/Homestay by the Government of India.

The Ministry of Tourism's Scheme for Regulation and Accreditation of Incredible India Bed and Breakfast/Homestay Establishments is purely voluntary. The scheme's major goal is to create a safe and economic environment for domestic and international tourists, including the option for international visitors to stay with an Indian family and learn about Indian culture and traditions while enjoying authentic Indian cuisine. The following are among the scheme's main attributes:

I Incredible India Bed and Breakfast/Homestay Facilities will be classified for certification and registration only if the landlord/entrepreneur of the operation and their family are physically residing in the same facility and renting out a least of one room and a total of six rooms (12 beds).
II The scheme is based on a bed and breakfast model, and rates will be assessed accordingly.
III The registration classification (Silver/Gold) will be active for two years from the date of order issuance.
IV The Regional Classification Committee of the respective states will examine and evaluate the excellence of the Bed and Breakfast/Homestay Establishment's infrastructure and services.

Homestay in Himachal Pradesh, India

Himachal Pradesh simply means Snowy Mountainous Region. Not only is the state known for its natural features, but it also has a long religious heritage. That is perhaps one of the reasons why the state is also known as Dev Bhoomi, which translates to Land of Gods. Himachal Pradesh is divided into twelve administrative districts, which are further divided into more than 75 tehsils. Travel to the state is mostly for relaxing, sightseeing, and religious purposes. Adventure tourism and community-based tourism (CBT) are two other types of tourism that are well-known. Homestay tourism operations are increasing in popularity around the world, especially in the rural areas (Sood et al., 2017). In the beautiful valleys of Sainj, Bir in Kangra, Kullu, Tirthan, Manali, Barot in Mandi, Sal in Chamba, and most of Spiti and Kinnaur, many homestays have sprung up. There are homestays to suit every budget, ranging from approximately Rs 1,500 per day to luxurious ones which cost over Rs 30,000 per day (Chauhan, 2021). In Himachal, there are 3,679 hotels and 2,305 homestays registered with the state tourist administration, respectively. Until December 31, 2019, there were 2,189 homestays in the state, tourism department sources have confirmed (Chauhan, 2021). However, the actual number of hotels and homestays in the state is much larger, with many of them operating without being registered with the tourism administration. Kullu district has the most homestays (638), followed by Shimla district (334), and Kangra district (268). Many have been startled by the small tribal district of Lahaul-Spiti, which boasts a comparatively large number of 258 homestays. The growing number of homestays in Lahaul-Spiti reflects travellers' desire to explore newer areas away from the bustle of city life. This year, 61 new homestays were registered in Kullu district, while 29 were registered in Kangra district, demonstrating the growing popularity of this new idea (Chauhan, 2021). However, a maximum of four guestrooms are permitted under Himachal Tourism's homestay program, without a restaurant for commercial reasons, six rooms are permitted under the Government of India's B&B scheme.

The role of the Himachal Pradesh government

Himachal Pradesh's state government is one of many in India that has embraced the notion of homestaying. The state government has already granted several exemptions in the procedural registration of such units, including a luxury tax, change of land use fee, sales tax, and commercial charges on energy, among others. The authorities have taken a number of permissive measures to promoting rural tourism. The state government has made initiatives to boost the homestay industry in Himachal Pradesh, including providing subsidies to owners, keeping interest rates low for those taking out loans for the development of homestays, and easing GST registration. The homestay concept is modelled after the Incredible India Bed and Breakfast Scheme announced by the Union Tourism Ministry. In Himachal Pradesh, there are a few steps to starting a homestay operation.

Homestay in Uttarakhand, India

The finest way to appreciate the Himalayas' scenic grandeur is to travel to Uttarakhand, an Indian state located in the Himalayan foothills. Staying at a homestay is the ideal approach to bring back some priceless memories. Many people are aware of this, making homestays a popular option for lodging. More people, particularly those from rural areas, have been inspired to establish their own homestay businesses as a result of this. This place is a great attraction for pilgrimages, adventurers, and visitors from all over the world, as it is surrounded by notable pilgrimages and lovely hill stations. Among the prominent attractions are Nainital, Mussoorie, Ranikhet, Chopta, Auli, Almora, Rishikesh, and Dehradun. UNESCO has also designated Nanda Devi National Park and the Valley of Flowers National Park as World Heritage sites (Chaudhary, Kumar, Pramanik, & Negi, 2022).

Not just that, but Uttarakhand also features Auli, which is known for its skiing, and Rishikesh, which is known for its yoga and river boating.

The role of the Uttarakhand government

This homestay scheme was started by the Uttarakhand government in order to develop the rural economy and raise the living standards of the people of Uttarakhand. Another motivation was to allow visitors to see the true colours of Uttarakhand, the God's Land. The administration had planned to establish over 5,000 homestays in Uttarakhand by 2020, but the initiative has been hampered by the current COVID-19 outbreak (S. Srivastava, 2021b). However, once it is feasible, the idea will bloom once more. There is also a provision for persons who are covered by this scheme to get subsidies and rebates.

The increasing research on this phenomenon shows a high demand for homestay hospitality (McIntosh, Lynch, & Sweeney, 2011; Shereni, 2019). While the idea of a homestay is not unique, it is seen as a tourist accommodation that allows visitors to stay in local residences while visiting a place. Since India's culture is so rich, the country encourages tourism through its rich culture. Cultural tourism can be classified as a sub-sector of tourism. Cultural tourism allows tourists to learn about the cultural identity of a particular place and the way of life of the Indigenous people, to meet their local people, and visit their geographic country in order to learn more about their customs, crafts, rituals, art, language groups, clothing and gastronomy experience about how they live their lives (Arunmozhi & Panneerselvam, 2013; Jenkins, 2015). Cultural tourism can be found in museums, theatres, and local streets in urban centres. Many urban areas have fascinating histories. However, when visitors find cultural tourism in rural areas, they need to participate in their way of life to understand their traditions and culture. It has been shown that the intensity of a tour by a cultural tourist is greater than that of an average leisure tourist. As a result, tourists prefer cultural tourism to a typical vacation, contributing to cultural tourism's growth.

Procedure of how to start a homestay business

There was a period when the term accommodation meant hotel by default, and the concept of a homestay was not widely accepted. However, people are increasingly opting for homestays. These accommodations are preferred by tourists who want to spend their vacations in tranquility and close to nature. Homestays have grown in popularity due to their family-friendly feel, good and nutritious meals, reasonable pricing, and the opportunity to see the nation's culture. When compared to the establishment of any other type of new housing, the cost of a homestay is relatively low. All that needs to be done in the name of investment is to spend money on renovating the extra rooms. Homestay operators can give their homestay a pleasant and natural vibe with a touch of simple customisation. There are a few basic steps that must be taken in order to begin a homestay. These stages can be thought of as a broad description of how to start a homestay business in any Indian state (Figure 8.2).

Drivers and challenges in the homestay business

There are several incentives or motivations for becoming a homestay host. Most of the people opt to manage homestays since it is a unique, interesting and engaging profession (Leung et al., 2021). It allows hosts to meet people of different ethnicities and cultures, so

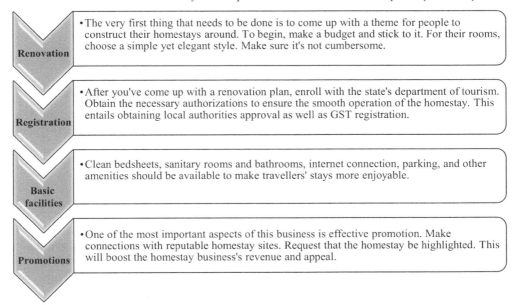

Figure 8.2 General outline of the procedure of how to start a homestay business.

Source: Author compilations (Srivastava, 2021a)

there is a good chance that this connection between tourists and hosts will blossom into a long friendship and relationships (Ikkala & Lampinen, 2015; Wang et al., 2019; Zhu, 2021). Relationship building with guests can make them more thankful and assist the operator to bring in much more business (Kayat, 2010; Pasanchay & Schott, 2021). Relationship and trustworthiness are essential in every connection, whether interpersonal or business (Donnelly, Wilson, Whillans, & Norton, 2021), since they create the path for people to understand, enjoy, and admire them. Relationship building with visitors may aid in the development of loyalty and a deep connection (Tran, Nguyen, Le, & Tran, 2021). Relationships are made up of two parts. The first is a pleasant interaction (Qamar, Mujtaba, Majeed, & Beg, 2021) (satisfaction, friendliness, connection, harmonisation, sense of humor, and comfortable). The second aspect is the special relationship, which consists of five aspects (bond, care, personal interest, relationship closeness and looking forward to seeing again) (Hao & Xiao, 2021). Homestay operators should work on developing and keeping positive relationships in order to get returning guests. Maintaining and retaining loyal users may help providers secure earnings. Relationship management is the process of developing and sustaining existing relationships, which includes the features of attracting, retaining, and expanding customers to be utilised to boost client loyalty, which mostly entailed accumulating and recording all retail and business information. After-sales service is defined as consistent connections with the brand following the completion of a transaction. The majority of businesses do not prioritise after-sales support, which has a negative impact on consumer satisfaction. The authors built a conceptual model based on the literature and considered two motivational derivers of homestay businesses in the Himalayan region of India.

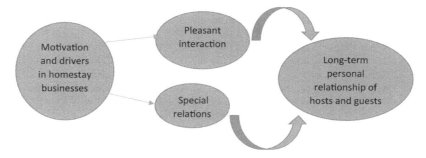

Figure 8.3 Conceptual model of long term relationship.
Source: Author creations.

Pleasant interactions

Homestays are places in someone's home that have been converted into accommodation for visitors for a service fee. The host, generally a local family, primarily provides tourists with accommodation at their residence, but they may also provide food, travel and local accommodation, pickup and other services depending on the homestay owner. For first-time visitors, a homestay is less challenging than staying in large guesthouses. Even for frequent travellers, a homestay is a great way to meet new people and experience a home away from home experience. Many people nowadays prefer host families because the services offered by the hosts are more personal and affordable. The best example of intercultural exchange is the pleasant interaction between guests and hosts, an excellent platform for promoting harmony between different ethnic groups and peoples. The delicious home-cooked food is undoubtedly the best thing about a homestay. Staying there allows visitors to learn about the preparation process, as most of the hosts are willing to share their secret recipes with visitors. If tourists have strict dietary restrictions, homestays give them the opportunity to create their own meals. Even if they choose to eat outside, homestays can provide information on some great local restaurants that may not be on the tourist trail. This simply means that visitors have more time for themselves, their family or friends.

Special relationships

The best thing about staying with a homestay is that visitors are always making new friends. Visitors will most likely end up having long, meaningful conversations with host family owners and perhaps even forming a new friendly relationship. For solo travellers, homestays are the best option. After spending the day exploring the city on your own, it is always nice to have some company.

Challenges in homestay businesses in Himalayan regions

In the Himalayan region of India, the authors interviewed some stakeholders and found some challenges based on of the interview by the stakeholders of the homestay businesses (Figure 8.4)

Degeneration of culture and cultural shock

The first question was regarding the culture. In this, we ask stakeholders how tourists distort local culture. The most common problem encountered by stakeholders in the Himalayan

Figure 8.4 Challenges in homestay businesses.

Region's homestay operators is cultural in nature. According to stakeholders, cultural degradation is occurring as a result of the advent of harmful societies. Many homestay owners will feel some sort of cultural difference at some point in their lives. The culture of Himachal Pradesh and Uttarakhand is very different from the metropolitan and Western parts of the country. Travellers smoking cannabis and drinking habits are not acceptable in these Himalayan states. They are afraid of their children imitating them. Married families from other countries who have little regard for local customs pose difficulties to a family-ly-run operations like homestays. Most homestay hosts were upset by their visitors' food patterns, their proclivity for extended baths, and their habit of keeping electric equipment turned on after usage.

Misuse and harsh treatment of household items

The next question in the interview was: how do tourists use the operators' household items and equipment? And in this we have seen that the female operator was not happy with the tourists.

In this problem, several female homeowners described feeling like servants in their own homes. There was also inappropriate behaviour and inappropriate use of house appliances during the visit. The cultural gap, however, does not seem to be a surprise to the hosts who are interested, and they are curious to learn. Even operators admit that they occasionally tolerated unacceptable behaviour from visitors in order for them to keep their employment and earn money. They serve as cultural interpreters, learning about the visitors' cultures and presenting their own culture.

Time schedule issues

In the next interview question, the authors asked the homestay operators about timetable management, and most of the operators were not happy with the time schedule. Although a few people become homestay owners to use their spare time, several operators have stated that it disrupts their whole-day routine. So, if the social engagement with the tourists is limited, making meals and responding to their requirements takes a significant amount of time, disrupting their typical schedules. The homestay business detracts the owners' time with family and privacy. Some operators also mentioned that overlapped surfaces in the residences were a concern and source of anxiety.

Language barrier

One of the interview questions related to language. Homestay owners had a mixed response regarding the language. According to some hosts, language problems do not arise with

Indian tourists, but they do occur with foreign tourists. Some homestay hosts also mentioned that, as a result of the lack of understanding in the language, sometimes they lose their customers. But this problem is not common; most foreign tourists understand hand gestures. The language issue appears to become more of a concern in rural homestays, due to the low educational opportunities for people. Urban hosts are likely to be fluent in English.

Lack of young generation involvement in this business

The next interview question was related to the participation of the younger generation, in which we found that a lot of young people are running towards the urban city from the Himalayan region. Some homestay operators said that the participation of the younger generation in the homestay business is decreasing day by day. According to some operators, experience towards the outside environment may motivate young people in rural regions to relocate to cities in quest of better professions and a better lifestyle. The majority of the homestay providers are female and elderly people. The most significant difficulty they faced was a shortage of young people to take on responsibilities and maintain operations. This appears to be another issue with the rural homestay programme. In reality, this has caused a shortage of potential entrepreneurs.

Insecurity

On one hand, tourists' security is a major concern for the hosts, and on the other hand, insecurity from tourists is also one of the major problem for hosts. In this survey, the majority of respondents, particularly the male visitors, felt uneasy about hosting persons of a different ethnic background. They feel more at ease receiving guests from their ethnic group, especially if the visitor is a female or a man accompanied by a female. We discovered a problem with hosts who felt duped by visitors. However, we learned from the hosts that the majority of them had no issues hosting because the homestay providers carried out a thorough check of the identity credentials of domestic tourists and notified foreign travellers to the nearest police station.

About the homestay scheme

In our last interview question, we asked all the operators about the government's bed & breakfast/homestay scheme. When we asked people whether or not they had information and knowledge about the scheme related to homestays, most of them answered yes, but less-educated operators knew little about the scheme. Most of them also cited a lack of information, only because of low education, and that they could get it if they knew how to read and write. The operators also believed that if the next generation takes interest in this business, then this business is good and profitable. A common problem that we saw in the Himalayan Region, especially in rural areas, was unregistered homestay businesses. Many people had not registered their homestay businesses because they were not aware of the registration process.

The homestay idea is widespread as it allows communication between the visitor and the homeowner, and the visitor learns about local culture and customs; requiring room and board for visitors at reasonable prices is an added benefit (Phoochinda, 2018). For example, this concept has great potential in the Malaysian context as it fits nicely into the Malaysian hospitality culture (Siti-Nabiha, Nordin, & Poh, 2021). Homestays, rural homestays, and bed and breakfasts are well established in other countries. In the following example, in Australia, homestay is often associated with farmhouse accommodations (Magar, 2021; Pfitzner, Fitz-Gibbon, & True, 2022), and in the U.K., the concept corresponds to bed and breakfast systems (Saraithong & Chancharoenchai, 2011). A homestay program is available in the U.S. for international students who are studying in the country for some time (Kwon, 2021). Interaction is generally limited in these setups, with no cultural engagement. Homestay tourism is now integral to community sustainability issues in Nepal (Jolliffe, 2022). Nepal has two types of homestay families: (1) community-based rural host families and (2) privately run rural or urban host families. World tourism can learn from the problems in India. In order to run a homestay in India, there are many issues to be dealt with. This problem can become a lesson for other countries.

Discussion

Homestay is a well-established idea in other countries, although it is still in its adolescence in the Indian tourism industry. Some individuals in India are hesitant to expose their residences to visitors and are also unwilling to stay in a homestay. Homeowners and visitors must be educated on the homestay concept. There are several incentives or drivers for becoming a homestay host. Many people opt to manage homestays since it is a unique and fascinating profession. It provides an opportunity to connect new lifestyle peoples and communities, and there is a good chance that the relationship between tourists and hosts will develop into a strong bond. Earlier, during festivals and holidays in India, tourist areas were overcrowded, due to which there was a shortage of rooms in hotels. To solve the problem of housing shortages that the thriving Indian tourism sector is experiencing, the Ministry of Tourism has authorised the Bed & Breakfast Scheme, which is a policy targeted at giving homestay services to domestic and global travellers. The Ministry of Tourism promotes homestays. It is also pressing the states to make it more attractive and valuable. According to global studies, profit and prestige are obvious motivating factors, and they are not the only ones in this sector. Regarding economic concerns, social and economic variables play a crucial role in motivating homestay owners. Most studies on this topic have focused on the function of house stays in community outreach, environmental sustainability, and the alleviation of poverty in rural regions.

Conclusion and limitations

Homestays could be a more effective approach for marketing tourism that is motivated by a desire to unwind in a peaceful and ethnically genuine setting. To boost the number of important tourist destinations in homestays, local authorities, industry experts, and homestay operators must develop and maintain positive connections with the local inhabitants. In India, especially in rural areas, many people are not aware enough about homestay schemes and programmes. India and state governments should make rural areas more aware; everyone should be aware of government schemes and schemes related to homestay business. The job of the government is not only to make schemes; the policy should also reach every citizen of the country, so that everyone can get its real benefit. The Central and state government should start an awareness programme through the homestay scheme, because all the operators working in this business are less educated, especially in the Himalayan Region. The accountability of tourists should also be measured. Tourists should respect the culture and values of the host and make good use of everyone's belongings. The language barrier is also a major problem in homestay business, especially in rural India. For this, the participation of the younger generation should be increased as we have seen that children of most operators were well educated.

This chapter also has some limitations. The first limitation is that the interview questions in the chapter were not asked in a structured manner. The second limitation is that the tourist perspective was not reflected in this chapter. What tourists think and experience about homestay businesses was not documented. The authors also consider the absence of government participation as a limitation. Future studies can ask questions about the development and problems related to the schemes from the authority of the respective state governments. Future scholars can collect data on challenges and motivational drivers at homestays from host and guest by creating a structured questionnaire.

References

Agarwal, S. (2022). Homestay and Community. In *Encyclopedia of Tourism Management and Marketing*: Cheltenham, UK: Edward Elgar Publishing.

Agyeiwaah, E. (2019). Exploring the relevance of sustainability to micro tourism and hospitality accommodation enterprises (MTHAEs): Evidence from home-stay owners. *Journal of Cleaner Production*, 226, 159–171.

Arunmozhi, T., & Panneerselvam, A. (2013). Types of tourism in India. *International Journal of Current Research and Academic Review*, 1(1), 84–88.

Basak, D., Bose, A., Roy, S., Chowdhury, I. R., & Sarkar, B. C. (2021). Understanding sustainable homestay tourism as a driving factor of tourist's satisfaction through structural equation modelling: A case of Darjeeling Himalayan region, India. *Current Research in Environmental Sustainability*, 3, 100098.

Bhuiyan, M. A. H., Siwar, C., & Ismail, S. M. (2013). Socio-economic impacts of home stay accommodations in Malaysia: A study on home stay operators in Terengganu state. *Asian Social Science*, 9(3), 42.

Chaudhary, S., Kumar, A., Pramanik, M., & Negi, M. S. (2022). Land evaluation and sustainable development of ecotourism in the Garhwal Himalayan region using geospatial technology and analytical hierarchy process. *Environment, Development and Sustainability*, 24(2), 2225–2266.

Chauhan, P. (Producer). (2021, Jan 4). Why Himachal homestays mean business. www.tribuneindia.com. Retrieved from https://www.tribuneindia.com/news/features/why-himachal-homestays-mean-business-192916

Chipumuro, J., & Lynette, L. (2011). The challenges of kwam emakana Community-based tourism homestay initiative In South Africa. *29th EuroCHRIE*, 152.

Danthanarayana, C., Amarawansha, T., & Gamage, P. (2021). Entrepreneurs Motivation for Selecting Homestay Businesses: Special Reference to Ella, Sri Lanka. In *Design for Tomorrow—Volume 2* (pp. 677–690): Cham, Switzerland: Springer.

Dash, S. B., & Sharma, P. (2021). Reviving Indian Tourism amid the COVID-19 pandemic: Challenges and workable solutions. *Journal of Destination Marketing & Management*, 22, 100648.

Dong, T. B. (2020). Cultural tourism: An ethnographic study of home stay in Briddim Village, Nepal. *The Gaze: Journal of Tourism and Hospitality*, 11(1), 10–36.

Donnelly, G. E., Wilson, A. V., Whillans, A. V., & Norton, M. I. (2021). Communicating resource scarcity and interpersonal connection. *Journal of Consumer Psychology*, 31(4), 726–745.

Escolar-Jimenez, C. C. (2020). Cultural homestay enterprises: Sustainability factors in Kiangan, Ifugao. *Hospitality & Society*, 10(1), 63–85.

Geary, D. (2013). Incredible India in a global age: The cultural politics of image branding in tourism. *Tourist Studies*, 13(1), 36–61.

Habeeb, S., Arya, V., & Ahmad, N. (2021). Home-based entrepreneuring for empowerment and sustainability of Muslim women: a study in the Indian context. *World Review of Science, Technology and Sustainable Development, 17*(4), 334–347.

Hao, F., & Xiao, H. (2021). Residential tourism and eudaimonic well-being: A 'value-adding'analysis. *Annals of Tourism Research, 87*, 103150.

Ikkala, T., & Lampinen, A. (2015). *Monetizing network hospitality: Hospitality and sociability in the context of Airbnb*. Paper presented at the *Proceedings of the 18th ACM conference on computer supported cooperative work & social computing*.

Ismail, M. N. I., Hanafiah, M. H., Aminuddin, N., & Mustafa, N. (2016). Community-based homestay service quality, visitor satisfaction, and behavioral intention. *Procedia-Social and Behavioral Sciences, 222*, 398–405.

Janjua, Z. U. A., Krishnapillai, G., & Rahman, M. (2021). A systematic literature review of rural homestays and sustainability in tourism. *Sage Open, 11*(2), 21582440211007117.

Jenkins, C. L. (2015). Tourism policy and planning for developing countries: Some critical issues. *Tourism Recreation Research, 40*(2), 144–156.

Jolliffe, L. (2022). Tea heritage and tourism as sustainable development in the Eastern Himalaya. In *Tourism and Development in the Himalaya* (pp. 225–241). London: Routledge.

Kayat, K. (2010). The nature of cultural contribution of a community-based homestay programme. *Tourismos: An International Multidisciplinary Journal of Tourism, 5*(2), 145–159.

Kayat, K. (2011). *Homestay Programme as a Malaysian Tourism Product (UUM Press)*: Sintok Kedah Darul Aman, Malaysia: UUM Press.

Kerrigan, F., Shivanandan, J., & Hede, A.-M. (2012). Nation branding: A critical appraisal of Incredible India. *Journal of Macromarketing, 32*(3), 319–327.

Kontogeorgopoulos, N., Churyen, A., & Duangsaeng, V. (2015). Homestay tourism and the commercialization of the rural home in Thailand. *Asia Pacific Journal of Tourism Research, 20*(1), 29–50.

Kunjuraman, V., & Hussin, R. (2017). Challenges of community-based homestay programme in Sabah, Malaysia: Hopeful or hopeless? *Tourism Management Perspectives, 21*, 1–9.

Kunjuraman, V., Hussin, R., & Yasir, S. (2015). Challenges of seaweed community-based homestay programme in Sabah, Malaysian Borneo. *Hospitality and Tourism 2015, Proceedings of HTC*, 123–126.

Kwon, J. (2021). Intercultural learning in the home environment: Children's experiences as part of a homestay host family. *Globalisation, Societies and Education, 19*(3), 274–286.

Lama, M. (2013). Community homestay programmes as a form of sustainable tourism development in Nepal. Thesis centria university of applied sciences Degree Programme in Tourism October 2013

Lama, W. B., & Sattar, N. (2002). Mountain tourism and the conservation of biological and cultural diversity. *MF Price, L, 24*.

Leung, D., Tuan Phong, L., Fong, L. H. N., & Zhang, C. X. (2021). The influence of consumers' implicit self-theories on homestay accommodation selection. *International Journal of Tourism Research, 23*(6), 1059–1072.

Long, F., Liu, J., Zhang, S., Yu, H., & Jiang, H. (2018). Development characteristics and evolution mechanism of homestay agglomeration in Mogan Mountain, China. *Sustainability, 10*(9), 2964.

Ly, T. P., Leung, D., & Fong, L. H. N. (2022). Repeated stay in homestay accommodation: An implicit self-theory perspective. *Tourism Recreation Research, 40*(5/6), 569–582.

Magar, D. A. (2021). Economic Contribution of Homestay Tourism: A Case Study of Magar Homestay of Naruwal, Lamjung. *Marsyangdi Journal*, 129–139.

McIntosh, A. J., Lynch, P., & Sweeney, M. (2011). "My home is my castle" defiance of the commercial homestay host in tourism. *Journal of Travel Research, 50*(5), 509–519.

Mohamed, R., & Aminudin, N. (2016). *Understanding homestay sustainability through successor motivational factors*. Paper presented at the *Regional Conference on Science, Technology and Social Sciences (RCSTSS 2014)*.

Pasanchay, K., & Schott, C. (2021). Community-based tourism homestays' capacity to advance the Sustainable Development Goals: A holistic sustainable livelihood perspective. *Tourism Management Perspectives, 37*, 100784.

Paul, T., & Patil, A. (2022). Sustainable agro tourism: A case study of "Farm of Happiness". *International Journal of Risk and Contingency Management (IJRCM)*, *11*(1), 1–11.

Pfitzner, N., Fitz-Gibbon, K., & True, J. (2022). When staying home isn't safe: Australian practitioner experiences of responding to intimate partner violence during COVID-19 restrictions. *Journal of Gender-Based Violence*, 1–18.

Phoochinda, W. (2018). Development of community network for sustainable tourism based on the green economy concept. *Journal of Environmental Management and Tourism (JEMT)*, *9*(06 (30)), 1236–1243.

Phunnarong, S. (2021). Factors affecting the success of community-based tourism (CBT) in homestay form. *Journal of Community Development Research (Humanities and Social Sciences)*, *14*(4), 14–27.

Promburom, T. (2022). Transformed gender relations in community-based tourism development: Performing gender in homestay tourism. *Humanities, Arts and Social Sciences Studies*, 155–173.

Qamar, S., Mujtaba, H., Majeed, H., & Beg, M. O. (2021). Relationship identification between conversational agents using emotion analysis. *Cognitive Computation*, *13*(3), 673–687.

Rai, S. S., Ansari, I. A., Ganguly, K., Giri, S., & Rai, S. (2021). Lean practices in homestay operations: A case study. *Journal of Quality Assurance in Hospitality & Tourism*, *22*(4), 395–424.

Rasoolimanesh, S. M., Dahalan, N., & Jaafar, M. (2016). Tourists' perceived value and satisfaction in a community-based homestay in the Lenggong Valley World Heritage Site. *Journal of Hospitality and Tourism Management*, *26*, 72–81.

Ristiawan, R., & Tiberghien, G. (2021). A critical assessment of community-based tourism practices in Nglanggeran Ecotourism Village, Indonesia. *Journal of Indonesian Tourism and Development Studies*, *9*(1), 26–37.

Samsudin, P. Y., & Maliki, N. Z. (2015). Preserving cultural landscape in homestay programme towards sustainable tourism: Brief critical review concept. *Procedia-Social and Behavioral Sciences*, *170*, 433–441.

Sapam, B. (Producer). (2019, Nov 18). MakeMyTrip bets on expanding homestays market to take on rivals. www.livemint.com. Retrieved from https://www.livemint.com/news/india/makemytrip-bets-bigger-on-home-stays-to-take-on-rivals-like-airbnb-11573980213249.html

Saraithong, W., & Chancharoenchai, K. (2011). Tourists behaviour in Thai homestay business. *International Journal of Management Cases*, *13*(3), 112–126.

Shereni, N. C. (2019). The tourism sharing economy and sustainability in developing countries: Contribution to SDGs in the hospitality sector. *African Journal of Hospitality, Tourism and Leisure*, *8*(5).

Siti-Nabiha, A., Nordin, N., & Poh, B. K. (2021). Social media usage in business decision-making: the case of Malaysian small hospitality organisations. *Asia-Pacific Journal of Business Administration*, *13*(2), 272–289.

Sood, J., Lynch, P., & Anastasiadou, C. (2017). Community non-participation in homestays in Kullu, Himachal Pradesh, India. *Tourism Management*, *60*, 332–347.

Srivastava (Producer). (2021a, May 16). How to Start a Homestay Business in Himachal Pradesh? *homestayinfo.com*. Retrieved from https://homestayinfo.com/how-to-start-a-homestay-business-in-himachal-pradesh/

Srivastava, S. (Producer). (2021b, May 15). How to Start a Homestay Business in Uttarakhand. *homestayinfo.com*. Retrieved from https://homestayinfo.com/how-to-start-a-homestay-business-in-uttarakhand/

Tran, P. K. T., Nguyen, P. D., Le, A. H. N., & Tran, V. T. (2021). Linking self-congruity, perceived quality and satisfaction to brand loyalty in a tourism destination: The moderating role of visit frequency. *Tourism Review*, *77*(1), 287–301.

Wang, L., Hu, M., Guo, Z., Sun, P., Geng, F., & Voon, B. (2019). China tourists' experiences with longhouse homestays in Sarawak. *International Journal of Service Management and Sustainability (IJSMS)*, *4*(2), 1–26.

Zhu, H. (2021). Chinese working holidaymakers in New Zealand: Adaptation to work culture. *Tourism Culture & Communication*, *21*(2), 109–121.

9 Cultural heritage tourism and ethical trends

Eleni Mavragani and Sofia Avramidou

Introduction

At present, cultural heritage is considered one of the main drivers of tourism development, helping to differentiate destinations from one another. Cultural heritage is an important part of social and community well-being, with national governments and international organisations increasingly recognising the value of cultural heritage (Tweed & Sutherland, 2007). Tourism has played an important role in highlighting and affirming the contemporary concept of heritage, where behind every object there is a narrative produced either for promotional or political reasons (Gravari-Barbas, 2020). The tourism and cultural sectors have mutual interests in the management, conservation and presentation of cultural heritage. In addition to being attractions for tourists, cultural heritage sites can also boost local communities and tourism in general (Figure 9.1). Often, however, the two sectors operate in parallel, maintaining a complex relationship with only limited scope for dialogue (Mavragani, 2015). There is a heated debate about whether tourism preserves or destroys cultures in an era of globalisation and homogenisation where cultures around the world are affected and the authenticity of cultural heritage is threatened.

The effort to preserve cultural property and manage cultural heritage is an immense task undertaken by the United Nations Educational, Scientific and Cultural Organization (UNESCO) with the assistance of its Member States. The main objective of management is not simply tourist exploitation of the cultural assets, but their protection and preservation with a view to be appreciated by future generations as well as to ensure access and understanding of the cultural heritage by present generations.

The difficulties that arise for UNESCO and other non-governmental organisations from different national legislations, and the reluctance of certain powerful states to implement the conventions they have signed, lead to the destruction of cultural heritage as a result of warfare or religious intolerance in war zones (e.g., Afghanistan, Iraq, Syria and Ukraine), causing destruction and the looting of cultural property. Furthermore, the management of memory for purposes related to tourism, which is used in order to increase destinations' visitor numbers, as well as to use culture as an instrument for nationalist purposes, raises ethical concerns and issues around the concept of heritage, with some arguing that heritage becomes a creation of the present, as its history is interpreted, staged and packaged to serve the purposes of the tourism industry and the ideology of the day (Payne & Dimanche, 1996).

Figure 9.1 Relationships in cultural heritage tourism.

Cultural heritage tourism and challenges

In recent decades, cultural heritage has been viewed as one of the most important and fastest-growing components of tourism. Some authors even call it the essence of tourism (Salazar & Zhu, 2015). The term heritage is defined as the link between the present and the future, which modern society chooses to inherit and pass on. Heritage carries meanings and values, by preserving material elements, from one generation to the next. Adequate understanding and interpretation of these values is therefore essential to ensure their appropriate use and to maintain their authenticity. Heritage creates a sense of collective membership in a nation, strengthens social relationships, and is used by nations as a powerful means of enhancing national identity and stimulating pride in national history, although it can often become entangled in a nation's efforts to emphasise the virtues of particular ideologies and to establish social, political, and religious norms (Mavragani, 2014; Salazar & Zhu, 2015).

Since the early 18th century, tourism has contributed to the identification of cultural heritage and the regeneration of cultural sites. It is considered a mega-industry highly desirable in every destination and country bringing significant positive effects on culture, such as conservation, restoration, enhancement, the protection of monuments, the general improvement of the image of the destination, the preservation of local customs and cultural events, intercultural interaction between tourists and local communities, the development of mutual understanding, mutual respect and tolerance for culture, increases in revenue for the local community and a sense of local pride in the community (Mavragani, 2022).

Tourism and cultural heritage can be considered as two phenomena which are acting in synergy and with mutual influences that contribute to the development of what has been defined as a tourism culture. However, it is true that the interaction between cultural resources and tourism is dynamic and ever-changing, since it creates opportunities and challenges, as well as negative effects. Cultural heritage tourism involves a multitude of incentives, resources and experiences and is different in the case of each individual and each place visited (Jelinčić & Senkić, 2017). Heritage tourism could be said to be a double-edged sword: on the one side, it can be a positive force for the preservation of cultural values and for the mitigation of threats; on the other, however, global tourism can itself become a threat to the sustainable management of cultural heritage (Pedersen, 2002).

Heritage and sustainable tourism focus on the same key phrase: future generations. Sustainable tourism is defined as an activity that can guarantee that assets are preserved and protected in order to be passed on to future generations, and heritage tourism is described as tourism that focuses on what we have inherited and want to pass on to future generations (Singh, 2014), that guarantee peace, justice and strong instructions (Sustainable Development Goals). Sustainable development of heritage tourism requires optimal policies in order to meet the needs of current visitors and local communities and respect the carrying capacity of each destination, thus protecting tourism resources for future generations. Sustainable heritage tourism, according to the Sustainable Development Goals (SDGs), contributes to the development of communities provided that all tourism stakeholders are effective, equitable and environmentally oriented (Singh, 2014).

Ethical issues and trends

A multitude of issues and problems in the tourism industry can be linked to ethics or to the lack of them (Payne & Dimanche, 1996). Therefore, trying to balance heritage management and protection with tourism development is considered a challenging process as planning and development policies can lead to the deterioration or degradation of heritage. It is also worth noting that sometimes tourism destinations face the dilemma between development, regeneration and modernisation rather than the preservation of cultural heritage. The challenge is not to threaten the architectural heritage and the built cultural environment during the process of development projects and tourism development, which would also mean destroying the integrity of cultural resources and the attractiveness of the destination.

The management of memory for tourist purposes, used in order to increase destinations' visitor numbers and the use of culture as an instrument for nationalistic reasons, creates ethical concerns around the concept of heritage, with the risk of heritage being transformed into a creation of the present, since its history is interpreted and packaged to serve the purposes of the tourism industry and the ideology of the time (Payne & Dimanche, 1996).

Destruction of monuments and cultural property is caused by direct or indirect human interventions, in times of either peace or war. States decide to destroy historical or religious buildings either as part of a redevelopment for economic exploitation, or for propaganda purposes, as well as in the context of state plans to assimilate or even eliminate minority groups. As Hofmann (2002) points out, there are states that even today treat minorities with suspicion and hostility, which results in an inability to accept their culture and monuments and thus either destroy or neglect them with the aim of their deterioration and collapse.

Examples of destruction of monuments during every historical war period are numerous, with typical examples being the capture of Constantinople by the Latins in 1204, the looting of cultural goods during the Napoleonic Wars, the destruction of monuments during World War II, the war in Yugoslavia and the destruction of monuments between warring ethnic groups. In recent decades, culture and cultural heritage have been regarded as instruments of war. The case of ISIS attacks causing moral and material damage to cultures and religious monuments is one example of cultural terrorism, with the systematic destruction of monuments and objects of cultural heritage (in countries such as Syria, Iraq and Yemen) in order to alter national identities, break the link between natural and intangible heritage and obliterate the cultural background of ethnic groups.

Authenticity and opportunities

Authenticity is a key element in the International Cultural Tourism Charter (ICOMOS, 1999) that explicitly includes tangible and intangible remains of the past, their presentation and interpretation (Doganer & Dupont, 2013). However, the issue is more complex since the word "real" can have different meanings in different parts of the world and in different cultural contexts. For other cultures, authenticity may be more closely associated with place or location than with material values, which may be regularly renewed or replaced. There are clearly multiple issues revolving around authenticity, ranging from the authenticity of the place or object itself, to the authenticity of the tourist experience (MacCannell, 1973; Orbaşlı & Woodward, 2009).

There is often a distinction between built heritage as used and treated by a community and the way it is packaged and promoted to tourists as a heritage attraction in order to cater for the tourist experience and to ensure satisfying touristic experiences (Figure 9.2), thus leading to varying degrees of mediation and staging of heritage (Orbaşlı & Woodward, 2009). A prime example of a staged and directed tourist gaze is the case of Bali. Many of the elements of Bali's culture and art are so alien to Western standards that they do not lend themselves easily to mass production. Eventually, tourist facilities and attractions are constructed, which, on the whole, are characterised by uniformity. In this way the tourist space is organised around what is called directed authenticity (Turner & Ash, 1975).

Heritage preservation begins with the aim of authenticity; it resorts to the practice of staged authenticity where nostalgic collective memory selectively reconstructs the past to serve the needs of the present. Heritage resources are subject to constant competition between different views of ownership, presentation, interpretation based on context, logic and interest. With a central question of who is interpreting and for whom (Figure 9.2), the process and the decisions of selection and presentation create an expectation of an offer that is authentic, but some of these presentations may be either contrived or directed (Doganer & Dupont, 2013).

Different social groups with dissimilar and/or often competing political interests and historical interpretations are rewriting the mnemonic landscape. What is mentioned and what is airbrushed about the past? To what extent does a monument silence certain narratives of

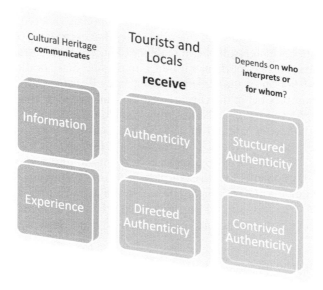

Figure 9.2 Outcomes of cultural heritage tourism.

the past while giving voice to others? Does treating histories differently mean anything about power relations and patterns of inequality within historical and contemporary societies? For instance, in New World narratives and monuments, history is often written by colonialists (Alderman et al., 2020). The challenge is to present cultural heritage in an authentic way so that its value is not undermined for tourists, the local community and the destination (Figure 9.2).

Inheritance involvement and property issues

Cultural heritage is about the past and the question that arises is who owns the past. At the same time, cultural heritage pertains to the present and the future and the engagement of culture in contemporary ethical debates about who owns the cultural heritage. The problem of ownership of intangible heritage seems more tractable, since intangible heritage is transferred by individuals and groups through time and from one generation to another, and therefore belongs to them, not to countries (Kamel-Ahmed, 2015). Even so, some conflicts have recently begun to emerge about ownership of intangible heritage (Hazucha & Kono, 2009).

The involvement of heritage in property issues further reveals the tension between universalism and cultural specificity. On the one hand, there is the trend of universal cultural heritage as universally valuable, which supports every person's right regarding its use and ownership; on the other hand, there is a pressure for culturally specific rights and restrictions that recognise the property claims of particular cultural groups. Heritage, on the one hand, can play an important role in fostering a sense of national identity around a national culture, but on the other hand many nations are not culturally homogeneous and there is a diversity of cultures and cultural groups (Plato.stanford, 2018). Therefore, conflicts may arise over issues of Indigenous land rights and cultural property rights or between ethnic minorities and dominant majorities that challenge the right to define and manage the minorities' cultural heritage. Thus, while heritage can unite, it can also divide and lead to violence and war (Silverman & Ruggles, 2007).

Apart from issues concerning the repatriation of art and cultural objects, further ethical questions arise about the way in which the cultural heritage preserved in museums is displayed. Similar to cultural property, museums may sometimes be in doubt for misrepresentation of cultures or lack of relevant participation by members of minority groups. The obligation of museums and heritage sites to preserve, and protect, the storylines of the past involves frequent attempts to combine all these storylines together through processes of selection, omission and emphasis (Mavragani, 2022; Whitehead et al., 2019). Therefore surviving monuments from the past select specific meanings of preservation and presentation to shape the dominant national identity.

When heritage is heavily politicised for reasons related to national pride and conducts the official interpretation, the control of the selection and interpretation of heritage has as a result cultural resources to appear in the way that ideological dogma governs. Interpretation, therefore, has been determined by supply rather than demand. The mismatch between what tourists want to see and how heritage is displayed is an example of this aspect (Bui & Lee, 2015). This is the so-called authorised heritage discourse, a kind of stamp of acceptance of the cultural elements that are considered to represent the community. Sometimes the façade of an authorised discourse is used to completely reject the heritage of other cultural elements, and sometimes a veil is used to allow for a different presentation and interpretation of the heritage of other minority cultural elements. Thus, heritage becomes a performance that focuses on the construction and negotiation of memories and meanings and a cultural process of establishing identity (Gravari-Barbas, 2020).

Stakeholders, catalysts and UNESCO

Interpretation and presentation are recognised as an integral part of the conservation process, underlining their importance in providing physical and intellectual access to cultural heritage. Providing all-embracing accessibility by taking into account all aspects of heritage would be the most ethical way not only to promote a better understanding of cultural heritage, but also to engage communities in joint conservation efforts (Georgieva, 2018). Cultural heritage should be considered as a key component of human rights, because the very concept of heritage requires respect and protection of individuals and groups. The link between cultural heritage and human rights is clear (Silverman & Ruggles, 2007). From a human rights perspective, cultural heritage represents the means by which communities and individuals develop culturally. Cultural rights and cultural heritage aim to strengthen and protect human identity; therefore, the destruction of cultural heritage can amount to a human rights violation when there are ulterior motives, such as the elimination of a group identity. The destruction of sites and objects essential to people's culture is a violation of people's collective and individual dignity.

Scholars of nationalism have pointed out how the sites, monuments and traditions that constitute national cultural heritage are symbolic condensations that provide concrete and tangible form to otherwise abstract ideas of nationhood (Astor et al., 2019). The creation of UNESCO in 1945 led to the development of international protocols that encouraged the concept of world heritage, bypassing nationalist ideologies. In 1978, UNESCO's World Heritage Committee began designating World Heritage Sites that are considered to be of global significance, thus providing protection through international treaties. In this way, culture became a tool for global cooperation and diplomacy, acting as a clever instrument for power and prestige diplomacy. In some cases, however, inscription on the World Heritage List becomes a political tool for nations to strengthen their sovereign interests, using World Heritage as a pawn in their international relations (Bertacchini et al., 2016).

The need to address the challenges of managing cultural heritage and heritage tourism and, by extension, the impacts these challenges bring to heritage assets and communities has led to the development and implementation of strategies and guidelines for identifying threats to heritage and the development of tools and codes of ethics that promote the ethical side of tourism and serve as guidelines for ethical decision-making (Kimball, 2017), such as the Code of Ethics for the interaction between cultural resources and tourism, which is dynamic and creates challenges and conflicts between stakeholders.

In order to achieve sustainability of the tourism industry and to ensure the protection of cultural resources for future generations, the contribution and cooperation of cultural heritage managers and tourism stakeholders is essential. The creation of codes of conduct for tourism is part of a general ethical trend of creating agreements and recommendations of a voluntary nature and acceptance in international relations and they are interesting examples of soft law that could be adopted in a more flexible way in the context of good faith and incorporated into national laws of states or contractual provisions between tourism stakeholders (Faure & Arsika, 2015). The application of ethical principles to cultural heritage relies on the good functioning of the tourism industry and the willingness of States to accept limits to their sovereign rights for the benefit of the environment, future generations and the international community as a whole, always under the umbrella of the ethical management and enhancement of the monuments it identifies and defines (Faure & Arsika, 2015).

One interesting case study about the ethical trends in cultural heritage management is Hagia Sophia, located in Constantinople, Turkey. This monument functioned as a Christian church for more than nine centuries and served as a religious centre for the Byzantine Empire until 1453, when it was converted into an Islamic mosque. Hagia Sophia was converted into a museum by Kemal Atatürk's decision in 1934, thus restoring the original Christian mosaics and beginning to display Christian and Islamic remains in the museum. The transformation of the Hagia Sophia into a museum was considered a very important event in the history of Turkey and, indeed all of humanity, because it took place in times of peace and not after battles between nations (Katipoğlu & Caner-Yüksel, 2010). In 1985, Hagia Sophia was included in the UNESCO list of monuments; it retained this status until 2020, when it was converted into a mosque again. Many argue that the conversion of Hagia Sophia into a mosque is a political act and a symbolic establishment of nationalist Islamic identity, a nationalist narrative based on the revival of the Ottoman past (Adar, 2020). Hagia Sophia has been one of the largest monuments in the world adapting to changing cultural and political environments throughout its history and continuing its current existence to the present day.

The conversion of Hagia Sophia into a mosque raises many questions and concerns regarding its compatibility with the World Heritage monument status and clearly highlights the tension between national sovereignty and the idea of world heritage (Lixinski & Tzevelekos, 2020). The conversion of Hagia Sophia into a mosque frames a typical dilemma between national sovereignty and intercultural values. Does this act alter Hagia Sophia's authenticity and, to some extent, its meaning and significance? Which chosen meaning of the past in the present is the most authentic representation of identity and whose identity does it refer to? More broadly, how will the experience of visiting the building remain, and how do tourists understand the universal value of the monument?

The management and promotion of cultural heritage is also a political issue, a matter of political choices and decisions. A sense of heritage is constructed and used in the present to support national, local and individual identities. Furthermore, the ways in which heritage objects are selected, assembled and presented to visitors have political effects as well as causes, and these effects take into account not only the object presented, but also the interpretation given to it by those who control it within a historical, cultural and social context. The questions that arise are many: for example, under future trends and catalysts like wars, politics and technology, who is going to make the decisions about the narrative and representation of the monument and what role is going to be played by UNESCO and other organisations?

Conclusions

Heritage tourism has specific sustainable objectives, such as preserving the authenticity and integrity of monuments, their accurate interpretation and presentation, the authentic experience of visitors and the use of profits for the conservation of monuments. As such, it is not only about engaging in heritage management and protection, but also about understanding the impact of tourism on local communities, achieving economic and social benefits and providing economic revenues to protect cultural heritage (Dangi, 2017). Moreover, trying to balance heritage management and protection with tourism development is considered a difficult process, as planning and development policies can lead to the damage, deterioration or degradation of cultural heritage. Cultural management is not always considered an easy task and various ethical dimensions of heritage are often raised concerning the protection and enhancement of monuments in times of war and peace.

Cultural heritage gives to each place its identifiable characteristics and is the essence of the human experience. Its potential has been confirmed by the ever-increasing number of World Heritage Sites added to the UNESCO list (Jelinčić & Senkić, 2017). The relationship between cultural heritage and tourism is dynamic and often changing. It creates opportunities and challenges as well as conflicts and could also pose a threat to the integrity and values of heritage if not planned sustainably.

It is clear that heritage, heritage conservation and heritage tourism often confront stakeholders and communities with issues of multiculturalism, national ideology, collective identity, cultural survival, authenticity, interpretation, heritage contestation, social exclusion, contested ownership, control and conservation (Orbaşlı & Woodward, 2009). Vandalism directed against material cultural heritage occurs as a result of malice, political protest, wars, religious intolerance and many other reasons (Silverman & Ruggles, 2007). Furthermore, the right to access and exclusion from sacred sites due to a particular political agenda falls within the realm of human rights and freedom of expression of religious and cultural identity.

The need to address the ethical issues of heritage and heritage tourism in general has led many international organisations to create and adopt codes of ethics for many sectors of the tourism industry that serve as advisory guidelines for ethical decision-making. The application of ethical principles to heritage tourism relies on the good functioning of the tourism industry and the willingness of states to accept limits to their sovereign rights for the benefit of the environment, future generations and the international community as a whole (e.g., SDGs), always under the umbrella of ethical management and promotion of the monuments it identifies and defines (Faure & Arsika, 2015).

One of the key ethical challenges for tourism stakeholders in the management and promotion of heritage tourism is the development of a management system where all interested cultural groups are represented and involved. Heritage rights will include cultural rights of participation, self-determination, diversity, expression, access and management rights (Meskell, 2010).

The UNESCO World Heritage List already provides the initial framework for the responsible management of cultural and natural heritage, but it also provides a platform by which participating State Parties can promote the integration of the moral obligation of humanity as a whole, a sense of global responsibility and the principle of good faith and consensus among all parties. This means that we need a culture of peace through tourism, a shared understanding and awareness of the responsibility that World Heritage Sites do not belong only to the community in which they are located, but belong to all the peoples of the world (Salazar, 2006). Perhaps peacekeeping, peacemaking and peacebuilding by individuals, nations, and organisations are the three realistic approaches to build peaceful societies and at the same time the first step towards solving ethical problems in heritage tourism. The creation of a culture of peace is a contemporary, topical agenda of humanity (Becken & Carmignani, 2016; Sempiga, 2017; Wintersteiner & Wohlmuther, 2014). Thus, it appears that future ethical trends and associated practices are heralding the role of heritage tourism in safeguarding the peace.

References

Adar, S. (2020). *A Nation in Fight with Itself: The Hagia Sophia between Ideas and Elites*. Hagia Sophia: From Museum to Mosque. Berkley Forum. Berkley Center for Religion, Peace & World Affairs.

Alderman, D., Brasher, J., & Dwyer, O. (2020). Memorials and Monuments in A. Kobayashi, (ed.), *International Encyclopedia of Human Geography*, 2nd edition, 9, 39–47. London: Elsevier.

Astor, A., Burchardt, M., & Griera, M. (2019). Polarization and the Limits of Politicization: Cordoba's Mosque-Cathedral and the Politics of Cultural Heritage. *Qualitative Sociology*, 42(3), 337–360.

Becken, S., & Carmignani, F. (2016). Does tourism lead to peace? *Annals of Tourism Research*, 61, 63–79.

Bertacchini, E., Liuzza, C., Meskell, L., & Saccone, D. (2016). The politicization of UNESCO World Heritage decision making. *Public Choice*, 167(1), No 6, 95–129.

Bui, H. T., & Lee, T. J. (2015). Commodification and politicization of heritage: Implications for heritage tourism at the Imperial Citadel of Thang Long, Hanoi (Vietnam). ASEAS – *Austrian Journal of South-East Asian Studies*, 8(2), 187–202.

Dangi, V. (2017). Heritage and tourism: Issues and challenges. *Research Journal of Humanities and Social Sciences*, 8(2), 217–222.

Doganer, S., & Dupont, W. (2013). Cultural heritage tourism and authenticity: San Antonio Missions Historic District in C.A. Brebbia (ed.), *Structural Studies, Repairs and Maintenance of Heritage Architecture*, vol 131, 15–27, WIT Transactions on the Built Environment, Ashurst Lodge.

Faure, I., & Arsika, M. (2015). Settling Disputes in the Tourism Industry: The Global Code of Ethics for Tourism and the World Committee on Tourism Ethics, *Santa Clara Journal of International Law*, 13(2), 375–415.

Georgieva, D. (2018). Ethical and Philosophical Dimensions of Accessibility to Cultural Heritage or Why We Need a Different Perspective in Serdica-Sredets-Sofia, Vol. VII, Faber, Sofia, 2018, 418–430.

Gravari-Barbas, M. (2020). *A Research Agenda for Heritage Tourism*. Elgar Research Agendas.

Hazucha, B., & Kono, T. (2009). Conceptualization of Community as a Holder of Intangible Cultural Heritage in T. Kono (ed.), *Intangible Cultural Heritage and Intellectual Property: Communities, Cultural Diversity and Sustainable Development* (pp. 145–157). Antwerp: Intersentia.

Hofmann, T. (2002). *Armenians in Turkey today. A critical assessment of the situation of the Armenian minority in the Turkish republic*. Brussels: The EU Office of Armenian Associations of Europe.

ICOMOS (1999). *International Cultural Tourism Charter: Managing Tourism at Places of Heritage Significance*. International Council on Monuments and Sites.

Jelinčić, D.A., & Senkić, M. (2017) Creating a heritage tourism experience the power of the senses. *Etnolosca Tribina*, 47(40), 109–126.

Kamel-Ahmed, E. (2015). What to conserve? Heritage, Memory, and Management of Meanings. *International Journal of Architectural Research*, 9(10), 67–76.

Katipoğlu, C., & Caner-Yüksel, Ç. (2010). Hagia Sophia 'Museum': A humanist project of the Turkish Republic. *Studi culturali*, 306, 21.

Kimball, M. (2017). Heritage Place Building Theory, Heritage Impact Assessment and the Role of the Sacred Dimension. *Journal of Heritage Management*, 2(1), 1–18.

Lixinski, L., & Tzevelekos, V. (2020).The Hagia Sophia, Secularism, and International Cultural Heritage Law. *American Society of International Law*. 24(25).

MacCannell, D. (1973). Staged Authenticity: Arrangements of Social Space in Tourist Settings. *American Journal of Sociology*, 79(3), 589–603.

Mavragani, E. (2014). National Archaeological Museums and the Growth of Tourism in Greece. *Journal of Regional Socio-Economic Issues*, 4(1), 61–74.

Mavragani, E. (2015). Greek Museums and Tourists' Perceptions: An Empirical Research. *Journal of the Knowledge Economy*, 12, 120–133.

Mavragani, E. (2022). Museum Services. In D. Buhalis (ed.), *Encyclopedia of Tourism Management and Marketing*, Cheltenham, UK and Northampton, MA: Edward Elgar Publishing.

Meskell, L. (2010). Social Thought & Commentary: Human Rights and Heritage Ethics. *Anthropological Quarterly*, 83(4), 839–859.

Orbaşlı, A., & Woodward, S. (2009) Tourism and Heritage Conservation. *The SAGE Handbook of Tourism Studies*, 314–332.

Payne, D., & Dimanche, F. (1996) Towards a Code of Conduct for the Tourism Industry: An Ethics Model. *Journal of Business Ethics*, 15(9), 997–1007.

Pedersen, A. (2002). *Managing Tourism at World Heritage Sites: A Practical Manual for World Heritage Site Managers*. Paris, UNESCO World Heritage Centre, coll. "World Heritage Manuals".

Plato.stanford. (2018). The Ethics of Cultural Heritage. *Stanford Encyclopedia of Philosophy*. Department of Philosophy, Stanford University. https://plato.stanford.edu/entries/ethics-cultural-heritage/

Salazar, N. (2006). Building a Culture of Peace through Tourism: Reflexive and Analytical Notes and Queries. *Universitas humanística*, 62. 319–333.

Salazar, N., & Zhu, Y. (2015). Heritage and Tourism. In L. Meskell (ed.), *Global Heritage: A Reader*. Chichester: Wiley Blackwell, 240–258.

Sempiga, O. (2017). Peacekeeping, peacemaking, and peacebuilding: Towards positive peace in a society that endured conflict. *World Environment and Island Studies*, 7(4), 185–200.

Silverman, H., & Ruggles, F. (2007). *Cultural Heritage and Human Rights*. New York, NY: Springer.

Singh, R. (2014). Heritage tourism and sustainability. *International Journal of Research in Engineering*, 4(4), 66–76.

Turner, L., & Ash, J. (1975). *The Golden Hordes—International Tourism in the Pleasure Periphery*. London, UK: Constable.

Tweed, C., & Sutherland, M. (2007). Built cultural heritage and sustainable urban development. *Landscape and Urban Planning*, 83(1), 62–69.

Whitehead, C., Eckerslay, S., Daugbjerg, M., & Bozoglu, G. (2019). *Dimensions of Heritage and Memory. Multiple Europes and the Politics of Crisis*. Routledge.

Wintersteiner, W., & Wohlmuther, C. (2014). Peace Sensitive Tourism: How Tourism Can Contribute to Peace. In C. Wohlmuther & W. Wintersteiner (Eds.), *International Handbook on Tourism and Peace*. Centre for Peace Research and Peace Education of the Klagenfurt University/Austria in cooperation with World Tourism Organization (UNWTO).

10 Challenges and opportunities in cultural tourism

Insights from Canada

Louis-Etienne Dubois, Shawn Newman and Frédéric Dimanche

Introduction

Arts and culture are an integral part of the tourism industry, not just a related sector. Some would even argue that they are a key driver for tourism: without attractions, many destinations would have little need for other services (Hughes, 2013). Cultural tourism describes the influx of travellers interested in heritage sites, and museums, in addition to more ephemeral activities such as festivals and concerts. Specifically, it denotes "the movement of persons to cultural attractions away from their normal place of residence, with the intention to gather new information and experiences to satisfy their cultural needs" (Richards & Richards, 1996, p. 24). As a concept, this brings attention to the things people do during their stays and the attractions with which they engage.

COVID-19 has made these sectors' interdependencies even more striking. In 2020, global arts and culture attendance collapsed following travel bans, border closures, and quarantine measures. The compound effect of empty venues, airports, local restaurants, and hotel lobbies was certainly not lost to many culturally vibrant destinations (Dubois & Dimanche, 2021, 2022; Muro et al., 2020; Roigé et al., 2021. However, if culture and tourism were hard-hit by virtue of restrictions of one impacting the other during the pandemic, their recovery is also bound to be intertwined.

This chapter explores some of those challenges, in addition to recent developments, and future trajectories in cultural tourism. To do so, it draws from an ongoing collaboration with Ontario Culture Days (ONCD), a non-profit organisation that supports arts and culture initiatives across the Canadian province. Following an overview of the cultural tourism literature, this chapter highlights key issues and trends, as well as practical and theoretical implications.

Historical and intellectual development of cultural tourism

Though generally accepted that cultural tourism involves the use of cultural heritage and the consumption of its offerings by visitors, there continues to be ongoing debate around the concept itself (McKercher & du Cros, 2002). Part of the challenge has to do with the difficulty of defining culture and tourism as separate terms (Richards & Richards, 1996); cultural tourism's dynamic nature and ongoing evolution add to the difficulty of defining it. The ambiguity also stems from how people identify – or do not – with the label cultural tourists, much like cultural workers often resist seeing themselves as mere tourist hosts (Bendixen, 1997).

Over the years, cultural tourism has grown from a niche pursuit that was the sole purview of an affluent and well-educated market (Tighe, 1986) to something with much greater mass appeal (Richards & Richards, 1996). As the market for cultural tourism gradually broadened, so too did its scope. From an initial focus on physical heritage sites and museums (Jovicic, 2016), it gradually meshed with more intangible offerings that encompass cultural practices and ways of life (Antón et al., 2019; Kim et al., 2019; Richards, 2018; Sharpley, 2013; Smith, 2022). More recently, the field has taken a creative turn that emphasises developing unique offerings in which tourists actively participate with locals (Richards, 2021a). It is no longer enough to see things from a distance or to merely be told about a given culture. Indeed, visitors now demand authentic experiences in which they can live like locals and ultimately co-create cultural experiences with their hosts (). As such, what can be considered cultural tourism also encompasses food, film, arts, music, language, and more, focused on local communities' ways of life. This also extends to gastronomy as a way to understand a given culture (Antón et al., 2019). Everything that constitutes a place can be turned into a tourist opportunity, lending credence to the idea that there is no real difference between tourism at large and cultural tourism (Noonan & Rizzo, 2017).

Richards and Richards (1996) identified the desire to gather new information as a key motivator in cultural tourism, thereby suggesting a focus on educational experiences and a deep engagement by tourists with the destination's culture(s). Indeed, cultural tourists are typically said to crave contact with the local community, to have genuine (Campos et al., 2018) interest in better understanding its customs, and to be more willing to make other smaller or shorter trips in the attractions' vicinity. They have also long been described as a rather homogeneous market of well-educated, rather affluent, frequent travellers that are comfortable with technologies (Hughes, 2013). However, recent research has shown a more nuanced understanding of who cultural tourists are, and consequently of the motivations and behaviours that underpin cultural tourism itself. Thus, cultural tourism is understood to be a heterogenous market not only about deep learning, but also driven by a host of more recreational motives (McKercher, 2020; McKercher & du Cros, 2003).

As such, destinations are expected to continuously roll out varied cultural offerings that can satisfy tourists' demands for authentic, co-created experiences, without losing sight of the intrinsic value of the community's identity separate from its economic potential (Bendixen, 1997; McKercher, 2020). As Jovicic argues, "the simple provision of information and services is not enough for realizing adequate cultural tourism benefits... [suppliers] should therefore focus their attention on the close interaction with consumers and co-creation of high-quality experiences" (2016, p. 606). In other words, cultural destinations must also think about the broader experience they provide to remain competitive in this ever-evolving tourism market.

Beyond defining what cultural tourism is, and who cultural tourists are, the field has also been widely discussed for its purported ability to stimulate economic growth and protect local heritage. Thus, in addition to reinvigorating cities and contributing to urban regeneration, cultural tourism has also drawn interest to relieve pressure on resources facing the strain of nature-based tourism, as well as a strategy to help foster community pride and belonging (Richards & Richards, 1996). However, the success of cultural tourism may lead to threats to identity and authenticity because of the increasing tourist influx (Bachleitner & Zins, 1999). Indeed, there is a growing realisation that the promise of cultural tourism may have been overstated (McKercher, 2020). Cultural tourism is proving to be just as prone to overtourism. Congestion within heritage sites not only leads to damage, but also results in negative experiences for tourists (Koç et al., 2022) and locals (du Cros, 2008). Moreover, cultural tourism can have significant impacts for local communities, which calls for a sensitivity to the way residents' quality of life is impacted by tourism (Uysal et al. 2016). Last, even though cultural tourism is said to be a key economic driver, its actual value has proven difficult to measure given how contested its parameters are and that gathering information on how tourists consume culture is complex (Galí-Espelt, 2012; Torre & Scarborough, 2017).

Issues in cultural tourism: Insights from the field

At the federal level, Canada's arts and culture sector is part of the Department of Canadian Heritage, whereas tourism is associated with Innovation, Science, and Economic Development. Yet at the provincial level, and much like in many other jurisdictions around the world, culture and tourism fall under the same department. This suggests, theoretically at least, some degree of proximity, shared insights, and collaboration between the two sectors. In the field, however, culture and tourism still mostly operate in silos, resulting in fragmented and old data that depict an incomplete picture of the magnitude and specificities of cultural tourism. The disconnect is also visible in the sector's funding mechanisms that, despite coming out of the same ministry, use different timelines and criteria, making it difficult to launch joint projects.

In addition, Ontario has yet to set up joint key performance indicators (KPIs) or to establish a formal top-down strategy to grow cultural tourism, as well to launch cross-sector research projects to support decision-making or dedicated training programmes to enhance career mobility and knowledge exchange. Consequently, the lack of shared vocabulary and understanding remains a hurdle to collaboration. Not knowing how each side operates, nor even who to potentially turn to, makes it difficult to envision joint initiatives. These issues are especially true for institutions in rural areas, which tend to be smaller and minimally staffed. In fact, they face a range of unique challenges, such as the lack of reliable Internet connection or transportation infrastructure, as well as others including their remoteness and the tourists' reluctance to travel long distances. Given that Ontario is over three times the size of Germany, and the bulk of its population is concentrated in the Greater Toronto Area, pushing cultural tourists further into the entire province has historically been difficult. While cities like Sudbury or Thunder Bay have a host of cultural attractors, many will balk at the five-hour drive. In other words, cultural institutions in rural areas cannot rely on a deep-drive radius pool of prospective visitors and face an uphill battle in convincing those outside of that radius that the drive is worth their while.

People who have attempted to develop cultural tourism also speak of the challenges of getting projects off the ground. For instance, those on the tourism side mention experiencing resistance and distrust from cultural organisations who are wary that teaming up will somehow lessen their authenticity. This reluctance to engage is also fueled by the impression that tourism actors are mostly interested in mainstream offerings rather than more traditional or fringe institutions, a lack of understanding of the benefits that a collaboration could yield, and tensions within sectors that can get in the way of finding connections across borders to arts and culture.

As in other destinations around the world, cultural tourism in Ontario increasingly is interfaced with other known issues in tourism. For instance, while the sheer size of the province makes it less prone to overtourism, its northern climate leads to packed offerings in the warmer months, thereby still creating some degree of strain on the local infrastructures and

Figure 10.1 Shaw Festival.

communities. Likewise, concerns over the sustainability of cultural tourism in Ontario become evident when developing itineraries that span thousands of kilometres, especially when targeted towards international visitors who have already travelled long distances simply to get to Canada.

Last, cultural tourism is becoming greatly intertwined with broader social justice issues. For example, Canada is facing numerous discoveries of unmarked graves in Indian residential schools. These sites of horrific violence were mostly led by churches but also directly funded by the federal government. The oldest and longest-running school in Canada was the Mohawk Institute Residential School, which was in operation until 1970. Two years later, the Woodland Cultural Centre opened to preserve and promote the history and culture of the Haudenosaunee people of the Eastern Woodlands. As the truth of residential schools has been revealed, the meaning of such institutions and the grounds upon which they stand have much more sombre meaning. This affects the ways that visitors frame their experiences and their engagement with the community at large. Such dark cultural tourism experiences – "the act of travel to sites associated with death, suffering and the seemingly macabre" (Stone, 2006, p. 146) bring visitors to local Indigenous businesses such as local restaurants, shops, and other aspects of the community.

Predictions for cultural tourism

The context of Indigenous–settler relations in Ontario, and the continuing work to uncover graves, demonstrates how cultural tourism is starting to account for problematic, if not outrightly violent, histories. There will undoubtedly be a tremendous increase in re-articulating how places and regions are marketed to tourists, and the ways that engaging with the

Figure 10.2 Woodland Cultural Center.

cultural histories of local communities will take on greater meaning for visitors. At the same time, this trend aligns with regenerative approaches to cultivating tourism ecologies in that visitors and locals come together to participate in the re-making of a place and contribute to its growth, not only in economic terms but by way of community healing and building or repairing bonds. The fact that locals have been shown to be less inclined to engage with areas impacted by disasters compared with tourists suggests a very real sensitivity issue (Huang et al., 2021). Thus, destinations will have to prioritise attractions that attend to local issues and honour the diversity of peoples who have historically inhabited a place, while also being attentive to the different knowledges that cultural tourists have about the broader contexts of the places they visit.

Looking ahead, demographic changes are bound to impact the content and the format of cultural attractions. Indeed, while Boomers have historically been the largest age group of cultural tourists, destinations will need to account for Millennials and Gen Zers, who crave different experiences. This begins with tailored communications, generally through social media, to give destinations an enticing brand with which new generations will want to engage (Peco-Torres et al., 2020). Destinations will have to develop a range of new offerings, some more participative than others, and increasingly account for accessibility considerations, as well as to bridge generations through collaborative programming that includes younger tourists in the activities while also providing more traditional forms of engagement for older audiences.

In addition, the rise of attention to equity issues in a variety of sectors will intersect with conventional approaches to understanding tourism along generational or socio-economic boundaries. Identity-based data related to race, gender, and disability, for example, will provide more nuanced documentation of who individual tourists are and better equip the cultural tourism sector to market its products to wider, yet more refined segments of the tourist ecology. Having a stronger understanding of the lived experiences of tourist populations, and how those experiences impact and shape interests in cultural tourism, will fundamentally change how organisations and communities can reach out to visitors. This is also likely to impact how attractions are designed and communicated in the first place as content co-creation with local communities is bound to become a core industry practice (Wiktor-Mach, 2020).

The pandemic has also laid bare the centrality of arts and culture to mental health, community-building, and economic recovery. In areas where lockdowns or restricted indoor capacity hampered gathering, outdoor spaces became places of connection. Arts and culture animate these spaces, and provide a point around which people can gather, exchange ideas, and escape the monotony of the pandemic. We have seen how arts and culture activities have been repositioned by local governments as a means of creating public liveliness, and these kinds of adaptations are likely to remain (Richards, 2021b). As a driver to get people out of their homes and participate in public life, we will likely see an increase in policy shifts (e.g., changes to permitting) at the local level to accommodate and encourage outdoor arts and culture activities.

At the same time, destinations overly dependent on their cultural sector, and on visitors flocking to partake in their offerings, are more likely to explore economic diversification strategies, or at the very least to develop new contingency plans (Dubois & Dimanche, 2021). For example, hospitality-related policy changes have already occurred in cities like Toronto, where the CaféTO program, initiated temporarily in summer 2020, has become permanent. This program makes it possible for restaurants to have seated patios on public sidewalks and even in the streets. Moving forward, such initiatives, which re-define how public space can legally be used, will undoubtedly continue throughout other branches of the cultural tourism sector.

Last, new technologies are bound to continue to reshape cultural tourism, be it to connect with prospective visitors and to empower tourists at all stages of the travel process, or for destinations to differentiate themselves and enhance the tourism experience in general (Neuhofer & Buhalis, 2014). There is also a growing interest in how cultural tourism can occur within the digital space, and how technologies such as virtual reality (VR) and augmented reality (AR) can offer tourists a way to experience destinations from a distance (Akhtar et al., 2021; Griffin et al., 2022). Interestingly, this move towards remote experiences is occurring alongside a turn towards placemaking. Indeed, today's enhanced mobility may have given rise to a renewed interest in a sense of place (Richards, 2021b). The cultivation of local and domestic tourist markets is another emerging trend motivated directly by the pandemic (Flew & Kirkwood, 2021), but also by a broader realisation that "smaller tourism" is a necessary response to overtourism as well as social, economic, and cultural sustainability (Dodds & Butler, 2019; Scherf, 2021).

Opportunities and challenges for cultural tourism

Arts and culture workers, and artists themselves, know how important this sector is to local communities. Indeed, it generates employment, spillovers and tax revenues, and stimulates economic activity. As those individuals and organisations get recognised for their attractiveness, they become stakeholders with a stronger voice around the community decision-making table. Tourism's economic impact, in a complementary way, provides a significant incentive for communities to protect and enhance local culture, and to generate more income to strengthen cultural heritage, production, and creativity.

Stepping back to see those offerings as part of a larger intersection of a variety of products, including food, shopping, and local history, also situates arts and culture organisations within a more adaptable framework from which to think about the tourist experience. Further, knowing how scarce resources in the arts and culture sector often are, developing attractions and new experiences through collaboration and partnership presents opportunities to pool talents and resources. While the benefits of tourism are plentiful, the closer arts and culture organisations work with tourism the likelier they are to be reaping rewards. Unfortunately, of all the segments that they cater to, tourists are often overlooked.

Yet these trends also paint a picture of increasingly tightly knit communities, tourist experiences couched in local histories and cultures, and cross-sectoral collaborative offerings. Thus, potential benefits include more authentic tourism products and stronger ties within local communities, including a better understanding of how to work across sectoral boundaries, greater stakeholder buy-in from residents, as well as job opportunities and revenues for organisations.

We are also seeing the beginning of a renewed purpose for charitable arts and culture organisations. Given the centrality of arts and culture to re-building community, charitable organisations have begun to re-articulate their missions and mandates. The emerging opportunity here is to demonstrate to existing and potential donors how their investment in smaller charitable arts organisations stand to impact the local community. Simultaneously, such activity supports growing interests for tourists around authentic local experiences that tell local stories.

Of course, in the Ontario case, this underutilised and quite promising way forward is only possible if and when the tourism and arts and culture sectors draw closer together. The need for collaborations such as these cannot be overstated. In fact, the United Nations' Sustainable Development Goals (SDGs) call for multi-stakeholder partnerships to tackle pressing economic, environmental, and social issues. While there is no stand-alone culture-related SDG, the assumption is that culture acts as a key enabler for this agenda as a whole (Wiktor-Mach, 2020). Indeed, when done right, arts and culture, together with tourism, can improve individuals' health, facilitate reconciliation, alleviate further prejudices, and provide jobs to communities. Yet, despite the great potential, these sectors need to attend to the strategic development of data-gathering tools that enable organisations and communities to demonstrate impact. Across Canada, these sectors lack robust data collection processes; the arts and culture sector, in particular, is tremendously under-equipped and under-skilled in research and impact assessment capacity. While there are various efforts underway to provide training and capacity for the sector to engage more consistently and rigorously with data, there remains a great risk that such initiatives and projects move too slowly to capitalise on the immediate opportunities for growth.

Stakeholders, business, and policy implications

At a policy level, these trends call for a renewed appreciation of both sectors' economic and social impacts, and a desire to grow cultural tourism as a distinct subsector. Targeted funding programmes, joint KPIs, and shared resource libraries should stem from a well-thought-out strategy that considers the many faces of cultural tourism: rural vs. urban, large vs. small attractions, ephemeral vs. permanent. As cultural tourism becomes enmeshed with communities, encompassing not just dedicated sites but also daily life activities, policy makers will also want to weigh in on issues such as ownership, cultural representation, and sustainability.

These trends also highlight how digital technologies are going to be integral for future cultural tourism. Yet the arts and culture sector in general, as well as many rural markets, often lack digital literacy and infrastructure. Without greater financial investment and training, many risk losing cultural tourists, and the money they spend, to other destinations that are on the vanguard of innovation. At the industry or institutional level, organisations should get together to develop events, identify cross-sector career pathways, and implement a range of smaller-scale initiatives such as cultural itineraries, while also actively assisting each other in planning, asset mapping, and advocating. New dedicated training programmes should also address collaboration skills, marketing, as well as equity, diversity, and inclusion considerations.

While some in the arts and culture sector still resist the attraction label, the reality is that people travel the world to view classical and contemporary art museums and galleries, see avant-garde and commercial live dance and theatre, and discover the works of local artisans and craftspeople. For this sector to reject tourism means that it is missing opportunities to reach, educate, and provide enjoyment for even more people. Thus, a mindset shift needs to occur for arts and culture to fully benefit from these trends. Indeed, regardless of how the cultural sector feels towards tourists in general, visitors can fill seats or explore museums, especially when local audiences or government funding begin to stagnate. There are key values and objectives of tourism and the arts and culture sector that are closely aligned, and the basic principles in drawing tourists are the same as drawing local audiences and patrons.

Certainly, there are many distinctions between arts, culture, and heritage, and notable structural differences between not-for-profit and commercial systems. However, on the ground, these elements are often related and closely intertwined. The same tourist that attends a not-for-profit theatre performance might also attend a commercial production, visit an arts market of independent artisans and craftspeople, or even go shopping at chain retail stores in a mall, all in the same visit. Thus, for cultural tourism to thrive, organisations should not emphasise one sector at the expense of another, but rather focus on the broader visitor experience.

Contributions and conclusion

Taking stock of cultural tourism reveals issues and opportunities that demand further actions (Figure 10.3). On the one hand, it highlights the interplay between top-down policy-level challenges, and bottom-up community-level tensions. Together, they show how cultural tourism is static and longing for change. On the other hand, this chapter lays out opportunities and underscores overlapping considerations with other key themes in the tourism literature, which together suggest that cultural tourism has yet to achieve its true potential.

As noted in the Ontario Culture strategy, "culture provides important social and economic benefits (…) it contributes significantly to our quality of life and economic development (…) and it is an essential part of individual and community wellbeing." The same can be said about tourism. Hence, with shared objectives, these sectors can work together to ensure the responsible restart of inclusive cultural tourism. The challenge here is to make cultural tourism relevant to, and significant in, recovery efforts, and to make sure that visitors and attractions abide by ethical principles and are concerned with helping host communities thrive.

This chapter does not offer 'one-size-fits-all' strategies for cultural tourism. Still, many of the issues experienced in Ontario will resonate elsewhere: the need to understand how

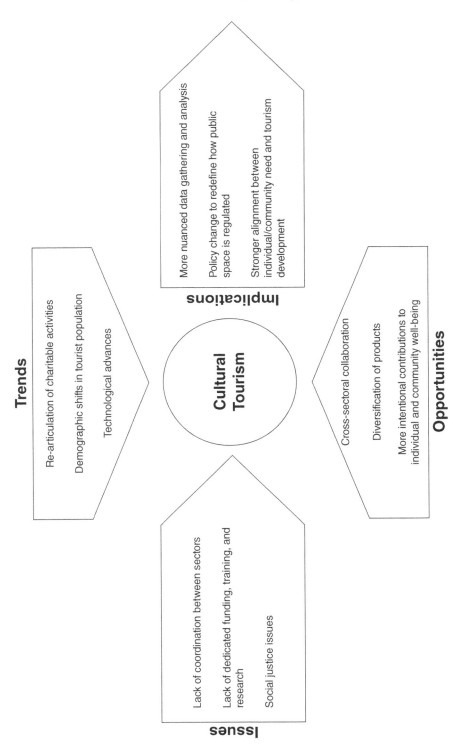

Figure 10.3 Cultural Tourism: A Canadian Perspective.

tourism and arts overlap; the necessity to reckon with injustice and trauma; the misalignment between and within various levels of government; and the importance of dedicated support mechanisms.

References

Akhtar, N., Khan, N., Mahroof Khan, M., Ashraf, S., Hashmi, M. S., Khan, M. M., & Hishan, S. S. (2021). Post-COVID 19 tourism: Will digital tourism replace mass tourism? *Sustainability*, *13*(10), 5352. https://www.mdpi.com/2071-1050/13/10/5352

Antón, C., Camarero, C., Laguna, M. and Buhalis, D. (2019). Impacts of authenticity, degree of adaptation and cultural contrast on travellers' memorable gastronomy experiences, *Journal of Hospitality Marketing & Management*, *28*(7), 743–764.

Bachleitner, R., & Zins, A. H. (1999). Cultural tourism in rural communities: The residents perspective. *Journal of Business Research*, *44*(3), 199–209. https://doi.org/10.1016/S0148-2963(97)00201-4

Bendixen, P. (1997). Cultural tourism: Economic success at the expense of culture? *International Journal of Cultural Policy*, *4*(1), 21–46. https://doi.org/10.1080/10286639709358061

Campos, A. C., Mendes, J., Valle, P. O. D., & Scott, N. (2018). Co-creation of tourist experiences: A literature review. *Current Issues in Tourism*, *21*(4), 369–400. https://doi.org/10.1080/13683500.2015.1081158

du Cros, H. D. (2008). Too much of a good thing? Visitor congestion management issues for popular world heritage tourist attractions. *Journal of Heritage Tourism*, *2*(3), 225–238. https://doi.org/10.2167/jht062.0

Dodds, R., & Butler, R. (Eds.). (2019). *Overtourism: Issues, realities and solutions*. Berlin: De Gruyter.

Dubois, L.-E., & Dimanche, F. (2021). The futures of entertainment-dependent cities in a post-COVID world. *Journal of Tourism Futures*, *7*(3), 364–376. https://doi.org/10.1108/JTF-11-2020-0208

Dubois, L.-E., & Dimanche, F. (2022). Brighter but not clearer: Entertainment-dependent destinations dealing with long COVID. *Journal of Themed Experience and Attractions Studies*, *2*(1). https://stars.library.ucf.edu/jteas/vol2/iss1/7

Flew, T., & Kirkwood, K. (2021). The impact of COVID-19 on cultural tourism: Art, culture and communication in four regional sites of Queensland, Australia. *Media International Australia*, *178*(1), 16–20. https://doi.org/10.1177/1329878X20952529

Galí-Espelt, N. (2012). Identifying cultural tourism: A theoretical methodological proposal. *Journal of Heritage Tourism*, *7*(1), 45–58. https://doi.org/10.1177/1329878X20952529

Griffin, T., Guttentag, D., Lee, S. H. (M.), Giberson, J., & Dimanche, F. (2022). Is VR always better for destination marketing? Comparing different media and styles. *Journal of Vacation Marketing*. https://doi.org/10.1177/13567667221078252

Huang, L., Zheng, Q., Yin, X., Luo, M., & Yang, Y. (2021). "Double-edged sword": The effect of cultural distance on post-disaster tourism destination recovery. *Tourism Review*, *77*(1), 146–162. https://doi.org/10.1108/TR-03-2021-0113

Hughes, H. (2013). *Arts, entertainment and tourism*. London: Routledge.

Jovicic, D. (2016). Cultural tourism in the context of relations between mass and alternative tourism. *Current Issues in Tourism*, *19*(6), 605–612. https://doi.org/10.1080/13683500.2014.932759

Kim, S., Whitford, M., & Arcodia, C. (2019). Development of intangible cultural heritage as a sustainable tourism resource: The intangible cultural heritage practitioners' perspectives. *Journal of Heritage Tourism*, *14*(5–6), 422–435. https://doi.org/10.1080/1743873X.2018.1561703

Koç, B., Küçükergin, G., & Dimanche, F. (2022). How destructive are negative tourist-to-tourist interactions despite the mitigating effect of optimism? *Journal of Destination Marketing and Management*. https://doi.org/10.1016/j.jdmm.2022.100693

McKercher, B. (2020). Cultural tourism market: A perspective paper. *Tourism Review*, *75*(1), 126–129. https://doi.org/10.1108/TR-03-2019-0096

McKercher, B., & du Cros, H. (2002). *Cultural tourism: The partnership between tourism and cultural heritage management*. London: Routledge.

McKercher, B., & du Cros, H. (2003). Testing a cultural tourism typology. *International Journal of Tourism Research*, 5(1), 45–58. https://doi.org/10.1002/jtr.417

Muro, M., Whiton, J. and Maxim, R. (2020). Why it will be difficult to restart the economy after COVID-19, Brookings Institute, https://www.brookings.edu/blog/the-avenue/2020/04/01/why-it-will-be-difficult-to-restart-the-economy-after-covid-19/

Neuhofer, B., & Buhalis, D. (2014). Experience, co-creation and technology: Issues, challenges and trends for technology enhanced tourism experiences. In S. McCabe (Ed.), *The Routledge handbook of tourism marketing* (pp. 146–161). London: Routledge.

Noonan, D. S., & Rizzo, I. (2017). Economics of cultural tourism: Issues and perspectives. *Journal of Cultural Economics*, 41(2), 95–107 https://doi.org/10.1007/s10824-017-9300-6

Peco-Torres, F., Polo-Peña, A. I., & Frías-Jamilena, D. M. (2020). Brand personality in cultural tourism through social media. *Tourism Review*, 76(1), 164–183. https://doi.org/10.1108/TR-02-2019-0050

Richards, G. (2018). Cultural tourism: A review of recent research and trends. *Journal of Hospitality and Tourism Management*, 36, 12–21. https://doi.org/10.1016/j.jhtm.2018.03.005

Richards, G. (2021a). Conclusion: Creative placemaking strategies in smaller communities. Creative Tourism in Smaller Communities. In K. Scherf (Ed.), *Creative tourism in smaller communities: Place, culture, and local representation* (pp. 283–298). Calgary, Alberta: University of Calgary Press. https://doi.org/10.2307/j.ctv1ks0d4d.15

Richards, G. (2021b). *Rethinking cultural tourism*. Edward Elgar.

Richards, G., & Richards, G. B. (Eds.) (1996). *Cultural tourism in Europe*. CABI.

Roigé, X., Arrieta-Urtizberea, I., & Seguí, J. (2021). The sustainability of intangible heritage in the COVID-19 era: Resilience, reinvention, and challenges in Spain. *Sustainability*, 13(11), 5796. https://doi.org/10.3390/su13115796

Scherf, K. (2021). Creative tourism in smaller communities: Collaboration and cultural representation. In K. Scherf (Ed.), *Creative tourism in smaller communities: Place, culture, and local representation* (pp. 1–26). University of Calgary Press, Calgary, Alberta.

Sharpley, R. (2013). In defense of tourism. *Tourism Recreation Research*, 38(3), 350–355.

Smith, M. K. (2022). Cultural tourism. In D. Buhalis (Ed.), *Encyclopedia of tourism management and marketing*. Cheltenham, UK: Edward Elgar.

Stone, P. R. (2006). A dark tourism spectrum: Towards a typology of death and macabre related tourist sites, attractions and exhibitions. *Tourism: An International Interdisciplinary Journal*, 54(2), 145–160. https://hrcak.srce.hr/161464

Tighe, A. J. (1986). The arts/tourism partnership. *Journal of Travel Research*, 24(3), 2–5. https://doi.org/10.1177/004728758602400301

Torre, A., & Scarborough, H. (2017). Reconsidering the estimation of the economic impact of cultural tourism. *Tourism Management*, 59, 621–629. https://doi.org/10.1016/j.tourman.2016.09.018

Uysal, M., Sirgy, M. J., Woo, E. and Kim, H. (2016). Quality of life (QOL) and well-being research in tourism. *Tourism Management*, 53, 244–261.

Wiktor-Mach, D. (2020). What role for culture in the age of sustainable development? UNESCO's advocacy in the 2030 Agenda negotiations. *International Journal of Cultural Policy*, 26(3), 312–327. https://doi.org/10.1080/10286632.2018.1534841

11 Edutainment interpretation trends in dark tourism

Brianna Wyatt

Introduction

Within the extensive range of trends and issues that reinforce the complexity of global tourism is interpretation – the strategic effort used to enhance visitor understanding and experiences through thought-provoking methods and media (Smith, 2016). Commonly used in the heritage industry to bring the past to life, interpretation has been at the centre of academic debate for decades. The dissension among historians and heritage practitioners concerning interpretation continues to percolate through academic writings. This is most often observed in publications concerning dark histories – that which is marked by past tragedies. Echoing early criticisms concerning the heritage industry's treatment of history (see Hewison, 1987), many dark tourism contemporaries (e.g., Kennell & Powell, 2021) have illustrated issues with edutainment interpretation (i.e., educational entertainment; entertaining education) at dark heritage attractions.

Dark heritage attractions sit at the core of dark tourism – travel to places representative of historic death, tragedy or macabre events (Stone, 2006), and are therefore designed with reflective, commemorative, or educational interpretation to help visitors cope and understand past events. However, as the temporal distance continues to grow between the past and the present (Stone, 2006), and with new media and technological developments, visitors to dark attractions are beginning to seek more immersive and engaging experiences (Alabau-Montoya & Ruiz-Molina, 2020; McKercher, 2020). Such experiences are possible with edutainment, which uses innovative and experiential techniques to create entertaining, educational and memorable experiences (Wyatt et al., 2021).

Recent studies (e.g., Ivanova & Light, 2018; Wyatt et al., 2021) have shed light on the increasing use of co-creation, immersion, and performance within dark tourism, and in effect have called attention to the evolving dark tourism experiencescape (Matečić et al., 2021) that is now an undeniable force within the global tourism market. Although much of the dark tourism experiencescape has been observed to create negative affective experiences (Qian et al., 2022), few scholars (see e.g., Light & Ivanova, 2021) have noted the positive affective qualities that dark tourism experiences can offer, particularly through edutainment interpretation, which can lead to a greater sense of appreciation and learning. Expanding on these developments, this chapter discusses edutainment interpretation within dark tourism practice. By illustrating the growing trend of edutainment interpretation, this chapter demonstrates the need for greater dialogue and collaboration between practitioners and scholars concerned with the use of dark pasts for the present and future.

Dark tourism experiences

Dark tourism is an expansive field for study and practice, which comprises a range of dark visitor attractions (DVAs) that offer commemorative, reflective, educational, and/or entertaining experiences. DVAs are recognised within the global tourism industry for their associations and/or representations of death, tragedy and seemingly macabre events (Stone, 2006). Some DVAs offer purely entertainment experiences for adrenaline-driven, thrill-seeking audiences wanting overstimulation and scare tactics (e.g., McKamey Manor, Summertown, USA). However, the majority of DVAs, on which this chapter focuses, are generally linked to historical events and have educational aims. These DVAs are most often typified by their individual characteristics defined by Stone's (2006) darkness spectrum – a scale that identifies an attraction by its level of darkness. According to this spectrum, darker DVAs are generally in situ and have a lower tourism infrastructure, stronger sense of authenticity, and are history-centric, offering commemorative, reflective and/or educational experiences. At the opposite end of the spectrum, lighter DVAs are shown to be more often purposefully created with a higher tourism infrastructure, commercial focus, and heritage-centric, offering more entertaining experiences. Between these two boundaries is a grey area where, according to the spectrum, some DVAs blur the darker and the lighter characteristics. Stone (2006) acknowledges that darker DVAs may become lighter over time due to the temporal distance that grows between the past and present, interpretation developments, and the public's increasing desensitisation to tragedy as a result of increased media.

It is evident that the identification of DVAs is largely based on their varying interpretation agendas (Figure 11.1). Darker DVAs that promote commemorative interpretation are generally designed to offer visitors a quiet space for reflection and a memorial to recognise and remember victims (e.g., Jeju Peace Park, South Korea). While commemorative experiences are often designed in collaboration with survivors and historians, as temporal distance increases between the past and the present, these experiences often submit to interpretation alterations that adopt educational objectives (Lennon & Weber, 2017). DVAs that promote educational interpretation may be considered grey in nature (with respect to the darkness spectrum), as they are generally designed with static exhibitions, displayed artefacts, text panels, and photographic or filmic imagery (Frew, 2011); for example, Dachau Concentration Camp Memorial Site (Germany). Some DVAs might find themselves at the crossroads of education and entertainment when using guided tours, staged scenes of period-inspired props and mannequins, and/or re-enactments (e.g., Eyam Museum, UK) (Skipalis, 2012). These DVAs maintain their interpretative efforts to foster deeper learning experiences, but often find themselves at the centre of academic debate concerning the appropriateness of re-enacting sensitive histories and their general white-washing and exploitation of the past (Alderman et al., 2016). Stepping further into the entertainment side of edutainment interpretation, lighter DVAs unapologetically use augmented reality, sensory stimulation, and amusement rides to create memorable encounters

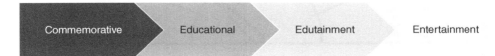

Figure 11.1 Dark visitor attraction interpretation.
(*Source:* Wyatt, 2022a).

with history (Wyatt et al., 2021); for example, the Titanic Museum and Attraction (USA). History still underpins lighter experiences; however, they lean into the gruesome details unabashedly, and because of this they are often labelled inauthentic and frivolous (Hertzman et al., 2008).

Edutainment interpretation

Edutainment interpretation is used in tourism to make visitor experiences more interesting, engaging and memorable. They often rely on simulation technologies, theming and storytelling to immerse visitors in an interactive and/or co-created experience (Åstrøm, 2020; Oren & Shani, 2012). However, they can also be non-immersive, with visitors merely watching live performances (Rapeepisarn et al., 2006). Figure 11.2 demonstrates fully immersive experiences may have a higher entertainment value and use virtual or augmented reality (VR/AR) to physically place visitors in virtual environments. Less immersive, but still interactive experiences may rely on character actors, sensory stimulated props (e.g., smell pods, ambient sounds), and some advanced technologies or amusement rides to create a simulation of the past and help visitors to connect with history. Non-immersive experiences may use re-enactment performances, thematic displays, and film footage to provide visitor learning and enjoyment through spectating. At the centre of these edutainment experiences is theming (Oren & Shani, 2012), which involves strategic staging and a strong central narrative to create coherence and added value in visitor experience, whilst helping to guide the aesthetic design (Åstrøm, 2020).

The proliferation of edutainment interpretation is not only a direct response to the growing public preference for realism but is also transforming how visitors engage with the past and their experiences (Little et al., 2020). Recent studies have shown experiential and interactive experiences provide visitors with a personalised way to consume the past, thereby increasing visitor engagement, enhancing visitor learning and understanding (Jin et al., 2020) and, in turn, creating a positive impact on visitor satisfaction and enjoyment

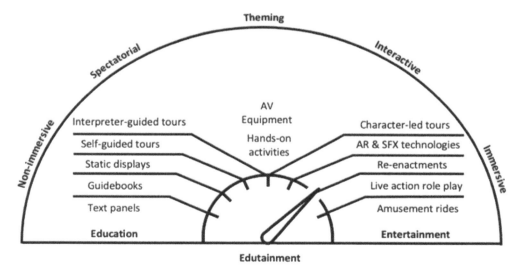

Figure 11.2 Edutainment scale.
(*Source:* Wyatt, 2022b).

(Lunardo & Ponsignon, 2020). While the use of edutainment, advanced technologies and immersive theming has increased, the core concept and practice of edutainment is fundamentally rooted in Disney practice.

Edutainment and Disney

Recognising the value of informal learning through film, Walt Disney (1954) promoted the mixing of education with entertainment in amusement parks to counteract what he found to be poor-quality experiences lacking educational values (D'Ambrosi, 2019; Oren & Shani, 2012). With his Imagineers, Disney combined set design, theming, storytelling, and technology to create the first edutainment visitor attraction, Disneyland, and the subsequent EPCOT Center, inspired by the World's Fair, which have since become the epitome of edutainment experiences given their use of emotive and sensory stimulating techniques to create imagined environments that seem real and authentic (Mittermeier, 2016).

Although edutainment helps stimulate visitor engagement, it is often challenged by heritage and dark tourism scholars because of its inherent association with Disney. When dealing with historical contexts, Disney regularly omitted or sanitised potentially controversial narratives to make them more palatable and uplifting for audiences (Scarbrough, 2021). While these actions were to maintain Disney's brand and image, they whitewashed historic truths, and, in consequence, reinforced stereotypes and myths that permeated public memory (Scarbrough, 2021). In 1994, for example, Disney proposed Disney's America, a new theme park that was to depict the American past and engage visitors in playlands representing America's past, including a re-enactment battle between Union and Confederate soldiers, immigrant treatment at Ellis Island, and Native American history 1600–1810 (Synnott, 1995). Following staunch criticisms of the proposal and Disney's inability to portray history accurately, Disney officials argued the new park would, for example, 'show the Civil War with all its racial conflict' and make visitors 'feel what slavery was like during that time period, and what it was like to escape the Underground Railroad' (Lukas, 2016, p. 229). Such statements were met with condemnation and arguments that there was no possible way Disney could honestly address these dark histories, particularly if the expectation were to have an enjoyable time (Lukas, 2016).

The controversy that underpinned Disney's America was that when the idea was proposed, the Disney brand had expanded across film, media, merchandising, and tourism, becoming an influential juggernaut in global business and resulting in the Disneyfication of the audience-focused and customer services industries (Sandlin & Garlen, 2017). Critics of Disney's monopoly argued its intention to accurately portray America's past was unbelievable as it would most certainly trivialise and commercially exploit the histories through its predictable and calculated methods of efficiency and control that prioritised patriarchy and innocence (Bryman, 2004). Defending their case, Disney officials likened their efforts to that of Colonial Williamsburg, suggesting Disney's America would encourage visitors to take up more learning of these histories in further reading or visiting historic sites (Synnott, 1995). However, Colonial Williamsburg was also faced with criticism and controversy in relation to their sanitised representations of colonialism and slave auction re-enactments.

Edutainment today

The use of dark histories for edutainment purposes has become increasingly part of mainstream culture. Darker histories are now experienced through tourism, film and television, and virtual gaming (Light & Ivanova, 2021). It is impossible to ignore the growing public preference for edutainment experiences. Society's desire for immersive and sensory stimulating experiences may be due to society becoming almost exclusively dependent on media and Internet communication technologies (Alabau-Montoya & Ruiz-Molina, 2020; Perry, 2020). While there are arguments that edutainment glorifies tragedy and often negates the truth, it generally creates visceral encounters with the past to create experiences that allow audiences to consider societal issues and public memory (Tschida, 2022).

Currently, edutainment interpretation within dark tourism attractions is generally used to present history with a greater temporal distance, thereby allowing for a more light-hearted approach. For example, the Black Death (14th–18th centuries) is often portrayed through a *Horrible Histories* style using embellished props, sensory technologies, jump scares, and thematic staging to create a more immersive experience (e.g., Gravedigger Ghost Bus Tour, Ireland). Similar treatment is observed for experiences of the 1666 Great Fire of London (e.g., London Bridge Experience, UK) and medieval torture (e.g., Tallin Legends, Estonia). The epitome of these types of edutainment experiences are perhaps found in the global Dungeon Experiences, which, across their Disneyfied themed attractions, depict scenes of death, persecution, disease, crime, and murder spanning the 14th–19th centuries, generally ending with a drop ride to simulate being hung. Because of their increased entertainment value, these attractions are often criticised for glorifying past horrors and mocking real suffering (Ivanova & Light, 2018). Stirring even greater controversy are experiences that amplify their edutainment approach through experiential opportunities, allowing visitors to co-create their experience (e.g., *Follow the North Star*, Connor Prairie, U.S.). While co-created experiences are fewer in number, they are responding to the growing public preference for realism and affective engagement in heritage and dark tourism experiences (Light & Ivanova, 2021). Further challenging the criticisms, their narratives are generally grounded in academic text, and rather than shying away from the historical realities of how cruel and punishing life could be, they lean into all of the horrific details to provide real and raw accounts (Wyatt et al., 2021).

Yet edutainment does not always use jump scares and special effects. Many edutainment experiences at DVAs depicting histories that span the 14th–19th centuries are often underpinned with a greater sense of gravity. For example, the persecution of witches (e.g., Feria de Brujeria y Magica, Trasmoz, Spain), witch trials (e.g., *Cry Innocent*, Salem, U.S.), plague (e.g., The Real Mary King's Close, Edinburgh, U.K.), famine (e.g., Dunbrody Famine Ship Experience, Wexford, Ireland), colonialisation (e.g., *Unto these Hills*, Cherokee, U.S.), and slavery (e.g., *What holds the future?* Colonial Williamsburg, U.S.) are examples of DVAs that use thematic staging and minimal sensory stimulating technologies to create engaging edutainment experiences. These experiences strive to memorialise events and educate audiences. While most do not mock history in a satirical way, some still face staunch criticisms for issues of whitewashing, sanitising, or omitting truths to make it more palatable for audiences, consequently exacerbating issues of absence, misrepresentation, stereotypes, social inequality, and racism within public memory (Tschida, 2022).

Until now, most edutainment experiences have been used to reflect bygone pasts of at least 100 years ago. While there are no hard-set rules as to when a dark event can be turned into a visitor attraction, 100 years appears to be the common timeframe (Wright, 2018). Yet DVAs using edutainment to represent 20th century events have started to emerge. For example, thematic storytelling in the 1914 Rise of the Rebel Bus Tour (Ireland); interactive exhibitions at the Titanic Museum and Attraction (U.S.); re-enactment at the Boggo Road Gaol (Australia); live virtual tours at the Lizzie Borden House (U.S.); and AR tours at

KZ-Gedenkstätte Dachau (Germany). Although these experiences seek to educate audiences, their use of staged scenes, theatricality and technology continue to incite debate concerning temporal distance and appropriateness.

Edutainment futures

Looking at the existing trends, mixing edutainment with dark histories will continue to exist as we move forward into the future. While some see edutainment as a means for visitors to engage more deeply with the past, there is a continuing fear and discussion over whether the edutainment interpretation of certain histories is appropriate (Mittermeier, 2016). Deciding when enough time has lapsed between death and suffering and the interpretation of it for tourism purposes remains debatable. However, Huang et al. (2022) suggest there are also issues of cultural distance, in which visitors who are generally not local may react and consume death-related spectacles differently as a result of their cultural backgrounds. This echoes Light and Ivanova (2021), who recognised Western societies are generally more interested in witnessing spectacles of death and tragedy because they are culturally removed from the realities of it. Demonstrated in their study of visitor perspectives on the use of edutainment at lighter DVAs, death is often observed as being absent from the public sphere, which consequently ignites a morbid curiosity among visitors (Light & Ivanova, 2021). Similarly, Qian et al. (2022) note the influence of media on visitor behaviours and engagement with darker histories, which can create expectations that further influence their level of emotion, shock, or awe, when confronted with the history on site.

Scholars (e.g., Light & Ivanova, 2021; Qian et al., 2022) have noted the changing trends towards death-related experiences and increasing visitor preferences for experiences that lead to self-satisfaction and enjoyment. Critical to this discussion is Light and Ivanova's (2021) findings, which revealed visitors to lighter DVAs acknowledge the seriousness of the stories but found the edutainment interpretation as a safe and socially acceptable way to engage with the history, death, and the reality of their own mortality. Although the appropriateness of using edutainment is still questionable at places of 20th- and 21st-century tragedies (Qian et al., 2022), the literature indicates the future of dark tourism practice is moving towards a greater use of edutainment interpretation to accommodate a wider spectrum of visitors seeking more interactive and sensory stimulating experiences (Alabau-Montoya & Ruiz-Molina, 2020).

Because society has become largely agreeable with engaging and consuming tragedy through more entertaining channels, Wright (2018) suggests future tourists could visit dark attractions that reflect our current tragedies. This is particularly true given there are no guidelines for how and when to establish a dark tourism experience, let alone one that promotes edutainment or even pure entertainment. In fact, Wright (2018) suggests by 2100, the 2015 Paris attacks, 9/11, and Hurricane Katrina, for example, could be experienced in an entertaining way. This may seem unimaginable at this point in time given the shorter temporal distance. However, it is plausible that victims of the plague, torture and punishment in the 14th–18th centuries would never have imagined their suffering and deaths would be a source for entertainment – and yet there are now a great number of attractions and media that do just that (e.g. Merlin Attraction's Dungeons Experience; *Horrible Histories* books and television shows). Thus, the passing of time is key to creating these experiences. Yet, we may not have to wait until 2100 to experience more recent tragedies. The Oklahoma City Bombing Memorial and Museum (U.S.), for example, promotes a sense of edutainment through its use of sensory stimulation technologies to immerse visitors in a simulation of the 1995 events before witnessing the aftermath and authentic artefacts. A less immersive example, but still provocative through thematic staging, is the Museum of Death in Los Angeles (USA), which depicts artefacts, images and film relating, but not limited, to high-profile serial killers and celebrity deaths of the 20th and 21st centuries.

As dark tourism experiences move further into the future, edutainment will surely be a prominent trend as a result of the increasing advancements in technology that continue to influence visitors' expectations and satisfaction. Wright (2021) suggests the future visitor will demand more from dark tourism experiences, including more choices and co-created opportunities to tailor their experiences. This could be possible through self-service and personal devices, augmented reality (AR) and virtual reality (VR) technologies, as well as wearable technologies, such as glasses, headgear or gloves, thereby intensifying experiences and allowing full immersion (Wright, 2018, 2021). Others have also suggested advancements in technology, such as 3D modelling and visualisation techniques, will help to implement greater innovation and enhanced visitor experiences and engagement (Alabau-Montoya & Ruiz-Molina, 2020; Lee et al., 2020). Although future DVAs will likely engage with advanced technologies on a greater level, some are already doing so, such as the Battle of Bannockburn Memorial and Museum in Stirling, U.K., where visitors use 3D glasses to engage kinaesthetically with VR characters. Similarly, the Auschwitz-Birkenau Memorial and Museum in Poland now offers a 360° virtual tour and on-site application that creates digital reconstructions of the grounds.

Given the increasing technical advancements, the future of edutainment experiences in DVAs will likely also encompass greater sustainability practices, such as increased use of recycling and renewable energy and water (Wright, 2018). To impact on society's understanding about the severity of climate change, DVA simulation experiences of natural disasters, such as the California wildfires and Hurricane Katrina, could also appear in the future edutainment experiences. This would be possible, and even in the very near future (e.g., 2025–2035), given the rise and preference for simulation rides and rollercoasters in theme parks around the world, most notably at Universal Studios (USA). This may be possible with IMAX simulation experiences to show visitors what a natural disaster feels and looks like from a bird's eye view (e.g., RiseNY, New York, U.S.; Soarin' Around the World, Disney California Adventure Park, U.S.). In fact, Wu et al. (2020) suggests 360° panoramic films of dark tourism experiences could use VR technologies to create immersive and interactive experiences. As earlier mentioned, such experiences are emerging in even the darkest of places. Such experiences would therefore support larger efforts to educate visitors of the realities of natural disasters, further engaging and encouraging them to participate in climate change action, thereby supporting the United Nation's Sustainable Development Goals (SDGs), specifically SDG13.

In addressing the SDGs, it is important to remember that edutainment is twofold, as it relies on education and entertainment. Many DVAs use edutainment to create affective and memorable experiences, but specifically emphasise the educational value. It is thus plausible that future edutainment experiences can also support actions for more inclusive societies, which will in turn support the UN's SDG16 for peace, justice and strong institutions. Šuligoj and Kennell (2021), for example, have discussed the impact dark tourism practices can have on bridging community divides and developing a peaceful coexistence in the Western Balkans, thereby supporting SDG16. While controversial, studies have shown that edutainment techniques, such as re-enactments and simulations of darker histories, can help visitors to engage with history on a deeper level, and as they can challenge dominant narratives established by elitist power-holders, they help to create a better-balanced understanding among visitors of historic truths (Magelssen, 2006; de Groot, 2016; Tschida, 2022). Given their observed preference among visitors and increasing use within dark tourism, it is expected that edutainment will continue to be a preferred method for visitor experiences as we move forward into the future.

Conclusions

Influenced by advancing technology and the proliferation of mass media, society is becoming more experience-driven (Perry, 2020). In response, more DVAs are offering engaging opportunities through immersion and simulations to provoke affective and visceral responses. These experiences exist through edutainment interpretation, which moves beyond the confines of Disney Imagineering to influence visitor engagement, learning and public memory. Concern for mixing dark histories with edutainment will remain a concern. However, dark tourism scholars and practitioners can no longer deny the public preference and growing expectation for, or benefits of, edutainment experiences. As society continues to demand hyper-real accounts of the past, there is an established expectation that edutainment experiences will flourish as we move into the future, particularly with greater advancements in technology. Thus, research should place greater attention onto the use of edutainment within future dark tourism contexts, particularly as DVAs are becoming increasingly liberated from societal concerns of morality and appropriateness.

References

Alabau-Montoya, J. & Ruiz-Molina, M. E. (2020). Enhancing visitor experience with war heritage tourism through information and communication technologies: Evidence from Spanish Civil War museums and sites. *Journal of Heritage Tourism*, *15*(5), 500–510. https://doi.org/10.1080/1743873X.2019.1692853

Alderman, D., Butler, D., & Hanna, S. (2016). Memory, slavery, and plantation museums: The river road project. *Journal of Heritage Tourism*, *11*(3), 209–218. https://doi.org/10.1080/1743873X.2015.1100629

Åstrøm, J. K. (2020). Why theming? Identifying the purposes of theming in tourism. *Journal of Quality Assurance in Hospitality & Tourism*, *21*(3), 245–266. https://doi.org/10.1080/1528008X.2019.1658147

Bryman, A. (2004). *The Disneyization of society*. London: Sage.

de Groot, J. (2016). *Consuming history: Historians and heritage in contemporary popular culture*. London: Routledge.

D'Ambrosi, J. R. (2019). The search for a great, big, beautiful tomorrow: Performing utopia with non-human bodies in the Hall of Presidents. In J. A. Kokai, & T. Robson (Eds.), *Performance and the Disney theme park experience* (pp. 171–192). London: Palgrave Macmillan.

Disney, W. (1954). Educational values in factual nature pictures. *Phi Delta Kappa International*, *33*(2), 82–84.

Frew, E. (2011). Interpretation of a sensitive heritage site: The Port Arthur Memorial Garden, Tasmania. *International Journal of Heritage Studies*, *18*(1), 33–48. https://doi.org/10.1080/13527258.2011.603908

Hertzman, E., Anderson, D., & Rowley, S. (2008). Edutainment heritage tourist attractions: A portrait of visitors' experiences at Storyeum. *Museum Management and Curatorship*, *23*(2), 155–175. https://doi.org/10.1080/09647770802012227

Hewison, R. (1987). *The heritage industry: Britain in a climate of decline*. London: Methuen.

Huang, L., Zheng, Q., Yin, X., Luo, M., & Yang, Y. (2022). "Double-edged sword": The effect of cultural distance on post-disaster tourism destination recovery. *Tourism Review*, *77*(1), 146–162. https://doi.org/10.1108/TR-03-2021-0113

Ivanova, P. & Light, D. (2018). 'It's not that we like death or anything': Exploring the motivations and experiences of visitors to a lighter dark tourism attraction. *Journal of Heritage Tourism*, *13*(4), 356–369. https://doi.org/10.1080/1743873X.2017.1371181

Jin, L., Xiao, H., & Shen, H. (2020). Experiential authenticity in heritage museums. *Journal of Destination Marketing and Management*, *18* https://doi.org/10.1016/j.jdmm.2020.100493

Kennell, J. & Powell, P. (2021). Dark tourism and World Heritage Sites: A Delphi study of stakeholder perceptions of the development of dark tourism products, *Journal of Heritage Tourism*, *16*(4), 367–381. https://doi.org/10.1080/1743873X.2020.1782924

Lee, H., Jung, T. H., Tom Diek, M. C., & Chung, N. (2020). Experiencing immersive virtual reality in museums. *Information & Management*, *57*, 103229. https://doi.org/10.1016/j.im.2019.103229

Lennon, J. J., & Weber, D. (2017). The long shadow: Marketing Dachau. In Glenn Hooper & J. J. Lennon (Eds.), *Dark tourism: Practice and interpretation* (pp. 27–39). Routledge.

Light, D., & Ivanova, P. (2021). Thanatopsis and mortality mediation within "lightest" dark tourism. *Tourism Review*, *77*(2), 622–635. https://doi.org/10.1108/TR-03-2021-0106

Little, C., Bec, A., Don Moyle, B., & Patterson, D. (2020). Innovative methods for heritage tourism experiences: Creating windows into the past. *Journal of Heritage Tourism*, *15*(1), 1–13. https://doi.org/10.1080/1743873X.2018.1536709

Lukas, S. A. (2016) Dark theming reconsidered. In S. A. Lukas, *A reader in immersive and themed spaces*. (pp. 225–238). ETC Press.

Lunardo, R. & Ponsignon, F. (2020). Achieving immersion in the tourism experience: The role of autonomy, temporal dissociation and reactance, *Journal of Travel Research*, *59*(7), 1151–1167. https://doi.org/10.1177/0047287519878509

Magelssen, S. (2006). "This is drama. You are characters": The tourist as fugitive slave in Conner Prairie's "Follow the North Star". *Theatre Topics*, *16*(1), 19–34. https://doi.org/10.1353/tt.2006.0011

Matečić, I., Rajić Šikanjić, P., & Perinić Lewis, A. (2021). The potential of forgotten and hidden Zagreb historical cemeteries in the design of 'dark' tourist experiences. *Journal of Heritage Tourism*, *16*(4), 450–468. https://doi.org/10.1080/1743873X.2020.1864384

McKercher, B. (2020). Cultural toruism market: A perspective paper. *Tourism Review*, *75*(1), 126–129. http://dx.doi.org/10.1108/TR-03-2019-0096

Mittermeier, S. (2016). Windows to the past: Disney's America, the culture wars, and the question of Edutainment. *Polish Journal for American Studies*, *10*, 127–146. ISSN: 1733-9154

Oren, G., & Shani, A. (2012). The Yad Vashem Holocaust Museum: Educational dark tourism in a futuristic form. *Journal of Heritage Tourism*, *7*(3), 255–270. https://doi.org/10.1080/1743873X.2012.701630

Perry, R. E. (2020). The Holocaust is present: Reenacting the Holocaust, then and now, *Holocaust Studies*, *26*(2), 152–180. https://doi.org/10.1080/17504902.2019.1578460

Qian, L., Zheng, C., Wang, J., de Los Ángeles Pérez Sánchez, M., Parra López, E., & Hanliang, L. (2022). Dark tourism destinations: The relationships between tourists' on-site experience, destination image and behavioural intention. *Tourism Review*, *77*(2), 607–621. https://doi.org/10.1108/TR-08-2020-0360

Rapeepisarn, K., Wong, K. W., Fung, C. C., & Depickere, A. (2006). Similarities and differences between "learn through play" and "edutainment." *Proceedings of the 3rd Australasian Conference on Interactive Entertainment (IE '06)*, 28–32.

Sandlin, J. A. & Garlen, J. C. (2017). Magic everywhere: Mapping the Disney curriculum, *Review of Education, Pedagogy, and Cultural Studies*, *39*(2), 190–219. https://doi.org/10.1080/10714413.2017.1296281

Scarbrough, E. (2021). Are Archaeological Parks the New Amusement Parks? UNESCO World Heritage Status and Tourism. In: Killin A., Allen-Hermanson S. (eds) *Explorations in Archaeology and Philosophy*. (pp 235–261). Cham: Springer.

Skipalis, B. (2012). *Construction of heritage and identity in the plague village: Examining the intersections of local identity, heritage tourism and local heritage museum in Eyam*. University of Manchester. Retrieved from https://www.research.manchester.ac.uk/portal/files/60988331/FULL_TEXT.PDF

Smith, M. (2016). *Issues in cultural tourism studies* (3rd ed). London: Routledge.

Stone, P. (2006). A Dark Tourism Spectrum: Towards a typology of death and macabre related tourist sites, attractions and exhibitions. *Tourism: An Interdisciplinary International Journal*, 54(2), 145–160. ISSN 1790-8418

Šuligoj, M. & Kennell, J. (2021). The role of dark commemorative and sport events in peaceful coexistence in the Western Balkans. *Journal of Sustainable Tourism*, 30(2–3), 408–426. https://doi.org/10.1080/09669582.2021.1938090

Synnott, M. G. (1995). Disney's America: Whose patrimony, whose profits, whose past? *The Public Historian*, 17(4). https://doi.org/3378384

Tschida, D. A. (2022). Rendevous with history: Grand Portage National Monument and Minnesota's North Shore. In C. Rex & S. E. Watson (Eds.), *Public memory, race, and heritage tourism of early America* (pp. 136–152). Routledge.

Turner, J. & Peters, K. (2015). Doing time-travel: Performing past and present at the prison museum. In K. M. Morin & D. Moran (Eds.) *Historical geographies of prisons: Unlocking the usable carceral past*. (pp. 71–87). London: Routledge.

Wright, D. W. M. (2018). Terror park: A future theme park in 2100. *Futures*, 96, 1–22. https://doi.org/10.1016/j.futures.2017.11.002

Wright, D. W. M. (2021). Immersive dark tourism experiences: Storytelling at dark tourism attractions in the age of 'the immersive death'. In M. H. Jacobsen (Ed.) *The age of spectacular death*, (pp. 89–109). Routledge.

Wu, H. C., Ai, C. H. & Cheng, C. C. (2020). Virtual reality experiences, attachment and experiential outcomes in tourism. *Tourism Review*, 75(3), 481–495. http://dx.doi.org/10.1108/TR-06-2019-0205

Wyatt, B. (2022a). Dark visitor attractions. In D. Buhalis (Ed.) *Encyclopedia of Tourism Management and Marketing*. Edward Elgar Publishing Ltd.

Wyatt, B. (2022b). Edutainment. In D. Buhalis (Ed.) *Encyclopedia of Tourism Management and Marketing*. Edward Elgar Publishing Ltd.

Wyatt, B., Leask, A., & Barron, P. (2021). Designing dark tourism experiences: an exploration of edutainment interpretation at lighter dark visitor attractions. *Journal of Heritage Tourism*. 16(4), 433–449, https://doi.org/10.1080/1743873X.2020.1858087

12 Modelling heritage justice for under-represented communities

Deepak Chhabra

Introduction

The entire notion of heritage is dialectical in nature. According to Harrison, heritage means

> "caring from, valuing and assuming an ethical stance toward the future" (2015, p. 52). Pishief describes heritage as: "… an intangible, emotional, imaginative, memory-laden, cultural performance around place(s) that are inherently political and dissonant, and concerned with the making, remaking, and, or maintenance of identity…"
>
> (2012, p. 52)

Harvey writes that heritage is "related to human action and agency and is an instrument of cultural power" (2001, p. 327). Johnston and Marwood write that,

> doing heritage… is not simply about the preservation or celebration of the past, it also involves negotiating and making decisions about the past in the present. The inherited past is part of political, community and personal discourses in the present.
>
> (2017, p. 818)

The ongoing dialogue between the past and the present has often compromised the cultural authenticity and heritage expressions of under-represented communities. Negotiating heritage and its claims is a complex and contentious issue (Baird, 2014). Therefore, it is important to develop a route that supports key pillars of heritage justice aimed at fostering the overall wellbeing of under-represented communities. What is required is an ethical, mindful and just approach centred on the dignity, identity and wellbeing of these communities whose heritage resources are popularly sought in the quest for 'othered' authentic experiences. In other words, there is a call for measures associated with heritage justice to protect the authentic inheritance and cultural expressions of marginalised communities across the globe. For the purpose of this chapter, heritage justice is defined as consideration/resolution of issues associated with social inequality, cultural rights and authenticity, misuse of cultural resources, and marginalisation of Indigenous voices and identity; it is a scrutiny to see if specific practices and claims are more privileged than the others (for instance, universal versus local claims over heritage expressions) (Association of Critical Heritage Studies, 2022; Baird, 2014; Chhabra, 2021; Harvey, 2001; Menzies & Wilson, 2020; Timothy, 2021).

Documented literature presents several connotations of authenticity which can be broadly delineated into four categories (Timothy, 2021): objective (legitimate, true to the origin), constructivist (commodified for income), existentialist (optimal and euphoric) and negotiated (that refers to a tradeoff between constructivist and essentialist or existentialist and essentialist ideologies, that is also referred as theoplacity) (Belhassen, Caton, & Stewart, 2008; Chhabra, 2021; DeSoucey, Elliott, & Schmutz, 2019; Kolar & Zabkar, 2010; MacCannell, 1992; Wang, 1999). The essentialist view supports the process of cultural continuity, that is, all that is considered authentic is symbolic of past happenings, time periods and/or lifestyles (Salamone, 1997; Timothy & Boyd, 2003). It can be postulated that the essentialist (or objective) perspective mirrors the true, original, genuine, actual, frozen and continuous perspective of heritage (Reeves et al., 2020). Having said that, extant literature argues about the futility of aiming for a perfectionist version of authenticity. It is contended that aiming for essentialist authenticity is an unviable goal (Belhassen et al., 2008; Chhabra, 2021; Timothy, 2021). Nevertheless, by using it as a point of reference, a delicately negotiated stance can be forged that echoes a sincere effort to retain objectively authentic elements of heritage. In this chapter, this tradeoff point is referred to as cultural authenticity.

One key purpose of heritage justice from the standpoint of cultural authenticity is to foster the wellness and wellbeing of host communities. Ryan and Deci (2001) present two dominating paradigms of wellbeing: the hedonic and the eudaimonic. Hedonic wellbeing emphasises attaining positive feelings such as happiness that also hold the potential to boost physiological health whereas the eudaimonic wellbeing refers to human flourishing and desire to reach Maslow's self-actualisation state. It aims at unveiling the best that lies within us and realising our true self and living in accordance with that authentic self (Ryan & Deci 2001; Waterman 1993). Wellbeing is an indicator of how well a person has been living his/her life. That is, "The realization of potentialities denotes how well a life has been lived". In this sense, people are living a quality of life when their life activities are congruent with and following their deeply held values, directed by meaningful orientations, and enable them to be true to themselves, and thereby, "feel intensely alive and authentic, existing as who they really are" (Ryan & Deci, 2001, p. 146). These articulations echo with theoretical postulations that wellbeing consists in self-actualisation and that fully functioning people live an authentic life (Rogers, 1961; Vainio & Daukantaitė, 2016; Yu, Li, & Xiao, 2020, p. 147). In tangible terms, overall wellbeing is facilitated by a sense of pride, rejuvenation, dignity, happiness, satisfaction, economic wellbeing, physiological wellbeing, sense of place and identity.

For wellness and wellbeing to flourish, favourable policies and conducive circumstances are required given the ongoing discontentment in the manner Indigenous voices are marginalised and their heritage is showcased to privilege those in power or from a lopsided Eurocentric perspective. In the context of heritage tourism in Indigenous and under-privileged landscapes, it is impertinent to scrutinise who gets to tell the story, for whom, and in what context. For instance,

> stories told through the lens of Indigenous peoples themselves enable better understanding of Indigenous cultural landscapes, identity and place attachment. With understanding comes respect, recognition and cultural cohesion that can enable Indigenous peoples to work collectively towards a more resilient future.
>
> (Menzies & Wilson, 2020, p. 55)

This chapter is contextualised in the nexus between authenticity, heritage justice and wellbeing. Potentially, the chapter aims to offer a new perspective on sustainable heritage tourism by integrating the overall wellness and wellbeing of under-represented subaltern communities such as Indigenous and other populations that have descended from Africa. By identifying the barriers and enablers of heritage justice, it suggests a heritage justice model aimed to sustaining cultural authenticity and overall wellbeing of under-represented communities in transformative times.

Contemporary heritage tourism trends point to the visitor quest for slow immersive experiences and an elevated sense of consciousness. Also, as we move to the post-pandemic times, stakeholders on the supply and demand sides are taking sustainability seriously (Ateljevic & Sheldon, 2022; Fusté-Forné, & Hussain, 2022; Sheldon, 2020) and advocating responsible behaviour by developing a sense of place and care of place (Nandasena, Morrison, & Coca-Stefaniak, 2022, p. 289). Recent studies postulate that both areas can stimulate profound transformations in visitors as well as the societies (Chhabra, 2021; Nandasena, Morrison, & Coca-Stefaniak, 2022; Pung & Chiappa 2020; Sheldon 2020). UNWTO's sustainable development goals clearly underline pillars associated with sustainable tourism in this regard: sustainable economic growth, social inclusiveness, employment and poverty reduction; cultural values, diversity and heritage, mutual understanding, peace and security (UNWTO, 2018). Emerging trends illustrate increasing emphasis on promoting and integrating these goals in heritage tourism (Luan, Hai, An, & Thuy, 2022; Nandasena, Morrison, & Coca-Stefaniak, 2022). As pointed out by Timothy, heritage tourism is an inclusive phenomenon and it is directly related to "living cultures, folklore, arts and handicrafts, faith traditions and the everyday life of people" (2021, p. 533). By suggesting a heritage justice model, this chapter makes an important contribution from the scholarship and practitioner perspectives. As stated earlier, research on this line inquiry is sparse. Also, this chapter is unique because it integrates wellness/wellbeing elements in the heritage justice model. Wellness and wellbeing perspectives have become crucial in the post-COVID times. By integrating these elements and by identifying barriers, the author suggests a holistic pathway that calls for a collaborative effort among different stakeholders of heritage tourism. As illustrated in the forthcoming paragraphs and shared examples, heritage justice is not a stand-alone phenomenon. It is a collective effort between various private and public sector stakeholders.

Contextualising heritage justice

Only a handful of studies have appeared that offer noteworthy insights on cultural/heritage justice issues, from the perspective of under-privileged communities, and offer a discourse on possible solutions to address them. Cultural justice refers to equitable rights with regard to the use, protection and valuation of cultural resources and any amendment that needs to be made to alter the cultural texture of Indigenous heritage (Camargo, Lane, & Jamal, 2007). Within this context, issues such as, "cultural consent, cultural compensation, allocation of cultural rights, and the right of the individual to determine their actions" need to be resolved to foster cultural equity (2020, p. 174). Attention, in documented literature, is mostly centred on multiple dimensions of justice such as procedural justice, distributional justice, social justice and cultural/heritage justice. A perusal of existing literature reveals that the majority of the justice discourse is focused on addressing questions related to the existence/depth of collaborative partnerships, fair and equitable distribution of community resources, and advocating the rights and authority of Indigenous peoples and/or other under-represented communities.

Numerous items of concern overlap across matters associated with procedural justice, social justice, distributive justice, recognition justice and environmental justice and, to some extent, cultural and heritage justice. As an instance, legitimacy and ethics fostering equality are reported to be the key elements of a socially just tourism paradigm (Higgins-Desbiolles, 2010; Hultsman, 1995). The conceptual work on justice theories can be traced to the environmental justice movement (Camargo & Vázquez-Maguirre, 2021; Lee & Jamal, 2008). Environmental justice scrutinises inequitable access to tourism resources and sites such as freshwater and the manner in which wildlife impacts are dispersed in rural communities (Cole, 2017; Schnegg & Kiaka, 2018). Camargo and Vazquez-Maguire also argue that elements of cultural justice exist in environmental justice because of connectedness with the tangible and intangible heritage of Indigenous communities. The recognition perspective in justice frameworks has also been recommended (Whyte, 2010) to facilitate participation and empowerment of Indigenous communities. Social environments of Indigenous communities significantly shape this justice standpoint.

Furthermore, Figueroa and Waitt (2010) recommend employing a restorative justice perspective which advocates fixing issues associated with unfairness by producing resolution strategies and transformative solutions for victims of injustice. Van Ness (2000) presents four fundamental tenets of restorative justice: encounter (meeting between all parties, the victims, the offenders and the community members impacted by the wrong doing), amends (tangibly compensating the marginalised people), reintegration (restoring to a previous harmonious position), and inclusion (just participation across victims, offenders and the remaining community). Reconciliation between historically segregated groups (in non-Indigenous settings) and initiatives, to enforce restorative justice, also need important consideration (Higgins-Desbiolles 2003).

Based on the aforementioned, it is clear that studies examining heritage tourism solely from the lens of heritage justice need to integrate other theories of justice. Among the meagre studies that have appeared on heritage justice, Harbor and Hunt (2021) uses a micro-level perspective to offer insights on how Indigenous peoples negotiate showcasing of cultural practices and goods in a preferred manner coupled with a desire to receive equitable compensation. The authors offer suggestions to ensure that the tourism agencies are mindful and attentive to the tangible and intangible heritage resources of the marginalised community. The following paragraphs offer insights on challenges constraining the identity, authority, voice, and dignity of under-represented communities.

Menzies and Wilson (2020) stress the importance of taking a comprehensive view of the distribution and tradeoffs between benefits and costs associated with showcasing Indigenous heritage expressions for the purpose of heritage tourism, from individual as well as community standpoints. The authors note that tourism holds potential to play a positive role in that it can slow down the erosion of fragile cultures which are threatened by globalisation, Eurocentric ideologies and/or by other external agencies and government policies. For instance, heritage tourism can serve a useful purpose for many Indigenous and under-represented communities by generating awareness of a painful past and mindfulness against colonial encroachment and exclusionary practices (Fortenberry, 2021; Timothy, 2021).

In several instances, it is noted that irresponsible tourism has been planned by particularly promoting Western ideologies, using neoliberal policies; this has compromised the cultural, social and natural environments of under-represented communities in countries such as Guatemala, Mexico, New Zealand, Australia, the Greater Caribbean and Canada (Camargo & Vázquez-Maguirre, 2021; Everingham, Peters, & Higgins-Desbiolles, 2021; Fortenberry, 2014; Harbor & Hunt, 2021; Menzies & Wilson, 2020). For example, Harbor and Hunt (2021) point out that irresponsible tourism is rampant in Indigenous areas and has led to the marginalisation, endangerment and continued loss of cultural resources in a Maya community in Guatemala. The communities, in that region, are confronted by numerous challenges as they struggle to adapt to macro-environment factors that have permeated colonial and neocolonial configurations of their cultural and natural spaces (Harbor & Hunt, 2021). Consequently, several expressions of Indigenous identity have become susceptible, including tangible and intangible aspects of their culture (such as language and garb). Another undesirable outcome is the demonstration effect which has compromised the sense of self-respect in that the wealthy tourists can make the locals feel backward and poor. Furthermore, several authors reiterate that fair and equitable benefits allude most Indigenous communities and in the process of appealing to tourists, they compromise their traditional learning, medicinal and healing ways (Camargo & Vázquez-Maguirre, 2021). Other examples include occupation of land and exclusionary attempts by neo-liberal agencies such as separating the nomadic tribes from their sacred land (most national parks were developed by segregating and excluding the local communities from the land) or disrespecting them (as in the case of Ayers Rock in Australia: incense burning and other tourist practices are not mindful of the Indigenous rituals) (Brown, 1999; Everingham et al., 2021). As pointed out by Harbor and Hunt, in such cases "historical and economic exploitation and exclusionary practices are exacerbated by tourism… and can contribute cumulatively to cultural disintegration, political disenfranchisement, discontent, increased violence, and conflict in Indigenous communities" (2021, p. 215).

Undeniably, colonial pasts have left a profound impression on numerous under-privileged communities across the globe and this has exacerbated social inequalities, resulting in hostility and contestation for local resources. Furthermore, redistribution of wealth has resulted in instability and leakages in scenarios where elites partner with outside agencies to stimulate profitability at the cost of local welfare. Also, unfair distribution of power can compromise the "ability of Indigenous groups to exert their agency in management decisions related to tourism" and tend to give priority to the more privileged (the elites) (Harbor & Hunt, 2021, p. 216). Another disastrous outcome is the compromise of the sense of community. According to Harbor and Hunt, "macro-level processes such as urbanisation, industrialisation and centralisation of bureaucratic power can weaken the economic autonomy of once-isolated rural and Indigenous communities, aligning them with the needs and decisions of mass society" (2021, p. 216). They become victims of 'institutionalised individualism' which implies that they feel compelled to adapt without the traditional support mechanisms (such as religion, family, status and culture), thereby encroaching on community trust and posing a threat. Prevailing issues also include commodification, encroachment and, possession and use of tribal lands without informed consent.

Along similar lines, Camargo and Vázquez-Maguirre (2021) write that the use of cultural resources of Indigenous communities without their permission or indiscriminant compensation of their use has led to an encroachment of justice rights. Other unjust acts reported are absent local voices in tourism narratives, exclusion and poor representation as stakeholders in tourism governance, and offering tourism on the sacred sites without their permission. The authors contend that "such examples of injustices can have devastating effects on their economic opportunities, culture, and relationships with the natural environment, affecting their wellbeing and dignity" (2021, p. 372). It is noted that the postcolonial dynamics have worsened and continue to disregard local perspectives, values and identity.

Contextual specifics of heritage justice

The aforementioned challenges and barriers associated with heritage justice can be evidenced in several key heritage tourism projects/cases. One example is the Maya Train Project in Southern Mexico. It spans a route of 1,525 kilometres and 15 towns across five states in the southern part of Mexico that share portions of the Mayan jungle. According to Camargo and Vázquez-Maguirre (2021), questions have been raised about its ability to protect the rights and preferences of the Mayan communities and capability to assess the capacity of the jungle to support mass tourism in a sustainable manner. This excessively advocated project has earned the resentment of several parties, such as environmental groups, researchers, and Indigenous groups, as well as some of the private sector. From a political standpoint, Mexico is required to provide the Mayan communities the authority to decide and determine the manner in which they wish to coexist socially, economically, politically and culturally. This project holds significance because of the support extended to it, at the government level and also because several stakeholders have become cognizant of the emerging challenges encountered by the Mayan communities; a variety of injustices have come to the fore – such as colonial and postcolonial harassment and marginalisation, wide-ranging impact on their ecological and cultural resources, and awareness that mass tourism and mega-level development is likely to impact the lifestyles and authentic values of the Indigenous communities (Camargo and Vázquez-Maguirre, 2021). Camargo and Vazquez-Maguire further report that:

> the efforts destined to create favourable conditions for the development of Indigenous communities in Mexico had often ended up reproducing colonial and postcolonial patterns of exploitations. Recently, the government has been accused of faking consultations with Indigenous communities. The invitations to roundtable discussions, which lasted less than a month, were issued by government bodies that did not have the legal status to do so, and they only reached 11 out of 28 Indigenous communities and discrimination towards Indigenous communities' rights and self-determination, and also bring into question how Indigenous communities will participate and be affected by the Mayan Train project.
>
> (2021, p. 379)

Another notable scrutiny is offered by Fortenberry (2014) in regard to two port towns in the Greater Caribbean: St. George's, Bermuda and Falmouth in Jamaica. St. George's, Bermuda and its early capital offer a strategic location of study in understanding the impacts of cultural heritage tourism on heritage representation in Greater Caribbean port towns. Its domestic affairs are self-governed with the help of an elected Parliament, although its defence and military affairs continue to be managed by the Crown. The urban landscapes of St. George have been the subject of numerous deliberations. Although the Bermuda National Park Trust has developed a database for the historic structures that exist on the island, inherent bias is noted; Fortenberry writes that,

> the challenges of inequitable representation are not due to a lack of knowledge, infrastructure, or architectural integrity. Instead, they relate to policy, programmatic foci, and the challenges of tourism clientele. The conservation policy is modeled on the foundations of the U.K.'s listing system. This system prioritises architectural integrity, the

> material remains of the past, meaning that, in many cases, buildings are protected only if they retain original fabric. But enslaved Bermudians often did not inhabit these spaces.
>
> (2021, p. 260)

The town of Falmouth (a cruise ship hub) is centrally located in Jamaica. It has witnessed retarded growth in heritage tourism initiatives due to the exclusionary agenda of the cruise ship industry coupled with its isolated location and poor oversight and conservation regulations, particularly regarding the demolition of historic structures (Bray & Redfearn, 2014). For the most part, local vendors are absent in the walled enclave zone, the so-called third controlled tourist space; the local market has been relocated outside the walled utopia built by the cruise ship industry. Fortenberry writes that

> this exclusion zone bifurcates the heritage tourism landscape of Falmouth. The cruise ship industry has created an island, similar to their 'private islands' that one can visit for the day before leaving again. Equitable representation in heritage tourism does not exist due to the lack of heritage programming infrastructure and the exclusionary and enclave practices of the cruise ship industry.
>
> (2021, p. 270)

According to the author, four linked processes have triggered the inequalities and poor representation of local residents: disagreement among different stakeholder groups; conservation ethics being poorly enforced, thereby compromising the cultural authenticity of the local community; limited local capacity and resources to develop inclusive heritage programmes; and missing dual purpose of inclusive agenda that simultaneously considers the needs of the visitors and the local residents.

Next, in discussing the Altai region (a World Heritage Site) in Mongolia, Baird (2014) offers an overview of the themes at a conference focusing on Altai cultural landscapes sponsored by UNESCO. The author writes that most narratives and reports were centred on climate change in the region and

> only a few conceptualised the region as a cultural landscape and few had explicitly outlined how nomadic herders or other communities would be impacted by a World Heritage designation. In the making of heritage in the Mongolian Altai, specific views of the region, largely aesthetic, archaeological, and material, dominated the discussions, and guided how the region would be managed and interpreted for a global audience. The question remains, what does this have to do with human rights or social justice? How can a relationship exist that on one hand recognises peoples' rights, and at the same time nullifies some of the same rights?
>
> (2014, pp. 144–146)

The voices of the local herders are absent in the heritage-making plans. By conferring the World Heritage site status to the region, heritage making is mostly decided from a Eurocentric standpoint, thereby disregarding the cultural authenticity of the local community. That is, the Western experts and international heritage agencies offer recommendation on how the heritage of Altai should be showcased to the world in the absence of participation of the Mongolian officers and local agencies. The discourse on Mongolia's heritage-building efforts excludes the country's minorities and other local stakeholders, including the Indigenous Altai groups.

Several recurring challenges can be identified. For instance, inadequate localised representation on the global stage as reiterated by several scholars: "Indigenous knowledge is still filtered by Western understandings" (Durie, 2005, p. 322; Menzies & Wilson, 2020). Attention is drawn to "topics associated with inequalities and marginalisation of Indigenous identities, voice and recognition in contemporary Western political frameworks" (Menzies & Wilson, 2020, p. 53). According to Baird (2014), mediation and negotiation of heritage rights by international organisations can compromise the rights of the people they strive to safeguard because the decisions are made by outside agencies. A global rights discourse does not always take the needs of the local communities into consideration. The most recurrent barriers of heritage justice include: compromise of cultural authenticity; surging inequalities in terms of participation, representation, and decision-making in heritage matters of concern to the communities; disregard of individual and collective identities; uneven distribution of economic benefits; establishment of enclave spaces driven by corporate and/or Eurocentric agenda and dislocation to peripheral areas; unfair employment practices; absence of local voices and heritage in marketing and heritage tourism plans on the national and global stage; direction selling and products and services predominantly designed for neocolonial markets; and damage to the local identity and spaces inflicted by the World Heritage status.

Contextualizing core elements of a heritage justice paradigm

Collective responsibility is required to initiate and get involved in educational and transformative practices that hold potential to unsettle colonial spaces such as by enabling and offering anatomy to the less-privileged people to protect their heritage (Menzies and Wilson 2020). Such communities deserve the right to participate and launch cultural knowledge programmes/content in educational institutions and online platforms in a manner that promotes a shared sense of pride, dignity and cultural continuity. As an instance, the local populations also need empowerment to uphold their cultural authenticity by keeping their "traditional names for landscapes and revered shared spaces" (Menzies and Wilson, 2020, p. 63). To deal with issues associated with heritage justice, Camargo and Vázquez-Maguirre (2021) suggest scrutiny from the lens of dignity and suggest integrating a humanist dimension in addition to procedural, distributive, procedural and recognition justice perspectives. That is, the authors argue that humanistic theory can offer unique insights on how to deal with injustice related to the manner in which tourism resources, from under-privileged environments, are utilised and promoted. Lee and Jamal (2008) proposed an environmental justice paradigm to deal with unfairness associated with human–environment relations that impacted marginalised and under-privileged Indigenous peoples. The paradigm presented several integrated justice perspectives to scrutinise the manner in which environmental effects of tourism spread across different populations and their degree of involvement and say in decision-making processes. The paradigm also integrated perspectives associated with procedural and distributive justice.

What is required is a viable strategy aligned with the SDGs (Sustainable Development Goals) that focus on the resolution of issues related to exclusion, fairness and authority, barriers restricting the design of products and experiences by those who belong to the community to honour the ecological and socio-cultural foundations and relationships (Harbor & Hunt, 2021, p. 217). Four independent innate drives (to acquire, to defend, to bond and to comprehend) were presented by Pirson and Steckler (2018) to inform managerial practices that foster human dignity and wellbeing. These regulations require support in terms of fair and honest exchanges, enhancement of existing properties, dissemination of relevant information in a timely manner and "respecting the other beliefs even when disagreeing and helping to protect rather than harm or abandon the other" (Camargo and Vázquez-Maguirre 2021, p. 378). Dignity can be compromised by unfavourable socioeconomic practices such as injustice, exclusionary practices, marginalisation and lack of recognition (Pirson et al., 2019). Therefore, a humanistic management approach can be a useful remedy and help to restore, protect and promote dignity.

Grounded in humanistic principles, Camargo and Vázquez-Maguirre (2021) posit that government and the tourism industry responsibilities should focus on three thresholds of dignity: restoration, protection and the promotion of dignity and justice. Restoration should be guided by principles such as decent and meaningful work and prioritisation of entrepreneurship opportunities for Indigenous people. This calls for government and industry initiatives and embracing responsibilities such as developing initiatives to integrate marginalised voices, ensuring the private industry complies with the labour laws and promoting the development of community-based tourism and prioritising the local enterprises in destination marketing strategies, and setting up an entrepreneurial ecosystem that fosters fair practices and the development of micro-businesses. Industry obligations, in this regard, need to ensure employment of Indigenous communities, adherence to labour laws, and integrating under-represented businesses in the value chain portfolio. Protection is guided by principles such as self-determination and self-control which require the government to ensure enforcement of human and Indigenous rights, respect the wish of Indigenous communities to participate or abstain in tourism development initiatives, ensuring participatory opportunities in tourism development agencies and protecting their interests and resources from mass tourism exploitation. The industry obligations with regard to protection call for respect for under-represented communities, taking permission before integrating the Indigenous narratives and resources in the tourism offerings, forging mutually respectful partnerships with local residents, taking views of the local communities on matters that impact their lifestyles and environment, developing environmentally sensitive programs and enhancing the ecological center in indigenous areas. With regard to the third dignity threshold (promotion), Camargo and Vázquez-Maguirre (2021) use the principle of recognition and suggest responsibilities for the government and the industry. Government obligations include: "developing cultural projects that reconnect local peoples with their cultural heritage and ecosystems; helping to advance an agenda of development according to local world views; and promoting cultural heritage and Indigenous knowledge internationally as a source of national pride" (2021, p. 384). The industry obligations include recognising the under-privileged groups as important partners in decisions related to the planning, development and management of tourism; promoting their products in tourism markets; and acknowledging the Indigenous groups are legal and important stakeholders of tourism.

Menzies and Wilson (2020) present a conceptual paradigm that captures various ways of deciphering Indigenous/under-privileged heritages such as from the standpoint of nature/culture, ethics of care, sustaining cultural spaces and cultural authenticity, and a sense of identity and safeguarding knowledge inherited from previous generations. They suggest key Indigenous narratives based on axiology, ontology and epistemology delineations. Evidently, nature and culture are closely inter-connected and this intertwining is the foundation of Indigenous heritage. The authors point out that the ten outstanding universal value (OUV) criteria that segregate cultural and natural heritage hold a neo-colonial perspective and this is detrimental to the protection of Indigenous heritage. It is pointed out that the idea of nature and landscape as personified and that Indigenous peoples understand that impacts create a hurt to that personhood. There is a deep connection of indigeneity with place that resonates with all Indigenous peoples; and which threatens their identity when place and people are separated.

(2020, p. 65)

For most Indigenous peoples across the globe, land and all it contains or "all that is therein conceived is integral of a mutually living entity" (Menzies & Wilson 2020, p. 66). It is important to recognise the significance of place naming and the notion of ancestral landscapes need recognition in the World Heritage status (WHS) designation process.

Fortenberry recommends "re-orientation of the heritage planning structures in several key areas:

1 The build heritage protection guidelines need to be altered to make them less focused on European colonial built heritage and these policies need to be enforced.
2 The heritage planning priorities need to include aspects of intangible heritage, with an equitable emphasis on oral histories and traditions that are vital to the cultural heritage of the Afro-Bermudians.
3 Incorporating a deeper civic engagement in the planning process will provide multiple, diverse voices for the protection of tangible and intangible heritage." (2021, p. 372)

Harbor and Hunt suggest a preliminary paradigm to inform the future agenda on heritage justice in the context of Indigenous tourism. This framework integrates compensation justice, recognition justice and procedural/participative justice and direct participation:

- *Compensation justice*: Processes and procedures need to be developed to organise and manage the tourist flows for more fair and equitable distribution of economic costs and benefits. However, in the context of cultural justice, much greater attention will need to be paid to addressing the intangible as well as tangible impacts of cultural tourism development.
- *Recognition justice*: Mechanisms are needed to ensure Indigenous peoples are accorded recognition status and due recourse if they experience discrimination and unfair treatment. This is closely related to procedural and participative justice, as well as direct participation.
- *Procedural/participative justice*: The Indigenous peoples need to be directly involved in tourism development as well as in the management and marketing of their tourism offerings. Tourism was playing a significant role to facilitate economic wellbeing as well as cultural wellbeing, facilitating not just agency but also autonomy to develop cultural tourism as they wished, through direct engagement and participation in the process. When asked how he learned the job skills he needed to be a guide, one respondent replied simply, "*It's my life. I lived it.*" (2021, p. 229)

In summary, the authors call for a local emic perspective that is mindful of fragile and sensitive aspects of under-represented communities. It is important to understand that their socio-cultural values and economic requisites shapes their viewpoint of

what constitutes fair and equitable outcomes of tourism. Institutional structures for the regulation of tourism, mechanisms for procedural justice as well as participatory planning to ensure that community members have voice and control over tourism development, may be needed as tourism continues to develop.

(2021, p. 230)

Baird (2014) suggests an upstream framework centred on the needs of the local communities within the parameters deemed important by them that empowers them to make decisions based on their priorities and values. In other words, one of the key aims should be to situate the custodians of local heritage within a place of power so that local contexts and voices can be connected to the external agencies. According to Baird, "by reclaiming power and by re-appropriating language or tactics or bringing to light just how certain policies or practices perpetuate inequalities, this approach allows for varied voices in the community to decide their categories of relevance" (2014, p. 150). Here, the significance of integrating a social justice perspective of rights is advocated; it is argued that it can assist in recognising that all heritage is subject to contestation and various perspectives of heritage can produce different tangible outcomes shaped by a variety of heritage procedures, such as policies, directives and a set of rules. The key challenge lies on how a narrative is interpreted and conveyed, by whom and for whom.

Conclusion

Undeniably, the pandemic halted heritage tourism across the globe. However, it also inspired the need for resiliency and led to technological adoption even by conventional tech-wary institutions. For instance, as Bertacchini et al. (2021) write that the COVID-19 crisis obligated museums to reconsider their tactics on strategies associated with audience engagement and economic sustainability. In fact, it speeded up the convergence between the digital and physical experience realms.

Demand patterns have been impacted with the surge in bleisure, workations, slow travel, staycations, transformational experiences and regenerative tourism. Regenerative tourism can be described as a form of tourism that is

about giving back more than we take. It is about understanding that soil, water and all living beings are a part of us and therefore our well-being. The regenerative paradigm brings nature and communities at the decision-making table as equal partners to create a flourishing local economy.

(Ateljevic & Sheldon 2022, p. 268)

According to Bhalla and Chawdhary, "regeneration has become a necessity for the planet's survival, but it requires restoring deep spiritual inner life and awakening" (2022, p. 388). These principles are aimed at various forms of special interest tourism and cultural/heritage tourism belongs to this niche category. Transformative experiences in heritage tourism settings rely on slow-paced immersions and bonding with the place and its host communities, thereby offering opportunities to elevate mindfulness towards ethical practices and support of inclusive strategies.

As postulated by Sheldon, visitors today are looking for a new type of experience that "is part of the awakening of consciousness, and creates more self-awareness, more self-inquiry into the purpose of life, living by a higher set of values, and making greater contributions to others" (2020, p. 2). As an instance, workcation trends have enabled workers to work remotely from a destination of their choice and this has led to a surge in bleisure

Modelling heritage justice for under-represented communities 159

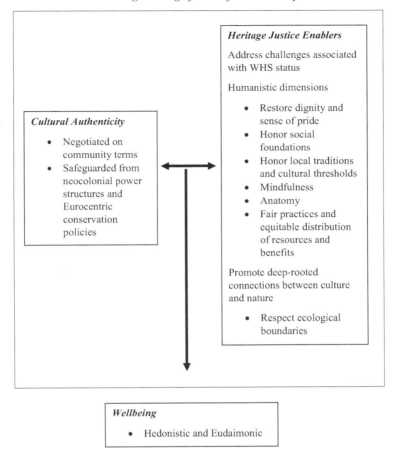

Figure 12.1 Heritage justice paradigm.

travelers. Digital nomads belong to this category. Digital nomads are traveling while they work (Aroles, Granter, & Vaujany, 2020) and are in quest of an authentic and meaningful life. There is an increase in demand for co-working spaces that offer work and travel packages for extended work stays. These spaces offer potential to stimulate authentic heritage tourism and rural regeneration processes that benefit the marginalized communities.

It has become crucial for heritage tourism stakeholders to plan and promote their cultural and heritage resources in a manner that the under-represented communities benefit equitably and have the autonomy to shape the manner in which the authenticity of their heritage is safeguarded and showcased. Figure 12.1 captures the key enablers/pillars of heritage justice that can uphold tangible and intangible attributes of cultural authenticity and are guided by a humanistic approach (by fostering dignity, fair treatment and compensation, identity, and interactive civic engagement), and sustainable planning of local capacity to foster the overall wellbeing of local communities in an ethical manner. Intersections exist between different enablers of heritage justice integrating the core elements of other dimensions of justice such as environmental, social, compensation, procedural, and recognition. Evidently, the extant literature suggests that several factors have challenged the cultural authenticity such as colonial and neo-colonial policies. Undeniably, if strategically planned, sustainable heritage tourism can act as a buffer to counter Eurocentric ideologies and assist in safeguarding the cultural authenticity of local heritage, mindfully improving/expanding local capacity to generate economic benefits and enhancing a sense of cultural identity. Such initiatives can be facilitated by "proactive stakeholder and community engagement through public forums and workshops that foster authentic dialogue among the parties" (Camargo and Vázquez-Maguirre, 2021, p. 372). This calls for a coordinated effort, dedicated towards inclusivity and wellbeing. Key responsibility lies on the shoulders of the cultural custodians, the government, and other stakeholders who represent ancillary sectors. For instance, the government needs to implement policies that are mindful towards the Indigenous perspective and ensure that these under-represented communities are equitably showcased in marketing messages.

As shown in Figure 12.1, cultural authenticity is crucial to inform and guide the enablers of heritage justice and vice versa. That is, heritage justice can help safeguard cultural authenticity in return. Cultural authenticity refers to a negotiated version of objective authenticity. As argued earlier in the chapter, culture evolves and the purest version of authenticity is an impossible feat. Hence, cultural authenticity is considered realistic and closest to the pristine version. The model also illustrates that cultural authenticity and heritage justice need to be integrated in the heritage tourism agenda to facilitate the overall wellbeing of the under-represented communities. It is also important to align all initiatives and goals with the SDGs. Many of the cultural landscapes of Indigenous communities have been or are in the process of being endorsed with the WHS. That said, WHS status has resulted in unfair practices triggered by Eurocentric ideologies. The SDGs can lend credence particularly to the humanistic enablers of heritage justice on the world stage. Its principles can assist in envisioning a rights-based approach by including those who are outside the global organisations to ensure that counter-narratives are heard and conflicts are mediated using localised perspectives (Baird, 2014). Structured on the aforementioned, the overarching goal of a heritage justice agenda holds potential to reorient heritage tourism programmes by looking to under-privileged communities and trusting their knowledge, instinct and competencies in heritage making that safeguard their cultural authenticity in a flourishing manner. This will ensure that they live their life well, staying true to themselves, nurturing a sense of being that is in congruence with their cultural and deeply held values.

References

Aroles, J., Granter, E., & Vaujany, F.-X. (2020). 'Becoming mainstream': The professionalisation and corporatisation of digital nomadism. *New Technology, Work and Employment*, 35(1), 114–129.
Association of Critical Heritage Studies (2022). Race and Heritage. Spring Symposium on Heritage Justice. https://www.criticalheritagestudies.org/heritage-justice-symposium-series.
Ateljevic, I., & Sheldon, P. J. (2022). Guest editorial: Transformation and the regenerative future of tourism. *Journal of Tourism Futures*, 8(3), 266–268.
Baird, M. F. (2014). Heritage, human rights, and social justice. *Heritage & Society*, 7(2), 139–155.
Belhassen, Y., Caton, K., & Stewart, W. P. (2008). The search for authenticity in the pilgrim experience. *Annals of Tourism Research*, 35(3), 668–689.
Bertacchini, E., Morelli, A., & Segre, G. (2021). The COVID-19 pandemic and structural change in the museum sector: Insights from Italy. In *Cultural Industries and the COVID-19 Pandemic* (pp. 177–193). Routledge.
Bhalla, R., & Chowdhary, N. (2022). Green workers of Himalayas: evidence of transformation induced regeneration. *Journal of Tourism Futures*, (ahead-of-print).

Bray, K., & Redfearn, C. H. (2014). Poverty in paradise. In Nelson, L. P. and Chappell, E. A. (Eds.), *Falmouth Jamaica: Architecture as history* (pp. 228–249). University of the West Indies Press.

Brown, T. J. (1999). Antecedents of culturally significant tourist behavior. *Annals of Tourism Research*, 26(3), 676–700.

Camargo, B., Lane, K., & Jamal, T. (2007). Environmental justice and sustainable tourism: The missing cultural link. *The George Wright Forum*, 24(3), 70–80.

Camargo, B. A., & Vázquez-Maguirre, M. (2021). Humanism, dignity and indigenous justice: the mayan train megaproject, Mexico. *Journal of Sustainable Tourism*, 29(2–3), 372–391.

Chhabra, D. (2021). *Resilience, Authenticity, and Digital Heritage Tourism*. Routledge.

Cole, S. (2017). Water worries: An intersectional feminist political ecology of tourism and water in Labuan Bajo. *Annals of Tourism Research*, 67, 14–24. https://doi.org/10.1016/j.annals.2017.07.018

DeSoucey, M., Elliott, M. A., & Schmutz, V. (2019). Rationalized authenticity and the transnational spread of intangible cultural heritage. *Poetics*, 75. https://doi.org/10.1016/j.poetic.2018.11.001

Durie, M. (2005). Indigenous knowledge within a global knowledge system. *Higher Education Policy*, 18, 301–312.

Everingham, P., Peters, A., & Higgins-Desbiolles, F. (2021). The (im) possibilities of doing tourism otherwise: The case of settler colonial Australia and the closure of the climb at Uluru. *Annals of Tourism Research*, 88, 103178.

Figueroa, R., & Waitt, G. (2010). Climb: Restorative justice, environmental heritage, and the moral terrains of Uluru-Kata Tjuta National Park. *Environmental Philosophy*, 7(2), 135–164.

Fortenberry, B. (2014). *Bermuda: Celebrating 400 years of history*. Routledge: London.

Fortenberry, B. R. (2021). Heritage justice, conservation, and tourism in the greater Caribbean. *Journal of Sustainable Tourism*, 29(2–3), 253–276.

Fusté-Forné, F., & Hussain, A. (2022). Regenerative tourism futures: a case study of Aotearoa New Zealand. *Journal of Tourism Futures*, (ahead-of-print).

Harrison, R. (2015). Beyond "natural" and "cultural" heritage: Toward an ontological politics of heritage in the age of Anthropocene. *Heritage & Society*, 8(1), 24–42.

Harbor, L. C., & Hunt, C. A. (2021). Indigenous tourism and cultural justice in a Tz'utujil Maya community, Guatemala. *Journal of Sustainable Tourism*, 29(2–3), 214–233.

Harvey, D. C. (2001). Heritage pasts and heritage presents: Temporality, meaning and the scope of heritage studies. *International Journal of Heritage Studies*, 7(4), 319–338.

Higgins-Desbiolles, F. (2003). Reconciliation tourism: Healing divided societies. *Tourism Recreation Research*, 28(3), 35–44. https://doi.org/10.1080/02508281.2003.11081415

Higgins-Desbiolles, F. (2010). Justifying tourism: Justice through tourism. In S. Cole & N. Morgan (Eds.), *Tourism and inequality: Problems and prospects*, (pp. 194–211). CABI.

Hultsman, J. (1995). Just tourism: An ethical framework. *Annals of Tourism Research*, 22(3), 553–567. https://doi.org/10.1016/0160-7383(95)00011-T

Johnston, R., & Marwood, K. (2017). Action heritage: Research, communities, social justice. *International Journal of Heritage Studies*, 23(9), 816–831.

Joy, C. (2020). *Heritage Justice* (Elements in Critical Heritage Studies). Cambridge: Cambridge University Press. doi:10.1017/9781108900669

Kolar, T., & Zabkar, V. (2010). A consumer-based model of authenticity: An oxymoron or the foundation of cultural heritage marketing? *Tourism Management*, 31(5), 652–664.

Lee, S., & Jamal, T. (2008). Environmental justice and environmental equity in tourism: Missing links to sustainability. *Journal of Ecotourism*, 7(1), 44–67. https://doi.org/10.2167/joe191.0

Luan, D. X., Hai, T. M., An, D. H., & Thuy, P. T. (2022). Transformation of heritage into assets for income enhancement: Access to bank credit for Vietnamese Community-based Tourism Homestays. *International Journal of Rural Management*, 09730052221101671.

MacCannell, D. (1992). Cannibalism today. In D. MacCannell (Ed.), *Empty meeting grounds*: The tourist papers (pp. 17–73). London: Routledge.

Menzies, D., & Wilson, C. (2020). Indigenous heritage narratives for cultural justice. *Historic Environment*, 32(1), 54–69.

Nandasena, R., Morrison, A. M., & Coca-Stefaniak, J. A. (2022). Transformational tourism–a systematic literature review and research agenda. *Journal of Tourism Futures* (ahead-of-print).

Pung, J., & Chiappa, G. (2020). An exploratory and qualitative study on the meaning of transformative tourism and its facilitators and inhibitors. *European Journal of Tourism Research*, 24, 2404–2404.

Pirson, M., & Steckler, E. (2018). A humanistic ontology for responsible management learning. *Available at SSRN 3162851*.

Pirson, M., Vázquez-Maguirre, M., Corus, C., Steckler, E., & Wicks, A. (2019). Dignity and the process of social innovation: Lessons from social entrepreneurship and transformative services for humanistic management. *Humanistic Management Journal*, 4(2), 125–153.

Pishief, E. D. (2012). Constructing the identities of place: An exploration of Māori and archaeological heritage practices in Aotearoa New Zealand.

Reeves, C. D., Dalton, R. C., & Pesce, G. (2020). Context and knowledge for functional buildings from the industrial revolution using heritage railway signal boxes as an exemplar. *The Historic Environment: Policy & Practice*, 1–26.

Rogers, C. R. (1961). *On becoming a person: A therapist's view of psychotherapy*. Constable: London.

Ryan, R. M., & Deci, E. L. (2001). On happiness and human potentials: A review of research on hedonic and eudaimonic well-being. *Annual Review of Psychology*, 52(1), 141–166. https://doi.org/10.1146/annurev.psych.52.1.141

Salamone, F. (1997). Authenticity in tourism: The San Angel inns. *Annals of Tourism Research*, 24(2), 305–321.

Schnegg, M., & Kiaka, R. D. (2018). Subsidized elephants: Community-based resource governance and environmental (in)justice in Namibia. *Geoforum*, 93, 105–115. https://doi.org/10.1016/j.geoforum.2018.05.010

Sheldon, P. J. (2020). Designing tourism experiences for inner transformation. *Annals of Tourism Research*, 83, 102935.

Timothy, D. (2021). *Cultural and heritage tourism*. Bristol: Channel View Publications.

Timothy, D., & Boyd, S. (2003). *Heritage tourism*. Harlow, UK: Pearson.

Vainio, M. M., & Daukantaitė, D. (2016). Grit and different aspects of wellbeing: Direct and indirect relationships via sense of coherence and authenticity. *Journal of Happiness Studies*, 17(5), 2119–2147. https://doi.org/10.1007/s10902-015-9688-7.

Van Ness, D. (2000). The shape of things to come: A framework for thinking about a restorative justice system [Paper presentation]. Paper Presented at the *Fourth International Conference on Restorative Justice for Juveniles*, Tubingen, Germany.

UNWTO. (2018). *Tourism and the sustainable development goals – Journey to 2030*. Madrid: UNWTO.

Wang, N. (1999). Rethinking authenticity in tourism experience. *Annals of Tourism Research*, 26, 349–370.

Waterman, A. S. (1993). Two conceptions of happiness: Contrasts of personal expressiveness (eudaimonia) and hedonic enjoyment. *Journal of Personality and Social Psychology*, 64(4), 678–691. https://doi.org/10.1037/0022-3514.64.4.678

Whyte, K. P. (2010). An environmental justice framework for indigenous tourism. *Environmental Philosophy*, 7(2), 75–92.

Yu, J., Li, H., & Xiao, H. (2020). Are authentic tourists happier? Examining structural relationships amongst perceived cultural distance, existential authenticity, and wellbeing. *International Journal of Tourism Research*, 22(1), 144–154.

13 Creative tourism trends

Diogo Moleiro and Lígia Ribeiro

Introduction

The emergence of the concept of creative tourism has been connected to the experience economy, which has led many researchers to compare creative tourism to experiential tourism (Baixinho et al., 2020). However, the characteristics of creative tourism make it more than just a tourist experience, as it involves a more active role for visitors and hosts through shared and co-created activities (Baixinho et al., 2020; Richards, 2014). One of the first formulations of creative tourism, by Richards and Raymond (2000), is defined as tourism that offers visitors the opportunity to develop their creative potential through active participation in experiences that are characteristic of the destination (Richards & Raymond, 2000). Creative tourism is therefore a subset of cultural tourism (Richards, 2014), as it exploits the tangible and intangible cultural resources of the destination (Galvagno & Giaccone, 2019).

The value of creative tourism lies in the integration of the tourism experience with creative content, which allows reaching new market segments (Galvagno & Giaccone, 2019). Interest in creative tourism is growing exponentially (Bakas, Duxbury, & de Castro, 2018; Chen & Chou, 2019; Galvagno & Giaccone, 2019; Remoaldo & Cadima-Ribeiro, 2019; Richards, 2014; Zhang & Xie, 2018). This growth calls for a restructuring of existing offerings, emphasising creativity as a key element of the offering (Galvagno & Giaccone, 2019). Creative experiences can be characterised according to their: (i) social dimension; (ii) skilled consumption; (iii) tourist engagement; (iv) tourist self-realisation; and (v) context specificity (Galvagno & Giaccone, 2019; Richards, 2014). The term creative refers to visitors' active interaction with the local community through participation in sharing local traditions and customs (Woosnam & Aleshinloye, 2018). The experience gained is represented as a memory, which can influence identity construction (Galvagno & Giaccone, 2019).

The first studies relating creativity to tourism were published at the end of the last century. In 1993, the production of artifacts and artistic experiences in the sphere of tourism activities was studied (Cohen, 1993). Recently, the role of co-creation in tourism has been investigated (Chathoth et al., 2016; Ross et al., 2017; Zatori, 2016), as a consumption process, made available by tourism companies (Giordano & Ong, 2017; Marques & Borba, 2017; Ottenbacher & Harrington, 2013; Prebensen & Foss, 2011; Ross et al., 2017). The literature on creative tourism focuses on two main themes: the first focuses on aspects related to the production of tourism services (Marques & Borba, 2017; Zatori, 2016) and the second highlights the need for visitors to co-create their experiences (Chathoth et al., 2016; Mossberg, 2007; Tan et al., 2013, 2014). Despite the relevance of creative tourism, there is still a need to reach a consensus on its main theoretical constituents as well as to develop further research (Chen & Chou, 2019).

This chapter analyses creative tourism at the level of key trends, with a focus on the influence of behaviour and motivation on the demand for creative tourism, stakeholders, including their economic and political implications, main catalysts, contributions of creative tourism to achieving the Sustainable Development Goals (SDGs), forecasts from 2032 to 2052, and the future opportunities and challenges inherent in creative tourism. Finally, in the conclusions, the implications and contributions of this chapter are presented. The authors believe that this chapter is very relevant because there is a clear growth in academic studies as well as an increase in practical efforts on the ground to promote creative tourism as a means of achieving sustainability.

Main trends and issues in creative tourism

Creative tourism is centred on four major areas (Figure 13.1). First, co-creation as a tourism experience, where research has focused on the management of the creative tourism experience and tourism behaviour, with a focus on defining the tourism experience, describing the processes of producing the tourism offer, and the active co-creation role of visitors in shaping their experiences, and the role of memorable experiences as an antecedent of return intentions (Calver & Page, 2013; Chathoth et al., 2016; Duxburg & Richards, 2019; Hung et al., 2016; Richards, 2014, 2020).

Second, creativity, where research has highlighted the concept and characteristics of the creative tourism experience, the role of experience as a driver for the development of a creative tourism offer (Duxburg & Richards, 2019; Tan et al., 2013, 2014), creativity as a basic element in the development of a destination, and the key factors of creative tourism experiences (Pappalepore et al., 2014; Richards, 2014); Third, cultural tourism, where research highlights the role of creative activities, based on local culture (Bec et al., 2019), as a way to engage and stimulate the visitor (Skavronskaya et al., 2020; Wood & Kenyon, 2018), with

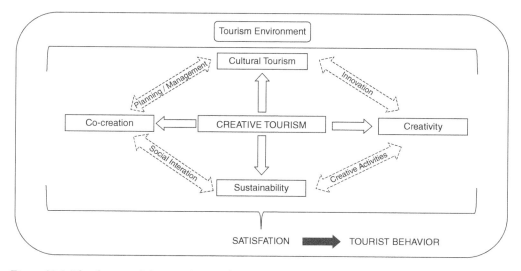

Figure 13.1 The themes of the creative tourism research.

an emphasis on authenticity, as an element that enhances visitor engagement and satisfaction with the experience (Coelho et al., 2018; Majeed & Ramkissoon, 2020).

Fourth, sustainability, where creative tourism is seen as a sustainable tourism segment that represents an opportunity for sustainable development (Hull & Sassenberg, 2012), through the provision of genuine experiences that combine local culture with learning and creativity (Duxbury, Silva, & de Castro, 2019), with a view to the wellbeing of the resident community, as an alternative to mass cultural tourism (Baixinho et al., 2020).

Creative tourism has seen a dual development, as it is either based on the traditional practices of communities or linked to more contemporary experiential industries (Pappalepore et al., 2014). This justifies that the initial concepts of creative tourism were based on learning experiences related to the traditional areas of culture and creativity (Richards, 2014). Currently, driven by the creative economy, concepts are based on the integration of tourism and the creative industries as a whole (Richards, 2014). The conceptual evolutionary stages of creative tourism therefore end up being overlapping (Duxbury & Richards, 2019).

The new conceptual trends follow the general trends in tourism (Richards, 2014). This is because conventional tourism distinctions between hosts and guests have been rapidly eroding, giving way to more dispersed networks of individuals and organisations involved in the co-creation of tourism experiences. As a result, tourism is increasingly being displaced from its conventional spaces to more dispersed, diverse, and everyday spaces (Richards, 2014). The evolution of creative tourism is dependent on the geographical context, tourism development, economic and political contexts, local cultural factors, and the public sector support of destinations (Duxbury & Richards, 2019; Richards, 2014). Hence, creative tourism no longer corresponds to a single definition, but rather to a cumulative set of interconnected concepts, reflected in a wide range of practices and contexts (Duxbury & Richards, 2019). In its definition the only constant is change, as creative tourism consists of a bundle of dynamic creative relationships between people, places, and ideas (Duxbury & Richards, 2019; Richards, 2020).

In the new tourism consumption models, visitors move beyond the traditional role of spectators to co-creators of the experience (Galvagno & Giaccone, 2019). This new trend has determined that many destinations differentiate their offer through products that give the opportunity to develop the creative potential of visitors (Richards, 2014; Zhang & Xie, 2018) and local sustainability (Duxbury, et al., 2019), since through co-creation, the visitor not only experiences the host's culture, but also fosters an attachment and appreciation of their own culture (Galvagno & Giaccone, 2019; Remoaldo & Cadima-Ribeiro, 2019).

Stakeholders and their interest and involvement in creative tourism

The creative industry holds the potential to create value, new possibilities of interaction, co-creation, the formation of new business models, the improvement of marketing strategies, the mobilisation of networks and new partnerships (Baixinho et al., 2020; Richards, 2011). In this context, local communities emerge, through the creation of small and medium-sized enterprises, as the main stakeholders in creative tourism. These apply business models that not only enhance the visitor's creativity, but also facilitate sustainability, as a daily management process of these businesses (Baixinho et al., 2020; Park, 2017; Lopes et al., 2021). In addition to the resident communities, local public entities emerge as the main stakeholders and enablers of creative tourism (Lopes et al., 2021; Ost & Saleh, 2021).

Although entrepreneurs see creative tourism as an opportunity to innovate (Park, 2017), most of these small and medium-sized businesses are essentially focused on maintaining operational activity and not so much on developing future strategies focused on customer behaviour patterns (Lopes et al., 2021). As such, public entities and policy makers should build a creative local environment and plan initiatives that can develop the creative skills of the local population and businesses operating in the sector (Li & Kovacs, 2022). Since, regardless of the type of surrounding environment, creativity is at the core of the relationship that will involve visitors, locals (Lopes et al., 2021), consumers, producers, policy makers and knowledge institutions (Richards, 2014), through networking and knowledge sharing (Baixinho et al., 2020; Ost & Saleh, 2021).

Creative tourism appropriates local cultural and heritage resources (Richards, 2014). Therefore, the management and conservation of heritage and culture have not only been vulnerable to strong economic and social disruptions but have also been challenged and reassessed from the perspective of sustainable development (Duxbury et al., 2019; Ost & Saleh, 2021). Here, it is up to policy makers to foster an environment where all stakeholders share a unified and adequate vision at the level of creative tourism management and planning, since its relevance and value is based on the close relationship with cultural heritage (Lopes et al., 2021).

Implemented policies should also build on sustainable processes based on the implementation of cross-sectoral partnerships among multiple and diverse partners (Baixinho et al., 2020), with a view to integrating peripheral regions into cross-border collaborations (Barzotto et al., 2020). Since creative tourism strengthens competitiveness and stimulates the local economy (Baixinho et al., 2020; Ost & Saleh, 2021), public entities should be the main enablers of innovation and creativity as management and planning models (Morgan, 2019).

Social contexts, institutional structures, the development of social awareness, and the effectiveness of legal regulations are what will drive creative tourism from discourse to practice (Boga & Topcu, 2020). Therefore, it is absolutely essential that the institutional arrangements that affect the institutionalisation of public policies enhance processes of innovation, sharing and competitiveness of the management and institutional structures of traditional creative businesses (Boga & Topcu, 2020; Morgan, 2019).

This sharing ideology is quite relevant since in most developing countries, traditional businesses are not considered as creative industries due to differences in concept, knowledge and application (Boga & Topcu, 2020). As such, approaches and policies are needed to ensure the implementation of participatory actions that increase cooperation between local stakeholders and entrepreneurs with public knowledge institutions (Fahmi et al., 2017).

This evidence has been observed in many countries that have already realised the value created by the relational dimension of creative tourism and its contribution to sustainable socio-economic development, and, in this context, we can highlight the U.S., the E.U. and the U.K. as they have implemented policies to develop and strengthen creative tourism in the post-2000 period through the integration of the cultural economy and the products, services and content, produced by the creative sectors, into bilateral trade agreements (Fahmi et al., 2017). Here, the relationship between tourism, development and creativity, while being guided by five different principles, environmental, economic, social, cultural and spatial or territorial, is also influenced by good governance (Pimenta et al., 2021).

Therefore, governance should guide public policies towards the development of creative product-building processes (Fahmi et al., 2017) and the creation of creative tourism links to territory, territory cohesion and competitiveness, through potential networks between economic actors and economic and cultural singularities (Barzotto et al., 2020; Boga & Topcu, 2020; Pimenta et al., 2021). These policies should intervene in culture and tourism through a set of normative resources that value and exploit co-creative experiences and the creativity of the destination (Fahmi et al., 2017; Pimenta et al., 2021).

In this dynamic, the possibility of creating synergies between the local community, visitors, and other tourism stakeholders should be central to the formulation of policies aimed at providing quality of life for populations and maintaining local authenticity (Pimenta et al., 2021). Valuing culture, experience, co-creation, community participation, and the relationship between visitors and the overall reality of destinations emerge as guiding pillars of creative tourism (Remoaldo & Cadima-Ribeiro, 2019), which materialises the notion of local in creative tourism (Pimenta et al., 2021).

Catalysts

As main catalysts of creative tourism we can highlight: (i) visitor behaviour, since tourism is influenced by human interactions and their behaviours (Fang, 2020; Kandampully et al., 2018; Lopes et al., 2021; Qiu et al., 2018; Scott, 2020), which influences the creative experience (Moyle et al., 2019; Prebensen et al., 2014; Wood & Kenyon, 2018; Skavronskaya et al., 2020); (ii) visitor motivation, as visitors are increasingly influenced by the authenticity of the experience (Cohen, 1979; Otto & Ritchie, 1996), which is enhanced through creativity (Coelho et al., 2018; Cropley, 1999; Lopes et al., 2021; Majeed & Ramkissoon, 2020). That is, behaviour as motivation will influence tourism demand, which is evident in the new dynamics of the sector (Coelho et al., 2018; Lopes et al., 2021; Moscardo, 2020; Richards, 2019; Sheldon, 2020; Teoh et al., 2021; Volo, 2021; Xiang et al., 2021); (iii) information and communication technologies, as they play an intermediary role in transforming creative intellectual capital into economic value, being the driving force of creative tourism (Pearson & Saunders, 2013); (iv) the Internet and digital technology are indispensable elements in creative tourism, as tools to enhance creativity, competitiveness and innovation (Chathoth et al., 2016; Della Lucia & Trunfio, 2018; Kirillova et al., 2017; Mossberg, 2007; Lopes et al., 2021; Tan et al., 2013, 2014; Richards, 2020; Ross, 2020; Wang et al., 2020); (v) social media, as they act as an intermediary in the promotion and distribution of creative products and the expansion of cultural values (Ahmad & Ribarsky, 2018); (vi) creative cities, as they add value to urban culture and socioeconomic life (Richards, 2020; Xiang et al., 2021); (vii) culture and territory, as these are the main resources of creative tourism (Garcês et al., 2018; Lopes et al., 2021; Majeed & Ramkissoon, 2020; Ramkissoon, 2020; Richards, 2020; Skavronskaya et al., 2020; Wen et al., 2020; Xiang et al., 2021); (viii) the role of local communities and entities, as they are the main stakeholders and enablers of creative tourism (Baixinho et al., 2020; Park, 2017; Lopes et al., 2021; Ost & Saleh, 2021); and (ix) sustainability, as this integrates and cohabits in the creative experience itself (Baixinho et al., 2020; Duxbury et al., 2019; Hull & Sassenberg, 2012).

Contributions of creative tourism to the sustainable development goals

Creative tourism can be seen as a tool that can achieve the SDGs (Baixinho et al., 2021). This is because creative tourism strengthens competitiveness and stimulates the economy (Baixinho et al., 2020; Ost & Saleh, 2021) and generates significant economic benefits (Blapp & Mitas, 2017). In other words, the goal of ending poverty can be achieved as economic growth, decent work, and development at all levels is promoted through job creation.

Creative tourism can be used as a tool to create stronger and more meaningful links between the social, economic, and environmental goals of the SDGs (Blapp & Mitas, 2017; Ost & Saleh, 2021). Since development starts from the communities' own latent needs, in the search for alternatives that provide benefits at all levels, creating conditions for the community to participate in the local development process, as an agent of its own development. This is indirectly related to the improvement of education, welfare, and health, since the revenues from tourism can be directed to the improvement of health, education, and training services.

Creative tourism facilitates building resilient infrastructure, promoting inclusive and sustainable industrialisation and innovation. As such, places are lived according to new expectations, images, and symbols where residents and visitors experience them through practices that offer new opportunities for interaction, integrating participatory activities that foster learning (Ost & Saleh, 2021). In this perspective, another SDG is achieved, as these new opportunities for interaction build the foundations for an inclusive and peaceful society, measured by multicultural and interfaith tolerance and understanding.

Creative tourism values the cognitive, cultural, symbolic capital and collective memory, which opens the way for a greater respect for the preservation of community characteristics, which will positively affect the cohesion of communities, self-confidence, cooperation and the pride of locals (Blapp & Mitas, 2017). To ensure this commitment, creative tourism, by distancing itself from mass tourism, decreases the tourist flow, which allows minimising negative impacts on the territory and the community, and thus meets the SDGs, namely, making cities more inclusive, safe, resilient and sustainable by ensuring sustainable production and consumption patterns (Blapp & Mitas, 2017; Della Lucia & Trunfio, 2018; Lopes et al., 2021).

In short, creative tourism is a strong promoter of the notion of cultural identity of residents and their creativity to create unique products that emphasise the contact of visitors with their local traditions. It is also an asset for creating jobs, training human resources, attracting resources, installing equipment, and developing infrastructure and accessibility. Creative tourism can contribute to ensure the revitalisation of the local economic fabric, through the integration of endogenous local resources, based on practices stimulated by innovation and reinforced by new support policies (Blapp & Mitas, 2017; Della Lucia & Trunfio, 2018; Duxbury & Richards, 2019).

Predictions for 2030, 2040 and 2050

The massification of cultural tourism has emerged as an opportunity for the development of creative tourism as a consequence of the changes in the motivations and profiles of the visitors in the present decade (Remoaldo & Cadima-Ribeiro, 2019). In this perspective, the management and planning of creative tourism emerges as a challenge for the next decades of 2030, 2040 and 2050.

Creative tourism will develop under the premise of sustainability to achieve local development since the concept of sustainability is a guiding principle capable of contributing to development focused on local resources (Galvagno & Giaccone, 2019). Creative tourism is therefore expected to value alternative and responsible practices that respect local identity, the needs and aspirations of local communities, their authenticity and environmental preservation (Majeed & Ramkissoon, 2020). It will likewise highlight its role as a link between local identity and local development, as an integrator/conciliator between the interests of the visitor and those of the resident community (Duxbury & Richards, 2019) since local development is understood as a process that involves local communities as the main beneficiaries of creative tourism.

In this perspective, local actors will be given a greater role in the formulation of strategies, decision-making and implementation of creative activities (Galvagno & Giaccone, 2019), which will ensure the development of the territory as a socio-cultural and natural support of the tourism activity. Therefore, creative tourism is expected to assume the role of an active agent in the enhancement of the territory and the preservation of the local cultural heritage (Richards, 2020; Xiang et al., 2021) through the implementation of partnerships, since sustainability, as the basis of creativity, requires efficient and cross-sector collaborations between multiple and diverse partners (Baixinho et al., 2020; Richards, 2011; Morgan, 2019). Thus, the influence of institutional support for innovative regions and regional resilience will be recognised since creativity will be increasingly grounded in innovation as a place-based approach, a result of changing resilience and competitive conditions (Ost & Saleh, 2021).

Finally, creative tourism is expected to be increasingly based on the integration of backward or peripheral regions into cross-border collaborations so that innovation synergies are achieved (Barzotto et al., 2020). Thus, reformulations in creative tourism planning are expected to occur so that it is focused on a socio-ecological model of innovation (Chathoth et al., 2016; Della Lucia & Trunfio, 2018; Kirillova et al., 2017; Mossberg, 2007; Lopes et al., 2021; Richards, 2020; Ross, 2020; Wang et al., 2020), which directly affects quality of life, experiential learning, implementation of entrepreneurial training and assistance models, encouragement of social training, innovation, and the revitalisation of regional and local stakeholder coalitions (Duxbury & Richards, 2019; Morgan, 2019).

Opportunities and challenges

Research on creative tourism has focused on a macro approach based on the creative economy and cultural development. It would be interesting to redirect studies towards the actors involved (Galvagno & Giaccone, 2019), in particular to empirically investigate how to manage the relationships between local actors and visitors (Li & Kovacs, 2021), their motivations (Galvagno & Giaccone, 2019) and the existential dimension of creativity (Tan et al., 2013).

Although there is a growing literature on identifying and exploring the key sub-dimensions of creative tourism experiences, namely, participation, learning, self-improvement of knowledge and experiencing different cultures (Li & Kovacs, 2021), research lacks a more integrated conceptual framework, a more explicit acknowledgement and critique of temporal, conceptual and geographical contexts, a critical analysis of trajectories, a critical review of previous work considering current situations and challenges, and a sustainable development perspective (Duxbury & Richards, 2019). As such, it would be pertinent to empirically address what the real impacts and benefits of creative tourism are for host communities, from a macro perspective of sustainable development in various territorial contexts.

Another relevant aspect that emerges in multiple approaches to creative tourism is the need for the adequate planning and development of creative tourism activities (Hull & Sassenberg, 2012), as an integrated tourism offer in articulation with broader local and regional development strategies (Stipanovic & Rudan, 2014). Therefore, it would be pertinent to empirically analyse the planning and management processes of creative tourism, from its conception to its practice.

Finally, it would also be important to analyse the role of stakeholders, at the supply level, with regard to uses of heritage and culture and how these are safeguarded since creative tourism integrates local heritage and culture (Burke, 2014; Duxbury & Richards, 2019; Richards, 2014). This analysis would be pertinent, since it may be necessary to (re)consider not only the links between the tangible and intangible cultural dimensions, but also how this interconnects with natural heritage sites and, in this perspective, the concept of cultural landscapes (Baixinho et al., 2020), and its relationship with creative tourism, also emerges as a theme that can be analyzed.

Figure 13.2 shows a possible conceptual map that interconnects these themes, as paths for future research.

Conclusions

Creative tourism is a promising and developing field of research (Li & Kovacs, 2021). There is a growing awareness that visitors actively seek participatory and learning experiences during their trips (Richards, 2014). From this perspective, and to respond to this new demand, creative tourism is seen as a clear solution to changes in tourism demand, as well as an antidote to the mass reproduction of culture, as the creativity generated between local people and visitors is harnessed to maximise the distinctiveness of places (Richards, 2010).

In this perspective of new uses of culture, as a key resource of creative tourism, human, social, natural and symbolic capital, good governance, respect for differences and diversity, solidarity, cooperation and appreciation of place, emerge as the main driving forces of creative tourism (Pimenta et al., 2021). The use of culture determines that creative tourism brings a new approach to the tourism industry, one that presupposes to benefit people, communities and the collective and cooperative work (Remoaldo & Cadima-Ribeiro, 2019).

However, despite growing academic interest, as well as increasing practical efforts on the ground to promote creative tourism, the literature to date has largely been confined to addressing the potential of creative tourism, and to a lesser extent how creative tourism experiences occur in places or across peoples (Chen & Chou, 2019; Galvagno & Giaccone, 2019; Wang et al., 2020; Zhang & Xie, 2018) as well as lacking an analysis of creative tourism from a local and regional development (Stipanović & Rudan, 2014) and sustainable development perspectives, particularly for the enjoyment of cultural intangibles (Duxbury & Richards, 2019; Richards, 2014).

The chapter expands the knowledge base of the field of creative tourism and offers three main contributions: first, it proposes a comprehensive overview of the existing literature on the topic, identifying the main strands of study: constructing the tourist experience; defining creative tourism and analysing the creative experience from the visitor's perspective, in which creativity and co-creation can be applied to a variety of different empirical contexts; cultural tourism as a basis for creative tourism; and the relationship of creative tourism to sustainability.

Secondly, it provides insight into the role of creativity in the development of places and destinations, as this is seen a key element in differentiating the destination's tourism offer, thus providing an incentive for tourism organisations and policy makers involved in destination policy formulation to enhance local specificities based on creative processes. Thirdly, it allows several paths for future research in creative tourism to be identified; namely, exploring a more targeted approach to those involved, impacts, benefits, role of co-creation as a creative experience with a view to sustainable and competitive development.

Creative tourism trends 171

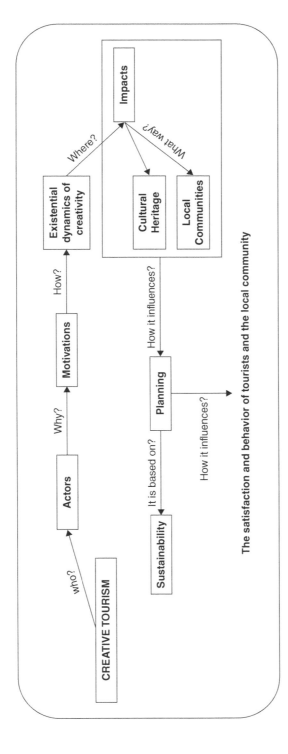

Figure 13.2 Opportunities and challenges of future research on creative tourism.

This chapter presents some practical implications regarding the research: (i) usefulness for scholars working in tourism but who are not sufficiently aware of this topic; (ii) exemplifies the general framework and academic development of creative tourism; and (iii) recognition by managers and policy makers that creative tourism experiences are the result of the co-creation process, based on creativity, in which collaboration among all stakeholders is necessary. Finally, it is relevant to justify that proper planning, management and development of creative tourism contributes to meet the growing demand for participatory and memorable experiences, to decrease the negative effects of the COVID-19 pandemic, and to differentiate and make a tourist destination competitive (Baixinho et al., 2020).

References

Ahmad, N. & Ribarsky, J. (2018). *Towards a Framework for Measuring the Digital Economy*. OECD Headquarters, Paris, France, 19–21 September 2018.

Baixinho, A., Santos, C., Couto, G., Albergaria, I., Silva, L., Medeiros, P., & Simas, R. (2020). Creative tourism on Islands: A review of the literature. *Sustainability 12*, 10313.

Bakas, F., Duxbury, N., & de Castro, T. (2018). Creative tourism: Catalysing artisan entrepreneur networks in rural Portugal. *International Journal of Entrepreneurial Behavior & Research*, 24, 731–752.

Barzotto, M., Corradini, C., Fai, F., Labory, A., & Tomlinson, P. (2020). *Revitalizing Lagging Regions: Smart Specialization and Industry 4.0*. London: Routledge.

Bec, A., Moyle, B., Timms, K., Schaffer, V., Skavronskaya, L., & Little, C. (2019). Management of immersive heritage tourism experiences: a conceptual model. *Tourism Management*, 72, 117–120.

Blapp, M., & Mitas, O. (2017). Creative tourism in Balinese rural communities. *Current Issues in Tourism*, 21(11), 1–27.

Boga, S., & Topcu, M. (2020). Creative economy: A literature review on relational dimensions, challenges and policy implications. *Economics*, 8(2), 149–169.

Burke, S. (2014). Creative clustering in small island states: the case of Trinidad and Tobago's carnival industry. *Journal of Caribbean Culture*, 60(1), 74–95.

Calver, S. and Page, S. (2013). Enlightened hedonism: exploring the relationship of service value, visitor knowledge and interest, to visitor enjoyment at heritage attractions. *Tourism Management*, 39, 23–36.

Chathoth, P., Ungson, G., Harrington, R., & Chan, E. (2016). Co-creation and higher order customer engagement in hospitality and tourism services: A critical review. *International Journal of Contemporary Hospitality Management*, 28, 222–245.

Chen, C., & Chou, S. (2019). Antecedents and consequences of perceived coolness for Generation Y in the context of creative tourism: A case study of the Pier 2 Art Center in Taiwan. *Tourism Management*, 72, 121–129.

Coelho, M., Gosling, M., & Almeida, A. (2018). Tourism experiences: core processes of memorable trips. *Journal of Hospitality and Tourism Management*, 37, 11–22.

Cohen, E. (1979). A phenomenology of tourist experiences. *Sociology*, 13, 179–201.

Cohen, E. (1993). The heterogeneization of a tourist art. *Annals of Tourism Research*, 20, 138–163.

Cropley, A. (1999). Creativity and cognition: producing effective novelty. *Roeper Review*, 21(4), 253–260.

Della Lucia, M., & Trunfio, M. (2018). The role of the private actor in cultural regeneration: Hybridizing cultural heritage with creativity in the city. *Cities*, 82, 35–44.

Duxbury, N., & Richards, G. (2019). Towards a research agenda for creative tourism: Developments, diversity, and dynamics. In Duxbury, N., Richards, G., (Eds.), *A Research Agenda for Creative Tourism* (pp. 1–14). Cheltenham, UK: Edward Elgar Publishing.

Duxbury, N., Silva, S., & de Castro, T. (2019). Creative tourism development in small cities and rural areas in Portugal: Insights from start-up activities. In D. A. Jelincic, & Y. Mansfeld (Eds.), *Creating and managing experiences in cultural tourism* (pp. 291–304). New Jersey: World Scientific.

Fahmi, F., Koster, S., & McCann, P. (2017). Creative Economy Policy in Developing Countries: The Case of Indonesia. *Urban Studies*, 54(6), 1367–1384.

Fang, W. (2020). Cultural Tourism in *Tourism in Emerging Economies: The Way We Green, Sustainable, and Healthy* (pp. 75–101). Berlin: Springer.

Galvagno, M. & Giaccone, S. (2019). *Journal of Hospitality & Tourism Research*, 43(8), 1256–1280.

Garcês, S., Pocinho, M., Jesus, S., & Rieber, M. (2018). Positive psychology and tourism: a systematic literature review. *Tourism & Management Stutdies*, 14(3), 41–51.

Giordano, E. and Ong, C.-E. (2017). Light festivals, policy mobilities and urban tourism. *Tourism Geographies*, 19(9), 1–18.

Hull, J., & Sassenberg, U. (2012). Creating new cultural visitor experiences on Islands: Challenges and opportunities. *Journal of Tourism Consumption Practice*, 4, 91–110.

Hung, W., Lee, Y., & Huang, P. (2016). Creative experiences, memorability and revisit intention in creative tourism. *Current Issues in Tourism*, 19, 763–770.

Kandampully, J., Zhang, T., & Jaakkola, E. (2018). Customer experience management in hospitality: a literature synthesis, new understanding and research agenda. *International Journal of Contemporary Hospitality Management 30*, 21–56.

Kirillova, K., Lehto, X., & Cai, L. (2017). What triggers transformative tourism experiences? *Tourism Recreation Research*, 42(4), 498–511.

Li, Q., & Kovacs, J. (2021). Creative tourism and creative spectacles in China. *Journal of Hospitality and Tourism Management*, 49, 34–43.

Li, Q., & Kovacs, J. (2022). Creative tourism and creative spaces in China. *Leisure Studies*, 41(2), 180–197.

Lopes, T., Palrão, T., & Rodrigues, R. (2021). Creativity as an opportunity to stimulate a cognitive approach to tourist demand. *Frontiers Psychology*, 12, 711930.

Majeed, S., & Ramkissoon, H. (2020). Health, wellness, and place attachment during and post health pandemics. *Frontiers in Psycholgy*, 11, 573220.

Marques, L., & Borba, C. (2017). Co-creating the city: Digital technology and creative tourism. *Tourism Management Perspectives*, 24, 86–93.

Morgan, K. (2019). The future of place based in innovation policy (as if lagging regions really mattered). In M. Barzotto, C. Corradini, F. Fai, S. Labory, & P. Tomlinson (Eds.), *Revitalizing Lagging Regions: Smart Specialization and Industry 4.0* (pp. 78–89). New York: Routledge.

Moscardo, G. (2020). Stories and design in tourism. *Annals of Tourism Research*, 83, 102950, https://doi.org/10.1016/j.annals.2020.102950

Mossberg, L. (2007). A marketing approach to the tourist experience. *Scandinavian Journal of Hospitality and Tourism*, 7(1), 59–74.

Moyle, B., Moyle, C., Bec, A., & Scott, N. (2019). The next frontier in tourism emotion research. *Current Issues in Tourism*, 22(12), 1393–1399.

Ost, C. and Saleh, R. (2021). Cultural and creative sectors at a crossroad: from a mainstream process towards an active engagement. *Built Heritage*, 5, 14. https://doi.org/10.1186/s43238-021-00032-y

Ottenbacher, M., & Harrington, R. (2013). A case study of a culinary tourism campaign in Germany: Implications for strategy making and successful implementation. *Journal of Hospitality & Tourism Research*, 37(1), 3–28.

Otto, J., & Ritchie, J. (1996). The service experience in tourism. *Tourism Management*, 17(3), 165–174.

Pappalepore, I., Maitland, R., & Smith, A. (2014). Prosuming creative urban areas: Evidence from East London. *Annals of Tourism Research*, 44, 227–240.

Park, K., Lee, J., & Lee, T. (2017). Residents' attitudes toward future tourism development in terms of community well-being and attachment. *Asia Pacific Journal of Tourism Research*, 22(2), 160–172.

Pearson, K., & Saunders, C. (2013). *Strategic Management of Information Systems*. New Jersey: John Wiley & Sons.

Pimenta, C., Cadima-Ribeiro, J., & Remoaldo, P. (2021). The relationship between creative tourism and local development: a bibliometric approach for the period 2009–2019. *Tourism & Management Studies*, 17(1), 5–18.

Prebensen, N., Chen, J., & Uysal, M. (2014). Co-creation of tourist experience: scope, definition and structure. In N. Prebensen, J. Chen, & M. Uysal (Eds.), *Creating Experience Value in Tourism* (pp. 1–10). Wallingford: CABI.

Prebensen, N., & Foss, L. (2011). Coping and co-creating in tourist experiences. *International Journal of Tourism Research, 13*, 54–67.

Qiu, R., Masiero, L., & Li, G. (2018). The psychological process of travel destination choice. *Journal of Travel & Tourism Marketing, 35*(6), 691–705.

Ramkissoon, H. (2020). Perceived social impacts of tourism and quality-of-life: a new conceptual model. *Journal of Sustainable Tourism 28*, 1–17.

Remoaldo, P., & Cadima-Ribeiro, J. (2019). Creative tourism as a new challenge to the development of destinations: The Portuguese case study. In M. Peris-Ortiz, M. Cabrera-Flores, & A. Serrano-Santoyo (Eds.), *Cultural and Creative Industries: Innovation, Technology, and Knowledge Management* (pp. 81–99). Cham, Switzerland: Springer.

Richards, G. (2010). Tourism development trajectories – from culture to creativity? *Tourism & Management Studies, 6*, 9–15.

Richards, G. (2011). Creativity and tourism: the state of the art. *Annals of Tourism Research, 38*(4), 1225–1253.

Richards, G. (2014). Creativity and tourism in the city. *Current Issues in Tourism, 17*, 119–144.

Richards, G. (2019). Creative tourism: opportunities for smaller places? *Tourism & Management Studies, 15*, 7–10.

Richards, G. (2020). Designing creative places: the role of creative tourism. *Annals of Tourism Research, 85*, 102922.

Richards, G., & Raymond, C. (2000). Creative tourism. *ATLAS News, 23*, 16–20.

Ross, D. (2020). Towards meaningful co-creation: a study of creative heritage tourism in Alentejo, Portugal. *Current Issues in Tourism, 23*(22), 2811–2824.

Ross, D., Saxena, G., Correia, F., & Deutz, P. (2017). Archaeological tourism: A creative approach. *Annals of Tourism Research, 67*, 37–47.

Scott, N. (2020). Cognitive psychology and tourism surfing the "cognitive wave": a perspective article. *Tourism Review, 75*, 49–51.

Sheldon, P. (2020). Designing tourism experiences for inner transformation. *Annals of Tourism Research, 83*, 1–12.

Skavronskaya, L., Moyle, B., Scott, N., & Kralj, A. (2020). The psychology of novelty in memorable tourism experiences. *Current Issues in Tourism, 23*(21), 2683–2698.

Stipanovic, C., & Rudan, E. (2014). Development concept and strategy for creative tourism of the Kvarner destination [Croatia]. In *Tourism and Hospitality Industry – Congress Proceedings* (pp. 507–517). Opatija, Croatia: Faculty of Tourism and Hospitality Management.

Stipanović, C. and Rudan, E. (2014). Development concept and strategy for creative tourism of the Kvarner destination. In *Tourism & Hospitality Industry 2014: Trends in Tourism and Hospitality Management*, Perić, J. (ed.), Fakultet za menadžment u turizmu i ugostiteljstvu, Opatija, pp. 1–8.

Tan, S., Kung, S., & Luh, D. (2013). A model of "creative experience" in creative tourism. *Annals of Tourism Research, 41*, 153–174.

Tan, S., Luh, D., & Kung, S. (2014). A taxonomy of creative tourists in creative tourism. *Tourism Management, 42*, 248–259.

Teoh, M., Wang, Y., & Kwek, A. (2021). Conceptualising co-created transformative tourism experiences: a systematic narrative review. *Journal of Hospitality and Tourism Management, 47*(4), 176–189.

Volo, S. (2021). The experience of emotion: directions for tourism design. *Annals of Tourism Research, 86*(1), 1–11.

Wang, C., Liu, J., Wei, L., & Zhang, T. (2020). Impact of tourist experience on memorability and authenticity: a study of creative tourism. *Journal of Travel & Tourism Marketing 37*(1), 48–63.

Wen, J., Wang, W., Kozak, M., Liu, X., & Hou, H. (2020). Many brains are better than one: the importance of interdisciplinary studies on COVID-19 in and beyond tourism. *Tourism Recreation Research, 46*(2), 1–4.

Wood, E., & Kenyon, A. (2018). Remembering together: The importance of shared emotional memory in event experiences. *Event Management*, *22*(2), 163–181.

Woosnam, K., & Aleshinloye, K. (2018). Residents' emotional solidarity with tourists: Explaining perceived impacts of a cultural heritage festival. *Journal of Hospitality & Tourism Research*, *42*, 587–605.

Xiang, Z., Stienmetz, J., & Fesenmaier, D. (2021). Smart Tourism Design: Launching the annals of tourism research curated collection on designing tourism places. *Annals of Tourism Research* *86*(C), 1–7.

Zatori, A. (2016). Exploring the value co-creation process on guided tours (the "AIM-model") and the experience-centric management approach. *International Journal of Culture, Tourism and Hospitality Research*, *10*, 377–395.

Zhang, Y., & Xie, P. (2018). Motivational determinates of creative tourism: A case study of Albergue art space in Macau. *Current Issues in Tourism*, *22*(20), 2538–2549.

1.3
Supply-side trends
Technology

Chapter 14 is by **Peter O'Connor** on *Intermediation, disintermediation and re-intermediation: Tourism distribution in the electronic age*. Two important and interrelated trends within tourism have been the transformation of intermediaries and the explosion of growth in sales through online channels. Together, these trends have resulted in the emergence of powerful online intermediaries, known as online travel agencies (OTAs) which have become one of the predominant forces influencing the success of tourism businesses. This chapter critically examines the role and development of intermediaries within tourism, critically analysing their growth, decline and subsequent reemergence as market makers holding massive sway over tourism suppliers, and assesses their corresponding implications for the sector and consumers.

Technology trends and trip planning is the topic of Chapter 15 by **Kim-Ieng Loi** and **Jose Weng Chou Wong**. With the advent and popularity of ICT adaptation and the virtual space, people tend to shorten their trip planning lead time and do more ad hoc planning during the trip. They are also more inclined to participate in sharing their trip experiences (information and advice) through social media during and post-trip, so that they themselves contribute to the repertoire of information sources from which they benefit; thereby forming a sustainable ecosystem. Acknowledging the opportunities and feasibility afforded by this phenomenon, this chapter explores the paradigm shift by: (i) reviewing the traditional trip planning literature; (ii) investigating the change in trip planning style alongside the evolution of ICTs; and (iii) identifying trends in the smart era. The chapter concludes with several potential directions that may continue to shape changes in trip planning behaviours such as immersive virtual trips, smart self-drive tourism, and impulsive travel stimulated by gamification concepts.

Wenjie Cai and **Brad McKenna** are the authors of Chapter 16 on *Digital-free tourism: The state-of-art and future research directions*. Technology is used for a wide variety of activities in tourism. However, the overwhelming use of technology in our everyday lives has resulted in a growing disconnection movement for people who desire to resist digital technology. Digital-free tourism (DFT) has become an increasingly popular phenomenon. The focus of DFT studies thus far is on the consumer side; for example, Millennials and digital wellbeing, escape, personal growth, mindfulness, technostress, relaxation, and emotions. This chapter suggests a future research agenda linking DFT with nature-based tourism, quality of life, digital wellbeing, and sustainability. Some practical applications of DFT are suggested, such as helping with Zoom fatigue, adopting DFT in tourism operations, and rebranding opportunities for destinations. The chapter closes with future trends of DFT, such as new business opportunities, growing adoption across tourism and hospitality services, and combined with other forms of tourism such as slow, rural, spa, and adventure tourism.

Metaverse as a new travel marketing platform is the title for Chapter 17 by **Min Jung Kim** and **Dae-Young Kim**. The evolution of the travel information technology (IT) systems brings the question, "what will be the next tourism information platform?" The Metaverse has attracted enormous attention because of the combination of the non-face-to-face lifestyles due to the prolonged pandemic and the convergent digital technologies such as virtual reality (VR) and augmented reality (AR). It is expected that the Metaverse will be vital for marketing toward tourists. This chapter discusses the definition of the Metaverse, some exemplary applications, and its four categories: AR, lifelogging, mirror worlds, and virtual worlds. This chapter provides meaningful insights into tourism marketing by understanding that the Metaverse can be used as a new travel IT platform and promotion channel in the digital environment.

Craig Webster and **Stanislav Ivanov** provide Chapter 18 on the *Challenges and opportunities for the incorporation of robots in hotels*. In this chapter, the authors discuss the issues that accommodation providers have to consider when transforming tasks in their operations from human labour to robotic labour. The chapter illustrates the major concerns of accommodation establishments with regards to the switchover to robotic labour, including discussions of operations, finance, human resource management, marketing, and the interior design of establishments. It highlights that the transformation will have critical implications concerning the design of establishments and the practicalities of the front-of-house and back-of-house operations. To conclude, the chapter discusses the implications of the new reality and the major concerns that the hospitality industry will have with the recruitment and management of a workforce that will service customers while at the same time working in concert with robots as co-workers.

14 Intermediation, disintermediation and reintermediation

Tourism distribution in the electronic age

Peter O'Connor

Introduction

Intermediaries, traditional and web-based, play a critical role in tourism, facilitating the marketing, distribution, and sale of travel in return for a share of the resulting revenues. Although, for strategic and financial reasons, tourism suppliers would prefer to sell directly to customers, challenges in terms of visibility and reach in today's highly competitive marketplace mean that intermediaries have attained an important role in facilitating the distribution of most tourism products, positioning themselves between customers and suppliers. The development of initially electronic and subsequently web-based distribution cemented this role, with specialisation, economies of scale/scope as well as superior market visibility allowing reinvigorated intermediaries to capture substantial market share.

While the growth of the Web initially offered the potential of a more level playing field, allowing smaller, independent, tourism suppliers to compete on an equal footing with intermediaries and their larger, frequently branded, peers, new forms of platform-based intermediaries, with substantially different business models, emerged in response to transforming consumer needs. These new players fundamentally altered the competitive landscape, gaining control of significant proportions of the travel marketplace, which has significant implications for how the sector operates in the future.

This chapter examines the role and development of intermediaries within tourism distribution, critically analysing their growth, decline and subsequent re-emergence from a consumer and supplier perspective. In particular, the value added by working with intermediaries is assessed to help demonstrate the net benefit of these players and the corresponding implications for tourism suppliers and consumers.

The importance of distribution in tourism

Due to heavy capital investments, most tourism businesses are characterised by high fixed costs, forcing them to focus on maximising gross revenues. As unsold airline seats, rooms or rental cars cannot be stored and subsequently reoffered for sale at a later date, this makes selling each product each night at the optimum rate critical to financial success (O'Connor, 1999). Tourism businesses typically use two techniques to achieve this goal – revenue management (manipulating room rates in response to demand to maximise achieved revenues) and distribution (using multiple distribution channels to maximise visibility, ease of booking and subsequent sales).

From the tourist's perspective, organizing travel is challenging at the best of times. With a myriad of options available, identifying the product or service that is right for them can be difficult and frustrating (Buhalis & Laws, 2001). Thus, for suppliers, gaining visibility in front of potential customers searching for solutions is a key issue. Even the best hotel in the world will not be successful if it cannot be found and booked by potential customers. The intangible nature of travel, which cannot be inspected or experienced prior to purchase and is thus completely reliant on information to help customers make purchase decisions, heightens this dependence (Bilgihan et al., 2014). With the consequences of a suboptimal choice in mind, travellers seek out as much detailed, relevant, and topical information as they can to minimise risk and make the right selection. Such information has traditionally been accessible in two ways; directly from suppliers or through a series of third parties known as intermediaries (Buhalis and O'Connor, 2005).

Traditional intermediaries include travel agencies, who typically sell individual travel components and vacation packages to consumers through high-street retail stores; tour operators, who assemble transportation, accommodation, and other travel elements into packages, selling the resulting packages for an all-inclusive price, thus simplifying travel planning for customers; travel management companies (TMCs), who manage travel on behalf of businesses and corporate travellers; and destination management organisations, public/private partnerships charged with promoting and managing tourism within a region (Leung et al., 2014). Each, in effect, acts as an information broker, leveraging their knowledge and experience to selectively filter supply to find the product/service most closely matching the customer's need (and frequently facilitating the resulting booking transaction), thus bridging the information gap between customers and suppliers (O'Connor and Frew, 2003).

In the past, intermediaries typically interacted with customers through either personal contact or print-based media. Both methods are inefficient, with print, in particular, being one-dimensional and becoming outdated quickly (O'Connor, 2008). While, since dynamic data can be included, personal contact is better, using it is time-consuming and expensive. As travel expanded, and the number of options/combinations possible exploded, intermediaries quickly found themselves lost in a sea of possibilities, leading to incomplete and inaccurate knowledge and lessening their utility to potential customers. This prompted the adoption of IT-based systems to help better service customers' information needs. Initially, these developed as electronic internal control systems introduced by the airlines in the 1970s to manage the multiplication of fare combinations following deregulation (O'Connor, 1999). Such systems offer many advantages, including fewer capacity limitations; lower marginal cost; and more efficient communication of dynamic data such as inventory and pricing. These systems were subsequently forwardly integrated into retail travel agencies and TMCs to allow agents to search for information and make bookings for themselves. From the agent's perspective, these Global Distribution Systems (GDS), as they became known, were considerably more efficient and cost-effective than working manually, prompting widespread adoption and causing other travel suppliers, such as hotel chains and car rental companies, to develop similar systems and link them to the GDS to facilitate distribution to the travel agent community.

While an improvement on manual processes, these new systems were not without their challenges. In particular, such systems were technical and expensive to develop, maintain and operate, causing a digital divide between larger operators and the small and medium-sized enterprises (SMEs) that typify much of the tourism sector (Buhalis & Kaldis, 2008). The latter, in particular, typically do not have the resources, expertise or finances to be able to participate in such initiatives (Schegg et al., 2013). Furthermore, built for transaction efficiency, GDSs' technology and user interfaces left little opportunity for product differentiation, while their overt travel agency focus meant that their potential audience was limited (O'Connor, 1999). Adoption of the Web as a consumer search and shopping medium in the mid-1990s offered tourism suppliers an alternative route to the marketplace, shattering pre-existing relationships in the travel value chain and prompting a wave of disintermediation by allowing suppliers of all sizes to reach out and transact directly with the consumer over online channels (Kim, Bojanic, and Warnick, 2009).

The Web as a driver of disintermediation

As a distribution channel, the Web offered many potential advantages (Murphy and Chen, 2014). Its interactive nature allowed detailed, pertinent, information to be placed directly into the hands of potential customers (Murphy et al., 1996). Direct web distribution also offered major cost savings as little capital investment was required to participate and fewer middlemen meant that GDS fees and travel agent commissions could be avoided (O'Connor and Frew, 2003). In effect, this meant that tourism businesses of all sizes and types could promote to, and sell directly to, customers without the need for intermediaries (Carroll and Siguaw, 2003). With low barriers to entry and low operating costs, direct Web distribution offered the myriad of small suppliers that characterise the tourism sector the possibility to be visible in front of, and bookable by, potential customers using the developing medium to book travel components for themselves (Thakran and Verma, 2013). Most tourism suppliers quickly began experimenting with the developing medium, providing detailed product information and reservation facilities on their branded websites, leading to speculative claims about disintermediation and the death of the travel agent (Sigala and Christou, 2006).

However, while initially moderately successful, many such suppliers quickly encountered a new series of challenges, particularly in terms of the budget, resources and technical expertise needed to drive business through direct Web channels (Schegg et al., 2013). Maintaining an effective Web presence requires specialised expertise; the implementation of technical systems such as booking engines; and committing scarce marketing funds to gaining visibility and driving traffic in a crowded online marketplace. Such efforts were often beyond the capabilities of smaller tourism suppliers, many of whom lacked the awareness, expertise, budget and technical competency to be able to compete effectively on online channels (Law and Jogaratnam, 2013). Furthermore, most supplier direct websites limit their offer to just their own products. For example, visitors to an airline's website frequently only find information about that company's flights. Consumers, however, typically do not purchase travel in this way, since someone booking a flight also usually needs a hotel or rental car, or to find out something about the destination. Similarly, they would like to know about visas and health requirements (Xiang et al., 2015).

To satisfy such diverse information needs, consumers increasingly (re)turned to intermediaries, in particular through their online presences. Travel agencies, tour operators, TMCs and DMOs all introduced consumer-facing websites, endeavouring to serve/transact with customers through the developing medium. Such intermediary sites typically offered not just a more complete product range but also broader choice as they could simultaneously list products from multiple suppliers (Lee, Guillet and Law, 2013). At the same time, a new range of pure-play online intermediaries (what we today call the OTAs) also emerged, hoping to exploit the developing online travel market (Jørgensen, 2017). With their origins outside the sector, these challengers were not blinkered by pre-existing relationships or traditional ways of doing business (Murphy and Chen, 2014). In contrast to traditional agencies, most positioned themselves as double-sided platforms, consolidating demand for suppliers and providing one-stop-travel-shop access to travel brands and trip components for customers (Beritelli and Schegg, 2016). Using a combination of powerful brands, high visibility through mastery of the online search environment, superior content and, in many cases, lower pricing, these companies drove a movement towards reintermediation, causing increased proportions of business to flow through these new indirect routes to the marketplace (Law, Leung, and Wong, 2013).

This movement towards reintermediation continues (Garcia et al., 2022). As innovations continue, new, potentially powerful, alternatives continue to develop (Fountoulaki et al., 2015). Peer-to-peer vacation rentals network Airbnb now provides distribution services to hotels and destination services, while e-commerce giants such as Taobao in China and Amazon in the U.S. periodically experiment with travel distribution. Other players have taken control of the discovery side of the distribution equation, including peer-review sites such as Tripadvisor, metasearch engines such as Kayak and Skyscanner, and the general search engine Google. Being listed on such sites has become a competitive necessity and, while, since they do not facilitate transactions, technically they are not distribution channels, pressure to monetise traffic means each is becoming increasingly commercial and more visible in the travel distribution process (O'Connor, 2010). While individually small in scope, each new development eats away at suppliers' distribution advantage, causing more bookings to flow through indirect channels.

Thus, rather than prompting simplification, direct distribution and disintermediation, the growth of the Web as a consumer search and shopping medium has ultimately resulted in a complex, interconnected, and increasingly crowded network of digital channels interlinking suppliers and customers (Kracht and Wang, 2010). Most of these add value by helping to navigate travellers through the extensive range of choices available to find the products and services most appropriate to their needs, while at the same time positioning suppliers in front of relevant, qualified audiences in a cost-effective manner. As a result, travel has become deeply (re)dependent on intermediaries for sales, marketing, distribution, and financial success.

Online travel agencies – Driving the reintermediation of travel

With most players wanting to both reach out directly to customers and, at the same time, work with other points-of-sale up and down the value chain, this has resulted in a very complicated network of distribution channels (Figure 14.1), with intermediaries of different types now playing a pivotal role in travel suppliers' sales, marketing and distribution processes (Koo, Mantin and O'Connor, 2011). They help make the market by aggregating disparate supply; assisting consumers to navigate the options available; and facilitating the resulting bookings. Within leisure travel, online travel agencies (OTAs) (for example, Booking.com, Expedia Group and Trip.com (Ctrip)) have become a key demand collection source for most travel suppliers, displacing more traditional intermediaries and cementing a key role at the centre of travel distribution.

Research has shown that consumers use online travel intermediaries for a variety of reasons, including having access to the best prices (Beldona et al., 2005), superior user experience (Rajaobelina, 2018), and easier facilitation of the somewhat complicated travel booking process (Fu et al., 2010). Thanks to their multi-product, multi-brand approach, OTAs also help reduce friction for consumers, allowing them to find and book the most appropriate products and services for their needs more easily (Mohseni et al., 2018).

Tourism distribution in the electronic age 183

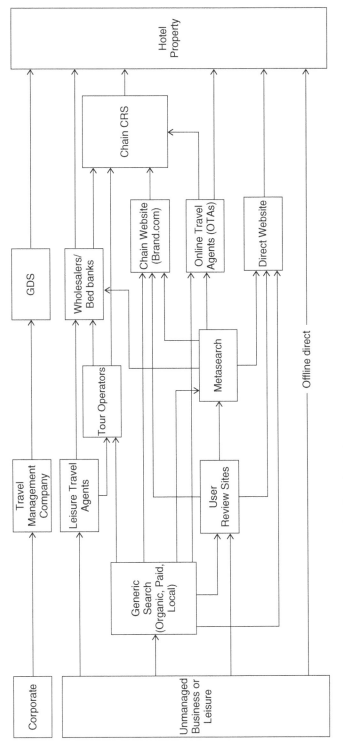

Figure 14.1 Overview of primary hotel distribution channels.

As a result, travel intermediaries tend to play a more significant role in more fragmented segments of travel such as hotels and car rentals (Toh et al., 2011). In contrast, within consolidated segments such as airline and lodging, suppliers are better able to leverage their brand power, marketing expertise and financial resources to drive more direct bookings (Stangl et al., 2016).

From the supplier perspective, OTAs bring a series of advantages. Chief among these is enhanced access to potential customers, allowing suppliers to gain visibility amongst (and be bookable by) customers, market segments and geographical markets difficult/expensive to address otherwise (Koo et al., 2011). For example, to sell to customers in China, a supplier would have to develop a Chinese-language version of their consumer-facing website, optimise it using paid search engine marketing on Chinese search engine Baidu, have a payment gateway that accepts payment from Chinese credit cards, as well as engage in promotional activities using social network WeChat. In contrast, selling through an OTA present in the Chinese market involves simply signing a contract and paying a commission for any business delivered. As a result, smaller suppliers, without the brand power, technology, and other resources to be able to drive sufficient business through direct channels, typically value the reach, visibility, and additional bookings they can gain from working with selected third-party intermediaries, allowing them to position themselves in front of a wider audience more quickly, more easily and more cost-effectively than they could do by working independently (Park et al., 2019).

Secondly, partnering with online travel intermediaries is perceived as a cost-effective way of driving additional bookings (Lv et al., 2020). Not only does it typically require little to no capital expenditure, but costs are usually pay-for-performance, with no bookings meaning no costs, which contrasts sharply with the significant, high-risk costs incurred when attempting to distribute directly. Thirdly, consumer expectations continue to evolve, forcing suppliers to relook at how they sell in the digital space. With many of their mission-critical systems decades-old and lacking the functionality or flexibility to power today's dynamic distribution environment, and with capital, cash flow and expertise strained following COVID-19, partnering with online travel agencies is seen as an easy and low-risk way to acquire the latest protocols, platforms and processes to satisfy the increasingly sophisticated needs of customers in a timely and cost-efficient manner. Lastly, since they service multiple suppliers and segments, OTAs can consolidate vast amounts of market data in real time, which can be shared with suppliers to provide valuable input into forecasting, capacity planning and revenue management.

However, working with online travel intermediaries does present some challenges. Despite evidence to the contrary, operationally the most widely cited limitation is the perceived high cost of driving bookings through online intermediary channels (Green & Lomanno, 2012). OTAs are typically compensated using commissions or through discounted net rates through the so-called merchant model (Enz & James, 2017), which many travel suppliers believe to be too high for the value delivered (ETTSA, 2018). However, proponents of this argument usually fail to consider the true cost of driving direct business. As Sabre (2018) point out, in addition to implementing and maintaining the technical infrastructure necessary to process direct bookings, to gain visibility suppliers must, at the very least, optimise Web pages for search engines in multiple geographic markets and market segments; engage in paid search campaigns; and leverage social media channels effectively to ensure they are present in customers' consideration sets (Paraskevas et al., 2011). Coupled with the low conversion rates that typify travel supplier websites, this results in substantial customer acquisition costs, typically far in excess of the pay-per-performance fees paid to online travel intermediaries. With the latter, however, highly visible, and the cost of direct bookings hidden in broader marketing and technology spending, misconceptions continue as to the high cost of working with online travel agency partners (Abdullah et al., 2022).

On a more strategic level, the tourism sector is characterised by long-standing historical relationships that result in resistance to change (Chang et al., 2019). In particular, many suppliers struggle to understand the changing nature of online travel intermediary relationships (Yin et al., 2019). Simultaneously competing and cooperating with third-party players, many smaller players struggle to adjust toward working in non-exclusive virtual alliances, leading to unnecessary conflict and lost opportunities (Beritelli & Schegg, 2016). Larger suppliers, in contrast, seem more progressive and to have embraced such partnerships with enthusiasm, squeezing as much value as possible out of these new symbiotic relationships, whilst also acknowledging that doing so does make it more difficult to differentiate in the long run (Cetin et al., 2016). With everyone working with the same portfolio of partners, and using the same technology, no one has the capacity to pull away from the pack and differentiate themselves through their distribution efforts. Suppliers, therefore, must carefully balance the relative advantages of partnering with online travel intermediaries – lower cost, faster time to market and reduced risk – with this need to find new and innovative ways to gain competitive advantage and win the customer.

Implications of reintermediation

With online travel intermediaries offering significant advantages for suppliers and consumers, it is little surprise that they have captured substantial market share and now form a key component of the distribution strategy of tourism suppliers globally (Leung, 2019). Phocuswright estimate that online travel intermediaries now represent the most significant source of indirect business for most travel suppliers, delivered over one-third of industry gross revenue in 2020 (Phocuswright, 2022). In addition to driving direct sales, OTAs also play an influencer role when travellers shop on their systems but subsequently book directly with suppliers – a phenomenon known as the billboard effect (Anderson & Han, 2017). As consumers shop for suitable products or services, many visit the supplier website having initially discovered its existence through an OTA site. Thus, in addition to being a source of indirect bookings, OTAs also act as a complement to direct sales, positioning potential solutions in front of customers and giving them a choice as to how they want to complete the subsequent transaction.

The effect of this dramatic growth on other intermediary players has been transformational. With their focus on leisure travel, retail travel agents have been the most dramatically affected (Fountoulaki et al., 2015). While previously these played an important role, acting as a key point-of-sale for tour operators and suppliers, they have largely been displaced by OTAs providing better functionality and service through digital channels (Díaz et al., 2015). Reintermediation has also prompted innovation in the tour operator sector. Traditionally vertically integrated, tour operators have increasingly divested physical assets and adopted business models that mimic the more flexible platform approach of the OTAs (Berne, Garcia-Gonzalez, and Mugica, 2012). While introducing flexibility, this, in effect, erodes their competitive advantage, calling into question their sustainability in a highly competitive digital marketplace.

In terms of the effect on suppliers, the domination of online sales by travel platforms is worrying from a strategic perspective. While larger travel suppliers may survive, potentially the big losers will be small and independent suppliers, most of whom lack the awareness, expertise, budget and technical competency to be able to compete effectively in a dramatically changed distribution environment (Law and Jogaratnam, 2013). The result will undoubtedly be more consolidation (Andreassen et al., 2018), driven by a need to gain scale to be able to compete more effectively in today's highly competitive marketplace. Such a move threatens the very fabric of tourism, which risks becoming standardised and homogenised without the multitude of small and medium-sized operators that have traditionally characterised the sector.

Conclusion

A key component of the travel value chain, the function, scope and methods of operation of intermediaries have evolved substantially over the past three decades. Once seen simply as distribution channels, simultaneously collaborating and competing with suppliers, their role has evolved into highly sophisticated commercial partners, allowing suppliers to more fully exploit the potential of the online marketplace by selectively targeting specific groups or segments on a highly efficient, pay-per-performance basis. At the same time, their role has further developed into technology platforms rather than just simple distribution facilitators. For example, the GDSs now generate a significant proportion of their revenue from provision of technology services rather than distribution fees, while many OTAs are positioning themselves as technology partners, selectively working with suppliers to enable functionality or features that would be difficult or costly for the latter to develop internally.

Driven by systemic changes arising from the COVID-19 crisis, travel distribution is entering a new phase, one where non-exclusive virtual partnerships between value chain participants are the name of the game. The most successful travel companies of this new era will be the ones who figure out how to work with the right portfolio of online travel intermediaries to not only gain broader distribution advantage but also supplement their technological capacities and better serve the customer.

References

Abdullah, M., Dias, C., Muley, D. and Shahin, M. (2022). Exploring the impacts of COVID-19 on travel behavior and mode preferences. *Transportation Research Interdisciplinary Perspectives*, 60, 251–258.

Anderson, C. K., & Han, S. (2017). The billboard effect: Still alive and well. *Cornell Hospitality Report*, 17(11), 3–10.

Andreassen, H., Diaz Andrade, A., & Milne, S. (2018). Integration in the New Zealand wholesale travel industry: A case of interoperability or inoperability? *CAUTHE 2018: Get Smart: Paradoxes and Possibilities in Tourism, Hospitality and Events Education and Research*, 682.

Beldona, S., Morrison, A. M., & O'Leary, J. (2005). Online shopping motivations and pleasure travel products: a correspondence analysis. *Tourism Management*, 26(4), 561–570. doi:10.1016/j.tourman.2004.03.008

Beritelli, P., & Schegg, R. (2016). Maximizing online bookings through a multi-channel strategy: Effects of interdependencies and networks. *International Journal of Contemporary Hospitality Management*, 28(1), 68–88.

Berne, C., Garcia-Gonzalez, M., & Mugica, J. (2012). How ICT shifts the power balance of tourism distribution channels. *Tourism Management*, 33(1), 205–214. doi:10.1016/j.tourman.2011.02.004

Bilgihan, A., Okumus, F., Nusair, K. and Bujisic, M. (2014). Online experiences: Flow theory, measuring online customer experience in e-commerce and managerial implications for the lodging industry. *Information Technology & Tourism*, 14, 49–71.

Buhalis, D., & Kaldis, K. (2008). eEnabled Internet distribution for small and medium sized hotels: the case of Athens. *Tourism Recreation Research*. https://doi.org/10.1080/02508281.2008.11081291

Buhalis, D., & Laws, E. (2001). *Tourism distribution channels: practices, issues and transformations*, Wallingford, UK: CABI, https://www.cabdirect.org/cabdirect/abstract/20023015404

Buhalis, D., & O'Connor, P. (2005). Information communication technology revolutionizing tourism. *Tourism Recreation Research*. https://doi.org/10.1080/02508281.2005.11081482

Carroll, B., & Siguaw, J. (2003). The evolution of electronic distribution: Effects on hotels and intermediaries. *Cornell Hotel and Restaurant Administration Quarterly*, 44, 38–50. https://doi.org/10.1016/S0010-8804(03)90257-6

Cetin, G., Aydogan Cifci, M., & Istanbullu Dincer, F. (2016). Coping with reintermediation: the case of SMHEs. *Information Technology in Tourism*, 16, 375–392. https://doi.org/ 10.1007/s40558-016-0063-2

Chang, Y. W., Hsu, P. Y., & Lan, Y. C. (2019). Cooperation and competition between online travel agencies and hotels. *Tourism Management*, 71, 187–196.

Díaz, E., Martín-Consuegra, D., & Esteban, Á. (2015). Perceptions of service cannibalisation: The moderating effect of the type of travel agency. *Tourism Management*, 48, 329–342.

Enz, C.A., & James, E.C. (2017). Beyond channel mix management: Building within online travel agencies (OTA) metrics and strategies. *Journal of Revenue & Pricing Management*, 16, 109–114.

ETTSA. (2018). Hotel Distribution Costs: Examination of the costs associated with direct and indirect distribution channels for Hotels, together with the impact of channel shift. Brussels: European Travel Technology Services Association. Brussels.

Fountoulaki, P., Leue, M. C., & Jung, T. (2015). Distribution channels for travel and tourism: The case of crete. In Tussyadiah, I. and Inversini, A. (eds), *Information and Communication Technologies in Tourism*, Vienna, New York: Springer International Publishing, pp. 667–680 (ISBN: 978-3-319-14342-2) DOI: 10.1007/978-3-319-14343-9_48

Fu Tsang, N. K., Lai, M. T., & Law, R. (2010). Measuring e-service quality for online travel agencies. *Journal of Travel & Tourism Marketing*, 27(3), 306–323.

Garcia, G., Dos Anjos, S. & Doğan, S. (2022). Online Travel Agencies and Their Role in the Tourism Industry. *Advances in Hospitality and Tourism Research (AHTR)*, 10(3), 361–386. DOI: 10.30519/ahtr.865546

Green, C. E., & Lomanno, M. V. (2012). *Distribution channel analysis: A guide for hotels*. McLean: HSMAI Foundation.

Jørgensen, M. T. (2017). Reframing tourism distribution-activity theory and actor-network theory. *Tourism Management*, 62, 312–321.

Kim, J., Bojanic, D. C. and Warnick, R. B. (2009). Price bundling and travel product pricing practices used by online channels of distribution. *Journal of Travel Research*, 47(4), 403–412.

Koo, B., Mantin, B., & O'Connor, P. (2011). Online distribution of airline tickets: Should airlines adopt a single or a multi-channel approach? *Tourism Management*, 32(1), 69–74. doi:10.1016/j.tourman.2009.11.008

Kracht, J., & Wang, Y. (2010). Examining the tourism distribution channel: evolution and transformation. *International Journal of Contemporary Hospitality Management*, 22(5), 736–757.

Law, R., & Jogaratnam, G. (2013). A study of hotel information technology applications. *International Journal of Contemporary Hospitality Management*, 17(2): 170–180 doi:10.1108/09596110510582369

Law, R., Leung, K., & Wong, R. (2013). The impact of the Internet on travel agencies. *International Journal of Contemporary Hospitality Management*, 16(2), 100–107. doi:10.1108/09596110410519982

Lee, H. A., Guillet, B. D., & Law, R. (2013). An examination of the relationship between online travel agents and hotels a case study of choice hotels international and Expedia.com. *Cornell Hospitality Quarterly*, 54(1), 95–107. doi:10.1177/1938965512454218

Leung, R. (2019). Smart hospitality: Taiwan hotel stakeholder perspectives. *Tourism Review*, 74(1). 50–62.

Leung, R., Guillet, B. D., & Law, R. (2014). The channel that offers the lowest online room rates: a case study of hotels in Hong Kong. *International Journal of Hospitality & Tourism Administration*, 15(2), 103–120. doi: 10.1080/15256480.2014.901050.

Lv, X., Li, N., Xu, X., & Yang, Y. (2020). Understanding the emergence and development of online travel agencies: a dynamic evaluation and simulation approach. *Internet Research*, 30(6), 1783–1810.

Mohseni, S., Jayashree, S., Rezaei, S., Kasim, A., & Okumus, F. (2018). Attracting tourists to travel companies' websites: the structural relationship between website brand, personal value, shopping experience, perceived risk and purchase intention. *Current Issues in Tourism*, 21(6), 616–645.

Murphy, H. C., & Chen, M.-M. (2014). Online Information Sources Used in Hotel Bookings Examining Relevance and Recall. *Journal of Travel Research*, (forthcoming). doi:10.1177/0047287514559033

Murphy, J., Forrest. E. J., Wotring, C. E. and Brymer, R. A. (1996). Hotel management and marketing on the Internet: An analysis of sites and features. *Cornell Hospitality Quarterly*, 37(3), 70–82.

O'Connor, P. (2010). Managing a hotel's image on TripAdvisor. *Journal of Hospitality Marketing & Management*, 19(7), 754–772.

O'Connor, P. (1999). *Electronic Information Distribution in Hospitality and Tourism*. Wallingford: CABI.

O'Connor, P. (2008). Managing hospitality information technology in Europe: issues, challenges and priorities. *Journal of Hospitality Marketing and Management*, 17(1–2), 59–77.

O'Connor, P., & Frew, A. J. (2003). An evaluation methodology for hotel electronic channels of distribution. *International Journal of Hospitality Management*, 23, 179–199.

Paraskevas, A., Katsogridakis, I., Law, R., & Buhalis, D. (2011). Search engine marketing: transforming search engines into hotel distribution channels. *Cornell Hospitality Quarterly*, 52(2), 200–208. doi:10.1177/1938965510395016

Park, S., Yin, Y., & Son, B. G. (2019). Understanding of online hotel booking process: A multiple method approach. *Journal of Vacation Marketing*, 25(3), 334–348.

Phocuswright (2022) The Critical Role of Independent Distribution in the U.S. Travel Industry. Travel Tech. Available at: https://www.traveltech.org/the-critical-role-of-independent-distribution-in-the-u-s-travel-industry/ (Accessed 1/2/23).

Rajaobelina, L. (2018). The impact of customer experience on relationship quality with travel agencies in a multi-channel environment. *Journal of Travel Research*, 57(2), 206–217.

Sabre. (2018). Sabre integrates Booking.com listings into its industry-first Content Services for Lodging platform, https://www.sabre.com/insights/releases/sabre-integrates-booking-com-listings-into-its-industry-first-content-services-for-lodging-platform/

Schegg, R., Stangl, B., Fux, M., & Inversini, A. (2013). Distribution channels and management in the Swiss Hotel Sector. In: Cantoni, L., & Xiang, Z. (eds) *Information and Communication Technologies in Tourism 2013*. Springer, Berlin, Heidelberg. https://doi.org/10.1007/978-3-642-36309-2_47

Sigala, M. and Christou, E. (2006). Investigating the impact of e-customer relationship management on hotels' website service quality. *Published Proceedings of 14th European Conference on Information Systems. ECIS 2006 Proceedings*, Goteborg, Sweden.

Stangl, B., Inversini, A., & Schegg, R. (2016). Hotels' dependency on online intermediaries and their chosen distribution channel portfolios: Three country insights. *International Journal of Hospitality Management*, 52, 87–96.

Thakran, K., & Verma, R. (2013). The emergence of hybrid online distribution channels in travel, tourism and hospitality. *Cornell Hospitality Quarterly*, 54(3), 240–247. doi:10.1177/1938965513492107

Toh, R. S., Raven, P., & DeKay, F. (2011). Selling rooms: Hotels vs. third-party websites. *Cornell Hospitality Quarterly*, 52(2), 181–189.

Xiang, Z., Wang, D., O'Leary, J. T., & Fesenmaier, D. R. (2015). Adapting to the internet: Trends in travelers' use of the web for trip planning. *Journal of Travel Research*, 54(4), 511–527. https://doi.org/10.1177/0047287514522883

Yin, C. H., Goh, E., & Law, R. (2019). Developing inter-organizational relationships with online travel agencies (OTAs) and the hotel industry. *Journal of Travel & Tourism Marketing*, 36(4), 428–442.

15 Technology trends and trip planning

Kim-Ieng Loi and Jose Weng Chou Wong

Introduction

The development and commercialisation of the Internet and thereafter information and communications technologies (ICTs) have not only enabled new business models but also augmented people's planning style in various areas, one of which being their trip planning behaviours. Travelling behaviours are typically divided into pre-trip, during and post-trip stages, where information search for planning purposes used to take place mostly in the pre-trip stage and via physical means. However, with the advent and popularity of ICT adaptation and the virtual space, people tend to shorten their trip planning lead times and do more ad hoc planning during trips. They are also more inclined to participate in sharing their trip experiences (information and advice) through social media during and post-trip, so that they themselves contribute to the repertoire of information sources from which they benefit; thereby forming a sustainable ecosystem. Acknowledging the opportunities and feasibility afforded by this phenomenon, this chapter explores the paradigm shift by: (i) reviewing the traditional trip planning literature; (ii) investigating the change in trip planning styles alongside the evolution of ICTs; and (iii) identifying trends in the smart era. The chapter concludes with several potential directions that may continue to shape changes in trip planning behaviours, such as immersive virtual trips, smart self-drive tourism and impulsive travel stimulated by gamification concepts.

Trip planning 1.0 (before 1990s): Pre-Internet era (traditional approaches)

Traditionally, trip planning was often affiliated with traffic/transportation, environment, and physical bearings via maps. Scholars have used different terms to express the concepts of trip planning, including travel demand management (TDM) plans (Taylor, Nozick, & Meyburg, 1997), trip reduction plans (Rye, 2002), mobility management plans (Enoch & Rye, 2006).

Gärling, Böök, and Lindberg (1984) define trip planning as "people's behavior in social and physical environments is determined by action plans, and, if the execution of such action plans requires traveling, plans for how to travel, termed travel plans, are formed and executed". They further propose four stages of trip planning in the 1980s: (i) the action stage that tourists confirm the certain place; (ii) formation of travel plan: decision about destination, localisation of destination and selection of route; (iii) acquisition of information about properties of the environment; and (iv) the choice of travel mode (Gärling, Böök, & Lindberg, 1986).

In the pre-Internet era, trip planning was the core work of tourists before travelling and an important element that specified how to get from one place to another, so tourists might plan what to do during the holidays, or how to spend their leisure time. Trip planning was particularly important for those who had no trip experiences or were not familiar with the destination and they mainly relied on travel catalogues and travel guides to plan trips prior to departure, in the hope that trip planning could largely enhance the overall quality of travel. However, the quality of trip planning is not inherently existent. In order to improve the plan, tourists need to notice three main aspects, including: a) travel mode, b) location activities, and 3) attractions (Filiatrault & Ritchie, 1980). These aspects require ample information search and as a result of various limitations, it was impossible for tourists to make the whole plan comprehensively by relying on manual operations. Tourists needed to spend much effort in devising a reasonably good plan way before the trip and making changes in the interim was difficult, if not impossible. Another challenge in trip planning was that information was not timely updated (e.g., recent closure or relocation of hotel, temporary changes in an exhibition or in a museum, or the closure of scenic spots due to renovation). Very often, tourists had to combine information from different sources and decide which information was most reliable before making decisions.

In the last few decades, destination choices evolved as per the development of modes of transportation. In the 1970s, tourists tended to choose destinations with shorter distances because of the underdeveloped transportation, and they usually planned those short-distance trips by themselves. For the mid- to long-distance trips this task would be handled by travel agencies. In the 1980s, due to the increase of travel distance in general, the involvement of travel agencies before departure became higher (Woodside & Ronkainen, 1980). Different types of tourists chose different trip planning methods in this period. There were three main types: self-planning, car clubs and travel agents. Tourists with a single travel purpose would plan their itineraries by themselves or through car clubs while tourists with multiple travel purposes would use travel agents (Gitelson & Crompton, 1983). This coincides with Schul and Crompton's (1983) classification of information sources (internal personal experiences and external travel agencies). In all cases, planning tended to happen way before departure.

Those with less tourism experience often used a wider range of information sources and authoritative management information, such as maps and materials of land management agencies, or neutral tourist information sources such as official visitor centres. As trip planning was gathered and made sense of through tourists' experience and interactions with materials, it was not always universally interpreted in the same way (Rao, Thomas, & Javalgi, 1992). Trip planning varied between individual tourists and particularly personal attitude segments, such as the attributes of the trip, including distance, length of stay, and budget; or personal attitudes: like the socio-economic characteristics of tourists, including age and education and disposable income.

Trip planning 2.0 (1990–2015): The era of the Internet, WWW and Web 2.0

The emergence of the Internet changed the way people plan their trips. Tourists are no longer confined to traditional travel agencies and frequently use the Internet to search for information and arrange their itineraries. Given that the Internet provides a convenient channel to people searching for tourism information without physical access to agents, there has been a transformation in the traditional travel agency–tourism relationship

(Gretzel, Yuan, & Fesenmaier, 2000) and provides more opportunities to foster the development of trip planning (Heung, 2003), all attributable to social information and technological advancements that come with evolution in information and communication technologies. Although the rise of the Internet has had a significant impact on trip planning, there were still some frustrating experiences in the 1990s. As users' searching abilities and educational backgrounds varied, not all were Internet-savvy; also, most of the travel websites at that time were not professional enough and therefore they often failed to reflect tourism information that tourists needed (Xiang & Fesenmaier, 2004). Moreover, it was not common for tourists to purchase travel products on the Internet in the 1990s because of payment security problems and limited functions on websites (Wolfe, Hsu, & Kang, 2005). Most travellers (especially the older generation) still preferred traditional paper materials, such as tourist magazines and brochures as the main source of information, and payments in person. Using websites was much more popular among younger generations than older generations.

Nonetheless, because of the search engine's carrying capacity and speed of information retrieval, travellers often used search engines to plan and experience their trips (Buhalis & Law, 2008). Subsequently, traditional information searching has been considered no longer efficient and effective to satisfy tourists' needs. The Internet during this period included a huge range of other tourist experiences and official tourist information, images, and introductions of tourism destinations. Such valuable and accurate tourism information greatly influenced tourists' pre-trip planning and Web pages were hence very influential at this stage. Furthermore, the Web 2.0 technology, with its emphasis on social networking sites (SNS) and user-generated content (UGC), has transformed the internet website from "publishing-browsing-platform" to "participation-interaction-platform" (Xiang, Wang, O'Leary, & Fesenmaier, 2015). As O'Connor (2010, p. 754) describes, "the Internet is evolving from a push marketing medium to one where peer-to-peer generation and sharing of data are the norms". This provided a communication platform for tourists all over the world on trip planning without geographical limitations. Websites have since then acted as an important trip planning source. Importantly, they make planning more personalised and provide more alternatives for tourists, and the efficiency of travel is hence greatly improved (Fernández-Herrero, Hernández-Maestro, & González-Benito, 2018). Web 2.0 continues to evolve by launching new functions in which tourists can upload images, text, and videos to share their planning. Through communications on websites, a virtual community can be built among travellers for information sharing and they are no longer relying solely on travel agents.

In addition, different from the traditional web search, people since then would use blogs to share their travel experiences. A large amount of interaction and sharing help travellers save their time and cost to know the real situations in the destination, and the information shared by bloggers is often believed to be more reliable than the information provided by travel agents or other parties with commercial agendas. With the continuous refinement of the website features, Web pages allow users to establish point-to-point communication with other users, or even multidirectional communications such as online communities, forums, and chat rooms (Țugulea, Bobalca, Andreea, & Liviu, 2013). Users are no longer in a passive role in the process of trip planning. They actively create and generate their own content, gradually changing from one-way output to two-way communication flow (Dellarocas, 2003). To conclude, Web 2.0 has influenced the searching modes, trip planning goals, actions, and arrangements for managing trip plans. Nevertheless, up to this stage planning remained mostly a pre-trip activity.

Trip planning 3.0 (status quo): Smart mobile device era

With the rapid development of science and technology, using smart mobile devices in lieu of computers has become a norm. From laptops, notebooks, and tablets to the most important of all, smartphones, smart mobile devices have dramatically changed the living style of many. Getting everything done via mobile applications on smartphones is recognised as a convenient approach in trip planning. The smartphone, an integrated electronic device, enables telephone conversations, emails, website browsing, online social media networking and e-shopping (Lai, 2015). In other words, the smartphone can be considered as a computer-on-the-go. It is a convenience enabler that can help tourists make decisions without much advance planning and reduces the time required for taking action. Many tourists now perform their trip planning entirely using smartphones because of the huge amount of information afforded by this technology.

The emergence of smartphones and mobile applications and the developments of social media and UGC allow travellers to communicate with other travellers without time and space obstacles. Using smartphone applications has gained competitive advantages in trip planning as people can map their trip routes and destinations anytime and anywhere. Trip information is presented in various forms by videos, blogs, vlogs (i.e., video blogs), photos, and social media posts and many of them are generated by travellers themselves (Fan, Buhalis, & Lin, 2019). Smartphones help travellers collect other tourists' information and experiences efficiently, meaning that travellers can now perform not only pre-trip planning but also during trip planning; and the role of travellers is not limited to information searchers, they also contribute themselves as information providers through social media, thereby providing a real-time "infostructure" for value co-creation in which trip planning depends a great extent on tourists' individual involvement in social media (Buhalis & Amaranggana, 2015). Social media applications on smartphones provide a platform for travel consumers to share their experiences and opinions online in the form of text, photos, and videos in real time (Buhalis & Sinarta, 2019; Xiang & Gretzel, 2010). Therefore, social media has not only fundamentally changed the way travel-related information is disseminated, but also the way people plan and consume travel (Buhalis & Law, 2008). Tourists do not need to do much preparation on trip planning before travel. The mobile technologies and various tourism mobile apps allow tourists to become more flexible when making travel decisions, such as choosing an appropriate mode of transport by providing real-time traffic information, assisting in ordering, or cancelling restaurants when they are browsing through the online travel agency (OTA) applications (Jamal & Habib, 2020; Zhang, Gordon, Buhalis, & Ding, 2018) without the limitations of time and space.

Tools such as Google and other social media provide instant access to the information at tourists' fingertips, and, as a result, people have now become increasingly reliant on them. The incorporation of a global positioning system (GPS) with smartphone and other wearable smart devices also replaces paper maps and allows navigation and planning on the road. The smart era empowers the dynamic and seamless interoperability of all stakeholders in the tourism industry (Buhalis, 2020) and enables tourists to secure accurate and reliable information, to do planning, as opposed to traditional information searching which was considered to be difficult or even impossible (Mihajlović, Krželj, & Milić-Beran, 2014). The smart era will continue to develop and grow in importance with new technologies and changing the ways of travel and trip planning. The implication is that tourists tend to plan their trip activities as they go, to implement ad hoc changes during trips, and to participate in information exchange during and after trips.

Trip planning: The way forward (2022–future)

The development of new technologies and concepts such as the 5th generation mobile networks, the big data Internet of Things (IOT) and blockchain have offered unprecedented opportunities to the tourism industry and will continue to cause significant impacts on trip planning in the future (Buhalis, 2020). Some latest developments are illustrated below as tentative food for thought. They are at their initial stage of application and are considered to have huge potential to be further developed and expanded in terms of tourism consumption.

Virtual tourism: the Metaverse

The term Metaverse has a history of 30 years, but has recently become a hot topic since the COVID-19 and the renaming of Facebook as Meta. The Metaverse is defined as "the hypothesized next iteration of the Internet, supporting decentralised, persistent online 3-D virtual environments" (Dionisio, III, & Gilbert, 2013). This technology can be used in a variety of settings, including personal computers, smartphones, augmented reality, virtual reality, and mixed reality. People can utilise wearable gadgets to enter the Metaverse, a virtual world connected to a range of digital surroundings, instead of sitting in front of a computer and perusing the Internet (BBC, 2021). One can visualise the Metaverse as a digital world accessible through smart applications via an avatar with 3D representation through relevant gadgets. Coupled with the penetration of the 5G network communication and Web 3.0, which give greater user empowerment, artificial intelligence and enhanced machine learning capability, significant changes have occurred in many fields including the tourism industry through influencing the patterns of travel and trip planning. For the tourism industry, which has been deeply affected by the pandemic, the integration with the Metaverse can come in handy and provides an outlet full of opportunities (Buhalis et al. 2023a, 2023b).

The Metaverse can be significantly integrated into the tourism industry, with a natural affinity, such as the virtuality of tourist scenery, scenes, props, as well as interactive participation and immersive experiences of tourists, and it can provide strong assistance to tourists in trip planning. Tourism destinations can collect not only tourists' demographic information, but also their multi-personal experiences with friends. Under the Metaverse technology, people can choose to 'visit' their destination directly without any planning in advance, and in the world of the Metaverse, all kinds of attractions are independent and the Metaverse technology can be complementary to the real world. For example, when visiting the Forbidden City, regardless of the weather and climate, it is possible to experience the landscapes of four seasons in the same spectacular site. This Metaverse concept is already in implementation. For example, Hunan province in China has established the world's first Scenic Spot Metaverse Research and Development Center in Zhangjiajie, the setting which inspired the movie *Avatar* and now that would make this experience a reality in the foreseeable future (Global Times, 2021). So, when the time comes (and it will come before long), people can pre-explore new destinations through virtual navigation or feel other people's travel experiences through this immersive platform. In fact, the primitive version of this has been happening, for example in the form of taking a virtual tour to a hotel room before one makes the booking. The Metaverse takes it to another level, one which is more immersive and participative.

Drive tourism: Smart vehicles

Drive tourism has always been a popular way of travelling in most Western countries since the last century and this mode has also gained widespread acceptance in Asia (especially China) in recent decades. With its growing market penetration, smart vehicles, specifically smart cars, may become the next revolutionary product to evolve the way people travel. Intelligent interaction, intelligent driving, and intelligent services are regarded as the three components of intelligent networked automobiles (Deloitte, 2018). Correspondingly, smart cars are smartphones, smart robots, AI, search engines, and voice-directed navigation all in one. Theoretically speaking, certain essential travel operations, such as ticketing, seat selection, hotel bookings, and route planning, can be handled by smart cars instead of human beings. The "brain" in the smart car can help optimise routing, stopovers, restaurant/hotel selection, preferred activities and scenic spots, and time scheduling with certain prescribed personalised considerations from a dataset. The results can be presented as best site-visit time windows, rest requirements, and preference for site-visiting sequences. Through the incorporation of real-time information, tourists will be able to avoid any potential hiccups that may dampen their travel plans, such as traffic, long queues, provisional closure and/or other unpredictable changes on the road, literally leading to a seamless travel "plan" that requires no plan at all.

The tourists' behaviour can be evaluated every time they use smart cars to plan their excursions. The itinerary that best suits the tourists will be recommended based on their own behaviours and the datasets of other similar users on the road. With some technological refinement and integration, it can be imagined that these itineraries and plans generated by the smart cars can be shared to any social network sites or online travel community instantly and effortlessly, adding to the information pool that can be consumed by other travellers or "learned" by machines. In this way, the dataset continues to grow and decisions refined with time through big data analysis and machine learning which will help the next round of vacation preparation and planning, forming an endless improvement cycle. In this case, tourists will spend less time on trip planning processes by simply pressing a few buttons on the smart vehicles, and they will be able to spend more time pondering over what they truly want by assessing the possibilities supplied by the smart cars which are now their best "travel buddies".

Gamification: Destination mystery boxes

Mystery boxes, also called blind boxes or grab bags, originated in Japan. They are a product filled with unknown random contents and sold at a substantial discount (BBC, 2019). It is estimated that the blind box economy in China will reach 30 billion Yuan (around US$4.6 billion) in 2024 (Daxueconsulting, 2021). Consumers feel excited when they are buying mystery boxes as they enjoy exploring something unknown, and 'destination blind box' campaigns in China become a novel marketing strategy in which customers can spend a small sum of money (98 Yuan or US$15) to purchase a domestic roundtrip air ticket with a set departure location at a random destination, and on a random date. If the ticket does not meet expectations, tourists can receive a full refund (Chinanews, 2021). This gamification concept is also used in other tourism products. For instance, Ctrip launched four categories of eat, live, play, and fly blind boxes corresponding to food, accommodation, tickets, and air tickets (Minnews, 2022). This recent marketing gimmick is, in part, a result of the prolonged COVID-19 pandemic which has generated massive losses for airlines and tourism product operators with excessive inventories of a highly perishable nature. Using an extremely attractive price as a loss leader to expand the customer base and stimulate consumption are among the clear motives of such campaigns. Another example, the TikTok blind box campaign, attracted more than ten million users on 3 April 2021 alone, and 100 million users on XiaoHongShu (Little Red Book, a leading SNS especially for key opinion leaders, KOLs) on the same day (Daxueconsulting, 2021). Travel blind boxes in China are targeted at young consumers who enjoy the thrill of not knowing where the final destination and the gamification concept alongside it. According to the 2021 Young People's Quality Tourism Report released by the famous Chinese travel community Mafengwo, the post-1990s and post-2000s are more willing to explore new ways to travel and are no longer confined to public travel channels as they are in an era where shared information is easily accessible, with new platforms frequently adding to the market. The excitement and heartbeat provided by blind boxes cater exactly to the preferences of these young people which have made them the "ace strategy" for many travel platforms and airlines to gain customers and clear inventory (Minnews, 2022).

In addition, domestic travellers dominate the market when many international borders are still closed or faced by restrictions. This growth in domestic tourism may continue even after the pandemic when people get used to and find the values from it. The extremely attractive prices provided by the blind box come with certain restrictions (regarding, for example, travel time and destination choices). As a result, the people who buy this concept are likely to be those who are experienced, more flexible in travel and require little (or even no) advance planning. If this fad continues into the future, tourists may choose to visit a tourism attraction or destination simply because of the mystery box ticket, without any prior agenda or planning, and enjoy the process of exploring the unknown, given that information search can take place anytime and anywhere. Under the experience economy, the general population has more travel experiences than before, and they can afford to add more flexible and customised elements in the journey. Also, under high working and living pressures, people may look forward to quick trips or impulsive trips without long time planning and considerations (Gong et al., 2012), and hence more tourists will make ad hoc decisions by consuming mystery boxes of integrated tourism products, even though they may not be their original best or most preferred choices.

Conclusions

The development in technology has dramatically changed the habitats of the tourism industry and the way people travel and plan. Figure 15.1 presents a summary of what has been discussed in this chapter. Real-time information, accessible on mobile or wearable devices, makes advance planning more of an option than a requirement. The several recent phenomena discussed in this chapter have brought implications for readers to ponder. Some people argue that the continuous development of the Metaverse may result in the disappearance of all business travel trips as they can be perfectly replaced by virtual trips and meetings. Leisure tourists may leverage the Metaverse in their planning stage (to sample the destination) in order to complement physical trips. Leisure tourism experiences are still largely considered as high-touch types of personal experiences that cannot be entirely replaced by high-tech elements. As such, personalisation is key to the maintenance of touch in the process and this is where the smart technology-enabled vehicles may come in handy. Self-drive domestic or cross-border tourism, assisted by smart cars which act as AI personal assistants, can help provide a highly personalised plan based on big data and machine learning, allowing for more impulsive travel. With the development of technology, trip planning has also injected a new impetus into the sustainable development of the tourism

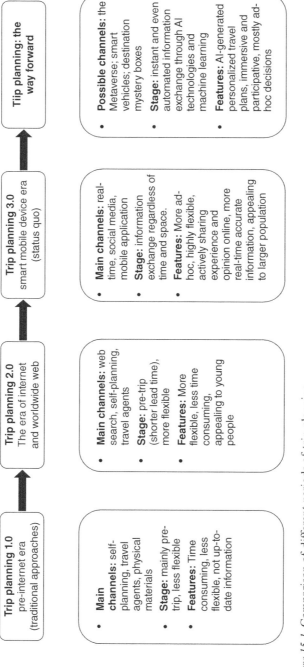

Figure 15.1 Comparison of different periods of trip planning.

industry. In terms of the United Nations SDGs, different ways of trip planning offer new perspectives on sustainable development; they may help foster infrastructure and innovation (SDG 9) and maintain the economic growth of tourism destinations (SDG 8).

Impulsive travel trips are further encouraged by the mystery/blind box craze which has recently been sweeping the China youngster market. Gaming on good value at low prices with uncertain products or services packaged in blind boxes is fun in itself, never mind the actual value received from them. Whether this fad will continue is still unknown, but price incentives have always been one of the most effective marketing gimmicks. It is likely that this gamification concept (or its adaptation) will spice up this highly seasonal tourism industry. So, what is next?

References

BBC. (2019, February 9). Fukubukuro: Why Japan Goes Crazy for "Lucky Bags". Retrieved from https://www.bbc.com/news/world-asia-46805873

BBC. (2021, October 18). Apparently, It's the next Big Thing. What Is the Metaverse? Retrieved from https://www.bbc.com/news/technology-58749529

Buhalis, D. (2020). Technology in tourism-from information communication technologies to eTourism and smart tourism towards ambient intelligence tourism: a perspective article. *Tourism Review*, *75*(1), 267–272.

Buhalis, D., & Amaranggana, A. (2015). Smart tourism destinations enhancing tourism experience through personalisation of services. In I. Tussyadiah & A. Inversini (Eds.) *Information and Communication Technologies in Tourism 2015* (377–389). Springer, Cham.

Buhalis, D., & Law, R. (2008). Progress in information technology and tourism management: 20 years on and 10 years after the Internet—The state of eTourism research. *Tourism Management*, *29*(4), 609–623.

Buhalis, D., Leung, D., & Lin, M. (2023a). Metaverse as a disruptive technology revolutionising tourism management and marketing. *Tourism Management*, *97*, 104724. https://doi.org/10.1016/j.tourman.2023.104724

Buhalis, D., Lin, M., & Leung, D. (2023b). Metaverse as a driver for hospitality customer experience and value co-creation: Implications for hotel and tourism management and marketing. *International Journal of Contemporary Hospitality Management*. https://doi.org/10.1108/IJCHM-05-2022-0631

Buhalis, D., & Sinarta, Y. (2019). Real-time co-creation and nowness service: lessons from tourism and hospitality. *Journal of Travel & Tourism Marketing*, *36*(5), 563–582.

Chinanews. (2021, April 21). The Time Route Is All Random, Is the Blind Box of the Ticket a Marketing Gimmick or a Real Benefit? Retrieved from https://www.chinanews.com.cn/sh/2021/04-21/9459705.shtml

Daxueconsulting (2021, May 10). Destination unknown: The newest addition to the blind box economy in China – Airplane tickets. Retrieved from https://daxueconsulting.com/blind-box-economy-in-china-airline-tickets/

Dellarocas, C. (2003). The digitization of word of mouth: Promise and challenges of online feedback mechanisms. *Management Science*, *49*(10), 1407–1424.

Deloitte. (2018, June). How to Build an Intelligent Networked Car for the Future. Retrieved from https://www2.deloitte.com/cn/zh/pages/consumer-business/articles/how-to-build-a-future-oriented-intelligent-networked-car.html

Dionisio, J. D. N., III, & Gilbert, R. (2013). 3D virtual worlds and the metaverse: Current status and future possibilities. *ACM Computing Surveys (CSUR)*, *45*(3), 1–38.

Enoch, M. and Rye, T. (2006). Travel plans: Using good practice to inform future policy, in B. Jourquin, P. Rietveld and K. Westin (Eds.), *Towards better performing transport networks*, pp. 157–177. London: Routledge.

Fan, D. X., Buhalis, D., & Lin, B. (2019). A tourist typology of online and face-to-face social contact: Destination immersion and tourism encapsulation/ decapsulation. *Annals of Tourism Research*, *78*, 102757.

Fernández-Herrero, M., Hernández-Maestro, R. M., & González-Benito, Ó. (2018). Autonomy in trip planning and overall satisfaction. *Journal of Travel & Tourism Marketing*, 35(2), 119–129.

Filiatrault, P., & Ritchie, J. B. (1980). Joint purchasing decisions: A comparison of influence structure in family and couple decision-making units. *Journal of Consumer Research*, 7(2), 131–140.

Gärling, T., Böök, A., & Lindberg, E. (1984). Cognitive mapping of large-scale environments: The interrelationship of action plans, acquisition, and orientation. *Environment and Behavior*, 16(1), 3–34.

Gärling, T., Böök, A., & Lindberg, E. (1986). Spatial orientation and wayfinding in the designed environment: A conceptual analysis and some suggestions for postoccupancy evaluation. *Journal of Architectural and Planning Research*, 55–64.

Gitelson, R. J., & Crompton, J. L. (1983). The planning horizons and sources of information used by pleasure vacationers. *Journal of Travel Research*, 21(3), 2–7.

Global Times (2021, November 19). China Zhangjiajie unveils 'world's first scenic spot metaverse R&D center,' aims to create the world of Avatar. Retrieved from https://www.globaltimes.cn/page/202111/1239404.shtml

Gong, P., Liang, S., Carlton, E. J., Jiang, Q., Wu, J., Wang, L., & Remais, J. V. (2012). Urbanisation and health in China. *The Lancet*, 379(9818), 843–852.

Gretzel, U., Yuan, Y. L., & Fesenmaier, D. R. (2000). Preparing for the new economy: Advertising strategies and change in destination marketing organizations. *Journal of Travel Research*, 39(2), 146–156.

Heung, V. C. (2003). Internet usage by international travellers: reasons and barriers. *International Journal of Contemporary Hospitality Management*, 15(7), 370–378.

Jamal, S., & Habib, M. A. (2020). Smartphone and daily travel: How the use of smartphone applications affect travel decisions. *Sustainable Cities and Society*, 53, 101939.

Lai, I. K. (2015). Traveler acceptance of an app-based mobile tour guide. *Journal of Hospitality & Tourism Research*, 39(3), 401–432.

Mihajlović, I., Krželj, Z., & Milić-Beran, I. (2014). Study of the impact of ICT on new trends in consumer behaviour in tourism when planning trips. *Mathematics and Computers in Contemporary Science*, 144–154.

Minnews (2022, February 20). Is the ticket blind box cool? There are many complaints! Practitioners in the tourism industry: may be helping the airlines to clear inventory. Retrieved from https://min.news/en/travel/4831417f01df3e7d2dfc893b1ffdd100.html

O'Connor, P. (2010). Managing a hotel's image on TripAdvisor. *Journal of Hospitality Marketing & Management*, 19(7), 754–772.

Rao, S., Thomas, E. G., & Javalgi, R. G. (1992). Activity preferences and trip-planning behavior of the US outbound pleasure travel market. *Journal of Travel Research*, 30(3), 3–12.

Rye, T. (2002). Travel plans: do they work? *Transport Policy*, 9(4), 287–298.

Schul, P., & Crompton, J. L. (1983). Search behavior of international vacationers: Travel-specific lifestyle and sociodemographic variables. *Journal of Travel Research*, 22(2), 25–30.

Taylor, C. J., Nozick, L. K., & Meyburg, A. H. (1997). Selection and evaluation of travel demand management measures. *Transportation Research Record*, 1598(1), 49–60.

Țugulea, O., Bobalca, C., Andreea, M., & Liviu, M. (2013). How do young people select information to plan a trip. *Revista de turism-studii si cercetari in turism*(16), 51–57.

Wolfe, K., Hsu, C. H., & Kang, S. K. (2005). Buyer characteristics among users of various travel intermediaries. *Journal of Travel & Tourism Marketing*, 17(2–3), 51–62.

Woodside, A. G., & Ronkainen, I. A. (1980). Vacation travel planning segments: Self-planning vs. users of motor club and travel agents. *Annals of tourism Research*, 7(3), 385–394.

Xiang, Z., & Fesenmaier, D. R. (2004). An analysis of two search engine interface metaphors for trip planning. *Information Technology & Tourism*, 7(2), 103–117.

Xiang, Z. and Gretzel, U. (2010). Role of social media in online travel information search. *Tourism Management*, 31, 179–188.

Xiang, Z., Wang, D., O'Leary, J. T., & Fesenmaier, D. R. (2015). Adapting to the internet: trends in travelers' use of the web for trip planning. *Journal of Travel Research*, 54(4), 511–527.

Zhang, H., Gordon, S., Buhalis, D., & Ding, X. (2018). Experience value cocreation on destination online platforms. *Journal of Travel Research*, 57(8), 1093–1107.

16 Digital-free tourism
The state of the art and future research directions

Wenjie Cai and Brad McKenna

Introduction

Digital technologies have transformed tourism in various aspects and have become increasingly adopted by providers (Cai et al., 2019) and integrated into tourist experiences (Neuhofer et al., 2014). Tourists use technology for a wide variety of activities such as trip planning (Ferrer-Rosell et al., 2017), live streaming (Deng et al., 2021), self-service (Liu & Hung, 2020), sharing experiences on social media (Munar & Jacobsen, 2014), making bookings (Murphy et al., 2016), voice assistants (Buhalis & Moldavska, 2021), smart tourism (Buhalis, 2020), real-time co-creation (Buhalis & Sinarta, 2019), and robotics (Pizam et al., 2022). Smartphones have long been an essential tool for travel (Lamsfus et al., 2015; Wang et al., 2016) and have impacted human interactions (Dickinson et al., 2014). However, the overwhelming use of technology has resulted in a growing disconnect movement (Syvertsen, 2020) for people who desire to resist the omnipresent power of digital technology (Cai & McKenna, 2021).

Ubiquitous connectivity in society has blurred the boundaries between work and life, causing negative impacts on travel experiences (Kirillova & Wang, 2016). Responding to the increasing wellbeing issues caused by the dark side of technology (Gao et al., 2018), in recent years digital-free tourism (DFT) has become an increasingly popular phenomenon in consumer demands and academic research. Many tourists voluntarily disconnect from their smartphones to set a clear boundary between home and away in order to reclaim their wellbeing on holiday. Although DFT is still a niche concept in the digitalised society, we can see its growth potential with the increasing emphasis on digital wellbeing (Vanden Abeele, 2021). In the tourism and hospitality sectors, several organisations and destination management organisations (DMOs) have incorporated the digital detox concept either through developing an unplugged experience or through marketing a remote destination. Current studies on digital detoxing in the tourism context are largely exploratory, focusing on media representation, motivation, perception, emotion, and character strength. Most studies to date focus on the consumer perspective.

The future of technology use in tourism includes smart tourism and the Metaverse, and we acknowledge the potential for technology for various stakeholders such as managers, operations, staff, and tourists (Buhalis et al. 2023a, 2023b). However, the perceived overuse of technology within society has led to increasing demand for DFT. From DFT, new tourism providers such as digital detox retreats have emerged, and tourists are partaking in their own digital-free trips. Therefore, this chapter aims to bring together the key discussions related to the issues of DFT by firstly introducing a working definition of digital-free tourism by building on existing academic work; secondly, providing a comprehensive and critical review of the state of the art of digital detox research in tourism; thirdly, situating digital-free tourism research within the umbrella term of digital wellbeing, and link it to the larger agenda of sustainability; and finally, the chapter outlines future research directions and practical implications.

The state of the art of digital-free tourism

Early studies on digital disconnection in the tourism context focus mainly on forced disconnection (e.g., technology dead zones) (Pearce & Gretzel, 2012) due to the constraints of Internet connection facilities. While some benefits were discussed, these studies focus on the negative aspects of digital disconnections on holidays, such as anxiety and social tensions (Paris et al., 2015). Other earlier studies placed disconnection as just one aspect of their studies on connectivity. For example, Dickinson et al. (2016) explored campsite connectivity, and the concept of disconnection arose through their data analysis. Their findings revealed that being completely disconnected was not universal among all tourists. Other studies of partial disconnection include Rosenberg (2019), who studied backpacker behaviour; Tribe and Mkono (2017), who conceptualised "e-lienation" and the negative consequences of technology; and Tanti and Buhalis (2016) presented five consequences of being disconnected.

Some earlier work began to partially discuss issues such as wellbeing and work–life balance (Dickinson et al., 2016). More recently, DFT research has begun to reflect on positive outcomes of disconnection, for example, increasing wellbeing issues due to technostress (Liu & Hu, 2021) and blurred boundaries between work and life (White & White, 2007). The term DFT is coined by Li et al. (2018) as "tourism spaces where Internet and mobile signals are absent, or digital technology usage is controlled" (p. 317). Differing from travel experience in the technology dead zone, DFT emphasises the voluntary aspect; in other words, tourists voluntarily engage in the digital detox experience.

DFT research has become more popular in recent years and has begun to explore various aspects of DFT. Despite a growing number of digital detox providers, for example, Unplugged (in the UK), studies focusing on the DFT provider side are scarce. Digital detox providers offer facilities to enable their guests to lock away their phones for several days and enjoy remote rural destinations free from the distractions of technology. As far as we are aware, Pawłowska-Legwand and Matoga (2020)'s study is the only one investigating the diverse offering of DFT experiences in Poland, such as farm stays, spa hotels, monasteries and convents, tour operators, and an addiction treatment centre.

The focus of DFT studies thus far is on the consumer side, ranging from perception and motivation to experiences and outcomes. Floros et al. (2021) found that Millennials tend to have positive perceptions towards DFT and believe the experience can help them improve their wellbeing; however, they also perceive constraints from social expectations, digitalised tourism infrastructure, and their high dependence on technology. Egger et al. (2020) identified escape, personal growth, health and wellbeing, and relationships as four key motivations for participating in DFT. Using a mixed-method approach, Jiang and Balaji (2021) found that mindfulness, technostress, relaxation, or self-expression motivate tourists to partake in digital-free holidays. In the same vein, Liu and Hu (2021) argued that techno-exhaustion and social-network-services-exhaustion positively affect the intention to participate in DFT.

In terms of the DFT experience, Cai et al. (2020) investigated the emotional journey of DFT. The study revealed that DFT participants suffered from withdrawal symptoms at the beginning, but later enjoyed and appreciated the experience. The study highlighted that

DFT leads to increased social interactions and greater engagement with the surroundings. From a positive psychology aspect, Li et al. (2020) revealed that DFT builds nine character strengths, including self-regulation, appreciation of beauty and excellence, spirituality, social intelligence, love, open-mindedness, creativity, perspective, and vitality. From a critical perspective, Cai and McKenna (2021) explored how individuals negotiated and resisted the omnipresence of digital technology. They found that leveraging strategies such as going for complete disconnections, negotiating punishments and rewards, recalling nostalgic memories, and engaging in self-reflections help digital detox participants to maximise the positive experience of DFT.

Different studies discussed above have various interpretations of DFT, with some other similar terms, such as unplugged tourism (Pawłowska-Legwand & Matoga, 2020) and digital detox holiday (Jiang & Balaji, 2021). Fan et al. (2019) provide a tourist typology for technology use at destinations. Among six tourist types, they suggest two which are relevant for DFT; a "disconnected immersive traveller" and a "digital detox traveller". Although Li et al. (2018) did not explicitly define DFT as voluntarily disconnecting, most DFT studies using this definition consider it as a voluntary disconnection. For example, Zhang and Zhang (2022) discussed voluntary disconnection with selective unplugging, where tourists decide to partially disconnect or connect to rethink their relationships with everyday life and travel. However, Jiang and Balaji (2021) differentiate the digital detox holiday from DFT and emphasise tourists' conscious, voluntary, and goal-directed behaviour. For the future theoretical development of the field, it is essential to have a universal understanding of the term. In this case, we suggest understanding DFT the same as Jiang and Balaji's (2021) definition of a digital detox holiday having an emphasis on voluntary disconnection. In this case, unplugged tourism and digital detox holiday should be considered as DFT, which is positioned within the umbrella term of disconnected tourism (both forced disconnection and voluntary disconnection).

The discussions of DFT have been embedded in digital wellbeing and sustainability. Floros et al. (2021) suggested that DFT can potentially contribute to psychological sustainability by aligning 'mental' away with 'physical' away. In Stankov and Gretzel's (2021) conceptualisation of digital wellbeing, they positioned DFT in the tech-scarce tourism category and the avoidance of tech-savvy living. By placing DFT in the broad scope of digital wellbeing and psychological sustainability and IT, it brought in a bigger picture of how the balanced use of digital technology can contribute to the quality of life.

Future research agenda

Firstly, future research can discuss how DFT can be connected with other forms of tourism with a similar wellness-centred focus. Further developing from Pawłowska-Legwand and Matoga (2020), we suggest future research can explore various nature-based tourism with DFT potentials such as forest tourism, coastal tourism, rural tourism, and adventure tourism. As these tourism forms strongly emphasise wellbeing and embodying experiences, it is worth exploring how the removal of disruptive digital technology contributes to the overall experience. Future DFT studies can develop a framework that includes various forms of tourism that can adopt DFT experiences with a focus on improving wellbeing and self-development. These discussions and conceptualisation of DFT should be connected to the quality of life, digital wellbeing, and the United Nations Sustainable Development Goals (SDGs), in particular, SDG 3 (good health and wellbeing) and SDG 11 (sustainable cities and communities). In addition, although several studies so far suggest the wellbeing benefit of DFT, there are no studies dedicated to investigating the long-term wellbeing benefits of digital detox. Therefore, we encourage more studies investigating the short-term and long-term wellbeing benefits of DFT.

Secondly, we call for more studies focusing on the provider side of DFT. Many tourism and hospitality providers are offering digital-free experiences. It is worth exploring how they design the product; in particular, how they help participants deal with the withdrawal symptoms (Cai et al., 2020), private and professional commitments (McKenna et al., 2020) and maximise the benefits such as developing character strengths (Li et al., 2020). It is also worth exploring the servicescape design in these digital detox holiday spaces and how they afford DFT consumers' experiences. In addition, future research can also explore how the providers co-create a digital-free experience with the consumers. We also suggest future research in hospitality and events can investigate the potential of using digital-free experiences in experience design.

Thirdly, we call for more studies on the dark side of DFT. The rationale of DFT is based on the awareness of the dark side of technology. Although DFT helps to address these issues, such as unbalanced technology use, technostress, and the lack of immersive engagements with social and environmental surroundings, the potential issues of DFT should not be neglected. So far, most DFT studies are still in the advocate stage. However, the nature of DFT, asking for a certain period of disconnecting from digital technology, might lead to some levels of adverse effects. By conceptualising the digital technology of disciplinary power, Cai and McKenna (2021) argued that being constantly connected has become a norm. Partaking in DFT experiences might improve the wellbeing during the trip and the number of emails to respond to, but issues to resolve after the disconnection might lead to more stress. As discussed in Cai et al. (2020), participants felt rather stressed and anxious when the DFT experience approached the end before the re-connection. In addition, without the disruptions of smartphones, DFT tourists have more time to engage with reflective thoughts, which might trigger some traumatised memories and experiences. In particular, the setting of many digital-free providers is in isolated locations, which also raise potential concerns for participants wellbeing and safety.

Fourthly, we invite more theoretical and epistemological discussions on DFT. One of the future research areas could discuss how DFT is positioned in today's postmodern world. One of the key characteristics of today's postmodern society results from disruptive technology, which compresses and detaches time and space (Harvey, 1999). This has shown in today's network sociality, which replaces the community-oriented sociality (Wittel, 2001). In the postmodern society, boundaries between work and life are blurred. In the tourism context, the emergence of a digital nomad (Olga, 2020) and bleisure (Chung et al., 2020) reflect travel in the postmodern era. The DFT, however, criticises and challenges this fluidity and aims to re-establish the boundary between work and leisure, everyday life, and holiday experiences. To reflect this trend, we can argue a new theoretical tendency of post-postmodernity, which also reflects other aspects of consumer behaviour and today's society. We encourage future research to reflect and discuss DFT within the wider context of the cultural and societal state.

Fifthly, we suggest that future DFT research reflect the development of new technologies and new consumers. The digital element in DFT today mainly focuses on smartphones. In the next few decades, we will witness the increasing adoption of new technologies and mobile devices such as augmented reality, service robots, virtual reality, mixed reality, and the Metaverse. There might be new portable devices designed to facilitate these new features. With the adoption of these new technologies in everyday lives, the withdrawal symptoms and challenges to disconnect could be somewhat different, which requires new studies to investigate. Future research should also acknowledge new consumers in a different demographic cohort. So far, most DFT studies have focused on Millennials (e.g., Cai et al., 2020; Floros et al., 2021). It is worth noting that Millennials grew up in a period without disruptive technology, in which they can recall their memories (Cai & McKenna, 2021). However, Generation Z, also known as digital natives (Vodanovich et al., 2010), has a very different relationship with technology which requires new evidence-based understandings of their perceptions and experiences of DFT.

Sixth, we call for future research to investigate the influential factors of DFT experiences. In Cai et al.'s (2020) study, they briefly discussed the type of destination, travel companions, commitments, reliance on technology, and motivation that affect the DFT experience. However, these factors should be further tested and validated in various contexts. Other factors, such as nationality and length of the trips, should also be considered. We encourage more studies investigating DFT in various contexts to bring more contextual and theoretical insights.

Seventh, we encourage future research to take on a more critical lens on investigating DFT. Cai and McKenna (2021) discussed Foucault's power and resistance in DFT. Future research can also embed DFT within today's geopolitical climate. For instance, the relationship between digital detox travel and the political view (Sutton, 2020), and the re-conceptualisation and rejuvenation of the concept of escape. As DFT is considered a new trend and 'resistance', we encourage future research to use DFT as a vehicle to push new theoretical development and paradigmatic boundaries.

Eighth, we call for more creative and advanced research methods to contribute to DFT studies. For instance, using physiological measurements will help to measure participants' objective responses during the digital detox experience. Methods such as interventions and focus groups are also encouraged to bring more empirical insights. So far, most studies in DFT are still qualitative by nature, and we thus encourage more quantitative contributions to deliver generalisable findings.

Future trends for digital-free tourism

With the increasing awareness of digital wellbeing and embedded experiences of the dark side of technology in everyday life, we expect substantial growth of the digital-free experience in tourism, hospitality, and leisure. There are already several successful businesses building on the concept of digital-free tourism, such as Unplugged in the U.K., Getaway in the U.S., and Buzzoffski in Serbia. These businesses share similar ideas of having digital detox cabins in the rural and natural environment (Figure 16.1). The target customers for these hospitality products are knowledge workers from urban areas. These customers struggle with overwhelming screentime and blurred boundaries between work and life. By observing the successful expansions of these businesses, we can expect the hospitality sector will develop more similar products by combining nature, idleness, and digital-free experiences with a focus on improving the digital wellbeing of their guests. There is also great potential for destinations to develop digital-free experiences. This is more suitable for destinations that are in rural areas. The design of such digital-free products should not detach from the unique offering of the destination and must engage in user-centric experience design to maximise the visitor's experience.

In addition to the dedicated digital-free experience, we are expecting to see many hospitality and tourism services incorporate the idea of a digital detox as part of their experience.

Figure 16.1 Digital detox cabin.
Photo Credit: Unsplash; Photographer: Nachelle Nocom.

For instance, restaurants can provide a phone lockbox on the dining tables to enhance social interactions without distraction from social media or work emails. Hotels and leisure centres can also create a phone-free zone that facilitates genuine interpersonal interactions and mindful reflections. Further development of technology could also facilitate tourists to be more mindful and present in their leisure experiences. For example, artificial intelligence could predict the activity types based on the location and the time and suggest the users turn the phone into the do not disturb mode.

We predict DFT will be further woven into specific tourism experiences such as slow tourism, rural tourism, spa tourism, and adventure tourism, as they share a similar focus on existential authenticity and tourists' wellbeing. These tourism operators and providers could introduce the awareness of digital wellbeing in their experience design to maximise tourists' overall experience of self-reflection, learning, and relaxation. In addition, the DFT, together with other sustainable tourism initiatives, will become an essential part of tourism and travel in the decades to come. The development and popularity of DFT is a counterculture with excessive technology use and its negative consequences. Therefore, we expect DFT and digital tourism to improve tourists' wellbeing in the decades to come.

We also expect an increasing number of tourists will participate in various forms of DFT, including selective unplugged periods or a full digital detox. Currently, participants of DFT are mostly Millennials who started to experience the dark side of technology.

With Gen Z joining the workforce in the next decade, their relationship with digital technology will shift from the advocate stage to a more critical and reflective one. In other words, we will witness more Gen Z consumers take action to look after their digital wellbeing and partake in leisure activities that separate them from the ubiquitous digital world. Differing from Millennials that grew up at a time without digital technology, Gen Z are digital natives who require a different experience design of DFT to maximise their wellbeing benefits.

Practical implications

The COVID-19 pandemic and working from home has resulted in several issues, such as Zoom fatigue and increased technostress (Waizenegger et al., 2020). Many people have started to pay more attention to their digital wellbeing in the post-COVID world (Blake et al., 2021). This creates many business opportunities for DFT. For DFT businesses, it is essential to understand the perceptions, motivations, concerns, experiences, and expected outcomes of DFT travellers. The understanding should be implemented into marketing communications, product and experience design, and additional supports. We encourage DFT start-ups to engage in professional training in digital wellbeing and mental health for looking after their guests. We also suggest DFT operators to avoid urban destinations, and work closely with the nature-related tourism activities.

There are also many opportunities for existing tourism and hospitality organisations to adopt the digital detox concept in part of their operations. For instance, some restaurants are already adopting this concept by offering a box to lock away guests' mobile phones. Museums, resorts and hotels can create some digital-free zones; whilst tour operators can design some trips with mindful reductions of technology use.

DFT is potentially an excellent marketing strategy or re-branding opportunity for destinations in remote areas. Examples already can be found on the Isle of Man and Scotland's marketing campaign with an emphasis on a digital detox. We encourage DMOs to recognise this potential, not only using unplug or digital detox' as buzzwords in the marketing messages, but also actively engaging with stakeholders to develop DFT destinations that are dedicated to improving people's wellbeing. For some destinations suffering from overtourism or being overwhelmed by one type of tourism, DFT could be a solution to diversify tourism offerings and encourage tourists to visit beyond Instagramable attractions and explore the hidden gems in the cities.

We encourage DMOs and DFT providers to recognise the alignment of DFT within the scope of sustainability. This requires DMOs and DFT providers to engage in various forms of socially sustainable tourism (e.g., community-based tourism, pro-poor tourism, voluntourism), seek green solutions in operational details, and empower women in employment and career development. We urge DFT providers to work closely with stakeholders to deliver a cohesive and consistent DFT experience. By aligning DFT with the sustainability agenda, a sustainable DFT experience should not only provide long-lasting wellbeing impacts to tourists but should also benefit local communities.

However, we should also acknowledge the challenge of operating and marketing digital-free experiences. Today's marketing is predominated by user-generated content through social media platforms such as Instagram and Snapchat. Using digital forms of marketing communications tools might be considered controversial to the idea of a digital-free experience. Therefore, an alternative, innovative marketing communication approach is required to promote such forms of tourism experiences and engage with customers.

Conclusion

In this chapter, we discussed the theoretical and contextual development of the DFT phenomenon. We have suggested a definition for DFT and suggest that it should be situated within the larger context of digital wellbeing and sustainability. We suggested eight future research directions, predicted future trends, and offered some practical implications for stakeholders. Looking forward, there will be an increasing demand for DFT due to the increasing awareness of digital wellbeing. However, researching and implementing DFT requires alternative theoretical lenses and operational/marketing strategies as outlined in this chapter.

References

Blake, H., Mahmood, I., Dushi, G., Yildirim, M., & Gay, E. (2021). Psychological Impacts of COVID-19 on Healthcare Trainees and Perceptions towards a Digital Wellbeing Support Package. *International Journal of Environmental Research and Public Health*, *18*(20), 10647.

Buhalis, D. (2020). Technology in tourism-from information communication technologies to eTourism and smart tourism towards ambient intelligence tourism: A perspective article. *Tourism Review*, *75*(1), 267–272.

Buhalis, D., Leung, D., & Lin, M. (2023a). Metaverse as a disruptive technology revolutionising tourism management and marketing. *Tourism Management*, *97*, 104724. https://doi.org/10.1016/j.tourman.2023.104724

Buhalis, D., Lin, M., & Leung, D. (2023b). Metaverse as a driver for hospitality customer experience and value co-creation: Implications for hotel and tourism management and marketing. *International Journal of Contemporary Hospitality Management*. https://doi.org/10.1108/IJCHM-05-2022-0631

Buhalis, D., & Moldavska, I. (2021). Voice assistants in hospitality: Using artificial intelligence for customer service. *Journal of Hospitality and Tourism Technology*, *13*(3), 386–403.

Buhalis, D., & Sinarta, Y. (2019). Real-time co-creation and nowness service: Lessons from tourism and hospitality. *Journal of Travel & Tourism Marketing*, *36*(5), 563–582.

Cai, W., & McKenna, B. (2023). Power and resistance: Digital-free tourism in a connected world. *Journal of Travel Research*, *62*(2), 290–304.

Cai, W., McKenna, B., & Waizenegger, L. (2020). Turning it off: Emotions in digital-free travel. *Journal of Travel Research*, *59*(5), 909–927.

Cai, W., Richter, S., & McKenna, B. (2019). Progress on technology use in tourism. *Journal of Hospitality and Tourism Technology*, *10*(4), 651–672. https://doi.org/10.1108/JHTT-07-2018-0068

Chung, J. Y., Choi, Y.-K., Yoo, B.-K., & Kim, S.-H. (2020). Bleisure tourism experience chain: Implications for destination marketing. *Asia Pacific Journal of Tourism Research*, *25*(3), 300–310.

Deng, Z., Benckendorff, P., & Wang, J. (2021). Travel live streaming: An affordance perspective. *Information Technology & Tourism*, *23*(2), 189–207.

Dickinson, J. E., Ghali, K., Cherrett, T., Speed, C., Davies, N., & Norgate, S. (2014). Tourism and the smartphone app: Capabilities, emerging practice and scope in the travel domain. *Current Issues in Tourism*, *17*(1), 84–101.

Dickinson, J. E., Hibbert, J. F., & Filimonau, V. (2016). Mobile technology and the tourist experience:(Dis) connection at the campsite. *Tourism Management*, *57*, 193–201.

Egger, I., Lei, S. I., & Wassler, P. (2020). Digital free tourism–An exploratory study of tourist motivations. *Tourism Management*, *79*, 104098.

Fan, D. X., Buhalis, D., & Lin, B. (2019). A tourist typology of online and face-to-face social contact: Destination immersion and tourism encapsulation/decapsulation. *Annals of Tourism Research*, *78*, 102757.

Ferrer-Rosell, B., Coenders, G., & Marine-Roig, E. (2017). Is planning through the Internet (un)related to trip satisfaction? *Information Technology & Tourism*, *17*(2), 229–244.

Floros, C., Cai, W., McKenna, B., & Ajeeb, D. (2021). Imagine being off-the-grid: Millennials' perceptions of digital-free travel. *Journal of Sustainable Tourism, 29*(5), 751–766. https://doi.org/10.1080/09669582.2019.1675676

Gao, W., Liu, Z., Guo, Q., & Li, X. (2018). The dark side of ubiquitous connectivity in smartphone-based SNS: An integrated model from information perspective. *Computers in Human Behavior, 84*, 185–193.

Harvey, D. (1999). Time-space compression and the postmodern condition. *Modernity: Critical Concepts, 4*, 98–118.

Jiang, Y., & Balaji, M. (2021). Getting unwired: What drives travellers to take a digital detox holiday? *Tourism Recreation Research*, 1–17.

Kirillova, K., & Wang, D. (2016). Smartphone (dis) connectedness and vacation recovery. *Annals of Tourism Research, 61*, 157–169.

Lamsfus, C., Wang, D., Alzua-Sorzabal, A., & Xiang, Z. (2015). Going mobile: Defining context for on-the-go travelers. *Journal of Travel Research, 54*(6), 691–701.

Li, J., Pearce, P. L., & Low, D. (2018). Media representation of digital-free tourism: A critical discourse analysis. *Tourism Management, 69*, 317–329.

Li, J., Pearce, P. L., & Oktadiana, H. (2020). Can digital-free tourism build character strengths? *Annals of Tourism Research, 85*, 103037.

Liu, C., & Hung, K. (2020). A comparative study of self-service technology with service employees: A qualitative analysis of hotels in China. *Information Technology & Tourism, 22*(1), 33–52.

Liu, Y., & Hu, H. (2021). Digital-free tourism intention: A technostress perspective. *Current Issues in Tourism, 24*(23), 3271–3274.

McKenna, B., Waizenegger, L., & Cai, W. (2020). The influence of personal and professional commitments on digitally disconnected experiences. In D. Kreps, T. Komukai, T. V. Gopal, & K. Ishii (Eds.), *Human-Centric Computing in a Data-Driven Society* (pp. 305–314). Cham, Switzerland: Springer.

Munar, A. M., & Jacobsen, J. K. S. (2014). Motivations for sharing tourism experiences through social media. *Tourism Management, 43*, 46–54.

Murphy, H. C., Chen, M.-M., & Cossutta, M. (2016). An investigation of multiple devices and information sources used in the hotel booking process. *Tourism Management, 52*, 44–51.

Neuhofer, B., Buhalis, D., & Ladkin, A. (2014). A typology of technology-enhanced tourism experiences. *International Journal of Tourism Research, 16*(4), 340–350.

Olga, H. (2020). In search of a digital nomad: Defining the phenomenon. *Information Technology & Tourism, 22*(3), 335–353.

Paris, C. M., Berger, E. A., Rubin, S., & Casson, M. (2015). Disconnected and unplugged: Experiences of technology induced anxieties and tensions while traveling. In *Information and communication technologies in tourism 2015* (pp. 803–816). Cham, Switzerland: Springer.

Pawłowska-Legwand, A., & Matoga, Ł. (2020). Disconnect from the digital world to reconnect with the real life: An analysis of the potential for development of unplugged tourism on the example of Poland. *Tourism Planning & Development*, 1–24.

Pearce, P. L., & Gretzel, U. (2012). Tourism in technology dead zones: Documenting experiential dimensions. *International Journal of Tourism Sciences, 12*(2), 1–20.

Pizam, A., Ozturk, A. B., Balderas-Cejudo, A., Buhalis, D., Fuchs, G., Hara, T., Meira, J., Revilla, R. G. M., Sethi, D., & Shen, Y. (2022). Factors affecting hotel managers' intentions to adopt robotic technologies: A global study. *International Journal of Hospitality Management, 102*, 103139.

Rosenberg, H. (2019). The "flashpacker" and the "unplugger": Cell phone (dis) connection and the backpacking experience. *Mobile Media & Communication, 7*(1), 111–130.

Stankov, U., & Gretzel, U. (2021). Digital well-being in the tourism domain: Mapping new roles and responsibilities. *Information Technology & Tourism, 23*(1), 5–17.

Sutton, T. (2020). *Digital re-enchantment: Tribal belonging, new age science and the search for happiness in a digital detoxing community*. University of Oxford.

Syvertsen, T. (2020). *Digital Detox: The Politics of Disconnecting*.

Tanti, A., & Buhalis, D. (2016). Connectivity and the consequences of being (dis) connected. In Inversini, A., and Schegg, R. (eds.), *Information and communication technologies in tourism 2016* (pp. 31–44). Cham, Switzerland: Springer. https://doi.org/10.1007/978-3-319-28231-2_3

Tribe, J., & Mkono, M. (2017). Not such smart tourism? The concept of e-lienation. *Annals of Tourism Research*, *66*, 105–115.

Vanden Abeele, M. M. (2021). Digital wellbeing as a dynamic construct. *Communication Theory*, *31*(4), 932–955.

Vodanovich, S., Sundaram, D., & Myers, M. (2010). Research commentary-Digital natives and ubiquitous information systems. *Information Systems Research*, *21*(4), 711–723.

Waizenegger, L., McKenna, B., Cai, W., & Bendz, T. (2020). An affordance perspective of team collaboration and enforced working from home during COVID-19. *European Journal of Information Systems*, *29*(4), 429–442.

Wang, D., Xiang, Z., & Fesenmaier, D. R. (2016). Smartphone use in everyday life and travel. *Journal of Travel Research*, *55*(1), 52–63. https://doi.org/10.1177/0047287514535847

White, N. R., & White, P. B. (2007). Home and away: Tourists in a connected world. *Annals of Tourism Research*, *34*(1), 88–104.

Wittel, A. (2001). Toward a network sociality. *Theory, Culture & Society*, *18*(6), 51–76.

Zhang, M., & Zhang, X. (2022). Between escape and return: Rethinking daily life and travel in selective unplugging. *Tourism Management*, *91*, 104521.

17 The metaverse as a new travel marketing platform

Min Jung Kim and Dae-Young Kim

Introduction

While overseas travel has been almost entirely halted due to the pandemic, the global tourism industry is doing its best to overcome the crisis. According to UNWTO (2022), international tourist arrivals in 2021 were below 72% compared to pre-COVID-19. However, real-world travel restrictions have given travellers new opportunities to discover the Metaverse. The Metaverse appears to have obtained momentum during the pandemic, which has shifted everything online. Some people, especially those from young generations who have been exposed to the online environment (e.g., video games or social media) for a long time, are gradually trending toward travel in the virtual world instead of the real world. In addition, as this virtual travel experience leads to the desire for actual tourism, the influence of the Metaverse is expected to grow in tourism in the future. The term Metaverse may seem unfamiliar to most people, but we are already experiencing the Metaverse in various ways, such as through Instagram, Facebook, Twitter, and Zoom meetings. For instance, we witnessed that Facebook changed its company name to Meta as it expanded beyond social media into areas such as virtual reality.

To date, the study of the Metaverse remains in its infancy. While it has great potential for development in tourism settings, there are few discussions about the Metaverse in academia to guide its development and application to the industry. As the technologies that deal with VR, AR, and virtual influencers develop rapidly, it is anticipated that the Metaverse will be vital for tourism marketing in the future. Young people, such as those of Generation Z, are the best example of how new users will adapt to the Metaverse-related technologies they pioneer. To understand how critical this developing stage of virtual reality is, having a solid grasp of what the Metaverse is and how it can be harnessed is essential. In this chapter, we highlight the definition, specific attributes, and representative applications of the Metaverse in various fields. Then, we illustrate existing Metaverse examples of tourist destinations and discuss how this new technology can be utilised to market to tourists (Buhalis et al. 2023a, 2023b).

What is the Metaverse?

Metaverse is a portmanteau of "meta," meaning beyond or transcendent, and "verse" from the universe. Studies suggest that in the decades to come the Metaverse will become more common in our daily lives. The term Metaverse first appeared in 1992 in a sci-fi novel by Neal Stephenson entitled *Snow Crash*; decades later, it gained attention in 2020 when

Nvidia's CEO proclaimed, "The Metaverse is coming." After that, Facebook, which can be said to be a representative of social media, changed its company name to Meta, thereby signalling its intention to use Metaverse as its main business model. Another major social media, Instagram, introduced 3D avatars in 2022. These examples show that the Metaverse has quickly emerged as a next-generation social media platform. Experts predict that the Metaverse industry will further expand with the development of related technologies, including AR and VR. Gartner, an information technology research firm, has reported that 25% of people will spend more than an hour a day on the Metaverse by 2026 (Gartner, 2022). The report postulates that 30% of organisations worldwide will provide their products and services on the Metaverse. In addition, the AR and VR market size is expected to grow significantly from about US$31 billion in 2016 to close to US$297 billion in 2024 (Alsop, 2021). In addition to social and entertainment purposes, the proportion of active Metaverse users in various fields such as education, fashion, and tourism is predicted to increase.

Individuals will start using the Metaverse for multiple purposes. According to a survey by the market and consumer research firm, Statista (2022), about three-quarters of U.S. adults were considering joining the Metaverse in 2021. They wanted to join the Metaverse mainly to experience things that cannot be done in physical reality and to communicate with others via the Metaverse platform. Nearly a quarter of respondents also mentioned that they wanted to become someone (e.g., an avatar) other than their real self in the Metaverse (Statista, 2022).

It is challenging to attempt to offer a full definition of the Metaverse because it is not a conceptual word derived from academic research, and its form is constantly evolving even at this time. Since the term Metaverse was first used in the book *Snow Crash* (Stephenson, 1992), there are multiple definitions in practice. Some describe it as "a fully realised digital world that exists beyond the analog one in which we live" (Herrman & Browning, 2021); "a set of virtual spaces where you can create and explore with other people who aren't in the same physical space as you" (Bosworth & Clegg, 2021); or "a massive virtual world where millions of people – or their avatars – will interact in real time" (Collins, 2021).

The Metaverse is more specifically defined as the post-reality world, a permanent and persistent multi-user setting amalgamating physical reality and digital virtuality (Mystakidis, 2022). Based on spatial and immersive technologies such as VR and AR, the Metaverse is a platform that enables people to interact with virtual environments. The first version of Metaverse was a web of virtual worlds that allowed users to communicate through avatars. After that, immersive VR platforms such as large-scale multiplayer online games appeared (Mystakidis, 2022).

In 2007, the Acceleration Studies Foundation (ASF) published a report entitled "Metaverse Roadmap," presenting the hypothetical components of the Metaverse. Thanks to this report, the Metaverse, which up to this point had only been a fantasy in novels, was conceptualised. This publication, and the scenarios it outlined, have become essential to researchers who study the Metaverse. The ASF classifies the Metaverse into four categories: AR, lifelogging, mirror worlds, and virtual worlds (Smart et al., 2007). As shown in Figure 17.1, the four types are distinguished by two dimensions. The X-axis relates to whether the technologies implementing the Metaverse are related to the user (intimate) or the user's external environment (external). The Y-axis relates to whether the technologies are based on physical reality (augmentation) or VR (simulation).

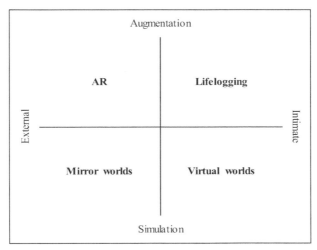

Figure 17.1 Classification of Metaverse.
Source: Smart et al. (2007).

Four categories of the Metaverse

Augmented Reality (AR)

AR is reality-based, but refers to a technology that enhances an individual's external physical world (Smart et al., 2007). It is a technology that has been implemented using GPS and Wi-Fi since the earliest days of smartphones, which overlays virtual images onto the real world. To use a fictional example, in the movie *Iron Man* the protagonist commands his AI assistant through glasses with AR technology. Through the AI assistant, Jarvis, in the movie, information such as terrain or missile speed is displayed overlaid on the screen, reflecting reality. This vision of AR is nothing new, and its popularity in media means that this Metaverse technology has already captured the human imagination.

Among the AR applications that are familiar to us in reality rather than movies are mobile games and QR codes. A prime example of an AR mobile game is *Pokémon Go*, released in the U.S. in 2016. The game aims to allows players to find and capture Pokémon characters that appear as if they are in the player's actual location and can be accessed by anyone using a mobile device with GPS (Pokémon GO, 2016). Another example of AR is scanning a QR (quick response) code with a smartphone camera to link to a brand website or product information. Numerous companies, such as Starbucks, have used it to advertise their brands or products because consumers can access their websites faster via QR codes than by entering a URL (Gybas et al., 2019).

Lifelogging

Lifelogging, a combination of the words "life" and "log," is an intimate and reality-based Metaverse where individuals disclose their lives (Smart et al., 2007). Literally, lifelogging refers to the activities in which individuals record and share their experiences or personal lives. It is a method of digitising users' personal data, such as emotions, movements, or experiences, and recording them in a digital space. Typically, social media such as Facebook,

Instagram, and Twitter are included in the lifelogging Metaverse. Checking in your location on Facebook or Instagram, tagging people who were with you, changing your relationship status, or even adding emojis to your posts to convey how you felt are among the examples of the ways we interact with the Metaverse in daily life.

Individuals participating in lifelogging can be divided into two types. One is people who share every moment that happens to them, such as daily life or travel, on social media platforms through the use of text, images, or videos. The other is people who comment or click "like" the content shared by other users and bring it to their lifelogging platform for later viewing or sharing. The former can be divided into two types again. One is a form in which individuals share content created by themselves on social media. The other is a form in which individuals share content recorded by a wearable device, such as their number of steps or heart rate.

Mirror worlds

Mirror worlds mean broadening information into the virtual world by reflecting the physical world around us (Smart et al., 2007). It is as if we look at ourselves in the mirror. We are in the real world, but we are also in the mirror, and other objects around us are in the mirror as well. Mirror worlds resemble reality as if they were reflected in a mirror. Still, it is characterised by an informationally enhanced world beyond simply replicating information in the physical world. It refers to replicating the real world into a virtual space, such as Google Earth, food delivery apps, or Zoom, and then adding relevant information.

Google Earth provides Street View and 3D imagery to see roads and buildings worldwide from eye level and aerial photography. People can feel as if they are travelling by looking at the streets of famous cities and tourist destinations such as UNESCO World Heritage Sites through Google Earth. Another example of mirror worlds is food delivery apps. By replicating restaurants that exist in the real world into the apps, people get information about the real world (e.g., food photos and menus provided in the apps) in a virtual space, order food, and share information with others through reviews. Zoom is an emerging video-conferencing and online education platform that has become the new normal of communication during the pandemic (Rospigliosi, 2022). It brings face-to-face meetings and classes to the digital world, providing chat, polls, and breakout rooms as well as video conferencing. As such, mirror worlds have the advantage of making the real world convenient and efficient by providing necessary information while reflecting the real world (Kye et al., 2021).

Virtual worlds

Virtual worlds, the most common category, are virtual spaces where the implemented information is individual-centred (Smart et al., 2007). Through the Metaverse and the Internet, we can access virtual worlds built with graphics technology. Although the terms look similar, it is necessary to distinguish the virtual world from virtual reality (VR). VR refers to a technology that allows access to the virtual world and is mainly produced in the form of a head-mounted display (HMD). Through the use of this head-mounted screen display, various experiences can be made real in a computer-generated space from a first-person perspective rather than a third-person perspective. The users can feel entirely immersed in VR because it is designed to feel like they are in a different time, space, and cultural background. It is also characterised by users creating an avatar to express themselves

Table 17.1 Dimensions of Metaverse

Dimensions	Definition	Examples	Characteristics
AR	Technologies of overlaying virtual images into the real world	– Pokémon GO – QR code	External/Augmentation
Lifelogging	Activities in which individuals record and share their experiences or daily lives	– Social media (e.g., Facebook, Instagram, and Twitter) – Wearable devices (e.g., Apple Watch)	Intimate/Augmentation
Mirror Worlds	Virtual spaces with enhanced information reflecting the real world	– Google Earth – Food delivery apps (e.g., Grubhub, UberEats, and Doordash) – Zoom	External/Simulation
Virtual Worlds	Virtual worlds that do not exist in reality in which users participate by creating avatars to express themselves	– Online games (e.g., Roblox and Fortnite) – Online communities (e.g., Second Life and Zepeto)	Intimate/Simulation

(Kye et al., 2021). The avatar, which was once predefined and exaggerated in the virtual worlds, has gradually changed into an ideal projection of the users' real-world appearance and personality (Park & Kim, 2022).

Virtual worlds are divided into game-based platforms (e.g., Roblox and Fortnite) and community-based platforms (e.g., Second Life and Zepeto). For example, Roblox is a platform where users can develop various games or enjoy games created by other users. As of November 2021, Roblox has nearly 50 million daily active users in 180 countries (Roblox, 2022), with 67% of them under 16 (Dean, 2022). Zepeto is an app that uses facial recognition, AR, and 3D technology to create an avatar with the user's personality and enjoy social activities in a virtual space. It is a global communication platform with 190 million users around the world. As such, virtual worlds appeared mainly in the entertainment industry, such as online games, which popularised the Metaverse. Table 17.1 summarises the definitions, examples, and characteristics of each type of Metaverse discussed above.

These four types developed independently, but gradually evolved into new applications integrated between Metaverses (Kye et al., 2021). For instance, Ghost Pacer is a gadget that allows users to run together and compete with a holographic running partner while viewing it through AR glasses (Mehar, 2020). The users can adjust the avatar's speed, link apps to analyse the exercise time and distance, and create a customised exercise based on the data. The gadget can also be connected to a smartwatch to record the user's heart rate. As such, Ghost Pacer is an example of the interaction of two Metaverses, such as AR (forming a virtual runner in reality) and lifelogging (recording lifelog data with a wearable device).

Digital natives and Metaverse

Since the young generation cohort (e.g., Gen Z) is considered as digital natives, using the Metaverse comes naturally to them. They were born when technology was rapidly developing, so the younger generation has grown up using the Internet and mobile devices from an early age. It is only natural that they are tech-savvy, even though they have not received any special technical training (Buhalis & Karatay, 2022). The younger generation cares about aesthetics, interactivity, ease of use, and communication (Buhalis et al., 2020), so the Metaverse can appeal to them. This digital native is particularly sensitive to the latest trends and value experiences, showing the characteristics of pursuing a unique experience different from others. As can be seen from the fact that about two-thirds of Roblox users are under the age of 16 (Dean, 2022), Gen Z actively communicates in virtual spaces. They play a role as producers in the Metaverse. For example, they can create content or events and profit through their avatars. In addition, they act as consumers who exert a powerful influence. Since consumption becomes a means of self-expression for Gen Z, they not only prefer customised products but are also pleased to pay a premium for products that emphasise their personality (Francis & Hoefel, 2018).

By identifying these characteristics of the digital native, global firms focus on marketing using Metaverse platforms to target them. For instance, in 2021 Gucci worked with Roblox to launch Gucci Garden, a virtual exhibit. In this space, unveiled on Roblox for two weeks, users could purchase Gucci's limited-edition virtual items such as handbags, sunglasses, or hats and wear them on their avatars. This experience induces the young Roblox users to be familiar with the world of luxury goods while spending their money on digital-only items. To explain the success of the event, the vice president for brand partnerships at Roblox said that Gen Z consumers "sometimes see virtual products as more valuable than physical products." As such, the way the young generation consumes brands and builds relationships with brands is different from that of older generations. As Gen Z is a value-driven cohort, actively communicates online, and consumes to express their individuality, they play an active role as key users of the Metaverse platforms. The brands they meet on the Metaverse can have a lasting impact on their lives. Taking everything into consideration, the Metaverse is expected to be a powerful marketing platform, especially for Gen Z beyond social media.

Metaverse applications in the travel industry

As in other industries, the use of the Metaverse is increasing in the tourism sector (Buhalis et al. 2023a, 2023b). We present some applications of the Metaverse to travel in South Korea using S-Map and Virtual SEOUL, the platforms developed by Seoul City and Zepeto, the existing Metaverse platform, and then explain virtual influencers.

Mirror worlds: S-Map

The Seoul City government launched S-Map (https://smap.seoul.go.kr/) in 2021. It is a 3D replica of a city identical to the real city of Seoul. It is a virtual world expanded in terms of information and reflects the real Seoul, so it can be called a mirror world Metaverse. People can prevent environmental and traffic problems that may occur in a metropolis through various simulations. Not only that, but the simulations allow us to travel around Seoul online. For example, S-Map provides VR images and descriptions of major tourist attractions in Seoul. Potential travellers can even view the currently destroyed cultural assets through 3D technology.

Virtual worlds: Virtual SEOUL and Hangang Park in Zepeto

Virtual SEOUL (https://virtualseoul.or.kr/) is a platform that can hold MICE events in a 3D virtual space launched in 2021. It provides nine virtual venues for participants to hold conferences, live sessions, exhibition booths, and more. The virtual spaces include major landmarks and tourist attractions of Seoul. Event organisers can select necessary functions, such as video or promotional material posting through a content management system and use a customised platform for event branding at no extra cost. As of December 2021, there were 11 events held on this platform, and the number of users reached about 30,000, In the Virtual Seoul Playground within the Virtual SEOUL, participants can select an avatar to experience Seoul with 3D Metaverse and communicate with others (Seoul Convention Bureau, 2020).

Another example of the virtual world is Hangang Park in Zepeto. The Korea Tourism Organization has introduced a virtual space for travel experiences in Korea since November 2020 using Zepeto, a mobile-based 3D avatar creation app aimed at Gen Z. The virtual travel destination was the Hangang Park, where K-pop boy group BTS used as a part of the live streaming background during the MTV awards ceremony. Their influence helped the park rank first in the survey of "The tourist site I want to visit through Zepeto." About

Figure 17.2 Hangang Park in Zepeto.
Source: Korea Tourism Organization.

257,000 users visited the virtual Hangang Park within a day of its launch, showing Gen Z's interest in travelling to Korea. They can experience all the possible virtual experiences identical to the real activities in the actual Hangang Park, such as flea markets and food trucks, cooking ramen at a convenience store, and riding a water leisure attraction. In particular, the convenience store opened in the virtual Hangang Park was very popular. The number of posts related to the virtual convenience store on the social networking service in Zepeto exceeded 2,900 and 2.7 million views in about a month. The convenience store-related items for Avatar sold over 220,000. In addition, the event held by the virtual convenience store drew a total of 720,000 participants within a week.

The Korea Tourism Organization utilises Zepeto, whose primary user is familiar with the mobile environment, as the optimal platform for content creation targeted at young people. For example, a K-pop girl group Blackpink held a virtual fan meeting at Zepeto, with more than 46 million people participating. Other than the special event, Zepeto users can create avatars that resemble their photos using AR technology, make friends, and socialise while communicating with each other in a 3D virtual world. Users can follow each other's characters just like on Facebook or Instagram and click "like." Because of these functions, Zepeto captured the heart of Gen Z, who tend to express themselves and show off.

Virtual influencers

Due to the expanding influence of the Metaverse, where the boundaries between reality and virtuality disappear, virtual humans who lead marketing trends in various industries are emerging. A virtual human is also called a digital human or a virtual influencer depending on how it is used. Virtual influencers created by synthesising virtual faces on real people or realising whole bodies with computer graphics go beyond just characters or avatars. They appear in actual advertisements, communicate with people through social media, and have been surfacing as a new marketing method. Rather than an avatar, which is a digitised image of an individual in the real world as an icon or figure (Rasmussen, 2021), a virtual influencer is a digital character but is given a personality defined by a first-person worldview. It is further characterised by being made accessible on social media platforms (Travers, 2020). Virtual influencers result from technological advances, including artificial intelligence, computer graphics, and the Metaverse, the space in which they operate.

Virtual influencers are artificial intelligence characters generated using computer graphics software. During the pandemic era, virtual influencers have emerged as alternative marketing channels on the Internet since the tourist destinations have difficulties collaborating with social media influencers creating travel content. They have a significant number of followers on image-based social media such as Instagram. Their appearance is designed to look like human beings. In addition, the influencers have anthropomorphic characteristics such as personality, expression, and behaviour, interacting with their followers (Moustakas et al., 2020). They are already driving impressive results for entertainment, fashion, beauty, and retail. Just as Prada collaborated with one of the most famous virtual influencers, Lil Miquela, virtual influencer marketing is one of the leading marketing methods of prestigious brands.

There are several advantages to using virtual influencers in the travel industry. According to new findings by Baklanov (2019), the average virtual influencer's post attracts four times more followers than real influencers. Unlike real influencers, every aspect of virtual influencers' content is controlled by marketers, guaranteeing an enhanced level of brand safety. What makes it attractive for marketers, above all, is that it is cost-effective to use

The metaverse as a new travel marketing platform 217

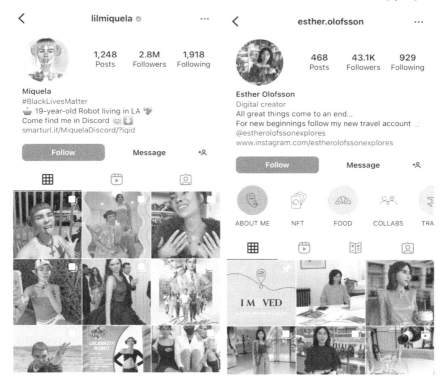

Figure 17.3 Virtual influencers.

virtual influencers in the travel industry, where there is usually an additional cost to execute influencer campaigns (Mak, 2020). Travel destinations have started new collaborations with virtual influencers thanks to these advantages. For instance, Kizuna AI, a Japanese virtual influencer, became a tourism ambassador for Japan, and Esther Olofsson, the first virtual influencer of the Netherlands, became a brand ambassador for Postillion Hotels (Xie-Carson et al., 2021).

Conclusion

The global tourism industry is in crisis due to the pandemic that occurred at the end of 2019 (Wut et al., 2021). While physical tourism is interrupted, potential travellers are looking forward to future trips by reminiscing about past trips and collecting information on destination websites and social media (Gretzel et al., 2020). Obtaining information is an essential process when potential travellers select a destination before travel and make various decisions during the trip (Buhalis, 2020; Kim et al., 2007). Social media, which has been rapidly increasing, has become a popular tool for ubiquitously collecting and sharing tourism information based on a mobile digital environment (Parra-Lopez et al., 2012) and allows travellers to simultaneously access online and physical (e.g., destination) networks during the trip (Fan et al., 2019). Because of their characteristics as experiential consumers, travellers are more likely to use social media to post, share, and comment on their trip experiences (Hays et al., 2013).

The evolution of the travel IT system brings a question, "What will be the next tourism information platform?" The Metaverse has attracted enormous attention because of the combination of the non-face-to-face lifestyles due to the prolonged pandemic and the convergent digital technologies such as VR and AR. The Metaverse is a space where we can travel freely, sustainably, and without boundaries (Sabil & Han, 2021). The expected Metaverse in tourism should be a realistic destination with more direct and virtual interactions. Risk factors for tourism, such as natural disasters, terrorism, cultural conflicts, high travel cost, seasonality, and even physical disability, would be weakened by the Metaverse, which would be either beneficial or harmful for the travel industry. Regardless of its positive and negative impact on tourism, it is obvious that the Metaverse can be utilised as a new travel IT platform and promotion channel especially targeting travellers familiar with the digital environment.

From a marketing perspective, AR can be the best Metaverse for travel marketing and advertising because the technology can connect desired content at any desired location. For instance, AR can be used with QR codes in a way that a popular celebrity appears and explains the destination. It is one of the most straightforward and accessible marketing methods as the users only need a smartphone. Destination marketers can also utilise the VR Metaverse to motivate potential travellers. For example, many museums have started offering virtual tours of full information about their collections (Guy, 2020). Likewise, various Metaverse platforms will enable destination marketers to attract potential travellers by offering virtual experiences of the destination before the trip (Huang et al., 2016). The Metaverse should go beyond simply reproducing tourist destinations or attractions. A wide range of possibilities to appeal to travelers should be further explored.

References

Alsop, T. (2021, November 23). VR and AR market size 2024. *Statista*. https://www.statista.com/statistics/591181/global-augmented-virtual-reality-market-size/

Baklanov, N. (2019, November 14). The top Instagram virtual influencers in 2019. *Hype-Journal*. https://hypeauditor.com/blog/the-top-instagram-virtual-influencers-in-2019/

Bosworth, A., & Clegg, N. (2021, September 27). Building the metaverse responsibly. *Meta*. https://about.fb.com/news/2021/09/building-the-metaverse-responsibly/

Buhalis, D. (2020). Technology in tourism-from information communication technologies to eTourism and smart tourism towards ambient intelligence tourism: A perspective article. *Tourism Review*, 75(1), 267–272.

Buhalis, D., Leung, D., & Lin, M. (2023a). Metaverse as a disruptive technology revolutionising tourism management and marketing. *Tourism Management*, 97, 104724, https://doi.org/10.1016/j.tourman.2023.104724

Buhalis, D., Lin, M., & Leung, D. (2023b). Metaverse as a driver for hospitality customer experience and value co-creation: Implications for hotel and tourism management and marketing. *International Journal of Contemporary Hospitality Management*. https://doi.org/10.1108/IJCHM-05-2022-0631

Buhalis, D., & Karatay, N. (2022, January). Mixed Reality (MR) for Generation Z in cultural heritage tourism towards metaverse. In *ENTER22 e-Tourism Conference* (pp. 16–27). Springer, Cham.

Buhalis, D., López, E. P., & Martinez-Gonzalez, J. A. (2020). Influence of young consumers' external and internal variables on their e-loyalty to tourism sites. *Journal of Destination Marketing & Management*, 15, 100409.

Collins, B. (2021, September 25). The metaverse: How to build a massive virtual world. *Forbes*. https://www.forbes.com/sites/barrycollins/2021/09/25/the-metaverse-how-to-build-a-massive-virtual-world/?sh=2b4663186d1c

Dean, B. (2022, January 5). Roblox user and growth stats 2022. *Backlinko*. https://backlinko.com/roblox-users

Gartner. (2022, February 7). *Gartner predicts 25% of people will spend at least one hour per day in the metaverse by 2026*. https://www.gartner.com/en/newsroom/press-releases/2022-02-07-gartner-predicts-25-%-of-people-will-spend-at-least-one-hour-per-day-in-the-metaverse-by-2026

Gretzel, U., Fuchs, M., Baggio, R., Hoepken, W., Law, R., Neidhardt, J., Pesonen, J., Zanker, M., & Xiang, Z. (2020). e-Tourism beyond COVID-19: A call for transformative research. *Information Technology & Tourism*, 22(2), 187–203.

Guy, J. (2020, December 16). *Online bidder pays $98K to get up close and personal with the 'Mona Lisa'*. CNN. https://www.cnn.com/style/article/louvre-auction-christies-drouot-scli-intl/index.html

Gybas, V., Klubal, L., & Kostolányová, K. (2019, April). Visual keyboards or QR codes in an inclusive school environment. In *Asian Conference on Intelligent Information and Database Systems* (pp. 221–229). Springer, Cham.

Fan, D. X., Buhalis, D., & Lin, B. (2019). A tourist typology of online and face-to-face social contact: Destination immersion and tourism encapsulation/decapsulation. *Annals of Tourism Research*, 78, 102757.

Francis, T., & Hoefel, F. (2018). True Gen': Generation Z and its implications for companies. *McKinsey & Company*, 12.

Hays, S., Page, S. J., & Buhalis, D. (2013). Social media as a destination marketing tool: Its use by national tourism organisations. *Current Issues in Tourism*, 16(3), 211–239.

Herrman, J., & Browning, K. (2021, July 10). Are we in the metaverse yet? *The New York Times*. https://www.nytimes.com/2021/07/10/style/metaverse-virtual-worlds.html

Huang, Y. C., Backman, K. F., Backman, S. J., & Chang, L. L. (2016). Exploring the implications of virtual reality technology in tourism marketing: An integrated research framework. *International Journal of Tourism Research*, 18(2), 116–128.

Kim, D.-Y., Lehto, X., & Morrison, A. M. (2007). Gender differences in online travel information search: Implication for marketing on the Internet. *Tourism Management*, 28(2), 423–433.

Kye, B., Han, N., Kim, E., Park, Y., & Jo, S. (2021). Educational applications of metaverse: Possibilities and limitations. *Journal of Educational Evaluation for Health Professions*, 18.

Mak, M. (2020, October 1). The evolution of the virtual influencer: No longer just a trend. *INCA*. https://www.inca-global.com/news/the-evolution-of-the-virtual-influencer-no-longer-just-a-trend/

Mehar, P. (2020, August 11). Ghost Pacer, an ultimate holographic training partner for runners. *InceptiveMind*. https://www.inceptivemind.com/ghost-pacer-ultimate-holographic-training-partner-runners/14631/

Moustakas, E., Lamba, N., Mahmoud, D., & Ranganathan, C. (2020, June). Blurring lines between fiction and reality: Perspectives of experts on marketing effectiveness of virtual influencers. In *2020 International Conference on Cyber Security and Protection of Digital Services (Cyber Security)* (pp. 1–6). IEEE.

Mystakidis, S. (2022). Metaverse. *Encyclopedia*, 2(1), 486–497.

Park, S. M., & Kim, Y. G. (2022). A metaverse: Taxonomy, components, applications, and open challenges. In *IEEE Access*, vol. 10, pp. 4209–4251.

Parra-López, E., Gutiérrez-Taño, D., Diaz-Armas, R. J., & Bulchand-Gidumal, J. (2012). Travellers 2.0: Motivation, opportunity and ability to use social media. In Marianna Sigala and Evangelos Christou (Eds.), *Social Media in Travel, Tourism and Hospitality: Theory, Practice and Cases*, 171–187. London: Routledge.

Pokémon GO. (2016, July 6). Pokémon. Retrieved February 13, 2022, from https://www.pokemon.com/us/pokemon-video-games/pokemon-go/

Rasmussen, M. (2021, September 27). What's the difference between virtual influencers, VTubers, artificial intelligence, avatars, and more? *Virtual Humans*. https://www.virtualhumans.org/article/whats-the-difference-between-virtual-influencers-vtubers-artificial-intelligence-avatars

Roblox. (2022, January 26). *A year on Roblox: 2021 in data*. https://blog.roblox.com/2022/01/year-roblox-2021-data/

Rospigliosi, P. A. (2022). Metaverse or simulacra? Roblox, Minecraft, Meta and the turn to virtual reality for education, socialisation and work. *Interactive Learning Environments*, 30(1), 1–3.

Sabil, J. W., & Han, D. D. (2021). Immersive tourism-state of the art of immersive tourism realities through XR technology. [White paper]. Breda University of Applied Science. https://pure.buas.nl/ws/files/10867716/Weber_Han_Immersive_Tourism_State_of_the_Art.pdf

Seoul Convention Bureau. (2020, December 18). *Seoul held UIA associations round table Asia-Pacific 2020 in 3D virtual Seoul*. https://www.miceseoul.com/successfulstories/view?succesEventSn=150&curPage=1#none

Smart, J., Cascio, J., & Paffendorf, J. (2007). *Metaverse roadmap overview: Pathway to the 3D web*. CA: Acceleration Studies Foundation. Retrieved February 13, 2022, from https://metaverseroadmap.org/MetaverseRoadmapOverview.pdf

Statista. (2022, February 7). *U.S. adults reasons for joining the metaverse 2021*. https://www.statista.com/statistics/1288048/united-states-adults-reasons-for-joining-the-metaverse/

Stephenson, N. (1992). *Snow crash*. New York: Bantam Books.

Travers, C. (2020, November 4). What is a virtual influencer? Virtual influencers, defined and explained. *Virtual Humans*. https://www.virtualhumans.org/article/what-is-a-virtual-influencer-virtual-influencers-defined-and-explained

UNWTO. (2022, January 18). *Tourism grows 4% in 2021 but remains far below pre-pandemic levels*. https://www.unwto.org/news/tourism-grows-4-in-2021-but-remains-far-below-pre-pandemic-levels

Wut, T. M., Xu, J. B., & Wong, S. M. (2021). Crisis management research (1985–2020) in the hospitality and tourism industry: A review and research agenda. *Tourism Management*, *85*, 104307.

Xie-Carson, L., Benckendorff, P., & Hughes, K. (2021). Fake it to make it: Exploring Instagram users' engagement with virtual influencers in tourism. *Travel and Tourism Research Association: Advancing Tourism Research Globally*, *17*.

18 Challenges and opportunities for the incorporation of robots in hotels

Craig Webster and Stanislav Ivanov

Introduction: History of robots and their incorporation into hospitality

The concept of the robot is now more than 100 years old and has moved from a concept to an integral part of the economy in just a few decades. Unimation (derived from "universal automation"), in 1956, was the first company founded to produce a robot that would do tasks that were dangerous and difficult for humans (Parekattil & Moran, 2010). Its first industrial robot was installed in 1961 at General Motors' plant in Trenton, New Jersey, where it unloaded high-temperature parts from a die-casting machine (Stone, 2005). Since then, robots have been produced and were first incorporated into various manufacturing, and, more recently, service industries. While the industrial robot has been with us for quite some time, the incorporation of robots into service industries has lagged behind. Academic research on the application of robots in travel, tourism, and hospitality has only recently begun to investigate the implementation of robotic technologies in hospitality and related industries (Ivanov et al., 2019), with the first-known academic article by Schraft and Wanner (1993), making the first foray into the new research field less than three decades ago.

A robot is an "actuated mechanism programmable in two or more axes with a degree of autonomy, moving within its environment, to perform intended tasks" (International Organization for Standardization, 2012: n.p.). There are several key issues in this definition that need attention:

- The robot is a *mechanism*, i.e., it has physical embodiment, unlike chatbots, which that exist solely in the digital space.
- The robot is a *task-oriented* device, i.e., it is produced to implement specific tasks (prepare a pancake, clean floor, provide information, deliver items).
- The robot is *programmable*, i.e., the tasks it implements and the way it operates can be determined and changed, as necessary.
- The robot has some *degree of autonomy*. The latter is defined as "the extent to which a robot can sense the environment, plan based on that environment, and act upon that environment, with the intent of reaching some goal (either given to or created by the robot) without external control" (Beer, Fisk and Rogers, 2014: 77). Autonomy means that the robot takes some of the decisions related to the implementation of its tasks independently without human supervision. For instance, a room service delivery robot communicates with the elevator system of the hotel to move across the floors and deliver the orders to the guests. It adjusts its movement trajectory based on the obstacles it detects en route (e.g., a person or a housekeeper cart in a hotel's corridor)

- The robot has some *degree of mobility*. Some robots are mobile (e.g., delivery robots, autonomous drones, autonomous vehicles) while others do not move around the premises of the hospitality company but still have some moving parts. For example, the robot Pepper is not a mobile robot but it can move its robotic hands and turn its head to the human to enhance the human–robot interaction experience.

From a technical perspective, robots have sensors and actuators. Sensors allow the robot to obtain data about some aspects of its surrounding environment. Robots can have a wide variety of sensors depending on their intended use, such as sensors for identifying objects, sound/voice, distance/location, pressure, temperature, power consumption, for communicating with other devices. Actuators help the robot affect its environment and include a motor, robotic arm, screen, light, loudspeaker, transmitter (Ben-Ari & Mondada, 2018).

Based on their application, robots can be industrial, service and social robots. Industrial robots are largely used in manufacturing, although recently they have been adapted for the service industries as well. For example, Makr Shakr (2022) has developed a robotic bartender based on an industrial robotic arm. Service robots perform "useful tasks for humans or equipment excluding industrial automation applications" (International Organization for Standardization, 2012: n.p.). They can be used for the provision of information (e.g., robotic receptionists, concierges, hosts in restaurants), cleaning (of floors, swimming pools), item delivery (e.g., room service), the disinfection of premises with ultraviolet light, and cutting grass in a hotel's garden/park, entertainment (e.g., dancing for guests during a hotel's animation programme). Those service robots designed to primarily interact with humans are called social robots. Usually, they are anthropomorphic in appearance (e.g., Pepper, Nao, Sophia, Promobot) (Figure 18.1), but some social robots are zoomorphic (e.g., Paro resembles a small seal) or caricatured (e.g., Amazon's Astro). Most service robots, however, have a functional design (Figure 18.2), i.e., they look more like a machine and their design is driven by the tasks they need to perform (e.g., the vacuum cleaning robots, most waiter robots, room service delivery robots, disinfection robots).

Robot technologies are being utilised in many different ways in tourism and hospitality services (Ivanov, Webster, & Berezina, 2017). While the hospitality industry uses a great deal of labour, there is a clear indication that in the most developed of countries the demographics will ensure that the current labour shortage is not a short-term problem but a longer-term issue with which employers will have to grapple (Webster, 2021). Robots will come to the rescue to compensate for the insufficient supply of human labour in the hotel industry (Webster & Ivanov, 2020b).

Here, we first discuss the major trends and issues related to the coming switchover to a more robotised hospitality. We then look at a prediction for what will come for hospitality in the next few decades. Finally, we conclude with a discussion of the contributions we have made to the issue.

Major trends and issues in the switchover to robot labour in hotels

While we march into a robonomic society (Ivanov, 2021), we will see the increasing automation of all industries. What makes the hospitality industry especially interesting is that it is very labour-intensive. In terms of the switchover from an industry that is largely based upon service provided by humans to one that is to a large extent supplied by robots, there

Challenges and opportunities for incorporation of robots 223

Figure 18.1 Pepper robot.
(Photo credit: Stanislav Ivanov).

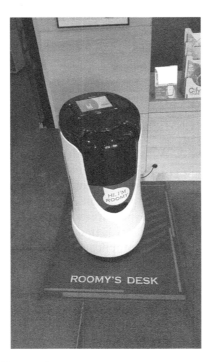

Figure 18.2 A room-service delivery robot.
(Photo credit: Stanislav Ivanov).

will be several concerns. Here, we delve into how the operations, finance, human resource management, marketing, and the interior design of accommodation establishments will have to be dealt with in the switchover in the coming decades.

Operations

From an operations management perspective, the implementation of robotic technologies in hotels has a wide array of impacts. On the positive side, robots contribute to the easier scheduling and planning of operations due to their advantages compared to human employees – they work 24/7, do not get ill, do not complain, do not shirk from work, and implement their tasks as they should. Robots malfunction but their behaviour is indeed largely predictable, which facilitates the planning of operations. Additionally, robots save employees time and energy. While robots implement dirty, dull, dangerous and repetitive tasks, employees can concentrate on customer service and other revenue-generating activities. In that way, robots may help hotels focus more on their core value – hospitality. On the negative side, robots decrease the flexibility of a hotel's service delivery system. For example, a robotic bartender will make a cocktail always as per the recipe; it will not understand a customer's request to put 'a bit more vodka' in the cocktail because 'a bit more' is a vague expression that the robot will be unable to translate into a specific quantity, while humans could interpret it. Furthermore, robots collect a great deal of information (e.g., a digital map of the hotel, faces of customers and employees); hence, their implementation raises privacy and security concerns of potential damage to customers, employees, the company and its partners in case of data leakage. Finally, as with any device robots require maintenance. Hotels also need to consider insurance for damages on and by the robots. From an accounting perspective, robots are assets. Due to their high costs (one room service delivery robot is within the range of 10,000–20,000 euros), it needs to be insured to protect the hotel's interests in case of damages to the robot. At the same time, as robots have some degree of autonomy, they may harm a guest or an employee or damage their property. That is why hotels that use robots need to consider insurance for damages caused by robots.

Finance

With regards to finance, the incorporation of robots into operations will have many ramifications. Robots will be incorporated into establishments when their expected value will outweigh their costs (Ivanov & Webster, 2019) although some studies do not find a link between perceived robot costs and hoteliers' intentions to adopt them in hotels' operations (Pizam et al., 2022). While the expectation is that the use of robots will make the running of hotels more profitable, due to the movement away from expensive human labour that may be in short supply, the capital expenditures and service costs could be substantial. One major positive aspect for the industry is that the movement away from human labour may, in some ways, make payroll less complicated, there will still be running costs associated with robots, including insurance, energy costs, service costs, and other hidden costs such as the cost of recovery following robot service failures (Choi, Mattila, & Bolton, 2021). From the perspective of the customer, the cost of robot services will be an issue, since the expectation is that robot-delivered services are linked with cost savings for customers (Ivanov & Webster, 2021). However, cost savings should not be the primary motivation of hotel managers because customers' perceptions that managers use robots to cut costs have a negative effect on their robot use intentions (Belanche, Casaló, & Flavián, 2021).

Although cost reduction is a legitimate reason for the implementation of robots in hotels, customers need to see that the service they get is enhanced as well. Belanche, Casaló, and Flavián (2021) find that customers' perceptions that managers use robots to enhance the service overcompensate the negative effect of cost-cutting on their intentions to use robots. From the perspective of the employees, what is important is the effect of robots on employees' salaries and social security payments. While previous studies have shown that robots lead to lower salaries (DeCanio, 2016), the lack of sufficient labour supply on the tourism and hospitality labour market may mitigate the negative effect of robotisation on salaries.

Human resource management

Human resource management will be massively influenced by the increasing incorporation of robots into hospitality. Many tasks will shift from actions largely dependent upon human labour to ones largely dependent upon robots. By automating dirty, dull, dangerous and repetitive tasks (e.g., cleaning, disinfection, provision of information, transporting items), robots in hotels create decent work environments for their employees (Tuomi et al., 2020). Since not all tasks can and will be automated in the near future, there will be a period of time in which there will be a great number of humans working side-by-side with robots. In many ways, this will result in a new workforce that will have to be receptive to the limitations and capabilities of robots. Such a shift in the workplace will have implications not just for the management of the workforce in the workplace but also for the quality of the education that employees will have before employment. In this way, we will see that universities and other training facilities will have to change their approach to education to be relevant in the new economy (Murphy, Hofacker, & Gretzel, 2017).

In addition, the future hospitality workplace will have to provide training for humans to work together with their robotic co-workers, since there will likely be Luddite reactions to the incorporation of such technologies into the workplace (Ivanov, Kuyumdzhiev, & Webster, 2020). Many employees and local residents (who are also hotel employees) may feel insecure about their jobs. Indeed, the research does indicate that many workers are concerned with being replaced by robots but that the ideology and political beliefs of individuals shape attitudes towards job replacement (Nam, 2019). However, there is an indication that there will be many employees who will welcome working together with robots and have no problem relegating some tasks to robots (van Looy, 2022).

Marketing

From a marketing perspective, robots can be used to develop experiences for hotel guests (Tung & Au, 2018; Tung & Law, 2017). Because service robots are still very rare in the hotel industry, the robotic service experience is considered novel and exciting (Ivanov, Webster, & Garenko, 2018). Hotels that use robots also boast positive word of mouth because their guests share their robotic experiences on social media. This will indirectly serve the interests of local residents because it will also improve the destination image. Another marketing benefit of robots for hotels is that they provide consistent service quality. A robotic bartender will prepare the cocktail in the same way as per the recipe. A room service delivery robot will deliver the purchased item as requested. They can also make the service delivery process funny and entertaining (e.g., a robot dancing for the guests in a hotel's restaurant). However, once robots become more widespread, their novelty advantage will disappear and guests will see them as part of the standard hotel offering. In that case, customers start seeing robots as cost-saving devices rather than as devices for experience enhancement and they may want part of hotels' cost savings to be transferred to them in the form of price discounts. A previous study by Ivanov and Webster (2021) showed that customers requested, on average, between an 8% and a 10% discount if they were to be served entirely by robots compared to an entirely human-delivered service for all travel, tourism and hospitality services included in the research, including hotel accommodation. Therefore, although hotels may save on costs when using robots, they may also save on revenue due to the lower willingness to pay for robot-delivered services of hotel guests. A cost–benefit analysis needs to be carefully implemented to check whether an investment in service robots will actually pay off.

Interior design of establishments

One of the critical changes that will be needed is that facilities will need to be friendly places for robots. Many different types of robots will be used in hotels for front-of-house and back-of-house operations. Some robots may be stationary, but others may be mobile (Ivanov & Webster, 2017). The stationary robots raise numerous concerns regarding health and safety to ensure that employees and customers can interact with the robots safely and effectively such as the supply of energy to the machines and design issues related to the servicing and supplying of goods for the robots. However, a more interesting case is the mobile robots in hotels. Companion robots, delivery robots, security robots, and other types of mobile robots will require additional design concerns to ensure that they can navigate the environment safely and effectively, so the design will have to create environments that are inclusive and welcoming venues for robots (Tan, Mohan, & Watanabe, 2016). Robots need to move freely in the hotels. Doors, doorsteps, and stairs are obstacles that hinder a robot's navigation within the premises of the hotel. The robot needs to be able to communicate with the elevator system of the hotel to move across the floors. For customers, a major concern will be that the interior design is not just appropriate and enables robots to operate but also that changes to the design do not hinder or undermine their customer experience and do not lead to anything unpleasant to any of the senses (sound, smell, temperature) that would undermine their otherwise pleasant time as guests.

Table 18.1 summarises the main trends and issues related to the implementation of service robots in hotels from the viewpoints of the various stakeholders.

Predictions for 2030 to 2050

With the increased use of robots in hotels, there will be issues about how the transformation of the hospitality environment will impact the industry and the customer experience. Here, we explore some of the major changes and make some predictions for how the increased incorporation into the environment will impact the industry and the customers.

The expectations of and experiences for customers

With the further incorporation of robots into hotels, we expect that there will be a bifurcation of the industry into high-tech and high-touch markets (Ivanov and Webster, 2021; Zeng, Chen, & Lew, 2020) because many guests expect that increased use of robots will result in cost savings for hoteliers and customers. While customers may underestimate the cost of robots and the significant running costs to keep them operational, the expectation

Table 18.1 Trends and issues with regards to the switchover to robot labour

	Trend	Major Concerns for Management	Major Concerns for Customers	Major Concerns of Shareholders / Owners	Major Concerns of Employees	Major Concerns of Local Residents
Operations	Greater provision of services in the back-of-house and front-of-house operations by robots	• Cost-effectiveness	• Service quality needs to be good despite the use of robot	• Cost-effectiveness	• Human-robot collaboration	• Service quality needs to be good despite the use of robot
Finance	Changes in capital expenditures and running expenses of the hotel	• Investment • Service and repair costs • Running costs	• Cost of services	• Profitability	• Salaries and social security payments	• Impacts of robots on the salaries and social security payments to employees • Impacts of robots on tax revenue
Human Resources	Incorporation of more robot labour in the workplace	• Training for humans to work with robots • Safety of human-robot interactions	• Service quality from robotic services	• Training for humans to work with robots • Safety of human-robot interactions	• Training for humans to work with robots • Safety of human-robot interactions • Decent work environment	• Jobs for local residents

(Continued)

Table 18.1 (Continued)

	Trend	Major Concerns for Management	Major Concerns for Customers	Major Concerns of Shareholders / Owners	Major Concerns of Employees	Major Concerns of Local Residents
Marketing	Greater stress on the quality of service by robots in marketing	• The use of robots to differentiate hotel products • The use of robots to attract visitors to particular establishments and chains	• The attractiveness of using robot services and the quality of such services	• The use of robots to differentiate hotel products • The use of robots to attract visitors to particular establishments and chains	• Pride in working with a robot	• Destination image
Interior Design	Mobile robots that move around the facilities of the hotel	• Ensuring that space and design account for stationary robots' needs • Ensuring that design allows mobile robots to navigate facilities with ease • Ensuring that design accounts for space allocation for charging, repair, and support services for robots	• Robot safety • Privacy from robot intrusions • Visitors experience good despite interior design changes to facilitate robots	• Investment in interior design	• Ensuring the design allows safe human-robot interactions	• Ensuring the design allows safe human-robot interactions

is that robot labour should result in lower costs for the customer. This expectation, coupled with the labour shortages in developed countries (Webster, 2021), means that services in most hotels will be provided by robots. However, with the increased automation and its expected income inequalities (Mao, Koide, Brem, & Akenji, 2020), we envision the growth of a market that demands high-touch service provision. Those customers with significant wealth (the minority) will tend to visit hotels delivering most services with humans and the rest will expect many of their services to be provided by robots. Therefore, the hotel market will likely be segmented into low-to-medium-priced high-tech hotels and medium-to-high-priced high-touch hotels. This bifurcation of the market, however, does not mean that high-tech hotels will not have employees or that high-touch hotels will not have robots – in both groups, various mixes of human employees and robots will implement the back-of-house tasks.

The expectations of and experiences for hoteliers

Hoteliers will have a very different working environment. The switchover to the use of robotic labour will mean that many of the issues that complicate human resources in hospitality as an industry (high labour turnover and seasonality) will largely be done away with. This, however, will lead to several new concerns. First, there will be an issue with navigating the financials of robots. There will be a need for cost–benefit analysis of robot implementation, including concerns regarding taxation issues (Webster & Ivanov, 2020a). Second, there will be concerns regarding human resources, since human employees will have to have the emotional intelligence and technical skills to work together with robots as co-workers in the workplace as these will be key skills in the future (World Economic Forum, 2020). These employees will likely be more highly paid but flexible and willing to be trained in the new technologies that are incorporated into the operations. Third, there will be new strategic concerns regarding whether a hotel would rather focus on the large high-tech market which uses predominantly automation to provide services or on the lucrative but smaller high-touch market. The wide spread of robots for the provision of various services in and outside tourism and hospitality and their improved technological capabilities, will contribute positively towards more realistic expectations of hoteliers about what robots can and cannot do and how to incorporate them effectively and efficiently in the service delivery process. This will help them not only avoid the problems faced by the first robotised hotel, Henn na hotel in Nagasaki, Japan, which was forced to turn off half of its robots (Hertzfeld, 2019), but experiment with innovative ways of robotic service delivery.

Other issues

The use of robots in hotels is closely connected to other issues that need to be considered when deciding on the use of robots. First, one of the recurring issues in the literature is the role of gender in terms of the perception of robots. The majority of studies find that females are more likely to be sceptical of robots (Ivanov, Webster, & Garenko, 2018; Katz & Halpern, 2014), although some studies do not find that there is a relationship between the gender and the attitudes towards robots (Dinet & Vivian, 2014). These findings based upon gender differences seem to support the general research findings that females are attracted to social endeavors and males are attracted to those things that are mechanical (Su, Rounds, & Armstrong, 2009). For hoteliers this implies that male employees are likely to be more receptive towards the implementation of robots than female employees and that female employees will be more resistant towards to the robotisation of hotel services.

Second, previous studies have shown that those who have generally positive attitudes towards robots are more likely to have more positive attitudes towards the use of robots for specific services (Ivanov, Webster, & Garenko, 2018), since there seems to be a segments of the population that are robophilic and robophobic. The greater exposure to robots in hotels and other service settings may soften the robophobic sentiments of hotel employees and hotel guests because they would experience first-hand what robots can and cannot do and form adequate expectations about robots' role in the hospitality industry.

Third, a major concern is the way that the incorporation of robots into hospitality will impact upon the workforce. While there will be resistance from some employees because they will see robots as their substitutes, many other employees will embrace the incorporation of the technologies because they will see the benefits of robots for their own job performance (Ivanov & Webster, 2019; Nam, 2019; van Looy, 2022). The implementation of robots will have different effects in different countries depending on their demographic contexts. For example, while there is a strong need for robots in economies in which there are declining birthrates (Webster, 2021), in developing countries in which there is substantial youth unemployment, attitudes towards the incorporation of technologies of the fourth industrial revolution may be quite different (Matli & Ngoepe, 2020).

Fourth, the new technologies have benefits such as improved communications and productivity there is also an indication that they lead to increasing inequalities and a surveillance society (Mao, Koide, Brem, & Akenji, 2020) and robots in hospitality are part of that ecosystem. With the development of a bifurcated hotel industry (high-tech and high-touch), there will be different types of customers with somewhat different demands. They will all expect high-quality services, but one will demand that humans provide services while the other expects to be served by a robot. One common expectation by all customers, though, is that there will be some sort of safeguards with regards to privacy and information security.

Conclusion

With demographic drivers in play that favour automation (Webster & Ivanov, 2020b; Webster, 2021) and the increased capability of technology, we are stepping into a robonomic society. Hotels, as with many other service providers, will make the switch over to the use of automation technologies of all sorts, including robots. With this, there are many fundamental issues that will change since the major providers of services will be machines and not human. However, we have the expectation that consumers will retain high standards so that hoteliers in the future will have to be mindful of the switchover, ensuring that customer satisfaction remains high while there are massive changes to the way that services are provided.

May the robots serve you well today and in the future!

References

Beer, J. M., Fisk, A. D., & Rogers, W. A. (2014). Toward a framework for levels of robot autonomy in human–robot interaction. *Journal of Human–Robot Interaction*, 3(2), 74–99. https://doi.org/10.5898/JHRI.3.2.Beer

Belanche, D., Casaló, L. V., & Flavián, C. (2021). Frontline robots in tourism and hospitality: service enhancement or cost reduction?. *Electronic Markets*, 31(3), 477–492. https://doi.org/10.1007/s12525-020-00432-5

Ben-Ari, M., & Mondada, F. (2018). *Elements of robotics*. Cham: Springer International Publishing.

Choi, S., Mattila, A. S., & Bolton, L. E. (2021). To err is human (-oid): how do consumers react to robot service failure and recovery? *Journal of Service Research*, 24(3), 354–371. https://doi.org/10.1177/1094670520978798

DeCanio, S. J. (2016). Robots and humans – complements or substitutes?. *Journal of Macroeconomics*, 49, 280–291. https://doi.org/10.1016/j.jmacro.2016.08.003

Dinet, J., & Vivian, R. (2014). Exploratory investigation of attitudes towards assistive robots for future users. *Le travail humain*, 77(2), 105–125.

Hertzfeld, E. (2019). Japan's Henn na Hotel fires half its robot workforce. Hotelmanagement.net. Retrieved 14 March 2022 from https://www.hotelmanagement.net/tech/japan-s-henn-na-hotel-fires-half-its-robot-workforce.

International Organization for Standardization (2012). *ISO 8373:2012(en) Robots and robotic devices – Vocabulary*. Retrieved from https://www.iso.org/obp/ui/#iso:std:iso:8373:ed-2:v1:en:term:2.2

Ivanov, S. (2021). Robonomics: The rise of the automated economy. *ROBONOMICS: The Journal of the Automated Economy*, 1, 11. Retrieved from https://journal.robonomics.science/index.php/rj/article/view/11

Ivanov, S., Gretzel, U., Berezina, K., Sigala, M., & Webster, C. (2019). Progress on robotics in hospitality and tourism: a review of the literature. *Journal of Hospitality and Tourism Technology*, 10(4), 489–521. https://doi.org/10.1108/JHTT-08-2018-0087

Ivanov, S., Kuyumdzhiev, M., & Webster, C. (2020). Automation fears: drivers and solutions, *Technology in Society*, 63, 101431. https://doi.org/10.1016/j.techsoc.2020.101431.

Ivanov, S., & Webster, C. (2017). Designing robot-friendly hospitality facilities. *Proceedings of the Scientific Conference "Tourism. Innovations. Strategies"*, 13–14 October 2017, Bourgas, Bulgaria, pp. 74–81.

Ivanov, S., & Webster, C. (2018). Adoption of robots, artificial intelligence and service automation by travel, tourism and hospitality companies – a cost–benefit analysis. In Marinov, V., Vodenska, M., Assenova, M., & Dogramadjieva, E. (Eds), *Traditions and Innovations in Contemporary Tourism*. Cambridge Scholars Publishing, pp. 190–203.

Ivanov, S., & Webster, C. (2019). Economic Fundamentals of the Use of Robots, Artificial Intelligence and Service Automation in Travel, Tourism and Hospitality Ivanov, S., & Webster, C. (Eds) (2019a). *Robots, Artificial Intelligence and Service Automation in Travel, Tourism and Hospitality*. Bingley, UK: Emerald Publishing, pp. 39–55.

Ivanov, S., & Webster, C. (2021). Willingness-to-pay for robot-delivered tourism and hospitality services – an exploratory study. *International Journal of Contemporary Hospitality Management*, 33(11), 3926–3955. https://doi.org/10.1108/IJCHM-09-2020-1078

Ivanov, S., Webster, C., & Garenko, A. (2018). Young Russian adults' attitudes towards the potential use of robots in hotels. *Technology in Society*, 55, 24–32. https://doi.org/10.1016/j.techsoc.2018.06.004

Ivanov, S. H., Webster, C., & Berezina, K. (2017). Adoption of robots and service automation by tourism and hospitality companies. *Revista Turismo & Desenvolvimento*, 27(28), 1501–1517.

Katz, J.E., & Halpern, D. (2014). Attitudes towards robots suitability for various jobs as affected robot appearance. *Behaviour and Information Technology*, 33(9), 941–953. https://doi.org/10.1080/0144929X.2013.783115

van Looy, A. (2022). Employees' attitudes towards intelligent robots: a dilemma analysis. *Information Systems and e-Business Management*. https://doi.org/10.1007/s10257-022-00552-9

Makr Shakr (2022). Official website. Retrieved from https://www.makrshakr.com/

Mao, C., Koide, R., Brem, A., & Akenji, L. (2020). Technology foresight for social good: Social implications of technological innovation by 2050 from a Global Expert Survey. *Technological Forecasting and Social Change*, 153, 119914. https://doi.org/10.1016/j.techfore.2020.119914

Matli, W. & Ngoepe, M. (2020). Persistently high levels of youth unemployment in the 4IR digital society: a structuration theory perspective. *Commonwealth Youth and Development*, 18(2), 21. https://doi.org/10.25159/2663-6549/6751

Murphy, J., Hofacker, C., & Gretzel, U. (2017). Dawning of the age of robots in hospitality and tourism: challenges for teaching and research. *European Journal of Tourism Research*, 15, 104–111. https://doi.org/10.54055/ejtr.v15i.265

Nam, T. (2019). Citizen attitudes about job placement by robotic automation. *Futures*, 109, 39–49. https://doi.org/10.1016/j.futures.2019.04.005

Parekattil, S. J., & Moran, M. E. (2010). Robotic instrumentation: evolution and microsurgical applications. *Indian Journal of Urology: IJU: Journal of the Urological Society of India*, 26(3), 395–403. https://doi.org/10.4103/0970-1591.70580

Pizam, A., Ozturk, A. B., Balderas-Cejudo, A., Buhalis, D., Fuchs, G., Hara, T., Meira, J., Revilla, M. R. G., Sethi, D., Shen, Y., State, O., Hacikara, A., & Chaulagain, S. (2022). Factors affecting hotel managers' intentions to adopt robotic technologies: A global study. *International Journal of Hospitality Management*, 102, 103139.

Schraft, R.D. & Wanner, M.C. (1993). The aircraft cleaning robot 'SKYWASH'. *Industrial Robot: An International Journal*, 20(6), 21–24.

Stone, W. L. (2005). The history of robotics. In Kurfess, T. R. (Ed.). *Robotics and automation handbook*. Boca Raton, FL: CRC Press, pp. 1–12.

Su, R., Rounds, J., & Armstrong, P. I. (2009). Men and things, women and people: A meta-analysis of sex differences in interests. *Psychological Bulletin*, 135(6), 859–884. https://doi.org/10.1037/a0017364

Tan, N., Mohan, R. E., & Watanabe, A. (2016). Toward a framework for robot-inclusive environments, *Automation in Construction*, 69, 68–78. https://doi.org/10.1016/j.autcon.2016.06.001.

Tung, V. W. S., & Au, N. (2018). Exploring customer experiences with robotics in hospitality. *International Journal of Contemporary Hospitality Management*, 30(7), 2680–2697. https://doi.org/10.1108/IJCHM-06-2017-0322

Tung, V. W. S., & Law, R. (2017). The potential for tourism and hospitality experience research in human–robot interactions. *International Journal of Contemporary Hospitality Management*, 29(10), 2498–2513. https://doi.org/10.1108/IJCHM-09-2016-0520

Tuomi, A., Tussyadiah, I., Ling, E. C., Miller, G., & Lee, G. (2020). x=(tourism_work) y=(sdg8) while y= true: automate (x). *Annals of Tourism Research*, 84, 102978. https://doi.org/10.1016/j.annals.2020.102978

Webster, C. (2021). Demography as a Driver of Robonomics. *ROBONOMICS: The Journal of the Automated Economy*, 1, 12.

Webster, C. & Ivanov, S. (2020a). Robotics, artificial intelligence, and the evolving nature of work. In George, B. & Paul, J. (Eds), *Digital Transformation in Business and Society Theory and Cases*. Cham: Palgrave-MacMillan, pp. 127–143.

Webster, C. & Ivanov, S. (2020b). Demographic change as a driver for tourism automation. *Journal of Tourism Futures*, 6(3), 263–270. https://doi.org/10.1108/JTF-10-2019-0109

World Economic Forum (2020). *The future of jobs report 2020*. Retrieved 11 May 2022 from https://www3.weforum.org/docs/WEF_Future_of_Jobs_2020.pdf

Zeng, Z., Chen, P. J., & Lew, A. A. (2020). From high-touch to high-tech: COVID-19 drives robotics adoption. *Tourism Geographies*, 22(3), 724–734. https://doi.org/10.1080/14616688.2020.1762118

1.4
Supply-side trends
Policies and issues

Cristina Maxim in Chapter 19 writes on *Urbanisation: Trends and issues in world tourism cities*. The chapter focuses on world tourism cities, which are important destinations that lately have received an increased attention from scholars. It specifically examines the current trends that are shaping tourism cities and the challenges faced by these environments. The chapter first discusses the rapid growth of urbanisation, with an emphasis on its effects on communities. Urbanisation is seen to be one of the megatrends that the global society is experiencing at present. The increased level of urbanisation that was seen over the past decade in many countries has contributed to the growth of the urban tourism phenomenon, which was one of the fastest-growing types of tourism before the COVID-19 pandemic. The implications of the pandemic on world tourism cities are briefly touched upon, with an emphasis on the major tourism crisis that many urban destinations have been or are still going through.

Overtourism: Trends, issues, impacts and implications is the topic for Chapter 20 by **Richard W. Butler** and **Rachel Dodds**. While the existence of overtourism as a phenomenon has been discussed and conceptualised, a key question remains as to whether or not there is a solution to such a 'wicked' problem. This chapter first outlines the defining trends and issues that have led to the use of the term and then briefly reviews the impacts of overtourism. It then discusses attempts at mitigating and preventing the occurrence of the phenomenon, and the reasons for their general failure to date. The chapter concludes with an overview of likely future implications and trends.

David L. Edgell, Sr. authors Chapter 21 about *Issues and policies that have an impact on future trends in global tourism*. There are many issues and policies that have an impact on future trends in global tourism. Such critical issues that need the immediate attention of the global tourism community include understanding the impact of transportation disruptions, climate change and global warming, traveller safety and security, global cooperation with respect to traveller barriers to travel, a well-educated and trained workforce, approaches to meeting natural and human-induced disasters, the introduction of new technology and dynamic plans for the overall management of sustainable tourism. The opportunity for positive future trends in global tourism will ultimately depend on international organisations, businesses, government, academia, not-for-profit entities, and local tourism leaders all working together to develop policies and plans to address the important current and future tourism issues that face the travel and tourism industry.

Tourism policies for the next normal: Trends and issues from global case studies are discussed in Chapter 22 by **Vanessa Gowreesunkar, Shem Wambugu Maingi**, and **Chris Cooper**. The aim of this chapter is to examine tourism policies adopted by tourism destinations following the pandemic. From a methodological point of view, collective case designs are chosen as these are widely used in tourism studies when it is not possible to separate the phenomenon being studied from its context. Drawing from 15 global case studies, this chapter proposes a synthesis of evidence-based tourism policies embraced by tourism destinations. Findings show that the crisis is an opportunity to rethink the tourism system; the COVID-19 pandemic is not solely a tourism issue. Rather, it is a health issue requiring whole-of-destination policies, including health and other sectors of the economy. Rebuilding tourism requires collective effort, global solidarity, and, more importantly, tourism policies that address structural weaknesses, advance key socio-economic priorities and take advantage of new opportunities. Information derived from the case studies is helpful to destination managers, policy makers and other tourism stakeholders interested in implementing tourism policies that are tested and trusted in a pandemic context.

19 Urbanisation

Trends and issues in world tourism cities

Cristina Maxim

Introduction

Nowadays over half of the world's population lives in towns and cities. Urbanisation is therefore considered by the United Nations a key megatrend alongside global population growth, ageing population and international migration (UN, 2019). Urban areas are places where wealth is created and innovation takes place, as well as places where workforce skills are developed. They are places where people live, shop, and enjoy other leisure activities, but also destinations that attract many visitors interested in experiencing those complex environments. Large cities, in particular, offer great transportation and accommodation infrastructure, which facilitates tourism activities. However, urban areas have been recognised as an important setting for tourism only a few decades ago.

Urban tourism used to be one of the fastest-growing tourism sectors before the COVID-19 pandemic and this form of tourism is expected to become popular again in the near future. Among the factors that contributed to the rapid growth of this sector are urbanisation, affordable transport and travel facilities, increased mobility, new technologies and digital platforms, as well as a growing middle class with more money to spend on holidays (UNWTO, 2020b).

World tourism cities, in particular, attract large number of visitors, as they perform various functions, and present specific features that differentiate them from other tourism cities. Morrison and Maxim (2022) identify five distinct characteristics of world tourism cities, which are briefly introduced here.

Firstly, world tourism cities are considered a key gateway for tourism in a country. They offer convenient access to various means of transportation, and often act as important nodes in the transportation system, such as hubs for airlines, railways, ships, or key points in the national highway systems. Secondly, world tourism cities are influential places that perform multiple functions. They are usually home to government bodies, are finance and banking centres, attract key industries and services, and tend to be hubs for the MICE (meetings, incentives, conferences, and exhibitions) market.

The third characteristic of world tourism cities is that they are impactful destinations, which tend to economically influence other regions in the country. They are key centres of culture and heritage, represent innovative and creative hubs, and can have political power as capital cities. Fourthly, they are cosmopolitan places that attract many international visitors besides domestic travellers, as they are lively and dynamic centres that bring together a mix of people and cultures. Finally, they are easily recognised destinations, not only for being famous for the attractions they offer, but also as a result of the social media attention they receive.

Major developments in the field of world tourism cities

Having briefly discussed the features and characteristics of world tourism cities, we look next at how this area of research has developed over the years.

Although considered to be one of the earliest forms of tourism (e.g., the pilgrims from the 14th centuries, the Grand Tours from the 17th and 18th centuries), urban tourism as a research area tended to be neglected by scholars for many years (Ashworth & Page, 2011). However, this situation changed over the past few decades when city tourism started to attract more attention from academics, and with new works contributing to developing this field of study. Therefore, this area of research has evolved from the initial studies that mainly looked at urban geography of seaside resorts (e.g., Barrett, 1958; Gilbert, 1939; Pearce, 1978; Pigram, 1977), to the works in the 1980s and 1990s that largely focused on understanding this complex phenomenon (e.g., Ashworth, 1989; Ashworth & Tunbridge, 1990; Getz, 1993; Jansen-Verbeke, 1986; Law, 1992; Page, 1995).

During the 2000s more studies on urban tourism emerged, part of them trying to address some of the criticisms towards earlier works related to the lack of integrated approaches in researching this topic. These include the works of Pearce (2001), who proposed an integrated framework for urban tourism research; Law (2002) on the visitor economy in large cities; Page and Hall (2003) on managing urban tourism; Beedie (2005) on the adventure of urban tourism; Connelly (2007) on urban governance and tourism competitiveness; Pearce (2007) on capital city tourism; Edwards, Griffin and Hayllar (2008), who developed a strategic framework for urban tourism research; Timur and Getz (2008), who look at managing stakeholders in urban destinations; Maitland and Ritchie (2009), who contribute to expanding the knowledge on national capital tourism; and Maitland and Newman (2009), who brought to attention the concept of world tourism cities.

The past decade has seen an increased attention from academics who looked at trends and issues faced by urban destinations. Among these studies we note Nunkoo and Ramkissoon (2010) on urban tourism in small islands; Ashworth and Page (2011) on paradoxes in urban tourism research; Richards (2014) on creativity and tourism in cities; Miller, Merrilees and Coghlan (2015) on sustainable urban tourism and pro-environmental behaviour; Gretzel, Zhong and Koo (2016) on the application of smart tourism to cities; Maxim (2016) on sustainable tourism implementation in urban areas; Wearing and Foley (2017) on how tourists explore and experience cities; Su, Bramwell and Whalley (2018) on urban heritage tourism; Koens, Postma and Papp (2018) on overtourism and the impact of tourism in cities; Romero-García et al. (2019), who conducted a literature review on systems approach in urban tourism research; Cohen and Hopkins (2019) on autonomous vehicles and urban tourism; and the *Routledge Handbook of Tourism Cities* edited by Morrison and Coca-Stefaniak (2021), which presents a comprehensive overview of emerging themes in urban tourism.

When looking specifically at the topic of world tourism cities, not much research has been published to date. Some of the most significant works include Maitland and Newman's (2009) book, which looks at urban neighbourhood development in several world cities; Simpson's (2016) work on "tourist utopia" in three post-world cities; Maitland's (2016) paper on how tourists experience world tourism cities; Maxim's (2019, 2021) works on challenges faced by world tourism cities; and Morrison and Maxim's (2022) book on world tourism cities that takes a systematic approach to analyse those environments.

Challenges faced by world tourism cities

Tourism is an integral part of many world cities as it contributes to their development, with policy makers generally encouraging the growth of this phenomenon as it is seen to bring economic and social benefits. Tourism, for example, contributes to job creation and infrastructure development; it is an important source of revenue for many local economies, and encourages cultural exchanges between hosts and visitors. Some examples include cities such as Macao, Cancún, Marrakech and Las Vegas, which, before the coronavirus pandemic, used to rely on a significant contribution of tourism to their GDP (WTTC, 2019). Other megacities for which tourism is an important source of revenue are Shanghai, Beijing, Paris, London, New York, Tokyo, Bangkok, Istanbul, Singapore, Sydney, and Rio de Janeiro.

However, as seen in many destinations, tourism development in cities is associated with several negative impacts that require careful planning and management. Among the challenges identified by scholars are a rise in the price of land, properties, and food; the deterioration of the natural and built environment as a result of the large numbers of visitors; an increase in crime rates and antisocial behaviour; a loss of cultural identity; conflicts that can arise between locals and visitors; displacement, gentrification or touristification in those areas; traffic congestion, littering, and increased pollution that is already an issue in many such destinations (Maxim, 2021; Morrison & Maxim, 2022). Therefore, policy makers in world tourism cities are faced with multiple challenges related to the complex nature of the urban tourism phenomenon, and how to better plan and manage this activity.

Among the most important challenges faced lately by world tourism cities are the sustainability debates, climate change, managing conflicts between visitors and hosts, preparing for crises and disasters, and implementing smart tourism solutions, all of which are briefly discussed here.

Sustainability

Sustainability is an important topic that deserves some consideration when discussing trends and issues in world tourism cities. Sustainable development is widely perceived as a tool that helps managers and policy makers in balancing the negative and positive impacts of tourism in a destination. This concept can be traced back to the debates around the conservation and management of resources in National Parks from the 1960s and 1970s. Despite its different interpretations and definitions, sustainable development is seen by many as a way forward and destinations are encouraged to implement its principles in practice. This is also the case with the Global Guidelines to Restart Tourism and the associated Restart Tourism campaign promoted by UNWTO (2020a), which name sustainability among the priorities for the recovery of tourism post COVID-19.

Implementing sustainability in practice is not an easy task, particularly in world tourism cities that are complex environments where various stakeholders have different needs and interests. Therefore, scholars looked at best practices that could help destinations in their efforts to implement sustainable tourism principles in practice (Maxim, 2015). Among the factors identified are designing policies and strategies for guiding sustainable tourism development in cities, with a clear vision and objectives, and a long-term view. Strong leadership and political will are needed to help allocate resources and promote regulations, which could ultimately push forward the sustainability agenda. In addition, stakeholder cooperation and partnerships are required to bring together the relevant resources and know-how, thus facilitating sustainable development of tourism in cities. Figure 19.1 presents the key stakeholders in a destination and the roles they play in sustainable tourism development.

The Sustainable Development Goals (SDGs), promoted in the 2030 Agenda for Sustainable Development (UN, 2015), are considered to be a useful framework to help destinations in implementing sustainable tourism practices. Tourism is seen as an important contributor to all SDGs, and cities are expected to play a key role in achieving these goals. This is reinforced by the fact that a specific goal was dedicated to cities – Goal 11: Make cities and human settlements inclusive, safe, resilient and sustainable.

Climate change

Climate change is another important challenge faced by tourism cities that cannot be overlooked when discussing about sustainability. The past few decades have seen an increased interest in this topic, with more international organisations and scholars asking for action to limit its negative consequence. The fast-growing levels of CO_2 emissions are expected to lead to changes in weather, which, in turn, can lead to more frequent natural disasters such as floods, storms, and heatwaves.

World tourism cities are among the main contributors to climate change, with estimates produced by UNEP (2017) suggesting that urban settlements are responsible for as much as 75% of the global CO_2 emissions. They are also expected to be among the most affected destinations, with many cities being vulnerable to extreme weather conditions and other negative impacts, particularly in the Global South. Climate change can therefore have major implications for the local infrastructure and the services offered to locals and visitors.

To address this challenge, a series of international events took place over the years with the intention of advancing the climate change agenda. Among the latest major events were the Conference of the Parties (COP21) that took place in December 2015, when the Paris Agreement on Climate Change was adopted, and the 26th UN Climate Change Conference of the Parties (COP26) in Glasgow that took place in November 2021. The aim of these events is to bring together the world leaders and try to agree on targets to reduce the greenhouse gas emissions, and thus limit global warming to certain levels. The tourism industry is seen to play an important part in this, and cities are expected to have an important role in implementing these agreements.

Support of local communities

The support of local communities in world tourism cities is essential for the sustainable development of tourism in these destinations. As seen in Figure 19.1, residents can play an important role in tourism development when they are involved in the planning process. In many city destinations, however, residents are only marginally (or even not at all) involved in tourism planning and policy formulation. This can lead to conflicts between visitors and hosts, as witnessed in several European cities before the COVID-19 pandemic (e.g., Barcelona, Amsterdam and Venice). This happens when the benefits associated with tourism development in a destination are exceeded by the negative consequences such as overcrowding, increased congestion and pollution, which impact the quality of life of residents.

This is how the concept of overtourism emerged, which is defined as "the excessive growth of visitors leading to overcrowding in areas where residents suffer the consequences of temporary and seasonal tourism peaks, which have caused permanent changes to their

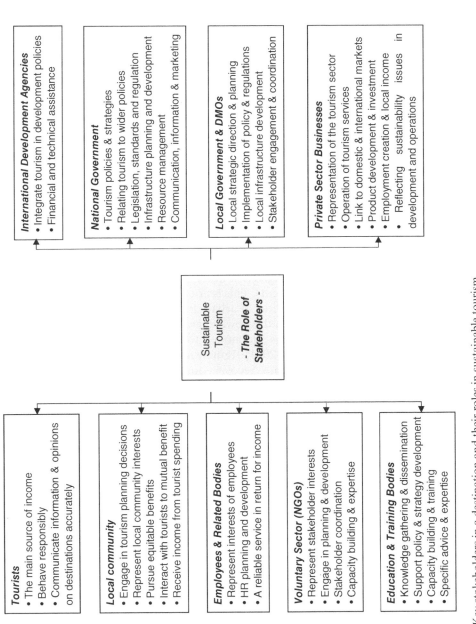

Figure 19.1 Key stakeholders in a destination and their roles in sustainable tourism.

Source: developed from Morrison and Maxim (2022) and UNWTO (2013).

lifestyles, denied access to amenities and damaged their general wellbeing" (Milano et al., 2019, p. 354). A number of strategies can be used by destination management organisations (DMOs) to address this issue, including dispersing visitors within a city; demarketing a certain destination; closing a site for a certain period of time to allow for recovery; applying restrictions such as banning large cruise ships or limiting their numbers and capacity; and pricing strategies to help control visitor numbers (Morrison & Maxim, 2022).

Crises and disasters

Crises and disasters are other important challenges faced by destinations worldwide, as witnessed over the past few decades. World tourism cities are even more vulnerable and more exposed to such events due to their characteristics, including their high connectivity and multifunctional nature, which were discussed earlier in the chapter. There are different types of crises that can affect tourism cities, among the most studied ones being economic and financial crises such as the global economic crisis in 2008–2009; health-related crises, such as the recent COVID-19 pandemic, which caused one of the most severe disruptions of the global tourism since the Second World War; terrorism events, which usually have serious consequences for city destinations as a result of an immediate decline in visitor numbers; political crises and instability; and natural disasters, such as earthquakes, hurricanes, tsunamis, bushfires or floods, that can create major property damage and even loss of life (Maxim & Morrison, 2022).

City destinations need therefore to design crisis and disaster management plans to help them better prepare for such unwanted events. This is not an easy task, however, due to the very fragmented nature of the tourism sector in urban destinations, and the various types of crises they may face, each of them with their own characteristics. Nevertheless, scholars have put together a number of frameworks and models to help destinations better manage crises and disasters, such as Faulkner's (2001) framework that includes six phases: pre-event, prodromal, emergency, intermediate, recovery and resolution. Efforts should be made by DMOs during the pre-crisis stage to identify possible risks and take actions to try to prevent, or at least minimise, the damage caused by a crisis or disaster.

Among the most recent crises that severely impacted the tourism industry worldwide is the COVID-19 pandemic, which resulted in strict travel restrictions imposed by many countries. World tourism cities were among the most affected destinations, with visitors trying to stay away from them due to the large number of infections they recorded. Some cities that were struggling with overtourism before the pandemic found themselves in a different situation – impacted by undertourism. Since then, more cities have opened their borders to international visitors, with the number of tourists expected to increase again and return to pre-pandemic levels over the next years. Still, some segments such as business travel and the MICE market are expected to see a slower recovery as many companies are still hesitant and consider the benefits of organising online or hybrid events.

Smart tourism solutions

As seen so far, tourism cities are dynamic destinations that continually evolve, facing many challenges that require smart tourism solutions. The rapid development in new technologies, including information and communication technologies (ICTs) and the Internet of Things (IoT), can help address these challenges. They can contribute to smart transport networks, energy efficiency, safer public spaces, better management of resources, improved

Table 19.1 Key roles played by new technologies in city destinations

- Help with the operation, structure and strategies of tourism organisations
- Contribute to the innovation of products, processes and management
- Enable opportunities for tourism organisations to attract and retain visitors
- Facilitate individual expression, e.g., visitors can more easily share information about their experiences, self-constructing their social images and identities
- Act as decision support tools for tourism companies and visitors, e.g., in setting and comparing prices, and providing meta-search engines
- Support market intelligence activities, e.g., collecting, analysing, sharing, and interpreting data
- Offer e-learning tools, e.g., education and knowledge management via collaborative and open learning models such as MOOCs (massive open online courses)
- Provide automation tools, e.g., substituting labour with programmable tasks such as in the case of self-driven cars
- Enable new business models, such as the sharing economy, and new management practices, including crowdfunding and gamification
- Transform tourism experiences, such as in the case of virtual tours and augmented experiences that are discussed later in this chapter
- Constitute a co-creation platform, with examples including review websites and wiki-based tourism guides

Sources: Morrison and Maxim (2022, p. 223), built on the works of Neuhofer, Buhalis and Ladkin (2012) and Sigala (2018).

productivity, and to better addressing the negative impacts of tourism. Other key roles played by ICTs and other new technologies are listed in Table 19.1.

The rapid advances of new technologies are changing the way city destinations and tourism businesses promote themselves and their products, and how they interact with visitors and various other stakeholders. As noted by Buhalis (2022), smart strategies are expected to transform destinations and make them more sustainable and inclusive societies.

The COVID-19 pandemic has pushed the industry to a faster adoption of the new technologies available, with a focus on smart solutions to counteract the restrictions in place and limit human interaction to avoid the spread of coronavirus. This has advantages and disadvantages, as it creates many opportunities for the industry, but can also affect the tourism experience due to a lack of engagement and human interaction. New technologies can also create disruption for existing structures and patterns, and may raise privacy issues, digital exclusion, and threaten languages and cultures (Buhalis, 2020).

Current and future trends in world tourism cities

This section considers the future of world tourism cities and in doing so discusses several current and future trends in urban tourism.

At the time of writing this chapter, tourism cities around the world were recovering from the severe effects of the COVID-19 pandemic. After two years of battling with the coronavirus, which saw destinations going through months of strict lockdowns, world tourism cities are looking for ways to bring back visitors. While some city destinations are focusing on increasing the numbers of tourists, targeting in particular international visitors and the economic advantages brought by tourism, other cities are debating the way they would like to see tourism develop in the future and are thus taking a more sustainable approach.

Planning and managing tourism remains an important aspect that should not be overlooked by local authorities and governments when developing tourism in a destination. This will help create better cities to live and work in, which in turn will lead to better experiences for visitors. But for this to happen, the key stakeholders in world tourism cities (including residents, visitors, private sector, and local and central government) need to work together in trying to address the challenges identified in the previous section. In addition, promoting policies and guidance to the tourism industry is key to the sustainable development of this sector. Advocates from international organisations, as well as scholars, are calling for a better integration of tourism in the wider urban agenda, which would contribute to "inclusive, resilient and sustainable cities" (UNWTO, 2020b, p. 4).

Sustainability will continue to be an important topic in the future, with city destinations expected to look into more efficient use of resources, reducing CO_2 emissions and waste, and addressing climate change. As mentioned earlier in the chapter, cities are expected to play an important role in achieving the SDGs, with several cities already producing Voluntary Local Reviews to show the progress made towards achieving these goals (e.g., New York, Los Angeles, Bristol, Helsinki, and Buenos Aires).

Policy makers in world tourism cities should focus more on understanding how tourism affects the quality of life of residents and their wellbeing. Researchers have emphasised the importance of having the support of local communities when developing tourism in a destination, to avoid possible future conflicts between visitors and hosts such as seen in the case of overtourism. A balance should be sought between the advantages brought by tourism development in world cities, including international reputation and economic positioning, and the negative impacts associated with this activity that are extensively discussed in the literature.

Being well prepared in the face of unexpected events and crises is now a necessity that no city destination should ignore. World tourism destinations have faced many crises over the years, including economic crises, natural disasters, epidemics and pandemics, and hopefully the industry and policy makers have learned lessons. To survive future crises and disasters, urban destinations need to make use of existing crisis management frameworks and build resilience, and thus better adapt and transform in the face of new challenges. One such example is the Real Time Response (RTR) framework proposed by Bethune, Buhalis and Miles (2022), a smart system approach aimed at enhancing destination resilience.

World tourism cities are expected to implement the concept of smart urban destinations, using smart solutions, big data and new technologies available to better plan and manage this activity. Some of the latest technologies include artificial intelligence, service robots, cloud computing, virtual reality, augmented reality, autonomous vehicles, personalised interactive real-time tours, ambient intelligence tourism, all discussed in more detail by Morrison and Maxim (2022). Being able to easily adjust to new realities and to implement smart solutions will help city destinations to improve their efficiency and enhance the experience of visitors, which will ultimately help them improve their competitiveness.

How would world tourism cities look in ten years' time? These environments will continue to be popular tourist destinations, smarter for sure, more connected, facing more frequent crises and climate change events, adopting more flexible working patterns, and hopefully more sustainable – although this is difficult to say. As we have seen over the past two years, despite many talks during the pandemic involving industry representatives, policy makers and academia on how to restart tourism and make it more sustainable, many

Urbanisation: Trends and Issues in World Tourism Cities		
Mega-trend: *Urbanisation* Growth of Urban Tourism	**World Tourism Cities** - key gateways - influential places - impactful destinations - cosmopolitan places - easily recognised destinations	**Key Trends & Issues** - planning & management - sustainability - climate change - overtourism - quality of life of citizens - crises and disasters - the progress of ICTs - smart tourism
How would world tourism cities look like in ten years' time? These environments will continue to be popular tourist destinations, smarter for sure, more connected, facing more frequent crises and climate change events, adopting more flexible working patterns, and hopefully more sustainable.		

Figure 19.2 Visual abstract – Urbanisation: Trends and issues in World Tourism Cities.

world tourism cities are already facing the same challenges as before the pandemic, such as overcrowding and conflicts between locals and visitors (e.g., Barcelona, Amsterdam). Therefore, more actions are needed from all stakeholders involved in tourism development in urban destinations to "walk the talk" and implement sustainable measures to make cities better places for locals and visitors.

To summarise, this chapter contributes to expanding the literature on world tourism cities, by discussing several key challenges and current and future trends in urban tourism. More interdisciplinary approaches are needed to further develop this field of study and to progress the urban tourism agenda, which could help policy makers in better addressing the challenges that world tourism cities are currently facing.

A visual abstract of this chapter is provided in Figure 19.2.

References

Ashworth, G. J. (1989). Urban tourism: An imbalance in attention. In C. P. Cooper (Ed.), *Progress in Tourism, Recreation and Hospitality Research* (pp. 33–54). London: Belhaven.

Ashworth, G. J., & Page, S. J. (2011). Urban tourism research: Recent progress and current paradoxes. *Tourism Management*, *32*(1), 1–15.

Ashworth, G. J., & Tunbridge, J. E. (1990). *The Tourist-Historic City*. Belhaven.

Barrett, J. A. (1958). *The seaside resort towns of England and Wales* [Thesis, University of London]. https://qmro.qmul.ac.uk/xmlui/handle/123456789/1380

Beedie, P. (2005). The Adventure of Urban Tourism. *Journal of Travel & Tourism Marketing*, *18*(3), 37–48. https://doi.org/10.1300/J073v18n03_04

Bethune, E., Buhalis, D., & Miles, L. (2022). Real time response (RTR): Conceptualizing a smart systems approach to destination resilience. *Journal of Destination Marketing & Management*, *23*, 100687. https://doi.org/10.1016/j.jdmm.2021.100687

Buhalis, D. (2020). Technology in tourism-from information communication technologies to eTourism and smart tourism towards ambient intelligence tourism: A perspective article. *Tourism Review*, *75*(1), 267–272. https://doi.org/10.1108/TR-06-2019-0258

Buhalis, D. (2022). Smart Tourism. In D. Buhalis (Ed.), *Encyclopedia of Tourism Management and Marketing*. Edward Elgar Publishing. https://doi.org/10.4337/9781800377486.smart.tourism

Cohen, S. A., & Hopkins, D. (2019). Autonomous vehicles and the future of urban tourism. *Annals of Tourism Research*, 74, 33–42. https://doi.org/10.1016/j.annals.2018.10.009

Connelly, G. (2007). Testing governance—A research agenda for exploring urban tourism competitiveness policy: The case of liverpool 1980–2000. *Tourism Geographies*, 9(1), 84–114. https://doi.org/10.1080/14616680601092931

Edwards, D., Griffin, T., & Hayllar, B. (2008). Urban tourism research: Developing an agenda. *Annals of Tourism Research*, 35(4), 1032–1052. https://doi.org/10.1016/j.annals.2008.09.002

Faulkner, B. (2001). Towards a framework for tourism disaster management. *Tourism Management*, 22(2), 135–147. https://doi.org/10.1016/S0261-5177(00)00048-0

Getz, D. (1993). Planning for tourism business districts. *Annals of Tourism Research*, 20(3), 583–600. https://doi.org/10.1016/0160-7383(93)90011-Q

Gilbert, E. W. (1939). The growth of Inland and seaside health resorts in England1. *Scottish Geographical Magazine*, 55(1), 16–35. https://doi.org/10.1080/00369223908735100

Gretzel, U., Zhong, L., & Koo, C. (2016). Application of smart tourism to cities. *International Journal of Tourism Cities*, 2(2). https://doi.org/10.1108/IJTC-04-2016-0007

Jansen-Verbeke, M. (1986). Inner-city tourism: Resources, tourists and promoters. *Annals of Tourism Research*, 13(1), 79–100.

Koens, K., Postma, A., & Papp, B. (2018). Is overtourism overused? Understanding the impact of tourism in a city context. *Sustainability*, 10(12), 4384. https://doi.org/10.3390/su10124384

Law, C. M. (1992). Urban tourism and its contribution to economic regeneration. *Urban Studies*, 29(3–4), 599–618.

Law, C. M. (2002). *Urban Tourism: The Visitor Economy and the Growth of Large Cities*. Cengage Learning EMEA.

Maitland, R. (2016). Everyday tourism in a World Tourism City: Getting backstage in London. *Asian Journal of Behavioral Studies*, 1(1), 13–20.

Maitland, R., & Newman, P. (Eds.). (2009). *World Tourism Cities: Developing Tourism Off the Beaten Track*. Routledge.

Maitland, R., & Ritchie, B. W. (Eds.). (2009). *City Tourism: National Capital Perspectives*. CABI Publishing.

Maxim, C. (2015). Drivers of success in implementing sustainable tourism policies in urban areas. *Tourism Planning and Development*, 12(1), 37–47.

Maxim, C. (2016). Sustainable tourism implementation in urban areas: A case study of London. *Journal of Sustainable Tourism*, 24(7), 971–989.

Maxim, C. (2019). Challenges faced by world tourism cities – London's perspective. *Current Issues in Tourism*, 22(9), 1006–1024. https://doi.org/10.1080/13683500.2017.1347609

Maxim, C. (2021). Challenges of World Tourism Cities: London, Singapore and Dubai. In A. M. Morrison & J. A. Coca-Stefaniak (Eds.), *Routledge Handbook of Tourism Cities* (1st Edition) (pp. 19–30). Routledge.

Maxim, C., & Morrison, A. M. (2022). Crisis in the city? A systematic literature review of crises and tourism cities. *Tourism Recreation Research*, 1–13. https://doi.org/10.1080/02508281.2022.2078063

Milano, C., Novelli, M., & Cheer, J. M. (2019). Overtourism and Tourismphobia: A Journey Through Four Decades of Tourism Development, Planning and Local Concerns. *Tourism Planning & Development*, 16(4), 353–357. https://doi.org/10.1080/21568316.2019.1599604

Miller, D., Merrilees, B., & Coghlan, A. (2015). Sustainable urban tourism: Understanding and developing visitor pro-environmental behaviours. *Journal of Sustainable Tourism*, 23(1), 26–46.

Morrison, A. M., & Coca-Stefaniak, J. A. (Eds.). (2021). *Routledge Handbook of Tourism Cities* (1st Edition). Routledge. https://www.routledge.com/Routledge-Handbook-of-Tourism-Cities/Morrison-Coca-Stefaniak/p/book/9780367199999

Morrison, A. M., & Maxim, C. (2022). *World Tourism Cities: A Systematic Approach to Urban Tourism*. Abingdon: Routledge.

Neuhofer, B., Buhalis, D., & Ladkin, A. (2012). Conceptualising technology enhanced destination experiences. *Journal of Destination Marketing & Management*, *1*(1), 36–46. https://doi.org/10.1016/j.jdmm.2012.08.001

Nunkoo, R., & Ramkissoon, H. (2010). Small island urban tourism: A residents' perspective. *Current Issues in Tourism*, *13*(1), 37–60. https://doi.org/10.1080/13683500802499414

Page, S. J. (1995). *Urban Tourism*. London: Routledge.

Page, S. J., & Hall, C. M. (2003). *Managing Urban Tourism*. Harlow: Pearson Education Limited.

Pearce, D. (1978). Form and function in French resorts. *Annals of Tourism Research*, *5*(1), 142–156. https://doi.org/10.1016/0160-7383(78)90008-7

Pearce, D. (2001). An integrative framework for urban tourism research. *Annals of Tourism Research*, *28*(4), 926–946.

Pearce, D. (2007). Capital city tourism. *Journal of Travel & Tourism Marketing*, *22*(3-4), 7–20. https://doi.org/10.1300/J073v22n03_02

Pigram, J. J. (1977). Beach resort morphology. *Habitat International*, *2*(5), 525–541. https://doi.org/10.1016/0197-3975(77)90024-8

Richards, G. (2014). Creativity and tourism in the city. *Current Issues in Tourism*, *17*(2), 119–144. https://doi.org/10.1080/13683500.2013.783794

Romero-García, L. E., Aguilar-Gallegos, N., Morales-Matamoros, O., Badillo-Piña, I., & Tejeida-Padilla, R. (2019). Urban tourism: A systems approach – state of the art. *Tourism Review*, *74*(3), 679–693. https://doi.org/10.1108/TR-06-2018-0085

Sigala, M. (2018). New technologies in tourism: From multi-disciplinary to anti-disciplinary advances and trajectories. *Tourism Management Perspectives*, *25*, 151–155. https://doi.org/10.1016/j.tmp.2017.12.003

Simpson, T. (2016). Tourist utopias: Biopolitics and the genealogy of the post-world tourist city. *Current Issues in Tourism*, *19*(1), 27–59.

Su, R., Bramwell, B., & Whalley, P. A. (2018). Cultural political economy and urban heritage tourism. *Annals of Tourism Research*, *68*, 30–40. https://doi.org/10.1016/j.annals.2017.11.004

Timur, S., & Getz, D. (2008). A network perspective on managing stakeholders for sustainable urban tourism. *International Journal of Contemporary Hospitality Management*, *20*(4), 445–461.

UN. (2015). *Resolution adopted by the General Assembly on 25 September 2015*. https://www.un.org/ga/search/view_doc.asp?symbol=A/RES/70/1&Lang=E

UN. (2019). *World Urbanization Prospects The 2018 Revision*. New York. https://population.un.org/wup/Publications/Files/WUP2018-Report.pdf

UNEP. (2017, September 26). *Cities and climate change*. UNEP – UN Environment Programme. http://www.unenvironment.org/explore-topics/resource-efficiency/what-we-do/cities/cities-and-climate-change

UNWTO (Ed.). (2013). *Sustainable Tourism for Development Guidebook: Enhancing capacities for Sustainable Tourism for development in developing countries*. World Tourism Organization (UNWTO). https://doi.org/10.18111/9789284415496

UNWTO. (2020a). *Global Guidelines to Restart Tourism*. https://webunwto.s3.eu-west-1.amazonaws.com/s3fs-public/2020-05/UNWTO-Global-Guidelines-to-Restart-Tourism.pdf

UNWTO. (2020b). *UNWTO Recommendations on Urban Tourism*. Madrid. https://www.e-unwto.org/doi/book/10.18111/9789284422012

Wearing, S. L., & Foley, C. (2017). Understanding the tourist experience of cities. *Annals of Tourism Research*, *65*, 97–107. https://doi.org/10.1016/j.annals.2017.05.007

WTTC. (2019). *City Travel and Tourism Impact 2019*. London: World Travel and Tourism Council.

20 Overtourism

Trends, issues, impacts and implications

Richard W. Butler and Rachel Dodds

Introduction

Although overtourism is a relatively new term, being coined in 2016 (Ali, 2016), the idea of too many tourists, and/or tourists of the wrong kind can be traced back over a century to the complaints of some Europeans about tourists brought on package tours by Thomas Cook, or numbers of architecturally unappreciative visitors to Venice by John Ruskin in the 19th century (Hanley and Walton 2011). In recent years, the concept of overtourism has received a great deal of attention and has become the gathering call for the opposition to tourism development and continued growth in a number of instances. Locations include cities such as Barcelona, Venice, Edinburgh, and Dubrovnik as well as natural areas such as the Scottish Highlands, U.S. parks and even islands, including Maya Bay and Boracay, which have generated a considerable number of academic and popular media publications (Dodds and Butler, 2019a, 2019b; Mihalic, 2020; Milano Cheer and Novelli, 2019a). Agreeing with O'Regan et al. (2021) in the use of 'discourse', a cogent and precise comment on the subject by Mihalic (2020, p. 6) is that "Generally, overtourism means unsustainable tourism", while the European Parliament (European Parliament, 2018, p. 19) defines it as "the situation in which the impact of tourism ... exceeds physical, ecological, social, economic psychologically and or political capacity thresholds". This last definition ties overtourism specifically to its effects on destinations and is of particular relevance as it includes the term "political capacity", which has been argued (Butler and Dodds, 2022) to be at the heart of the failure to deal effectively with the problems of too many tourists.

There is also considerable opposition to the concept and the term, as Mihalic (2020) points out, with many of the promoters of tourism, such as United Nations World Tourism Organization (UNWTO) and World Travel & Tourism Council (WTTC), arguing that the difficulties are simply a problem of management and not of excessive numbers of tourists. Other researchers (e.g., Buhalis, 2020) have argued that the phenomenon does not really exist and is a reflection of crowding and poor management, while others (Koens et al., 2018) have queried if the term is overused. It is clear, however, that the problems associated with overdevelopment of tourism and what are perceived as excessive numbers of tourists are not new. There is almost half a century of academic commentary on issues relating to the carrying capacity of tourism and recreation destinations, and many papers and books that have illustrated the problems of undesirable levels of tourism in specific destinations (Krippendorf, 1982; Mathieson and Wall, 1982; Turner and Ash, 1975; Young, 1973). A number of models and concepts have also explored the nature and effects of overdevelopment and the subsequent changes in destinations and the attitudes of their residents towards tourism (Butler, 1980; Doxey, 1975; Plog, 1973). The conclusion has to be that there can be too much tourism in specific places and that such a situation causes undesirable impacts on residents of those destinations and on their physical and cultural environment. One pertinent question is why this situation has emerged and continues to remain a serious problem in many locations throughout the tourist world. The next section discusses some of the causes and trends of this phenomenon.

Trends causing overtourism

The causes or trends influencing what is called overtourism are clear: continually increasing numbers of tourists since figures have been collected, rising general affluence, developments in technology, and in most tourist-generating and reception countries, a growth mindset. Allied to these four major causes, one can add a generally more peaceful world, increased education levels, and lack of political will to seriously move to applying sustainable principles on many related issues (Dodds and Butler, 2019a, 2019b).

The relationships between these elements are portrayed in Figure 20.1. An ever-increasing world population provides the base for more tourists. Increasing levels of world affluence and education allow more of those people to attain a financial level from which they can engage in tourism. Such people are more informed than their predecessors about tourism and travel, have the funds and time to engage in travel, and find many inducements encouraging them to do so. Improvements in technology have made the necessary increase in mobility become a reality. Travel has become safer, more reliable, more accessible, cheaper and available to a far greater number of destinations than ever existed before. The infrastructure necessary for mass movement is continuously being improved and enlarged, from airplanes and airports to passenger ships, to high-speed trains. In addition, a more peaceful world has meant many restrictions on tourist travel have been removed or relaxed,

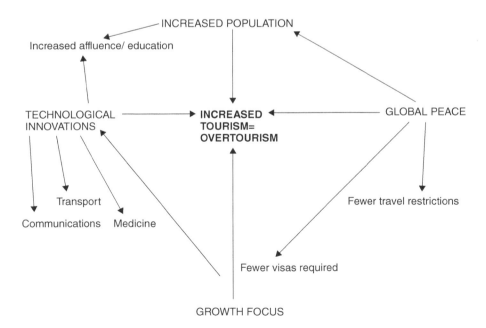

Figure 20.1 Elements leading to overtourism.

and thus many more destinations are available to be visited. The communications revolutions have allowed almost instant reservations for travel, made widespread information (and disinformation) about destinations available, allowed influencers to direct (and misdirect) potential visitors to specific, often iconic sites and sights, encouraging major sudden increases in tourist numbers, and, finally, have allowed costs to be reduced drastically. Thus, for several decades the trend has been towards ever-increasing numbers of tourists, domestic and international, because of these developments.

Finally, the overall attitude of the tourism industry, and many agencies and governments, has been that growth is the primary goal and that increasing numbers of tourists are beneficial to all concerned, including local residents, tourists, the private sector and public finances. Such growth has enabled the global distribution of capital, provided millions of jobs and is often the only source of economic development and growth in more remote and poor countries which have either limited or no other opportunities. There can be little disagreement that having more people reach a financial threshold which enables them to partake in tourism is a positive result. Tourism development in many places has seen an alleviation of poverty and much-needed infrastructure development that has proved of benefit to residents as well as tourists. Unfortunately, such growth and development has mostly been unchecked with overtourism the result in an increasing number of locations (Milano et al., 2019a; Seraphin et al., 2021).

With the exception of the years 2020 and 2021, tourism growth has continued every year in the post-war period; only the advent of COVID 19 has caused this growth to cease. The pandemic has removed overtourism from the popular lexicon for the duration of its course, but there are few signs that it will not reappear once the pandemic and the restrictions on travel that it has brought come to an end. The following section discusses future trends and what the impacts of overtourism have and will be; the subsequent section focuses on why efforts to mitigate and prevent overtourism before the advent of COVID 19 failed and may continue to fail in the future.

Future trends

There are a number of short-term and long-term trends which may affect whether overtourism will return or not. One short-term positive factor may be that the cost of air travel will increase as airlines rush to recoup the US$52 billion revenue lost due to COVID (IATA, 2021). This may only limit air travel-related overtourism in some destinations, however, as more localised areas may suffer as pent-up demand may overpower cost (Butler, 2022). Another positive trend may be that many destinations have realised the benefit of reservation systems which were implemented during the COVID era to manage capacity. This relatively simple effort may continue into the future and therefore capacity may be better managed and a destination understanding of the visitor will increase. Venice officials, for example, have been tracking movements in the city, monitoring including who and how many enter and leave and have installed a network of 468 security cameras, ticketing and smartphone tracing which will help with visitor flow management (Bubola, 2021). Although sustainability and regenerative and experiential travel seem to be touted as the new trend (American Express, 2022), there is little concrete evidence to support this and recent effects of consumerism such as daily Amazon deliveries begs the question as to who exactly this experiential traveller is. Additionally, although residents who benefitted from tourism may hope travel rebounds quickly, other residents who have felt the effects of overtourism may be even more vocal as they have now experienced two plus years of peace and quiet.

Long-term, more sustainable travel may be achieved as governments have come to accept the importance of climate change and many have developed policies for future reduction of carbon emissions, including those from transportation, while implementing the SDGs may also impact positively on tourism development and management. Action and implementation, however, remain to be seen. In New Zealand's case, an earlier decision had been made to attempt to change the composition of tourism to the country to attract higher-spending longer-staying visitors, compensating for a reduction in numbers by an increase in per capita spending (Insch, 2020), but whether this would be successful or not has not yet been tested. It is clear, however, that the desired type of tourist in that case is limited in numbers and highly sought after, making for a highly competitive situation which could not be achieved by all destinations wishing such a change in their market.

Another positive trend is towards the imposition of destination taxes. Destination tax has come a long way since it was first trialed in destinations such as Spain (Dodds, 2007), and is quickly becoming the norm, possibly increasing prices and therefore driving down demand. Finally, a common trend is the increased awareness of sustainability. Although there are many articles to suggest that travellers care more about experiences and the authenticity of place, there is little actual evidence that this will impact the also prevalent motivations such as last-chance tourism where participants feel they must visit a destination before it is gone (e.g., visiting polar bears before they become extinct or visiting Venice before it sinks) (Lemelin et al., 2010).

Results of overtourism

The impacts of overtourism have been reported widely in non-academic sources as being damaging to the quality of life of residents of destination communities, generally ascribed to overcrowding of often iconic tourist sites and disturbance or the disruption of traditionally non-tourist, often residential, areas (Goodwin, 2017). Many of the forms of annoyance and discomfort to local residents are those noted by Doxey (1975) and others, namely, noise, the interruption of normal activities, crowding in shops and parking areas, increased traffic, and the transformation of functions and services from those aimed at local residents to those serving the needs and preferences of tourists. At the core of the complaints and charges is a general feeling amongst local residents that they have lost control of their ways of life and their communities through the increasing presence of ever more tourists. Such reactions have been documented for several decades (for example, Boissevain, 1979; Young, 1973) and given the above-mentioned trends, such dissatisfaction is likely to continue into the future. In a number of cases, it is a reaction against tourists rather than tourism, the latter being recognised as bringing employment and income to communities, as well as improved services and increased infrastructure often desired by long-term, as opposed to new, residents of destination communities, while tourists are the personification of the perceived loss of quality of life.

Changes in the attitudes of residents have been documented over an equally long period, and excessive and inappropriate development have been proposed as agents creating new markets and displacing old ones in tourist destinations (Plog, 1973). Many of these problems have been aggravated in recent years by the enablers of overtourism (Dodds and Butler, 2019a), including low-cost airlines opening new communities up to tourism and bringing in lower-income and lower-spending tourists than may have been desired, the World Wide Web allowing the growth of Airbnb and similar agencies introducing tourists to formerly exclusively local residential parts of communities, and social media generally popularising destinations quickly, often mindlessly and to unrealistic levels, turning them into trending 'must visit' destinations (Gretzel, 2019; Ruck, 2021).

Along with the resultant impacts in the social-cultural realm have been increased impacts upon the natural or physical environment with increased erosion, reduction in wildlife owing to increased disturbance, and increased litter and garbage. Many of these impacts are found at lower levels of visitation in destinations not appearing to experience overtourism, or at least not complaining of overtourism and support the general discussion of the impacts of tourism, as summarised so well by Mathieson and Wall (1982) some decades ago.

Overtourism occurs not just in large urban areas, but also in smaller cities. Although urban areas have a more media-conscious population better able to utilise the media to gain attention and desired action from authorities, many iconic sites and natural areas have also been overpopularised and suffered accordingly. Overtourism also clearly exists in rural areas, islands and elsewhere globally (Butler, 2021a, 2021b; Kim et al., 2020; Maingi, 2019; Nadheema and Habeeb, 2020; Peterson and DiPietro, 2021; Ruck, 2021), but generally numbers of tourists are much smaller and rural areas tend to get much less media coverage than urban centres. This may explain why UNWTO (2018) discussed the subject only in an urban context. It is difficult to identify specific impacts of overtourism that are not part of the overall effects of excessive tourist numbers in general, and thus it may well be that Koens et al. (2018) were correct to ask "Is overtourism overused?" although their research too was urban in focus. The COVID-related recent trend of an increase in domestic tourism has also led to overuse being complained about in rural areas in several European countries, although this may disappear with the decline in COVID-related travel restrictions.

The nature of the discussion of overtourism and its effects have very much been in the context of numbers of tourists, their behaviour, and their location, rather than overdevelopment of tourism *per se*. This raises the issue and trends noted above, of the type of tourist being linked to overtourism. For the most part, it is the mass tourist that is being targeted in discussions of overtourism, the passengers on the large cruise liners visiting coastal tourism ports, for example, or short-term visitors arriving on low-cost airlines. The characteristics such groups have in common are large numbers, short visits in terms of time spent in destinations, low spending per capita, and, frequently, inappropriate behaviour, sometimes based on ignorance about the destination and its culture/way of life. This raises the issue of xenophobia, or, as Milano et al. (2019b) have described it, "tourismophobia", reflecting a general dislike of tourists amongst local residents. Such attitudes have existed, often at a low level, towards specific groups of tourists such as second home owners (Coppock, 1977) for many years, but in the present the feelings are being expressed against all forms of tourist. In many respects, the establishment of strong, even potentially violent, negative attitudes towards tourists may represent the most serious and potentially long-term negative impact of overtourism and could lead to tourists and tourism promoters avoiding some specific locations. While this may seem a satisfactory response to some residents in those communities, the dramatic illustration of what happens when tourism stops, provided by the COVID-19 pandemic, reveals how dependent many communities and regions, and even states, have become on tourism for incomes and employment (Wang et al., 2021). Proponents of degrowth and radical reforms, including the reduction of tourism generally (e.g., Andriotis, 2021; Fletcher et al., 2019; Higgins-Desbiolles et al., 2019), need to be careful that their aims do not do more damage to destinations than overtourism, as Butcher (2021) has argued.

To summarise, many, if not all, of the impacts and trends of overtourism are common to tourism in general, and mass tourism in particular. They are the result of unsustainable practices in provision of the supply and stimulation and creation of the demand for tourism. Mitigating or preventing the negative impacts of tourism have been attempted in many areas, mostly with limited success at best, and the application of sustainable principles has also only been successful in specific and often small areas. To achieve success in preventing or even mitigating overtourism will require more than the imposition of a few controls or slightly reducing tourism numbers in specific places. The following section reviews attempts that have been made to reduce or avoid the negative effects of overtourism and explains why there has been so little success in this regard.

Stakeholders and their efforts to combat overtourism

Given that overtourism is incorrectly viewed as a recent phenomenon, steps to mitigate or prevent its occurrence have only been instituted over the past few years. Many stakeholders have a role to play. Communities that have been focused on building, or at least maintaining, their level of tourism must become more concerned with trying to limit numbers of tourists. Agencies such as destination management organisations (DMOs) have traditionally been focused not on the actual management of tourism or tourists, but on the promotion of their destinations in order to maintain or increase numbers of visitors, and success has normally been expressed and viewed as increased tourist visitation (Dwyer, 2018). These agencies have played a different role in the time of COVID-19 and acknowledgement of data-driven decision-making and the need to involve a wider stakeholder base are increasing in some destinations. DMOs need to refocus their attention from a priority on growth to less economic-driven issues such as quality of life and actually managing rather than promoting tourism. They could be valuable in mitigating the effects of overtourism and have the advantage of operating and being controlled at the local level (Mihalic and Kuščer, 2021).

The argument that "overtourism is driven by global and domestic policy factors", as stated by Peterson and DiPietro (2021 n.p.), is sadly true, as few policies ever identify potential limits to tourism, particularly in specific terms, and the implicit assumption is therefore that the growth of tourism is not only likely, but desirable.

Part of the reason for this is that the economic argument in favour of tourism development invariably is given priority over the other elements of sustainable development. Opposing arguments (e.g., Everingham and Chassagne, 2020) in favour of a greener and more sustainable form of tourism, tend to fail because tourism is seen as an economic activity rather than a potential social-cultural or environmental problem. Governments, national and local, must play a larger role in tourism development and marketing in order to mitigate the negative effects. Although those residents and enterprises in destination communities that are economically involved with tourism are hesitant to take any steps which might result in a reduction in tourist numbers and expenditure and thus a resulting reduction in their incomes and employment possibilities (Ghoochani et al., 2020; Walmsley et al., 2021), perhaps as negative effects continue to rise, even they will realise that they must think long rather than short-term.

There are a number of factors to consider when examining measures which could be, and have been, taken to mitigate overtourism. One is the level at which any measures might or should be implemented. As overtourism is generally seen as a location-specific problem rather than a global one (although the day may come when that view is incorrect), then measures are most appropriate at the local level, a view shared by Kuščer and Mihalič (2019, n.p.) who stated that "... new system-wide challenges may be effectively tackled only through tailored, sophisticated forms of local cooperation between key stakeholders". Such local policies, even when implemented, are rarely successful in isolation. For example, this was illustrated in Calvia, Spain when the municipality was unsuccessful in securing national-level support for its efforts to implement sustainable measures (Dodds, 2007). If regional and national agencies do not support local actions, and, for example, still promote destinations despite local efforts to restrain tourism growth, then little will be gained.

The variety of approaches to preventing overtourism have been discussed in some detail elsewhere (Novelli et al., 2019b; Dodds and Butler, 2022) and include attempts to control and limit tourism by identifying and implementing carrying capacity limits, dispersion, pricing to reduce demand, modifying the destination image to make it more focused on the desired forms of tourism, and by implementing policies in coordination with other levels and through smart tourism initiatives. Unfortunately, as Ivars-Baidal et al. (2019, p. 122) note, "the management of overtourism is not a priority in the smart strategies of the cities considered". The failure of the above approaches reflects a variety of reasons. One is the inevitable failure of all stakeholders in a destination to share a common goal, particularly when that goal is aimed at halting or even reducing growth of tourism, thus threatening individual incomes and employment. Another is the failure, noted above, of successful coordination of different levels of government, understandable when it is clear that overtourism is seen as a local problem, while attracting tourists at a national level is viewed as an economic priority.

The COVID-19 pandemic has demonstrated that national governments can restrict tourism numbers when they choose. New Zealand and Australia are notable examples of locations which closed down international tourism to their countries in response to the COVID-19 pandemic. The economic impacts on their tourism and hospitality industries have been severe, and while a re-opening of their borders to tourists is likely to see a rapid resumption of visits, numbers may take a while to reach pre-pandemic levels.

The principal reason for overtourism continuing to exist (at least until 2019 and the onset of the pandemic) is the reluctance of industry and government to take any measures which might reduce the appeal and/or the actual volume of tourism. The same reluctance has been shown to introduce measures which would make tourism significantly more sustainable in the majority of cases. While individual enterprises in many countries have become more sustainable, they are mostly the results of individual efforts, and facing the global scenario of ever-increasing numbers of tourists, most public sector agencies see that as an opportunity for continued growth in tourism to their destinations, regardless of whether those individual destinations want such growth or may, in fact, choose to put a higher priority on quality of life of their residents and their local environment. The delimitation of carrying capacity levels of all types (economic, social, cultural, physical and environmental) for destinations has been toyed with for over half a century, but rarely adopted in principle and even less frequently applied in practice (Wall, 2020). Until the principles of sustainable development, including capacity limits, are adopted and implemented for tourism at all levels, efforts to mitigate or prevent overtourism are almost inevitably going to fall short.

Implications and conclusions

The COVID-19 pandemic has dominated tourism for the past two years (at the time of writing in March 2022) and during this period overtourism has scarcely been mentioned in the academic or the popular press. In the ongoing absence of realistic efforts to prevent its return, however, overtourism as a trend or discourse is almost certain to reappear once the pandemic is over, or at least once the current restrictions and quarantines are relaxed or removed. The increasing desire for people to travel has not abated, however; the trend of regenerative tourism that ensures destinations are better after tourism than before may see a slight shift in some visitor behaviour, although it is unlikely unless economic practices are shifted (Cave and Dredge, 2020; O'Regan et al., 2021). This, and the many calls for a major revision and shaping of tourism at the global level (see, for example, papers in the special edition of *Tourism Geographies*, 2020), combined as some are with the abandonment of the capitalist and growth approaches to economic development, are unlikely to be responded to positively by governments for two reasons. One is that to abandon the free-market neoliberal arrangements of the past few decades runs counter to the ideologies of most states that are involved in tourism, either as originating markets, or, even more, as destinations. The second is that the desire to reduce tourism inevitably means a reduction in employment and income generated for some countries and destinations, even if some were to be successful in re-orienting to a higher-spending visitor segment. History has shown such a step is unlikely to be supported, and in the immediate post-COVID 19 period, most, if not all, destinations and countries will be trying their utmost to repair and restore their tourism industries to pre-COVID-19 levels as quickly as possible to overcome the economic downturn and hardships suffered by those industries. The probability of accepting reduced economic benefits, coupled with making the additional expenditures that would be required to become more sustainable and increasing capacity limits through development and refitting infrastructure, is extremely low.

It is possible that the impacts of tourism may shift due to the increased competitive landscape and new countries opening up to tourism which would lead to possible wider global dispersal of tourists. Another contributing factor may be that tourism may be limited by the sheer impacts of poor development. For example, perpetuated destruction of mangroves or building on dunes in coastal areas have ruined entire tourism coastal areas (Hall, 2001). Extreme weather may also be a long-term trend, which may make it harder for destinations to plan and manage tourists therefore crowding may indeed become a risk management issue.

Despite all the pronouncements and claims about supposed sustainable tourism, the fact remains that few places or countries have done much to move towards such a state. As long as that remains the norm, given the links between sustainability and overtourism, the future is gloomy. The conclusion is that overtourism will continue to create problems for destinations, for visitors and for residents for some time to come. Perhaps only when tourists become so dissatisfied with levels of crowding, inadequate services, delays and shortages, that they vote through their choice of destinations to visit quieter and less overcrowded locations, will serious and effective action be taken.

References

Ali, R. (2016). Exploring the coming perils of overtourism. *Skift*. Retrieved July 7, 2019.

American Express Travel (2022) 2022 Global Travel Trends Report. Retrieved March 26, 2022, from https://www.americanexpress.com/en-us/travel/discover/get-inspired/global-travel-trends

Andriotis, K. (2021). *Issues and Cases of Degrowth in Tourism*. CABI: Wallingford.

Boissevain, J. (1979). The impact of tourism on a dependent island: Gozo, Malta. *Annals of Tourism Research*, 6(1), 76–90.

Bubola, E. (2021). Venice, overwhelmed by tourists, tries to track them. https://www.nytimes.com/2021/10/04/world/europe/venice-tourism-surveillance.html

Buhalis (2020). http://buhalis.blogspot.com/2020/02/there-is-no-overtourism-only-badly.html Feb 19, 2020.
Butcher, J. (2021). COVID-19, tourism and the advocacy of degrowth. *Tourism Recreation Research*, 1–10.
Butler, R. W. (1980). The concept of a tourist area cycle of evolution: Implications for management of resources. *The Canadian Geographer*, 24(1), 5–12.
Butler, R. (2021a). Measuring tourism success: alternative considerations. *Worldwide Hospitality and Tourism Themes*, 14(1), 11–19.
Butler, R.W. (2021b). Overtourism in Rural Areas. In Seraphin, H., Gladkikh, T, and Vo Thanh, T. *Overtourism Causes, Implications and Solutions* pp. 27–43. London: Springer.
Butler, R. (2022). Managing Tourism – A Missing Element? *PASOS Revista de Turismo y Patrimonio Cultural*, 20(2), 255–263.
Butler, R.W. & Dodds, R. (2022). Overcoming overtourism: A review of failure. *Tourism Review*, 77(1), 35–53.
Cave, J., & Dredge, D. (2020). Regenerative tourism needs diverse economic practices. *Tourism Geographies*, 22(3), 503–513.
Coppock, J. T. (ed.) (1977). *Second Homes: Curse or Blessing?* Oxford: Pergamon.
Dodds, R., & Butler, R. (Eds.). (2019a). *Overtourism: Issues, Realities and Solutions* (Vol. 1). Berlin: Walter de Gruyter GmbH & Co KG.
Dodds, R., & Butler, R. (2019b). The phenomena of overtourism: A review. *International Journal of Tourism Cities*, 5 (4), 519–528.
Dodds, R., & Butler, R. W. (2022). Over-tourism mitigation. In Buhalis, D. (Ed.) *Encyclopedia of Tourism Management and Marketing*. Edward Elgar E-Publishing.
Dodds, R. (2007). Sustainable tourism and policy implementation: Lessons from the case of Calvia, Spain. *Current Issues in Tourism*, 10(4): 296–322.
Doxey, G. V. (1975). *A causation theory of visitor/resident irritants: Methodology and research inferences. Proceedings of the Travel Research Association 6th Annual Conference* (pp. 195–198). San Diego: Travel Research Association.
Dwyer, L. (2018). Saluting while the ship sinks: the necessity for tourism paradigm change. *Journal of Sustainable Tourism*, 26(1), 29–48.
European Parliament (2018). Overtourism*: impact and possible policy responses* TRAN Committee, Policy Department for Structural and Cohesion Policies" Brussels.
Everingham, P., & Chassagne, N. (2020). Post COVID-19 ecological and social reset: moving away from capitalist growth models towards tourism as Buen Vivir. *Tourism Geographies*, 22(3), 555–566.
Fletcher, R., Mas, I.M., Blanco-Romero, A., & Blázquez-Salom, M. (2019). Tourism and degrowth: an emerging agenda for research and praxis. *Journal of Sustainable Tourism*, 27(12), 1745–1763.
Hall, C. M. (2001). Trends in ocean and coastal tourism: the end of the last frontier? *Ocean & Coastal Management*, 44(9–10), 601–618.
Hanley, K., & Walton, J.K. (2011). *Constructing Cultural Tourism: John Ruskin and the Tourist Gaze*. Channel View Publications: Bristol.
Higgins-Desbiolles, F. Carnicelli, S. Krolikowski, C. Wijesinghe, G., & Boluk, K. (2019). Degrowing tourism: rethinking tourism. *Journal of Sustainable Tourism*, 271(2), 1926–1944.
Ghoochani, O. M., Ghanian, M., Khosravipour, B., & Crotts, J. C. (2020). Sustainable tourism development performance in the wetland areas: a proposed composite index. *Tourism Review*. 75(5): 745–764.
Goodwin, H. (2017). The challenge of overtourism, Responsible Tourism Partnership Working Paper 4. http://haroldgoodwin.info/pubs/RTP'WP4Overtourism01'2017.pdf
Gretzel, U. (2019). 5. The role of social media in creating and addressing overtourism. In Dodds, R. and Butler R. (Eds.) *Overtourism* (pp. 62–75). Berlin: De Gruyter.
IATA (2021). Director General's Report on the Air Transport Industry, AGM 2021, Boston. https://www.iata.org/en/pressroom/speeches/2021-10-04-01/
Insch, A. (2020). The challenges of over-tourism facing New Zealand: Risks and responses. *Journal of Destination Marketing & Management*, 15, 100378.

Ivars-Baidal, J.A., Hernández, M.G., de Miguel, S.M. (2019). Integrating overtourism in the smart tourism cities agenda *e-Review of Tourism Research* (eRTR), 17(2), 122–139.

Kim, M., Choi, K. W., Chsng, M., & Lee, C. H. (2020). Overtourism in Jeju Island: The Influencing Factors and Mediating Role of Quality of Life. *The Journal of Asian Finance, Economics, and Business*, 7(5), 145–154.

Koens, K., Postma, A., & Papp, B. (2018). Is overtourism overused? Understanding the impact of tourism in a city context. *Sustainability*, 10(12), 4384.

Kuščer, K., & Mihalič, T. (2019). Residents' attitudes towards overtourism from the perspective of tourism impacts and cooperation – The case of Ljubljana. *Sustainability*, 11(6), 1823.

Krippendorf, J. (1982). Towards new tourism policies. *Tourism Management*, 3(3), 135–148.

Lemelin, H., Dawson, J., Stewart, E. J., Maher, P., & Lueck, M. (2010). Last-chance tourism: The boom, doom, and gloom of visiting vanishing destinations. *Current Issues in Tourism*, 13(5), 477–493.

Mathieson, A., & Wall, G. (1982). *Tourism, economic, physical and social impacts*. Longman: Harlow.

Maingi, S. W. (2019). Sustainable tourism certification, local governance and management in dealing with overtourism in East Africa. *Worldwide Hospitality and Tourism Themes*, 11(5), 532–551.

Mihalic, T. (2020). Conceptualising overtourism: A sustainability approach. *Annals of Tourism Research*, 84, 103025.

Mihalic, T., & Kuščer, K. (2021). Can overtourism be managed? Destination management factors affecting residents' irritation and quality of life. *Tourism Review*, 77(1), 16–34.

Milano, C., Cheer, J. M., & Novelli, M. (Eds.). (2019a). *Overtourism: Excesses, discontents and measures in travel and tourism*. CABI: Wallingford.

Milano, C., Cheer, J. M., & Novelli, M. (2019b). Overtourism and tourismophobia: A journey through four decades of tourism development, planning and local concerns *Tourism Planning and Development*, 16(4), 353–357.

Nadheema, A., & Habeeb, Z. (2020). Managing overtourism in Asian cities. In Dixit, S.K. (Ed.) *Tourism in Asian Cities* (pp. 249–262). London: Routledge.

O'Regan, M., Salazar, N. B., Choe, J, & Buhalis, D. (2021). Unpacking overtourism as a discursive formation through interdiscursivity. *Tourism Review*.

Peterson, R., & DiPietro, R. B. (2021). Is Caribbean tourism in overdrive? Investigating the antecedents and effects of overtourism in sovereign and non-sovereign small island tourism economies (SITEs). *International Hospitality Review*. 10.1108/ihr-07-2020-0022

Plog, S. C. (1973). Why destination areas rise and fall in popularity. *Cornell Hotel and Restaurant Administration Quarterly*, 13–16.

Ruck, A. (2021). "Overtourism" on Scotland's North Coast 500? Issues and Potential Solutions in Seraphin, H., Gladjikh, T. & Vo Thanh, T. *Overtourism Causes, Implications and Solutions* (pp. 208–227). London: Palgrave Macmillan.

Seraphin, H., Gladjikh, T., & Vo Thanh, T. (2021). *Overtourism Causes, Implications and Solutions*. London: Palgrave Macmillan.

Turner, L., & Ash, J. (1975). *The golden hordes: International tourism and the pleasure periphery*. London: Constable & Robinson.

UNWTO (2018). *Overtourism? Understanding and Managing Urban Tourism Growth beyond Perceptions*. Madrid: UNWTO.

Wall, G. (2020). From carrying capacity to overtourism: a perspective article. *Tourism Review*, 75(1), 212–215.

Walmsley, A., Koens, K., & Milano, C. (2021). Overtourism and employment outcomes for the tourism worker: impacts to labour markets. *Tourism Review*. (In-press). https://doi.org/10.1108/TR-07-2020-0343

Wang, L, Tian, B, Filimonau, V, Ning, Z, & Yang, X. (2021). The impact of the COVID-19 pandemic on revenues of visitor attractions: An exploratory and preliminary study in China. *Tourism Economics*. doi:10.1177/13548166211027844

Young, G. (1973). *Tourism: Blessing or blight?* Penguin: Harmondsworth.

21 Issues and policies that have an impact on future trends in global tourism

David L. Edgell, Sr.

Introduction

Worldwide tourism will be faced with difficult challenges over the next several years, but, overall, the future for international growth in travel is positive. Most countries will develop policies for increasing and sustaining their tourism programmes. A non-technical review of certain issues that will impact future trends in international tourism policy is presented in this chapter.

Global tourism was most recently confronted with a major crisis that included the worldwide impact of COVID-19, the Omicron variant, and other strains of the virus. The results of the COVID-19 pandemic have been particularly devasting for the travel and tourism industry. However, even with the virus running rampant in some parts of the world, the global travel and tourism industry is optimistic that the future will see renewed growth. The key to such growth will depend on resolving many of the issues currently facing the travel and tourism industry.

Research produced by the World Travel & Tourism Council (WTTC) noted a strong positive growth trend in the global travel and tourism industry from 2015 to 2019. For example, in 2018 the travel and tourism industry was among the world's largest industries, accounting for more than 319 million jobs (one in ten of the world's total jobs). This trend continued in 2019 with the global tourism industry accounting for 10.4% of global GDP (US$9.2 trillion), 10.6% of all jobs (334 million). However, in 2020 COVID-19 struck the world and the global travel and tourism industry suffered accordingly, with losses of almost US$4.5 trillion, a reduction to only 3.7% of GDP and a loss of 62 million jobs. 2021 saw limited relief to the global travel and tourism industry with an increase to 284 million jobs or one in 11 of the world's total jobs. Forecasts by the WTTC predict that the global travel and tourism industry will grow by about 4% over the next several years and that by 2026 the travel industry will account for 370 million jobs, or one in nine of the world's total jobs. Unless some major global catastrophe envelops the world, this positive growth trend will likely continue throughout the next decade.

The opportunity that tourism offers for positive economic and social benefits for tomorrow will depend on the decisions being made today. International tourism arrivals and receipts often account for a significant portion of a country's local economy and are of critical importance as an export for industrialised and developing nations. The key factors for the growth of the global travel and tourism industry are the understanding of how to sustain the industry when the world is confronted with addressing health issues; economic disruptions; transportation concerns; changes in travel industry sustainability; safety and

Table 21.1 Ten important current and future world tourism issues

1.	Responding appropriately to the global impacts of the COVID-19 pandemic viruses which are continuing to cause international stress in the tourism industry
2.	Determining the most effective anti-pandemic approaches to regain the contributions of international tourism to the global economy
3.	Researching and understanding the impact of transportation disruptions, especially those of airlines and cruise ships, related to current and future pandemics
4.	Investigating the long-term impacts on the travel and tourism industry of climate change, global warming and environmental adjustments
5.	Identifying concerns related to safety and security that remain important issues to address within the world travel and tourism industry
6.	Recognising the need for increased global cooperation, coordination, and leadership in developing effective policies and strategies for managing a global tourism society
7.	Working toward consistent and positive rules and regulations that all countries can utilise for entry and exit procedures for international travellers during pandemics
8.	Maintaining a well-educated, trained, engaged, skilled and experienced workforce in order to deliver quality tourism experiences
9.	Understanding the effect on the travel and tourism industry from natural and human-induced disasters, new technologies, consumer behaviour and political disruptions
10.	Seeking to develop sustainable tourism policies, strategies and management guidelines aimed toward protecting the natural and built environments for future tourists to enjoy

security needs; shortcomings in global leadership and cooperation; confusion with travel entry procedures; a lack of an educated workforce; disasters and political upheavals; and environmental, climate change, and global warming conditions. These issues and concerns will be presented and discussed in this chapter as they pertain to future trends in international tourism policy.

The following list of "Ten Important Current and Future World Tourism Issues" helps to illustrate the complexities involved in forecasting future trends in international tourism growth (Table 21.1).

Responding to the global impact on the travel industry of SARS-CoV-2 viruses

To sustain the global travel and tourism industry in the future may very well mean a better adjustment and management of current and future responses to types of infectious diseases caused by the "Severe Acute Respiratory Syndrome Coronavirus 2" (SARS-CoV-2) virus or variant mutations (like the Omicron variant, which appeared in late 2021 and the new Omicron subvariant of 2022) that may present additional problems. Over the past few years (2020–2022), the travel industry has been grappling with responses to what is commonly called COVID-19, an infectious disease caused by SARS-CoV-2 which first appeared late in 2019. As the world faces an unprecedented global health, social, and economic crisis, resulting from the COVID-19 pandemic, the international travel and tourism industry, being among the most affected sectors, must develop plans and policies to minimise the negative impact on the tourism industry due to such global epidemics.

Over the history of the world, we have seen numerous situations in which health issues impacted on people's ability to travel. For example, the great Plague of Justinian in 541–542 C.E. killed somewhere between 30 and 50 million people or about half the population of

Europe and, in effect, it closed down travel. Then, in 1347–1350 (and beyond), the well-known Black Plague appeared and killed more than 20 million people. Also, in the 18th and 19th centuries the Europeans brought to the Americas diseases such as the deadly smallpox disease, which wiped out about half the Native American populations throughout North and South America. A more recent plague was the 1918 Flu Pandemic which was caused by an H (hemagglutinin)1N (neuraminidases)1 virus with genes of avian origin. Over two years, 1918–1919, this pandemic, sometimes referred to as the Spanish Flu, killed at least 50 million people worldwide. While the COVID-19 deathrate seems mild, with over six million deaths, compared to the past pandemics mentioned above, the impact on the travel industry has been enormous.

Early in 2020, the COVID-19 crisis led to a downturn in domestic tourism and a collapse in international travel. For example, the United Nations World Tourism Organization (UNWTO) estimated that international tourist arrivals declined globally by 73% in 2020, with one billion fewer travelers compared to 2019. As noted earlier, from data from the WTTC, COVID-19 caused massive losses in international revenues and jobs. In some tourism-dependent countries, and particularly in many small island nations, where tourism accounts for more than 50% of their economy, the impact was catastrophic with few options for relief. Such economies went into heavy debt with few resources to depend on for economic growth. This travel shock continued into 2022. The question is: when the next pandemic appears, is it possible for the world's travel and tourism industry to have developed policies and plans to alleviate much of the negative impact of such a phenomenon on global travel? Critical decisions about the sustainability of tourism in a world subject to potential pandemics must be made today – at the local, national, regional, and international levels – if tomorrow is to present a bright future for the tourism industry. If the world leaders will come together to work toward appropriate policies and solutions to the impact that COVID-19 and other viruses have on the global travel and tourism industry, then international tourism can fulfill its role in stimulating global improvements in the social, cultural, economic, political, and ecological dimensions of future lifestyles.

Global health issues, and especially COVID-19-related viruses, are extremely critical and worrisome with respect to their potential impact on international tourism. Ironically, international travellers can be the individuals responsible for spreading epidemics of certain diseases. These crises with respect to the impact of viruses on international tourism must be dealt with on a rational basis. In working toward global solutions to the negative downturn in travel that pandemics have had on the global tourism industry, we must investigate what has taken place in the past, and what has worked and what has not worked. Globally, there have been many different approaches to deal with COVID-19 and its impact on the travel industry. This would be expected as the pandemic was more severe in some countries than others and the severity and intensity of lockdowns did not always resolve problems related to the tourism industry. While this section of the chapter will not look at the individual decisions being made by each country regarding COVID-19, it will highlight a few of the general directions taken to reduce the impact of the pandemic on international tourism.

In initially dealing with COVID-19, some countries moved toward a country lockdown of most industries (including the tourism industry) and strict border measures to keep international travellers from entering the country and potentially spreading the virus. There was a heavy cost involved in such a policy and gradually most such countries moved toward an emphasis on vaccinations (Figure 21.1), the wearing of masks, and a limited and restrictive opening of their borders for international visitors as a preventative measure to the

Future trends in global tourism 259

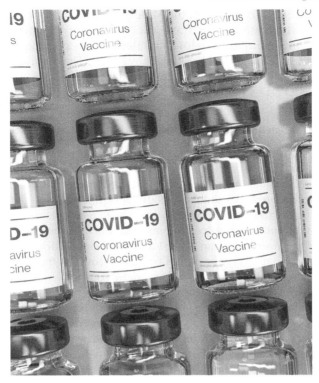

Figure 21.1 Vaccinations were part of the global strategy to stimulate travel and tourism.
Photo: Courtesy, Unsplash.com.

spread of the COVID-19 virus. Many other countries had a somewhat mishmash of policies ranging from a laissez-faire attitude toward developing a consistent COVID-19 prevention programme to one of gradually reopening hospitality and tourism businesses with stringent limitations on receiving international visitors. The only consistency in such policies was a strong emphasis on vaccinations, social distancing, and the wearing of protective masks. A search for a policy that protects against the spread of the COVID-19 virus and still allows for international tourism is still being researched and studied by academic institutions, governments at all levels, businesses, and global organisations.

It is clear that international cooperation will be necessary to eventually develop a consistent policy for dealing with the issue of the impact of pandemics on global tourism. The United Nations, and most certainly the UNWTO, must conduct research and present general guidelines for coping with this issue. In addition, the World Health Organization could be more forthcoming with presentations of their information, analysis, and data about pandemics that might shed light on how best for international tourism entities to better manage policies to prevent the disastrous results seen most recently. It might mean a global education programme aimed at citizens in all countries. There are also numerous regional organisations that can conduct studies and share their results for the better handling of international tourism responses to pandemics. To name just a few would certainly include the Organization for Economic Co-operation and Development, the Organization of American States (Inter-American Travel Congress), the Caribbean Tourism Organization, the Asia Pacific Economic Cooperation, the Middle East–Mediterranean Travel and Tourism Association, the International Air Transport Association, the International Civil Aviation Organization, the International Hotel and Restaurant Association, the World Bank, the International Monetary Fund (IMF) and many others. The question remains as to how best to share the information these organisations might generate toward handling international travel due to COVID-19 or other pandemics.

Post-pandemic era approaches toward the economic contributions of tourism

As noted earlier, global tourism had been on a continuous growth pattern until the pandemic hit the world in 2020. A certain panic and rash of unwarranted decisions were made across the globe that impacted negatively on most related international industries, including the global travel and tourism industry. Nations began imposing harsh policies in the entry and exit of visitors to their respective countries. In a few instances, nations, in effect, locked down their international borders and imposed onerous restrictions for travel within their own country. The result was that tourist arrivals dropped dramatically and domestic tourism declined. It is no mystery the global travel and tourism industry suffered more intensely than was the case for other industries in many country economies. Unemployment in the travel and tourism industry became rampant, even more so than in most other industries. Employers made changes to keep some employees on the payroll by moving toward online employment with computer workstations to operate in a home environment. Such a movement was minimally effective within the tourism industry.

The very makeup of the travel and tourism industry made it most vulnerable to the negative impact of the pandemic. If there are severe limitations on the number of international destinations available to the public, then the airline sector of the travel industry must lay off most of its employees. Restrictions on where people can travel has a major impact on the international hotel sector of the tourism industry. If restaurants are not allowed to serve food on their premises, then many will disappear or go bankrupt. In other words, with the heavy restrictions imposed by governments in 2020 because of COVID-19, much of the travel and tourism industry closed down and employees lost their jobs. As noted earlier, globally in 2020 international tourist arrivals declined by 73% and 62 million employees lost their jobs. What the global travel and tourism industry needs is consistency in terms of governmental responses to COVID-19 or with respect to other catastrophes that might impact the industry.

While the prospects for containing the pandemic were promising in 2022, it will likely take 3–4 years for the global tourism industry to recover. As noted earlier, the WTTC predicts the global tourism industry will be healthy and robust by 2026. What needs to happen now is for the public and private sectors to join forces and develop new policies and plans for the recovery of the global travel and tourism industry. The impact of the travel and tourism industry on the economies of countries and communities is now well known by most major leaders of the world. During World Tourism Day in 2021, Antonio Guterres, Secretary General of the United Nations, noted that it is "Time to rethink, transform, and safely restart tourism." Success for the global tourism industry's recovery from COVID-19 will depend on international cooperation, coordination, and collaboration by the public and private entities involved in tourism development and promotion. Leaders in the tourism industry must regain the confidence of travellers, push hard for country policies toward increased vaccinations, wearing of masks, social distancing, easing entry restrictions, and greater support for sustainable destinations while protecting their populations' health and safety. The future for global tourism will be positive if governments continue to open their borders, remove onerous restrictions, implement simple rules, and allow for the use of digitalisation to speed up the reservation of transportation conveyances, entry procedures, and identification. The global travel and tourism industry has endured the worst of the pandemic and is now headed toward a positive future.

Reviewing solutions to transportation issues related to the pandemic

Of major concern for the global travel and tourism industry is how to resolve issues regarding the transportation of international visitors whether by airlines, boats, buses, cars, and trains across borders. The lack of being able to travel during the height of the pandemic produced a pent-up demand for leisure tourism and business travel. The key for the international visitor is safety no matter what form of transportation. Flight availability, airline restrictions and rules, and country entry procedures will determine the number of long-haul tourists within the global tourism market. Cruise ship bookings will also depend on rules and regulations regarding health measures as well as new approaches to marketing and making changes in itineraries. Business travel will mean fewer trips but possibly longer stays. Also, different countries in the short term will likely approach the entry of visitors in different ways. This may very well end up creating competition for visitors to determine which destination they want to visit. This is particularly true with respect to many of the island nations. Whatever happens with respect to resolving the transportation issues will have a substantial bearing on how hotels and other accommodations and eating establishments respond. Ultimately, it is the local community that is most impacted based on the decisions made by the travel and tourism industry components.

Prior to the pandemic, international visitors were complaining about the poor service of many airlines (not all of them, but a goodly number), and the trend of airlines to impose numerous fees on travellers. There are fees for luggage, extra leg room, seating location, snacks, and a blanket. The seats are narrower and closer to the seat in front than in years past. Many tourists complained that the worst part of their vacation was the negative treatment by the airlines. Some of the older passengers hark back to the good old days of the 20th century when passengers were treated with respect and looked forward to their flights instead of dreading them. Most passengers would just like to be treated according to the Golden Rule… treat passengers as you would want to be treated… Then, with the onset of the pandemic, the lack of hospitality by the airlines was exacerbated to a new level. Some countries have laws, rules, or regulations to help passengers get better services from the airlines. For example, the U.S. has needed for some time similar protection ever since the Civil Aeronautics Board was abandoned many years ago. Finally, in 2022 the U.S. Senate introduced (S. 3222) the Airline Passenger Bill of Rights, which, if passed, should help improve airline services to passengers. In addition, it was noted that during the pandemic, the U.S. government provided air carriers with Us$80 billion, but unfortunately did not impose penalties for the airlines lack of good service. An interesting article titled "Purchase the Best Airline Seat" by Sam Kemmis, explains in detail the complicated rules and costs associated with airline seat selection by many airlines.

As a major growth sector within the travel and tourism industry, cruise ships were hit the hardest during the pandemic. In 2020, for example, the cruise line business was, in effect, shut down. However, today, with certain restrictions imposed, cruise ships have mainly been given the green light to operate in most areas of the world. Basically, the crews must be fully vaccinated as well as the passengers. What has often been lacking is good communication by the crew in letting passengers know about cases of COVID-19 aboard their ships. This causes undue nervousness and stress for the passengers. In addition, the crew members are not always properly notified when the ship is denied entry at a selected port. Finally, some countries, from time to time, issue advisories to their people not to take a cruise. However, in spite of the confusion, the cruise lines are sailing again.

Tourism impacts: climate change, new technologies, and consumer behaviour

Much of the discussion thus far has been related, in some form or another, with COVID-19. However, the development of post-pandemic strategies for increased travel may very well be heavily impacted by how the world or a destination approaches responses to climate change. Climate change policies in the future will have a major impact on decision-making in global tourism and will be an important factor affecting all nations, especially many of the small island countries where tourism accounts for a major part of their economy.

Climate change, and its direct or potential impact on tourism, are among the most controversial issues within the tourism industry and elsewhere with respect to other industries. There is reasonably good information on climate change and global warming. Two U.S. agencies that conduct research, produce scientific studies, and release enormous amounts of information to the global community on climate change and global warming are the National Aeronautics and Space Administration (NASA) and the National Oceanic and Atmospheric Administration. According to a NASA Global Climate Change Report, 97% of climate scientists agree that climate-warming trends over the past century are very likely to be due to human activities, and most of the leading scientific organisations worldwide have issued public statements endorsing this position.

One regional group, the European Academics' Science Advisory Council (EASAC) and Leopoldina-Nationale Akademie der Wissenschaften issued a report on 21 March 2018, noting in summary that "New data show that extreme weather events have become more frequent over the past 36 years, with a significant uptick in floods and other hydrological events compared even with five years ago…" EASAC noted further that: "… Given the increase in frequency of extreme weather events, EASAC calls for stronger attention to climate change adaptation across Europe; leaders and policy-makers must improve the adaptability of Europe's infrastructure and social systems to a changing climate." Other countries and regions throughout the world have issued similar statements and warnings regarding their concerns for climate change and global warming.

All sectors of the tourism industry must address the climate change impacts as a part of a broad international agenda. The tourism industry, particularly with respect to the transportation and accommodation sectors, is a major source of greenhouse-gas emissions. The critical challenge is to develop a dynamic tourism policy plan now in order to thwart the negative impacts of climate change in the future. Such a plan must be developed in conjunction with scientific organisations, business leaders, and government policy makers. Climate change impacts a broad spectrum of the travel and tourism industry, including destinations, the travelling public, individual tourism and hospitality businesses, energy-related tourism supply companies, transportation and accommodation sectors and eating establishments. In effect, climate change is already impacting destinations such as mountain regions and coastal destinations. With recent meetings and conferences taking place regarding climate change and tourism, strategies are beginning to be developed, especially with respect to island nations. A recent United Nations report noted that "Countries must cut emissions faster than originally agreed to avoid dire consequences…"

The tourism industry is exposed to numerous direct and indirect impacts from climate change. Climate change, for example, may lead to changes in biodiversity, thus affecting sustainable tourism. If climate change causes additional storms and hurricanes, coastal areas and islands will be threatened with short- and long-term damage. Melting ice and snow due to climate change and global warming could increase the water levels of oceans, causing some island nations to simply disappear. In addition, it could exacerbate wave and storm surge effects that occur with hurricanes, which, in turn, may damage major tourism destinations. It is already clear that many islands will remain vulnerable to impacts from climate change with possible drastic consequences.

Addressing concerns for safety and security within the tourism industry

Concern for the safety and security of world travellers remains an extremely important issue for the travel and tourism industry. A global study by Cable News Network, titled: "How Safe is your Holiday Destination?" (12 July 2017), asked consumers about their travel perceptions and behavioural trends. Respondents from more than 70 countries identified key influencing factors in their decision-making processes before travelling for leisure or business. The survey found that for more than two-thirds of global respondents, safety and security were of greatest concern when choosing an international travel destination. Providing safety and security in the travel industry will continue to be a major challenge for tourism policy, planning and management. In brief, safety and security are vital elements in the provision of quality tourism. A tourism destination that is not considered to be safe and secure is not going to survive very long.

The first item on many safety and security agendas is the universal issue of the relationship of terrorism to tourism. Over the years, there has been considerable discussion about safety and security with respect to terrorism. While terrorism has existed throughout history, the terrorist attacks that took place in the U.S. on September 11, 2001 became a rallying cry in terms of a need for national and international tourism policies to counteract the impact of terrorism on the tourism industry. While many nations have been subjected to terrorism attacks that impacted on the tourism industry, the September 11 attacks have possibly been the most powerful in galvanising policy changes in many nations. In the U.S. alone, the U.S. Government changed drastically. The U.S. responded by developing a brand-new governmental department: the Department of Homeland Security. For those seasoned international travellers who were used to arriving at an airport a few moments before their flights, the world turned upside down after September 11, 2001. Globally, we now have an onerous inspection system at airports, which is a continual reminder of just how important safety and security concerns are for the travel and tourism industry. The process of travel has become increasingly complicated with inspections of international visitors related to terrorism, with respect to COVID-19, and other issues such as illegal drugs. To help visitors choose safe destinations, most countries have installed warning systems to help their citizens determine which destinations are safe and which destinations may present concerns for safety and security. These warning systems suggest to its citizens countries or destinations that may present a problem with respect to a traveler's safety and security.

Once seen as an encumbrance to travel, measures to support security, are now endured, if not welcomed and demanded by many tourists. Accordingly, safety and security requirements for transporting travellers are now one of the segments of the responsibility of transporters such as airlines and cruise lines. Likewise, the destination of the traveller must assure the visitor of a safe and sound vacation, meeting place, or business experience. While the issue of terrorism often permeates the agenda for safety and security, perceived crime, civil disorder, and other crisis situations at a destination are often more of a concern for many visitors. Those international destinations that have a positive reputation for safety and security will benefit in multiple ways as the word about their peaceful destination spreads throughout the world. Research on safety and security in the tourism industry clearly supports the old adage that "When peace prevails, tourism flourishes" (author unknown).

Develop tourism polices to increase global leadership and cooperation

In spite of some crises along the way, there is every indication that tourism will grow in the future. However, the nature of this growth may be quite different from that seen in the past. According to most global forecasts and information from leaders in the tourism industry, the future of the tourism industry will be one of change, unknown challenges, vibrancy, new outcomes, and growth. Travellers are demanding high-quality tourism experiences, variety, and flexibility in their tourism products along with a clean and healthy environment. Innovative tourism policy, strategic planning, good management, and strong leadership will be the hallmarks crucial to economic prosperity, sustainability and quality-of-life opportunities for most communities, destinations, and countries of the world. A key to the prospective quality growth of tourism is to ensure that careful planning, effective policies, and creative management take place.

Leadership, tourism policy and strategic planning should usually start at the local level so that the community where tourism is taking place or the location of the destination involved allows for all of the stakeholders to have an opportunity to express their views. It is also important that the stakeholders at all levels have the opportunity to input their views on what a national tourism policy should include so that guidelines are available to follow at all levels of government and industry. The point is that tourism policy and planning may take different avenues of approach with the goal of ultimately providing improvement in the quality of life to the local citizenry.

The global tourism industry will face many different issues over the coming years, and, quite certainly, tourism policy and strategic planning will drive many of the dynamics of tourism well into the future. We can expect to see a greater global focus on the tourism industry's potential for quality growth. In tandem, sustainable benefits of tourism for local communities will continue to grow in priority and importance. There will be greater efforts toward partnerships between the private and public sectors in facilitating tourism, and supporting the economic, socio-cultural, and environmental contributions of tourism for the benefit of world citizens.

Developing new tourism projects, maintaining present destinations, and improving travel-related facilities and service, require comprehensive policies and detailed strategic plans that combine local needs, market competitiveness, and tourism sustainability. Those destinations, localities, and nations that prepare good policies and implement detailed strategic plans will reap the benefits for sustaining their tourism products in the future. When the policies and plans are multi-faceted to include all aspects of tourism, the opportunities for future success will be greatly enhanced. Leadership in dynamic tourism policy and planning for the future must link the political goals and local plans for tourism into a concrete set of guidelines to give us positive direction for the tourism industry as we move ahead. If there is one thing the global tourism industry has learned from coping with COVID-19 in

2020–22 is the need for greater local, regional, and national leadership, cooperation, and coordination within the travel and tourism industry. At the global level, the tourism industry looks to the WTTC for leadership within the private sector and to the UNWTO for help in coordinating governmental efforts for country tourism programs.

Promote international cooperation and consistency in visa/entry procedures

Countries throughout the world are seeking innovative approaches to attract visitors but still maintain vigilance with respect to potential outbreaks of viruses or other problem areas. COVID-19 was a clarion call for action to develop innovative policies and creative solutions for international traveller entry procedures. One policy and procedure that has gained international recognition resulting from COVID-19 was to encourage travellers to get vaccinated before arriving at their destinations. In addition, many countries require the traveller to be tested for COVID-19 either prior to boarding an airline or cruise line in their home country or being tested after arriving at the port of entry of the destination country. It would greatly facilitate international travel if there was a degree of consistency for such policies across the world.

The issue of obtaining a visa and properly following entry procedures has been a barrier to travel for many years, way before the COVID-19 pandemic. Countries often have different rules and procedures for entering and exiting the destination country that sometimes confuse international travellers or cause considerable delay in planning a vacation or business trip. Common impediments include travel costs, visa and passport requirements, travel allowance restrictions, duty-free allowances, travel delays and inconveniences, use of credit cards in international travel, foreign currency exchange, and other barriers and obstacles. In the past, for example, the U.S. had one of the worst records in terms of long delays for international visitors to obtain a visa to travel to the U.S. Until the pandemic hit, the U.S. had worked toward an expanded visa waiver program and had expedited the visa process. It remains to be seen what policies countries will develop to reduce the barriers to international travel in the post-pandemic era of travel'

Another impediment in recent years has been the increase in fuel prices which can wreak havoc on the travel and tourism sector. All forms of transportation, be it automobiles, airlines, or other transportation modes, are immediately affected by changes in fuel prices. Also, the volatile nature of changes in fuel prices has made it difficult to develop transportation policies to alleviate the negative impact on the tourism industry. The mercurial and erratic price changes will likely continue, causing a need for the travel industry to find better ways to adjust.

Many countries that depend on tourism to spur their economies were hit unduly hard with the recent pandemic. Such countries' economies have turned sour with few alternatives for revival and growth. They simply lack the finances to build back their once-prosperous tourism revenues and do not have the wherewithal to move toward other industries. One international organisation working with countries needing financing is the International Monetary Fund (IMF). An innovative paper developed by the IMF to respond to the pandemic or post-pandemic suggests, among other ideas, that the government of a tourism-dependent country concentrate its promotions on greater visitation by tourists to more remote or ecotourism destinations within the country. In addition, the WTTC, in a study, noted that the pandemic has shifted travellers to focus on nature and adventure travel away from crowded resorts and cities. Other international organisations are working toward ways and means to help the global tourism industry regain its footing and to move in a positive format for the future. To better prepare for the future, the global travel and tourism industry needs to develop protocols that regain the public's confidence to travel while at the same time developing policies to facilitate such travel.

Increase the efforts toward a well-educated and trained workforce

There is a need to understand the dynamics of a constantly changing world and the impact on workforce development in the global travel and tourism industry. Rapidly changing technology and a highly competitive environment have contributed to an evolving workplace, which places new demands on the skills, knowledge, and attributes workers will need to bring to their jobs. This is particularly true for those employees expected to deliver quality sustainable tourism products now and in the future.

Sustaining the tourism industry for the future puts a heavy emphasis on the needs of education and training. Many training centres and universities have stepped forward to offer programmes specifically designed to meet the demands of the global travel and tourism industry. There have been more degree curricula, certifications and workshops supporting the broad parameters of the travel and tourism industry over the past ten years than in all the years past. There have been more books written about tourism-related subjects within the past five years than has taken place in the past 25 years. In addition, there are now many online education offerings providing many different courses in travel and tourism. In a 2013 the *Journal of Tourism & Hospitality* article titled "Online Education and Workforce Development: Ten Strategies to Meet Current and Emerging Workforce Needs in Global Travel and Tourism," Kristen Betts and David Edgell discussed many of the opportunities for applying online education to the travel and tourism industry. The article noted that "Quality education and training is crucial to the growth of the global tourism industry…" The article also noted one of the ten strategies identified included "…conservation and sustainable tourism…" In addition, in response to tourism education needs during the pandemic, many universities expanded their online tourism courses, many educators and organisations added webinars, and additional articles and books were produced.

As would be expected, the UNWTO offers numerous opportunities for global tourism education through their "Tourism Human Capital Development" initiatives. There is the UNWTO Academy, which is a leading institution for education and training in the tourism industry. UNWTO also has a special Executive Education programme for tourism professionals throughout the globe. An excellent executive education program in tourism is the University of Hawaii's Executive Development Institute for Tourism (EDIT) Program. EDIT has been around for more than 40 years providing professional development for career-minded tourism professionals. The 11-day institute offers a rigorous and interactive curriculum, preparing leaders to develop strategic approaches in global destination marketing, product development, and international tourism policy.

An area of education that needs greater attention at this time, as well as in the future, is tourism courses, research, and training in the intricacies of sustainable tourism development, planning, and marketing of current and potential sustainable tourism destinations. Another area that is deficient in most academic institutions is the attention to the history of the travel and tourism industry. In addition, a problem area that arises quite often when people travel is misinformation due to a language barrier. With a world full of linguistic experts and computer technology innovations, it should be possible to develop a simple international language for travellers.

Tourism impacts from natural disasters, new technologies and consumer behaviour

Global issues such as natural disasters, humanitarian crises, and political disruptions are extremely critical and worrisome concerns with respect to their potential impact on tourism. As mentioned earlier, the recent pandemic changed the travel patterns of international visitors. There is information through the Internet that allows the international visitor opportunities for cancelling or adjusting their travel itineraries depending on the circumstances taking place in their desired destination.

Earthquakes, tsunamis, floods, storms, mudslides, hurricanes, tornados, droughts, and fires take place every year and possibly at an increased rate due to climate change. Such disasters, along with political upheavals and temporary shutdowns due to strikes and other conflicts, impact heavily on the travel and tourism industry. The results often pose great problems for destinations but may also cause airline disruptions and many other types of problems. Potential visitors avoid areas that have been impacted by disasters, which in turn means tourism as an economic development tool to those areas is negated. Conflicts, and the increases in the number of natural disasters continue to impede development, peace, and security worldwide, dimming the prospects of achieving the sustainable development goals in many countries fraught with humanitarian concerns.

Another major disaster in the making, and certainly a problem for the future, is the endless flow of trash into the ocean, which not only affects the health of humans and wildlife, but also impacts on destinations near to the problem areas and compromises the livelihoods that depend on a healthy ocean. This is a crisis that is resolvable. It might take a global education effort aimed at citizens in all countries or greater international cooperation or the imposition of new laws and regulations.

An academic paper presented by authors Jaume Rossello, Susanne Becken, and Maria Santana-Gallego titled "The effects of natural disasters on international tourism: A global analysis", in *Tourism Management* (Volume 79, August 2020) provides an excellent discussion of the impact of disasters on international tourism. The authors noted that

> … Findings provide evidence that the occurrence of different types of event (disaster) change tourism flows to varying degrees… in general the impacts are negative, resulting in reduced tourist arrivals following an event… Understanding the relationship between disaster events and tourism is helpful for destination managers who make critical decisions in relation to recovery, reconstruction and marketing…

Another major impact on the future of the tourism industry has been the recent introduction and use of new technologies. A simple illustration of how technology is changing the future of the tourism industry is the current emphasis on space tourism. Another innovation making use of new techniques in computer technology is its application in the social media frontier.

Manage policies for maintaining a sustainable tourism industry in the future

Before the pandemic was in full swing, there was considerable global interest in all aspects of managing sustainable tourism development. For example, in 2016, the United Nations 70th General Assembly declared that "2017 is the United Nations International Year for Sustainable Tourism Development." In 2017, the UN issued a detailed document titled *Transforming Our World: 2030 Agenda for Sustainable Development* with a list of 17 goals. Then on 27 September 2018, UN Secretary General Antonio Guterres said (in summary)

> The wide reach of tourism into many sectors, from infrastructure and energy to transport and sanitation, and its huge impact on job creation make it a vital contributor to the 2030 Agenda for Sustainable Development... tourism plays a pivotal role in advancing cultural understanding and bringing people together...

The global tourism industry, like many other industries, has latched onto the word sustainable as if it were the panacea for all future achievements within the travel and tourism industry. In its shorthand definition, it is all-encompassing to include a balance between economic progress, environmental wellbeing, protection of the Earth, and positive community development. It supports the old adage "We have not inherited the Earth from our ancestors, we have only borrowed it from our children" (author unknown).

A recent article (3 June 2022), "The Confusing State of 'Sustainable' Travel", Arnie Weissmann attempts to explain some of the misnomers about the word sustainable and its application to the travel industry. He notes at the beginning of the article that: "The term 'sustainable' has become so elastic that, ironically, its continued effectiveness as an indicator of vital issues may not be sustainable." The most comprehensive discussion of "sustainable tourism" is contained in David Edgell's book *Managing Sustainable Tourism: A Legacy for the Future* (third edition, 2020). Edgell traces the history of his approach to sustainable tourism through the ages, starting with the great Greek historian, geographer, and worldly traveler Herodotus (484 BCE–425 BCE). His discussions introduce the underpinnings of sustainable tourism, which include ecotourism, geotourism, responsible tourism and cultural tourism. The key is being able to manage sustainable tourism, thus: "Sustainable Tourism, when properly managed, can become a major vehicle for the realization of humankind's highest aspiration in the quest to achieve economic prosperity while maintaining social, cultural, and environmental integrity."

Conclusion

From the discussion in this chapter, it is clear that issues in the tourism industry must be resolved if future trends in international tourism are to yield positive economic and sustainable growth. To avoid future negative impacts from health issues means that all the stakeholders in the travel and tourism industry must come together to work toward solutions to such pandemics. This will require creative and innovative decision-making by the leadership at the local, national, regional, and international levels. In the post-pandemic era, countries seeking to recoup the economic contributions of the tourism industry must work together with the public and private entities involved in tourism development and promotion. An issue that keeps appearing year in and year out is how to improve transportation within the global tourism industry. There needs to be a complete analysis of the airline industry to find better ways and means in providing quality service to the passengers. An area the global travel and tourism industry is still grappling with is how to respond to climate change issues. Climate change, and its direct or potential impact on tourism, is fraught with political innuendos globally, as well as within the local travel and tourism industry. Climate change, and its impact on global tourism, will continue to be an important issue in the future. Safety and security will always be an issue that must be dealt with if the future of the tourism industry is to have quality growth. Those destinations that provide a safe and secure vacation for international visitors will be rewarded with repeat visitation. Possibly the number one issue for a positive industry in the future is the provision of good leadership at all levels of government and the private sector. This leadership will be challenged to develop positive policies regarding the entry procedures of international tourists. The future of the tourism industry may very well depend on well-educated and trained staff in all aspects of the industry. Such training must include the best approaches to handling potential disasters and disruptions in the business of travel and tourism. The evidence is clear that disasters have a negative impact on a destination where the disaster occurred. Since disasters will take place in the future, it behooves the international travel industry and the local community to be prepared with proactive plans to reduce the negative impact of such events. Finally, the global travel and tourism industry must realise that, in the long run, managing sustainable tourism is most critical to a quality experience for a tourist at the destination. Sustainability is possibly the most important contemporary issue facing the tourism industry in the 21st century and, as a result, the stakeholders in the tourism industry must take the lead to ensure destinations are sustainable.

It is well recognised in the tourism community that we have a finite planet that must be conserved, protected, and nurtured and that we all have a stake in assuring that future tourism growth be of high quality and sustained for future generations to enjoy. This is an acknowledgement that sustainable tourism is a part of an overall shift that recognises that orderly economic growth, combined with concerns for the environment and quality-of-life social values, will be the driving force for long-term progress in tourism policies for development. This will only happen if international organisations, businesses, government, academia, not-for-profit entities, and local tourism leaders focus their attention on the need to develop and promote sustainable tourism development. All who work in the tourism industry, and those who travel, want to manage the sustainability of the tourism products as a legacy to ensure that their children and grandchildren can enjoy a wide variety of quality tourism destinations.

Bibliography

World Travel & Tourism Council (2021) *Economic Impact 2021*, "Global Economic Impact & Trends", June.

Edgell, D. L. (2015) "International Sustainable Tourism Policy" in *The Brown Journal of World Affairs*, Volume XXII Issue 1 Fall/Winter.

Edgell, D. L. (1990) "Trends in International Tourism Through the Year 2000" in *Trends: Travel and Tourism*, U.S. Department of the Interior, National Park Service, National Recreation and Park Association Volume 27, Number 3, 1990.

World Health Organization (2021) *Coronavirus Disease (COVID-19) Situation Reports*. 28 December, 2021.

Centers for Disease Control and Prevention (2021) "1918 Pandemic (H_1N_1 virus)".

United Nations World Tourism Organization "2021 news release".

Guterres, A. (2021) "Time to rethink, transform, and safely restart tourism." *World Tourism Day*, 2021, United Nations.

Kemmis, S. (2022) "Purchase the Best Airplane Seat" in *The Daily Reflector*, 11 March.

Edgell, D. L. and Swanson, J. R. (2019a) *Tourism Policy and Planning: Yesterday, Today, and Tomorrow*, 3rd edition, London: Routledge, pp. 314–315.

Edgell, D. L. (2020a) *Managing Sustainable Tourism: A Legacy for the Future*, 3rd edition, London: Routledge, pp. 117–120.

National Aeronautics and Space Administration "Global Climate Change Report", 6 February 2019.

European Academics' Science Advisory Council "Climate Report", March 21, 2018.

Jordan, F. and Borenstein, S. (2022) "U.N. Issues Major Climate Warming", in *The Daily Reflector*, April 15, 2022.

Cable News Network (2017) "How Safe is your Holiday Destination", July 12, 2017.

Edgell, D. L. and Swanson, J. R. (2019b) *Tourism Policy and Planning: Yesterday, Today, and Tomorrow*, 3rd edition, London: Routledge, pp. 163–172.

Edgell, D. L. (2020b) *Managing Sustainable Tourism: A Legacy for the Future*, 3rd edition, London: Routledge, p. 267.

International Monetary Fund, "Tourism in a Post-Pandemic World", February 28, 2021.

Betts, K. and Edgell, D. L. (2013) "Online Education and Workforce Needs in Global Travel and Tourism", *Journal of Tourism & Hospitality*, 2013.

Edgell, D. L. (2020c) *Managing Sustainable Tourism: A Legacy for the Future*, 3rd edition, London: Routledge, p. 270.

Rossello, J., Becken, S. and Santana-Gallego, M. (2020) "The effects of natural disasters on international tourism", *Tourism Management*, Volume 79, August 2020.

70th United Nations General Assembly (2016) "2017 is the United Nations International Year for Sustainable Tourism Development."

United Nations (2017) "Transforming Our World: 2030 Agenda for Sustainable Development."

Guterres, A. (2018) "World Tourism Day: harnessing new technologies to transform travel", 27 September.

Pololikashvili, Z. "International Tourism Highlights" (2019 edition), UNWTO.

Weissmann, A. (2022) "The Confusing State of 'Sustainable' Travel" in *Travel Weekly*, 3 June.

Edgell, D. L. and Kogos, B. (2023) *The Worldly Travelers: Their Lives and Journeys Changed the World*. London: Routledge.

22 Tourism policies for the next normal
Trends and issues from global case studies

Vanessa G. B. Gowreesunkar, Shem Wambugu Maingi and Chris Cooper

Introduction

Historically, the tourism industry has shown remarkable resilience in the aftermath of any crisis and disaster (Gowreesunkar et al. 2021; Çakar, 2018; Bremser et al., 2021). As the world is moving towards the '*next normal*' of an ongoing pandemic, recovery plans of several tourism destinations are still not yielding desired results. Globally, the COVID-19 crisis has exposed long-standing structural weaknesses and gaps in tourism policy measures. To further complicate the process, destinations and segments of the tourism sector are re-opening and recovering at different speeds, and this is impacting on the global economy, as tourism is a multi-sectoral business. This is a grave concern, as due to lockdown and travel constraints, field research and collection of data in order to formulate appropriate tourism policies have not been possible. As well documented by now, tourism evolves in a non-linear way (Baggio, 2008), and, therefore, tourism policies may no longer be debated along the classical tourism area life cycle of Butler (1980). With climate change, globalisation and sophistication, several unpredictable events and calamities have been hitting the tourism industry to such an extent that the COVID-19 pandemic, perceived as a by-product of sophistication and globalisation, led to a critical transformation in perception and behaviour of tourism stakeholders. Consequently, since the effectiveness of existing tourism policy is being called into question, evidence-based policy has been seen to be a viable option to help destinations still struggling with the pandemic. It is important to document current trends in tourism and understand future tendencies in order to develop an effective tourism policy that is realistic and powerful enough to cope with unpredictable calamities and events.

Tourism policy research ideologically draws from different disciplines, ranging from social sciences, political sciences, public administration to economics and law, among others (Dredge, Jenkins and Whitford, 2011). So far, existing tourism policies have been quite effective in balancing the global economy, the society and the environment. For instance, the Sustainable Development Goals (SDGs) are a collection of 17 global goals set to end poverty and ensure that all people enjoy peace and prosperity (Gowreesunkar, 2018). Thus, the focus was mainly set on economic, social and environmental sustainability. Based on this universal, integrated and transformative vision, the United Nations World Tourism Organization (UNWTO) joined hands with governments, private partners, development banks, international and regional finance institutions, the UN agencies and international organisations to help achieve the SDGs, thus placing an emphasis on Goals 8, 12 and 14, in which tourism is featured. Sustainability was therefore the driving force of any national policy position. This is also clearly evidenced in the UNEP

(United Nations Environment Programme) and UNWTO report on "making tourism more sustainable: a guide for policy makers". According to the document, economic, social and environmental sustainability were the main components of any good tourism policy and the following factors would guide the policy:

- Economic viability
- Local prosperity
- Employment quality
- Social equity
- Visitor fulfilment
- Local control
- Community wellbeing
- Cultural richness
- Physical integrity
- Biological diversity
- Resource efficiency

In fact, policy planning for tourism has always been challenging due to the fragmented and interdependent nature of the industry. The arrival of the pandemic has further complicated the process. The crisis has exposed long-standing structural weaknesses in the tourism system and gaps in tourism policies. For instance, tourism-dependent countries such as the Maldives, Seychelles and Mauritius *inter alia* are still struggling as they were never prepared to face a pandemic, and their policies were mainly based on competition (http://tourism.gov.sc/policies/). In contrast, collaboration has now become their guiding principle (Gowreesunkar et al., 2021; OECD, 2021). This point is also echoed in the study of Buhalis and Cooper (2000): "… tourism suppliers at destinations need to mature and understand that they should not compete with each other at destination level. Instead, they should join forces and pool resources…" (Buhalis and Cooper, 2000, p. 21). This observation from Buhalis and Cooper, now a quarter-century old, has become relevant to the current pandemic status of the industry. Raising this argument to another level, it would seem that countries are using different approaches to confront the pandemic (Gowreesunkar et al., 2021). Destinations and segments of the tourism sector are re-opening and recovering at different speeds, and this is impacting on the global economy, as tourism is a multi-sectoral business. For example, when India was ready to open its tourism economy, Mauritius was not willing to take the risk and attract more COVID cases. Likewise, tourism businesses in Mauritius continued to suffer as no visitors were allowed onto the island for a very long period of time. Similarly, when South Africa opened its airport, many countries were not willing to accept South African visitors. In the process, several tourism businesses were affected due to their dependency on other countries. As a result, their coping capacity is seen in terms of stages and in terms of lessons from other destinations (Hall et al., 2020). Tourism policies of the new normal were therefore formulated on a case-by-case basis. This implies that while some destinations were coming out of the crisis, others were still struggling. The ability of stakeholders to forecast the future is critical for a strong tourism revival (Ritchie and Jiang, 2019), hence the reason policy for future trends needs to be articulated around future trends.

Based on these observations, the aim of this chapter is to examine tourism policies adopted by different tourism destinations following the pandemic outbreak. The objective is to propose some best practices that may serve as lessons to destinations interested to rebuild or update their tourism policies. The research design is based on multiple case studies, as recommended by Yin (1994) and Stake (2006). In this respect, the main source of data for this study is derived from the authors' edited book – *Tourism Destination Management in a Post-Pandemic Context* (Gowreesunkar et al., 2021). Case studies from this book offer a rich insight of how different countries developed their coping capacities and built resilience against the pandemic. Drawing from 15 areas (Africa, the Baltic States, the U.K., Asia, the U.S. and the Middle East), this chapter offers a synthesis of evidence-based tourism policies adopted by tourism destinations worldwide.

The overall impression from the case studies indicates that the pandemic is not a tourism issue. Rather, it is a health issue. As a result, cross-cutting tourism policies are working best for most destinations. There is also a need to strengthen multilateral cooperation, as actions taken by one government have implications for travellers and businesses in other countries, and hence in the global tourism system. The pandemic has provided evidence of the multi-dimensional impacts on different aspects of society: from the psychological comfort to health issues, social, economic, cultural, political, technological and environmental impacts, all of which contribute to a complex scenario as the interplay of the many elements leads to unexpected outcomes. This point is also echoed by Aldao et al. (2021), who reiterate that policy post-pandemic shows a major metamorphosis with a shift from reality to virtuality. The study of Aldao et al. (along with case studies proposed in this chapter) is a major eye-opener with regard to how the future of tourism might look. The information derived from the case studies is helpful to destination managers, policy makers and other tourism stakeholders interested in implementing tourism policies that are tested and trusted in a pandemic context.

The chapter is organised as follows. The first section sets the context and introduces the research gap. Then the chapter provides a brief review of the existing literature on tourism policies. The third section describes the methodology and then we present policies from different countries. Finally, there is a short section on some conclusions and implications.

Literature review

Tourism policy: A conceptual overview

Tourism policies during crisis situations have been an area of key concern in tourism research and development globally. Indeed, the role of government policies in influencing tourism development has been of great importance to tourism scholars (Hall, 2011; Stevenson, Airey and Miller, 2008; Spirou, 2022). Tourism development that ultimately ignores ecological, social, health and economic limits and capacities precipitates a crisis and may not be viable in the long term. This contextual approach to tourism has been considered by policy network theorists as more significant in contexts where public sector resources are more interdependent with other societal actors. Policy network theory (PNT) assumes that the resources are exchanged with interdependent actors (Compston, 2009). However, policy scholars and theorists have advocated for policy change vis-à-vis policy stability, with the fundamental concern that some of the policy makers and institutions may have long-term interests and dominance in the public sector (Galey and Youngs, 2014). More recently, specific interest has been on sustainable development (Santos, et al., 2022; Pigram, 1990), policy-making process and implementation (McKercher, 2022; Sedarati, Serra and Jakulin, 2022), evolution of tourism policy directions (Gao et al., 2022), and rebuilding tourism post-pandemic (Gowreesunkar et al., 2022). In times of global tourism evolution, the need for tourism policies to be adaptable to the global forces seeking to influence tourism change has been a major concern for tourism academics (Tyler and Dinan, 2001). Hall (2000) examines the functional roles of tourism policies in terms of coordination, planning, legislation, entrepreneurial support, demand stimulation, public interest protection as well as promotion. To a particular extent, the functional roles of tourism policies have a significant impact on the sustainable development of tourism at the destination level. Indeed, as noted by Henriques and Elias (2021), there is a critical link between tourism policies, modes of governance and sustainable tourism product development. However, the challenge of sustainability has evolved to a challenge of resilience, equity, balance and trade-offs. According to Tyrrell and Johnston (2008), tourism planners have had to address these tourism dynamics through optimising tourism policies to address the resilience of destinations and related socio-ecological systems. Ecological and social limits within destinations define the quality of life of communities and the economic prosperity of destinations.

Tourism policies and governance in crisis situations

A number of dominant paradigms in tourism policy research have emerged, ranging between political, stakeholder and network approaches. Political approaches, in a way, have questioned the rationality of institutional decisions and adopted the normative thinking underlying political decisions (Stevenson, Airey and Miller, 2008). In order to understand the complexity of political change at the different scales of analysis, Earl and Hall (2021) note that the political theorists acknowledge that institutions are fundamental towards driving change in the tourism sector and therefore provide the political basis for policy development in the tourism sector. However, as noted by Falaster, Zanin and Guerrazzi (2017), the institutional theorists assume isomorphism and the homogenisation of practices where institutions are expected to take similar actions and strategies. However, the stakeholder approaches to tourism policy focus on the competing stakeholder interests and demands in environments of economic turmoil. Contemporary turbulent economic times have brought to the forefront ethical issues on wealth distribution, thereby placing more emphasis on the welfare of the citizenry (Nicolaides, 2014). Much more emphasis in this approach had been on the diversity of interests within the sector. However, the limitations of the resources with which tourism is dependent upon has created the need to review and reflect on tourism policy-making practice. Despite the fact that tourism has been viewed as a pathway for economic development and social transformation (Harilal, Tichaawa and Saarinen, 2019; Walton, 2013), the sector has had to deal with myriad of challenges from global, regional and local contexts.

The concept of governance has been associated with the tourism policy-making process and in the particular context of steering and/or regulating the sector (Bramwell and Lane, 2011). In crisis situations, discourse on the roles of tourism policies and governance becomes crucial in response to the crises. Britton's (1991) perspective on the tourism production system took the perspective that tourism policies were more focused on the production capacities designed for the commodification of touristic experiences. Through his perspective, the different actors within the destination were more focused on the intensification of tourism production systems within actor networks. However, during crises, there has been a need to shift policy orientation towards resolving the crisis (Jóhannesson and Huijbens, 2013; Persson-Fischer and Liu, 2021). In the recent past, various scholars have proposed stakeholder-coordinated interventions to mitigate the effects of the COVID-19 pandemic (Barkas et al., 2020), economic stimulus measures (OECD, 2020) as well as organisational learning and reflection (Blackman and Ritchie, 2008). The COVID-19 pandemic has, however, exposed the systemic and long-standing structural weaknesses in tourism policies worldwide. Lessons from the Ebola-induced tourism crisis areas, such as the Gambia, have shown that crisis management policies and strategies and policies are crucial towards tourism growth and development (Novelli et al., 2018). According to Gowreesunkar et al. (2021), rebuilding tourism requires policies that foster global solidarity and advance key priorities during and post the pandemic period.

New trends and future tendencies

Globally, tourism policies have played a key role in advancing the fact that the tourism sector cuts across a number of industries and service sectors and that, therefore, tourism policies have to be multi-sectoral. The new tendency shows that tourists are looking for destinations following health protocols and that tourist behaviour has not really changed but has rather evolved alongside the pandemics' evolution. As pointed out in an earlier study of Gowreesunkar and Dixit (2017), customers of the 21st century are busy and demanding and they display unpredictable behaviour. The new tendency shows that customers are even more unpredictable and they have developed a sharper flair in making online decisions. Whenever they need information on a particular product or service, they resort to sources that are practical, convenient, less time-consuming and cost-efficient, and they can also change their decisions and act otherwise at last minute. Following the pandemic, the same tendency has been reinforced. The study of Aldao et al. (2021) clearly shows that companies that invest in digitalisation and social media are the ones that obtain the higher benefits. The Internet satisfies the needs of consumers as it covers the entire variety of choices of travel, accommodation, transportation and leisure services, holiday packages, prices and availability (Buhalis, 1998). This interactive medium not only gives information, but also provides feedback of holiday experiences of tourists is considered as a reliable source of information. The tourism industry urges for a worldwide unified criteria for restrictions and policies. Non-homogenous setup of protocols and the lack of trust in governments and travel services has turned into tourists' lack of confidence. Before the pandemic, terrorism and natural disasters were a concern; after the outbreak, however, the pandemic was placed as the foremost concern, overtaking terrorism and other disasters at the top of any tourist's worry list (Aldao et al., 2021). The COVID-19 pandemic has exposed the long-standing policy gaps that require to be addressed to enhance the resiliency of the sector in future. This requires adequate coordination between the market actors and industry segments towards the formulation of a comprehensive and inclusive tourism policy. So, each national or local government would select those policies and tools that were deemed most suitable to its particular circumstances and adapt them to the conditions prevailing in its country, region or local jurisdiction. The pandemic has highlighted the need of safe travel and hence tourism policies need to imperatively mention health protocol. Likewise, travel packages now imperatively comprise health protocols, failing which travel is not possible. From a destination management point of view, cooperation amongst all stakeholders and a clear governance structure, as well as an effective balance between public health concerns and economic imperatives are being prioritised by policymakers (Aldao et al., 2021).

Policy formulation remains the main tool to help the tourism industry remain aligned worldwide. For instance, if, as regulatory bodies, the WHO and the UNWTO did not impose conditions and regulations for tourism, the industry would have probably been completely devastated by now. Health and safety now play a pivotal role in any travel and

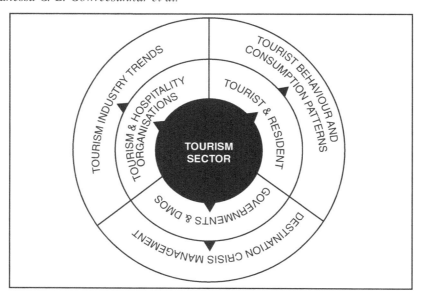

Figure 22.1 Future tourism policy pillars.
Source: Aldao et al. (2021).

tourism business and will remain so (as prevailing conditions show). This is well explained in the study of Wen et al. (2021). According to this study, high standards of medical facilities helped enhance the reputation of a country, and therefore, they represented a powerful feature for attracting tourists. Future tourism policy should therefore be based on three important pillars, as shown in the diagram provided by Aldao et al. (2021):

According to Aldao et al. (2021), the complexity of the tourism system needs to be addressed by analysing the factors that drive towards a crisis and its impact. In this way, it is possible to evaluate mitigation steps for a fast-forward recovery on an empirical level. Destination resilience is important for tourism managers and policy makers in the development of more adaptive strategies in the face of vulnerabilities, growing risks and the uncertainty of crises and disasters. Risks at the local, national and international levels are becoming ever more systemic and unpredictable, with high (and rising) costs for recovery. Tourism managers and stakeholders at the local and national level must be empowered through greater information sharing and responsiveness during the crisis/disaster. In the post-COVID-19 era, resilience in the tourism sector was highly linked to crisis management in order to reset the industry. Thus, crisis management represents the tool for implementing measures aimed at preparedness and planning strategies, response to crisis and recovery and crisis learning and long-term resilience actions (Ritchie and Jiang, 2019). With constant uncertainty being the main characteristic of a disruptive event such as a pandemic, the tourism sector experienced never-ending backwards and forwards activities that cause unstable behaviour and consumption patterns, as well as adaptive trends in an attempt to revive the sector.

Methodology

Following the pandemic, case studies analysis became a common method of investigation, due to restrictions on movement and mobility of people to public places. For the current chapter, the multiple case study approach as proposed by Stake (2006) was deemed appropriate. Case studies are, in fact, widely used in tourism research as they permit analysis of several contexts and, therefore, can make reflections beyond the cases (see Yin 1994; Stevenson et al., 2008; Stake, 2006; Kerr et al., 2001; Xiao and Smith, 2006). Multiple case studies provide a fast and reliable diagnosis that is helpful in producing evidence-based policies. Stake (2006) further explains that multiple case studies allow a combination of specific and general views on policy decisions which are helpful in analysing a greater range of elements with special attention being paid to social and political influences and other contexts in which each case is embedded. This approach is also recommended by Jafari (1987) and Kerr et al. (2001), who put forward that case-specific studies are useful to develop thick descriptions and improve understanding in a specific context rather than attempting to develop universal models. Multiple case studies are widely used in tourism studies when it is not possible to separate the phenomenon being studied from its context. For the present chapter, secondary data were obtained from the authors' edited book *Tourism Destination Management Post Pandemic* (Gowreesunkar et al., 2021). The rationale behind the choice was that these were the only accessible case studies available for analysis after the pandemic. Since the current chapter deals with multiple case studies, the following guidelines were followed:

- Case studies from Gowreesunkar et al. (2021) were broadly analysed
- This particular book was selected as it is one of the first text books published during the pandemic (December 2020)
- Fifteen case studies were chosen for the analysis as they were representative of each of the following areas: the Baltic States, Africa, the U.K., the U.S., Asia, the Middle East
- The policy decisions of each of the case studies were extracted and then analysed
- The summarised policy decisions were then compared against policy guidelines from UNWTO

Although case study research is useful as a means of studying information, it has several limitations. For example, policy statements (secondary sources of data for this chapter) might have changed as, after the initial COVID-19 infections, new realities such as the Omicron and other mutations emerged, thus forcing new policy decisions by different countries. Darke et al. (1998) argue that the case studies method has strengths and weaknesses. Nevertheless, the researchers can effectively manage this to justify the credibility of a research outcome. Xiao and Smith (2006) lends support to this claim and the authors affirm that the prevalent arguments of case studies as conceptually and analytically weak are not justified. Stereotypical perceptions as such can be misleading and may consequently exert a negative impact on the righteous application of case study methodology in tourism research. Thus, it is recognised that for the present chapter, policy decisions reflected in the 2020 case studies may be less reflective of the prevailing time.

Findings: Lessons from global case studies

Destination management policies

Tourism destinations globally have borne the brunt of the COVID-19 pandemic. Most destinations were unprepared for the pandemic. UNWTO reports indicate a loss of US$910 billion to US$1.2 trillion on visitor spend, with 100 to 120 million direct tourism jobs at risk globally (UNWTO, 2021). This coupled with the unprecedented socioeconomic impacts owing to the initial government responses to slow down the spread of the pandemic on the tourism sector were immense. The intensity and impacts of the COVID-19 pandemic on tourism destinations meant that governments had to develop coordinated actions aimed at reducing tourism vulnerability and enhancing the resilience of destinations as well as controlling the socioeconomic impacts and related ecological dimensions. Specifically, well-resourced strategies are important to shield the destination from the impacts of the pandemic in the future. Drawing on lessons from Chiappa (2021), in the short term, macro-based interventions such as financial, fiscal, health and welfare interventions are essential for shielding the destinations from such pandemics. However, in the long term, more coping and adaptable approaches are required to ensure that destinations are more agile in addressing the impacts of pandemics. Specifically, Livina et al. (2021) examine the roles of stakeholders and an integrated business strategy in the process of tourism recovery. Subadra (2021) also proposed collaborative management in mitigating the effects of the spread of COVID-19 across the destinations. Further, drawing on lessons from Egypt by Elgammal and Refaat (2021), the incorporation of human carrying capacity for tourism facilities and attractions is important in curbing the spread of the virus. Mugizi et al. (2021) propose a focus on sustainability pathways for destinations as a way of tourism recovery. Ideally, long-term tourism recovery measures for destinations call for stakeholder-driven approaches, a sustainability focus and public health regulations to provide a sustainable tourism business recovery in the post-pandemic era.

Disaster management policies

Disasters have persisted in the tourism sector for years, ranging from natural, chemical, biological, virus outbreaks to human-made disasters. Disaster management has been seen as the organisation and management of resources towards dealing with the early warning systems, disaster risk reduction, preparedness, response and recovery from disasters. It is important that the tourism sector acts before, during and after a disaster strikes. The focus of disaster management is to save lives and livelihoods as well as to reduce the risks faced by the adjacent communities from future effects of the disasters. Drawing from lessons from Argentina, tourism sector preparedness involves addressing the political differences, anti-tourism fears, lockdown deprivations and inter-class rivalries, as well as the narratives that largely swayed the public opinions on the pandemic (Korstanje, 2021). The rise of anti-tourist discourse at these times created a need to develop a much more differentiated marketing and image of tourism destinations in future. There is need to address the infodemic and negative news on such pandemics as they have an effect on the images of destinations. Further, Dale et al. (2021) focus on the adoption of contingency strategies in terms of health, safety certification and financial security protocols for the sector as prerequisites for disaster preparedness for such virus outbreaks and pandemics. However, drawing on lessons from previous outbreaks, the Ugandan case, as detailed by Mugizi et al. (2021), demonstrates the need for a structural mainstreaming of crisis management in tourism policy, planning and development frameworks to ensure preparedness, response, recovery and sustainability after virus outbreaks in future. Resilience measures, as evidenced by the Ugandan Government surveillance and control measures in past outbreaks, are important in guaranteeing the safety and security of visitors. In addition, drawing from lessons from Bangladesh, Rahman et al. (2021) state that there is a need to develop more integrated adaptive capacity and resilience by focusing on six domains of tourism resilience: engineering, social, economic, environmental institutional, individual and governance resilience.

Roles of local communities and destination recovery

Local communities are considered as important stakeholders in the tourism sector. Studies have also confirmed that the local community is an important agent for sustainable tourism development in any destination. In the wake of the COVID-19 pandemic, the role of local communities in flattening the infections curve was much more pronounced. Lessons from Mauritius from Hurnath and Dookhony-Rampul (2021) indicate that emotional solidarity and local community wellbeing was critical for the survival of community-dependent destinations in Mauritius. Social fears were imminent as a result of the COVID-19 outbreak and residents' perceptions were important to address in the future so as to promote post-pandemic destination recovery. It is important that social welfare considerations are considered for tourism-dependent communities to enhance tourism recovery. Further, lessons from Villena-Alarcon and Cabarello-Galeote (2021) from the territory of Andalusia show that communities and residents can play an active, participatory and vital role in expressing their opinions and influencing destination recovery amidst lockdowns and movement control orders. Communities can overcome crises through their power of networks and their collective voices in promoting destinations. The research further noted the protagonist roles of communities in social media networks and their influences on destination recovery. As a matter of policy, there is need to engage the local communities' endorsements through community-driven online marketing campaigns. In a similar context, Munene (2016) examines the roles of civil society organizations (CSOs) in the destination recovery process in the Kenyan context. The study examines the role of vulnerable communities and the need to formulate structural policies that highlight their plight, as well as their stories in the light of the COVID-19 pandemic. Social inclusivity in destination recovery is a win–win strategy for the tourism industry and communities. In a similar case, Chipurumo et al. (2021) further note inequalities and gender disparities in employability in the South African context as a result of the pandemic. There is a need to address gender issues in this context and develop protective policies that ensure protection of vulnerable workers in the sector.

Marketing and promotion of destinations post-pandemic

Within the context of marketing destinations in the pandemic and post-pandemic era, there has been a need to change marketing orientation and approach. The major factor is rebuilding visitor confidence as well as image on health and safety issues as a paramount concern. In order to weather the socio-economic storm of the pandemic, there is a need to alter the tourism experience and health risk perceptions, as noted by Yagci et al. (2021) from a Turkish context. The researchers further note that lower risk perception levels have a greater impact on travel-related behavioural intentions of visitors. Destination management organisations need to provide greater assurance in their marketing of destinations through effective communication strategies in the marketplace. However, lessons from the Italian context by Varriale et al. (2021) emphasise the importance of digital and social media marketing strategies during and after the pandemic era. According to Gowreesunkar et al. (2021), post-pandemic tourism destination marketing will be content-based and therefore will need to reengineer traditional marketing approaches to factor pandemics into the context of the tourism marketing mix. In addition, diversification of tourism offerings, as well as offering incentives for sustainable tourism and local development in the post-pandemic era, will be key in the promotion of mass appeal sports events (Bizzarri and Giuntarelli, 2021).

Sustainable tourism policies in the post-pandemic period

Sustaining tourism in the post-pandemic era will involve addressing issues such as economic viability, social inclusivity as well as environmental conservation measures. It will indeed be a tall order to achieve these three aspects amidst the adverse socio-economic and ecological impacts of the COVID-19 pandemic. According to Lama and Rai (2021), these challenges are vividly addressed through planning for sustainable tourism development in the destination. Within the context of social sustainability, the need for sustainability programmes is key to restoring tourism sustainably in the post-COVID-19 era (Mishra and Mishra, 2021). Governments need to focus on community wellbeing and enhanced opportunities for the locals as an important agent for redistributing wealth and developing social cohesion (Indu, Bindu and Singh, 2021). Wahome and Gathungu (2021) focus more on redefining sustainability from a post-pandemic perspective. An effective post-pandemic tourism definition needs to factor in the health and safety of the visitors, industry and communities as an important aspect of sustainability in a tourism context.

Tourism education policies in the post-pandemic period

The tourism education system is critical for the overall tourism recovery and resilience measures within the pandemic and post-pandemic period. Retooling and reviewing curricula in the sector are vital towards achieving desired competencies and skill sets in the industry. As a matter of priority, Sunneeth et al. (2021) advocate for the adaptation of resilience and disaster management courses in tourism education curricula for the post-COVID-19 era. Further, Gupta and Sahu (2021) propose mandatory management and industry training programmes as a basis for tourism revival in the Indian context. Overall, the education sector in the Mauritius context according to Abbass et al. (2021) will require an overhaul of tourism education policies, curricula, and pedagogy adopting online and remote learning methods so as to cope with the disruption to educational learning environments.

Discussion and conclusion

The objective of this chapter is to provide an insight into policy decisions adopted by tourism destinations during the pandemic. The selected cases studies derived from the authors' edited book *Tourism Destination Management in a Post-Pandemic Context* provide several interesting lessons. The crisis reveals the need to rethink tourism policies based on collaboration and not competition. The next normal of the tourism industry will be about confronting the historical role of tourism in perpetuating structural inequalities and consider how best to protect the rights and livelihoods of tourism workers rather than exploiting them in the post-pandemic recovery plan (Benjamin et al., 2020). Rebuilding tourism requires collective effort, global solidarity, and, more importantly, tourism policies that address structural weaknesses, advance key socio-economic priorities and take advantage of new opportunities. The case studies show that the crisis is an opportunity to rethink the tourism system. As a result, struggling destinations need to implement tourism policies that are cross-cutting. The impact of the crisis is being felt throughout the entire tourism ecosystem and reopening and rebuilding destinations will require a joined-up policy approach (OECD, 2021). As the world is still navigating within the pandemic, evidence-based policies derived from global studies may be used as valuable lessons to destinations still struggling with the pandemic. Local, regional and national governments have all played a part in assisting recovery after any crisis. Likewise, after two years of coping with the pandemic, the industry has also moved on with new set of coping capacities and policies that are really proving to be effective (Gowreesunkar et al., 2021). The COVID-19 pandemic is a wakeup call to re-strategise and re-think tourism policies that are flexible and adaptable to changing dynamics. Tourism planners should learn from mistakes made elsewhere and realise that policy making is not static but, rather, a continuous process which has to integrate exogenous changes (Airey, 2015; Hall, 2000). Tourism policy for the 'next normal' has to be based on coordination and collaboration.

References

Abbass, N. S., Essmallgee, F., & Cooshna-Gunputh, P. (2021). Adopt, Adapt or Perish: Re-building Support Systems for Travel and Tourism Education in COVID-19 Educational Crisis. In *Tourism Destination Management in a Post-Pandemic Context* (pp. 315–327). Emerald Publishing Limited.

Airey, D.W. (2015). Developments in understanding tourism policy. *Tourism Review*, 70(4), 246–258.

Aldao, C., Blasco, D., Espallargas, M.P. and Palou Rubio, S. (2021). Modelling the crisis management and impacts of 21st century disruptive events in tourism: the case of the COVID-19 pandemic. *Tourism Review*, 76(4), 929–941. doi: 10.1108/TR-07-2020-0297

Baggio, R. (2008). *Network analysis of a tourism destination*. Australia: University of Queensland.

Barkas, P., Honeck, D., and Rubio, E. (2020). International trade in travel and tourism services: economic impact and policy responses during the COVID-19 crisis (No. ERSD-2020-11). *WTO Staff Working Paper*.

Benjamin, S., Dillette, A. and Aldermann, D. (2020). "we can't return to normal", committing to tourism equity in the post pandemic age. *Tourism Geographies*, 22(3), 476–483.

Bizzarri, C. and Giuntarelli, P. (2021). Sport Events and Tourism for the Sustainable Local Development Post COVID. In Gowreesunkar, V.G., Maingi, S.W., Roy, H. and Micera, R. (Ed.) *Tourism Destination Management in a Post-Pandemic Context (Tourism Security-Safety and Post Conflict Destinations)*, Emerald Publishing Limited, Bingley, pp. 49–65. https://doi.org/10.1108/978-1-80071-511-020211004

Blackman, D., and Ritchie, B.W. (2008). Tourism crisis management and organizational learning: The role of reflection in developing effective DMO crisis strategies. *Journal of Travel & Tourism Marketing*, 23(2–4), 45–57.

Bramwell, B. and Lane, B. (2011) Critical research on the governance of tourism and sustainability. *Journal of Sustainable Tourism*, 19(4), 411–421.

Bremser, K., Crowley-Cyr, L., Abraham, V., Moreno-Martin, M.J. and Carreno, M. (2021). Application of the health belief model to explain public perceptions, travel intentions and actions during COVID-19: a sequential transformative design. *Journal of Hospitality and Tourism Insights*, Vol. ahead-of-print, doi: 10.1108/JHTI12-2020-0235

Britton, S. (1991). Tourism, capital, and place: Towards a critical geography of tourism. *Environment and Planning D: Society and Space*, 9(4), 451–478.

Buhalis, D. (1998). Strategic use of information technologies in the tourism industry. *Tourism Management*, 19(5), 409–421.

Buhalis, D. and Cooper, C. (1998) 'Competition or Co-operation: The needs of small and medium sized tourism enterprises at a destina tion level', in Laws, E., Faulkner, B. and Moscardo, G. (eds), *Embracing and Managing Change in Tourism*, London: Routledge, pp. 324–346.

Buhalis, D. and Cooper, C. (2000). Marketing the competitive destination of the future – Growth strategies for accommodation establishments in alpine regions. *Tourism Management*, 20(1), 91–116.

Butler, R. W. (1980). The concept of a tourist area cycle of evolution: Implications for management of resources. *Canadian Geographer*, 24(1), 5–12.

Çakar, K. (2018). Critical success factors for tourist destination governance in times of crisis: a case study of Antalya, Turkey. *Journal of Travel and Tourism Marketing*, 35(6), 786–802, doi: 10.1080/10548408.2017.1421495

Campiranon, K. and Scott, N. (2014). Critical success factors for crisis recovery management: a case study of Phuket hotels. *Journal of Travel and Tourism Marketing*, 31(3), 313–326. doi: 10.1080/10548408.2013.877414

Chiappa, G.D. (2021). COVID-19 Pandemic and the Accommodation Sector in Sardinia, Italy: Impacts and Response Actions. In Gowreesunkar, V.G., Maingi, S.W., Roy, H. and Micera, R. (Ed.) *Tourism Destination Management in a Post-Pandemic Context* (Tourism Security-Safety and Post Conflict Destinations), Emerald Publishing Limited, Bingley, pp. 49–65. https://doi.org/10.1108/978-1-80071-511-020211004

Chipurumo, J. Mihailescu, R. and Rinaldi, A. (2021). Gender Disparities in Employability in the Tourism Sector Post COVID-19 Pandemic: Case of South Africa. In Gowreesunkar, V.G., Maingi, S.W., Roy, H. and Micera, R. (Ed.) *Tourism Destination Management in a Post-Pandemic Context* (Tourism Security-Safety and Post Conflict Destinations), Emerald Publishing Limited, Bingley, pp. 99–112. https://doi.org/10.1108/978-1-80071-511-020211007

Compston H. (2009). Policy Network Theory as a Theory of Policy Change. In *Policy Networks and Policy Change*. Palgrave Macmillan, London. https://doi.org/10.1057/9780230244320_4

Cresswell, J. (2011). *Qualitative Inquiry and Research Design: Choosing among five traditions*. Thousand Oaks, CA; Sage.

Dale, C., Robinson, N. and Sheikh, F. (2021). Tourist Safety and Security Post COVID-19: Global Perspectives In Gowreesunkar, V.G., Maingi, S.W., Roy, H. and Micera, R. (Ed.) *Tourism Destination Management in a Post-Pandemic Context (Tourism Security-Safety and Post Conflict Destinations)*, Emerald Publishing Limited, Bingley, pp. 99–112. https://doi.org/10.1108/978-1-80071-511-020211007

Darke, P., Shanks, G., and Broadbent, M. (1998). Successfully completing case study research: combining rigour, relevance and pragmatism, *Information System Journal*, 4(4), 273–289.

Dredge, D. and Jenkins, J. (2007). *Tourism Planning and Policy*, Milton: Wiley, 2007.

Dredge, D., Jenkins, J. and Whitford, M. (2011). Tourism Policy and Planning: Historical Development and Contemporary Challenges In Dredge, D. and Jenkins, J. (eds.) *Stories of Practice: Tourism Planning and Policy*, Ashgate Publishing, Aldershot, pp. 13–34.

Earl, A. and Hall, C.M. (2021). *Institutional Theory in Tourism and Hospitality*, 1st edition. Routledge. https://doi.org/10.4324/9781003051206

Elgammal, I. and Refaat, H. (2021). Heritage Tourism and COVID-19: Turning the Crisis into Opportunity within the Egyptian Context. In Gowreesunkar, V.G., Maingi, S.W., Roy, H. and Micera, R. (Ed.) *Tourism Destination Management in a Post-Pandemic Context (Tourism Security-Safety and Post Conflict Destinations)*, Emerald Publishing Limited, Bingley, pp. 37–48. https://doi.org/10.1108/978-1-80071-511-020211003

Falaster, C., Zanin, L. M., & Guerrazzi, L. A. (2017). Institutional theory in tourism research: new opportunities from an evolving theory. *Revista Brasileira de Pesquisa em Turismo*, 11, 270–293.

Galey, S. and Youngs, P. (2014). *Moving Towards an Integrated Theory of Policy Networks: A Multi-Theoretical Approach for Examining State-Level Policy Change in U.S. Subsystems*. East Lansing, Michigan: The Education Policy at Michigan State University.

Gao, J., Ryan, C., Zhang, C., and Cui, J. (2022). The evolution of Chinese border tourism policies: an intergovernmental perspective on border tourism in Xishuangbanna. *Asia Pacific Journal of Tourism Research*, 27(2), 157–172.

Gowreesunkar, V., & Dixit, S. (2017). Customer Information Search Behaviour. In S. K. Dixit (Ed.), *Handbook of Consumer Behavior for Hospitality and Tourism* (pp 165–178). Oxford, UK: Routledge.

Gowreesunkar, V.G., Maingi, S.W., Roy, H., and Micera, R. (2022). Rebuilding tourism post pandemic–Policy recommendations from global case studies. *Emerald Open Research*, 4(2), 2.

Gowreesunkar, V.G.B., Maingi, S.W., Roy, H. and Micera, R. (2021). Introduction: Destination Management Solutions Post Pandemic: A Need of the Hour. Pandemic and the Accommodation Sector in Sardinia, Italy: Impacts and Response Actions. In Gowreesunkar, V.G., Maingi, S.W., Roy, H. and Micera, R. (Ed.) *Tourism Destination Management in a Post-Pandemic Context (Tourism Security-Safety and Post Conflict Destinations)*, 1st Edition, Emerald Publishing Limited, Bingley, pp. 49–65. https://doi.org/10.1108/978-1-80071-511-020211004

Gupta, V. and Sahu, G. (2021). Reviving Tourism in India Post COVID-19 Pandemic: Role of Tourism Education and Training. In Gowreesunkar, V.G., Maingi, S.W., Roy, H. and Micera, R. (Ed.) *Tourism Destination Management in a Post-Pandemic Context (Tourism Security-Safety and Post Conflict Destinations)*, Emerald Publishing Limited, Bingley, pp. 49–65. https://doi.org/10.1108/978-1-80071-511-020211004

Hall, C.M. (2000). Rethinking collaboration and partnership: A public policy perspective. *Tourism Collaboration and Partnerships: Politics, Practice and Sustainability*, 2(14), 3.

Hall, C.M. (2011). A typology of governance and its implications for tourism policy analysis. *Journal of Sustainable Tourism*, 19(4–5), 437–457.

Hall, C.M. and Jenkins, J. (1995). *Tourism and Public Policy*, Routledge: London, UK, pp. 523–540.

Hall, C.M., Scott, D., and Gössling, S. (2020). Pandemics, transformations and tourism: Be careful what you wish for. *Tourism Geographies*, Online. https://doi.org/10.1080/14616688.2020.1759131.

Hall, M. (2008). *Tourism Planning: Policies, Processes and Relationships*, 2nd Edition. Harlow: Pearson Education.

Harilal, V., Tichaawa, T.M. and Saarinen, J. (2019). "Development without Policy": Tourism planning and research needs in Cameroon, Central Africa. *Tourism Planning and Management*, 16(6), 696–705.

Henriques, C.H. and Elias, S.R. (2021). Interconnections between the cultural and creative industries and tourism: Challenges in four Ibero-American capital cities. *International Journal of Culture, Tourism and Hospitality Research*, 16(1), 337–351. https://doi.org/10.1108/IJCTHR-02-2021-0036

Hurnath, C. and Dookhony-Rampul, K. (2021). Exploring impacts of a health crisis on Emotional solidarity and support for Tourism: Case of Mauritius. In Gowreesunkar, V.G., Maingi, S.W., Roy, H. and Micera, R. (Ed.) *Tourism Destination Management in a Post-Pandemic Context (Tourism Security-Safety and Post Conflict Destinations)*, Emerald Publishing Limited, Bingley, pp. 99–112. https://doi.org/10.1108/978-1-80071-511-020211007

Indu, Bindu and Singh, K. (2021). Does your Post COVID-19 Travel Dream Talk about Sustainability? Insights from Potential Tourists in India. In Gowreesunkar, V.G., Maingi, S.W., Roy, H. and Micera, R. (Ed.) *Tourism Destination Management in a Post-Pandemic Context (Tourism Security-Safety and Post Conflict Destinations)*, Emerald Publishing Limited, Bingley, pp. 49–65. https://doi.org/10.1108/978-1-80071-511-020211004

Jafari, J. (1987). Tourism Models: The socio-cultural aspects. *Tourism Management*, 9(1), 82–84.

Jóhannesson, G.T., and Huijbens, E.H. (2013). Tourism Resolving Crisis? In *New Issues in Polar Tourism*, Springer, Dordrecht, pp. 133–147.

Kerr, B., Barron, G., and Wood, R. (2001). Politics, policy and regional tourism administration: A case examination of Scottish Area Tourist Board Funding. *Tourism Management*, 22(6), 649–657

Korstanje, M.E. (2021). Tourism Disaster [Preparedness Post COVID-19 pandemic: The Example of Argentina]. In Gowreesunkar, V.G., Maingi, S.W., Roy, H. and Micera, R. (Ed.) *Tourism Destination Management in a Post-Pandemic Context (Tourism Security-Safety and Post Conflict Destinations)*, Emerald Publishing Limited, Bingley, pp. 99–112. https://doi.org/10.1108/978-1-80071-511-020211007

Lama, R. and Rai, A. (2021). Challenges in Developing Sustainable Tourism Post COVID-19 Pandemic. In Gowreesunkar, V.G., Maingi, S.W., Roy, H. and Micera, R. (Ed.) *Tourism Destination Management in a Post-Pandemic Context (Tourism Security-Safety and Post Conflict Destinations)*, Emerald Publishing Limited, Bingley, pp. 49–65. https://doi.org/10.1108/978-1-80071-511-020211004

Livina, A., Bukovska, G., Abols, I. and Reddy, G.M. (2021). The Recovery Tactics of the Tourism Industry Amid COVID-19 Pandemic Conditions in the Baltic States. In Gowreesunkar, V.G., Maingi, S.W., Roy, H. and Micera, R. (Ed.) *Tourism Destination Management in a Post-Pandemic Context (Tourism Security-Safety and Post Conflict Destinations)*, Emerald Publishing Limited, Bingley, pp. 11–23. https://doi.org/10.1108/978-1-80071-511-020211001

Marshall, C. and Rossman, G.B. (2011) *Designing Qualitative Research* (5th ed.). Thousand Oaks, CA: Sage.

McKercher, B. (2022). The politics of tourism: The unsung role of trade associations in tourism policymaking. *Tourism Management*, 90, 104475.

Mishra, N. and Mishra, A. (2021). Impact of COVID-19 pandemic on Social Sustainability in Tourism: A Study of Uttarakhand State of India. In Gowreesunkar, V.G., Maingi, S.W., Roy, H. and Micera, R. (Ed.) *Tourism Destination Management in a Post-Pandemic Context (Tourism Security-Safety and Post Conflict Destinations)*, Emerald Publishing Limited, Bingley, pp. 49–65. https://doi.org/10.1108/978-1-80071-511-020211004

Mugizi, F., Ayorekire, J. and Obua, J. (2021). Uganda Tourism Sector COVID-19 Response, Recovery and Sustainability Strategies: Lessons from Previous Virus Disease Outbreaks. In Gowreesunkar, V.G., Maingi, S.W., Roy, H. and Micera, R. (Ed.) *Tourism Destination Management in a Post-Pandemic Context (Tourism Security-Safety and Post Conflict Destinations)*, Emerald Publishing Limited, Bingley, pp. 99–112. https://doi.org/10.1108/978-1-80071-511-020211007

Munene, M. B. (2016). *Urban resilience in Nairobi: Civil society's role and interaction with climate and risk science under devolution*. Urban Africa Risk Knowledge (ARK).

Nicolaides, A. (2014). Tourism stakeholder theory in practice: Instrumental business grounds, fundamental normative demands or a descriptive application? *African Journal of Hospitality, Tourism and Leisure*, 4(2), 1–26.

Novelli, M., Burgess, L. G., Jones, A., & Ritchie, B. W. (2018). 'No Ebola… still doomed'–The Ebola-induced tourism crisis. *Annals of Tourism Research*, 70, 76–87.

OECD (2020). Tourism policy responses, Tackling Coronavirus (COVID-19), Contributing to a global effort, 31 March 2020, Retrieved on 16 April 2022 at: https://www.oecd.org/coronavirus/policy-responses/tourism-policy-responses-to-the-coronavirus-COVID-19-6466aa20/

OECD (2021). Mitigating the impacts of COVID-19 on tourism and supporting recovery.

Persson-Fischer, U., and Liu, S. (2021). The impact of a global crisis on areas and topics of tourism research. *Sustainability*, 13(2), 906.

Pigram, J.J. (1990). Sustainable tourism-policy considerations. *Journal of Tourism Studies*, 1(2), 2–9.

Rahman, M., Muzareba, A.M., Amin, S., Faroque, A.R., and Gani, M.O. (2021). Tourism Resilience in the Context of Tourism Destination Management in Post-COVID-19 Bangladesh. In Gowreesunkar, V.G., Maingi, S.W., Roy, H. and Micera, R. (Ed.) *Tourism Destination Management in a Post-Pandemic Context (Tourism Security-Safety and Post Conflict Destinations)*, Emerald Publishing Limited, Bingley, pp. 99–112. https://doi.org/10.1108/978-1-80071-511-020211007

Ritchie, B. W., & Jiang, Y. (2019). A review of research on tourism risk, crisis and disaster management: Launching the annals of tourism research curated collection on tourism risk, crisis and disaster management. *Annals of Tourism Research*, 79, 102812.

Santos, M.C., Veiga, C., Santos, J.A.C., and Águas, P. (2022). Sustainability as a success factor for tourism destinations: A systematic literature review. *Worldwide Hospitality and Tourism Themes*, 14(1), 20–37. https://doi.org/10.1108/WHATT-10-2021-0139

Sedarati, P., Serra, F.M.D., and Jakulin, T.J. (2022). Systems approach to model smart tourism ecosystems. *International Journal for Quality Research*, 16(1), 285.

Spirou, C. (2022). Municipal Advancement and Tourism Policy in the United States: Economic Development and Urban Restructuring. In Jan Ver Der Borg (eds.) *A Research Agenda for Urban Tourism*. Edward Elgar Publishing. https://doi.org/10.4337/9781789907407

Stake, R.E. (1995). *The art of case study research*. London: SAGE Publications.

Stake, R.E. (2006). *Multiple case study analysis*. New York: The Guilford Press

Stevenson, N., Airey, D., and Miller, G. (2008). Tourism policy making: The policymakers' perspectives. *Annals of Tourism Research*, 35(3), 732–750.

Subadra, I.N. (2021). Destination Management Solution Post COVID-19: Best Practice from Bali – A World Cultural Tourism Destination. In Gowreesunkar, V.G., Maingi, S.W., Roy, H. and Micera, R. (Ed.) *Tourism Destination Management in a Post-Pandemic Context (Tourism Security-Safety and Post Conflict Destinations)*, Emerald Publishing Limited, Bingley, pp. 25–36. https://doi.org/10.1108/978-1-80071-511-020211024

Sunneeth, B.G., Suneeth, G., Kashyap, S., Reddy, G.M. and Kaushal, V. (2021). Resilience Adaptations in Tourism Education for the Post COVID-19 Era – A Study of India. In: Gowreesunkar, V.G., Maingi, S.W., Roy, H. and Micera, R. (Ed.) *Tourism Destination Management in a Post-Pandemic Context (Tourism Security-Safety and Post Conflict Destinations)*, Emerald Publishing Limited, Bingley, pp. 49–65. https://doi.org/10.1108/978-1-80071-511-020211004

Tyler, D., and Dinan, C. (2001). The role of interested groups in England's emerging tourism policy network. *Current Issues in Tourism*, 4(2–4), 210–252.

Tyrrell, T.J., and Johnston, R.J. (2008). Tourism sustainability, resiliency and dynamics: Towards a more comprehensive perspective. *Tourism and Hospitality Research*, 8(1), 14–24.

United Nations World Tourism Organization (2021). Tourism and COVID-19: Unprecedented economic impacts. Retrieved from https://www.unwto.org/tourism-and-COVID-19-unprecedented-economic-impacts

Varriale, Volpe and Noviello (2021). Enhancing Cultural Heritage at the Time of the COVID-19 Outbreak: An Overview of the ICT Strategies Adopted by Museums in the Campania Region of Italy. In Gowreesunkar, V.G., Maingi, S.W., Roy, H. and Micera, R. (Ed.) *Tourism Destination Management in a Post-Pandemic Context (Tourism Security-Safety and Post Conflict Destinations)*, Emerald Publishing Limited, Bingley, pp. 49–65. https://doi.org/10.1108/978-1-80071-511-020211004

Villena-Alarcon, E. and Cabarello-Galeote, L. (2021). Residents as Destination Influencers during COVID-19. In Gowreesunkar, V.G., Maingi, S.W., Roy, H. and Micera, R. (Ed.) *Tourism Destination Management in a Post-Pandemic Context (Tourism Security-Safety and Post Conflict Destinations)*, Emerald Publishing Limited, Bingley, pp. 99–112. https://doi.org/10.1108/978-1-80071-511-020211007

Vucetic (2021). *Tourism Policy*. Research Gate www.researchgate.net/publication/349102511

Wahab, S.E.A. (2000). Trends and Implications of Tourism Policy in Developing Counties. In Gartner, W.C. and Lime, D.W. (eds.) *Trends in Outdoor Recreation, Leisure and Tourism*, CABI Publishing, pp. 103–110.

Wahome, E. and Gathungu, J. (2021). Redefining Sustainability in the Conservation and Promotion of the Cultural Heritage Tourism Product in Kenya. In Gowreesunkar, V.G., Maingi, S.W., Roy, H. and Micera, R. (Ed.) *Tourism Destination Management in a Post-Pandemic Context (Tourism Security-Safety and Post Conflict Destinations)*, Emerald Publishing Limited, Bingley, pp. 49–65. https://doi.org/10.1108/978-1-80071-511-020211004

Walton, J.K. (2013). 'Social tourism in Britain': History and prospects. *Journal of Policy Research in Tourism, Leisure and Events*, 5(1), 46–61

Wen, J., Kozak, M., Yang, S., & Liu, F. (2021). COVID-19: potential effects on Chinese citizens' lifestyle and travel. *Tourism Review*, 76(1), 74–87.

Xiao, H.J., Smith, L.J. (2006). Case studies in tourism research: A state-of-the-art analysis, *Tourism Management*, 27, 738–749

Yagci, M.I., Dogrul, U, Ozturk, L and Yagci, A.C. (2021). Effect of perceived risk on Tourists 'Behavioural Intentions Post COVID-19 in Turkey. In Gowreesunkar, V.G., Maingi, S.W., Roy, H. and Micera, R. (Ed.) *Tourism Destination Management in a Post-Pandemic Context (Tourism Security-Safety and Post Conflict Destinations)*, Emerald Publishing Limited, Bingley, pp. 99–112. https://doi.org/10.1108/978-1-80071-511-020211007

Yin, R. (1994). *Case study research: design and methods*. 2nd edition. Thousand Oaks, CA: Sage.

1.5
Supply-side trends
Destination management

Pedro Vaz Serra and **Cláudia Seabra** in Chapter 23 discuss *Tourists' behaviour in a post-pandemic context: The consumption variables – A meta-analysis*. Tourism, as a system, faces important challenges, following events of wide scope and significance, with structural implications at the economic, social, and environmental levels. In this context, the chapter and the analysis of tourists' behavioural trends is particularly important, as, in addition to constituting an unavoidable basis for demand, it implies changes in terms of offer. To identify the main behavioural trends of tourists, through a long-term perspective, for the 2030s, 2040s and 2050s, an approach was carried out through a literature review, pointing out the most significant variables for the future. A special emphasis was given to Generations Y and Z, given their expression in the market over a long-term horizon, as well as a review of the compatibility between tourism and sustainable development goals, focusing on the responsibilities and opportunities of the various stakeholders.

Professionalisation destination management trends and issues is the topic of Chapter 24 by **Alastair M. Morrison**. Destination management is a profession that is gaining more recognition worldwide. The field is also becoming increasingly professional, and this is a significant trend in tourism. After an introductory review of destination management and its key events and influential publications, there is a discussion of recent trends. The chapter then articulates the roles and competencies in professional destination management and issues and challenges facing destination management are discussed. Various stakeholder interests and roles in destination management are elaborated. The conclusion is made that professional destination management can and should make a substantial contribution to the achievement of the Sustainable Development Goals (SDGs). Future trends in professional destination management are projected. The chapter ends by suggesting how this work can contribute to the literature and professional practice.

23 Tourist behavioural intention trends

Pedro Vaz Serra and Cláudia Seabra

Introduction

The evolution of tourism, which is currently facing global and challenging scenarios, requires stringent and committed responses. Given the impact of climate change, the COVID-19 pandemic, the need to contribute to economic efficiency and social justice, and the new horizons induced by technology (Xiang, Stienmetz, & Fesenmaier, 2021), it is crucial to reinterpret the way this activity is planned, integrating tangible and intangible elements to be capable of reading, anticipating and balancing market trends (Beritelli, Reinhold, & Laesser, 2020).

Destinations must therefore produce a response, based on creativity and innovation, which will materialise in services, products, and experiences (Hall & Williams, 2019). Since the tourism experience is a core component of tourism and considering that it is shaped and influenced by supply and demand, the nature of this interaction is a fundamental concept that forms the sphere of experience configurations based on objectives, goals, and types of markets (Uysal, Berbekova, & Kim, 2020).

Up until the beginning of 2020, globalisation and technological development have led to a remarkable growth in tourism (Gössling, Scott, & Hall, 2021). Tourists have enjoyed more competitive and affordable transportation, and particularly air transport fares (IATA, 2019), they were offered the possibility to plan, book, and share their trips using technology-based tools and platforms that were able to provide a more intense sensory involvement (Lv, Li, & McCabe, 2020) and the multiphase nature of the tourist experience – before, during the research phase; during, during the experience itself; and after and during the sharing of that given experience (Pirolli, 2018) – has been more valued than ever.

In this manner, the importance of social networks and digital content (Vaz Serra & Seabra, 2021), in the short and long term (Song & Yoo, 2016), is undeniable since they act as a vehicle for interaction, inducing value, for those who live, promote, and consume a destination (Hua, Ramayah, Ping, & Hwa, 2017).

However, the COVID-19 pandemic brought the world to an abrupt halt in 2020 and 2021 and caused the biggest economic crisis since the Great Depression and raised serious public health issues (Gössling et al., 2021). This dreadful situation forced countries around the world to adopt a set of measures that included the imposition of curfews and quarantines (Hartley & Perencevich, 2020), which had a serious impact on travel and on the entire tourism system (Folinas & Metaxas, 2020). In fact, the pandemic generated a remarkable, direct, indirect, and induced shock, given: i) its global character (UNWTO, 2021a); ii) its intensity compared to previous disruptive events (OECD, 2020); and iii) its potential to generate structural changes (Dolnicar & Zare, 2020).

The aim of this chapter is to obtain more detailed knowledge of the tourists' behavioural intentions when they have to deal with such atypical scenarios, considering a time horizon that will contemplate several decades and will therefore imply a step-by-step approach. We will, therefore, focus on demand.

The first stage, focusing on 2020 and 2021, is dedicated to behavioural trends arising from the COVID-19 pandemic, from a short-term perspective. At this stage, the research structure adopted includes the recollection of data related to the topic, its subsequent meta-analysis, in the discussion section, and, finally, the main similarities and differences found are highlighted during the sections where the conclusions, limitations, and relevance of this approach are described. In a second stage, the time horizon is much broader, up to 2050, and take into account the literature review that considers perspectives for the next decades.

Objective and methodology

The main objective of this chapter is to identify, based on a long-term perspective, the tourist behavioural trends for the 2030s, 2040s, and 2050s. The literature review was the method of choice, and then the most relevant aspects and those with the greatest potential for impact in the coming decades were highlighted. In this context, and even though all segments are addressed, special attention is given to the youngest generations, Generations Y and Z, given their relevance for tourism in the future and, complementarily, special emphasis is placed on the relationships with the SDGs – Sustainable Development Goals (Tourism for SDGS, 2021), considering the needs, concerns and expectations expressed by tourists concerning this major topic.

The new tourists: A generational approach for 2030, 2040 and 2050

For the coming decades, four megatrends that will shape the future of tourism are: the evolution of tourist behaviour; sustainable growth; enabling technologies; and travel mobility. Thus, demographic changes, environmental conditions, and technological innovations are among the variables that will have a strong impact on the future (OECD, 2018).

In this context, Generation Y, or Millennials, those born between 1980 and 1995, and Generation Z, born between 1996 and 2010 (Expedia Group, 2018), will play a decisive role in the tourism of the 2030s, 2040s, and 2050s, and will therefore require special attention (Postma et al., 2020). These fast-growing generations already represent 40% of the travel customers in Europe; by 2025, they will account for 50% (Postma et al., 2020). They were born and raised in the digital world and are consequently users and connoisseurs of technology. The way they communicate, their need for consumption and the way they seek tourism experiences set them apart from the previous generations and enable them to generate leading trends with meaning and scope (Carty, 2020).

Millennials prefer to live experiences than to acquire goods, i.e., should they have to choose between enjoying a holiday or buying the latest model of a television set or a special piece of clothing, they will go for the first option, and they are more demanding when it comes to taking decisions related to the orientation and acquisition phase of a trip (Postma et al., 2020). They value the relationship between tourism services and their daily lives, and favour a combination of conventional, locally based socialisation and the achievement of differentiating and highly personalised experiences (Nomads, 2017) that will contribute to a perfect trip experience (Manuell, 2017).

This generation enjoys travelling with family or with friends, but they do not rule out travelling with people with whom they simply share some sort of interest, like yoga, gastronomy, entrepreneurship, mountain biking, or bird watching, for instance. They are fans of slow tourism, although they embrace this sort of tourism when driven by a purpose: it may be a way to boost their physical performance (Health and Fitness Travel, 2018), or their married life (Iron Mountain Hot Springs, 2018), or to experience digital detox (Unyoked, 2021) following periods of intense work.

Millennials are attracted to several types of activities, preferring to visit less-frequented places, and it is worth noting that 54% of global travellers want to contribute to reducing overtourism and 51% are interested in switching destinations for a lesser-known, but similar place (Booking.com, 2019). These experiences may therefore include less predictable destinations, such as second cities, surf routes, and ecotours, where they can experience authenticity and immersion in the local culture (Eatwith, 2021).They look forward to combining the opportunity to share knowledge and developing different sorts of skills; several hotel chains have already developed sub-brands specifically for this generation: Radisson RED, Moxy by Marriott, Hyatt Centric and Hilton's Canopy are among the examples to date (Postma et al., 2020).

Generation Z is very dependent on social media (Fontein, 2019), susceptible to digital comments and influencers, but, compared to Millennials, they are careful about their online exposure, so privacy settings are important. They pay particular attention to prices and promotions, spending more on what they consider important and spending less, sometimes substantially less, on what they consider less meaningful (Postma et al., 2020). Generation Z values spaces where experiences with other consumers are enhanced, where they can meet people, but also stylish accommodation in a fun, modern, and smartly designed environment (Veeve, 2021). They are also eager to get the chance to combine business and leisure (WeWork, 2017), or engage on an epic journey on a luxurious, historic, and scenic train (Expedia Group, 2018).

The behaviour of Generation Z is not that different from that of the Millennials, although they are much more sensitive to prices, sustainability, and ethics. They also value real-time information, short and clarifying messages that use photographs or videos, and channels that allow interaction, co-creation, and sharing of information and that will therefore favour the use of image, a multiplatform communication, socially responsible attitude and personalisation (McMahon, 2021).

In fact, driven by the growing impact that Generation Y and Generation Z have on the tourism market, the demand for technologically supported experiences will continue to increase, boosted by the ease with which they use mobile devices, such as smartphones and tablets that will generate an interest for personalisation, i.e., seeing their preferences matched, from destinations to accommodation, will help develop the so-called smart tourism (Koens, Smit, & Melissen, 2021), where 90% of travellers expect a personalised experience (Stfalcon.com, 2018). Studies show that 69% of those customers are more loyal to a service provider that is ready to personalise their experiences (Ascolese & Llantada, 2019).

Generation Y and Z tourists are increasingly aware and concerned about sustainability (King's College London, 2021). Destination choice is influenced by ethics, moral values, concerns for the environment, animal welfare, production, and labour practices, as well as by the desire to have a positive impact on communities and people. These travellers require affordable, green, eco-friendly, climate-neutral, and organic products and services and show growing reluctance to fly or sail and seem to prefer other forms of mobility, like rail travel (King's College London, 2021). Growing concern for personal wellbeing and for the environment is also making air quality an increasingly important motivation when they have to choose a destination (Horwath HTL, 2016).

Health and a healthy lifestyle play equally important roles in tourists' decision-making. Older costumers and those who belong to Generation Y and Generation Z, who represent a growing middle class with a lifestyle compatible with the technological and digital revolution, contribute to the growing importance of the tourism health trend (Postma et al., 2020).

The market for multigenerational travel, where children, parents, and grandparents travel together, is growing as people are searching for experiences that contribute to a strengthening of family ties and the sharing of lasting memories. This development has led to increasing demand for larger accommodations to host those extended families (Covington Travel, 2014).

Unlike traditional family holidays, where grandparents used to take their children and grandchildren, in this current tourism trend the parents of the Baby Boomer generation, who were born between 1946 and 1964 and are currently aged between 57 and 75, take their adult children and their grandchildren on family trips. Consequently, many young people are given the chance to embark on trips they could not afford if they had to travel on their own. In this context, young adults from Generation Z play a relevant role in the planning of holidays and have a decisive influence on the choice of the destination and on the type of trips, which results in more exotic and adventurous trips (Postma et al., 2020).

The trend is reinforced by the increase in reconstituted families and the verticalisation of family structure: increased life expectancy means that grandparents are living longer than a few decades ago and therefore have more time to be with their grandchildren. These combined trends mean that grandparents join parents and their children on holiday and that the number of grandparents and grandchildren doubles in the case of blended families (Traveller, 2009).

Tourism and sustainable development

The increase in demand for sustainable travel and destinations, identified with the SDGs (Tourism for SDGS, 2021), cannot be considered separately from the rise of Generations Y and Z in tourism markets.

In fact, the trends described represent opportunities and, simultaneously, important challenges for tourism, since they have become inducers of broader and impactful changes that will lead to a reorientation of the system, namely towards the SDGs (Gössling et al., 2021) and away from growth at all costs, an abstract notion that benefits only a few (Piketty, 2015). If that is to happen, a more demanding, determined, and resilient tourism will be necessary, a new paradigm where climate actions, such as the sharp decrease in greenhouse gas emissions (Hall, Scott, & Gössling, 2013), combined with destination models that are capable of optimising local resources, are used to generate and distribute tourism value (Gössling et al., 2021). In this sense, the defence of a sustainable kind of tourism that will ensure the economic growth of its activity, and that will, at the same time, safeguard social and environmental impacts, current and future, it will cause, that will consider the needs of the visitors, of the tourism system and of the host communities is inevitable (UNWTO, 2021b).

To this end, compliance with the 2030 Agenda for Sustainable Development, approved by the United Nations General Assembly held on 25 September 2015, and where a list of global commitment SDGs was adopted has become a necessary and urgent global design (Coccia, 2021). These 17 goals and 169 targets were adopted to help the different States, civil society and the private sector guide and monitor their respective contributions (Tourism for SDGS, 2021).

In the SDGs, tourism is referenced, specifically, in paragraphs 8, 12 and 14, which focus, respectively on: i) inclusive and sustainable economic growth – given the impact it has on employment levels, exports and service provision; ii) sustainable consumption and production – as one of the main users of intermediate consumption for final products; and iii) the sustainable use of oceans and marine resources – due to the interaction with these realities, and these principles should be addressed in a holistic perspective, i.e., as a result of processes that exist and interact simultaneously (Lenzen, Sun, Faturay, Ting, Geschke, & Malik, 2018).

To achieve sustainability, it is essential to coordinate stakeholders (Heslinga, Hillebrand, & Emonts, 2019), whose interactions, to obtain synergies, are essential in governance processes, because they are structural in planning, monitoring, and sharing of results (Rivera & Gutierrez, 2018). The best practices of multistakeholder actions result from the combination of national and international actors, as well as from various regions and local communities (Crowe-Delaney, Koščak, & O'Rourke, 2019), favouring the involvement of the value chain, to the detriment of approaches top-down (Roxas, Rivera, & Gutierrez, 2020).

The various stakeholders must, therefore, make their contribution, adopting new behaviours, given an opportunity to critically reconsider the growth trajectory of tourism. For example, because of the significant decline in demand that has occurred in the recent past due to the pandemic, airlines have started phasing out old and inefficient planes (Simple Flying, 2020). Videoconferencing, a valuable resource in reducing the demand for means of transport (Banister & Stead, 2004), has become widely adopted by home office workers, avoiding non-essential travel (Cohen and Kantenbacher, 2020). Even in international instances, such as the G20 leaders' meeting in March 2020, videoconferencing was the preferred means (European Council, 2020).

In a more general and everyday manner, the view of mobility can change, also among tourists, opting for walking routes, outdoor activities, as well as the use of bicycles for short-distance trips (Gössling et al., 2021). Open spaces, in contact with nature, closer to rural tourism than to the urban environment, with fewer mass mobility solutions have become prominent options (SumWhere, 2020; Interface Tourism, 2020). The use of online transactions is also more and more expressive, and online sales and services are becoming increasingly significant (GlobalData, 2020), which highlights the growing importance of information and communication technologies.

There is a great concern with sustainable tourism and respondents are asking the different booking platforms to implement a system of incentives and rewards, when possible (Booking.com, 2020). The identification, defence, and promotion of sustainability, highlighting the authenticity of the experiences, the respect for the local communities, and the judicious use of resources, suggest the emergence of attitudes of greater responsibility that will have a multiscale impact and will increasingly rely on technology (The Condé Nast Johansens, 2021).

Governments should therefore have a long-term vision (Wang & Huang, 2021), supported by policies that enhance the development of the economy and a renewed vitality in tourism (Nicola et al., 2020), creating optimal conditions for the emergence of sustainable models, in line with the needs of citizens and companies, and based on new, agile, effective, and efficient business systems that can meet a constantly changing environment (Shakil, Munim, Tasnia, & Sarowar, 2020).

Underlying these public policies is the need to avoid a return to protectionism, which history suggests would be harmful to overall global growth; ensuring that the potential benefits of globalisation are shared more equitably across society; as well as supporting the development of new green technologies to ensure that long-term global growth is environmentally sustainable (PWC, 2021). To this end, it is essential to promote responsible management (Fenner & Cernev, 2021), i.e., limiting the consumption of natural resources, focusing on strategies identified with biodiversity protection, reasoned energy, and water use (Wang, Gao, Xu, & Wang, 2020), waste management (Shammi & Tareq, 2021) and economic and social development (Bontempi & Coccia, 2021).

There are, however, some potential problems in the way markets are still handling these trends, since the global economy, which is undergoing a slow readjustment after a disruptive period, keeps on influencing tourists' purchasing power, and therefore their behaviour, which remains overdependent on economic realities. That way, understanding the factors that affect the world scenario, in tourism and beyond, such as the growth of Gross Domestic Product (GDP), is very important for the implementation of appropriate strategies since it fosters the growth of private consumption and, consequently, a greater propensity to travel (European Travel Commission, 2021).

Conclusions

For the coming decades, emphasis will be placed on senior tourism, the emergence of new generations, an increasingly significant middle class, the affirmation of new destinations, the importance of political and security issues, technology and digital channels, loyalty, health, wellbeing, and sustainability (Horwath HTL, 2016). In 2050, individuals over 65 years old will account for approximately 20% of the world's population (UN, 2019), thanks mainly to countries such as China, India, and the U.S. who, with financial resources and time on their hands, will seek specific, highly personalised experiences (CBI, 2021).

The new generations, the Millennials and their successors, who will represent half of the travellers (OECD, 2018), will dictate the tourism activity and driven by technology, will seek interaction and multisensory experiences at the destination. Empathy and connection between tourism services and everyday life will then be a priority (McMahon, 2021).

An emerging and more informed middle class, which will correspond to more than 4.9 billion people in 2050 and originating mainly in Asia, will have greater control over the entire travel process (PWC, 2021).

New destinations will become top tourism choices, notably in Asia, South America, and the Middle East (Figure 23.1), and will attract more tourists who seek new cultures and new experiences (OECD, 2018).

Issues associated with unpredictable political and security-related risks pose a real threat to the tourism potential of any destination, and evidence shows that it takes a long time to regain tourists' confidence when it is affected by a threat situation (Seabra, AlAshry, Çınar, Raja, Reis, & Sadiq, 2021).

Technology will significantly and increasingly change tourism, providing more options and variables in tourists' behaviour and will open the way to more differentiating and personalised experiences (Fesenmaier & Xiang, 2017). Digital channels are a privileged and influential gateway to social networks, generating faster decision-making processes and benefiting from shared economy platforms (Cheng, Mou, & Yan, 2021).

Figure 23.1 Saudi Arabia is a Middle Eastern destination that plans to attract more tourists.
Photo: Courtesy, Unsplash.com.

Loyalty programs will become less and less relevant or, at least, their structure will change, as they will move from an accumulating to win format, to another that will favour access to exclusive experiences (Limberger, Pereira, & Pereira, 2021).

Health and hygiene aspects will become increasingly relevant in the decision-making process, and products and services that include treatments, relaxation, exercise, and healthy eating will become travellers' priorities (OECD, 2018).

Sustainability will represent a vital dimension that will be highly valued by tourists, not only due to environmental issues, but also because of the respect they have for the resident community, with their habits, values, and customs, and because they will more than ever before value the richness of their identity and local heritage (Gössling et al., 2021).

The truth is that technology allows an increasingly expressive interaction and the experience of virtual reality and augmented reality will become more and more prevalent. However, these virtual getaways will not allow tourists to live a full experience: they will never, for instance, be able to taste the cuisine, meet the local people, take excursions away from the well-trodden routes, or wrap themselves in tangible and intangible cultural treasures. As a result, the development of virtual tourism will stimulate the demand for real trips (Hammond, 2019).

In this evolution process, the following trends are easily recognised (Ianioglo & Rissanen, 2020): (i) digitalisation, where technology is highly used. Generation Y and Generation Z, as well as the following generations, stand out, as they are digital natives and their relationship with technology will continue to influence the provision of tourism services; ii) responsibility and sustainability, as people are increasingly aware of the value of nature, and favour destinations where the community is respected and where the local economy benefits from the presence of tourists; iii) health and wellbeing that will meet the travellers' main expectations;

iv) sustainable mobility; v) outdoor activities; and vi) business travel, that tend to be replaced by video conferences (Postma et al., 2020).

Implications and limitations of the research

A new paradigm may be emerging as new models, methods, and processes are summoned. This model has a deep impact on the configuration of the demand and on the organisation of tourism supply that will lead to an implicit reformulation of means and interactions and to an added value, on the design of instruments, the implementation of solutions and on the management of expectations.

All the above must be considered, but we are fully aware that we are dealing with behavioural intentions and that these are likely to change in the face of current or future events. This uncertainty is a limitation of this approach.

It is therefore important to figure, as a challenge for future research, if all these findings are the reflection of conjunctural facts and circumstances, or if, on the contrary, they represent the first sign of structural changes.

References

Ascolese, G., & Llantada, J. (2019). *The Next Great Tourism Revolution: A Report on Travel and Tourism Trends*. https://www.wearemarketing.com/uploads/media/default/0001/21/be54a5f27191d02797ff03aaacd4b799f25beb11.pdf

Banister, D., & Stead, D. (2004). Impact of information and communications technology on transport. *Transport Reviews*, *24*(5), 611–632. https://doi.org/10.1080/0144164042000206060

Beritelli, P., Reinhold, S., & Laesser, C. (2020). Visitor flows, trajectories and corridors: Planning and designing places from the traveler's point of view. *Annals of Tourism Research*, *82*, 102936. https://doi.org/10.1016/j.annals.2020.102936

Bontempi, E., & Coccia, M. (2021). International trade as critical parameter of COVID-19 spread that outclasses demographic, economic, environmental, and pollution factors. *Environmental Research*, *201*, 111514. https://doi.org/10.1016/j.envres.2021.111514

Booking.com (2019). *Booking.com Predicts the Top Travel Trends for 2020*. Booking.Com Predicts the Top Travel Trends for 2020. https://globalnews.booking.com/bookingcom-predicts-the-top-travel-trends-for-2020/

Booking.com (2020). *Everything we know about Future of travel here at Booking.com!* Booking.Com. https://www.booking.com/articles/category/future-of-travel.en-gb.html

Carty, M. (2020). *Millennial Parents Are Bringing a New Generation to Family Travel: New Skift Research*. Skift. https://skift.com/2020/02/25/millennial-parents-are-bringing-a-new-generation-to-family-travel-new-skift-research/

CBI – Centre for the Promotion of Imports from developing countries (2021). *Which trends offer opportunities?* https://www.cbi.eu/market-information/tourism/trends#the-disruptive-impact-of-COVID-19-on-global-tourism

Cheng, X., Mou, J., & Yan, X. (2021). Sharing economy enabled digital platforms for development. *Information Technology for Development*, *27*(4), 635–644. https://doi.org/10.1080/02681102.2021.1971831

Coccia, M. (2021). The relation between length of lockdown, numbers of infected people and deaths of COVID-19, and economic growth of countries: Lessons learned to cope with future pandemics similar to COVID-19. *Science of the Total Environment*, *775*, 145801. https://doi.org/10.1016/j.scitotenv.2021.145801

Cohen, S. A., and Kantenbacher, J. (2020). Flying less: personal health and environmental co-benefits. *Journal of Sustainable Tourism*, *28*(2), 361–376.

Covington Travel (2014). *The Who, What, Why and Where of Multigenerational Travel*. Covington Travel. https://www.covingtontravel.com/2014/08/the-who-what-why-and-where-of-multigenerational-travel/

Crowe-Delaney, L., Koščak, M., & O'Rourke, T. (2019). *Ethical and Responsible Tourism: Managing Sustainability in Local Tourism Destinations*. https://doi.org/10.4324/9780429200694

Dolnicar, S., & Zare, S. (2020). COVID19 and Airbnb – Disrupting the disruptor. *Annals of Tourism Research*, *83*, 102961. https://doi.org/10.1016/j.annals.2020.102961

Eatwith (2021). *Food experiences with local chefs and hosts in your city or abroad*. Eatwith. https://eatwith.com

European Council (2020). Statement by President Michael and President von der Leyen after the extraordinary G20 video conference on COVID-19. https://www.consilium.europa.eu/en/press/press-releases/2020/03/26/statement-by-president-michel-and-president-von-der-leyen-after-the-g20-video-conference-on-COVID-19

European Travel Commission (2021). *European Tourism: Trends & Prospects*. https://etc-corporate.org/uploads/2021/02/ETC-Quarterly-Report-Q4-2020_Public-1.pdf

Expedia Group (2018). *A look ahead: How younger generations are shaping the future of travel*. https://info.advertising.expedia.com/hubfs/Content_Docs/Premium_Content/pdf/2018%20-%20Gen%20Z%20Travel%20Trends%20Study.pdf?hsCtaTracking=a63196b4-62b8-4673-93e2-7d3ad0dc73e3%7Cfd9915c8-dc7f-492d-b123-265614cef08a

Fenner, R., & Cernev, T. (2021). The implications of the COVID-19 pandemic for delivering the Sustainable Development Goals. *Futures*, *128*, 102726. https://doi.org/10.1016/j.futures.2021.102726

Fesenmaier, D. R., & Xiang, Z. (Eds.). (2017). *Design Science in Tourism: Foundations of Destination Management*. Springer International Publishing. https://doi.org/10.1007/978-3-319-42773-7

Folinas, S., & Metaxas, T. (2020). *Tourism: The Great Patient of Coronavirus COVID-2019* [MPRA Paper]. https://mpra.ub.uni-muenchen.de/103515/

Fontein, D. (2019). Generation Z: Everything Social Marketers Need to Know. *Social Media Marketing & Management Dashboard*. https://blog.hootsuite.com/generation-z-statistics-social-marketers/

GlobalData (2020). COVID-19. *GlobalData*. https://www.globaldata.com/COVID-19/

Gössling, S., Scott, D., & Hall, C. M. (2021). Pandemics, tourism and global change: a rapid assessment of COVID-19. *Journal of Sustainable Tourism*, *29*(1), 1–20. https://doi.org/10.1080/09669582.2020.1758708

Hall, C., Scott, D., & Gössling, S. (2013). The Primacy of Climate Change for Sustainable International Tourism. *Sustainable Development*, *21*. https://doi.org/10.1002/sd.1562

Hall, C. M., & Williams, A. M. (2019). *Tourism and Innovation*. Routledge & CRC Press. https://www.routledge.com/Tourism-and-Innovation/Hall-Williams/p/book/9781138060821

Hammond, R. (2019). *The world in 2040: The future travel experience*. https://www.rayhammond.com/wp-content/uploads/The-Future-Travel-Experience_The-World-in-2040-Series.pdf

Hartley, D., & Perencevich, E. (2020). Public Health Interventions for COVID-19: Emerging Evidence and Implications for an Evolving Public Health Crisis. *JAMA*, *323*. https://doi.org/10.1001/jama.2020.5910

Health and Fitness Travel (2018). *Mumcation: A Healthy Retreat Every Mum Needs*. Health and Fitness Travel. https://www.healthandfitnesstravel.com.au/blog/mumcation-retreat

Heslinga, J. H., Hillebrand, H., & Emonts, T. (2019). How to improve innovation in sustainable tourism? Five lessons learned from the Austrian Alps. *Journal of Tourism Futures*, *5*(1), 35–42. https://doi.org/10.1108/JTF-09-2018-0054

Horwath HTL. (2016). *The link between wellness and sustainability*, https://horwathhtl.com/publication/industry-report-the-link-between-wellness-and-sustainability/

Hua, L., Ramayah, T., Ping, T., & Hwa, C. (2017). Social Media as a Tool to Help Select Tourism Destinations: The Case of Malaysia. *Information Systems Management*, *34*. https://doi.org/10.1080/10580530.2017.1330004

Ianioglo, A., & Rissanen, M. (2020). Global trends and tourism development in peripheral areas. *Scandinavian Journal of Hospitality and Tourism*, *20*(5), 520–539. https://doi.org/10.1080/15022250.2020.1848620

IATA (2019). *More Connectivity and Improved Efficiency – 2018 Airline Industry Statistics Released*. https://www.iata.org/en/pressroom/pr/2019-07-31-01/

Interface Tourism (2020). *Etude InterfaceTourism: les prévisions de voyage post-COVID-19 – Tendance Hotellerie*. https://www.tendancehotellerie.fr/articles-breves/communique-de-presse/13451-article/etude-interfacetourism-les-previsions-de-voyage-post-COVID-19

Iron Mountain Hot Springs (2018). What's a Painmoon? Why Take One? *Iron Mountain Hot Springs*. https://www.ironmountainhotsprings.com/whats-a-painmoon-why-take-one/

King's College London. (2021). *Who cares about climate change? Attitudes across the generations*. https://www.kcl.ac.uk/policy-institute/assets/who-cares-about-climate-change.pdf

Koens, K., Smit, B., & Melissen, F. (2021). Designing destinations for good: Using design roadmapping to support pro-active destination development. *Annals of Tourism Research*, *89*, 103233. https://doi.org/10.1016/j.annals.2021.103233

Lenzen, M., Sun, Y.-Y., Faturay, F., Ting, Y.-P., Geschke, A., & Malik, A. (2018). The carbon footprint of global tourism. *Nature Climate Change*, *8*. https://doi.org/10.1038/s41558-018-0141-x

Limberger, P. F., Pereira, L. A., & Pereira, T. (2021). The impact of customer involvement in airline loyalty programs: a multigroup analysis. *Tourism & Management Studies*, *17*(3), 37–49. http://www.tmstudies.net/index.php/ectms/article/view/1375

Lv, X., Li, C. (Spring), & McCabe, S. (2020). Expanding theory of tourists' destination loyalty: The role of sensory impressions. *Tourism Management*, *77*, 104026. https://doi.org/10.1016/j.tourman.2019.104026

Manuell, R. (2017). *No longer passenger experience; It's now seamless travel | Reflections from PTE*. International Airport Review. https://www.internationalairportreview.com/article/33223/seamless-travel-pte/

McMahon, K. (2021). *Gen Z and millennials are expected to inherit over $60 trillion in wealth by 2050. Cowen shares 10 stocks to capture the wealth transfer – including 3 expected to surge over 70%*. Business Insider. https://www.businessinsider.com/stocks-picks-cowen-gen-z-millennial-wealth-transfer-massive-upside-2021-10

Nicola, M., Alsafi, Z., Sohrabi, C., Kerwan, A., Al-Jabir, A., Iosifidis, C., Agha, M., & Agha, R. (2020). The socio-economic implications of the coronavirus pandemic (COVID-19): A review. *International Journal of Surgery (London, England)*, *78*, 185–193. https://doi.org/10.1016/j.ijsu.2020.04.018

Nomads (2017). Flashpacker or Backpacker? What type of traveler are you? *Nomads - Discover Different*. https://nomadsworld.com/what-type-of-traveler-are-you/

OECD (2018). *Megatrends shaping the future of tourism*. https://www.oecd-ilibrary.org/docserver/tour-2018-6-en.pdf?expires=1634654641&id=id&accname=guest&checksum=D7C9855927CAD6F110FF02D8B44FE2FB

OECD (2020). *Focus on the global economy*. OECD. https://www.oecd.org/coronavirus/en/themes/global-economy

Piketty, T. (2015). Putting Distribution Back at the Center of Economics: Reflections on Capital in the Twenty-First Century. *Journal of Economic Perspectives*, *29*(1), 67–88. https://doi.org/10.1257/jep.29.1.67

Pirolli, B. (2018). Travel information online: navigating correspondents, consensus, and conversation. *Current Issues in Tourism*, *21*(12), 1337–1343. https://doi.org/10.1080/13683500.2016.1273883

Postma, A., Heslinga, J. and Hartman, S. (2020). *Four futures perspectives of the visitor economy after COVID-19*. Breda, Netherlands: Centre of Expertise in Leisure, Tourism and Hospitality.

PWC (2021). *The World in 2050*. https://www.pwc.com/gx/en/research-insights/economy/the-world-in-2050.html

Rivera, J. P., & Gutierrez, E. (2018). A framework toward sustainable ecotourism value chain in the Philippines. *Journal of Quality Assurance in Hospitality & Tourism*. https://doi.org/10.1080/1528008X.2018.1492495

Roxas, F. M. Y., Rivera, J. P. R., & Gutierrez, E. L. M. (2020). Mapping stakeholders' roles in governing sustainable tourism destinations. *Journal of Hospitality and Tourism Management*, *45*, 387–398. https://doi.org/10.1016/j.jhtm.2020.09.005

Seabra, C., AlAshry, M., Çınar, K., Raja, I., Reis, M., & Sadiq, N. (2021). Restrictions' acceptance and risk perception by young generations in a COVID-19 context. *International Journal of Tourism Cities*, *7*(2), 463–491. https://doi.org/10.1108/IJTC-08-2020-0165

Shakil, M. H., Munim, Z. H., Tasnia, M., & Sarowar, S. (2020). COVID-19 and the environment: A critical review and research agenda. *Science of the Total Environment*, *745*, 141022. https://doi.org/10.1016/j.scitotenv.2020.141022

Shammi, M., & Tareq, S. (2021). Environmental Catastrophe of COVID-19: Disposal and Management of PPE in Bangladesh. *Global Social Welfare*, *8*. https://doi.org/10.1007/s40609-020-00195-z

Simple Flying (2020). United could follow American with early 757 & 767 retirement. https://simpleflying.com/united-757-767-early-retirement/

Song, S., & Yoo, M. (2016). The role of social media during the pre-purchasing stage. *Journal of Hospitality and Tourism Technology*, *7*, 84–99. https://doi.org/10.1108/JHTT-11-2014-0067

Stfalcon.com (2018). Top 10 Travel Industry Trends in 2019. *The Startup*. https://medium.com/swlh/top-10-travel-industry-trends-in-2019-d43d157de7b9

SumWhere (2020, May 13). Etude sur le tourisme post-COVID menée en mai 2020. *SumWhere*. https://www.sumwhere.co/2020/05/13/etude-sur-les-voyages-et-le-tourisme-post-COVID19/

The Condé Nast Johansens (2021). *Portugal one of the preferred destinations of luxury travellers after the coronavirus pandemic*. Idealista. https://www.idealista.pt/en/news/luxury-real-estate-in-portugal/2021/03/17/905-portugal-one-of-the-preferred-destinations-of-luxury-travellers-after

Tourism for SDGS (2021). *Tourism & Sustainable Development Goals – Tourism for SDGs*. https://tourism4sdgs.org/tourism-for-sdgs/tourism-and-sdgs/

Traveller (2009). *Large family holidays: nuclear explosion*. Traveller. https://www.traveller.com.au/large-family-holidays-nuclear-explosion-aofg

UN (2019). *World Population Ageing 2019*. https://www.un.org/en/development/desa/population/publications/pdf/ageing/WorldPopulationAgeing2019-Highlights.pdf

UNWTO (2021a). *2020: Worst Year in Tourism History with 1 Billion Fewer International Arrivals*. Retrieved April 2, 2021, from https://www.unwto.org/news/2020-worst-year-in-tourism-history-with-1-billion-fewer-international-arrivals

UNWTO (2021b). *Sustainable Tourism*. https://www.unwto.org/sustainable-development

Unyoked (2021). *For those times you wish you were out there but aren't*. https://www.unyoked.co

Uysal, M., Berbekova, A., & Kim, H. (2020). Designing for Quality of life. *Annals of Tourism Research*, *83*, 102944. https://doi.org/10.1016/j.annals.2020.102944

Vaz Serra, P., & Seabra, C. (2021). Digital Influencers and Tourist Destinations: Cristiano Ronaldo and Madeira Island, from Promotion to Impact. In T. Guarda, F. Portela, & M. F. Santos (Eds.), *Advanced Research in Technologies, Information, Innovation and Sustainability* (pp. 302–317). Springer International Publishing. https://doi.org/10.1007/978-3-030-90241-4_24

Veeve (2021). *Short Term Holiday & Vacation Luxury Apartment Rentals*. Veeve. https://www.veeve.com/en-gb/

Wang, Y., Gao, S., Xu, W., & Wang, Z. (2020). Nanogenerators with Superwetting Surfaces for Harvesting Water/Liquid Energy. *Advanced Functional Materials*, *30*(26), 1908252. https://doi.org/10.1002/adfm.201908252

Wang, Y., & Huang, B. (2021). Analysis on the Government Countermeasures of Regional Tourism Service Trade in Zhejiang Province under the Epidemic Situation. *Design Engineering*, 01–08. http://thedesignengineering.com/index.php/DE/article/view/1189

WeWork (2017). WeWork: "A Platform for Creators." *Digital Innovation and Transformation*. https://digital.hbs.edu/platform-digit/submission/wework-a-platform-for-creators/

Xiang, Z., Stienmetz, J., & Fesenmaier, D. R. (2021). Smart Tourism Design: Launching the annals of tourism research curated collection on designing tourism places. *Annals of Tourism Research*, *86*, 103154. https://doi.org/10.1016/j.annals.2021.103154

24 Professional destination management trends and issues

Alastair M. Morrison

Introduction to destination management

History of destination management

Destination management and destination marketing are terms that are used interchangeably by practitioners and academics. The initial mention of destination marketing was in Gartrell's (1988) pioneering book and he states that the first convention bureau was established in 1896 in Detroit (p. 4). Destination management is a somewhat newer phenomenon in tourism; Heller (1996) was among the first to use the term destination management in the academic literature. Table 24.1 is an approximate historical timeline of major developments (events and influential publications) in destination management.

At the time of writing, therefore, the destination marketing term has been in use for around 35 years, and destination management for approximately 27 years. It can be argued that there still remains confusion about the differences between destination management and destination marketing. Even some of the major industry groups are perpetuating this confusion; however, there is a growing acceptance that destination management is a multi-role profession that is not limited to just marketing.

From the academic publishing viewpoint, the volume of publishing on destination management and destination marketing is steadily growing. This trend is shown in Table 24.2, with the majority of publications being in the last ten years.

Definitions of destination management

Destination management is "the coordinated management of all the elements that make up a tourism destination (attractions, amenities, access, marketing and pricing)" (UNWTO, 2007). Another definition of destination management is provided by Morrison (2019) as:

> Destination management is a professional approach to guiding all of the efforts in a place that has decided to pursue tourism as an economic activity. Destination management involves coordinated and integrated management of the destination product (attractions and events, built facilities, transportation, infrastructure, and service quality and friendliness). Destination management organisations (DMOs) are teams of tourism professionals that lead and coordinate all tourism stakeholders. Effective destination management involves long-term tourism planning and continual monitoring and evaluation of the outcomes from tourism efforts.

Table 24.1 Historical timeline of major events and publications in destination management

Years	Events and authors	Details and titles
19th century	First convention bureau established in USA	Detroit, Michigan
1914	New DM organisation created	International Association of Convention Bureau
1988	Gartrell book published	*Destination marketing for convention and visitor bureaus*
1989	Burke & Lindblom article in Journal of Travel research	*Strategies for evaluating direct response tourism marketing*
1990s	IACVB launched certification program	Certified Destination Management Executive (CDME)
1996	Heller article in *Journal of Vacation Marketing*	*Designing a tourism marketing assessment for San Antonio, Texas*
2000	Buhalis article in *Tourism Management*	*Marketing the competitive destination of the future*
2000	Gretzel, Yuan, & Fesenmaier article in *Journal of Travel Research*	*Preparing for the new economy: Advertising strategies and change in destination marketing organisations*
2003	Ritchie & Crouch book published	*The competitive destination: A sustainable tourism perspective*
2003	Dwyer & Kim article in *Current Issues in Tourism*	*Destination competitiveness: Determinants and indicators*
2005	Blain, Levy, & Richards article in *Journal of Travel Research*	*Destination branding: Insights and practices for destination management organisations*
2005	International Association of Convention and Visitors Bureaus changed name	Destination Marketing Association International (DMAI)
2005	DMAI launched accreditation program	Destination Marketing Accreditation Program (DMAP)
2006	Fyall & Leask article in *Tourism & Hospitality Research*	*Destination marketing: Future issues, strategic challenges*
2007	Pritchard, Morgan & Pride book published	*Destination branding: Creating the unique destination proposition*
2007	UNWTO book published	*A practical guide to tourism destination management*
2007	Beritelli, Bieger, & Laesser article in *Journal of Travel Research*	*Destination governance: Using corporate governance theories as a foundation for effective destination management*
2008	Ford & Peeper book published	*Managing destination marketing organisations*
2009	Pollock paper published	*Speculation on the future of destination marketing organisations (DMOs)*
2011	Wang & Pizam edited book published	*Destination marketing and management: Theories and applications*
2012	New dedicated journal launched	*Journal of Destination Marketing & Management*
2013	Morrison book published	*Marketing and managing tourism destinations*
2014	Destinations International launched analysis of future of DMOs	*Destination NEXT Futures Study*

Table 24.1 (Continued)

Years	Events and authors	Details and titles
2014	Pike & Page article published in *Tourism Management*	Destination marketing organisations and destination marketing: A narrative analysis of the literature
2018	Gursoy and Chi edited a handbook on destination marketing	Routledge handbook of destination marketing
	Gowreesunkar et al. book chapter	Destination marketing organisations: Roles and challenges
2018	Gardiner & Scott article published in *Journal of Destination Marketing & Management*	Destination innovation matrix: A framework for new tourism experience and market development
2019	Kozak & Kozak edited book published	Tourist destination Management: Instruments, products, and case studies
2022	European Cities Marketing changed its name	Cities Destination Alliance (2022)

Source: Buhalis (2022).
Note: This is only a partial account of key events and influential publications. Many other valuable contributions were made during this time period.

Table 24.2 Academic publishing on destination management and destination marketing

Topic	Article title, abstract, keywords (all)	Article title, abstract, keywords 2013–2022	Article title only (all)	Article title only 2013–2022
Destination management	1,629 (100.0%)	1,281 (78.6%)	271 (100.0%)	201 (74.2%)
Destination management organi(s)zation	530 (100.0%)	436 (82.3%)	67 (100.0%)	50 (74.6%)
Destination marketing	1,678 (100.0%)	1,167 (69.5%)	332 (100.0%)	203 (61.1%)
Destination marketing organi(s)zation	541 (100.0%)	400 (73.9%)	50 (100.0%)	34 (68.0%)

Note: Based on a Scopus search, 8 April, 2022 (Author calculations).

These two definitions emphasise the role of the DMO as a coordinator of tourism stakeholders and that these organisations have multiple functions. It is noticeable again that they view a DMO as doing considerably more than marketing.

Recent trends for destination management

Destination management is experiencing many trends, globally and locally. The catalysts for these trends are external (such as changing customer demands and advancing technologies) and internal (including greater desire for partnering and requirements for more effective governance). Table 24.3 presents a listing of 25 current trends and their catalysts.

Table 24.3 Recent trends for destination management

Trends	Catalysts or factors causing trends
1. Greater industry, community and government alignment is driving destination competitiveness and brand	Partnering and collaboration; multi-stakeholder; branding
2. Customers are increasingly seeking a unique, authentic travel experience	Customer demands; authenticity, experiences
3. Content creation and dissemination by the public across all platforms drives the destination brand and experience	Technology; content creation
4. Video becomes the new currency of destination marketing and storytelling	Technology; video, storytelling
5. Travelers are demanding more personalised information, control and interaction	Customer demands; information; control; interaction
6. Travelers are seeking more personal enrichment and wellbeing	Customer demands; wellbeing; enrichment
7. Social media's increasing prominence in reaching the travel market	Technology; social media
8. Mobile devices are becoming the primary engagement platform for travelers	Technology; mobile
9. Customers increasingly expect highly curated and customised destination content	Customer demands; content; curation
10. Travelers want assurances of high standards of cleanliness and hygiene	Customer demands; safety and cleanliness
11. Better data management platforms are helping optimise strategy	Technology; data
12. Air access to a destination is key factor in attracting business travelers	Air access
13. The destination brand is a more important factor for choosing a destination	Destination branding; destination selection
14. Greater demand for more dynamic outdoor experiences	Customer demands; outdoor experiences
15. Business event customers are looking for better collaboration with destinations to achieve greater business outcomes	Partnering and collaboration; business events and destinations
16. New data management platforms provide 360-degree view of customers and marketplace	Technology; data management
17. Geotargeting and localisation becoming more prevalent	Technology; localisation and geotargeting
18. Organisations are increasingly developing strategic alliances across multiple economic sectors to leverage resources	Partnering and collaboration; strategic alliances; multi-sector
19. Governments approaching tourism from an integrated, multi-departmental perspective focused on economic development	Partnering and collaboration; public sector
20. Risk management now a top priority	Risks and crises
21. Venues are making significant investments in hygiene and spacing protocols	Safety; venues
22. More communities are aware of importance of tourism to local economy and job growth	Economic development and awareness; communities
23. COVID-19 dramatically accelerated e-commerce	Technology; COVID-19
24. Governments are more aware of the visitor economy's impact on jobs, tax base and the overall economy	Economic development and awareness; public sector
25. Increasing importance of transparency and building partnerships to secure business to a destination	Governance; partnerships

Source: Destinations International (2022b).

An analysis of the catalysts in Table 24.3 indicates that the three principal ones are technology, customer demands, and partnering and collaboration. While Table 24.3 provides a comprehensive, excellent list of recent trends, there is at least one major trend that is missing and that is the increasing emphasis being given by DMOs to social and environmental responsibility. According to a major tourism consulting firm, "*contrary to popular belief, the overall objective for a DMO isn't only to bring more tourists to the destination. It is to make tourism more sustainable and thus enjoyable for visitors for years to come*" (Hartog, 2021). This is a topic that will be raised again later in the chapter in the discussions of the SDGs and future trends.

Roles and competencies of professional destination management

Figure 24.1 shows eight roles of destination management, and these are the ones recommended for all DMOs, whether run by governments or not. These have been articulated by UNWTO (2007) and Morrison (2019, 2023). A brief description of each of the roles follows:

Leadership, governance, and coordination. DMOs set the agenda for tourism and coordinate all stakeholder efforts toward achieving the destination vision, goals and objectives. DMOs are the leaders for the tourism sector in their areas. They must follow good governance principles especially in terms of accountability and transparency.

Partnership and team-building. DMOs must collaborate with other organisations and individuals in their areas. They need to encourage cooperation among government agencies and within the private sector and establish partnerships to attain specific goals and objectives. DMOs achieve much more when they work in tandem with others.

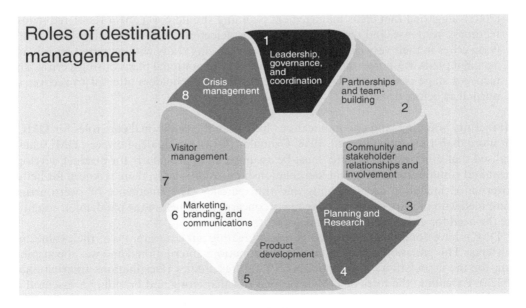

Figure 24.1 Roles of destination management (author).

Community and stakeholder relationships and involvement. It is crucial that community residents are supportive of tourism and know about its contributions as an economic sector. They also must be fully apprised of potential negative impacts of tourism. DMOs need to involve local community leaders and residents in tourism and continuously monitor resident attitudes. DMOs must frequently communicate and engage with stakeholders and community residents.

Planning and research. Typically, DMOs play the lead role in tourism planning and research. They must ensure that the planning and research is completed to achieve the destination vision, goals and objectives. DMOs need to view research as a strategic investment.

Product development. DMOs are not usually involved in physical tourism development; however, they are required to oversee tourism development planning to ensure the appropriate development of physical products and services. All aspects of destination products need to be considered, including tangible and intangible.

Marketing, branding, and communications. DMOs should lead the efforts to create destination positioning and branding, select the most appropriate markets, and communicate the destination. This includes marketing planning, market research, market segmentation, marketing strategy, marketing plan, integrated marketing communications (IMC), and marketing control and evaluation. DMOs are now putting more emphasis on e-marketing.

Visitor management. DMOs must monitor and manage visitors in different ways and mostly when they are within the destinations. A main concern is for resource protection within natural areas and cultural-heritage attractions. Visitor management has implications for the visitors, especially to ensure their safety and security. Also, there are economic yield reasons for considering visitor volumes and mixes. The most important lesson learned from the COVID-19 pandemic is that visitor management is needed to better balance economic goals and environmental and social-cultural priorities.

Crisis management. The COVID-19 pandemic should have convinced DMOs to be more actively involved in crisis management and to develop crisis management plans. PATA (2003) suggested that crisis management planning should cover the 4 Rs of reduction, readiness, response, and recovery. Reduction is detecting the early warnings and identifying crises in their very early stages. Readiness is being ready with prepared crisis management plans. Response is the implementation of operational plans during a crisis. The recovery stage is when the DMO and destination stakeholders attempt to recover to normal as before or better.

Marketing, branding, and communications have been the traditional core roles for DMOs for more than 100 years (Gartrell, 1988; Grimaldi, 2014). Gradually, however, DMOs have realised that other responsibilities must be assumed and particularly for product development and community and stakeholder relationships. Additionally, there is a need for better governance, including accountability and transparency. The emergence of overtourism, combined with increased safety and security concerns (even before the pandemic), accentuate the need for visitor and crisis management.

DMOs have done a less-than-average job of creating public awareness of their value and existence. This situation was recognised by Destinations International and was the inspiration for the association's DestinationNEXT futures studies (Destinations International, 2022a). Extending the roles of DMOs beyond just marketing and branding is essential in creating greater public recognition and acceptance of DMOs.

The eight roles of destination management provide a solid foundation for the specification of professional competencies. The professional competencies must be a close match to the roles of DMOs. Globally, there is not yet a standard set of competencies for destination management. This is attributable to a number of reasons, including the fact that it is a rather new and often-unrecognised profession. The variability in DMO structures and reporting responsibilities is a second reason. There is a lack of a broad consensus on the roles of DMOs as well, and that would represent the basic foundation for specifying the professional destination management competencies. A suggested list of competencies is provided in Table 24.4.

Table 24.4 Competencies for professional destination management (author)

Years	Events and authors	Details and titles
19th century	First convention bureau established in USA	Detroit, Michigan
1914	New DM organisation created	International Association of Convention Bureau
1988	Gartrell book published	Destination marketing for convention and visitor bureaus
1989	Burke & Lindblom article in *Journal of Travel Research*	Strategies for evaluating direct response tourism marketing
1990s	IACVB launched certification program	Certified Destination Management Executive (CDME)
1996	Heller article in *Journal of Vacation Marketing*	Designing a tourism marketing assessment for San Antonio, Texas
2000	Buhalis article in *Tourism Management*	Marketing the competitive destination of the future
2000	Gretzel, Yuan, & Fesenmaier article in *Journal of Travel Research*	Preparing for the new economy: Advertising strategies and change in destination marketing organisations
2003	Ritchie & Crouch book published	The competitive destination: A sustainable tourism perspective
2003	Dwyer & Kim article in *Current Issues in Tourism*	Destination competitiveness: Determinants and indicators
2005	Blain, Levy, & Richards article in *Journal of Travel Research*	Destination branding: Insights and practices for destination management organisations
2005	International Association of Convention and Visitors Bureaus changed name	Destination Marketing Association International (DMAI)
2005	DMAI launched accreditation program	Destination Marketing Accreditation Program (DMAP)
2006	Fyall & Leask article in *Tourism & Hospitality Research*	Destination marketing: Future issues, strategic challenges
2007	Pritchard, Morgan & Pride book published	Destination branding: Creating the unique destination proposition
2007	UNWTO book published	A practical guide to tourism destination management
2007	Beritelli, Bieger, & Laesser article in *Journal of Travel Research*	Destination governance: Using corporate governance theories as a foundation for effective destination management
2008	Ford & Peeper book published	Managing destination marketing organisations
2010	Pollock paper published	Speculation on the future of destination marketing organisations (DMOs)

(*Continued*)

Table 24.4 (Continued)

Years	Events and authors	Details and titles
2011	Wang & Pizam edited book published	*Destination marketing and management: Theories and applications*
2012	New dedicated journal launched	*Journal of Destination Marketing & Management*
2013	Morrison book published	*Marketing and managing tourism destinations*
2014	Destinations International launched analysis of future of DMOs	*Destination NEXT Futures Study*
2014	Pike & Page article published in *Tourism Management*	*Destination marketing organisations and destination marketing: A narrative analysis of the literature*
2018	Gursoy and Chi edited a handbook on destination marketing	*Routledge handbook of destination marketing*
	Gowreesunkar et al. book chapter	*Destination marketing organisations: Roles and challenges*
2018	Gardiner & Scott article published in *Journal of Destination Marketing & Management*	*Destination innovation matrix: A framework for new tourism experience and market development*
2019	Kozak & Kozak edited book published	*Tourist destination Management: Instruments, products, and case studies*
2022	European Cities Marketing changed its name	*Cities Destination Alliance*

Source: Buhalis (2022).

Note: This is only a partial account of key events and influential publications. Many other valuable contributions were made during this time period.

Trade associations, governmental agencies (e.g., UNWTO), and NGOs are the main instigators of the growth in professional destination management. These initiatives include Destination International's *Destination Marketing Accreditation Program* (DMAP), with its accreditation standards (Destinations International, 2022b), and the Certified Destination Management Executive (CDME) credential (Destinations International, 2022c). While not completely covering all the eight destination management roles, these two initiatives in North America are helpful in identifying the scope of the profession and what DMOs and their executives should be doing. The CDME is a certification programme for individual professionals, although Destinations International calls it a credential.

Another pioneering effort in professional destination management capacity-building and training was conducted in Indonesia with assistance from Swisscontact, the international development agency (NGO) of Switzerland. This resulted in modules being developed and tested on *Community Relationships and Involvement*; *Crisis and Disaster Management for Destinations and DMOs*; *Destination and DMO Leadership and Coordination*; *Destination Marketing and Promotion*; *Destination Research and Information*; *Governance and Finance for DMOs*; *Human Resource Management for DMOs*; *Introduction to Destination Management*; *The Management of Visitors at Destinations*; and *Tourism Destination Planning*.

Issues and challenges

The following quote sums up one of the major challenges facing DMOs in the future– *"the need and legitimacy of destination management organisations (DMOs) are increasingly questioned"* (Reinhold, Beritelli, & Grünig, 2019). Another quote from the practitioner side questions the longer-term sustainability of DMOs in their present form – *"the current DMO model (in the U.K.) is unsustainable for many organisations – particularly for those that rely heavily or entirely on subscriptions and funding from the private sector"* (Stratford, 2021). The COVID-19 magnified DMO issues and challenges; however, most of the issues and challenges existed well before the pandemic as several academic scholars discussed (e.g., Fyall & Leask, 2006; Gretzel et al., 2006; Morrison, 2019; Pollock, 2009). There is a need to unpack the reasons for the uncertainty surrounding the future of DMOs and now some of these are reviewed:

Funding and governance

Securing operating funds is a perennial issue for DMOs and this issue was exacerbated by the COVID-19 pandemic in 2020–2022. The health crisis and the drop in hotel and tourism revenues forced many DMOs to furlough or lay off staff members (Destinations International/NorthStar Meeting Group, 2020; Schoening, 2020). The governance side of this issue is that DMOs are often seen as not being accountable and transparent enough, e.g., absence of visible KPIs or performance measurement (Llewellyn McLaren Consulting, 2021).

Visibility and public recognition

As mentioned earlier, these organisations do not have high recognition by the general public and are not particularly visible within their own communities. Traditionally, they focussed communication efforts outside of their destinations. They are often confused with chambers of commerce and other business associations.

Myopia

There is a significant level of myopia within the DMO profession that their scope of responsibility is limited to just marketing, branding, and communications. Ironically this was the basis for the establishment of the first DMOs; today, it is a major criticism levelled against DMOs.

Overtourism

The coining of the term overtourism is attributed to Skift and its founder, Rafat Ali (Ali, 2018). This occurs when there are excessive numbers of tourists at a specific destination that result in negative impacts of all types on the community involved (Dodds & Butler, 2019). A research study based on Barcelona categorised DMOs as having tourism-philia, meaning pushing the economic benefits of tourism while not revealing the negative effects (Zerva et al., 2019). This connects with the earlier comment on myopia within some DMOs. The narrow conception on a DMO's role is reflected in the following definition of a destination management organisation: "A destination management organization (DMO) is an organization whose primary function is to attract visitors for the purpose of enhancing the local economy through purchase of room nights, food and beverage, retail items, transportation or visitor services" (Travel Oregon, 2022).

Villeneuve (2021) presents an opposing view of the DMO saying that "DMOs can vary in their official names (visitors bureau, tourist boards, organization of tourism, chambers of commerce) and geographic competence (local, regional, national, or multi-country) but they all have a pivotal role to play in sustainable tourism management".

Technology

As highlighted in Table 24.3, technological advances are the major recent trend affecting destination management. Hays, Page, and Buhalis (2013) reviewed the engagement on social media platforms by DMOs and saw the benefit of using such technologies as traditional funding sources were becoming more limited. User-generated content uploaded online can become a reservoir of crucial data (big data) for DMOs and can be built into a destination quality control system (Pan, MacLaurin, & Crotts, 2007). More recently, Gretzel (2022) has put forward six smart DMO functions in mobilising, match-making, managing, sensing, shapeshifting and stewardship as part of smart tourism governance that are partly, not wholly, supported by technology.

Consolidation

Communities have multiple agendas and not just tourism. They want to attract all forms of investment and quality human talent, as well as being more sustainable and better places to live. One of the future challenges for DMOs is that they may be consolidated into other agencies for cost-saving or strategy reasons. The coupling of tourism with film development is already happening and other such combinations are likely to continue in the future. Another instance is the absorption of the former China National Tourism Administration into the Ministry of Culture and Tourism. There is a potential danger that tourism will receive lesser priority when integrated into organisations with broader portfolios of responsibilities.

Creativity and innovation

There has been a tendency for DMOs to try to maintain the status quo and to closely guard existing budgets and activities. Most DMO managers follow a "stay as we are" strategy as this is the most efficient, safest and least controversial approach (Gardiner & Scott, 2018, p. 122). The challenge for DMOs is that they must change in the future due to a mixture of external and internal factors.

Stakeholder interests and roles

The main stakeholders for destination management are tourists, tourism operators and organisations, community residents, government, and NGOs and the environment. As Table 24.3 suggests, DMOs are reaching out more to form partnerships with traditional and non-traditional stakeholders and this implies that stakeholders will be more engaged with DMOs in the future. This is opening up many more opportunities for co-creation involving DMOs with their stakeholders. A more detailed itemisation of stakeholder roles and initiatives with DMOs and destination management is given in Table 24.5.

Table 24.5 Roles and initiatives of stakeholders with DMOs and destination management

Stakeholders	Roles and initiatives
Tourists	• Co-create tourism experiences with DMOs • Engage in crowdsourcing of materials with DMOs • Participate in environmentally oriented initiatives with DMOs
Tourism operators and organisations	• Co-create tourism experiences with DMOs • Provide inputs and recommendations to DMOs • Serve on DMO Boards of Directors • Financially support DMOs • Engage in crowdsourcing of materials with DMOs
Community residents	• Co-create tourism experiences with DMOs • Engage in crowdsourcing of materials with DMOs • Participate in environmentally oriented initiatives with DMOs • Serve on DMO Boards of Directors • Provide inputs and recommendations to DMOs
Government (public sector)	• Provide DMO funding • Develop policies in support of tourism and DMOs • Assist DMOs with planning and research • Provide industry training for DMOs
NGOs and the environment	• Engage with DMOs in pro-environmental programmes • Prepare guidelines for protection and conservation of natural areas

Potential contributions to SDGs

There are several calls for DMOs to be active agents in the achievement of the UN's Sustainable Development Goals (e.g., Bowen & Sotomayor, 2022; Morgan, 2021; Rivera et al., 2021; UNWTO, 2018). Table 24.6 shows suggested potential contributions of DMOs to the achievement of the SDGs.

Future trends for DMOs and destination management

Several commentators are predicting turbulent times ahead for DMOs in the next ten years and beyond, and the future challenges are already highlighted in this chapter. While it is acknowledged that there are now fears for the survival of DMOs, it must be asked how did these organisations manage to exist for more than 100 years? (Gartrell, 1988; Grimaldi, 2014). The answer that seems to have been forgotten by many academics is that DMOs have already been flexible and changed with different circumstances (e.g., broadening focus beyond business events, adapting to e-marketing).

There are future trends on the horizon that will call upon DMOs to be flexible once again and change to be effective and sustainable. Some of these future trends are now highlighted:

Changing workforce

As more members of Generation Z gain employment in DMOs, there could be a sea change in attitudes about organisational roles and responsibilities. This cohort of younger employees will demand that DMOs strictly follow social responsibility guidelines, for example.

Table 24.6 Potential contributions of DMOs to SDGs

SDG numbers and titles	SD goal explanations	DMO potential contributions to SDGs
SDG 1. No poverty	End poverty in all its forms everywhere	Supporting pro-poor tourism and community-based tourism programs
SDG 2. Zero hunger	End hunger, achieve food security and improved nutrition and promote sustainable agriculture	Encouraging food waste recycling by restaurants that feed the hungry
SDG 3. Good health and wellbeing	Ensure healthy lives and promote wellbeing for all at all ages	Encouraging local residents and tourists to improve lifestyles and wellbeing
SDG 4. Quality education	Ensure inclusive and equitable quality education and promote lifelong learning opportunities for all	Providing training and education on tourism for community residents
SDG 5. Gender equality	Achieve gender equality and empower all women and girls	Supporting women-owned and managed tourism enterprises
SDG 6. Clean water and sanitation	Ensure availability and sustainable management of water and sanitation for all	Encouraging reductions in the use of water
SDG 7. Affordable and clean energy	Ensure access to affordable, reliable, sustainable and modern energy for all	Encouraging the use of alternative and clean energy sources
SDG 8. Decent work and economic growth	Promote sustained, inclusive and sustainable economic growth, full and productive employment and decent work for all	Supporting community-based and pro-poor tourism businesses and projects
SDG 9. Industry, innovation and infrastructure	Build resilient infrastructure, promote inclusive and sustainable industrialisation and foster innovation	Encouraging the wise use of infrastructure in a sustainable manner Advocating sustainable tourism developments
SDG 10. Reduced inequalities	Reduce inequality within and among countries	Discouraging all forms of discrimination Being an equal opportunity employer
SDG 11. Sustainable cities and communities	Make cities and human settlements inclusive, safe, resilient and sustainable	Encouraging sustainable actions and initiatives within urban areas
SDG 12. Responsible consumption and production	Ensure sustainable consumption and production patterns	Purchasing and consuming responsibly
SDG 13. Climate action	Take urgent action to combat climate change and its impacts	Reducing carbon footprints
SDG 14. Life below water	Conserve and sustainably use the oceans, seas and marine resources for sustainable development	Encouraging the following of environmental guidelines and protocols in water
SDG 15. Life on land	Protect, restore and promote sustainable use of terrestrial ecosystems, sustainably manage forests, combat desertification, and halt and reverse land degradation and halt biodiversity loss	Encouraging the following of environmental guidelines and protocols on land

(*Continued*)

Table 24.6 (Continued)

SDG numbers and titles	SD goal explanations	DMO potential contributions to SDGs
SDG 16. Peace, justice and strong institutions	Promote peaceful and inclusive societies for sustainable development, provide access to justice for all and build effective, accountable and inclusive institutions at all levels	Advocating peace and harmony Being an effectively governed organisation
SDG 17. Partnerships for the goals	Strengthen the means of implementation and revitalise the global partnership for sustainable development	Co-creating innovations and projects that support achievement of the SDGs

Increasing organisational consolidation and integration

Place marketing and branding are receiving more attention in practice and in the academic literature. Destinations are becoming increasingly engaged in attracting inward investment, human talent, creative industries, university and other students, and major events. DMOs are increasingly targets for consolidation into integrated multi-sector economic development agencies. This consolidation of place marketing and branding entities seems inevitable in the difficult economic times ahead.

Digitalisation of marketing

DMOs have moved toward e-marketing since the late 1990s and digital is fast becoming a major part of what they do. This will continue and be the primary way that DMOs communicate with all audiences, especially through social media platforms and mobile devices.

Funding sources

The funding of DMOs was flagged earlier as a traditional issue and challenge that became even worse as a result of COVID-19. Staff costs are the major expenditures, and it is very likely that many DMOs will have to make do with lower budgets than they have been accustomed to. For example, full-time jobs set in offices may be replaced by contract work done from home.

More DMO partnering and collaboration

Greater collaboration and more partnerships among DMOs and other entities seem to be highly likely and needed. DMOs will increasingly be sharing resources to achieve common goals and desired outcomes. As suggested by Ford and Peeper (2008), associations that are active in destination management will need to work more collaboratively in the future to support the efforts of DMO practitioners.

New DMO business models

Many DMOs will have to make radical changes in their business models in the future (Destination International, 2022a; Ford and Peeper, 2008; Reinhold, Beritelli, & Grünig, 2019). The latter set of authors suggest four new DMO business models in the destination factory, destination service centre, value orchestrator and value enabler (pp. 1145–1146).

Professionalisation of destination management

The past three decades have witnessed increasing professionalism in destination management. Destination management associations, government agencies, and NGOs have been pioneering this movement to better prepare DMO professionals for the future. Academic institutions need to join in this effort by offering degree programmes in destination management.

DMO social responsibility

It is customary for companies to have corporate social responsibility (CSR) strategies and plans; however, these are not commonly found in DMOs. They are starting to appear in some DMOs, and this will be an even stronger trend in the future.

Sustainable tourism development and the SDGs

In some countries (e.g., Costa Rica), DMOs are placing a high priority on environmental concerns as well as the social-cultural impacts of tourism. However, many DMOs are yet to fully engage in this movement and seem to be giving it lip service rather than allocating resources to sustainability. This must change as DMOs need to accord sustainable tourism development a much higher priority.

A caveat needs to be offered here along with these future trends and that is that not all DMOs are alike. These trends are more applicable to Western and more developed nations. Countries such as China and Indonesia have huge national (governmental) DMOs with thousands of employees. These organisations are less likely to be adversely affected by worsening economic conditions in the future.

Contributions

This chapter provides a useful status report on destination management and DMOs for practitioners and academic scholars. The timeline of events and influential publications, and statements of DMO roles and competencies, recent and future trends, challenges and issues, stakeholder roles, and SDG initiatives will assist in evolving policies and strategies for the future.

There is a need for more research into professional destination management on a global basis. Assuming that a uniform definition can be agreed upon, a basic census of DMOs is needed. One estimate is that there are 4,200 DMOs in the world, 1,450 of which are in the U.S. (Hall, 2016). While the U.S. figure seems reasonable, the global estimate is well below the true number of DMOs globally, which the author suggests are in the tens of thousands.

An agreed-upon definition of a destination management organisation must be reached as the current confusion is inhibiting their recognition and minimising the status of DMOs in society. How such a consensus will be reached is an enigmatic proposition; however, it will be a worthwhile venture for destination management.

Conclusions

Destination management is becoming more professional; however, it is still struggling for broader recognition in society. Despite surviving in one form or another for more than a century, DMOs appear to be now facing the greatest threats to their existence. With global economic conditions expected to deteriorate further due to the pandemic and the Russia-Ukraine conflict, these organisations may be facing a greater struggle than in 2020–2022.

The changing labour pool, working habits (e.g., working from home and digital nomadism), and advancing technologies (e.g., IoT, Metaverse, extended reality, and artificial intelligence) will also have profound influences on destination management and DMOs in the decades ahead. The bottom line is that DMOs will have to change and, of course, continue to be even more professional at what they do.

References

Ali, R. (2018). The genesis of overtourism: Why we came up with the term and what's happened since, Skift, 14 April, https://skift.com/2018/08/14/the-genesis-of-overtourism-why-we-came-up-with-the-term-and-whats-happened-since/

Beritelli, P., Bieger, T., & Laesser, C. (2007). Destination governance: Using corporate governance theories as a foundation for effective destination management. *Journal of Travel Research*, 46, 96–107.

Blain, C., Levy, S. E., & Ritchie, J. R. B. (2005). Destination branding: Insights and practices from destination management organizations. *Journal of Travel Research*, 43(4), 328–338.

Bowen, J., & Sotomayor, S. (2022). Including residents in the rebranding of tourist destinations to achieve sustainable development goals. *Worldwide Hospitality and Tourism Themes*, 14(1), 56–64.

Buhalis, D. (2000). Marketing the competitive destination of the future. *Tourism Management*, 21(1), 97–116.

Buhalis, D. (ed.) (2022). *Encyclopedia of tourism management and marketing*. Cheltenham, UK and Northampton, MA: Edward Elgar Publishing. https://doi.org/10.4337/9781800377486

Burke, J. F., & Lindblom, L. A. (1989). Strategies for evaluating direct response tourism marketing. *Journal of Travel Research*, 28(2), 33–37.

City Destinations Alliance. (2022). City Destinations Alliance, https://citydestinationsalliance.eu/

Destinations International/NorthStar Meetings Group. (2020). Planning for post-COVID-19: Convention sales and services, https://www.northstarmeetingsgroup.com/uploadedFiles/Articles/News/Convention_and_Visitors_Bureaus/DI-Northstar-4-8-20.pdf

Destinations International. (2022a). A strategic road map for the NEXT generation of destination organizations, https://destinationsinternational.org/sites/default/files/DestinationNEXT_2021FuturesStudy_FINAL2.pdf

Destinations International. (2022b). Destination Marketing Accreditation Program (DMAP), https://destinationsinternational.org/destination-marketing-accreditation-program-dmap

Destinations International. (2022c). Certified Destination Management Executive (CDME) Credential, https://destinationsinternational.org/cdme

Dodds, R., & Butler, R. (2019). The phenomena of overtourism: A review. *International Journal of Tourism Cities*, 5(4), 519–528.

Dwyer, L., & Kim, C. (2003). Destination competitiveness: Determinants and indicators. *Current Issues in Tourism*, 6(5), 369–414.

Ford, R. C., & Peeper, W. C. (2008). *Managing destination marketing organizations*. Orlando, FL: ForPer Publications.

Fyall, A., & Leask, A. (2006). Destination marketing: Future issues, strategic challenges. *Tourism and Hospitality Research*, 7(1), 50–63.

Gardiner, S., & Scott, N. (2018). Destination innovation matrix: A framework for new tourism experience and market development. *Journal of Destination Marketing & Management*, 10, 122–131.

Gartrell, R. B. (1988). *Destination marketing for convention and visitor bureaus*. Dubuque: Kendall/Hunt Publishing Company.

Gretzel, U. (2022). The smart DMO: A new step in the digital transformation of destination management organizations. *European Journal of Tourism Research* 30, 3002.

Gretzel, U., Yuan, Y.-L., & Fesenmaier, D. R. (2000). Preparing for the new economy: Advertising strategies and change in destination marketing organizations. *Journal of Travel Research*, 30(2), 146–156.

Gretzel, U., Fesenmaier, D. F., Formica, S., & O'Leary, J. T. (2006). Searching for the future: Challenges faced by destination marketing organizations. *Journal of Travel Research*, 45, 116–126.

Grimaldi, L. A. (2014). DMAI: 100 years of service, Meetings & Conventions, 1 August, https://www.meetings-conventions.com/News/Third-Party/DMAI-100-Years-of-Service

Hall, A. (2016). 16 things to know about DMOs and DMCs, MeetingsNet, 3 October, https://www.meetingsnet.com/site-selectionrfps/16-things-know-about-dmos-and-dmcs

Hartog, Z. (2021). What is a DMO? Solimar International, https://www.solimarinternational.com/what-is-a-destination-management-organization-dmo-and-why-should-destinations-care/

Hays, S., Page, S. J., & Buhalis, D. (2013). Social media as a destination marketing tool: Its use by national tourism organisations. *Current Issues in Tourism*, *16*(3), 211–239.

Heller, V. L. (1996). Designing a tourism marketing assessment for San Antonio, Texas. *Journal of Vacation Marketing*, *2*(2), 163–175.

Kozak, N., & Kozak, M. (eds.). (2019). *Tourist destination management: Instruments, products, and case studies*. Cham, Switzerland: Springer Nature Switzerland.

Llewellyn McLaren Consulting. (2021). DMO review responses: Full report, https://assets.publishing.service.gov.uk/government/uploads/system/uploads/attachment_data/file/1011687/DMO_Review_Responses_Report_-_accessible.pdf

Morgan, N. (2021). Time for 'mindful' destination management and marketing. *Journal of Destination Marketing & Management*, *1*, 8–9.

Morrison, A. M. (2019). *Marketing and Managing Tourism Destinations*, 2nd ed. London: Routledge.

Morrison, A. M. (2023). *Marketing and Managing Tourism Destinations*, 3rd ed. London: Routledge.

Pacific Asia Travel Association (PATA). (2003). Crisis. It won't happen to us. Bangkok: PATA.

Pan, B., MacLaurin, T., & Crotts, J. C. (2007). Travel blogs and the implications for destination marketing. *Journal of Travel Research*, *46*, 35–45.

Pike, S., & Page, S. (2014). Destination marketing organizations and destination marketing: A narrative analysis of the literature. *Tourism Management*, *41*, 1–26.

Pollock, A. (2009). *The future of destination marketing: Why all marketing is social marketing*. Presentation to BIT Reiseliv, Oslo, Norway.

Pritchard, N., Morgan, A., & Pride, R. (2007). *Destination branding: Creating the unique destination proposition*. Oxford: Elsevier Butterworth-Heinemann.

Reinhold, S., Beritelli, P., & Grünig, R. (2019). A business model typology for destination management organizations. *Tourism Review*, *74*(6), 1135–1152.

Ritchie, J. R. B., & Crouch, G. I. (2003). *The competitive destination: A sustainable tourism perspective*. Wallingford, UK: CABI.

Rivera, J., Pastor, R., & Punzón, J. G. (2021). The impact of the COVID-19 on the perception of DMOs about the sustainability within destinations: A European empirical approach. *Tourism Planning & Development*, https://doi.org/10.1080/21568316.2021.1914149

Schoening, E. (2020). CVBs cut staff members as Coronavirus crisis continues, NorthStar Meetings Group, 23 April, https://www.northstarmeetingsgroup.com/News/Convention-and-Visitor-Bureaus/Coronavirus-CVB-DMO-Layoffs-Furlough-Staff-Employee-Reductions

Stratford, A. (2021). Future of DMOs = future of English tourism, Go To Places, 29 March, https://www.gotoplaces.co.uk/insights-and-resources/future-of-dmos-future-of-english-tourism/

Travel Oregon. (2022). Destination management organizations, https://industry.traveloregon.com/resources/tourism-in-oregon/destination-management-organizations/

UNWTO. (2007). *A practical guide to tourism destination management*. Madrid: UNWTO.

UNWTO. (2018). *UNWTO guidelines for institutional strengthening of destination management organizations (DMOs): Preparing DMOs for new challenges*, https://www.e-unwto.org/doi/epdf/10.18111/9789284420841

Villeneuve, V. (2021). The value of DMOs to destinations, Solimar International, https://www.solimarinternational.com/the-value-of-dmos-to-destinations/

Wang, Y., & Pizam, A. (eds.) (2011). *Destination marketing and management: Theories and applications*. Wallingford, UK: CABI.

Zerva, K., Palou, S., Blasco, D., & Donaire, J. A. B. (2019). Tourism-philia versus tourism-phobia: residents and destination management organization's publicly expressed tourism perceptions in Barcelona. *Tourism Geographies*, *21*(2), 306–329.

Part II
External factor trends

Cláudia Seabra in Chapter 25 reviews the *Terrorism threat and its influence on leisure and travel behaviours of Millennials*. The subject of this chapter was to evaluate the impact of terrorism on Millennials' travel and leisure behaviors. Using a survey approach, with a sample of more than 1,000 Millennials living and studying in the EU28, it was possible to evaluate their perceptions of risk when travelling and consuming leisure activities in their own countries, in Europe and worldwide. Results indicated that Millennials are mostly fearless but alert: i) only organisational and terrorism risk are significant, also they fear crime and violence and being lost; and ii) they feel that is safe travelling in Europe and outside the continent but agree that safety measures are very important. Also, findings prove that terrorism is part of Millennials' lives: i) Millennials are interested in information about terrorism in the media but they do not actively search for that information; ii) they feel that it is possible that there will be terrorist attacks in Europe and in their own country in the near future; however, they do not think of changing any aspect of their life because of that; and iii) Millennials feel safe carrying out most of their daily activities, except for activities with big crowds: concerts and festivals, discos, sport and religious events.

Multi-crisis destinations (MCDs) – Towards a future research agenda is the focus of Chapter 26 by **Sofia Lachhab, Alastair M. Morrison, Tina Šegota**, and **J. Andres Coca-Stefaniak**. Crisis events of various types (e.g., natural disasters, terrorism attacks, pandemics, economic downturns, political instability) can adversely affect the development of tourism destinations in the short to medium term. However, more scholarly research needs to be carried out on the classification attributes, spatial distribution, and impact structure of global tourism crises and how tourism destinations develop resilience as a result of these processes. This recommendation is particularly applicable in destinations subject to recurring crises over extended periods. This chapter argues the need for scholarly activity to pay greater attention to multi-crisis destinations. The multi-crisis destination concept is defined with suggestions for developing an index for measuring and classifying multi-crisis destinations. Finally, examples of such destinations are provided and discussed.

Yeonsook (Angie) Im and **Dae-Young Kim** are the authors of Chapter 27 on *Gen Z as a future workforce in the hospitality and tourism industry*. The global tourism and hospitality industry is anticipating the entry of another younger cohort of workers. As the industry fundamentally depends on human capital, understanding the workforce and its evolution over time has been an important and ongoing endeavour. Born between 1997 and 2012, those individuals who have been termed Generation Z currently account for the largest single age group in the U.S. Born into the digital age, this generation cannot be separated from technological advancement and innovation. Given that the future of the tourism and hospitality industry will be accompanied by technology, this tech-savvy demographic has great potential and will be a vital asset in the future. Having witnessed social turmoil and economic recessions, this generation will likely have different perspectives and traits in the workplace, such as being more independent, resilient, responsible, and tolerant of others. Being more radically diverse compared to previous generational cohorts, Generation Z will bring diversity and inclusion in the workplace to the next level. With a desire and anticipation of Generation Z's important contributions to the industry, this chapter discusses the trends and issues of this emerging workforce.

Chapter 28 on *Forced displacement: The 'refugee crisis' and its impact on global tourism* is written by **Shima B. Afshan, Cheryl Cockburn-Wootten**, and **Alison J. McIntosh**. Over the last decade, the number of people forcibly displaced from their homes and fleeing from war, persecution, and violence has nearly doubled, from 41 million in 2010 to 82.4 million in 2020. Of these, 26.4 million are refugees under international protection. The number of forcibly displaced people will increase in the future. Amid these global concerns, there has been a rise in the number of tourism scholars investigating the impact of refugees on tourism. To date, much of this work has excluded the involvement of refugee voices and experiences in the research processes. More worryingly, this type of orientation adopts an 'add refugees and stir' approach and perpetuates a conventional view of refugees as 'outsiders' and 'issue-generating' to the host country. To counter this approach, this chapter advocates theoretical and practical contributions that shift our orientation for the more inclusive study with, rather than only on, refugees, and takes a proactive approach to examining the trend of forced displacement and global tourism.

Maria Gebbels, Alison J. McIntosh, and **Tracy Harkison** provide Chapter 29 about *Leading social change through prison fine dining as a new form of global tourism*. Although tourism in decommissioned prisons is nothing new, tourists' fine dining in a working prison is. In this chapter, the authors discuss fine dining in prisons not only as a new form of global tourism but also as leading social change. Hospitality training programmes in the form of fine dining restaurants help prisoner rehabilitation and enable social purpose to change the public perception of prisoners. One example is The Clink Charity, U.K., which is successfully running four training restaurants in prisons. This chapter suggests a replication of the Clink model domestically and internationally, so that, in future, more tourists will be able to experience fine dining in prisons globally. Over the next 30 years, fine dining restaurants could have the ability to reduce reoffending, increase the hospitality workforce, change the stigma that prisoners face at present, and become a popular niche tourism experience.

Sharing economy legislation: Regulating peer-to-peer tourism platforms such as Airbnb and Uber is the topic of Chapter 30 by **Daniel Guttentag**. The chapter explores the regulation of sharing economy platforms like Airbnb and Uber, which epitomise the rapid, recent emergence of the peer-to-peer short-term rental and ride-hailing industries. The existing literature on such regulation is quite limited, particularly within the tourism field. Nevertheless, it is an important subject, as the services offered by these platforms were initially illegal in many jurisdictions, and the opportunities these platforms have created have been complemented by a myriad of negative impacts. More jurisdictions, therefore, have introduced new regulations specific to these platforms, often sharing a fairly similar underlying framework. The primary stakeholders in the legislative battles producing such regulations include the policy makers, the platform companies, their hosts and drivers, their customers, and their incumbent industries. Over time, it is likely that regulations will become tighter and more effective as jurisdictions learn from one another about successful strategies for better regulating the platforms.

David Newsome in Chapter 31 elaborates on ***Re-imagining tourism in a world of declining nature***. The chapter provides an overview of the tourism–environment relationship set in the context of declining nature. Furthermore, at the same time there is an increasing number of people wishing to enjoy and benefit from what the natural world has to offer. While global environmental degradation is a concerning trajectory, tourism can offer solutions if managed sustainably. The current tourism in nature scenario is reviewed and actual and potential problems identified. With greater awareness there is room for a re-imagined tourism, but this depends on action at all levels in human society. Governments and agencies can play a pivotal role in designating more protected areas and in the provision of management effectiveness. The role of individuals and the way people think about their relationship with nature will determine the quality and success of nature tourism into the future.

25 Terrorism threat and its influence on leisure and travel behaviours of Millennials

Cláudia Seabra

Introduction

Terrorism and political tensions are among the top concerns of all generations; however, Millennials ranked "war, terrorism and political tension" as their foremost concerns. For them, those issues are more important than healthcare, hunger, unemployment, or the environment, to mention some of the other high-ranked categories. In addition, the same study showed that this sentiment was more dominant among young people in mature economies, particularly in Europe (Deloitte, 2017). Even in the presence of the COVID-19 global pandemic, terrorist attacks are pointed to as the most imminent threats, along with employment and livelihood crises, widespread youth disillusionment, digital inequality, economic stagnation, human-made environmental damage, and the erosion of societal cohesion (World Economic Forum, 2022).

The Millennial generation is playing an increasingly important role in the development of all economic sectors, especially in tourism. Recent studies confirm that this generation will account for about half of the demand for tourism sector services in 2025 and they will represent 75% of the global workforce, which gives them considerable spending power (Seabra, AlAshry, Çınar, Raja, Reis, & Sadiq, 2021). In 2020, this generation represented 16% of the European population (Eurostat, 2020).

Millennials are those born in the late 1980s and 1990s and grew up during the Millennium period, a time of rapid change (Ketter, 2021). Their adolescence and young adulthood were marked by important and unique events that shaped their values and behaviours (Cavagnaro, Staffieri, & Postma 2018). In fact, this is the generation who have witnessed a greater number of traumatic events (Debevec, Schewe, Madden, & Diamond, 2013), each one of them having a high global impact, such as natural disasters, wars and conflicts, social changes, and especially terrorist events all over the globe (CBI, 2021).

This is the generation that has watched big conflicts and disruptive events broadcast live on TV, including the 9/11 terrorist attacks, the second Gulf War, the Arab Spring and a war in Ukraine; who witnessed pandemics such as the H1N1 flu and the Avian Flu, SARS; who watched gigantic natural catastrophes: tsunamis, earthquakes, catastrophic forest fires, typhoons, volcano eruptions, among others. But mostly, this is the generation who witnessed the growth and rise of transnational and global terrorist organisations, such as al-Qaida, ISIL, Boko Haram, Al-Shabaab, Muslim and Jihadi-inspired extremists (World-Data, 2022), among others. It has been estimated that such groups have perpetrated almost 30,000 terrorist attacks across the world in the decade between 2000 and 2010 (START, 2022).

Recently, European countries have been the targets of several attacks that are shaking important pillars of European identity: freedom, mobility, culture fruition and a happy way of life. Over the past two decades, more than 9,000 attacks have targeted people who just wanted to live the European way of life: to be happy and have fun, and to be allowed to work, live, and travel freely around the old continent. Those attacks (START, 2022) targeted specifically tourism targets: Beaches, museums, resorts, airports, train and subway stations, restaurants, cafés, festivals and concerts, and tourist sites (streets, terraces, and squares). The terrorist events in Madrid, Spain (2004), London, UK (2005), Tuusula, Finland (2007), Apeldoorn, Netherlands (2009), Utoya, Norway (2011), Paris, France (2015), Brussels, Belgium (2016), Nice, France (2016), Sousse, Tunisia (2015), Berlin, Germany (2016), Istanbul, Turkey (2016, 2017), Manchester, UK (2017), and London, UK (2017, 2018, 2019, 2020) show how tourist sites represent very important targets to terrorists who seek to achieve strategic and ideological goals (Seabra, 2019).

Following the calls of the United Nations (UN) to contribute to sustainable development based on the promotion of just, peaceful and inclusive societies in its 16th Sustainable Development Goal (SDG) (UN, 2022), it is important to understand the real effects of terrorism on people's lives, and to address the material and the psychological impact of terrorism in civilian behaviour. The aim of this chapter is to evaluate the impact of terrorism on Millennials' travel and leisure behaviours. Despite the importance and impact of the phenomenon, no studies have yet been conducted to assess the impacts of terrorism on people's lives in Europe, the receiving region that represented more than 50% of international tourism over the past decades (WTO – World Tourism Organization, 2020), especially as far as the younger generations are concerned. This chapter attempts to fill that gap.

Terrorism impacts and Millennials

Safety is one of the most fundamental conditions granted to human beings; it is an anthropological need and a vital part of the human condition (Maslow, 1943). So, it is important to understand the real effects of terrorism on people's lives, and to address the material and the psychological impact of terrorism on someone's behaviour. This requires a full analysis and the extension and improvement of our knowledge on the terrorists' intrinsic nature (Llussá & Tavares, 2007).

The majority of the previous studies focus on individuals or tourists in general; only a few studies analyse the reactions and attitudes of specific sociodemographic groups (Chen & Noriega, 2003). Millennials, in addition to being the biggest market segment for all products over the next five years, represent more than half of the global demand for the tourism sector (Seabra et al., 2021) and will therefore define and condition the main trends in the tourist market in the near future. So, understanding Millennials' perceptions, attitudes, behaviours and intentions is a crucial conern.

These young people were born in the 1980s and 1990s and are composed of individuals with specific sociological, motivational, and behavioural features. Millennials are the first generation of digital natives (Figure 27.1), always connected (Skinner, Sarpong, & White, 2018) and tech-savvy: they frequently view two screens at once (CBI, 2021). Technology is a central issue in their lives as they are very active in social and cultural terms, using Internet-based technologies in their daily lives, depending heavily on the use of apps, mobile phones, and social media (Ketter, 2021; Nielsen, 2017; Skinner et al., 2018). They are technologically innovative, globally conscious, and much more available when it comes to try new products and eager to acquire new cultural experiences (Gen C Travel, 2018). They prefer experiences over possessions (Ketter, 2021). In addition, Millennials are focused on the present, have an optimistic disposition and their main aspirations are freedom and flexibility (CBI, 2021).

In their consumer habits they show two specific features (CBI, 2021): i) they prefer to acquire experiences over goods; for example, they choose travelling over buying the latest TV; and ii) they invest more in what's meaningful to them, such as high-end travel experiences over luxury hotels.

Naturally, leisure, travel and tourism are top priorities for this age cohort (Cavagnaro et al., 2018). In fact, Millennials travel more than any other generation; something that will evolve significantly as their incomes and professional status grow (Nielsen, 2017). When travelling this generation eagerly searches for novelty. They are very motivated to try new experiences and so they are always looking forward to exploring different cultures and lifestyles, visiting new places, or practicing off-the-beaten-track tourism (Ketter, 2021). Thus, they look for excitement, and are ready to accept higher risks, but always in controlled environments.

Methodology

The focus of this chapter is to evaluate the impact of terrorism on Millennials' travel and leisure behaviours. Using a survey approach, with a sample of more than 1,000 Millennials living and studying in the EU28, it was possible to analyse their perceptions of risk when travelling and consuming leisure activities in their own countries, in Europe and worldwide.

The research setting included a survey approach. Data were collected from September 2017 to March 2020 using snowball sampling. The questionnaire was disclosed online through social media. Only individuals living, studying, or working in an EU country were allowed to answer the questionnaire. Those complying that premise and agreeing to participate in the study were redirected to an online platform to fill out the questionnaire. The respondents were asked to share the questionnaire with at least seven friends, colleagues, or family members. 1,800 of the 2,321 questionnaires collected were considered valid. From those, 1,160 are questionnaires from Millennials (born between 1980 and 2000).

Survey instrument development

The measurement instrument was developed based on scales previously established in relevant literature. The scales intended to capture the analysed concepts:

"Risk perception when travelling" was measured using a scale adapted from Seabra, Dolnicar, Abrantes and Kastenholz (2013), in which subjects were asked to indicate their perceptions regarding several risks that might occur during their travels, related to equipment, organisation and satisfaction issues, cultural and social aspects, crime and violence, terrorism and political turmoil, accidents, among others.

To assess the "Feelings of (un)safety when travelling", respondents were invited to rate their safety feelings considering their travels in Europe and outside Europe and the importance of aditional safety measures, with scales adjusted from Wong and Yeh (2009) and Seabra et al. (2014, 2021).

The concept of "Interest about terrorism in media" was measured using scales adapted from Jin (2003) and Seabra et al. (2012). Respondents were questioned about their interest and attention paid to news about terrorism in the media.

The "Feelings about terrorism threat" was evaluated by asking respondents to rate, using a five-point Likert scale, their perceptions and feelings about the threat posed by terrorism in daily life and future plans based on the works of Huddy, Feldman, Capelos and Provost (2002), Huddy, Khatib and Capelos (2001), and Jeuring and Becken (2013).

"Terrorism threat in tourism and leisure activities" concept was measured using an exploratory scale. Respondents were invited to rank, using a five-point Likert scale, their level of safety as they take part in several leisure and tourism activities that are threatened by terrorist actions.

After selecting the scales from the literature, the final instrument was discussed with experts. After that, the initial scales were translated into several EU languages – Portuguese, Spanish, German, Bulgarian, Czech, Croatian, Slovak, Finnish, French, Greek, Hungarian, Italian, Polish, Romanian, and Swedish – and then the instrument was back-translated to English. After revision, we used a pre-test sample of 30 university students to test the scales' reliability (through Cronbach's alpha). The pre-test results were used to further refine the questionnaire.

Data profile

The Millennials are mainly from EU countries (85%), but they also came from non-EU countries, including African, Asian, and South American countries. The countries of residence, work or study belong to the EU28 nations, and respondents were mainly from Portugal, Poland, Spain, France, Croatia, and the UK (72%). Most of the participants were female (65%). They were highly educated since 87% have university degrees and 12% had about 12 years of school; 53% were students; 17.5% were middle and senior managers; 9% worked in administration and commerce; 8.5% were unemployed; and 6% were either freelancer/self-employed or unemployed. The respondents' incomes were low for the most part: 67% earned less than 1,000€ of individual net income/month, 21% between 1,001€ and 2,000€, and only 12% earned more than 2,001€. The respondents are used to travel: 28.7% had already travelled five to ten times outside the country over the last ten years; 25.4% had travelled less than five times; 14.5% between ten and 15 times; and 11.6% 15 to 20 times. When asked about how many countries they know or have travelled to, the respondents from the ample showed a great travel experience: 36.3% were familiar with five to ten countries, 31.3% with less than five, 14.4% with ten to 15 countries; and 6.5% with more than 25 countries.

Data analysis

The main goal was to analyse the impact of the terrorism threat on European Millennials' risk perceptions and travel behaviours. To address the main goal, Millennials were asked to express their risk perceptions when travelling in general and the feelings of being safe or unsafe when travelling in Europe and outside the continent. In a different section, the participants were invited to describe their feeling about terrorism, namely: their interest about the issue in the media, the feeling of threat regarding terrorist attacks and their perception of safety or unsafety when taking part in leisure and tourism activities. To understand if there were any correlation between the risk perceptions when travelling and the feelings about the terrorism threat, a correlation analysis was performed.

Risk perceptions when travelling

Table 25.1 summarises the results regarding the risk perceptions of European Millennials when travelling. Respondents cited the organisation risk (the possibility of having

Table 25.1 Risk perceptions when travelling

When travelling, how often do you think about the following? (1= Never; 5= Always)	1+2	3	4+5
I am afraid I may experience mechanical, equipment, organisational problems…	35	26.5	**53.7**
I fear that the experience will not be worth the money spent	**72.5**	18.4	9
I fear I could get sick or have an accident	**66.5**	21.1	12.4
I am afraid of becoming involved in political turmoil	**78.7**	13.4	8
I fear that my travel experience will not reflect my personality	**83**	12.4	4.5
I fear that the travel experience will not provide personal satisfaction	**72.5**	15.5	11,9
I am afraid that my travel choice/experience can affect the opinion that others have of me	**91.1**	5.9	2,9
I fear being involved in a terrorist act	**40.8**	16.5	42.8
I am afraid of being victim of crime or violence	**62.4**	20.9	15.8
I worry about getting lost in places or losing contact with my travel companions	**65**	21.8	13.2
I am afraid I will find the local culture too strange or that I will not fit in	**81.9**	13.7	4.4
I am afraid it will take too long or will be a waste of time	**84.5**	11.6	3.8

Source: The authors.

mechanical, equipment, or organisational problems) and terrorism as their deepest fears when traveling. By contrast, the risks related to money, political turmoil, personality, satisfaction, social image, cultural aspects or time are ranked were the least significant risks. Health and accidents, violence, and crime, and getting lost or being separated from travel companions are risks that are less valued but were still pointed out in a great number of answers.

Table 25.2 shows that the feelings of safety travelling in Europe and outside the continent are mixed. When asked if general travels are risky and if they feel comfortable when they have to travel, respondents agree that it is safer and that they feel more confident and less nervous when they travel inside Europe. However, in specific types of travels, such as

Table 25.2 Feelings of (un)safety travelling in Europe vs outside Europe

What are your safety perceptions travelling in Europe and outside Europe? (1=Very Unsafe; 5 = Very safe)	In Europe			Outside Europe		
	1+2	3	4+5	1+2	3	4+5
Travelling is risky right now	**58.3**	27.5	14.2	34.6	39.6	25.9
I feel very comfortable traveling right now	9.7	17.9	**72.3**	17.3	29.6	53.1
Vacation travel is perfectly safe	**15**	27.7	57.4	20.4	39.8	39.9
Travelling for business or work is perfectly safe	**13,6**	26.0	60.3	19.3	35.6	45.2
Travelling to visit friends or relatives is perfectly safe	**10.9**	21.2	67.9	16.4	29.3	54.2
Travelling with my family is very safe	**13.6**	25.9	60.6	19.9	35.7	44.5
I feel nervous about traveling right now	**76.4**	12.9	10.7	67.5	18.4	14.3
Additional security measures at airports make travelling safer	12.5	**21.3**	66.2	12.8	**22.1**	65
Safety is the most important attribute a destination can offer	17.9	**24.8**	57.2	16.8	**25.0**	58.2
Safety is a serious matter to me	5.8	16.5	**77.7**	4.2	15.5	**80.2**

Source: The authors

vacation or business trips, when they travel to visit friends and family and when they travel with their family, the answers are more scattered, even though Millennials feel safer travelling within the European continent. With regard to safety, the participants in the study agree that this is a serious matter, that it is the most important attribute a destination can offer, and that additional security measures at airports will make travelling safer. These feelings are stronger when travelling outside Europe than in intraregional trips.

Feelings about the terrorism threat

With regard to the respondents' interest in terrorism in media, it is clear that European Millennials are not particularly interested in that kind of content in the media. In fact, they tend not to read or search for those contents, but in a moderate way they also do not ignore news about terrorism and pay some attention to content about terrorist attacks (Table 25.3). When asked if they forward information about the issue, mainly participants answer negatively and even claim that they do not waste time consuming information about terrorism or do not actively seek information about the topic.

Table 25.4 shows that European Millennials have a moderate level of fear when it comes to terrorism threats. Respondents seem to believe that tourists, as well as normal citizens, are not likely to be targets of terrorist attacks, but they also agree that they need more information about how to protect themselves from a terrorist attack, since they are worried that a terrorist attack may happen in Europe or in their country and that either they themselves or someone from their family could be one of the victims. They also claim that they have no trouble sleeping, are not willing to change any aspect of their lives or travel plans or to renounce any of their civil liberties or freedoms because of the terrorism threat.

Table 25.5 summarises the Millennials' feelings of safety when they engage in leisure and tourism activities. The analysis of the answers shows that activities that take place in crowded spaces, such as going to theme parks, concerts, and festivals, visiting city centres, shopping malls and markets, going to casinos or discos, going out at night, attending sport events, and going to religious places are among the activities that pose a higher risk when people think about the threat of terrorism. Leisure and tourism activities that take place in open spaces and sites with organised activities are considered safer. This is the case with

Table 25.3 Interest about terrorism in media

Regarding information and contents about terrorism would you say that… (1= strongly disagree; 5=strongly agree)	1+2	3	4+5
I am really interested in news and contents about terrorist attacks	30.5	26,1	35.8
When I have the opportunity, I watch/read/listen and search for news and contents about terrorist attacks	54.3	25.9	19.8
I never ignore a report or content about terrorist attacks	27	30.1	42.9
I pay great attention to news and/or contents about terrorist attacks	29.4	31.2	39.4
I tend to share information with my friends when I find interesting topics about terrorist events	67.7	19.5	12.8
When I am watching/reading some information about terrorist events, I tend to get so involved that I lose track of time	81.4	13.0	5.6
Whenever I can, I actively seek information about terrorist events	83.8	12.0	4.2

Source: The authors.

Table 25.4 Feelings about terrorism threat

Personally, would you say that… (1= strongly disagree; 5=strongly agree)	1+2	3	4+5
Tourists are not likely to be targets of terrorism	**42.2**	32,8	25
Normal citizens are not likely to be targets of terrorism	**41.5**	30,4	28
I need more information on how to protect myself from a terrorist attack or event	23.9	29,0	**47.2**
I am concerned that I, myself, or someone from my family could be a victim of terrorism	24.4	24,4	**51.2**
I am concerned that a terrorist attack may happen in my country in a near future	25.3	25,3	**49.3**
I am concerned that a terrorist attack can happen in Europe in a near future	14	20,9	**65,1**
I have been troubled and felt nervous for fear of some terrorist attack	**58.1**	24,8	17.1
I have had trouble sleeping because of my fear for terrorism	**91.2**	5,4	3.3
I am thinking about changing many aspects of my life and routines because of my fear of terrorism	**88.4**	8,3	3.3
I am thinking about changing travel or vacation plans due to fear of terrorism	**73.3**	16,5	10.2
I wouldn't mind giving up some civil liberties and freedoms to make my country safer from terrorist attacks	**63**	21.5	15.5

Source: The authors.

Table 25.5 Terrorism threat in tourism and leisure activities

Taking into account the threat of terrorism, how safe would you feel in the following situations? (1=very unsafe; 5=very safe)	1+2	3	4+5
Going to amusement or theme parks	10.1	24.7	65.2
Going to natural areas such as national parks or forests, hiking…	2.8	10.6	86.6
Visiting art galleries, museums, monuments	8.3	20.3	71.4
Going to the beach, rivers or lakes	5	11.5	83.5
Going to concerts, festivals, shows	28.4	25.3	46.3
Visiting historical and cultural sites, city centres	13	25.0	62
Having dinner in restaurants	5	14.3	80.7
Shopping in shopping malls, streets, markets	12.4	23.0	64.6
Going to casinos or gambling	13.3	25.5	61.3
Going out at night, dancing, going to nightclubs or discos	20.7	23.2	56.1
Sightseeing and participating in organised visits	7.8	21.4	70.9
Attending sport events	17.6	24.4	58
Staying in hotels, resorts, camping sites	6.1	14.9	79
Doing sport in closed spaces (sports halls, stadiums)	5.5	17.5	77
Going to religious places, doing pilgrimages or participating in religious events	22.2	27.8	50

Source: The authors

going to natural areas, visiting art galleries and museums, going to the beach, dining in restaurants, participating in organised visits, staying in hotels, and doing sports, which are considered safe activities.

Correlations between risk perceptions when travelling and the feelings about the terrorism threat

Before performing the correlation analysis, a factor analysis was conducted, specifically for items "Feelings of (un)safety travelling in Europe", Feelings of (un)safety travelling outside Europe", "Interest about terrorism in media", and "Feelings about terrorism threat". The risk perception variables were analysed independently due to the complexity of each risk perception type.

Tables 25.6–25.9 summarise the factor loadings, variance percentages, and Cronbach's alphas of the several exploratory factorial analyses. The factor extraction was made through the Kaiser method and the varimax rotation method was executed.

The final model for "Feelings of (un)safety travelling in Europe" (Table 25.6) showed a Kaiser–Meyer–Olkin measure of sampling adequacy was satisfactory at 0.844 and the results obtained from Bartlett's sphericity test showed that the variables were significantly correlated ($p = 0.000$), indicating that the use of factor analysis is adequate (Sharma, 1996). One variable was removed for showing a factor saturation above 0.5 in more than one factor. Two factors emerged with eigenvalues above 1.0. The rotated model explained 69.8%

Table 25.6 Factorial analysis of feelings of (un)safety travelling in Europe

Dimensions	Item	Communalities	Loadings	Cronbach's alpha	% of variance
Is safe to travel	I feel very comfortable traveling right now	0.459	0.676	0.917	48.4
	Vacation travel is perfectly safe	0.821	0.905		
	Travelling for business or work is perfectly safe	0.845	0.919		
	Travelling to visit friends or relatives is perfectly safe	0.844	0.919		
	Travelling with my family is very safe	0.800	0.893		
Importance of safety measures	Additional security measures at airports make traveling safer	0.439	0.604	0.609	21.4
	Safety is the most important attribute a destination can offer	0.713	0.843		
	Safety is a serious matter to me	0.669	0.797		
Total Variance Explained (%)					69.8

Source: The authors.

Table 25.7 Factorial analysis of feelings of (un)safety travelling outside Europe

Dimensions	Item	Communalities	Loadings	Cronbach's alpha	% of variance
Is safe to travel	Travelling isn't risky right now	0.412	0.603	0.886	43.6
	I feel very comfortable traveling right now	0.557	0.744		
	Vacation travel is perfectly safe	0.737	0.857		
	Travelling for business or work is perfectly safe	0.781	0.879		
	Travelling to visit friends or relatives is perfectly safe	0.767	0.872		
	Travelling with my family is very safe	0.750	0.856		
	I don't feel nervous about traveling right now	0.447	0.597		
Importance of safety measures	Additional security measures at airports make traveling safer	0.403	0.590	0.607	18.3
	Safety is the most important attribute a destination can offer	0.701	0.830		
	Safety is a serious matter to me	0.631	0.783		
	Total Variance Explained (%)				61.9

Source: The authors.

Table 25.8 Factorial analysis of interest about terrorism in media

Dimensions	Item	Communalities	Loadings	Cronbach's alpha	% of variance
Passive interest	I am really interested about news and contents about terrorist attacks	0.682	0.749	0.799	35.9
	I never ignore a report or content about terrorist attacks	0.699	0.835		
	I pay much attention on news and/or contents about terrorist attacks	0.814	0.858		
Active interest	I tend to forward information for my friends when I find interesting topics about terrorist events	0.579	0.702	0.771	35.5
	When I am watching/reading some information about terrorist events. I tend to get so involved that I lose track of time	0.757	0.849		
	Whenever I can. I actively seek information about terrorist events	0.751	0.861		
Total Variance Explained					71.4

Source: The authors.

Table 25.9 Factorial analysis of feelings about terrorism threat

Dimensions	Item	Communalities	Loadings	Cronbach's alfa	% of variance
Fear of being a target	Tourists are not likely to be targets of terrorism	0.869	0.924	0.820	27.3
	Normal citizens are not likely to be targets of terrorism	0.867	0.929		
Concern about terrorism attacks	I need more information about how to protect myself from a terrorist attack or event	0.350	0.553	0.765	24.2
	I am concerned that I. myself. or someone from my family could be a victim of terrorism	0.759	0.857		
	I am concerned that a terrorist attack can happen in my country in a near future	0.758	0.850		
	I am concerned that a terrorist attack can happen in Europe in a near future	0.757	0.865		
Changing behaviours regarding terrorism	I have had trouble sleeping because of the terrorism fear	0.684	0.822	0.848	17.5
	I am thinking about changing many aspects of my life and routines because of the terrorism fear	0.771	0.868		
	I am thinking about changing travel or vacation plans by terrorism fear	0.605	0.747		
	I think all the time that I wouldn't mind to give up some civil liberties and freedoms to make my country safer from terrorist attacks	0.485	0.579		
Total Variance Explained (%)					69.0

Source: The authors.

of the total variance. It was possible to obtain two factors: "Is safe to travel" (Cronbach's alpha, 0.917) and "Importance of safety measures" (Cronbach's alpha, 0,70).

To measure "Feelings of (un)safety travelling outside Europe" the same 10 questions mentioned above were considered (Table 25.7). These questions were retained in two factors or domains with eigenvalues above 1.0. The considered model showed a Kaiser–Meyer–Olkin measure of sampling adequacy satisfactory at 0.867 and the results obtained from

Bartlett's sphericity test showed that the variables are significantly correlated (p = 0.000), indicating that the use of factor analysis was appropriate (Sharma, 1996). The rotated model explained 61.9% of the total variance. The first factor was labelled as "Is safe to travel" (Cronbach's alpha, 0.886) and the second as "Importance of safety measures" (Cronbach's alpha, 0.607). In general, it is established that the ideal lower limit for the Cronbach's alpha is 0.70, still values near 0.60 can be considered acceptable (Streiner, 2003).

The factorial analysis was performed with the items concerning the interest about terrorism information in the media (Table 25.8). The variable "When I have the opportunity I watch/read/hear and search for news and contents about terrorist attacks" has been removed because it was associated with more than one factor. The use of factor analysis was appropriate (Sharma, 1996), since the final model showed a Kaiser–Meyer–Olkin measure of sampling adequacy was satisfactory at 0.761 and the results obtained from Bartlett's sphericity test showed that the variables were significantly correlated (p = 0.000). The rotated model explained 71.4% of the total variance. The construct was divided in two dimensions; the first factor was named as "passive interest" explaining 35.9% of the variance and the second was "active interest" explaining 35.5%. The Cronbach's Alpha were 0.799 and 0.771 for the first and second factors, respectively.

The construct "feelings about terrorism threat" was submitted to a factorial analysis (Table 25.9). The variable "I have been bothered and feel nervous by terrorism fear" was removed because it was associated with more than one factor. The use of factor analysis was appropriate (Sharma, 1996), since the final model showed a Kaiser–Meyer–Olkin measure of sampling adequacy satisfactory at 0.762 and the results obtained from Bartlett's sphericity test showed that the variables were significantly correlated (p = 0.000). The rotated model explained 69.0% of the total variance. It was possible to derive three factors: "fear of being a target" explaining 27.3% of the variance with a Cronbach's alpha 0.820; the second was dubbed as "concern about terrorism attacks" explaining 24.2% with a Cronbach's alpha 0.765; and the third "changing behaviours regarding terrorism" explaining 17.5% with a Cronbach's alpha of 0.848.

In order to evaluate the association between the variables/dimensions a correlation analysis was performed. The Spearman and Pearson correlation coefficients were used. Table 25.10 shows the values of the Spearman correlation coefficient between the risk perception types and the dimensions of safety perceptions and interest about terrorism information in media (Table 25.10).

The association between the different "risk perception types" and "is safe to travel" were significant and negative. The greater the perception that it was safe to travel, the lower the perception of risk. However, these associations, in general, are weak. Even though, those correlations are stronger when travelling outside Europe compared to travelling inside Europe. Note that the stronger associations are between terrorism risk, crime, and violence, and "is safe to travel", independently if considering travelling in or outside Europe.

Regarding the correlations for the importance of safety measures and the different risk perception types, the associations were significant for the following risk types: organisational, health, political turmoil, terrorism, crime, and violence, getting lost and cultural risk. These correlations were positive; the higher is the importance attributed to safety measures, the higher were the perceptions of the risks. Again, the associations were stronger for travelling outside Europe when compared to travelling in Europe. The stronger associations were between terrorism risk, crime, and violence, and "importance of safety measures", independently if considering travelling in or outside Europe. Note that these risk types were the same as reported as having stronger associations with "is safe to travel".

Table 25.10 Correlations between risk perception types and the dimensions of feelings of (un)safety and interest about terrorism information in media

Risk Perception Types	Feelings of (un)safety Travelling in Europe		Feelings of (un)safety Travelling outside Europe		Interest about terrorism information in media	
	Is safe to travel	Importance of safety measures	Is safe to travel	Importance of safety measures	Passive Interest	Active Interest
Organizational Risk	−.230**	.118**	−.252**	.146**	.084**	.046
Financial Risk	−.153**	.004	−.171**	.018	.135**	−.157
Health Risk	−.257**	.129**	−.345**	.144**	.152**	−0.006
Political turmoil Risk	−.268**	.095**	−.331**	.111**	.138**	−0.003
Psychological Risk	−.121**	−0.005	−.156**	.002	.181**	−0.039
Satisfaction Risk	−.160**	.032	−.165**	.055*	.131**	−0.041
Self-image Risk	−.136**	.000	−.141**	−0.036	.244**	−0.026
Terrorism Risk	−.339**	.223**	−.377**	.247**	.197**	.154**
Crime and Violence Risk	−.310**	.214**	−.400**	.239**	.127**	.103**
Getting lost Risk	−.220**	.145**	−.323**	.158**	.140**	.035
Cultural Risk	−.222**	.067*	−.294**	.069**	.187**	−0.010
Time risk	−.223**	.021	−.273**	.011	.128**	−.173

** Correlation is significant in the level 0.01 (unilateral).
* Correlation is significant in the level 0.05 (unilateral).
Source: The authors.

The passive interest about terrorism information in the media was positively associated to all the different risk perception types in analysis. The higher correlations were observed in associations with the risk of self-image and terrorism. The active interest about terrorism information in media was positively associated only terrorism risk and crime and violence risk. For the other kinds of risks, no significant correlations were found.

Table 25.11 reports the values of the Pearson correlation coefficient between the several dimensions of feelings of safety travelling in and outside Europe and the different dimensions of feelings about terrorism threat and terrorism information in the media.

For travelling in Europe, on average, the higher was the "fear of being a target" the lower was the perception of "is safe to travel". The same was observed when considering travelling outside Europe, but in this case the relationship was stronger. The relationship between "fear of being a target" and the "importance of safety measures" was stronger, but in this case it was positive. On average, the higher was the "fear of being a target" the higher was

Table 25.11 Correlations between feelings of (un)safety travelling in and outside Europe and the dimensions of feelings about terrorism threat and interest about terrorism information in the media

		Feelings about terrorism threat			Interest about terrorism information in media	
		Fear of being a target	Concern about terrorism attacks	Changing behaviours regarding terrorism	Passive Interest	Active Interest
Feelings of (un)safety Travelling in Europe	Is safe to travel	−.183**	−.238**	−0.017	−0.048	−.077**
	Importance of safety measures	.394**	.118**	.015	.061*	.210**
Feelings of (un)safety Travelling outside Europe	Is safe to travel	−.191**	−.275**	.003	−.108**	−.060*
	Importance of safety measures	.383**	.100**	.024	.041	.227**

** Correlation is significant in the level 0.01 (unilateral).
* Correlation is significant in the level 0.05 (unilateral).
Source: The authors.

the "importance attributed to safety measures". In this case the correlation was slightly stronger in travelling in Europe when compared with travelling outside Europe.

The "concern about terrorist attacks" was negatively associated to the construct of "is safe to travel", as expected, in travel in and outside Europe, being stronger for the latter. The relationship between the "importance of safety measures" and "concern about terrorist attacks" was positive and very weak. Regarding the relationship between "changing behaviours regarding terrorism" and the two dimensions of "feelings of (un)safety travelling in and outside Europe", no significant correlations were found.

It was possible to find a significant and positive association between the "active interest about terrorism information in the media" and the "importance of safety measures", for travelling in and outside Europe. For travel in and outside Europe, the association with the "active interest about terrorism information" were negative and very weak. In travel in Europe, the "passive interest about terrorism information" was positively associated to the "importance of safety measures". For travel outside Europe, no significant correlation was found. The dimension "is safe to travel" was negatively associated to "passive interest about terrorism information in the media", in the case of travelling outside Europe. For travelling inside Europe no significant relationship was found.

Conclusions, discussion, and implications

The results of this study bring some light on how the younger generations are facing the permanent presence of the terrorism menace and the impact it has on the way they travel, face daily life, consume information in the media, and future behaviours and decisions. This is an important contribution by bringing some light on the generation that will account for more than half of the tourism market until 2050. Their feelings, perceptions, and behaviours towards a threat that is constantly in daily life worldwide is an important asset to create a more resilient tourism industry.

Results indicated that most Millennials were not afraid; nonetheless, they are vigilant and worried. Only organisational and terrorism risk were significant, but they also fear crime and violence and are afraid they might get lost. In fact, for Millennials, the risks of terrorism, crime, and violence are strongly connected with the feelings of (un)safety travelling in, and especially outside, Europe. This is an interesting result showing that European Millennials are worried especially with two types of risks: violence and practical issues regarding their travels as having problems with organisation or being lost. These results confirm past studies evidencing the practical characteristics of this generation (Deloitte, 2017; EUROSTAT, 2020; Gen C Travel, 2018). Considering this result, it is expected that these consumers, as being the future of the tourism market, will be more and more attentive to organisational issues and crime and violence in the destinations, especially when they are getting older. In the near future, destination management organisations (DMOs) should focus on communication campaigns to make travelers feel safer regarding those risks in the destinations visited. Also, tour operators should prevent those risks by offering travel insurance regarding organisational risks and additional information to avoid sites where tourists could be more menaced in terms of violence and crime.

European Millennials feel that travelling within Europe and outside the continent is safe but they agree that further safety measures are crucial. The importance attributed to safety measures is also related with the fear of being a target and the concern about terrorism attacks. Since European Millennials are very aware of the importance of those measures, in consequence, they fear more being targets of terrorism attacks, augmenting their concern with this kind of violence. The different types of risk perceptions have a negative correlation with the feelings of safety. This is more evident when people travel within Europe than when they travel outside of the continent, this perhaps should be understood in the sense that Millennials feel that the old continent is, at the end of the day, the safest region to travel. In this line, it is crucial that tourism infrastructure, and especially airports, continue to develop safety measures in order to make tourists feel safer regarding terrorism events. Some of the safety measures implemented in the airports after the 9/11 events, public transportation and tourism sites are getting obsolete and weaker. Tourists need to feel that their safety is being assured, especially in a more and more uncertain future.

Risk perception has a positive correlation with the passive interest in terrorism information in the media and the active search is positively correlated with the risk of terrorism and crime/violence. Also, the more passive interest in information about terrorism in the media, the higher is on average the perception of all risk types when travelling. This can be suggested as a way for European Millennials to show that they are conscious of the menace since they are always connected. Also, news about terrorism and violence are a constant factor in the media, provoking an increased awareness of this danger in public opinion, and confirming past research (Hall, 2002; Klein, 2018; Schmid & DeGraaf, 1982; Seabra et al., 2012; Weimann & Winn, 1994). Certainly, this interest about terrorism in the news will continue, not only for this generation, but especially for the youngsters that are always online. Media play an important role by offering wider information about terrorism and other events of crime; however, excessive news coverage could create a general climate of fear with impacts for travelling. DMOs should invest in crisis comunnications in order to balance the constant negative media discourse.

Findings also prove that terrorism is part of European Millennials' life experiences. Millennials are interested in information about terrorism in the media, but they do not actively seek out that information. This generation feel that terrorist attacks might happen in Europe and in their own country in the near future; however, they do not consider changing any aspects of their lives because of that. Surprisingly, despite the concern about terrorism and the feelings of (un)safety when travelling, there is no evidence that Millennials plan to change their behaviours in the future. In fact, Millennials feel generally safe doing most of their daily activities, except for activities involving large crowds: concerts and festivals, discos, sport events and religious events, perhaps because most of the recent attacks of terrorist organisations happened in places highly frequented by sizable crowds (START, 2022). They feel that travelling inside and outside Europe is safe, and this is negatively correlated with the fear of being a target, the protection measures against terrorist threats and the active search for information about the topic in the media. In addition, safety measures' importance was positively connected with the passive and active interest of information about terrorism in the media, reinforcing the attention that Millennials give to safety measures. These are very interesting results, allowing us to conclude that European Millennials are aware of the terrorism risk, but, because of the frequency of attacks during their existence, they relativise this risk and learn to live with it, confirming past studies (Uriely, Maoz, & Reichel, 2007; Uriely, Yonay, & Simchai, 2002).

In conclusion, DMOs and tourism industry stakeholders are very aware of Millennial consumers' importance in the present and near future. Terrorism fear is a constant in the present day and this chapter's results prove its influence on consumer behaviour and decisions. So, tourism destinations and the respective stakeholders must be prepared with different action plans to make tourists feel safer. An interesting result is the unanimous opinion that it is safe to travel inside Europe, meaning that this is an important opportunity for European countries to promote their destination to the domestic regional market. In addition, the importance of media in the public opinion formation regarding terrorism is emphasised by the results, meaning that media, promotion, and crisis communication are crucial to deal with this menace, placing the emphasis on safety (Avraham, 2013; Avraham, 2021). In fact, safety should be considered as a brand for successful destinations (Avraham, 2018).

Funding

This research received support from the Centre of Studies in Geography and Spatial Planning (CEGOT) and Research Center in Digital Services (CISeD) funded by national funds through the Foundation for Science and Technology (FCT) under the reference UIDB/04084/2020 and UIDB/05583/2020.

References

Avraham, E. (2013). Crisis communication, image restoration, and battling stereotypes of terror and wars: media strategies for attracting tourism to middle eastern countries. *American Behavioral Scientist*, *20*(10), 1–18.

Avraham, E. (2018). Nation branding and marketing strategies for combatting tourism crises and stereotypes toward destinations. *Journal of Business Research*.

Avraham, E. (2021). Combating tourism crisis following terror attacks: Image repair strategies for European destinations since 2014. *Current Issues in Tourism*, *24*(8), 1079–1092.

Cavagnaro, E., Staffieri, S., & Postma, A. (2018). Understanding millennials' tourism experience: Values and meaning to travel as a key for identifying target clusters for youth (sustainable) tourism. *Journal of Tourism Futures*, *4*(1), 31–42.

CBI – Ministry of Foreign Affairs. (2nd de February de 2021). *Which trends offer opportunities or pose threats on the European outbound tourism market?* Obtido em 20th de January de 2022, de Ministry of Foreign Affairs: https://www.cbi.eu/market-information/tourism/trends

Chen, R., & Noriega, P. (2003). The impacts of terrorism: Perceptions of faculty and students on safety and security in tourism. *Journal of Travel & Tourism Marketing*, *15*(2/3), 81–98.

Debevec, K., Schewe, C., Madden, T., & Diamond, W. (2013). Are today's Millennials splintering into a new generational cohort? Maybe! *Journal of Consumer Behaviour*, *12*(1), 20–31.

Deloitte. (2017). *The Deloitte Millennial Survey 2017: Apprehensive millennials: seeking stability and opportunities in an uncertain world*. London: Deloitte. Obtido de www2.deloitte.com/uk/en/pages/about-deloitte-uk/articles/millennial-survey.html

EUROSTAT. (July de 2020). *Being young in Europe today – demographic trends*. Obtido em 20th de January de 2022, de EUROSTAT: https://ec.europa.eu/eurostat/statistics-explained/index.php?title=Being_young_in_Europe_today_-_demographic_trends

Gen C Travel. (April de 2018). *Gen C Travel – Intelligent insights on connected travellers*. Obtido em 17 de November de 2021, de Travel and tourism for the millennial generation: https://genctraveller.com/travel-and-tourism-for-the-millennial-generation/

Hall, C. (2002). Travel safety, terrorism and the media: The significance of the issue-attention cycle. *Current Issues in Tourism*, *5*, 458–466. doi:10.1080/13683500208667935

Huddy, L., Feldman, S., Capelos, T., & Provost, C. (2002). The consequences of terrorism: Disentangling the effects of personal and national threat. *Political Psychology*, *23*(3), 485–509.

Huddy, L., Khatib, N., & Capelos, T. (2001). Trends: Reactions to the terrorist attacks of September 11. *The Public Opinion Quarterly*, *66*(3), 418–450.

Jeuring, J., & Becken, S. (2013). Tourists and severe weather – An exploration of the role of 'locus of responsibility'in protective behaviour decisions. *Tourism Management*, *37*, 193–202.

Jin, H. (2003). Compounding consumer interest: Effects of advertising campaign publicity on the ability to recall subsequent advertisements. *Journal of Advertising*, *32*(4), 29–41.

Ketter, E. (2021). Millennial travel: tourism micro-trends of European Generation Y. *Journal of Tourism Futures*, *7*(2), 192–196.

Klein, A. (2018). Negative spaces: Terrorist attempts to erase cultural history and the critical media coverage. *Media, War & Conflict*, *11*(2), 265–281.

Llussá, T., & Tavares, J. (2007). The economics of terrorism: What we know, what we should know and the data we need. Em P. Keefer, & N. Loayza (Edits.), *Terrorism, economic development, and political openness* (pp. 233–296). Cambridge: Cambridge University Press.

Maslow, A. (1943). A theory of human motivation. *Psychological Review*, *50*, 370–396.

Nielsen. (2017). *Young and ready to travel: a look at millennial travelers*. New York: Nielsen. Obtido de https://www.nielsen.com/wp-content/uploads/sites/3/2019/04/nielsen-millennial-traveler-study-jan-2017.pdf

Schmid, A., & DeGraaf, J. (1982). *Violence as communications: Isurgent terrorism and the western news media*. Beverly Hills: Sage.

Seabra, C. (2019). Terrorism and tourism consumption revisited. In A. Correia, A. Fyall, & M. Kozak (Eds.), *Experiential Consumption and Marketing in Tourism: A cross-cultural contex* (pp. 58–75). Oxford: Goodfellow Publishers.

Seabra, C., Abrantes, J., & Kastenholz, E. (2012). TerrorScale: A scale to measure the contact of international tourists with terrorism. *Journal of Tourism Research & Hospitality*, *1*(4), 1–8.

Seabra, C., Abrantes, J., & Kastenholz, E. (2014). The influence of terrorism risk perception on purchase involvement and safety concern international travellers. *Journal of Marketing Management*, *30*(9–10), 874–903.

Seabra, C., AlAshry, M., Çınar, K., Raja, I., Reis, M., & Sadiq, N. (2021). Restrictions' acceptance and risk perception in a COVID-19 context by young generations. *International Journal of Tourism Cities*, *7*(2), 463–491. doi:https://doi.org/10.1108/IJTC-08-2020-0165

Seabra, C., Dolnicar, S., Abrantes, J., & Kastenholz, E. (2013). Heterogeneity in risk and safety perceptions of international tourists. *Tourism Management*, *36*, 502–510.

Sharma, S. (1996). *Applied multivariate techniques*. New York: John Wiley & Sons.

Skinner, H., Sarpong, D., & White, G. (2018). Meeting the needs of the Millennials and Generation Z: Gamification in tourism through geocaching. *Journal of Tourism Futures*, *4*(1), 93–104.

START – Maryland National Consortium for the Study of Terrorism and Responses to Terrorism. (2022). *Global Terrorism Database*. Obtido em 10th de January de 2022, de http://www.start.umd.edu/gtd/

Streiner, D. (2003). Starting at the beginning: An introduction to coefficient alpha and internal consistency. *Journal of Personality Assessment*, *80*(1), 99–103.

UN – United Nations. (2022). *Sustainable Development Goals – Goal 16: Promote just, peaceful and inclusive societies*. Accessed in May 2022, from United Nations Sustainable Development: https://www.un.org/sustainabledevelopment/peace-justice/

Uriely, N., Maoz, D., & Reichel, A. (2007). Rationalising terror-related risks: The case of Israeli tourists in Sinai. *International Journal of Tourism Research*, *9*, 1–8.

Uriely, N., Yonay, Y., & Simchai, D. (2002). Backpacking experiences: A Type and form analysis. *Annals of Tourism Research*, *29*(2), 520–538.

Weimann, G., & Winn, C. (1994). *The theater of terror: Mass media and international terrorism*. New York: Longman.

Wong, J.-Y., & Yeh, C. (2009). Tourist hesitation in destination decision making. *Annals of Tourism Research*, *36*(1), 6–23.

World Economic Forum. (2022). *The Global Risks Report 2021 – 16th Edition*. Cologne/Geneva: World Economic Foruam.

WorldData. (2022). *Comparison of the largest terrorist groups*. Accessed on 19 January 2022, from WorldData: https://www.worlddata.info/terrorism/groups.php

WTO – World Tourism Organization. (2020). *Tourism Highlights*. Madrid: World Tourism Organization.

26 Multi-crisis destinations (MCDs)
Towards a future research agenda

Sofia Lachhab, Alastair M. Morrison, Tina Šegota and J. Andres Coca-Stefaniak

Introduction

Tourism studies have generally focused on the impact of one crisis at a time. For example, Škare et al. (2021) and Chin and Musa (2021) examined the effect of the COVID-19 crisis. Corbet et al. (2019) reviewed the impacts of terrorism on European tourism. Rossello et al. (2020) addressed the effect of natural disasters on international tourism. However, researchers have also realised that international tourism is frequently faced with multiple crises simultaneously (Page et al., 2012). For instance, in 2009, the world faced a global financial crisis, topped up by the start of the Swine flu pandemic. Furthermore, Avraham (2021) describes the U.S. as a multi-crisis destination, which suffers from various crises such as terrorism, a health crises, and natural disasters. Avraham (2021) also asserts that the frequency and the multiplicity of crises and their adverse effects have increased over time. However, a literature gap exists regarding destinations that experience multiple crises for prolonged periods. This chapter introduces the construct of the multi-crisis destination (hereinafter MCD) and presents potential avenues for future research on MCDs.

Definition of a multi-crisis destination (MCD)

A brief and precise working definition of the construct is indispensable to conceptualise and identify the term 'multi-crisis destination'. Based on the tourism crisis literature (e.g., Avraham, 2021; Duan et al., 2022; Morakabati, 2013), this chapter proposes the first-known definition of an MCD as "a destination prone to frequent and substantial crises, often socio-economic in nature though not excluding other typologies, over a period that may span decades and often resulting in negative outcomes".

Developing an index for MCDs – the MCDI

Looking at the above-proposed definition of an MCD, the following question arises: what destinations classify as MCDs? Unfortunately, the answer to this question is complex, as there is no scale or index for measuring the phenomenon. It is simple to identify places where there are wars and civil unrest based on news reports; however, this is insufficient given the broader range of crises and the need to take a longer-term perspective.

There is a need to develop a scale or index for measuring MCDs, which is a crucial element of the future research agenda. The first step is to choose between creating a scale or an index for MCDs. Both are viable options and should be considered. However, scale development would require more time and input from multiple perspectives. Therefore, developing a Multi-Crisis Destination Index (MCDI) is more expedient. In addition, Diamantopoulos and Winklhofer (2001) suggest the use of formative (causal) indicators in creating indexes. The next step, therefore, is for researchers to identify these indicators.

The variable or domain to be investigated is crises. Churchill, Jr. (1979, p. 67) suggests that "the literature should indicate how the variable has been defined previously and how many dimensions or components it has". Here, the starting point for delineating the dimensions (indicators) of MCDs could be the various types of crises, which include: 1) natural disasters; 2) security crises; 3) economic and financial crises; 4) health safety crises; 5) environmental safety crises; 6) accidents and calamities; and 7) public opinion crises (Duan et al., 2022). Next, countries could be measured based on their proneness to these crises and their actual performance during a specified period (e.g., the immediately preceding ten years).

The next step in the research process to develop the MCDI would be to identify the measurement data that address the proneness and performance of countries for the seven types of crises. Fortunately, multiple country rank indexes are available; 20 of them are presented in Table 26.1. There are undoubtedly other candidate indexes, and future researchers should systematically identify them.

The results in these indexes are measured in different units, making it challenging to harmonise these into an MCDI. For example, Egypt received a score of 43.3 on the Environmental Performance Index 2020 (ranking 94th in the world), while it scored 89.87 on the Quality of Life Index (ranking it 80th in the world). Scores, therefore, will have to be standardised for calculating the MCDI positions of countries. Researchers will also have to determine which index scores to include and if any weighting of crises and index scores will be necessary. The main steps in developing the MCDI are visualised in Figure 26.1.

Another important question arises: why should researchers devote their time to developing the MCDI? To determine the functions and applications of MCDI, the Travel & Tourism Competitiveness Index (TTCI) provides valuable insights (World Economic Forum, 2022). TTCI is widely used by countries to benchmark their tourism against other countries and to develop policies and strategies to receive higher rankings in forthcoming editions. Egypt, for example, ranked 65th among 140 countries on the 2019 version of TTCI. In addition, national destination management organisations (DMOs) use the TTCI rankings to identify their closest competitors and benchmark. MCDI scores may also be helpful to consumers in determining the relative risks of travelling to different countries. Finally, government agencies issuing travel advisories would also find MCDI scores helpful when advising their residents about the levels of safety concerns for visitations to specific countries.

There is a need for tourism researchers to develop a Multi-Crisis Destination Index (MCDI) that will be of value to several audiences on the supply and the demand sides of tourism. The presence of the MCDI would advance the research on tourism crises and provide a platform on which tourism researchers can build to add further depth to the literature. The development of the MCDI will be challenging and complex; however, it is undoubtedly a worthwhile research endeavour.

Examples of multi-crisis destinations

Without an established index or scale, it is challenging to identify MCDs. All regions of the world suffer from tourism crises. However, different geographic areas experience particular problems, and crisis frequencies vary. A systematic review of the tourism crisis literature

Table 26.1 Potential indicator indexes by type of crisis

Crisis types	Names of index	Source	Website
Overall	The Crisis Index	The Organization for World Peace	https://theowp.org/our-work/crisis-index/
	INFORM Global Crisis Severity Index	INFORM	https://drmkc.jrc.ec.europa.eu/inform-index/Portals/0/InfoRM/GCSI/GCSI%20Beta%20Brochure%20Single.pdf
Security and political	Political Stability Index	TheGlobalEconomy.com	https://www.theglobaleconomy.com/rankings/wb_political_stability/
	Global Peace Index	Vision of Humanity	https://www.visionofhumanity.org/maps/#/
	Global Terrorism Index	Vision of Humanity	https://www.visionofhumanity.org/maps/global-terrorism-index/#/
	Safety Index	Numbeo	https://www.numbeo.com/crime/rankings_by_country.jsp?title=2021&displayColumn=1
	Positive Peace Index	Vision of Humanity	https://www.visionofhumanity.org/maps/positive-peace-index/#/
Natural and environmental	Environmental Performance Index	Yale University	https://epi.yale.edu/about-epi
	Ecological Threat Register	Vision of Humanity	https://www.visionofhumanity.org/maps/ecological-threat-register-2021/#/
	World's Most Polluted Countries	IQAir	https://www.iqair.com/world-most-polluted-countries
Health and safety	Global Health Security Index	Economist – NTI – Johns Hopkins	https://www.ghsindex.org/
Economic and financial	Global Multidimensional Poverty Index	Oxford Poverty & Human Development Initiative	https://ophi.org.uk/global-mpi-2021/
	Behavioral Finance and Financial Stability	Harvard Business School	https://www.hbs.edu/behavioral-finance-and-financial-stability/data/Pages/global.aspx
Other	Human Development Index	UNDP	https://hdr.undp.org/en/content/human-development-index-hdi
	World Happiness Report	World Happiness Report	https://worldhappiness.report/ed/2021/
	Gross National Happiness Index	Government of Bhutan	https://ophi.org.uk/policy/gross-national-happiness-index/
	Country Opinion Survey	World Bank	https://countrysurveys.worldbank.org/
	Quality of Life Index	Numbeo	https://www.numbeo.com/quality-of-life/rankings_by_country.jsp
	Country Brand Ranking (Tourism)	Bloom Consulting	https://www.bloom-consulting.com/en/country-brand-ranking
	FutureBrand Country Index	FutureBrand	https://www.futurebrand.com/futurebrand-country-index

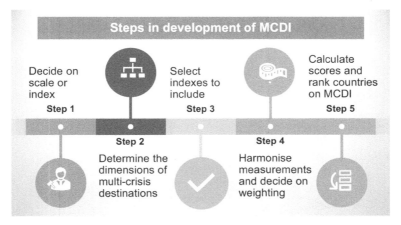

Figure 26.1 Steps in developing the multi-crisis destination index (MCDI)
Source: Authors.

conducted by Duan et al. (2022) showed that Asia and the Middle East were the most researched regions (Southeast Asia, East Asia, West Asia/Middle East, and South Asia). This study revealed that the West Asia/Middle East crises were connected to security (e.g., terrorist attacks, political unrest, and wars). Morakabati (2013) identified the Middle East as a multi-crisis region characterised by repeated crises over extensive periods. As mentioned earlier, Avraham (2021) denoted the U.S. as a multi-crisis destination. Another example of a multi-crisis destination is Turkey. This country has been through several incidents in a short period. These crises affected international tourist arrivals in 2002–2006 and 2016. Figure 26.2 shows the relationship between international tourist arrivals in the world, Turkey, and Egypt, between 1995 and 2019. Data were indexed with 1995 set at one hundred. The upper line is the world tourist arrival index, the middle line is the Turkey arrival index, and the lower line is the Egypt arrival index. Several differences in arrival levels can be seen in Figure 26.2. For example, it is noticeable that between 2011 and 2017, Egypt experienced declining visitor arrivals, while arrivals in Turkey and the world were more stable and increasing.

The multi-crisis destination is a unique and under-researched topic. Three initial characteristics of MCDs based on the literature and actual experiences are: 1) high frequency of crises over short periods; 2) multiple crises of different types; and 3) negative impacts on tourism and reputation. The countries that do not fit the definition of MCDs and their characteristics are considered non-MCDs. However, there is still a need to expand upon the dimensions of MCDs, and this will be accomplished through the development of the MCDI, as outlined earlier.

Traditionally, it was assumed that tourism is about selling landscapes. However, there is now the notion that safety should also be marketed (Fernández-Morales, Cisneros-Martínez, & McCabe, 2016). The absence of safe environments may be another characteristic or dimension of MCDs. Tourism is highly interconnected with all other aspects of society (political, economic, social-cultural, technological, environmental, and legal). Therefore, tourism destinations are more vulnerable to all crisis types and are impacted by political unrest, natural disasters, economic downturns, and acts of terrorism (Paraskevas et al., 2013). Asia, Africa, and the Middle East are known to have faced multiple crises (Shaheer, 2017). In the Middle

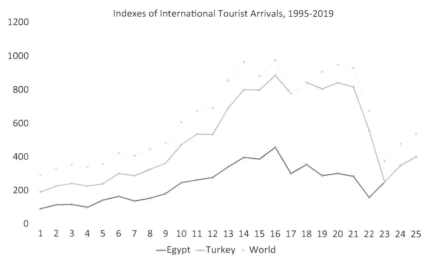

Figure 26.2 Indexes of international tourist arrivals, 1995–2019.
Sources: World Bank (2021), UNWTO (2011).

East, Egypt has been ruled by several presidents over the years. After the end of the monarchy in Egypt in 1952 (Islami, 2016), the first president was Abdel Nasser (1956–1970), followed by Anwar El Sadat (1970–1981), Hosni Mubarak (1981–2011), Mohamed Morsi (2012–2013) and the current president, Abdel Fattah El Sisi (2014–2022). During this period, from 1956 to 2021, Egypt experienced several crises. Figure 26.3 presents all the different crises Egypt has encountered since 2004.

From the timeline in Figure 26.3, it is noticeable that most events occurring in Egypt were terrorist acts or political events born of uncertainty. However, since 2014 after the election of President Abdul Fattah al-Sisi, the political sector has been more stable as the same president was elected for a second term in March 2018. Nevertheless, the crisis affected many Egyptian industries, mainly tourism, which experienced a significant decline. For example, after the 2011 revolution, the revenue of Egyptian monuments dropped by 95%, the number of hotel stays decreased by five million overnights in three years, and overall tourism revenue was reduced by 54% (Kingsley, 2014).

Spatial distribution of MCDs

Crises are progressively crossing geographical, infrastructural, and cultural boundaries (Ansell et al., 2021). As a result, the world has experienced several crises over time. However, individual countries perform differently regarding crisis impacts due to their frequency and extent of impacts.

The Global Peace Index (2021) ranks all countries according to levels of peace. It is noticeable from Table 26.2 that most low-peace-level nations are situated in countries with frequent crises in Africa (South Sudan, Somalia, the Democratic Republic of the Congo, Central African Republic), the Middle East (Yemen, Syria, Iraq), Asia (Afghanistan) and Russia. Although all these countries have similarities, most are developing nations and experience civil unrest.

Multi-crisis destinations (MCDs) 343

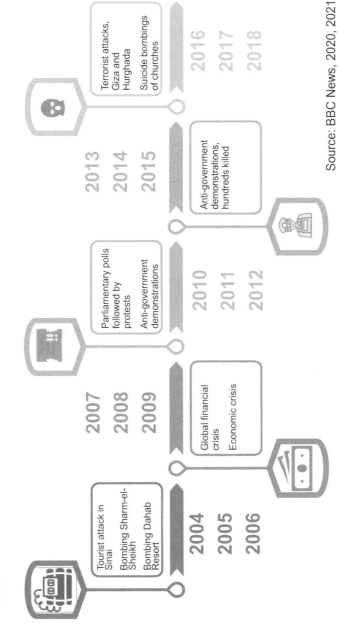

Figure 26.3 Egypt events timeline, 2004–2018.
Source: Modified from BBC News information, Knell (2020), Bowen (2021).

Table 26.2 Global Peace Index ratings for 2021

Country rank	Country	2021 overall GPI score
163	Afghanistan	3.631
162	Yemen	3.407
161	Syria	3.371
160	South Sudan	3.363
159	Iraq	3.257
149	Turkey	2.843
126	Egypt	2.397
1	Iceland	1.100

Source: Global Peace Index (2022).

Table 26.3 The five most negatively ranked countries for safety and security and ongoing conflicts

Country rank overall	Country	Safety and security domain	Ongoing conflict domain
163	Afghanistan	4.258	3.641
	Venezuela	4.089	
162	Yemen	3.944	3.559
161	Syria		3.828
160	South Sudan	3.891	
159	Iraq	3.888	
149	Turkey		
126	Egypt		
158	Somalia		3.474
156	Libya		3.3

Source: Global Peace Index (2022).

Tables 26.2 and 26.3 show the five least peaceful countries in terms of safety and security and ongoing conflict. Afghanistan, Yemen, Syria, South Sudan, and Iraq are ranked as the least peaceful countries. In addition, Venezuela is negatively ranked for safety and security, while Somalia and Libya are negatively ranked for ongoing conflicts.

Duan et al. (2022) developed a world map showing the geographical distribution of tourism crises based on the frequency of published studies on tourism crises. Although Asia and the Middle East were the most studied regions for tourism crises, Morakabati (2013) also mentioned that problems in these regions were prolonged and frequent. This information suggests that several Asian and Middle Eastern countries are MCDs.

Impacts of crises on tourism in MCDs

The significant growth tourism has experienced in the past 70 years, and due to the recent unplanned events and multiple crises happening in the world (terrorism, war, financial crises, natural disasters), a significant interest in the crisis topic has developed. Research on tourism crises intensified further after the beginning of the COVID-19 pandemic (Li et al., 2022). The tourism industry is particularly prone to external shocks such as wars, disease, extreme weather conditions (cyclones, tornadoes, mudslides, hurricanes, droughts), elections, adverse publicity, terrorist attacks, transport accidents, pollution, earthquakes, volcanic eruptions, political events, strikes (e.g., airline strikes), electricity shortages, recessions, and fluctuations in economic conditions (George, 2013).

The existing literature shows an apparent demand for knowledge about crises in tourism destinations, their impacts, and how to deal with them (Rindrasih et al., 2019; Duan et al., 2022; Jin et al., 2019). Dealing with a crisis in tourism as a fragile domain needs more attention when it comes to crisis management because it revolves around tourist experiences that are intangible and perishable, making it an open system (Tayeh & Mustafa, 2018). A crisis that affects tourism is an event or range of situations that destroy the market potential, reputation, and image of destinations or a whole region (PATA, 2011). Accordingly, there are five main types of crises that affect the tourism sector (UNWTO, 2011): 1) environmental crisis (Kim et al., 2006); 2) social and political events; 3) health-related crises (Hitchcock & Putra, 2005); 4) technological crises; and 5) economic events (Chu, 2008). These crises are characterised by a high-threat level, a short time to make decisions, and urgency (Faulkner, 2001). Hall (2010) asserts that financial and economic crises are the most researched in the tourism literature, followed by research on natural disasters due to their implications for travel and tourism at various levels as well as their substantial capacity to influence destination image (Huang & Min, 2002; Baade & Matheson, 2007; Wu & Shimizu, 2020). Several studies have shown an interest in the impact of crises on tourism. However, these publications were usually related to single-crisis impacts, often in small regions and single destinations (Rindrasih et al., 2019).

Related to the study of multi-crisis destinations (MCDs), Rindrasih et al. (2019) examined the impact of long-term, multi-disaster events on the performance of Indonesia's tourism industry. The authors present Indonesia as a multi-disaster destination that has experienced many natural and non-natural disasters over the past two decades. The findings showed that a destination has a different impact based on whether it is a single crisis or a multi-layered disaster. These elements influence the degree of effect on the tourism industry and the recovery period. Tourism is an industry that depends intensely on destination image (Morakabati, 2013), and crises significantly negatively influence the reputation and image of destinations (Rittichainuwat et al., 2018). The negative impacts are more significant for destinations with more than one crisis at a time, or sequentially. For MCDs, this may require more time to recover and regain reputational status. Unfortunately, existing studies do not examine the differing impacts of crises for single and multi-crisis destinations and whether crises last longer in MCDs. For this reason, researchers need to focus more on this topic, especially since many destinations suffer multiple crises and need advice and support.

How do MCDs develop resilience?

Several definitions of resilience have emerged within the literature. A general agreement is that resilience is the ability of a system to deal with change (Berkes & Ross, 2013; Cheer & Lew, 2017). Tourism is one field where resilience has been recognised, and this involves investigating a system's resilience level and ability to respond to short-term crises (Eakin et al., 2012; Guo et al., 2018; Bethune et al., 2022). However, various publications have stated that there is a need for more studies focusing on resilience within multi-crisis destinations (Koronis & Ponis, 2018).

Resilience is commonly linked with a system's ability to rebuild after a disturbance (Fath et al., 2015). Holling's (2001) adaptive cycle model (Figure 26.4) is a strong and valuable metaphor for system dynamics. The model engages the "infinity loop" pattern around the

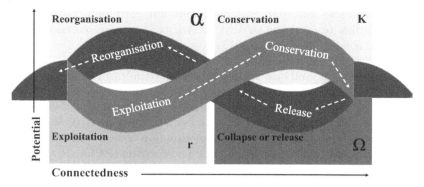

Figure 26.4 The adaptive cycle or "Holling Loop".
Source: Holling (1973). Authors' design.

four critical resilience variables and draws analytical attention to highlighting the relationship between the four factors. The adaptive cycle aptly depicts the continuous nature and recurring crises within MCDs.

Reddy et al. (2020) present a framework for building tourism resilience in a post-conflict destination. They assert that the proposed framework guides the destination authorities while recovering from a crisis. From the organisational resilience background, Kantur and İşeri-Say (2012) created a framework to suggest a new outcome concept of organisational evaluability. In their framework, Kantur and İşeri-Say (2012) categorised the sources of organisational resilience as strategic capacity, contextual integrity, perceptual stance and strategic acting. From a destination resilience perspective, Cahyanto and Pennington-Gray (2017) formulated a conceptual framework containing indicators that help tourism destinations to measure tourism crises. Similarly, Alves et al. (2020) revealed the crucial role of cooperation among businesses in a tourism destination, especially SMEs, in building individual and collective resilience.

The unique characteristics of MCDs require particular resilience strategies, helping them cope with the high frequency and overlapping crises. There is an urgent necessity for tourism scholars to investigate MCD resilience strategies that will be beneficial for many such destinations. This need is particularly true given recent world events, including COVID-19 and the Ukraine war.

Future trends and perspectives for MCDs

Here are several future trends for MCDs during the outstanding call for more significant research on the concept. These are as follows:

- The number of MCDs worldwide will increase rather than decrease.
- Crisis recovery times will be prolonged in MCDs.
- There will be reputational and other spillover effects of MCDs on neighbouring territories.
- Tourists will increasingly avoid MCDs as concerns for safety and security intensify.
- Individual governments and multi-country alliances will pay greater attention to the exceptional circumstances of MCDs.
- Tourism businesses and trade associations will develop special training and assistance programmes for colleagues operating in MCDs.

From the research perspective, although crisis management and resilience development are established fields in tourism, much of this scholarship has adopted a linear approach to these concepts. Thus, the overall lifecycle of a crisis affecting a tourism destination consists of the following: a crisis is usually foreseen (or unexpected); the crisis develops slowly or quite suddenly; the crisis affects the destination, and management plans are implemented to deal with it, and a retrospective analysis is completed with a focus on building resilience to future problems. Some destinations tend to be more prone to a sequential repeating of this cycle as one crisis is followed in time by another and then further crises. The lifecycle for economic crises lasts about ten years to coincide with the general trend of significant global economic downturns. For other crises, the peaks and troughs of the cycle are separated by more protracted and, at times, unpredictable timescales. This situation is particularly the case of natural disasters linked to geological processes such as earthquakes, volcanic eruptions, and tsunamis. Timescales for other natural events more closely related to climate, such as extreme weather events, significant floods, or wildfires, appear to be shortening, too, with research showing that they are closely related to global climate change patterns influenced by human activity rather than merely natural processes. However, recent events have brought a new dimension to the MCD concept posited in this chapter. As the global COVID-19 pandemic continues to take its toll on destinations globally despite early signs of a tentative recovery, new crises have emerged in countries along with the global health crisis.

For instance, Sri Lanka is facing the genuine possibility of a significant economic failure due to a default in the country's public debt interest payments while COVID-19 infections continue to rise. Ukraine, which suffered high infection rates and deaths during COVID-19, is facing a major crisis of its own as a result of the invasion by Russia, which has led to thousands of casualties, nearly five million people displaced due to the conflict, and several million people facing shortages of food, potable water, electricity, and heating in besieged cities, which are being bombed regularly. Although the conflict has not spread to other parts of Europe, its fallout has resulted in over three million refugees fleeing the country and seeking temporary sanctuary in Poland, Romania, Moldova, Slovakia, and Hungary before further travel to other European countries. Parallel to all this, high hydrocarbon prices worldwide have led to the genuine threat of an impending economic crisis triggered by growing consumer price inflation trends in Europe, North America, and much of the Western world. The advent of the MCD concept may have to be redrawn soon since destinations may not only face different crises over time in a linear format but, indeed, have to contend with several crises concurrently. In addition, it is worth considering that even for other concurrent crises, each crisis may be subject to its lifecycle with different peaks, troughs, timescales, and impacts on tourism. Thus, research and practice regarding MCDs need to address several questions and issues, namely:

1 How do linear MCDs differ from other MCDs where crises take place concurrently? Do potential visitors perceive the former types of destinations as safer?
2 How should planning and strategy formulation differ between both types of MCDs regarding the complexity of crisis management planning and future-proofing resilience strategies?
3 Should managing crises foster a higher degree of regional competition between destinations to remain competitive in global markets? For instance, would Sri Lanka be willing to promote India as a destination during a significant crisis, knowing that India will

reciprocate as soon as conditions are more favourable for Sri Lanka? Would that likely happen between other countries at the regional level, too (e.g., Italy and Spain), to prevent the loss of tourists to other competing regions (e.g., Morocco, Turkey, Egypt)? In times of life-threatening crises (e.g., significant droughts) facing wildlife, predators and prey cooperate to improve their collective chances of survival. However, is this an option that political leaders and key decision-makers in tourism would entertain in the highly competitive – and more civilised – global tourism ecosystem?

4 Are MCDs more resilient and better at managing crises than tourism destinations that have been less prone historically to crises? More generally, could MCDs' regular crisis management make them more competitive in a future scenario involving a more unstable world from a geopolitical perspective?

5 How to calculate MCDI for countries (diagnosis) and suggest strategies (prognosis)?

Similar arguments apply to the impact of multiple crises on the sustainable development of destinations. Over the last ten years, a consensus has slowly emerged on the need for destinations to develop future-proofing strategies to contend with climate change in terms of its short-term impacts (e.g., freak weather events) and longer-term threats (e.g., sea level rises). However, this consensus over the potential importance of the issue, rather than necessarily specific action and investment, has been centred on one type of crisis – climate change. If recent events linked to the armed conflict in Ukraine and high hydrocarbon prices are anything to go by, it would appear that, given a choice, political leaders will tend to prioritise economic development over environmental or even social issues. So, if the ongoing climate change debate is to be sidelined in favour of more pressing (financial) issues, how does this bode for managing multi-crisis processes (linear or not) in destinations? Just as we thought that the COVID-19 pandemic was under control and the focus could return to the UN SDGs, shorter-term crises divert the attention of policy makers, not without reason, from longer-term threats. Overall, humankind has much to learn from nature regarding how to read the signs of an impending crisis and, crucially, how to deal with it.

Stakeholder actions, initiatives, and the SDGs

What are the interests of and implications for various stakeholders in addressing the future trends and issues for multi-crisis destinations? In tourism, the stakeholders include the tourists, tourism operators (e.g., enterprises, SMEs) and organisations (e.g., DMOs, trade associations), community (host population), government (public sector), and the environment (Buhalis, 2000; Morrison, 2019). Table 26.4 provides recommendations for actions and initiatives to be undertaken by these stakeholders in the future, and researchers and scholars are added as the sixth group of stakeholders.

Do MCDs contribute to the SDGs now and on the path toward 2030–2040–2050? This is a new topic; however, if MCDs do not manage crises appropriately and build greater resilience, there will be a negative effect on achieving specific SDGs. For example, continuing and unresolved crises will exacerbate poverty (SDG 1), hunger (SDG 2), and health and wellbeing (SDG 3); they will also negatively impact infrastructure and industry (SDG 9), cities and communities (SDG 11), and peace and justice (SDG 16). In addition, specific crises will also degrade the land (SDG 15), oceans, and other water bodies (SDG 14). However, if MCDs can overcome crises and build superior resilience, the opposite will be true, and these places will move closer to meeting the SDGs.

Table 26.4 Recommended stakeholder actions and initiatives

MCD stakeholders	Required actions and initiatives
Tourists	• Increase awareness of multi-crisis destinations • Support MCDs whenever possible
Tourism operators and organisations	• Build up resilience to crises • Form collaborative partnerships to counter crises
Community	• Co-create innovative solutions to crisis recovery and resilience
Government	• Advise SMEs on how to cope with crises and build resilience • Consult MCDI when developing travel advisories • Establish policies addressing the particular circumstances of multi-crisis destinations
Environment	• Form environmental sustainability guidelines that support crisis recovery and resilience
Researchers and scholars	• Compare the effects of linear (one by one, sequential) versus concurrent crises in MCDs • Conduct more research studies on MCDs • Develop the Multi-Crisis Destination Index (MDCI) • Periodically report on MCDI results

Source: Authors.

Conclusions

This chapter calls for the recognition of multi-crisis destinations by the tourism industry and academic scholars. MCDs are a neglected yet crucial topic in tourism. There is a need to construct a multi-crisis destination index (MCDI) to determine which nations fit into this category. After that, more fine-grained research on MCDs is required in the decades to follow, and policy initiatives are needed to facilitate crisis recovery and resilience building. It has been insinuated that countries such as Egypt, Indonesia, Turkey, and the U.S. might be MCDs; this remains to be corroborated.

There is perceived to be a connection between MCDs and UN Sustainable Development Goals (SDGs). MCDs may find it more challenging to achieve the SDGs as resources become depleted owing to continuing crises, and recovery may be slower in these nations. Some MCDs are likely among the poorest and most unstable countries in the world and improving their status vis-à-vis the SDGs will be critical to achieving the UN's overall objectives.

References

Alves, J. C., Lok, T. C., Luo, Y. B., and Hao, W. (2020). Crisis challenges of small firms in Macao during the COVID-19 pandemic. *Frontiers of Business Research in China*, *14*, 26. https://doi.org/10.1186/s11782-020-00094-2

Ansell, C., Sørensen, E., and Torfing, J. (2021). The COVID-19 pandemic as a game changer for public administration and leadership? The need for robust governance responses to turbulent problems. *Public Management Review*, *23*(7), 949–960.

Avraham, E. (2021). From 9/11 through Katrina to COVID-19: crisis recovery campaigns for American destinations. *Current Issues in Tourism*, *24*(20), 2875–2889.

Baade, R. A., and Matheson, V. A. (2007). Professional sports, Hurricane Katrina and the Economic Redevelopment of New Orleans. *Contemporary Economic Policy*, *25*, 591–603.

Berkes, F., and Ross, H. (2013). Community resilience: toward an integrated approach. *Society and Natural Resources*, *26*(1), 5–20.

Bethune, E., Buhalis, D., and Miles, L. (2022). Real time response (RTR): Conceptualising a smart systems approach to destination resilience. *Journal of Destination Marketing & Management*, *23*, 100687.

Bowen, D. (2021). Arab Spring: How the uprisings still echo, 10 years on, BBC News, 12 February, https://www.bbc.com/news/world-middle-east-56000950

Buhalis, D. (2000). Marketing the competitive destination of the future. *Tourism Management*, *21*, 97–116.

Cahyanto, I., and Pennington-Gray, L. (2017). Toward a comprehensive destination crisis resilience framework. *Travel and Tourism Research Association: Advancing tourism research globally*. 21. https://scholarworks.umass.edu/ttra/2017/Academic_Papers_Oral/2

Cheer, J. M., and Lew, A. A. (2017). Sustainable tourism development: Towards resilience in tourism. *Interaction*, *45*(1), 10–15.

Chin, W. L. and Musa, S. F. P. D. (2021). Agritourism resilience against COVID-19: Impacts and management strategies. *Cogent Social Sciences*, *7*(1), https://doi.org/10.1080/23311886.2021.1950290

Chu, F. (2008). A fractionally integrated autoregressive moving average approach to forecasting tourism demand. *Tourism Management*, *29*(1), 79–88.

Churchill, Jr., G. A. (1979). A paradigm for developing better measures of marketing constructs. *Journal of Marketing Research*, *16*(1), 64–73.

Corbet, S., O'Connell, J. F., Efthymiou, M., Guiomard, C., and Lucey, B. (2019). The impact of terrorism on European tourism. *Annals of Tourism Research*, *75*, 1–17.

Diamantopoulos, A., and Winklhofer, H. M. (2001). Index construction with formative indicators: An alternative to scale development. *Journal of Marketing Research*, *38*(2), 269–277.

Duan, J., Xie, C., and Morrison, A. M. (2022). Tourism Crises and Impacts on Destinations: A Systematic Review of the Tourism and Hospitality Literature. *Journal of Hospitality & Tourism Research*, *46*(4), 667–695. https://doi.org/10.1177/1096348021994194

Eakin, H., Benessaiah, K., and Morales, H. (2012). Livelihoods and landscapes at the threshold of change: disaster and resilience in a Chiapas coffee community. *Regional Environmental Change*, *12*, 475–488.

Fath, B. D., Dean, C. A., and Katzmair, H. (2015). Navigating the adaptive cycle: an approach to managing the resilience of social systems. *Ecology and Society*, *20*(2), 24. http://dx.doi.org/10.5751/ES-07467-200224

Faulkner, B. (2001). Towards a framework for tourism disaster management. *Tourism Management*, *22*(2), 135–147.

Fernández-Morales, A., Cisneros-Martínez, J. D., and McCabe, S. (2016). Seasonal concentration of tourism demand: Decomposition analysis and marketing implications. *Tourism Management*, *56*, 172–190.

George, R. (2013). *Marketing tourism in South Africa*. 4th Edition. Cape Town: Oxford University Press.

Guo, Y.-F., Luo, Y.-H., Lam, L., Cross, W., Plummer, V., and Zhang, J.-P. (2018). Burnout and its association with resilience in nurses: A cross-sectional study. *Journal of Clinical Nursing*, *27*(1/2), 441–449.

Hall, C. M. (2010). Crisis events in tourism: Subjects of Crisis in tourism. *Current Issues in Tourism*, *13*(5), 401–417.

Hitchcock, M., and Putra, I. N. D. (2005). The Bali bombings: Tourism crisis management and conflict avoidance. *Current Issues in Tourism*, *8*(1), 62–76.

Holling, C. S. (1973). Resilience and stability of ecological systems. *Annual Review of Ecology and Systematics*, *4*(1), 1–23.

Huang, J. H., and Min, J. C. H. (2002). Earthquake devastation and recovery in tourism: the Taiwan case. *Tourism Management*, *23*(2), 145–154.

Islami, I. (2016). Political history of modern Egypt. *ILIRIA International Review*, *6*(1), 189–206.

Jin, X. C., Qu, M., and Bao, J. (2019). Impact of crisis events on Chinese outbound tourist flow: A framework for post-events growth. *Tourism Management*, *74*, 334–344.

Kantur, D., and İşeri-Say, A. (2012). Organisational resilience: A conceptual integrative framework. *Journal of Management and Organization*, *18*(6), 762–773.

Kim, H. Y., Chen, M. H., and Jang, S. S. (2006). Tourism expansion and economic development: The case of Taiwan. *Tourism Management*, *27*(5), 925–933.

Kingsley, P. (2014). Egypt's tourism revenues fall after political upheavals, The Guardian, https://www.theguardian.com/world/2014/aug/29/egypt-tourism-revenue-falls-95-percent

Knell, Y. (2020). Egypt desperate to revive coronavirus-hit tourism industry, BBC News, 15 July, https://www.bbc.com/news/world-middle-east-53402983

Koronis, E., and Ponis, S. (2018). Better than before: the resilient organisation in crisis mode. *Journal of Business Strategy*, *39*(1), 32–42.

Li, Z., Zhao, Q., Huo, T., Shao, Y., and Hu, Z. (2022). COVID-19: Management focus of reopened tourist destinations. *Current Issues in Tourism*, *25*(1), 14–20.

Morakabati, Y. (2013). Tourism in the Middle East: Conflicts, crises and economic diversification, some critical issues. *International Journal of Tourism Research*, *15*(4), 375–387.

Morrison, A. M. (2019). *Marketing and managing tourism destinations*, 2nd ed. London: Routledge.

Pacific Asia Travel Association (PATA). (2011). *Bounce back. Tourism risk, crisis and recovery management guide*, Bangkok: PATA.

Page, S., Song, H., and Wu, D. C. (2012). Assessing the impacts of the global economic crisis and swine flu on inbound tourism demand in the United Kingdom. *Tourism Management*, *51*(2), 142–153.

Paraskevas, A., Altinay, L., McLean, J., and Cooper, C. (2013). Crisis knowledge in tourism: Types, flows and governance. *Annals of Tourism Research*, *41*, 130–152.

Reddy, M.V., Boyd, S. W., and Nica, M. (2020). Towards a post-conflict tourism recovery framework. *Annals of Tourism Research*, *84*, 102940.

Rindrasih, E., Witte, P., Spit, T., and Zoomers, A. (2019). Tourism and disasters: Impact of disaster events on tourism development in Indonesia 1998–2016 and structural approach policy responses. *Journal of Service Science and Management*, *12*(02), 93–115.

Rittichainuwat, B., Nelson, R., and Rahmafitria, F. (2018). Applying the perceived probability of risk and bias toward optimism: Implications for travel decisions in the face of natural disasters. *Tourism Management*, *66*, 221–232.

Rossello, J., Becken, S., and Santana-Gallego, M. (2020). The effects of natural disasters on international tourism: A global analysis. *Tourism Management*, *79*, https://doi.org/10.1016/j.tourman.2020.104080

Shaheer, I. (2017). Tourism marketing for developing countries: Battling stereotypes and crises in Asia, Africa and the Middle East. *Place Branding and Public Diplomacy*, *13*, 98–99.

Škare, V., Soriano, D. R., and Porado-Rochoń, M. (2021). Impact of COVID-19 on the travel and tourism industry. *Technological Forecasting and Social Change*, *163*, https://doi.org/10.1016/j.techfore.2020.120469

Tayeh, S. N. A., and Mustafa, M. H. (2018). Tourism crisis management in Jordan: An overview. *Advances in Social Sciences Research Journal*, *5*(2), 283–290.

UNWTO. (2011). *Toolbox for crisis communications in tourism: Checklist and best practices*. Madrid: UNWTO.

World Bank. (2021). *International tourism, number of arrivals*, https://data.worldbank.org/indicator/ST.INT.ARVL

World Economic Forum. (2022). *Travel & Tourism Competitiveness Index*, https://reports.weforum.org/travel-and-tourism-competitiveness-report-2019/rankings/

Wu, L., and Shimizu, T. (2020). Analysing dynamic change of tourism destination image under the occurrence of a natural disaster: Evidence from Japan. *Current Issues in Tourism*, *23*(16), 2042–2058.

27 Understanding Gen Z as a future workforce in the hospitality and tourism industry

Angie Yeonsook Im and Dae-Young Kim

Introduction

The tourism and hospitality industry accounts for more than 10% of the global GDP, providing more than 330 million employment opportunities worldwide in 2019 (World Travel & Tourism Council, 2020). Younger workers – specifically those composing Generation Z (or "Gen Z") who were born between 1997 and 2012 – will be the largest demographic cohort joining the entry-level workforce over the next few years, largely replacing older retirees. In Europe, about 20% of the industry's workforce is 25 years old or under, and young talent accounts for over 30% of the industry in the U.S. and over 40% in Australia (Goh & Okumus, 2020). As Generation Z accounts for more than one-third of the world's population, the involvement of this cohort will have a profound impact on the global tourism and hospitality industry. This generational change and workforce trend, in particular, have prompted the industry to better understand this new generational cohort so as to better attract and retain talented individuals within it.

The industry fundamentally relies on human interaction, suggesting that its employees play the most critical role in delivering services, representing companies, and interacting with, satisfying, and delighting customers (Baum, 2019). Nevertheless, the sector has long suffered from high staff turnover, as its jobs are stigmatised as offering low pay, limited career opportunities, emotional labour, and long and irregular working hours (Baum, 2019). Jobs in the sector are often seen as precarious, and thus sustaining young human assets can be challenging for the industry (Robinson et al., 2019). With an emerging Gen Z workforce with idiosyncratic characteristics entering the industry, it is critical to contemplate how to invite and develop this new talent to make favourable contributions to the global tourism and hospitality industry. This chapter extends the understanding of the future Gen Z workforce by discussing their idiosyncratic perspectives with regard to life, careers, and society. It also provides a moment to think about how to attract and foster these significant human assets in the industry.

Generational differences in the workplace

A generation is commonly defined as a cohort of individuals who were born and have lived during the same time period, but generational research has elaborated that, beyond having proximate birth years, a generation shares the influence of historical, social, political, economic, and cultural events during their impressionable adolescence and early adulthood (Schuman & Corning, 2014). As major events experienced as children shape the commonalities of a generation in terms of beliefs, perceptions, values, attitudes, and behaviours, understanding generational cohorts requires knowing how they learn, think, interact, communicate, and take part in the world. Although there is no unanimous agreement on the cut-off points of generations, this chapter uses widely adopted, conventionally accepted brackets of generational cohorts in its discussions.

Generation Z is the latest generation to enter the workplace. Consisting of individuals born in the period 1997–2012, it accounted for about 20.35% of the U.S. population as of July 2020 (Statista, 2020). Currently comprising 30% of the global population, Generation Z will make up a significant part of the workforce in the next few years (Koop, 2021). Notably, this generation has experienced a capricious social, political, and economic landscape. For instance, in the U.S., school violence has been a salient issue for this generation, making it more focused on the importance of safety and security. Bullying, whether off- or online, has become a major societal concern. Furthermore, this generation witnessed an intense competition for the U.S. presidency between a woman and an African American candidate for the first time in history. Similarly, Generation Z grew up watching many debates related to LGBTQ tolerance and same-sex marriage.

Generations have different attitudes and perspectives toward jobs (Lyons & Kuron, 2014). Baby Boomers (those born in 1946–1964) tend to be sensitive to job status, security, and stability (Kupperschmidt, 2000). Generation X (those born in 1965–1980) is likely to pursue a work–life balance, has less respect for authority than previous generations, and tends to be more accepting of changes and challenges for higher pay (Gursoy et al., 2008). Generation Y (those born in 1981–1996, also known as Millennials) has higher expectations for the work environment and is more comfortable with changes in the workplace. To a greater extent than is the case with Baby Boomers, Generations X and Y regard challenges and development opportunities as important. While Baby Boomers and Generation X tend to have a greater organisational commitment (and thus lower turnover intention), Generation Y feels less of a reciprocal obligation to organisations and is therefore more prone to turnover (Lub et al., 2012). An important question, then, is how this newer cohort, Generation Z, will differ from the majority of the industry's current workforce.

Table 27.1 Comparisons of generations

	Baby Boomers	Generation X	Generation Y	Generation Z
Also known as	Boomers	Gen X, Xers, Post Boomers	Millennials, Gen Y, Nexters	Gen Z, Gen Zers
Born	1946–1964	1965–1980	1981–1996	1997–2012
Influencing Events	Post-war TV Economic growth and prosperity	Political transition Increase in crime Decrease in birth rate Cable TV and pop culture Recessions Financial insecurity	Globalisation Emergence of Internet Increase in school violence Economic expansion	Smartphone Artificial intelligence and technological disruption Social media Gun violence Bullying at school Natural disasters Worst recession
Characteristics	Collectivist Revolutionary	Materialistic Individual	Globalist Oriented to self	Undefined ID Diverse and inclusive
Value	Ideology	Status Luxury goods	Experience Flagships	Uniqueness Ethics Diversity

Note. Adopted from Sakdiyakorn et al. (2021) and Francis & Hoefel (2018).

Characteristics of Generation Z

Digital natives

Given the exponential growth of technology in the late 20th century, a discussion of Generation Z's characteristics cannot neglect the close relationship between the cohort and technology. Unlike the experience of previous generations, digital technology has suffused the entire life cycle of Generation Z (Kim & Park, 2020). They were born into a world in which the Internet and the World Wide Web had already been established. As a generation, they grew up with smartphones, iPads, and the rise of social media. It is unsurprising that these digital natives have a strong emotional bond to technology that helps create their life experience on a daily basis, from education, exercise, and entertainment to social interaction (Turner, 2015). While previous cohorts witnessed the advent of smartphones and social media, Generation Z has always known these technologies and cannot imagine a world that does not allow seamless, constant connection to others, even in other parts of the world.

Concerns have also been raised about this digital generation. Because they live with constant online communication through multiple devices, its members are not likely to secure quality time in which to contemplate important matters without interruption. In addition, the generation's environment promotes the instantaneous and contemporaneous nature of online communication, which does not engender a focus on a single critical issue (Turkle, 2017). A deluge of communication via online social media has shaped the generation's multitasking behaviour; consequently, its members seem to pay continuous attention to what they do, but the attention is only partial (Berkup, 2014). That is, they may be physically present, but their attention may be elsewhere. Extensive technology consumption has also influenced the cohort's apparent curtailed attention span.

Electronic communication

A close relationship with technology has influenced Generation Z's communication style, which may present challenges and opportunities in the workplace across industries, including the hospitality and tourism sector. One distinct characteristic of the cohort is its preference for emails or text messages over face-to-face communication. This generation tends to spend less time with in-person social interactions, preferring to be alone and relying on electronic communication (Twenge et al., 2019). However, it is important to recognise that Gen Zers are also radically inclusive in their communication (Francis & Hoefel, 2018). Because its members have followed various online communities based on their interests and causes, they are naturally more comfortable having dialogues with those from different backgrounds and circumstances.

Entrepreneurial mindset

Generation Z is accustomed to finding answers and solutions independently using resources on the Internet, so it is unsurprising that the cohort perceives itself as self-sufficient and independent. Generation Z displays characteristics similar to those of entrepreneurs, who are self-reliant, confident, innovative, and goal-oriented (Ozkan & Solmaz, 2015). This generation was born into a culture of active leisure and regards productive activities as important routines in their lives, even during free time. The cohort enjoys freedom and independence, as they were largely influenced by parents who encouraged them to think and make decisions independently (Sakdiyakorn et al., 2021). More than 60% of Generation Z indicates an interest in starting their own businesses (Merriman, 2015). Its members want to become entrepreneurs because they aspire to live purposeful lives with enhanced control and create an environmentally and socially better future with enhanced control.

Solitary learners

Being accustomed to solitary learning, Generation Z uses technology as a tool to learn alone (Seemiller & Grace, 2016), obtaining information and knowledge through various online resources, such as social media, web pages, and videos. Compared to previous generations, Gen Zers are self-reliant in their learning, as reflected in their negative attitudes toward group projects in higher education (Schlee et al., 2020). The Gen Z cohort is significantly less likely to appreciate projects involving team activities and more likely to be anxious about the quality of work produced this way (Schlee et al., 2020), which may prompt organisations to consider how to foster a team environment that the tourism and hospitality industry requires with these individuals as productive members.

Diversity and inclusion

Gen Z is known as the most ethnically and racially diverse cohort within the U.S. A bare majority of the generation in the U.S. (52%) is non-Hispanic White, which is significantly less than in previous generations; this same category accounts for 61% of Millennials and 82% of Baby Boomers (Fry & Parker, 2018). However, diversity is not limited to ethnicity and race for Gen Z, but also includes a range of individual identities. For example, the LGBTQ community has a larger representation in this generation compared to previous ones as a result of its propensity to be more open about disclosing sexual orientation (Fry & Parker, 2018). This generation exhibits non-traditional perspectives on identity and gender, refusing to check boxes for demographic questions (Francis & Hoefel, 2018). The generation's gender fluidity and refusal to accept easily defined identities reflect its ceaseless effort to experiment and change the self while assessing a plethora of information and influences from non-physical virtual communities (Francis & Hoefel, 2018). Because the cohort upholds the value of supporting identity-related causes, it more genuinely cares about human rights related to race, sexual orientation, gender, and ethnicity. The generation is truly global. In its wireless world, Generation Z enjoys diverse cultural expressions of a planet without boundaries, including movies, foods, trends, fashion, and blogs. Consequently, its members believe that the ideals of inclusion and tolerance for others are crucial to society. This perception of the importance of openness and diversity also applies to their desired workplaces.

Meaningful work

Having witnessed the hardship of family members during the Great Recession, Gen Z is viewed as a generational cohort whose desired work is determined by salary and compensation. Although money is a prime motivator for this generation, it is imperative to note that it has more important values when it comes to the meaning of work. Generation Z prizes work-life balance, work flexibility, and various perks. Salary may initially attract this cohort, but an organisation may not retain them if the work is not perceived as meaningful (Peters et al., 2019). Furthermore, corporate values and ethics are pivotal factors that attract Generation Z (Goh & Lee, 2018). Unlike previous generations, Gen Z has distinct standards for evaluating a company and its brand. For instance, the quality of a product or service alone is not sufficient to generate a positive opinion about a firm for Gen Zers (Merriman, 2015). Instead, this generation considers whether a company has a positive social and environmental impact on the community. This propensity is likely to be observed in the generation's attitudes toward consumers and employees. For instance, Gen Z employees feel guilty about food waste, knowing its negative impact on the environment (Goh & Jie, 2019). When a company has a positive culture, ethics, and genuine concern for society and acts accordingly, Generation Z forms a positive opinion about it as a potential employer.

Psychological vulnerability

While the technological revolution has benefited Gen Z in many ways, it has also negatively impacted the generation's mental health. Studies suggest that its heavy reliance on electronic devices has resulted in addictions to those devices, attention deficits, anxiety, loneliness, and depression (Duffy et al., 2019; Twenge, 2017). For instance, the rates of attempted suicide and self-injury among college students doubled from 2007 to 2018 (Duffy et al., 2019). As this generation tends to be more psychologically vulnerable than previous generations (Twenge, 2017), organisational interest in the enhancement of their wellness will play a critical role in accommodating Gen Z in the industry. Furthermore, although Gen Z employees acknowledge the major influence of technology in their lives, they desire social connections and genuine friendships beyond digital devices (Sakdiyakorn et al., 2021). This emphasises the importance of the industry offering this new cohort a supportive working environment that creates social connections.

Limited work experience

Gen Zers have relatively less work experience than previous generations when they enter adulthood. In the U.S., approximately 60% of teenagers had jobs in 1979, while that figure dropped to 34% in 2015 and is expected to fall even more by 2024 (Fry & Parker, 2018). Although there have not been significant changes in terms of schoolwork and extracurricular activities, there has been a decrease in Gen Z students with paid jobs (Twenge, 2017). While about 30% of Millennial teenagers aged 15–17 reported having a job in 2002, only 19% of the same age group in Gen Z had a job in 2018 (Fry & Parker, 2018), suggesting that the Gen Z cohort may have unrealistic expectations about entry-level work when they are employed (Schroth, 2019). Furthermore, the COVID-19 pandemic resulted in the furloughing or firing of many of the cohort who had just begun their career journey, which may influence how they view work and careers in the future. Experience with entry-level jobs in the tourism and hospitality industry as teens would be beneficial in terms of examining personal-job fit, as well as having realistic expectations for a career path within the industry. However, this generation's limited work experience might add concerns to the future of the industry because little work experience prior to an official debut to the industry can lead to a lower level of organisational commitment and a higher level of turnover. These have long been issues of concern in the tourism and hospitality industry, so this change in the future workforce may require more aggressive interventions.

Figure 27.1 Gen Z are digital natives.
Photo by Cagle (2018) on Unsplash.

What does this generation mean to the industry?

Attracting, developing, and retaining Gen Z talent in the hospitality and tourism industry is an emerging priority in a sector that suffers particularly from a human resource shortage and the limited retention of personnel. The industry might wish to revisit its current organisational practices and culture to welcome the next wave of available talent (Figure 27.2). The industry should aim to enhance Generation Z's competencies (such as technological and social-media intelligence, and embrace of cultural diversity, confidence, innovation, and independence), while addressing its weaknesses (such as apparently short attention spans and a tendency to avoid of face-to-face conversation and social interaction).

Recruiting

The industry should rely on a two-way dialogue to attract Generation Z individuals. While job applicants must promote their strengths and competencies for positions, companies should actively communicate their values and positive cultures to Gen Z, which prioritises a fun, positive, fair, and socially responsible company culture rather than relying solely on job descriptions to reach those seeking employment opportunities (AHLA, 2018). As digital natives, this generation's members continually seek information on a company's reputation online before accepting a position (McCrindle & Fell, 2019). In addition, companies should pay attention to their interactions with customers and potential talent on social media because Gen Z is more likely than the previous cohorts to examine a company's presence on social media platforms, including visual information on the workplace and organisation (McCrindle & Fell, 2019).

Training

Generation Z has been exposed to the idea of lifelong learning and ongoing personalised training based on their needs. Importantly, they expect training to lead to enhanced

Figure 27.2 The process of human resource management for Gen Z.

employee retention and improved productivity, as a majority of the cohort has expressed that the provision of training for professional development is extremely important in determining which company they join (McCrindle & Fell, 2019). Furthermore, Generation Z tends to have limited work experience compared to preceding generations (Goh & Lee, 2018). In the tourism and hospitality industry, in which employee interactions with customers are crucial to business success, a lack of experience in customer interaction can disadvantage an organisation and its employees. Thus, the industry needs to develop the new generation's people skills, as well as its technical skills. People skills make better understanding, interaction, communication, and collaboration with others possible. Enhanced people skills will help individuals from Generation Z in their fundamental interactions with customers, peers, and other members of the organisation. Companies need to invest in training programmes that are suitable to the new generation and instil in Gen Z a service mindset that is essential to the industry.

Socialisation programmes

Hospitality and tourism organisations should enhance their socialisation programmes to attract young talent and harmonise the new cohort with the industry's current workforce. One challenge the industry may face with young employees is their individualism, which influences their learning, interaction, and communication preferences. As the cohort, in general, prefers to work independently rather than collaboratively, the tourism and hospitality industry, in which teamwork is essential, should design a socialisation program to bridge gaps between generations who will be working together on teams. Socialisation programs can help to clarify one's view of a person-organisation fit (Cable & Pearson, 2001), which describes an individual's perception of whether their background (including personality, preferences, and values) is a good fit with the culture of an organisation (Cable & Pearson, 2001). Through such a programme, an organisation should introduce healthy norms of teamwork and help young employees understand their contribution to the organisation, as well as the advantages they will receive from being part of a team.

Furthermore, the industry should focus on developing employee relations efforts through which trust and genuine care for others can be established among members of the organisation. As they have been undergoing steady demographic changes, companies have a mix of generations in the workplace. A failure to understand differences between generations is likely to increase intergenerational employee conflict and threaten productivity and healthy work conditions. It is vital that generational diversity be respected by all individuals. The tourism and hospitality industry should consider its unique yet prevalent organisational structure, in which younger generations often serve as leaders of older workers. Companies should provide ongoing socialisation programs that offer knowledge and practical skills that foster a positive work environment for all generations.

Mentoring

Mentoring becomes even more important in sharing knowledge and values among employees to increase opportunities to connect various generations of an organisation, enabling them to learn from one another in formal and informal ways. Mentoring, which is based on reciprocity, often connects senior and junior members of an organisation for the purpose of professional development and personal growth (Eissner & Gannon, 2018). Mentoring is an important tool in the hospitality and tourism industry, effectively addressing prevalent concerns about employee motivation, engagement, and retention by enabling mentors and mentees to share personal stories and values, as well as organisational goals and culture (Eissner & Gannon, 2018; Sharples & Marcon-Clarke, 2019).

Moreover, companies can invest in the emerging practice of reverse mentoring, an unconventional approach that allows the new generation to contribute to the organisation and industry by sharing its knowledge of technology and current trends (Murphy, 2012). Reverse mentoring can benefit companies by creating a personalised opportunity for diverse generations to learn from others' perspectives. Older employees can gain insights into technological and social trends, while the younger cohort expands its industry knowledge and develops interpersonal and communication skills (Murphy, 2012). In an industry that encounters capricious changes, a reverse mentoring programme can be expected to broaden the industry talent's spectrum of viewpoints and foster meaningful relationships across generations.

Healthy workplaces and positive contributions to communities

Diversity management and workplace inclusivity have been crucial topics in the tourism and hospitality industry. Extensive minority representation with regard to race, gender, sexual orientation, and ethnicity provides an indispensable human resource in the sector. Embracing diversity within an organisation fosters a safe, positive work environment that supports individual and group performance (Kalargyrou & Costen, 2017). For an industry that has been addressing strategic diversity management and inclusion in organisational cultures, the entrance of Gen Z requires additional investment in these areas. As this new generation values human rights and inclusivity to a greater extent than previous cohorts, firms may wish to revisit and improve their current practices in these areas. From another perspective, individuals from Gen Z are expected to benefit the industry by serving as role models in accepting differences among members of an organisation. Gen Zers, who already value empathy and diversity, will help the industry become a better global citizen that serves others as well as its customers.

With a new generation joining the industry, companies' social and environmental activities are even more important in building sound, healthy relationships with internal and external customers and in positively affecting communities. Corporate social responsibility (CSR) embraces organisational initiatives designed to have favourable social and environmental impacts on society and that contributes to establishing public trust and a positive company image. Employees in the hospitality and tourism industry reacted positively to their employers' CSR initiatives, which enhanced their psychological resources, such as self-efficacy, resilience, hope, and optimism (Mao et al., 2020). CSR initiatives during the COVID-19 pandemic enhanced Gen Zers' cognitive and affective trust in organisations and thus increased their willingness to work for firms (Leung et al., 2021). Because Gen Z believes that human values are a pivotal concern that businesses must address, the industry should revisit current CSR initiatives and ensure that they resonate with the values of Gen Z employees (Leung et al., 2021; Sakdiyakorn et al., 2021). Well-designed and implemented CSR activities can effectively attract young industry talents who want to contribute positively to their communities and the world.

Conclusion

Proper work opportunities in healthy environments yields favorable socio-economic impacts worldwide. When management strategies consider employees' characteristics, motivations, and preferences, tourism and hospitality companies can attract and retain the right talent. It is essential that this labour-intensive industry pays continuous attention to the uniqueness of the new generation and how it may disrupt the entire human resources management process in the sector. Generations are inherently complex but understanding them is crucial to fostering a healthy workplace in which a mix of generations harmoniously and effectively collaborate. Influenced by "always-on" technology, this generation's heavy reliance on online communities through social media platforms highlights the cohort's distinct aspects of social connectedness and digital communication. This urges the industry to put in place proper strategies to attract and harmonise the group with the existing workforce. The Gen Z workforce is anticipated to bring empathy, resilience, humanity, and inclusiveness to the global tourism and hospitality industry. These independent, innovative, and confident Generation Z employees will display a greater demand for social and environmental responsibility from the industry. Notably, Gen Z views the hospitality and tourism sector as offering a fun, exciting, and fulfilling profession, contrary to the perspectives of previous cohorts, who often described the industry's jobs as having low pay and poor conditions. It is critical that the tourism and hospitality industry offer a meaningful work environment to this new generation, thus fostering its future leaders. In addition, the existing knowledge of generations has tended to primarily focus on Western culture. It is pivotal to expand the understanding of this generation to include in various cultures and societies. It remains unclear whether the unique qualities of Gen Z employees in the industry will persist or will become more muted over the course of their lives. The academic community and the industry together must continue to track and research this cohort in the coming years.

References

American Hotel and Lodging Association (2018, November 14). *Over half of Gen Z wants to work in the hospitality industry*. https://www.ahlafoundation.org/node/130

Baum, T. (2019). Does the hospitality industry need or deserve talent? *International Journal of Contemporary Hospitality Management*, *31*(10), 3823–3837.

Berkup, S. B. (2014). Working with generations X and Y in generation Z period: Management of different generations in business life. *Mediterranean Journal of Social Sciences*, *5*(19), 218–218.

Cable, D. M., & Pearsons, C. K. (2001). Socialization tactics and person-organization fit. *Personnel Psychology*, *54*(1), 1–23.

Cagle, B. (2018). [Photography]. https://unsplash.com/photos/-uHVRvDr7pg

Duffy, M. E., Twenge, J. M., & Joiner, T. E. (2019). Trends in mood and anxiety symptoms and suicide-related outcomes among US undergraduates, 2007–2018: Evidence from two national surveys. *Journal of Adolescent Health*, *65*(5), 590–598.

Eissner, S., & Gannon, J. (2018). Experiences of mentoring in the UK hospitality sector. *Journal of Human Resources in Hospitality & Tourism*, *17*(3), 296–313.

Francis, T., & Hoefel, F., (2018). *'True Gen': Generation Z and Its Implications for Companies*. McKinsey and Company. https://www.mckinsey.com/industries/consumer-packaged-goods/our-insights/true-gen-generation-z-and-its-implications-for-companies

Fry, R., & Parker, K. (2018). *Nearly half of post-millennials are racial or ethnic minorities*. Pew Research Center. https://www.pewsocialtrends.org/2018/11/15/early-benchmarks-show-post-millennials-on-track-to-be-most-diverse-best-educated-generation-yet/psdt-11-15-18_postmillennials-00-00

Goh, E., & Lee, C. (2018). A workforce to be reckoned with: The emerging pivotal Generation Z hospitality workforce. *International Journal of Hospitality Management*, *73*, 20–28.

Goh, E., & Jie, F. (2019). To waste or not to waste: Exploring motivational factors of Generation Z hospitality employees towards food wastage in the hospitality industry. *International Journal of Hospitality Management*, *80*, 126–135.

Goh, E., & Okumus, F. (2020). Avoiding the hospitality workforce bubble: Strategies to attract and retain generation Z talent in the hospitality workforce. *Tourism Management Perspectives*, *33*, 100603.

Gursoy, D., Maier, T. A., & Chi, C. G. (2008). Generational differences: An examination of work values and generational gaps in the hospitality workforce. *International Journal of Hospitality Management*, *27*(3), 448–458.

Kim, D.-Y., & Park, S. (2020). Rethinking Millennials: How are they shaping the tourism industry? *Asia Pacific Journal of Tourism Research*, *25*(1), 1–2.

Leung, X. Y., Sun, J., Zhang, H., & Ding, Y. (2021). How the hotel industry attracts Generation Z employees: An application of social capital theory. *Journal of Hospitality and Tourism Management*, *49*, 262–269.

Lub, X., Bijvank, M. N., Bal, P. M., Blomme, R., & Schalk, R. (2012). Different or alike? Exploring the psychological contract and commitment of different generations of hospitality workers. *International Journal of Contemporary Hospitality Management*, *24*(4), 553–573.

Lyons, S., & Kuron, L. (2014). Generational differences in the workplace: A review of the evidence and directions for future research. *Journal of Organizational Behavior*, *35*(S1), S139–S157.

Mao, Y., He, J., Morrison, A. M., & Andres Coca-Stefaniak, J. (2020). Effects of tourism CSR on employee psychological capital in the COVID-19 crisis: from the perspective of conservation of resources theory. *Current Issues in Tourism*, 1–19.

McCrindle, M., & Fell, A. (2019). *Understanding Generation Z: Recruiting, Training and Leading the Next Generation*. McCrindle Research Pty Ltd. https://generationz.com.au/wp-content/uploads/2019/12/Understanding_Generation_Z_report_McCrindle.pdf

Murphy, W. (2012). Reverse mentoring at work: Fostering cross-generational learning and developing millennial leaders. *Human Resource Management*, *51*(4), 549–573.

Merriman, M. (2015). *What if the next big disruptor isn't a what but a who*. Ernst & Young.

Kalargyrou, V., & Costen, W. (2017). Diversity management research in hospitality and tourism: past, present and future. *International Journal of Contemporary Hospitality Management*, *29*(1), 68–114.

Koop, A. (2021). *Chart: How Gen z employment Levels compare in OECD countries*. World Economic Forum. https://www.weforum.org/agenda/2021/03/gen-z-unemployment-chart-global-comparisons

Kupperschmidt, B. R. (2000). Multigeneration employees: Strategies for effective management. *The Health Care Manager*, *19*(1), 65–76.

Ozkan, M., & Solmaz, B. (2015). The changing face of the employees: Generation Z and their perceptions of work (a study applied to university students). *Procedia Economics and Finance*, *26*, 476–483.

Peters, M., Kallmuenzer, A., & Buhalis, D. (2019). *Hospitality entrepreneurs managing quality of life and business growth. Current Issues in Tourism*, Taylor & Francis, https://doi.org/10.1080/13683500.2018.1437122

Robinson, R. N. S., Baum, T., Golubovskaya, M., Solnet, D. J., & Callan, V. (2019). Applying endosymbiosis theory: tourism and its young workers. *Annals of Tourism Research*, *78*, 102751

Sakdiyakorn, M., Golubovskaya, M., & Solnet, D. (2021). Understanding Generation Z through collective consciousness: Impacts for hospitality work and employment. *International Journal of Hospitality Management*, *94*, 102822.

Schlee, R. P., Eveland, V. B., & Harich, K. R. (2020). From Millennials to Gen Z: Changes in student attitudes about group projects. *Journal of Education for Business*, *95*(3), 139–147.

Schroth, H. (2019). Are you ready for Gen Z in the workplace? *California Management Review*, *61*(3), 5–18.

Schuman, H., & Corning, A. (2014). Collective memory and autobiographical memory: Similar but not the same. *Memory Studies*, *7*(2), 146–160.

Seemiller, C., & Grace, M. (2016). *Generation Z goes to college*. New York: John Wiley & Sons.

Sharples, L., & Marcon-Clarke, G. (2019). Collaborative approach to mentoring in the tourism sector: Embracing new partners to enhance an industry program. *Tourism and Hospitality Research*, *19*(1), 132–136.

Statista (2020). *Population distribution in the United States in 2020, by generation*. https://www.statista.com/statistics/296974/us-population-share-by-generation

Turner, A. (2015). Generation Z: Technology and social interest. *The Journal of Individual Psychology*, *71*(2), 103–113.

Turkle, S. (2017). *Alone together: Why we expect more from technology and less from each other*. London: Hachette UK.

Twenge, J. M. (2017). *iGen: Why today's super-connected kids are growing up less rebellious, more tolerant, less happy-and completely unprepared for adulthood-and what that means for the rest of us*. New York: Simon and Schuster.

Twenge, J. M., Martin, G. N., & Spitzberg, B. H. (2019). Trends in US Adolescents' media use, 1976–2016: The rise of digital media, the decline of TV, and the (near) demise of print. *Psychology of Popular Media Culture*, *8*(4), 329.

World Travel & Tourism Council. (2020). *Travel and Tourism: Global Economic Impact and Trends 2020*. https://wttc.org/Portals/0/Documents/Reports/2020/Global%20Economic%20Impact%20Trends%202020.pdf?ver=2021-02-25-183118-360

28 Forced displacement

The 'refugee crisis' and its impact on global tourism

Shima B. Afshan, Cheryl Cockburn-Wootten and Alison J. McIntosh

Refugees, a global phenomenon: Major trends and issues

Many people have been forcibly displaced from their homes due to global issues such as oppression, human rights violations, climate change, disasters, and geographical events. Recently, this has increased "from 41 million in 2010 to 82.4 million in 2020" (UNHCR, 2021, p. 6). Of these displaced people, 26.4 million were granted international protection and recognised as refugees (UNHCR, 2021). Bloch (2020, p. 439) summarised international key sites of displacement since the 1950s (Figure 28.1).

These historical and continuing conflicts lead to one per cent of the global populations, or 1 in 95 people displaced by force (UNHCR, 2021). Table 28.1 summarises the major sources of refugees since 2000 (Desilver, 2022). As shown in the table, the Ukraine 'refugee crisis' is now the second-largest 'refugee crisis' after Syria. It is also the fastest-growing 'refugee crisis' since World War II in which more than 5.3 million refugees were displaced from their country within only two months. A further 7.7 million people have been displaced internally within Ukraine (UNHCR, 2021). As tourism businesses have faced increased oil prices, plus disruption and uncertainty over travel due to the pandemic, the current war in Ukraine presents another challenge. Despite these negative consequences, it has provided opportunities for other destinations as tourists turn their attention to safer countries away from the conflict (UNWTO, 2022a). This crisis illustrates that the displacement of people is not limited to poor countries and even European countries are not immune from this global issue.

Predictions for the future for 2030 and beyond indicate that the future trends for the number of displaced populations will far out-exceed current figures. The World Bank's report in 2021 predicts that climate change could force 216 million people to move by 2050. This figure could be exacerbated as food crises have worsened since 2020 due to prolonged conflicts, extreme weather conditions, and the economic ramifications due to COVID-19 (Safi, 2021). Climate change stimuli do not qualify a person for refugee status and existing statistics exclude those who are forcibly displaced due to climate change. Despite this restriction, an Al Jazeera report in 2020 noted that 55 million people had been forced to move due to having no access to food, water, or jobs, as well as violence and conflict resulting from extreme climate change. Changing weather patterns also illustrate that richer countries are not safe from potential displacement due to climate change (Taylor, 2017).

There are wider social implications that need to be considered when trying to examine the crisis and its impact for global tourism. In this vein, this chapter provides a broad overview of the global impact of the 'refugee crisis' for tourism and discusses tourism academic discourses that have been significantly shaped by refugee studies. First, we define and explain

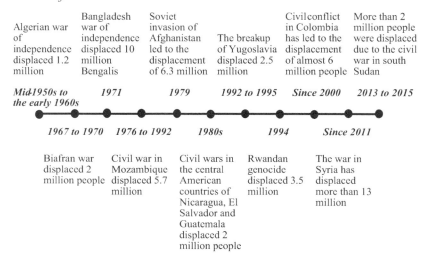

Figure 28.1 International key sites of displacement globally since the 1950s.

Table 28.1 Major sources of refugees since 2000 (number of refugees is in millions)

Source country	Event	Year	Number of refugees
Afghanistan	Taliban insurgency	2002–2021	3
Iraq	U.S occupation and insurgency	2003–2012	2.4
Syria	Syrian civil war	2011–present	6.8
South Sudan	South Sudanese civil war	2013–2020	2.5
Venezuela	Venezuelan economic-political turmoil	2014–present	5
Ukraine	Russian invasion	2022	5.3

Note: The number of Ukrainian refugees was updated based on the last report by UNHCR (2022).

the language that is typically used to label people within this global issue to reveal its political and marginalising nature. As other tourism scholars have argued, it is crucial to address this as the language used to label a group of people is neither neutral nor unpolitical (McIntosh & Cockburn-Wootten, 2019). As Gillovic, McIntosh, Darcy, and Cockburn-Wootten argue, "[l]anguage has the power to create, describe, condone or justify attitudes and behaviour" and we would argue shape tourism research agendas too (2018, p. 615). Next, stakeholders and their interests in the topic are discussed, along with potential future trends and drivers. Finally, we suggest avenues for future work advocated by critical tourism scholars, who have argued that we can reflect and change our social practices, communities, and societies to become a force of hope (Cockburn-Wootten, McIntosh, Smith, & Jefferies, 2018).

Crucial for understanding the topic is to unravel definitions. The definition of a 'refugee' draws from the United Nations Refugee Convention (1951) which states that the term relates to

> any person who owing to well-founded fear of persecution for reasons of race, religion, nationality, membership of a particular social group or political opinion, is outside the country of his/her nationality and is unable or, owing to such fear, is unwilling to avail

himself/herself of the protection of that country; or who, not having a nationality and being outside the country of his/her former habitual residence as a result of such events, is unable or, owing to such fear, is unwilling to return to it.

(Weis & Cambridge University, 1995, p. 6)

Prior to a person's request for refugee status being formally approved by the host country, they are referred to as an 'asylum seeker'. This is defined as someone seeking international protection. There can be a certain amount of confusion and overlap between the terms refugee and migrant, particularly within the tourism context. The difference is that migrants usually have freedom of movement and can leave their home to seek better opportunities in a host country. In comparison, a refugee's freedom to move is significantly restricted, plus, they are more likely to encounter physical and mental health issues as a result of experiencing or witnessing violence.

The use of the category 'refugee' is often generalised to imply a common identity and is mainly due to frequent stereotyping of groups in the media and other sources. Zetter (1988, p. 1) highlights that the term 'refugee' is "one of the most powerful labels" currently used in any discussions involving humanitarian concerns as well as in national and international public policies. It is often used to create social differentiation which results in both perpetuating stereotypes and cements a particular status for the individual. This issue is evident in tourism studies, particularly those that tend to present refugees as a homogeneous common community that ends up projecting a one-dimensional representation rather than acknowledging the diverse realities and experiences (e.g., Pappas & Papatheodorou, 2017). Lenette (2019) and other scholars have highlighted the negativity surrounding these terms and suggests terms like "'people with lived experiences', 'people from refugee and asylum seeker backgrounds', and 'knowledge holders'" (p. 14). These terms acknowledge an individual's rich lived expertise and their agency to articulate these experiences. All this would help to redress some of the power imbalances that often frame research that focuses on refugee-background communities.

Tourism scholars have approached the global 'refugee crisis' essentially in two key ways. Some scholars have investigated the impact of this crisis and problems for the host country and business of tourism. While scholars from critical and social justice orientations have approached the crisis in a broader manner, as one that involves us all to be accountable and proactively involved in changing this situation for the better. Research that has positioned refugees as a problem for the business of tourism has lamented that refugee inflows have severely affected a destination's image, resulting in negative tourism profits (e.g., Zenker, von Wallpach, Braun, & Vallaster, 2019). Figure 28.2 illustrates the word frequency used in research about refugees in the tourism literature. The majority of this work aims to provide policy recommendations to governments about how to deal with the 'problems' generated by refugees (e.g., Pappas & Papatheodorou, 2017). This is illustrated in the study by Tsartas et al. (2020) on the effects of refugee inflows on a tourist destination. They examined the reactions of local stakeholders to the presence of refugees in Chios and Lesvos Island. Their findings illustrated the negative attitudes from local stakeholders around the presence and perceived effects of the refugees' inflows on tourism. In a European study, Zenker et al. (2019) focused on the effects of 'refugee crisis' on tourists' decision structure in four countries: Austria, Germany, U.K., and U.S. They inferred that "tourists place greater importance on perceived security [than] perceived openness of a destination" (p. 207). All these researchers tend to be doubtful in their conclusions about whether the refugee crisis is actually beneficial for tourism.

Figure 28.2 Word frequency used in research about refugees in the tourism literature.

Within this body of research, scholars have examined possible ways that the 'refugee crisis' could be managed. Remedial actions and cooperation among tourism stakeholders has been offered as one possible solution to restore the positive image of a destination (e.g. Tsartas et al., 2020). Some scholars have illustrated positive impacts for the host country by identifying the economic opportunities that the 'refugee crisis' presents for tourism businesses, which may also develop a "culture of hospitality' based on diversity, tolerance, and compassion" (Pappas & Papatheodorou, 2017, p. 38). These economic opportunities may arise as the influx of international volunteer tourists and refugee aid workers arrive to a destination to offer their humanitarian services and use tourism services during the low season which brings positive economic impacts (e.g. Tsartas et al., 2020). Ultimately, these studies position refugees as groups that are detrimental to the economic values within a capitalist framework as well as promoting depersonalising 'othering' discourses (Freedman, Kivilcim, & Baklacıoğlu, 2017).

The rise of critical and advocative-orientated tourism research toward refugees is particularly significant. These studies argue that tourism must stop providing opportunities only for privileged tourists to travel and enjoy leisure activities which generate profits for large corporations. They also state that any research about or with refugee background communities should practice an inclusive, proactive manner that enhances agency for change. Within this perspective, scholars view tourism as a mechanism for facilitating economic empowerment and the social inclusion of refugees. For instance, Higgins-Desbiolles, Carnicelli, Krolikowski, Wijesinghe, and Boluk (2019) argue that "refugees are not welcome while tourism (for those privileged) is developed" (p. 1927) and criticise the "discriminating applications of mobility" in tourism "as an assertion of power and privilege" (p. 1927). They conclude that the right to travel for some communities needs to be reconsidered, especially as we face a future scenarios of challenges caused by global climate change.

Researchers within this perspective, such as Scheyvens and Biddulph (2018), examine the exclusive nature of tourism and critique its tendency to objectify and exoticise the 'other'. They discuss the importance of making tourism more inclusive and hospitable by including marginalised people in the production, representation, and consumption of tourism. Pechlaner, Nordhorn, and Poppe (2016) examined tourism and hospitality features associated with asylum seekers in order to evaluate the culture of welcome, quality of service, and relational aspects of a host country. Their study concludes that substantial improvements need to be made around creating a welcoming hospitality climate for refugees. Gibson (2016) also questioned the limited and exclusive nature of hospitality in her work examining the response shown in the U.K. and argues that the threshold of hospitality is revealed by the tolerance of strangers. According to this study, "a true 'welcome' involves accepting the unexpected visitation; it is much more than inviting a guest who conforms to the expectations of the host" (Gibson, 2016, p. 696).

To achieve equity and justice, tourism needs to provide opportunities for marginalised populations, including refugees, to participate in decision-making and receive the benefits of tourism development. Within these studies, researchers criticise the current definition of hospitality, as an inseparable part of tourism, in which it accepts the foreigner, the 'other' only up to a certain point, and usually with restrictions. Tourism offers hospitality only if the 'other' follows our rules, culture, and political system (Borradori, 2013). According to these critical studies, tourism must be returned to the original concept of hospitality and the political and business processes that designate some people as stranger than others must be avoided (Ahmed, 2000). Despite their advocacy toward refugees, some of these studies in this orientation still have limitations. Some of this research does not include empirical research that includes the voices of refugees, for instance. So refugees' perspectives, experiences, and agency as key stakeholders in this issue remain rather absent.

Stakeholders and their involvement

A variety of stakeholders are involved in tourism. Key stakeholders involved in the tourism and 'refugee crisis' include the media, refugee-service organisations, tourism businesses, and refugees. Within certain tenants of the media, the term 'refugee' is used as a quick and easy hook for their audiences, with a tendency to draw on easy stereotypes, labels, and negative images of crisis. Additionally, refugees are often discriminated and negatively framed in the media as a threat to security, jobs or viewed as an ethnic threat by those with nationalist tendencies (Abid, Manan, & Rahman, 2017). This type of news coverage can sometimes exaggerate negative consequences, and influence audience perceptions of refugees as a crisis, all of which can impact perceptions of a tourist destination by tourists and authorities in tourist-generating countries. This might result in declining numbers of tourists from certain areas. However, positive media reports depicting a destination's openness, hospitality from residents, and narrations of concrete support that include integration initiatives, all have the potential to positively influence the perception of a tourist destination and may shape future decisions to travel (Zenker et al., 2019).

Other stakeholders in this issue are refugee aid and refugee-service organisations that exist outside and within host countries. International refugee aid agencies often position refugees not as individuals, but as a homogenised group of clients with "an assumed set of needs" (Zetter, 1991, p. 44). Western humanitarian organisations "frequently resort to a vocabulary of trauma and vulnerability to describe the condition of refugees who have survived conflict and persecution" (Sigona, 2014, p. 372). Refugee-focused service providers in the host country can help refugees with education, employment, social engagement, mental health and wellness to successfully integrate into the new country. McIntosh and Cockburn-Wootten (2019) conducted research to understand the type and level of welcome provided by refugee-focused organisations in New Zealand. They concluded that refugee service organisations within the host country can also inevitably end up portraying refugees as vulnerable others, deserving humanitarian assistance. The media, in their quest for readers, and refugee aid organisations, in their quest for donors (Ludwig, 2016) create this stereotypical construction of human suffering, which affirms notions of refugees as victims without agency (Zetter, 1991). Researchers and activists within tourism have argued that these images, stereotypes, and labelling perpetuate refugees as victims of their own individual circumstances rather than as an outcome of international political and climate change global events (Ludwig, 2016). Critical postcolonial scholars further argue that these constructs reaffirm refugees as colonial subjects, and re-colonise them in a second way, after the violence of their displacement and dispossession (Ahmed, 2000).

Tourism businesses are another stakeholder affected by 'refugee crisis'. Some tourism researchers try to understand the effect of 'refugee crisis' on tourism businesses. For example, Pappas and Papatheodorou (2017) investigated complexity in their study focusing on tourism accommodation providers and their decision processes within the current Greek 'refugee crisis'. This study concluded that the significant influx of refugees may have a detrimental impact on the tourism sector, since sun-seeking tourists are discouraged from visiting places where refugees are waiting to be relocated. Ivanov and Stavrinoudis (2018) examined the impact of refugees in their study of the accommodation industry on four Greek islands. They discussed how hotels adopted coping mechanisms to reduce the negative consequences of the 'refugee crisis'. Much of this research is orientated around positioning refugees as a problem for the business of tourism and laments that refugee inflows have severely affected a destination's image, resulting in negative tourism profits (e.g. Ivanov & Stavrinoudis, 2018; Zenker et al., 2019).

Refugees are an important stakeholder for consideration of this global issue on tourism yet can often feel excluded and frustrated by how they are represented. This continuous focus on this feature of their identities, which is no longer salient to their current realities, tends to ignore their resilience, contributions, and talents. Shneikat and Alrawadieh (2019) investigated the role of entrepreneurship in the hospitality sector and how it had the potential to integrate refugees into the host country. They concluded that the term refugee was perceived negatively by the respondents and tended to affect the quality of the data by promoting a defensive attitude among them. It is clear that "definitions of categories of people, such as 'refugees' arising from the refugee and humanitarian regime are not necessarily meaningful in the academic field" (Scalettaris, 2007, p. 37), nor are they meaningful for the person with a refugee background. "These are policy related labels, designed to meet the needs of policy rather than scientific enquiry" and "bear assumptions which reflect the principles underlying the [bureaucratic policy] system" (Scalettaris, 2007, p. 37). For these reasons, using categories imposed by international policy, which have wider negative connotations, may actually inhibit the development of theory, hinder solutions, limit understandings, and reduce possibilities for engagement with social processes for positive change (Bloch, 2020).

Trends and Issues

The refugee crisis does present some challenges, as is already evident in the Ukraine refugee crisis; nevertheless, tourism businesses could transform this crisis into a positive opportunity by employing refugees. This would provide individuals with an income and security, and also improve their prospects for integration while addressing the current skills gaps for the sector. According to *The Times*, Ukrainian refugees could offer solutions rather than challenges for the U.K., since the country is facing the worst staffing crisis the tourism sector has ever seen, with about 230,000 vacant positions in holiday parks, visitor attractions, motels, hotels, restaurants, pubs, cafes, and guesthouses (Haslam, 2022). This allows hospitality businesses to actively seek staff from Ukrainian refugees. Similarly, Greece has turned to the Ukrainian refugees to help fill staff shortages of more than 50,000 for the tourism sector (Magra, 2022). The 'refugee crisis' can become an opportunity for tourism businesses if restrictions are lifted, so people can be employed in the sector. If individuals form a refugee background gain access to employment opportunities, then they will be less dependent on any government benefits or aid provided by their host countries. It will result in a win-win situation for refugees and tourism businesses.

A concerning forecasted trend and issue for 2021 has been the consequences of COVID-19. COVID-19-related travel restrictions have had far-reaching impacts on both tourists and refugees' mobility. By mid-July 2020, IOM estimated that the pandemic had left nearly three million people stranded abroad (Benton, Batalova, Davidoff-Gore, & Schmidt, 2021). The worst year for the tourism sector had been 2020, with a 73% decrease in arrivals from international tourists (overnight visitors) compared to 2019 (UNWTO, 2022b). COVID-19 has also exacerbated the situation of globally displaced people, as they constitute one of the most vulnerable populations affected by pandemic. Despite the fact that 1.44 million refugees worldwide need to be resettled immediately, due to COVID-19 restrictions, only 22,770 were resettled in 2020. This is an 80% decrease from 2019 and the lowest resettlement in almost two decades. To reduce the spread of COVID-19, many countries restricted movements in and out of their borders. This has made it difficult for those fleeing war and persecution to reach safe destinations. In addition to governments restricting opportunities to leave their country, in some cases, COVID-19 may have also been a key factor in triggering new movement of people in 2020. For instance, in Yemen, displaced people have started to report the pandemic as a reason for their displacement (UNHCR, 2021).

Climate change is an ongoing issue for tourism and the 'refugee crisis'. The global forecast for population has identified that, by 2050, nearly 10 billion people will be in conflict over the scarce resources (Baker, 2020). Those factors, combined with the likelihood of increased natural disasters, mean even stable countries will be vulnerable by 2050 (Baker, 2020). Due to the increasing number of international forcibly displacements, the United Nations added refugees as a new dedicated Sustainable Development Goals (SDGs) indicator framework in 2020. This dedicated refugee indicator highlights the importance of the prevention of situations that create forced displacement and the need for durable protection for those already displaced (UNHCR, 2019).

Within academia, there remains an issue and tensions around labelling and knowledge production. As our earlier examples illustrate, some articles focus on addressing the political, socio-cultural, and economic impacts of refugees from the perspectives of the host community and often refer to the phenomenon as a 'refugee crisis'. Using the term 'crisis' has deliberate implications. Usually defined as a negative event, a crisis is seen as a deviation from normality that has negative effects on destinations' or organisations' activities (Pforr & Hosie, 2008). According to Freedman et al. (2017), describing something as a 'crisis' emphasises the events exceptionality. Exceptionality legitimises any governmental decisions and measures aimed at enforcement, policing, and increasing control at its borders. The 'crisis' labelling which has been perpetuated in mainstream tourism research also diverts attention away from the underlying causes of migration and from related political problems, focusing attention on the urgent need for humanitarian relief (Freedman et al., 2017).

Institutions in wealthier nations typically fund and conduct academic research, and critical researchers argue that this maintains the hegemonic state in power within the postcolonial world order. In this mainstream economic orientation, researchers have tended to exclude the voices and experiences of refugees, leaving them voiceless in their research. As Māori scholar Tuhiwai Smith (2021) notes, "research is probably one of the dirtiest words in the Indigenous world's vocabulary" (p. 1), as, traditionally, it has been a colonising practice even when occurring in decolonising spaces. To counteract this tension, critical tourism and social justice researchers have advocated for more inclusive research with, rather than only on, refugees to open up opportunities for communities to illustrate hidden or ignored community-led knowledge about a topic. Such approach might reshape the current discourse around refugees as competent co-researchers, rather than portraying them merely as objects to be sampled and analysed.

Contributions, future work and conclusions

To improve the future, tourism businesses can play an important role in 'refugee crisis' situations by providing services to refugees. It is an emerging response to the situation in Ukraine in which tourism businesses in neighbouring countries supported the Ukrainian refugees by providing them with free accommodation, transportation, and food. The U.K. *Guardian* newspaper, for instance, reported that accommodation providers across 19 countries have signed up to offer free accommodation to Ukrainian refugees (Bowes, 2022). These initiatives have shown that the tourism sector can collaborate and unite for the greater good. Another way in which tourism businesses can improve the future is through employing refugees. This would involve reducing government restrictions to allow tourism businesses to employ refugees. Refugee inflows could provide opportunities for tourism businesses to compensate for the shortage of employment in the sector.

Mainstream tourism scholars also need to reconsider their framing to reflect on their assumptions that tend to represent refugees as a threat and passive. Rather, there could be an acknowledgement that there is possible value of refugees' inflows for the tourism sector. Similarly, within the research design processes, it is crucial that tourism scholars apply the principle of "nothing about us, without us" (Charlton, 2000) and consider the equal involvement of diverse stakeholders in their scholarship. "Tourism stakeholder collaboration, creative thinking, dialogic communication, and planning is crucial for enabling problem-solving around complex, unconsidered, and polysemous issues" (Cockburn-Wootten et al., 2018, p. 1491) – like refugee inflows.

This chapter has identified the historical, current, and future predictions of the global issue of the 'refugee crisis'. We then moved to highlight that the global 'refugee crisis' has been approached by tourism researchers in two ways. Some academics have examined the impact of the 'refugee crisis' and the challenges it has caused for the host country and the tourism businesses. Others from a critical social justice approach advocate for an inclusive and proactive research. They further argue that any research conducted on or with refugee-background communities should enhance agency for change. Following on from this section, we turned to identify different stakeholders in the topic and how some tourism researchers colonise the space of research by excluding the voices of refugees. While the number of refugees will increase in the future, we discussed the possibilities and the positive role tourism businesses and tourism scholars could play to improve the future situation for displaced people.

References

Abid, R. Z., Manan, S. A., & Rahman, Z. A. A. A. (2017). 'A flood of Syrians has slowed to a trickle': The use of metaphors in the representation of Syrian refugees in the online media news reports of host and non-host countries. *Discourse & Communication*, *11*(2), 121–140.

Ahmed, S. (2000). *Strange encounters: Embodied others in post-coloniality*. London: Routledge.

Baker, L. (2020, September 16). More than 1 billion people face displacement by 2050 – report. *Reuters*. Retrieved from https://www.reuters.com/article/ecology-global-risks-idUSKBN2600K4

Benton, M., Batalova, J., Davidoff-Gore, S., & Schmidt, T. (2021). COVID-19 and the State of Global Mobility in 2020. *International Organization for Migration*.

Bloch, A. (2020). Reflections and directions for research in refugee studies. *Ethnic and Racial Studies*, 43(3), 436–459.

Borradori, G. (2013). *Philosophy in a time of terror: Dialogues with Jurgen Habermas and Jacques Derrida*. Chicago: University of Chicago Press.

Bowes, G. (2022, March 15). How your holidays can help the people of Ukraine. The Guardian, https://www.theguardian.com/travel/2022/mar/15/how-your-holidays-can-help-the-people-of-ukraine.

Charlton, J. I. (2000). *Nothing about us without us: Disability oppression and empowerment*. Berkeley, CA: University of California Press.

Cockburn-Wootten, C., McIntosh, A. J., Smith, K., & Jefferies, S. (2018). Communicating across tourism silos for inclusive sustainable partnerships. *Journal of Sustainable Tourism*, 26(9), 1483–1498.

Desilver, D. (2022). *After a month of war, Ukrainian refugee crisis ranks among the world's worst in recent history*. Pew Research Center. https://www.pewresearch.org/fact-tank/2022/03/25/after-a-month-of-war-ukrainian-refugee-crisis-ranks-among-the-worlds-worst-in-recent-history/

Freedman, J., Kivilcim, Z., & Baklacıoğlu, N. Ö. (Eds.). (2017). *A gendered approach to the Syrian refugee crisis*. Abingdon and New York: Routledge.

Gibson, S. (2016). 'Abusing Our Hospitality': Inhospitableness and the politics of deterrence. In *Mobilizing hospitality* (pp. 159–175). London: Routledge.

Gillovic, B., McIntosh, A., Darcy, S., & Cockburn-Wootten, C. (2018). Enabling the language of accessible tourism. *Journal of Sustainable Tourism*, 26(4), 615–630.

Haslam, C. (2022, March 20). Hotels look to Ukrainian refugees to solve the hospitality staffing crisis. *The Times*. https://www.thetimes.co.uk/article/hotels-look-to-ukrainian-refugees-to-solve-hospitality-staffing-crisis-krbkbjn7l

Higgins-Desbiolles, F., Carnicelli, S., Krolikowski, C., Wijesinghe, G., & Boluk, K. (2019). Degrowing tourism: Rethinking tourism. *Journal of Sustainable Tourism*, 27(12), 1926–1944.

Ivanov, S., & Stavrinoudis, T. A. (2018). Impacts of the refugee crisis on the hotel industry: Evidence from four Greek islands. *Tourism Management*, 67, 214–223.

Lenette, C. (2019). *Arts-based methods in refugee research*. Singapore: Springer.

Ludwig, B. (2016). "Wiping the refugee dust from my feet": advantages and burdens of refugee status and the refugee label. *International Migration*, 54(1), 5–18.

Magra, L. (2022, May 9). Tourism poised to absorb job-seeking Ukrainian refugees. *Ekathimerini*. https://www.ekathimerini.com/news/1183832/tourism-poised-to-absorb-job-seeking-ukrainian-refugees/

McIntosh, A., & Cockburn-Wootten, C. (2019). Refugee-focused service providers: improving the welcome in New Zealand. *The Service Industries Journal*, 39(9–10), 701–716.

Pappas, N., & Papatheodorou, A. (2017). Tourism and the refugee crisis in Greece: Perceptions and decision-making of accommodation providers. *Tourism Management*, 63, 31–41.

Pechlaner, H., Nordhorn, C., & Poppe, X. (2016). Being a guest–perspectives of an extended hospitality approach. *International Journal of Culture, Tourism and Hospitality Research*, 10(4), 424–439.

Pforr, C., & Hosie, P. J. (2008). Crisis management in tourism: Preparing for recovery. *Journal of Travel & Tourism Marketing*, 23(2–4), 249–264.

Safi, M. (2021, May 7). Revealed: 46m displaced people excluded from COVID jab programmes. *The Guardian*. Retrieved from https://www.theguardian.com/world/2021/may/07/at-least-46m-displaced-people-excluded-from-COVID-jabs-who-study-shows

Scalettaris, G. (2007). Refugee studies and the international refugee regime: A reflection on a desirable separation. *Refugee Survey Quarterly*, 26(3), 36–50.

Scheyvens, R., & Biddulph, R. (2018). Inclusive tourism development. *Tourism Geographies*, 20(4), 589–609.

Shneikat, B., & Alrawadieh, Z. (2019). Unraveling refugee entrepreneurship and its role in integration: empirical evidence from the hospitality industry. *The Service Industries Journal*, *39*(9–10), 741–761.

Sigona, N. (2014). The politics of refugee voices: Representations. In Elena Fiddian-Qasmiyeh, Gil Loescher, Katy Long, Nando Sigona (eds.), *The Oxford handbook of refugee and forced migration studies*, 369–382. Oxford: Oxford Academic.

Smith, L. T. (2021). *Decolonizing methodologies: Research and Indigenous peoples* (3rd ed.) Bloomsbury Publishing.

Taylor, M. (2017). Climate change 'will create world's biggest refugee crisis'. *The Guardian*. Retrieved from https://www.theguardian.com/environment/2017/nov/02/climate-change-will-create-worlds-biggest-refugee-crisis

Tsartas, K., Stavrinoudis, D., Doumi, S., & Tsilimpokos, K. (2020). Refugees and tourism: a case study from the islands of Chios and Lesvos, Greece, *Current Issues in Tourism*, *23*(11), 1311–1327.

UNHCR (2019). Including Forced Displacement in the SDGs: A New Refugee Indicator. Retrieved from https://www.unhcr.org/blogs/including-forced-displacement-in-the-sdgs-a-new-refugee-indicator

UNHCR (2021). *Global trends: Forced displacement in 2020*. Geneva: UNHCR.

UNWTO (2022a). Impact of the Russian offensive in Ukraine on international tourism. UNWTO Tourism Market Intelligence and Competitiveness Department Issue 4 Retrieved from https://webunwto.s3.eu-west-1.amazonaws.com/s3fs-public/2022-05/16-05-22-impact-russia-ukraine.pdf?q7kCpUZsLi4Su_Zlo1d2b08bH0_L0Pln=

UNWTO (2022b). Tourism Grows 4% in 2021 but remains far below pre pandemic. Retrieved from https://www.unwto.org/news/tourism-grows-4-in-2021-but-remains-far-below-pre-pandemic-levels

Weis, P., & Cambridge University. (1995). Research Centre for International Law. *The refugee convention, 1951* (Vol. 7). Cambridge, UK: Cambridge University Press.

Zenker, S., von Wallpach, S., Braun, E., & Vallaster, C. (2019). How the refugee crisis impacts the decision structure of tourists: A cross-country scenario study. *Tourism Management*, *71*, 197–212.

Zetter, R. (1988). Refugees and refugee studies – A label and an agenda. *Journal of Refugee Studies*, *1*(1), 1–6.

Zetter, R. (1991). Labelling refugees: Forming and transforming a bureaucratic identity. *Journal of Refugee Studies*, *4*(1), 39–62.

29 Leading social change through prison fine dining as a new form of global tourism

Maria Gebbels, Alison J. McIntosh and Tracy Harkison

Introduction

This chapter evaluates in-prison dining as a new trend in global tourism. This trend contributes to a wider social purpose of reducing reoffending rates and changing public perceptions of prisoners. The issues of rising crime, incarceration and reoffending rates in the developed world have led to the creation of hospitality training and employment programmes in working prisons to rehabilitate, reduce recidivism, engender social impact, and help offenders find employment in the hospitality industry. These programmes can be seen as relating globally to the United Nation's Sustainable Development Goals (SDGs) of Quality Education (Goal 4), Decent Work and Economic Growth (Goal 8) and Peace, Justice and Strong Institutions (Goal 16). Specifically, the programmes position education and training as a means to rehabilitate prisoners, provide employment opportunities to stabilise their lives away from crime, and reducing recidivism and crime rates to increase public safety. Examples of such training programmes include The Clink Charity in the UK; restaurant Interno in Columbia, and the Gate to Plate event in New Zealand (Harkison & McIntosh, 2019a; Thomas-Graham, 2019).

The Clink Charity successfully runs four training restaurants open to the public in working prisons in Brixton, Cardiff, High Down and Styal. Since 2009, it has noted a 65.6% reduction in reoffending among its former prisoners who participated in the training programme (The Clink Charity, 2022). This chapter evaluates the success of The Clink Charity's training programme as a means to understand the new trend for fine dining in prison restaurants. The trend for responsible hospitality experiences tackles the concerning issue of recidivism and reveals a niche culinary tourism product. Working prisons are not usually places tourists choose to visit, yet research shows an increase in interest for these culinary experiences (Gebbels, McIntosh, & Harkison, 2021).

We draw on our evaluation of 3,951 TripAdvisor online customer reviews to reveal the positive memorable experiences reported by The Clink restaurant customers and the potential of this new tourism trend to change deep-set negative public assumptions about prisoners and help ameliorate the global dilemma of rising crime rates and recidivism.

Hospitality training programmes in prisons: A response to the dilemma in the developed world

Recent statistics record 11.5 million people being held in prisons around the world (ICPR, 2021). The focus of this chapter is to provide a response to the dilemma caused by the global issue of rising crime and recidivism. Recidivism, – or reoffending, rearrested, reconvicted, and re-entering the prison system – is a major policy challenge for countries in the developed world. It describes a repetitive cycle of reoffending and reincarceration for crimes committed. Recidivism is seen as important for improving public safety. Unfortunately, research continues to show that time spent in prison for crimes committed does not successfully rehabilitate offenders. In the UK, for example, statistics show that a high majority (75%) of inmates reoffend within nine years of release from prison, nearly 40% within 12 months (SP&CC, 2020). The reoffending rate for those sentenced to less than 12 months is greater. Reimprisonment of ex-offenders costs the UK taxpayer between £9.5 and £15 billion per year and continues to be a worldwide dilemma (Newton, May, Eames, & Ahmad, 2019). This is compounded by continuing increases in the size of the prison population year-on-year, consequently also leading to the problem of overcrowding in prisons and increased costs associated with incarceration and reducing crime rates. As such, rehabilitation is entrenched in social and criminal justice policies throughout the developed world. Reforms to the prison system and national crime prevention strategies or change programmes initiated by government justice departments aim to create long-term programmes that reduce crime (Full Fact, 2016). The aim of rehabilitation is to provide learning to change debilitating behaviour to live a life free from crime and to stabilise the lives of the formerly incarcerated and their families.

The social situation of the offender, including education, employment, and peer association, is found to have a major influence on increasing the likelihood of recidivism (Buckman, 2015). As such, incorporating education and employment opportunities into incarceration is seen among the suite of proposed rehabilitation methods implemented by national justice systems, alongside support for mental health, addiction counselling and community reintegration services. This arises because of policy changes to consider prisons as providing purposeful activity. The main objective of the Prison Reform Programme in England and Wales set out by the government in 2016 is to provide prisoners with access to training and education in prisons. Thus, purposeful activity is such that "prisoners are able, and expected, to engage in activity that is likely to benefit them" (HM Inspectorate of Prisons, 2018, p. 6). Examples include vocational training and work, work placements, as well as education, art classes, and peer support (Graham, 2020).

In 2018/19, over 4,500 prisoners in New Zealand participated in vocational short courses or industry qualification training provided through 70 vocational short courses available for prisoners during incarceration by New Zealand's Department of Corrections, covering skills including first aid, and health and safety (Department of Corrections, 2019). Education and training programmes during incarceration are shown to increase offenders' motivation for change, support learning needs like literacy and numeracy skills, as well as offer formal qualifications. They provide practical training, skills and experience before prisoners finish their sentences and re-enter society (McIntosh, Gebbels, & Harkison, 2020). They can provide employment pathways to support them economically and socially upon release (Gebbels et al., 2021). Importantly, research shows that prisoners who participate in education and training programmes, combined with counselling, life skills, work experience and post release support are less likely to recidivate (Buck, 2000; Collins, 2011). The delivery of in-prison training and education also comes with the challenges posed by the security, policy barriers, and practical confines of a working prison and the potential for changing financial and personnel resourcing (Collins, 2011; Hunter & Boyce, 2009).

The types of training and education programmes offered in prisons to rehabilitate prisoners include hospitality and culinary qualifications (Goodger, 2003; Werblow & Dischino, 2015; Peled-Laskov & Timor, 2018). Hospitality and culinary programmes are seen as effective in prisoner rehabilitation because they facilitate good employment opportunities in an industry where employees are in high demand; provide important social interaction and teamwork skills that the industry requires; and deliver transferable skills to other jobs. One of the main reasons ex-offenders choose to work in hospitality is because of their belief that it enables them to (re)connect socially, act as their true self, and derive a perception of themself as a "normal" person away from the stigma of their crime (Beier, 2015).

One notable in-prison training programme aiming to reduce recidivism was initiated by The Clink Charity in the UK. The original concept of The Clink restaurants in the UK, the case study focus of this chapter, will be discussed in detail in the next section.

In-prison dining: The Clink model

In-prison dining is certainly not a new concept. Over the last twenty years, many decommissioned prisons, jails and other correctional facilities have been transformed into tourism attractions such as boutique hotels, restaurants and bars. However, dining in working prisons is certainly a new concept. Traditional 'prison tourism' encompasses a varying degree of attractions from 'dark tourism' right through to fine dining restaurants – minus the alcohol and silverware being replaced with plastic cutlery (McIntosh & Harkison, 2022).

As previously discussed, high incarceration and reoffending rates have prompted several initiatives in working prisons focusing on prisoner rehabilitation. Many correctional facilities around the world have started initiatives in the form of restaurants within the prison where inmates can work and train while still in prison. An example of this is the Ingalera, based in Milan, Italy. Initially, this gourmet restaurant was set up to train 1,200 inmates in catering skills; now the public must book up to two months in advance to get a table. The Fife and Drum, in Concord, Massachusetts, has offered culinary training for inmates for the past 25 years; they use their own produce for their menu and are currently the only such restaurant open to the public in the U.S. The Idianathi, in Cape Town, South Africa, has a casual eatery that serves breakfast and lunch. Although the reviews of this eatery are positive, this prison has been cited as having some of the worst overcrowding and unsanitary living conditions. The Interno, Cartagena, Columbia, is the first restaurant to be located in a woman's prison; it helps women to gain valuable skills to help them find work when they are released.

Another example is The Clink Charity, which has restaurants in four locations in working prions in the UK, alongside a vast and growing portfolio of other activities (Thomas-Graham, 2019). In 2009, while HMP prison High Down, a male Category B prison in Surrey, UK was going through an expansion, Alberto Crisci OBE (then the catering manager) and his trustees, petitioned to have an under-utilised part of the prison's property turned into a restaurant. As a result, the first Clink restaurant was opened in 2009. Based on the success of the first Clink, a further three training restaurants were established. The second restaurant opened in HMP Cardiff within the grounds of the Category B prison (Figure 29.1). The third restaurant opened in HMP Brixton, Category C/D prison, and in 2015 the fourth Clink restaurant opened in HMP Styal, a Category D prison – the only restaurant to train female prisoners (Graham, 2020). For a full explanation of prison categories, please see Table 29.1.

At the time of setting up the first Clink training restaurant, there was a 48% reoffending rate and a 60% recidivism rate within the first year of release for inmates. The initiative aimed to provide more formal training for inmates and the ability to complete formal qualifications. One of the wider aims of this initiative was to provide an alternative option that

Figure 29.1 Clink restaurant at HMP Cardiff.
Photo: Courtesy, Alamy.com.

Table 29.1 Prison categories

Category A:	'Prisoners whose escape would be highly dangerous to the public or the police or the security of the State and for whom the aim must be to make escape impossible.'
Category B:	'Prisoners for whom the very highest conditions are not necessary but who do not have the resources and will to make a determined escape attempt.'
Category C:	'Prisoners who cannot be trusted in open conditions but who do not have the resources and will to make a determined escape attempt.'
Category D:	'Prisoners who present a low risk; can reasonably be trusted in open conditions and for whom open conditions are appropriate.'

(MoJ, 2011, p. 6).

would aid in the reduction of recidivism within prisons. Secondly, this initiative would provide students who participated an education, which would inevitably lead to job prosperity and a chance for them to enrich and support their lives without resorting to crime again (The Clink Charity, 2022; Harkison & McIntosh, 2019b). The Clink Charity has been working in partnership with Her Majesty's Prison and Probation Service (HMPPS) since its inception to deliver a unique integrated training programme for inmates on the inside and on release.

The success of the Clink Charity lies in the well-established formal, five-step integrated programme (Recruit, Train, Support, Employ, Mentor). The Clink works with men and women in prisons who have between six and 18 months left to serve, preparing them to be 'work-ready' upon their release. Students gain a formal qualification and soft skills, such as improving their communication and social skills. The training restaurants cater for between 90 and 120 customers at a time who, according to the anecdotal evidence from The Clink, come from all over the world. The Clink Charity works and supports Clink Graduates after release too. Thus, the programme continues beyond the sentence period; they continually work with the graduate post-release for a minimum of 12 months to help them secure full-time employment and accommodation.

Over the last decade, The Clink Charity has set the scene for using hospitality as a source for good. By replicating this exemplary model four times, they have also started other ventures – Clink Events, Clink Gardens, The Clink Café in Manchester, and Clink@Home, a home-delivery service from the Brixton restaurant, which was offered during the COVID-19 pandemic. The Clink Kitchens is the newest addition to the Clink portfolio, with three Clink Kitchen pilot sites (HMP Bristol, HMP Risley and HMP Styal) being set up in 2018. These sites are part of the Clink Integrated Rehabilitation Programme (CIRP). The course is available for inmates who volunteer for training whilst working in the prison kitchens preparing and cooking meals for their fellow prisoners. In April 2021 HMP Eastwood Park, HMP Send and HMP Downview started to deliver this programme and there will be a steady roll-out of this programme, ultimately aiming to have it in 70 prison kitchens by the end of 2023. Overall, the Clink Kitchen programme has proven to significantly cut the rates of reoffending of inmates. 32% of inmates who have done this programme so far are less likely to reoffend (Frazer, 2021).

Research has thus shown that The Clink model works, and that recidivism has dropped for the graduates of the Clink programme. Their reputation and success to date means that The Clink model could also be replicated in other prisons domestically and internationally (McIntosh et al., 2020). However, to ensure that the model is successful, every establishment that 'signs' up to run a 'Clink' would need to follow all of the franchise standards of procedures meticulously. At present, this model is a successful social enterprise concept that trains inmates while in prison, giving them invaluable skills, which includes getting them 'work ready' (Gebbels et al., 2021). The hospitality industry has so much to gain from the Clink model as there is a huge worldwide skills shortage in these industries. Therefore, the Clink model could help to produce a well-trained and qualified workforce (The Clink Charity, 2022; Gebbels et al., 2021). The Clink portfolio of training restaurants is a great way of highlighting the range of benefits of hospitality that could be introduced to other prisons, from fine dining to making everyday meals for the inmates. The portfolio provides a new way in which hospitality can be used for social change, through in-prison dining and beyond.

Hospitality and social purpose: Changing public's perceptions

In this section, we discuss how in-prison dining, apart from helping to tackle the concerning issue of recidivism, is also an example of responsible, conscious hospitality – a vehicle of social change (Cockburn-Wootten, McIntosh, & Phipps, 2014). As such, in-prison dining is conceptualised as a niche culinary tourism product and a new future tourism trend. Before discussing this any further, it is necessary to highlight that the delivery of culinary programmes requires cooperation between different stakeholders such as government justice departments, prison staff, in-house and/or external training providers, funding agencies, programme mentors, social enterprises and/or wrap-around support service agencies and potential employers. In-prison dining, a niche culinary tourism product, benefits three stakeholder groups: prisoners, customers, and hospitality employers. These benefits include the opportunity for prisoners to gain qualifications, work experience and employment prospects, a unique fine dining experience for customers and a work-ready, qualified workforce for the industry (Table 29.2).

From a stakeholder's perspective, the Institute of Hospitality UK, for instance, advocates that ex-offenders are a potentially untapped resource for labour challenges experienced

Table 29.2 Benefits of employing Clink graduates

Resolving skills shortage	Working with Clink Graduates makes good business sense, as well as it helps ex-offenders get their lives back on track.
Reducing recruitment costs	The cost to fill the average non-managerial vacancy costs around £2,000. Work inclusion initiatives, such as recruitment of ex-offenders can help reduce those overheads and save organisations substantial sums.
Increasing staff retention	81% of hospitality businesses that employ ex-offenders say they have helped their businesses. The higher value of having a job means a stronger desire to stay out of prisons, which can lead to higher levels of loyalty and retention.
Reducing staff absence	Employers' concern around hiring ex-offenders is a worry that they might be dishonest and untrustworthy. However, over half of employers of ex-offenders would positively rate their attendance at work, as being motivated and reliable.
Making a difference	Over two-fifths of employers say hiring ex-offenders has helped their company become socially responsible. Actively hiring former prisoners as such Clink Graduates is proven to reduce reoffending.

(Institute of Hospitality, 2022, p. 2).

within the hospitality industry (Institute of Hospitality, 2022). The Institute not only promotes hiring an ex-offender as potential and trustworthy labour source but also helps a hospitality business meet their Corporate Social Responsibility (CSR) initiatives, and provide financial, moral, and societal benefits to the employee.

With any new trend, tourists are known to share their experiences via social media and user-generated content. One of the most popular platforms for hospitality and specifically dining out is Tripadvisor. It is also considered the most relevant online review site for hospitality (Garrido-Moreno & Lockett, 2016). Gebbels et al. (2021)'s research revealed that 1) customer reviews positively support fine dining in prisons, 2) fine dining in prisons creates an outstanding and memorable culinary experience, and 3) customers fully support The Clink's cause of changing public perception of prisoners and giving them a second chance (Gebbels et al., 2021).

The evident success of The Clink Charity and its growing popularity among customers can be attributed to its strong reliance on the concept of hospitality and hospitableness. Broadly defined, hospitality is about making others feel welcome and comfortable, whether guests or customers (Ashness & Lashley, 1995; Farkić & Gebbels, 2021). Hospitableness, according to Telfer (2000, p. 39), is "the trait possessed by hospitable people". One can argue that The Clink has become the space where hospitality is practised and delivered, since Clink customers have noted the feeling of welcome. The main attraction for visiting a Clink restaurant is its high-quality food, professional welcome, and excellent service which contribute to a memorable dining experience. Many customers commented on the excellent service delivered by the prisoners, and their dining experience considered comparable to any non-training fine dining restaurant (Gebbels et al., 2021).

Almost all reviews mentioned being left with a memorable dining experience, despite strict security in place even before entering restaurant premises, the no-alcohol policy, and plastic cutlery. There is also an element of curiosity in relation to dining within a working prison and this can be seen as another motivation to dine at a Clink restaurant. The physical environment, including sophisticated décor, modern furniture, artwork created by prisoners, and the atmosphere (relaxed, friendly, and professional) were also important tangible and intangible factors that were highlighted in the customers' reviews. The desire to share their memorable experiences in the Clink restaurants saw reviews finishing with phrases like 'worth a visit' or 'highly recommend', and including details of the booking process, a step-by-step explanation of the security screening, details on nearby car parks or public transport. Therefore, visitors to the Clink can potentially be compared to brand ambassadors, who willingly and enthusiastically share their personal dining experiences.

Community support for rehabilitation via tourism

The success of the Clink training restaurants and its popularity evident in the large number of positive Tripadvisor reviews allows us to consider in-prison dining as a responsible conscious form of hospitality and a niche tourism product. Niche products can make a lasting contribution to meaningful and sustainable tourism (Novelli, 2005), and gastronomy or culinary tourism can help to differentiate tourist experiences within destinations (UNWTO, 2012). Therefore, training restaurants in prisons could become an ideal environment for prisoner rehabilitation because prisoners can experience what life outside of the prison walls will be like, through engaging with the public inside the prison. Training restaurants would partake in (re)educating the public and the prisoners in a unique location; that of a working prison. Built on the social capital of customers, the offer of hospitality is being reciprocated, so much so that hospitality becomes the source for social good (Cockburn-Wootten et al., 2014).

Yet, the literature on the importance of vocational training to reduce recidivism across the globe is scarce (Giousmpasoglou, Brown, & Marinakou, 2019), and there is little research that considers potential issues such programmes have on the various stakeholders, including tourists. Graham's (2020) research sought to understand what challenges the prisoners were dealing with while working in one of The Clink restaurants. She found that, for instance, prisoners had to constantly negotiate their identity in front of dining guests, and deal with challenges of being imprisoned whilst experiencing some level of freedom ('invisible walls') during working hours in the restaurant. She concluded that The Clink prepares its trainees for life in the community, however, not without its challenges. This is where tourism, as a vehicle for social change, can bring about awareness and change of public perceptions through active support of communities and different stakeholders to further showcase the purpose of The Clink Charity. By dining in The Clink restaurants and receiving exceptional hospitality service, we witness not only satisfied customers and increase in tourist activities but more importantly a positive change in public perception and opinion towards offenders.

Towards a new trend in global tourism

The Clink Charity has certainly contributed to a new trend toward a form of responsible, socially conscious hospitality (McIntosh, Gebbels, & Harkison, 2021). So much so, that visiting a working prison has become a tourist attraction, building on the recognised phenomenon of former prisons, now museums, as popular tourist experiences worldwide (Strange & Kempa, 2003). This chapter introduced and evaluated in-prison dining as a new trend in global tourism by using the case study of The Clink Charity and its successful running of four fine-dining, training restaurants staffed by prisoners themselves. The in-prison dining tourism trend contributes to a wider social purpose of reducing reoffending rates and changing public perceptions of prisoners. However, there is a need to track and measure these culinary experiences and their contribution to the wider social purposes of how hospitality can rehabilitate prisoners.

As cuisine can be a reason for tourists to visit a particular destination, it is necessary to better understand the gastro experience of dining in one of the Clink restaurants and the interactions. It is interactions, which enable the concept of hospitality, that the tourists are able to engage with prisoners and learn more about who they are and how this novel hospitality enterprise is changing their lives inside, and later outside the prison walls. Engendered as the 'inside and outside divide' by Gebbels et al. (2021), the physical space of restaurants inside prisons gives customers a chance to see inside how the prison functions, whilst for prisoners, the same physical space is the outside, an opportunity to engage with the public before release. Therefore, visiting a Clink restaurant and subsequently supporting the cause of the Clink Charity is the niche tourism product that becomes a conduit between the inside and outside, contributing to prisons fulfilling their role as spaces for purposeful activity.

Future research will need to unveil the customer decision-making process for visiting these restaurants with a focus on pre-, during-, and post-dining experiences, and how visitors' perceptions of offenders have changed as a result. Hospitality and tourism researchers have concentrated on the training and education aspect of this new trend using The Clink Charity as the case study, however, there is a lack of literature on this global trend and how it benefits the various stakeholders: prisoners, communities, employers, and prison services.

Lastly, relating globally to United Nations SDGs 4, 8, and 16, the new trend of prison fine dining has potential to become a global social initiative that unites tourists around the world. Therefore, as a tourism product and a prisoner rehabilitation initiative, prison fine dining can lead to social change as a new form of global, niche tourism.

To conclude, we propose the following suggestions on how this new trend can grow over the next 30 years, based on the evidence presented and discussed in this chapter.

- Encouraging key stakeholders to employ Clink graduates as part of their CSR initiatives and stop the global shortage of hospitality staff.
- The Clink model is adopted globally, starting with the domestic roll-out. This is to also include the roll-out of Clink@Home, food-delivery services across the U.K.
- Start media campaigns, involving influencers, to showcase The Clink chefs and front of house staff graduates, and by doing so changing public perceptions and breaking down the barriers of stigma in relation to ex-prisoners.

References

Ashness, D., & Lashley, C. (1995). Empowering service workers at Harvester Restaurants, *Personnel Review*, 24(8), 17–32.

Beier, S. (2015). An analysis of the potential restaurant operations have for rehabilitating offenders. *The Routledge Handbook of Sustainable Food and Gastronomy*. Oxon, UK: Routledge, 187–195.

Buck, M. (2000). *Getting back to work: Employment programs for ex-offenders*. Philadelphia: Public/Private Ventures.

Buckman, L. (2015). *Predictors of recidivism for offenders with mental illness and substance* use disorders (Doctoral dissertation, Walden University).

Cockburn-Wootten, C., McIntosh, A., & Phipps, A. (2014). Hospitality as advocacy and vulnerability. *Hospitality and Society*. 4 (2), 111–114.

Collins, G. R. (2011). A hospitality training model for prison inmates: Lessons learned from a pilot implementation. *International CHRIE Conference-Refereed Track*, *11*. http://scholarworks.umass.edu/refereed/ICHRIE_2011/Wednesday/11

Department of Corrections (2019). *Annual Report*, 1 July 2018 – 30 June 2019. https://www.corrections.govt.nz/__data/assets/pdf_file/0008/38852/Annual_Report_2018_2019_Web_Version_Final.pdf

Farkić, J., & Gebbels, M. (2021). *The Adventure Tourist: Being, knowing, becoming.* Bingley, UK: Emerald Publishing.

Frazer, L. (2021). *Expansion of prison kitchen training scheme to cut reoffending* https://www.gov.uk/government/news/expansion-of-prison-kitchen-training-scheme-to-cut-reoffending

Full Fact (2016). *Prisons: re-offending, costs and conditions*. https://fullfact.org/crime/state-prisons-England-Wales/

Garrido-Moreno, A., & Lockett, N. (2016). Social media use in European Hotels: Benefits and main challenges. *Tourism & Management Studies*, *12*(1), 172–179. doi:10.18089/tms.2016.12118

Gebbels, M., McIntosh, A. & Harkison, T. (2021). Fine-dining in prisons: Online TripAdvisor reviews of The Clink training restaurants. *International Journal of Hospitality Management 95*, 1–11. doi:10.1016/j.ijhm.2021.102937

Giousmpasoglou, C., Brown, L., & Marinakou, E. (2019). Training prisoners as hospitality workers: The case of the CLINK charity. *In: TTRA Europe 2019, 8-10 April 2019*, Bournemouth University, UK.

Goodger, A. (2003). A brief introduction to training prisoners within the British justice system in practical catering skills. *Nutrition & Food Science*, *33*(1), 6–8.

Graham, A. (2020). *Serving time: An ethnographic study of the Clink restaurant, Cardiff* (Doctoral dissertation, Cardiff University).

Harkison, T., & McIntosh, A. (2019a). *Changing lives through hospitality training for prison inmates: A case study of the 'Gate to Plate' event in New Zealand. 'Transforming hospitality': 28th Council for Hospitality Management Educational (CHME) Annual Research Conference*, London, 21–24 May 2019.

Harkison, T., & McIntosh, A. (2019b). Hospitality training for prisoners. *Hospitality Insights*, *3*(1), 5–6.

HM Inspectorate of Prisons (2018). *Annual Report 2017–2018*. London: HM Inspectorate of Prisons.

Hunter, G., & Boyce, I. (2009). Preparing for employment: Prisoners' experience of participating in a prison training programme. *The Howard Journal of Criminal Justice*, *48*(2), 117–131.

ICPR, Institute for Crime and Justice Policy Research (2021). *Prison Populations Continue To Rise In Many Parts Of The World*, New Report Published By The Institute For Crime & Justice Policy Research Shows. https://www.icpr.org.uk/news-events/2021/prison-populations-continue-rise-many-parts-world-new-report-published-institute

Institute of Hospitality (2022). *Management Guide: Employing Ex Offenders, Making the right choice*. https://www.instituteofhospitality.org/wp-content/uploads/2019/12/Employing-Ex-Offenders-Guide-2019.pdf

McIntosh, A., Gebbels, M., & Harkison, T. (2020). Serving time: How fine dining in jail is helping prisoners and satisfying customers. *The Conversation*, 19 November 2020.

McIntosh, A., Gebbels, M., & Harkison, T. (2021). In Focus. Fine dining in a prison: Case study of The Clink restaurants. In Marina Novelli, Joseph Cheer, Claudia Dolezal, Adam Jones, Claudio Milano (eds.), *Handbook of Niche Tourism*. Cheltenham, UK: Edward Edgar Publishing Ltd.

McIntosh, A., & Harkison, T. (2022). Prison Tourism. In *Encyclopaedia of Tourism Management and Marketing*. Edward Elgar Publishing.

MoJ, Ministry of Justice. (2011). *Categorisation and Recategorisation of Adult Male Prisoners*. PSI 40/2011, London: Ministry of Justice.

Newton, A., May, X., Eames, S. & Ahmad, M. (2019). Economic and social costs of reoffending analytical report. *Ministry of Justice*, https://assets.publishing.service.gov.uk/government/uploads/system/uploads/attachment_data/file/814650/economic-social-costs-reoffending.pdf

Novelli, M. (2005). *Niche tourism: Contemporary Issues, Trends and Cases*. Routledge.

Peled-Laskov, R. & Timor, U. (2018). Working bars: Employed prisoners' perception of professional training and employment in prison. *International Journal of Criminology and Sociology*, 7, 1–15.

SP&CC, Sussex Police & Crime Commissioner (2020). *PCC cash boost to help prisoners adjust back into the community* https://www.sussex-pcc.gov.uk/about/news/pcc-cash-boost-to-help-prisoners-adjust-back-into-the-community/

Strange, C. & Kempa, M. (2003). Shades of dark tourism: Alcatraz and Robben Island. *Annals of Tourism Research*, 30(2), 386–405.

Telfer, E. (2000). The philosophy of hospitableness. In C. Lashley and A. Morrison (Eds.), *In search of hospitality: Theoretical perspectives and debates*, Oxford: Butterworth-Heinemann, 38–55.

The Clink Charity (2022) *The Clink support us*. https://theclinkcharity.org/support-us

Thomas-Graham, P. (2019). The gourmet restaurants in the world inside a prison. *Dandelion Chandelier*, https://www.dandelionchandelier.com/2019/08/09/restaurants-inside-prisons/

UNWTO (2012). *Affiliate Members Global Report, Volume 4 – Global Report on Food Tourism*, Madrid, Spain: UNWTO.

Werblow, J. & Dischino, M. (2015). *Program Evaluability Study of Culinary Arts Programs in the Connecticut Department of Correction*, New Britain, CN: The Institute for Municipal and Regional Policy.

30 Sharing economy legislation

Regulating peer-to-peer tourism platforms such as Airbnb and Uber

Daniel Guttentag

Introduction

The recent emergence of the modern, technology-driven "sharing economy" has forever altered the landscapes of the tourism lodging and ride-hailing industries due to the ascent of new peer-to-peer platform marketplaces. There exists a wide variety of such sharing economy platforms, but Airbnb and Uber represent two particularly important posterchildren for this business model, and their evolution over the past decade and a half has epitomised the broader rise of their respective industries. Far removed from their days as scrappy start-ups, Airbnb and Uber have grown into massive, publicly-traded companies with market capitalisations of tens of billions of dollars, and which have even rebounded quite successfully from the challenges of the COVID-19 pandemic. They also have achieved the rare feat of becoming colloquial verbs (e.g., "I'm going to Uber to the condo where I'm Airbnb-ing tonight."). Nonetheless, the rise of Airbnb and Uber has been marked by a myriad of and seemingly perpetual regulatory battles that continue to this day.

This chapter examines the regulation of sharing economy platforms for short-term rentals (STRs) and ride-hailing, with particular attention paid towards Airbnb and Uber. These companies will be focused upon due to their dominant size, and because they have garnered far more research attention than their various smaller counterparts. The chapter begins by describing the extant literature on sharing economy platform regulation. It then examines the various issues that have spurred regulation, and the historical trends in the evolution of such regulation. Next, the chapter explores the primary stakeholders who are involved in the legislative battles that produce the regulation. The chapter then looks several decades ahead to consider how the regulation of sharing economy platforms may advance in the future. Lastly, this chapter explores some of the challenges and opportunities associated with sharing economy platform regulation and provides recommendations for future research in this field.

Key issues and regulatory trends

Existing literature

The regulation of STR companies and transportation network companies (TNCs; also, often called "ridesharing" companies), which this chapter refers to in aggregate as "sharing economy platforms," is not an esoteric legal topic pertinent only to government bureaucrats; rather, it is an issue that is incredibly relevant to nearly everyone. These platforms are routinely used by a very large share of the population, and STR units and TNC vehicles can be found in the communities and on the streets where most people live. Nevertheless, the existing scholarly literature on sharing economy platform regulation remains fairly limited. Moreover, this literature is especially sparse within the hospitality and tourism field. Even though Airbnb has become an incredibly popular research subject for tourism scholars, Airbnb research has tended to focus on topics like consumer motivation and pricing factors, rather than regulation (Dann, Teubner, & Weinhardt, 2018; Guttentag, 2019). Research on TNC regulation by hospitality and tourism scholars is even less common, with papers on Uber and other TNC companies appearing much more frequently in transportation journals. Moreover, a large portion of the literature exploring sharing economy platform regulation has appeared in law journals.

The existing literature on sharing economy platform regulation can mostly be divided into a handful of categories. Firstly, numerous papers have compared different jurisdictions' legislative approaches to either Airbnb or Uber (e.g., Beer, Brakewood, Rahman, & Viscardi, 2017; Crommelin, Troy, Martin, & Pettit, 2018; Tham, 2016; Thelen, 2018; von Briel & Dolnicar, 2020). Secondly, various papers have presented case studies about the establishment of sharing economy platform regulations in a single destination, such as New York City (Seidl, 2022), London (Ferreri & Sanyal, 2018), and Tasmania (Grimmer, Vorobjovas-Pinta, & Massey, 2019). Thirdly, several studies have examined a particular topic related to sharing economy platform regulation, such as taxation (Dalir, Mahamadaminov, & Olya, 2021) and enforcement (Leshinsky & Schatz, 2018). Lastly, numerous papers have taken a more conceptual approach to exploring the theory of business regulation and how sharing economy platforms represented a disruption to existing regulatory frameworks (e.g., Biber, Light, Ruhl, & Salzman, 2017; Tedds, Cameron, Khanal, & Crisan, 2021). Together, this body of literature provides many valuable insights into the various topics associated with the regulation of sharing economy tourism platforms.

Key regulatory issues

When the modern sharing economy was born, roughly around the time of the 2008 recession, by leveraging new "Web 2.0" technology that suddenly made it simple for anyone to publish online via Internet platforms, it heralded the arrival of a new form of peer-to-peer "collaborative consumption" that offered the promise of redefining consumer activity in a more sustainable, more collective, and less wasteful way (Belk, 2014; Botsman & Rogers, 2010). The emergence of the sharing economy contributed to and benefited from consumers' increasing comfort in using online interactions to arrange offline interactions (e.g., online dating). While the sharing economy model has been applied to countless activities and industries, ranging from hardware tools to financial loans, it was within the realms of home-sharing and ride-hailing in which this new Internet-based peer-to-peer model became especially disruptive and transformational (Guttentag, 2015). With regards to home-sharing, Airbnb and other similar companies (e.g., VRBO, Tujia, FlipKey, and OneFineStay) suddenly allowed ordinary people to transform their residences or investment properties into peer-to-peer STRs, with the ability to unlock new revenue from potentially underutilised space in residential properties. Likewise, Uber and other TNCs (e.g., Lyft and DiDi) suddenly allowed ordinary people to flexibly earn money driving private vehicles that may otherwise be sitting idle. Unlike many traditional lodging and transportation enterprises, Airbnb and Uber do not own or even manage any of the lodgings or vehicles being used; rather, they are matchmaking platforms through which buyers and sellers find one another (Figure 30.1). These platforms precipitated an explosion in peer-to-peer lodging and ride-hailing by dramatically lowering the barriers to entry; by facilitating transactions; and

Figure 30.1 Uber does not own the vehicles that are used.
Photo: Courtesy, Unsplash.com.

by establishing trust, which was achieved primarily through reputation management systems based on online reviews.

Despite how popular their products have become, when Airbnb, Uber, and other similar companies first emerged, their services were largely illegal. Just like countless other industries that are typically regulated and zoned to specific areas, in most jurisdictions people have not traditionally been permitted to simply rent out their homes as de facto hotels in a residential neighborhood, or to transform their personal cars into de facto taxis. Nevertheless, the existing laws governing the short-term lodging and ride-hailing industries predated the arrival of peer-to-peer online platforms, and therefore the laws typically did not properly map onto the contours of the new sharing economy platforms, thereby creating an example of "regulatory fracture" (Tedds, Cameron, Khanal, & Crisan, 2021). Rather than adapting their business models to the existing laws, Airbnb and Uber embraced a much more aggressive, "don't ask permission, ask forgiveness," approach (Thelen, 2018). The basic playbook they implemented involved establishing and growing their services in a community while waiting for policy makers – who generally were caught flatfooted by the rapid growth of these services – to catch up (Thelen, 2018). To defend their tactics, the platforms customarily highlighted ambiguities in existing ordinances; claimed that existing regulations were anachronistic and irrelevant to their new technology-driven services, and therefore needed to be modernised; and argued that they were simply third-party platforms that were not responsible for any illicit transactions between their platform users.

While these sharing economy platforms provided valuable entrepreneurial opportunities to hosts and drivers and created an innovative product that was highly desirable to many customers, it quickly became apparent that the optimistic promises of the sharing economy did not always match reality. It has frequently been highlighted that the economic transactions being facilitated are not "sharing" at all, but rather a form of "platform capitalism" in which profit-driven interactions are fuelling the growth of Silicon Valley behemoths (Stabrowski, 2017). Moreover, it has become clear that beneath the surface of the buzzwords and optimism of the sharing economy lay a troublesome underbelly characterised by myriad negative consequences caused by the services (Buhalis, Andreu, & Gnoth, 2020; Dredge & Gyimóthy, 2015; Slee, 2017).

These consequences have been summarised by a variety of researchers (e.g., Bivens, 2019; Collier, Dubal, & Carter, 2018; Gurran, 2018; Gurran & Phibbs, 2017; Guttentag, 2017; Thelen, 2018), and can be divided into several categories. Firstly, issues arise as a result of supply changes, as residences are transformed into tourism lodging and private vehicles are transformed into taxis. With STRs, research suggests that this transformation can reduce the available housing stock for locals and thereby increase housing costs. This concern is based on evidence that a large percentage of STR listings are "commercial" units that are used permanently or semi-permanently as tourism lodging. With TNCs, research has suggested that the companies exacerbate road congestion by filling the streets with more vehicles, which are often devoid of riders. Secondly, the sharing economy platforms can detract from everyday quality of life. Although many people enjoy using STRs when they travel, far fewer people desire to live next to an STR house or beneath an STR condominium. Commonly cited complaints include loud noise or partying, excess trash, and reduced parking availability. Moreover, when STRs become quite prevalent, they can alter the fabric of a community with the presence of more tourists and fewer residents; they can also drive gentrification. A third important concern is consumer safety. For example, STRs generally are not required to abide by the same licensing and safety standards that apply to hotels (e.g., carbon monoxide detectors and fire extinguishers), and TNC drivers may not be subject to the same background checks as taxi drivers. More generally, the sharing economy shifts the regulatory paradigm away from permission and towards accountability, which is provided via online reviews (Grossman, 2015), but research has highlighted a variety of limitations regarding such reviews (Stemler, 2017). A fourth concern relates to the status of the hosts and drivers. Because they operate in a somewhat grey area of "gig economy" employment, and exhibit significant internal diversity (e.g., an STR host who rents a spare bedroom a few weeks each year versus a host operating several permanent STR units), questions arise regarding the degree to which their revenues should be taxed (e.g., with accommodation taxes) and regarding whether TNC drivers should receive rights and benefits as "employees" rather than "contractors." Lastly, the newfound competition that sharing economy platforms create for their incumbent industries can be viewed as problematic. While regulation should not be designed to shield incumbents from innovative new forms of competition, hotel and taxi companies support countless jobs and livelihoods, and they contend that the sharing economy platforms are allowed to play by a different – and looser – set of rules.

Regulatory trends

While many policy makers initially were caught off-guard by the rapid rise of Airbnb and Uber, jurisdictions all across the world have since made efforts to either update existing regulations or establish new regulations to manage STRs and TNCs. Although there are some examples of full prohibition, STRs and TNCs are prevalent in most communities today, where they are increasingly regulated and therefore legitimised. This regulatory evolution consequently represents a fairly remarkable transformation from the informal economy towards adaptation and legitimisation. Nevertheless, the particular rules that policy makers have enacted to govern these sharing economy platforms vary significantly between jurisdictions, as a reflection of the characteristics and issues defining each place. For example, the STR regulations that are appropriate for a beachfront town with lots of second homes that have historically been rented out as vacation rentals are very different from the STR regulations that are appropriate for a city like Barcelona, which is struggling with overtourism and housing affordability. Likewise, Thelen (2018) provides an insightful examination of how the U.S., Germany, and Sweden have approached Uber regulation very differently as a function of each country's traits; for instance, in the U.S. there has been much more focus on drivers' employment status because citizens receive many supports through employment rather than from the federal government, whereas in Sweden a bigger issue has been taxation because such taxes form the basis of the country's robust social welfare system. It also is important to note that many jurisdictions have not simply enacted sharing economy platform regulations and kept them static but have instead continued to adjust them in order to enhance their effectiveness and implement new regulatory ideas that previously have been proven elsewhere.

Despite such significant variability between jurisdictions, the basic framework of such legislation tends to be fairly uniform (Cameron, Khanal, & Tedds, 2022). With regards to STRs, regulations commonly dictate how many nights per year a unit can be rented out and/or whether it needs to be the host's primary residence. Such rules are intended to prevent residential homes from being converted into full-time commercial STRs that are removed from the local housing stock. Regulations also commonly require some sort of license or registration, such as a business license or a unique STR license, and they additionally stipulate what taxes need to be paid, such as an accommodation tax or an affordable housing tax. There also are often rules regarding details such as how many individuals can be lodging simultaneously or whether parking spaces are required. Lastly, and slightly tangential to the regulations themselves, jurisdictions also must determine how they are going to enforce their rules. This element is critical, but often has received insufficient

Table 30.1 Key stakeholders in the regulation of Airbnb and Uber, and their primary interests

Stakeholder	Primary interests
Platform companies	They desire limited regulation that offers stability and legitimacy without significantly curtailing their business activities.
Hosts/drivers	They often are most interested in their ability to earn revenue on the platforms, and therefore desire limited regulation, licensing, and fees. Like the platforms, they desire stability and legitimacy without significantly curtailing their business activities.
Consumers	They want to have access to peer-to-peer services that are safe and that assure a satisfactory level of quality.
Policy makers	They generally wish to craft regulations that mitigate the negative impacts of these platforms, while typically still allowing them to operate.
Incumbent competing industries	They often advocate for stricter regulations for the platforms, generally arguing that the platforms should be subject to the same rules and regulations as operators in the incumbent industries.

attention when legislation is first being crafted. Enforcement almost always involves responding to complaints, and sometimes additionally entails tasking a specific government entity with identifying violators. Jurisdictions also sometimes hire third-party companies that use web scraping technology and other techniques to bolster such identification efforts. Enforcement methods also may entail requiring the platforms to be responsible for the enforcement of some rules (e.g., pausing a host's reservations after an annual quota has been reached), or sharing data with the jurisdiction. With regards to TNCs, typical regulations focus on licencing and permitting, external vehicle displays, background checks (sometimes together with fingerprinting), pricing, taxation, and data sharing.

Primary stakeholders

Just like the basic regulatory framework is similar between different jurisdictions, even if the actual rules are distinct, it is nearly always the same collection of stakeholders who are involved in these regulatory battles, even though the people are different. The first three stakeholders worth noting are the platform companies, their hosts/drivers, and their customers. Together, these three stakeholders represent the three-sided nature of sharing economy markets, which differ from the more typical two-sided markets (industry and consumers) with which regulators traditionally work (Tedds et al., 2021). The sharing economy platforms predictably are deeply involved in the regulatory debates. They strive to shape the narratives being discussed, and, as McKee (2017) and Stabrowski (2017) describe regarding Airbnb and Seidl (2022) describes regarding Uber, the companies have often succeeded in positioning themselves as aligned with efficient and open markets, innovation and technology, sustainability, individual economic empowerment, and progress in the face of sclerotic and protectionist industries. In addition, the companies play legal hardball and are aggressively litigious, with deep pockets to fund significant lobbying efforts (Cox & Haar, 2020; Martineau, 2019). The platform companies frequently leverage potential tax revenue as a carrot to offer in exchange for desirable regulations, while simultaneously shielding detailed data about platform activity that could reveal illegal transactions (Cox & Haar, 2020). Rather than opposing any regulation at all, which in most jurisdictions would now be unrealistic and which leaves the platforms in a state of legal ambiguity, the platforms generally push to craft a loose legal framework that proffers legitimacy and stability without significantly impinging on their ability to conduct business (Cox & Haar, 2020). Moreover, the platforms claim they are neutral, third-party technology platforms, not lodging or transportation companies, and therefore cannot be held responsible for how people use their platforms or the (potentially illegal) economic transactions that result.

To assist their lobbying efforts, Airbnb and Uber have frequently harnessed support from the other two entities in their three-sided markets – the hosts/drivers and the customers. Airbnb routinely enlists the support of its hosts to advocate on behalf of the service, including through the fostering of "host groups" that are mobilised for political purposes (Stabrowski, 2022). The company has surely found that such residents' voices can be compelling and persuasive in a way that out-of-town corporate lobbyists cannot. With regards to customers, Uber has practiced "clicktivism," in which its mobile app provides riders with the opportunity to easily click a link to advocate for Uber's service and regulatory position.

Outside of this three-sided market, policy makers represent an additional stakeholder category that is, by definition, central to the platforms' regulation. Sharing economy platform regulations are typically set by policy makers at the city level, but the relevant entities can be as granular as a homeowners' association or a condominium board, or as broad as a multi-national coalition (i.e., the European Union). As was mentioned, most policy makers were unprepared for the explosive growth of sharing economy platforms, and they have been faced with the difficult task of regulating a modern, technology-driven phenomenon that continues to evolve, and which has many competing vested interests. Moreover, the platforms are frequently uncooperative and highly litigious, with significant war chests available for courtroom contests. Nonetheless, over the past five years or so policy makers have become more adept at establishing effective regulatory frameworks to better manage these platforms, often learning from one another in the process.

The incumbent competing industries represent another important stakeholder category. Hotel associations and hotel workers' unions have long been critical of Airbnb, commonly arguing that Airbnb is not "competing on a level playing field" because of differences regarding zoning, taxation, licencing, and safety regulations. For example, the American Hotel and Lodging Association's webpage on STRs is titled "Illegal hotels" and it links to a member toolkit "that can be used to engage and advocate on common-sense regulations and accountability of the short-term rental industry to ensure a level and legal playing field within the lodging sector" (AHLA, 2022). Likewise, taxi drivers and their advocacy groups have opposed the rise of TNCs. This latter opposition has actually been much stronger than the hoteliers' opposition to Airbnb, likely because even though Airbnb is often used as a substitute for hotels (Guttentag & Smith, 2017), hotels have continued to thrive during the rise of Airbnb. In contrast, taxi drivers have been hit extremely hard by the rise of Uber, experiencing a significant decline in income, ridership, and the value of the medallions that previously functioned as taxi permits (Collier et al., 2018). In places like New York City, such medallions used to be prized assets that were worth hundreds of thousands of dollars and could be sold at the end of one's driving career to fund a comfortable retirement, meaning that as the medallions' value has plummeted it has plunged many drivers into debt and financial insecurity (Salam, 2021). For reasons such as these, there are a myriad of worldwide examples of taxi driver protests against Uber, which have sometimes even turned violent. When the incumbent competitors like taxi drivers and hoteliers advocate against the sharing economy platforms, these efforts sometimes can prove productive, but they also trigger inevitable attacks from the platform companies that such opposition represents incumbents' protectionist efforts to shield themselves from innovation and competition via "rent control."

The regulatory future

The sharing economy's regulatory history has been one of expanding legitimisation, as these services increasingly have transitioned from the informal economy to the formal economy. Airbnb, VRBO (through its parent company Expedia), Uber, and Lyft are all publicly-owned companies with investors who desire stability. The current phase of large-scale regulatory readjustment is certainly far from over, but the early "Wild West" days are past, and over the coming decades the rules governing sharing economy platforms will become more rigidly established as the remaining issues are increasingly resolved. As this transition unfolds, the overlap between the sharing economy platforms and their incumbent competitors will further grow. Airbnb already lists hotels on its platform and owns the online travel agency Hotel Tonight, and Uber has established itself as a software platform for hailing traditional taxis in some jurisdictions, including New York City. Moreover, the sharing economy platforms will continue diversifying their revenue streams, such as Airbnb's forays into "Experiences" and Uber's success with food delivery (i.e., "UberEats"). As the companies become more mature, diversified, and traditional, and as their ability to operate outside the bounds of legality shrinks, the platforms will gradually gravitate more towards accepting regulation, even while resisting costly changes like removing commercial hosts from Airbnb or recognising Uber drivers as employees.

Despite such inevitable resistance, each time a jurisdiction succeeds in more effectively regulating a sharing economy platform, it provides a blueprint for other jurisdictions to follow, so over time policy makers will gain more of an upper hand than they have enjoyed thus far. Policy makers also will become more adept at framing the narrative around sharing economy platform regulation in a way that is compelling to voters, as previously led to more stringent TNC regulations in New York City (Seidl, 2022). While some jurisdictions will seek to further restrict sharing economy platforms, others will increasingly embrace them and support their expansion. In stricter jurisdictions, the platforms will want to avoid being completely shut out of the market or having to endure aggressive crackdowns on hosts and drivers, so whether due to pressure or courtroom mandates, cooperation with local governments will grow. Cities will become more effective at policing the platforms and catching violators. Enforcement can be surprisingly challenging, but technologies like web scraping can help bolster these efforts (Leshinsky & Schatz, 2018; Wegmann & Jiao, 2017). The STR platforms ultimately will need to share more detailed data than they currently volunteer. Such data sharing is central to establishing any sort of genuine cooperation with a jurisdiction, and it is hard to imagine a future in which policy makers are comfortable with the regulatory situation until they have such data access.

As cooperation with cities deepens, the platforms increasingly will be required to help enforce the established rules. For example, if there is a quota on the number of nights a unit can be rented out or the number of drivers who can be licensed, then the platforms are best equipped to enforce these rules, and they will be obligated more to do so. The debates about the degree to which sharing economy platforms are neutral third parties veers into complex laws regarding Internet publishing and censorship, and mirrors similar discussions that are presently engulfing social media companies. Some sort of middle ground will be reached which acknowledges the unique status of platforms without completely absolving them of responsibility for their content. For example, Facebook is certainly different from *The New York Times*, yet recent events have demonstrated policy makers' desire to limit misinformation regarding topics like politics and health, Facebook has a proven ability to police content (e.g., pornography), and the proprietary algorithms used to craft personalised feeds and promote certain content underscore how Facebook is not a wholly neutral actor (Galloway, 2021). Similarly, Airbnb may not be Marriott, but it is intimately involved in the transactions that arise from its platform (it processes the payments, provides insurance), it can fairly easily remove bad actors from its platform, and its algorithm determines what listings an individual is most likely to see. Once the notion of complete platform neutrality is rejected, and the platforms' liability therefore expands, policy makers increasingly will demand that the sharing economy platforms act as partners in enforcing rule compliance.

Nearly all general recommendations for sharing economy platform regulation acknowledge the importance of allowing for local ordinances that account for local differences between jurisdictions. Different cities have different needs, so a one-size-fits-all approach is misguided (e.g., Reinhold & Dolnicar, 2017). Higher government bodies have increasingly become involved in these matters and will likely play a more prominent role in the future. For example, several U.S. states have established rules regarding STRs; several countries have established federal regulations for TNCs; and the U.S. federal government and the European

Union are considering the previously described question of platform neutrality. Interestingly, when U.S. states have become involved in STR regulation, it has frequently been to prohibit their cities from establishing certain restrictions on STRs, whereas many of the national policies regarding TNCs have been focused on curbing their activity.

Looking even further ahead into the future, the most pressing regulatory issue for Uber eventually will become the regulations surrounding autonomous (i.e., self-driving) vehicles. Uber has long expressed interest in transitioning its fleet to autonomous vehicles, and the demand for ride-hailing may increase significantly with the emergence of fully autonomous vehicles, as the ownership of privately-owned vehicles likely will shrink. The regulation of autonomous vehicles represents its own incredibly complex subject. Policy makers will have to, for example, establish a new liability framework to assign responsibility in the case of accidents, and, together with manufacturers, address difficult problems like what an automobile should do in circumstances when it is forced to select between crashing into one object or another (e.g., another car or a pedestrian) (Roe, 2019).

Challenges and opportunities

The future path of regulating sharing economy platforms promises to be as bumpy as the past. Regulating these platforms is particularly tricky because such regulations involve highly sensitive matters – people's finances, people's rights regarding how they can use their most valuable assets (homes and cars), and the daily rhythm of life within people's neighbourhoods and communities. There is, quite simply, no single solution that will please everyone in a community. Communities can still strive to craft regulations that best preserve the benefits of STRs and TNCs, while simultaneously mitigating the negative impacts. Such benefits should not be overlooked – the platforms have leveraged new technology to generate valuable entrepreneurial opportunities within the hospitality and tourism sector, to create a desirable product for consumers, and to provide flexible supply to help meet demand. They also have pushed their competing incumbent industries forward, encouraging product and service innovations. The negative consequences of platform activity also need to be recognised, as issues such as traffic congestion, rising housing costs, and hollowed out neighbourhoods are serious problems that must be addressed. Policy makers' efforts to resolve these matters should represent elements of broader tourism management practice, which is proving especially important in popular destinations that are wrestling with issues of overtourism.

As policy makers continue their work of crafting and refining regulations for sharing economy platforms, they will benefit from additional academic research, and there are numerous existing research gaps waiting to be filled. To begin, tourism scholars, who have devoted considerable attention to other aspects of Airbnb, should increase their examination of Airbnb regulation. Likewise, the dearth of tourism scholarship on TNC regulation represents a major gap in the literature, and an opportunity to apply tourism theories and concepts to a very important topic. Also, researchers focused on sharing economy regulation should increasingly expand beyond simply comparing the distinct regulatory frameworks that exist in different jurisdictions, to also examine the impacts and effectiveness of these regulations, thereby allowing for more valuable recommendations to be offered. In addition, there is a need to better understand the varying perspectives of the key stakeholders involved. For example, what are the similarities and differences between how the hosts/drivers, customers, incumbent industries, and policy makers view regulation?

Conclusion

This chapter provides an examination of sharing economy platform regulation, with a particular focus on Airbnb and Uber, the two quintessential sharing economy companies. The chapter explores the key issues driving this regulation, the prior trends in legislation, and the key stakeholders involved. The chapter also makes the unique contribution of providing a forward-looking analysis of how these regulations may evolve over the coming decades, together with a description of some of the challenges and opportunities that such future legislation will bring. Suggestions for future research are also provided, and greater knowledge on the recommended research topics would help to guide future policy making. Such a forward-looking perspective is critical because, despite how much has changed since the sharing economy platforms first emerged not long ago, the road ahead is much longer than the road behind.

References

AHLA. (2022). Illegal hotels. *AHLA*. Retrieved from https://www.ahla.com/issues/illegal-hotels on 24 May 2022.

Beer, R., Brakewood, C., Rahman, S., & Viscardi, J. (2017). Qualitative analysis of ride-hailing regulations in major American cities. *Transportation Research Record*, *2650*(1), 84–91.

Belk, R. (2014). You are what you can access: Sharing and collaborative consumption online. *Journal of Business Research*, *67*(8), 1595–1600.

Biber, E., Light, S. E., Ruhl, J. B., & Salzman, J. (2017). Regulating business innovation as policy disruption: From the Model T to Airbnb. *Vanderbilt Law Review*, *70*, 1561.

Bivens, J. (2019). The economic costs and benefits of Airbnb. *Economic Policy Institute*. Retrieved from https://www.epi.org/publication/the-economic-costs-and-benefits-of-airbnb-no-reason-for-local-policymakers-to-let-airbnb-bypass-tax-or-regulatory-obligations/

Botsman, R., & Rogers, R. (2010). *What's mine is yours. The rise of collaborative consumption*. New York: Harper Business.

Buhalis, D., Andreu, L., & Gnoth, J. (2020). The dark side of the sharing economy: Balancing value co-creation and value co-destruction. *Psychology & Marketing*, *37*(5), 689–704.

Cameron, A., Khanal, M., & Tedds, L. M. (2022). Managing Airbnb: A cross-jurisdictional review of approaches for regulating the short-term rental market. *MPRA* Paper No. 111535. Retrieved from https://mpra.ub.uni-muenchen.de/111535/

Collier, R. B., Dubal, V. B., & Carter, C. L. (2018). Disrupting regulation, regulating disruption: The politics of Uber in the United States. *Perspectives on Politics*, *16*(4), 919–937.

Cox, M., & Haar, K. (2020). Platform failures: How short-term rental platforms like Airbnb fail to cooperate with cities and the need for strong regulations to protect housing. *The Left*. Retrieved from https://left.eu/content/uploads/2020/12/Platform-Failures-Airbnb-1.pdf

Crommelin, L., Troy, L., Martin, C., & Pettit, C. (2018). Is Airbnb a sharing economy superstar? Evidence from five global cities. *Urban Policy and Research*, *36*(4), 429–444.

Dalir, S., Mahamadaminov, A., & Olya, H. G. (2021). Airbnb and taxation: Developing a seasonal tax system. *Tourism Economics*, *27*(2), 365–378.

Dann, D., Teubner, T., & Weinhardt, C. (2018). Poster child and guinea pig – insights from a structured literature review on Airbnb. *International Journal of Contemporary Hospitality Management*, *31*(1), 427–473.

Dredge, D., & Gyimóthy, S. (2015). The collaborative economy and tourism: Critical perspectives, questionable claims and silenced voices. *Tourism Recreation Research*, *40*(3), 286–302.

Ferreri, M., & Sanyal, R. (2018). Platform economies and urban planning: Airbnb and regulated deregulation in London. *Urban Studies*, *55*(15), 3353–3368.

Galloway, S. (2021, November 5). Facebook … What to do?. *No Mercy/No Malice*. Retrieved from https://www.profgalloway.com/facebook-what-to-do/

Grimmer, L., Vorobjovas-Pinta, O., & Massey, M. (2019). Regulating, then deregulating Airbnb-The unique case of Tasmania (Australia). *Annals of Tourism Research*, 75, 304–307.

Grossman, N. (2015). Regulation, the internet way: A data-first model for establishing trust, safety, and security. *Ash Center for Democratic Governance and Innovation*. Retrieved from https://datasmart.ash.harvard.edu/news/article/white-paper-regulation-the-internet-way-660

Gurran, N. (2018). Global home-sharing, local communities and the Airbnb debate: A planning research agenda. *Planning Theory & Practice*, 19(2), 298–304.

Gurran, N., & Phibbs, P. (2017). When tourists move in: How should urban planners respond to Airbnb? *Journal of the American Planning Association*, 83(1), 80–92.

Guttentag, D. (2015). Airbnb: Disruptive innovation and the rise of an informal tourism accommodation sector. *Current Issues in Tourism*, 18(12), 1192–1217.

Guttentag, D. (2017). Regulating innovation in the collaborative economy: An examination of Airbnb's early legal issues. In D. Dredge and S. Gyimóthy (Eds.), *Collaborative economy and tourism: Perspectives, politics, policies and prospects* (pp. 97–128). Frankfurt: Springer.

Guttentag, D. (2019). Progress on Airbnb: A literature review. *Journal of Hospitality and Tourism Technology*, 10(4), 814–844.

Guttentag, D., & Smith, S. L. (2017). Assessing Airbnb as a disruptive innovation relative to hotels: Substitution and comparative performance expectations. *International Journal of Hospitality Management*, 64, 1–10.

Leshinsky, R., & Schatz, L. (2018). "I don't think my landlord will find out:" Airbnb and the challenges of enforcement. *Urban Policy and Research*, 36(4), 417–428.

Martineau, P. (2019, March 20). Inside Airbnb's 'guerrilla war' against local governments. *Wired*. Retrieved from https://www.wired.com/story/inside-airbnbs-guerrilla-war-against-local-governments/

McKee, D. (2017). The platform economy: Natural, neutral, consensual and efficient? *Transnational Legal Theory*, 8(4), 455–495.

Reinhold, S., & Dolnicar, S. (2017). The sharing economy. In S. Dolnicar (Ed.) *Peer-to-peer accommodation networks: Pushing the boundaries* (pp. 15–26). Oxford: Goodfellow Publishers.

Roe, M. (2019). Who's driving that car: An analysis of regulatory and potential liability frameworks for driverless cars. *Boston College Law Review*, 60, 317–348.

Salam, E. (2021, October 2). 'They stole from us': The New York taxi drivers mired in debt over medallions. *The Guardian*. Retrieved from https://www.theguardian.com/us-news/2021/oct/02/new-york-city-taxi-medallion-drivers-debt

Seidl, T. (2022). The politics of platform capitalism: A case study on the regulation of Uber in New York. *Regulation & Governance*, 16(2), 357–374.

Slee, T. (2017). *What's yours is mine: Against the sharing economy*. New York: OR Books.

Stabrowski, F. (2017). 'People as businesses': Airbnb and urban micro-entrepreneurialism in New York City. *Cambridge Journal of Regions, Economy and Society*, 10(2), 327–347.

Stabrowski, F. (2022). Political organizing and narrative framing in the sharing economy: Airbnb host clubs in New York City. *City*, 26(1), 142–159.

Stemler, A. (2017). Feedback loop failure: Implications for the self-regulation of the sharing economy. *Minnesota Journal of Law, Science & Technology*, 18(2), 673–712.

Tedds, L. M., Cameron, A., Khanal, M., & Crisan, D. (2021). Why existing regulatory frameworks fail in the short-term rental market: Exploring the role of regulatory fractures. Retrieved from https://papers.ssrn.com/sol3/papers.cfm?abstract_id=3807492

Tham, A. (2016). When Harry met Sally: different approaches towards Uber and AirBnB—an Australian and Singapore perspective. *Information Technology & Tourism*, 16(4), 393–412.

Thelen, K. (2018). Regulating Uber: The politics of the platform economy in Europe and the United States. *Perspectives on Politics*, 16(4), 938–953.

von Briel, D., & Dolnicar, S. (2020). The evolution of Airbnb regulation – An international longitudinal investigation 2008–2020. *Annals of Tourism Research*, 87, 102983.

Wegmann, J., & Jiao, J. (2017). Taming Airbnb: Toward guiding principles for local regulation of urban vacation rentals based on empirical results from five US cities. *Land Use Policy*, 69, 494–501.

31 Re-imagining tourism in a world of declining nature

David Newsome

Introduction: Environment and tourism

The purpose of this chapter is to provide an overview of problems associated with the current state of the natural environment and its relationship with tourism. The author goes on to reinforce/suggest a better way of thinking about the way we see nature as a tourism product and to identify a form of nature-orientated tourism that benefits us and the environment.

Judeo-Christian thinking, regarding the human relationship with the natural world, as written in the book of Genesis is stated, "Be fruitful and increase in number; fill the earth and subdue it. Rule over the fish in the sea and the birds in the sky and over every living creature that moves on the ground" (Holy Bible, 2011). Martin (1975) reminds us of this perspective and its modern-day consequences in his pessimistic view on the future of humanity, where he provides an analysis of humanity's failure to deal with over-population, pollution, resource consumption and the loss of nature. Moreover, Martin (1975) is of the view that we will be the last generation to enjoy a healthy life and biodiverse natural environment. It would be profoundly naïve not to affirm that the natural world has been badly degraded and is in a state of decline and the overwhelming evidence is that humanity has many problems (climate change, loss of biodiversity, land degradation and pollution) that need urgent attention (e.g. Aplin et al., 1999; Marlier et al., 2016: UNSDG, 2019; BGCI, 2021; Ebi et al., 2021: McGrath, 2021; Laurance, 2022). On the positive side, more people care about the state of the environment and there are calls for action directed at tackling climate change, halting biodiversity loss, working towards halting land degradation, and dealing with pollution (e.g. Reyers et al., 2018; Attenborough, 2020; European Wilderness Society, 2021). An emotional impetus for caring about the fate of the natural world was previously articulated by Adams and Carwardine (1990)

> There is one last reason for caring, and I believe no other is necessary. It is certainly the reason so many people have devoted their lives to protecting the like of rhinos, parakeets, kakapos, and dolphins. And it is simply this: the world would be a poorer, darker, lonelier place without them.

Lemelin et al. (2012), in the text *Last Chance Tourism*, provide a combined perspective where some degree of pessimism intersects with a push for conservation and environmental integrity. Various chapters document declines in wildlife and quality of the natural environment and even substantial changes to large-scale features, such as glaciers, forest cover and coral reefs, which have always been part of the human experience. The role of tourism is carefully considered as to what it can offer as a means of recognition that we have a problem and a call for action. This is exemplified in the book's foreword, where Kenneth Shapiro states: "Working together, the travel industry is in the best position to appeal to governments to take measures to slow down and possibly even reverse some of the destruction we are seeing."

The above considerations beg the question: where are we today regarding the tourism–environment nexus? In recent decades, tourism has played an ever-increasing role in recognising the value of nature and protecting wildlife (Buckley, 2003, 2010; Newsome and Hassell, 2014). Furthermore, tourism focusing on nature and wildlife has become an increasingly important part of the overall tourism sector (Holden, 2016). Buckley (2020) and Buckley et al. (2018, 2019) have explored the tourism–environment nexus in the context of mental health benefits for tourists and recreationists engaging with nature. Buckley (2004), Newsome (2014), Newsome et al. (2013) and Newsome and Hughes (2017) have attempted to alert tourism decision-making authorities, protected area managers, interest groups and researchers to the impacts of tourism on natural vegetation, wildlife, and environmental features of tourism interest. Attendant to this are the negative impacts of tourism on visitor experience, such as in crowded situations or when tourists are behaving badly. In recent times there has been a whole conversation about the social and environmental impacts of overtourism (e.g., Wall, 2020; Insch, 2020; Koh and Fakfare, 2020; Cahyadi and Newsome, 2021).

The most recent big issue facing tourism has been the COVID-19 pandemic. Recognised as a disaster for all sectors of the global tourism industry the pandemic has highlighted our relationship with nature and the place of tourism within it (Spenceley et al. (2021). The pandemic is widely thought to relate to human encroachment and the damage and exploitation of nature (Carrington, 2020; IPBES, 2020; Vidal, 2020; McNeely, 2021). Some environmental benefits were recognised when the pandemic forced the closure of industry and halted travel, but in many cases the pandemic uncovered the reliance of wildlife conservation on tourism (Newsome, 2020a; Hockings, 2021). Work conducted in Europe, by McGinlay et al. (2020), following the easing of restrictions and lockdowns also brought out our reliance on nature as a safe, rejuvenating, and healthy place to be. McGinlay et al. (2020) also revealed a rise in negative domestic tourism-related impacts associated with crowding and inappropriate behaviours.

A view on the current tourism in nature situation

The potential impacts of tourism on the natural environment are many and varied and include trampling, construction and operation of access roads, use of vehicles, disturbance of wildlife, noise and other forms of pollution, development of accommodation and unsustainable practices such as poor waste management and excessive water and power consumption (Liddle, 1997; Buckley, 2004; Newsome et al., 2013). Whether impacts occur or not their severity depends upon the degree of tourism planning, management of tourism activity, funding, staffing, the effort put into monitoring change and the capability to deal with congested and crowded situations (Newsome et al., 2013; Cahyadi and Newsome, 2021). Such practices vary according to different situations and geographical contexts in that the severity of impact may depend on local environmental conditions, seasonal factors, sensitivity of wildlife and amount of use (Pickering, 2010).

Other complicating factors that are at play involve the blurring between recreational pursuits not directly connected with nature appreciation that take place in natural settings.

Included here is the rise of adventure racing and sporting activities in protected areas which may take place alongside more passive recreational activities such as bird watching and hiking (Newsome, 2014; Newsome and Hughes, 2017). The post-COVID-19 relaxation of lockdowns, while international borders remained closed, has seen a massive rise in domestic tourism (Cahyadi and Newsome, 2021; Spenceley et al., 2021). The increased domestic tourism cohort has put further pressure on natural areas as many have brought an ethic more attuned to 'having outdoor fun and play' which has led to crowding, apparent disregard for the environment and social conditions not conducive to nature appreciation (McGinlay et al., 2020). It may be that a sizeable portion of the post-COVID domestic tourism demographic never had an eco-centric and respectful view of nature.

While there are many examples of best practice and sustainable nature-based tourism enterprises around the world there is still much room for improvement (e.g., Newsome, 2013; Wong et al., 2019; Cahyadi and Newsome, 2021). There are several reasons why nature tourism fails to be sustainable, especially in terms of impact mitigation. The first reason is the failure of decision-making authorities and tourism providers to understand the core components of ecotourism. Ecotourism is a form of tourism that explicitly states it to be based upon the natural environment, educative in practice and sustainable through informed environmental and visitor management (Newsome et al., 2013). The second reason relates to poorly planned and coordinated tourism development which has led to overdevelopment and overtourism (e.g., Newsome et al., 2019). Attendant to this is a lack of funding, training, and human resources to manage tourism access and activities (e.g., Prakash et al., 2019). The third reason concerns target areas/tourism destinations that are under pressure. For example, Leverington et al. (2010), in a comprehensive world study of protected area management effectiveness, found that 40% of protected areas had major deficiencies. Lack of funding for management was identified as a particular problem and given that protected areas support important wildlife tourism industries around the world the situation generates concern. Schulze et al. (2018) identify tourism has a major threatening process to the integrity of protected areas into the future. Threatening processes come in the form of excessive development, inappropriate activities, and overtourism (e.g., Newsome and Hughes, 2017; Mandić and Marković Vukadin, 2021). Given the rise in global population along with increased wealth and mobility for many, nature-based tourism resources will be under increasing pressure. This is especially the case when wider environmental issues such as climate change, environmental degradation connected with resource consumption, competition for land and water, ever-growing energy demand, waste management issues and pollution are coming to the fore. In some cases, and particularly in Africa, severe poverty, natural disasters, civil unrest, and war pose major obstacles to the security of resident human populations, management of protected areas, conservation of nature and in the protection of iconic species of wildlife such as rare ungulates, primates, elephants, and large carnivores (Gaynor et al., 2016; Mimbale, 2020).

Major trends and issues up to the period 2021–2022 therefore include a decline in the extent and quality of natural ecosystems worldwide, a growth in tourism development projects and a rapid increase in visitation, putting the integrity of natural areas at risk (Goodwin, 2017; Schulze et al., 2018; UNSDG, 2019; Cahyadi and Newsome, 2021; McGrath, 2021). At the same time, the COVID-19 pandemic has highlighted the dependence of many protected areas on tourism and vice versa (Newsome and Perera, 2022). The recent pandemic has also brought the pressures associated with many people 'flocking to' protected areas to the fore underlining the need for implementing key sustainable development goals (McGinlay et al., 2020; Spenceley et al., 2021).

A re-imagined approach for tourism in a world of declining nature

Sustainable development

The 2030 Agenda for Sustainable Development is an ambitious project with the aim of tackling major problems such as world poverty and securing a sustainable future for humanity. It therefore includes goals and targets aimed at mitigating environmental degradation and climate change (UN, 2015). Furthermore, while general tourism is frequently mentioned regarding SDGs 8 (Decent Work and Economic Growth), 12 (Responsible Consumption and Production) and 17 (Partnerships for the Goals) when it comes to nature tourism SDGs 13 (Climate Action), 14 (Life below Water) and 15 (Life on Land) are also extremely important because of the current and predicted impacts of climate change and biodiversity loss (UNWTO/UNDP, 2018). Additionally, in considering the place of tourism within the 2030 Agenda for Sustainable Development, Hall (2019) articulates that tourism is currently less sustainable than it ever has been. Hence, he calls for a re-think in terms of the human–environment relationship. Accordingly, this chapter has already acknowledged many of big picture environmental issues that need to be addressed which is indeed a major task for all people and their governments. Nevertheless, there are many concerned and motivated people and an increasing call for action regarding developing solutions in tackling unsustainable and inappropriate tourism practices. Moreover, as part of offering a way forward in modifying the previously described situation, the following section acknowledges the positive actions of governments and later considers some tangible recommendations for adjusting our moral and ethical stance in nature-based tourism situations.

The role of governments and their agencies

The nature we have left is precious and governments have a responsibility in recognising the services nature provides and designating protected areas for wildlife and all people to enjoy. To this end protected areas are vital nature-based tourism resources and play a critical role in combating climate change, mitigating land degradation and conserving biodiversity. Protected areas, natural green space and wildlife habitats are also vital land uses in providing ecosystem services that are linked to the quality of life for a continually increasing urban human population (Newsome, 2020b). It is also well established that there are considerable ecological and health benefits to be derived from the retention and conservation of green space in cities (Irvine et al., 2010). Moreover, there is an increasing body of evidence that contact with, and experience of, nature confers mental health benefits to participants (White et al., 2019, Buckley, 2020).

Governments and their agencies play a critical role in the creation of protected areas and in the administration of environmental protection that fosters effective protected area management. For example, the Western Australian State Government agency, the Department of Biodiversity, Conservation and Attractions, has recently developed a plan to expand the State's protected area network. The project involves the creation of an extra five million hectares of new conservation reserves, national and marine parks across the State (DBCA, 2021). An important aspect of this programme will be the creation of the Helena Aurora Range National Park and the identification of additional nature reserves. It is, however, important to note that the creation of reserves is not enough to ensure the holistic protection of nature. For example, Costa Rica has substantial areas (around 26%) of landcover under protection, but this is still insufficient to conserve a full range of Cota Rica's mammal fauna (Gonzalez-Maya et al., 2015). Furthermore, Tafoya et al. (2020) report on a programme to reverse deforestation in Costa Rica but also make the point that it is vital to include payments for ecosystem services, employ ecotourism programmes and have a comprehensive portfolio of protected areas because different ecosystems can have different rates of disturbance, deforestation impact and representative wildlife.

Once protected areas have been gazetted there needs to be suitable management and resourcing in place to deal with perturbations sourced from the wider landscape, manage visitor pressure and illegal activities and control weed invasion and feral animals. There may be a particular need for wildlife recovery programmes targeting the conservation of rare, endangered, and charismatic species. The importance of paying special attention to charismatic species can be highlighted by examining the situation with the numbat (*Myrmecobius fasciatus*), which is endemic to Australia (Figure 31.1). The numbat exemplifies the issues faced by many species today, such as the impacts of habitat loss and predation by introduced and feral predators. Threatening processes, such as habitat loss, highlight the importance of conserving and restoring natural habitats for wildlife. The recently gazetted Dryandra National Park is one of only two areas in southwestern Australia that contains a natural population of numbats. The Dryandra ecosystem represents the largest viable remnant of wandoo (*Eucalyptus wandoo*) forest that remains and is an important conservation reserve for mammals (26), birds (100+), reptiles (41) and flora (850 species). Further to the conservation of remaining natural areas the numbat recovery programme involves controlling predation by the fox and feral cats and restoring numbat numbers via breeding and translocation programmes (DPW, 2017). In recognising the numbat as an animal of tourism interest there is much scope for interpretation programmes where visitors can learn about species recovery and conservation. Moreover, Dryandra National Park is already a well-recognised tourism resource with a range of nature-based tourism offerings, such as

Figure 31.1 The numbat is an endangered small marsupial with only two naturally occurring remnant populations in southwestern Australia. About 800 mature individuals survive in the wild.

Photograph courtesy of James Bennett.

the Barna Mia experience (occurring inside a predator proof mammal sanctuary), self-guided walk trails and a drive trail (Hughes et al., 2005).

As previously highlighted by the work of Leverington (2010), the gazettal of parks is usually not enough for achieving conservation outcomes and avoiding degradation. All protected areas require adequate and ongoing management of ecological communities, threatening processes and human usage. In Australia progress, or otherwise, in the condition of the natural estate can be tracked via State of the Parks Reporting (e. g. Parks Victoria, n.d.). Such programmes report on the status of threats and track whether management objectives have been met. It is a useful way of gauging management effectiveness as data inputs are provided by park staff and reported by protected area mangers. When data is collected for categories, such as nature conservation and management and management for visitors and community, an overall assessment can be made of where there have been successes or targets have not been met. Affected components can then be allocated additional resources to rectify underperforming areas. It is important to note, however, that resource management agencies may or may not use State of the Parks Reporting to evaluate management effectiveness.

Given that nature-based tourism relies on conservation and protected areas, governments and their agencies could do more to embrace the Green List global standard for area-based conservation. The Green List certification programme was developed by the International Union for the Conservation of Nature (IUCN) with the aim of increasing the number of protected areas that deliver successful conservation outcomes through good governance and best practice planning and management (IUCN, 2018). The programme is voluntary and requires national and local commitment. By 2021 more than 30 countries were participating with the goal of managing threats to protected areas such as climate change, invasive species, hunting, infrastructure development and tourism. A key pillar of the Green List Standard is in the delivery of conservation outcomes such as the recovery of endangered species, the re-establishment of previously lost local populations of wildlife and preventing any further declines of vulnerable and threatened species.

The role of individuals: Ways of thinking about nature and wildlife

Morris (1990) writes "every animal, every single living species, is the fascinating end-point of millions of years of evolution. Each uniquely adapted to its own way of life and each deserves our respect." However, in the same text Morris also states, "many fascinating species of wildlife are on the verge of extinction and the list of animals that are likely to vanish for ever during the twenty-first century is depressingly long." The human–environment relationship is complex and involves diverse cultural interpretations and histories, geographical contexts, and lifestyle scenarios. Humans also have a relationship with animals that goes back thousands of years, which has changed according to religious thinking and increasing urbanisation (Morris, 1990). Because most of us live in highly urbanised societies many people today have become far removed from contact with nature, but also in recent years broadcasters like the BBC, in combination with high-profile naturalists like David Attenborough, have profiled the natural world to millions of people. Increasing wealth and mobility for many and a new heightened awareness of nature, derived from television and social media, is the reason nature-based tourism continues to increase as a leisure activity. Holden (2016) has explored the tourism–environment relationship from the view of belief systems, the promotion of nature as an attraction and environmental ethics. While a full consideration of the aforementioned topics is beyond the scope of this chapter the intention here is to focus in on some aspects of human morals, ethics and attitudes and identify some behavioural issues that can be changed in the quest for sustainable tourism.

While there are many people who care and 'do the right thing' in the tourism context there are many that do not! Examples from zoos and collections include collecting rare species from the wild, keeping animals under poor conditions, collecting for the exotic pet industry, and exploiting animals for entertainment. In the natural environment there may be overt disturbance to wild animals, trampling of vegetation, accessing wildlife sanctuary areas, the use of drones at wildlife breeding sites and the selfie phenomenon. Charismatic wildlife is often subject to considerable tourism attention and the practice of tourists being photographed with wildlife is of concern (World Animal Protection, 2017; Hasanah Abd Mutalib, 2018; Rizzolo, 2021). It is important to acknowledge here that animals have personality and emotion, feel pain and distress, suffer from boredom, have group attachment, and need comfort and safety. They also have extraordinary sensory perceptions and adaptations to their environment and un-natural situations disrupts their lives (Neiwert, 2016).

In realising that the previously described negative scenarios may be due to a lack of understanding and ignorance about the effects that tourism can have on wildlife, revisiting and re-thinking moral and ethical standpoints can offer a way forward (Moorhouse et al., 2015, 2017). Table 31.1 identifies human behavioural standpoints where negative issues are compared with educated and informed moral and ethical standpoints. Promoting a tourism future that changes attitudes and expectations that are good for the environment is the responsibility of tour operators, guides, wardens and protected area and tourism managers. These actors, in charge of providing information, interpretation and supervision, thus have a key role to play.

The way that nature tourism is marketed and presented to the public by tourism agencies and companies is also in need of attention. Lenzi et al. (2020) highlight how social media can influence public perceptions of wildlife and often promotes inappropriate human behaviour which goes on to impact on wildlife. Social media can also be used to identify problems stemming from poor management practices, unethical tour operators and visitor behaviour in the presence of wildlife (Prakash et al., 2019).

The role of governments and their agencies has already been considered but it is still useful to make the point that individuals responsible for tourism management and environmental protection can do more in terms of embracing an aspirational tourism and nature relationship (Table 31.1) and allocate more funding for ranger presence and in the enforcement of codes of practice (Table 31.2).

Non-government organisations (Worldwide Fund for Nature, Birdlife International, IUCN) play an important collaborative role in advocacy, developing, refining, and promoting codes of ethics, setting goals, and developing guidelines (Table 31.2). Ethical codes and conservation actions as indicated in Table 31.2 are vital tools in re-imagining tourism in a world of declining nature.

Conclusion

This chapter has presented a case for designing a future where nature tourism is increasing while the quality and extent of the natural environment is declining. Nature is important to humans not only as a resource for leisure, inspiration, and psychological rejuvenation but for all the ecosystem services it provides. Tourism is the world's largest industry and activities in nature are not benign. Nature tourism thus needs to be enjoyed and managed according to a sustainable future. This future needs to include a significant wildlife conservation

Table 31.1 Understanding the tourism–nature relationship and a vision for the future

Behavioural standpoint	Meaning/definition	Current behavioural issues associated with the human condition	An aspirational future tourism and nature relationship
Morals	Acceptable codes of behaviour in a society. Principles of right or wrong	Abuse, exploitation and disregard for wildlife and the natural environment	Being 'present' to pro conservation messages when being guided. Respectful behaviour in the presence of wildlife
Ethics	Moral principle that governs a person's behaviour	View that animals have no consciousness, personality or rights and that human are superior. Lack of awareness or concern about the state of the environment	Respect for nature. Awareness that we are part of nature. Wild places are important, and that wildlife should be free.
Attitude	Settled in a way of thinking	There is no hope in stopping environmental destruction. Sustainability is a fallacy or impossible to achieve. That we can do what we want in the natural environment. Apathy and potential hedonistic attitudes.	Awareness that protection and appreciation of nature is good for us and important for our mental and physical health. Fosters a view that we are not superior and above nature. Realise that we are disrespecting wildlife. Realise that COVID-19 is an environmental problem. Learning about the environment helps us to predict and realise our future
Expectations	Strong belief that something will be the case	That we can do what we want in the natural environment.	Nature is wild and free and deserves respect
Experience	Practical contact with observed facts or events. An event or occurrence that leaves an impression	Negative perceptions associated with disrespect for wildlife, congestion, crowding, pollution, and environmental degradation.	Evokes a sense of awe, 'excitement' and wonder. Awareness that we are responsible for environmental damage

effort, the restoration of damaged ecosystems, scientifically informed tourism planning, best practice management and attention to the human–nature relationship according to an enlightened moral and ethical standpoint. Moreover, such actions are the collective and personal responsibility of governments, agencies, and individuals. Achieving such a goal requires re-examining and changing our way of thinking about the way we value the natural world and subsequently behave when visiting natural environments. Predicting the future is thus not easy. Will nature tourism of the future be 'business as usual'? Currently, some nature tourism enterprises strive for sustainability while other destinations are under pressure from overtourism, competing interests and/or subject to values and behaviour that degrades the natural world. Given that natural ecosystems continue to be damaged, and wildlife is declining globally the time for a re-imagined form of nature tourism is right now.

Table 31.2 Behavioural codes and practices designed to promote appropriate individual and community responsibility and relevant action plans and policies pertaining to the future of tourism and the natural environment

Codes and practice	Relevance for nature tourism futures	Relevant sources
Animal Ethical Code	Promotion and management of respectful and appropriate wildlife tourism, especially regarding wildlife interactions, wildlife photography and dealing with the selfie phenomenon	Fennell, D. A. (2014). Exploring the boundaries of a new moral order for tourism's global code of ethics: an opinion piece on the position of animals in the tourism industry. *Journal of Sustainable Tourism*, 22 (7), 983–996. Von Essen, E., Lindsjö, J., & Berg, C. (2020). Instagranimal: animal welfare and animal ethics challenges of animal-based tourism. *Animals*, 10: 1830 doi:10.3390/ani10101830
Plant Ethical Code	Botanical tourism, management of hiking, camping, mountain biking, adventure racing and events that take place in natural settings	Cohen, E., & Fennell, D. (2019). Plants and tourism: Not seeing the forest [n] or the trees. *Tourist Studies*, 19 (4), 585–606.
Geo-ethics	To guide geotourism and geopark visitation. Management of hiking, adventure racing, events, rock, and mountain climbing, prevention of graffiti and preventing excessive modification and loss of geodiversity.	The International Association for Promoting Geoethics (IAPG). https://www.geoethics.org/copia-di-homepage Gordon, J. E., Crofts, R., Gray, M., & Tormey, D. (2021). Including geoconservation in the management of protected and conserved areas matters for all of nature and people. *International Journal of Geoheritage and Parks* 9: 323–334.
Sustainable Development Goals	Guidelines for tourism DMA's regarding tackling climate change and fostering role of ecosystem services. Appropriate development, management, and role of education. Promotion of conservation	https://www.un.org/sustainabledevelopment/blog/2021/07/a-new-global-framework-for-managing-nature-through-2030-1st-detailed-draft-agreement-debuts/
Aichi Targets	Conservation of ecotourism resources. Government support for the creation and protection of natural areas	https://www.iucn.org/theme/species/our-work/influencing-policy/convention-biological-diversity-cbd/aichi-targets
Re-wilding programmes	Guidelines for conservation agencies Conservation and recovery of ecotourism resources	Hall, C. M. (2019). Tourism and rewilding: an introduction–definition, issues, and review. *Journal of Ecotourism* 18: 297-308. https://www.iucn.org/sites/dev/files/content/documents/principles_of_rewilding_cem_rtg.pdf
IUCN motion Marseille 2020/2021	Highlight importance of tourism conducted in a sustainable way and in protecting biodiversity	Mader (2021) Strengthening sustainable tourism's role in biodiversity conservation and community resilience, Motion 130 https://www.planeta.com/iucn2020-motion130/

This chapter offers a way forward in that it describes the problem and offers solutions that lie with the responsibility of governments and individuals. The biggest challenge of all will be in re-examining and changing our thinking about the way we value the natural world and subsequently behave when we are participating in tourism programmes that sit within a world of declining nature.

References

Adams, D. & Carwardine, M. (1990). *Last Chance to see*. London, UK: Heinemann Ltd.
Aplin, G., Beggs, P., Brierley, G., Cleugh, H., Curson. P., Mitchell. P., Pitman, A. & Rich, D. (1999). *Global Environmental Crises*. Oxford, UK: Oxford University Press.
Attenborough, D. (2020). *A life on our planet*. London: Witness Books.
Buckley, R. (2003). *Case studies in ecotourism*. Oxford, UK: CABI Publishing.
Buckley, R. (2004). *Environmental impacts of ecotourism*. Oxford, UK: CABI Publishing.
Buckley, R. (2010). *Conservation tourism*. Oxford, UK: CABI Publishing.
Buckley, R. (2020). Nature tourism and mental health: Parks, happiness, and causation. *Journal of Sustainable Tourism*, 28(9), 1409–1424.
Buckley, R. C., Brough, P., & Westaway, D. (2018). Bringing outdoor therapies into mainstream mental health. *Frontiers in public health*, 6, 119.
Buckley, R., Brough, P., Hague, L., Chauvenet, A., Fleming, C., Roche, E., Sofija, E., & Harris, N. (2019). Economic value of protected areas via visitor mental health. *Nature Communications*, 10(1), 1–10.
BGCI (2021). *State of the World's Trees*. Richmond, UK: Botanic Gardens Conservation International.
Cahyadi, H. S. & Newsome, D. (2021). The post COVID-19 tourism dilemma for geoparks in Indonesia. *International Journal of Geoheritage and Parks*. https://doi.org/10.1016/j.ijgeop.2021.02.003
Carrington, D. (2020) Pandemics result from destruction of nature, say UN and WHO https://www.theguardian.com/world/2020/jun/17/pandemics-destruction-nature-un-who-legislation-trade-green-recovery (accessed 4/12/21)
DBCA (2021). Plan for Our Parks. https://www.dbca.wa.gov.au/parks-and-wildlife-service/plan-for-our-parks. Department of Biodiversity, Conservation and Attractions, Perth, Western Australia.
DPW (2017). Numbat (*Myrmecobius fasciatus*) Recovery Plan. Western Australia Department of Parks and Wildlife, Perth, Western Australia.
Ebi, K. L., Vanos, J., Baldwin, J. W., Bell, J. E., Hondula, D. M., Errett, N. A., Hayes, K., Reid, C., Saha, S., Berry, P., & Spector, J. (2021). Extreme weather and climate change: Population health and health system implications. *Annual Review of Public Health*, 42, 293–315.
European Wilderness Society (2021) UN published a draft plan to halt biodiversity loss by 2030 https://wilderness-society.org/un-publishes-a-draft-plan-to-halt-biodiversity-loss-by-2030/ (accessed Sept 3, 2021).
Gaynor, K. M., Fiorella, K. J., Gregory, G. H., Kurz, D. J., Seto, K. L., Withey, L. S., & Brashares, J. S. (2016). War and wildlife: Linking armed conflict to conservation. *Frontiers in Ecology and the Environment*, 14(10), 533–542.
Goodwin, H. (2017). The challenge of overtourism. *Responsible Tourism Partnership Working Paper*, 4, 1–19.
Gonzalez-Maya, J. F., Víquez-R, L. R., Belant, J. L., & Ceballos, G. (2015). Effectiveness of protected areas for representing species and populations of terrestrial mammals in Costa Rica. *PloS one*, 10(5), e0124480.
Hall, C. M. (2019). Constructing sustainable tourism development: The 2030 agenda and the managerial ecology of sustainable tourism. *Journal of Sustainable Tourism*, 27(7), 1044–1060.
Hasanah Abd Mutalib, A. (2018). The photo frenzy phenomenon: How a single snap can affect wildlife populations. *Biodiversity*, 19(3–4), 237–239.

Hockings, M. (2021). COVID-19 wasn't just a disaster for humanity – new research shows nature suffered greatly too. https://theconversation.com/COVID-19-wasnt-just-a-disaster-for-humanity-new-research-shows-nature-suffered-greatly-too-156838 (accessed 4/12/21).

Holden, A. (2016). *Environment and tourism*. London and New York: Routledge.

Holy Bible (2011). New International Version. *Genesis*, *1*, 28.

Hughes, M., Newsome, D., & Macbeth, J. (2005). Visitor perceptions of captive wildlife tourism in a Western Australian natural setting. *Journal of Ecotourism*, *4*(2), 73–91.

Insch, A. (2020). The challenges of over-tourism facing New Zealand: Risks and responses. *Journal of Destination Marketing & Management*, *15*, 100378.

IPBES (2020). Workshop Report on Biodiversity and Pandemics of the Intergovernmental Platform on Biodiversity and Ecosystem Services. In Daszak, P., das Neves, C., Amuasi, J., Hayman, D., Kuiken, T., Roche, B., Zambrana-Torrelio, C., Buss, P., Dundarova, H., Feferholtz, Y., Foldvari, G., Igbinosa, E., Junglen, S., Liu, Q., Suzan, G., Uhart, M., Wannous, C., Woolaston, K., Mosig Reidl, P., O'Brien, K., Pascual, U., Stoett, P., Li, H. & Ngo, H. T. *IPBES secretariat*, Bonn, Germany, DOI:10.5281/zenodo.4147317 (accessed 4/12/21).

Irvine, K. N., Fuller, R. A., Devine-Wright, P., Tratalos, J., Payne, S. R., Warren, P. H., Lomas, K. J., & Gaston, K. J. (2010). Ecological and psychological value of urban green space. In *Dimensions of the sustainable city*. Springer, Dordrecht (pp. 215–237).

IUCN. (2018). IUCN Green List of Protected and Conserved Areas https://www.iucn.org/theme/protected-areas/our-work/iucn-green-list

Koh, E., & Fakfare, P. (2020). Overcoming "over-tourism: The closure of Maya Bay", *International Journal of Tourism Cities*, *6*(2), 279–296.

Laurance, B. (2022). Why environmental impact assessments fail. *Therya*, *13*(1), 67–72.

Lemelin, H., Dawson, J., & Stewart, E. J. (2012). *Last chance tourism: Adapting tourism opportunities in a changing world*. London: Routledge.

Lenzi, C., Speiran, S., & Grasso, C. (2020). "Let Me Take a Selfie": Implications of Social Media for Public Perceptions of Wild Animals. *Society & Animals*. https://doi.org/10.1163/15685306-bja10023

Leverington, F., Costa, K. L., Pavese, H., Lisle, A., & Hockings, M. (2010). A global analysis of protected area management effectiveness. *Environmental Management*, *46*(5), 685–698.

Liddle, M. (1997). *Recreation ecology: The ecological impact of outdoor recreation and ecotourism*. Melbourne, Australia: Chapman and Hall.

Mandić, A., & Marković Vukadin, I. (2021). Managing Overtourism in Nature-Based Destinations. In: A. Mandic & L. Petric (eds) *Mediterranean Protected Areas in the Era of Overtourism* (pp. 45–70). Cham: Springer.

Marlier, M. E., Jina, A. S., Kinney, P. L., & DeFries, R. S. (2016). Extreme air pollution in global megacities. *Current Climate Change Reports*, *2*(1), 15–27.

Martin, A. (1975). *The last Generation*. Glasgow, UK: Collins.

McGrath, M. (2021). Climate change: IPCC report is 'code red for humanity' https://www.bbc.com/news/science-environment-58130705 (accessed Sept 3, 2021).

McGinlay, J., Gkoumas, V., Holtvoeth, J., Fuertes, R. F. A., Bazhenova, E., Benzoni, A., Botsch, K., Martel, C., Sánchez, C., Cervera, I., Chaminade, G., Doerstel, J., García, C., Jones, A., Lammertz, M., Lotman, K., Odar, M., Pastor, T., Ritchie, C., Santi, S., Smolej, M., Rico, F., Waterman, H., Zwijacz-Kozic, T., Kontoleon, A., Dimitrakopoulos, P., & Jones, N. (2020). The impact of COVID-19 on the management of European protected areas and policy implications. *Forests*, *11*, 1214. https://doi.org/10.3390/f11111214

McNeely, J. A. (2021). Nature and COVID-19: The pandemic, the environment, and the way ahead. *Ambio*, *50*, 767–781.

Mimbale, J. (2020). Political Economy of War and Nature Conservation in the DRC: Strategic Approaches and Prioritization of Actions. *International Journal of Empirical Finance and Management Sciences*, *2*(4), 43–58.

Moorhouse, T. P., Dahlsjö, C. A., Baker, S. E., D'Cruze, N. C., & Macdonald, D. W. (2015). The customer isn't always right—conservation and animal welfare implications of the increasing demand for wildlife tourism. *PloS one*, *10*(10), e0138939.

Moorhouse, T., D'Cruze, N. C., & Macdonald, D. W. (2017). Unethical use of wildlife in tourism: What's the problem, who is responsible, and what can be done? *Journal of Sustainable Tourism*, *25*(4), 505–516.

Morris, D. (1990). *The animal contract*. London, UK: Virgin Books.

Neiwert, D. (2016). *Of orcas and men*. London, UK: Duckworth Overlook.

Newsome, D. (2013). An 'ecotourist's recent experience in Sri Lanka. *Journal of Ecotourism 12*, 210–220.

Newsome, D. (2014). Appropriate policy development and research needs in response to adventure racing in protected areas. *Biological Conservation 171*, 259–269.

Newsome, D. (2020a). The collapse of tourism and its impact on wildlife tourism destinations. *Journal of Tourism Futures*. https://doi.org/10.1108/JTF-04-2020-0053

Newsome, D. (2020b). Sustainability can start with a garden! *International Journal of Tourism Cities*. https://doi.org/10.1108/IJTC-04-2020-0084

Newsome, D., & Hassell, S. (2014). Tourism and conservation in Madagascar: The importance of Andasibe National Park. *Koedoe 56*, 1–8.

Newsome, D., & Hughes, M. (2017) Jurassic World as a contemporary wildlife tourism theme park allegory. *Current Issues in Tourism*, *20*, 1311–1319.

Newsome, D., & Perera, P. (2022). Nature-based tourism: Before, during and after COVID-19. In: Mandić, A., Valia, S.K. *Routledge Handbook of Nature-based Tourism Development*. London and New York: Routledge.

Newsome, D., Moore, S. A., & Dowling, R. K. (2013). *Natural area tourism*. Bristol, UK: Channel View Publications.

Newsome, D. Rodger, K. Pearce, J., & Chan, J. (2019). Visitor satisfaction with a key wildlife tourism destination within the context of a damaged landscape. *Current Issues in Tourism*. *22*, 729–746 (published on-line 2017).

Parks Victoria (n.d.). Fourth Edition Key Findings. https://www.parks.vic.gov.au/get-into-nature/conservation-and-science/science-and-research/state-of-the-parks/fourth-edition-key-findings. Government of Victoria, Australia.

Pickering, C. M. (2010). Ten factors that affect the severity of environmental impacts of visitors in protected areas. *Ambio*, *39*, 70–77.

Prakash, S. L., Perera, P., Newsome, D., Kusuminda, T., & Walker, O. (2019). Reasons for visitor dissatisfaction with wildlife tourism experiences at highly visited national parks in Sri Lanka. *Journal of Outdoor Recreation and Tourism*, *25*, 102–112.

Reyers, B., Folke, C., Moore, M. L., Biggs, R., & Galaz, V. (2018). Social-ecological systems insights for navigating the dynamics of the Anthropocene. *Annual Review of Environment and Resources*, *43*, 267–289.

Rizzolo, J. B. (2021). Wildlife tourism and consumption. *Journal of Sustainable Tourism*. https://doi.org/10.1080/09669582.2021.1957903

Schulze, K., Knights, K., Coad, L., Geldmann, J., Leverington, F., Eassom, A., Marr, M., Butchart, S.H., Hockings, M., & Burgess, N.D. (2018). An assessment of threats to terrestrial protected areas. *Conservation Letters*, *11*(3). https://doi.org/10.1111/conl.12435

Spenceley, A., McCool, S., Newsome, D., Báez, A., Barborak, J., Blye, C-J., Bricker, K., Cahyadi, H., Corrigan, K., Halpenny, E., Hvenegaard, G., Malleret King, D., Leung, Y-F., Mandić, A., Naidoo, R., Rüede, D., Sano, J., Sarhan, M., Santamaria, V., Sousa, T., & Zschiegner, A. (2021) Tourism in protected and conserved areas amid the COVID-19 pandemic. *Parks*, *27*, 108–118.

Tafoya, K. A., Brondizio, E. S., Johnson, C. E., Beck, P., Wallace, M., Quirós, R., & Wasserman, M. D. (2020). Effectiveness of Costa Rica's conservation portfolio to lower deforestation, protect primates, and increase community participation. *Frontiers in Environmental Science*, *8*, 212.

United Nations. (2015). Transforming our world: The 2030 Agenda for sustainable development (A/RES/70/1). New York, NY: UN General Assembly. Retrieved from https://sdgs.un.org/2030agenda

UNSDG (2019). UN Report: Nature's dangerous decline' unprecedented'; species extinction rates accelerating. https://www.un.org/sustainabledevelopment/blog/2019/05/nature-decline-unprecedented-report/ (accessed Sept 3, 2021)

UNWTO/UNDP (2018). Tourism and sustainable development goals – journey to 2030. United Nations World Tourism Organisation and United Nations Development Programme. https://www.undp.org/publications/tourism-and-sustainable-development-goals-journey-2030 (accessed 12/5/22)

Vidal, J. (2020). 'Tip of the iceberg': Is our destruction of nature responsible for COVID-19? https://www.theguardian.com/environment/2020/mar/18/tip-of-the-iceberg-is-our-destruction-of-nature-responsible-for-COVID-19-aoe (accessed 4/12/21)

Wall, G. (2020). From carrying capacity to overtourism: A perspective article. *Tourism Review*, 75(1), 212–215. https://doi.org/10.1108/TR-08-2019-0356

World Animal Protection. (2017). A close up on cruelty: The harmful impact of wildlife selfies in the Amazon. https://dkt6rvnu67rqj.cloudfront.net/sites/default/files/media/au_files/wap_wildlifenotentertainers_report_final_uk_092617lr.pdf (accessed 4/12/21).

White, M. P., Alcock, I., Grellier, J., Wheeler, B. W., Hartig, T., Warber, S. L., Bone, A., Depledge, M., & Fleming, L. E. (2019). Spending at least 120 minutes a week in nature is associated with good health and wellbeing. *Scientific Reports*, 9(1), 1–11.

Wong, C. M., Conti-Jerpe, I., Raymundo, L. J., Dingle, C., Araujo, G., Ponzo, A., & Baker, D. M. (2019). Whale shark tourism: Impacts on coral reefs in the Philippines. *Environmental Management*, 63(2), 282–291.

Part III
Market-led trends

Chapter 32 is by **Gokce Ozdemir** and **Duygu Celebi** on *Bleisure trends: Combining business and leisure travel*. Business travel containing leisure components is not a new phenomenon, but it is a new concept in tourism marketing strategies. With the bleisure concept, destination management organisations (DMOs) strive to create new markets and constantly develop innovative and creative offerings to keep up with the global competition. This chapter contributes to the literature by examining the bleisure offerings based on the information provided by DMOs on their websites. The content analysis was employed through data generated from 541 websites of DMOs that are members of Destinations International Foundation. This chapter fills an important gap in the literature and provides valuable insights for DMOs currently targeting bleisure travellers through a comprehensive marketing perspective. The current study also demonstrates strong motives to target bleisure tourists and offers several practical implications for DMOs.

Glamping: Camping in its "green" and luxurious version is the topic of Chapter 33 by **Spyridoula Dimitra Souki**. The chapter introduces and defines the subject matter of "glamping". Initially, it identifies the importance of glamping's new travel trend for consumers, businesses in the tourism sector, but also the impact that such a form of tourism can have on the environment, and its sustainability. Secondly it investigates the role of glamping in the global economy of the 21st century, as well as its potential of growth during the next decades.

Elisa Zentveld in Chapter 34 describes *VFR travel: opportunities, trends and issues*. The chapter addresses four key matters. Firstly, it outlines in what ways visiting friends and relatives (VFR) travel is highly relevant; especially in the years moving forward from the COVID-19 pandemic that consumed the world. Secondly, it explains the way in which VFR travel data are tracked and interpreted and how that influences VFR travel in scholarship as well as in practice. The chapter also discusses the definition of VFR and how misunderstandings of the definition in scholarly circles and in tourism industries have limited the development and adoption of VFR travel. Fourthly, the chapter highlights the major trends and issues and outlines what this may mean for scholarship and tourism industries.

Chapter 35 is on *Transformational tourism: A visionary approach to sustainable tourism?* by **G.L.W. Roshini N. Nandasena, Alastair M. Morrison, Wenjie Cai**, and **J. Andres Coca-Stefaniak**. The main purpose of the chapter is to propose a conceptual model of transformational tourism. The transformational process for tourists is explored through an analysis of tourism experiences in Sri Lanka. Based on a thematic analysis of in-depth interviews, two themes were identified: (1) The healing and inspiration of Sri Lanka; and

(2) self-reflective actions towards encountering poverty in tourism destinations. Future trends and research directions for transformational tourism are proposed.

In Chapter 36, **Katrina Glebova, Fateme Zare, Robert Book, Michel Desbordes**, and **Gabor Geczi** focus on *Sport tourism in times of VUCA world*. VUCA is an acronym constructed to embrace volatility, uncertainty, complexity, and ambiguity. Today's world maintains a constant state of VUCA conditions, affecting many industries, including sports and tourism. Today sport tourism is facing numerous changes, challenges, and, consequently, opportunities. The chapter begins with a brief section on the definition, taxonomy, and history of sport tourism. In addition, why sport tourism deserves special attention is explained and is of particular interest in the contemporary tourism context. Second, the recent changes in sport tourism are described, and challenges for this industry are seen. This is followed by a few vivid examples from the business. Subsequently, the opportunities and perspectives for sport tourism management and marketing are defined and developed for the foreseeable future. Multifaceted conclusions are drawn about reshaping sport tourism and its place in the tourism industry in general, about borders, obstacles, challenges, and following opportunities brought about by this complex situation. The current chapter can be of interest to a wide audience – students, scholars, and tourism and sport managers – in order to understand trends and issues in the field and to turn described challenges into an advantage.

German holiday travel demand trends are reviewed in Chapter 37 by **Dirk Schmücker, Anne Köchling**, and **Martin Lohmann**. Based on a larger trend study, this chapter describes key drivers and central future developments in German holiday travel demand. A main driving factor for the future demand is the immense stability of demand in the past. Holiday travel is a commonplace item in the consumption portfolio of most people in Germany. However, this stability does not promise major growth fantasies for the future. The effects of the COVID-19 pandemic disrupt this stability, at least for some time. Nevertheless, a return to previous patterns is what is expected for future tourism demand in Germany. Yet different dynamic forces could drive future demand into a different direction, compared to the stable patterns the industry was used to: Perception of climate change issues in society, labour market for the tourism industry, and new developments in communication technology. These aspects could lead to lower growth in air travel, rising prices and shifts in information and booking channels in the future.

Melanie Kay Smith discusses the *New trends in wellness tourism: Post-COVID restoration* in Chapter 38. The aim of the chapter is to analyse new trends in wellness tourism following the post-COVID era, where the focus shifted from hedonic to more restorative forms of tourism. Some authors predicted an increasing interest in health and wellness tourism post-COVID. Pocinho, Garcês and Neves de Jesus (2022, p. 7) stated that "Wellbeing and wellness can be attractive factors for new tourists and thus open doors to developing new products and activities in destinations". This, they argued, can make it possible to 'refresh' tourism, to change tourists' behaviour and to help solve pre-COVID problems such as overtourism. Discussions about the future of tourism include the concept of resilience which applies not only to destinations but also to residents and tourists. Pocinho et al. (2022) argue that resilience is a concept that is intimately related to wellbeing and helps to deal effectively with adversity. This is a broad subject that naturally lends itself to essential discussions about the impacts of tourism, resident wellbeing and sustainable destination development. One of the Sustainable Development Goals focuses specifically on Good Health and Wellbeing (SDG3) with several others emphasising, in particular, resident wellbeing (e.g., SDG 11 Sustainable Cities and Communities). In the future, it is predicted that wellbeing will become more central to government and stakeholder policy. Sustainable destination management will prioritise resident wellbeing and tourism businesses and industry will offer more wellness programmes for tourists. This chapter focuses more on the latter than the wellbeing of local residents, but it is recognised that the two should be inextricably connected in a more resilient and regenerative future.

Accelerated trends in tourism marketing and tourist behaviour are featured in Chapter 39 by **Metin Kozak**. Despite its much longer historical background, particularly since the 1980s, the world of marketing has entered a new era, becoming more consumer-oriented. Thus, consumers have begun to be at the centre of all production and marketing activities in the business world. In the first wave, commencing from the early 2000s, mass consumption has gained more emphasis in line with developments in technology. The tourism and hospitality industry has also been directly affected by such developments, and we have seen new ways of marketing methods and new types of tourism activities/products. As a second wave, one more feature of the 21st century is that it has principally been dominated by either regional or global incidents such as terrorism and pandemic. Together with disseminating the latest pandemic worldwide, marketing methods and consumer behaviour have undergone another dramatic transformation. Its initial outcomes have been reflected in present-day practice, e.g., more individualised lifestyles, more personalised marketing and consumerism, more concerns with safety and security, a more fashion-oriented approach, and greater engagement with social media. Consequently, this chapter aims to examine the new trends that are likely to be encountered in tourism marketing based on the possible changes in consumer behaviour in the light of the developments of the last two decades and two waves.

Brianna Wyatt provides Chapter 40 on *Re-enacting dark histories*. The growing temporal distance from death-related events and the increased presence of death and tragedy in media has influenced society to become desensitised to the image and presentation of death. In fact, studies have shown society has become more curious about death, resulting in an increased desire to learn about past pain and suffering. This, coupled with advancements in technology, have further influenced visitors to seek out more unique, memorable experiences that are engaging, personal, and even immersive. In response, there has been an increasing development of lighter dark visitor attractions – places considered lighter with respect to Stone's (2006) Darkness Spectrum on the basis of their higher commercial and tourism infrastructure and use of edutainment interpretation, which, as a strategic effort, that blurs education with entertainment, helps to create the more memorable and engaging experiences that visitors seek.

32 Bleisure trends

Combining business and leisure travel

Gokce Ozdemir and Duygu Celebi

Introduction

Since COVID-19 has devastated all travel forecasts (Walia, Kour, Choudhary, & Jasrotia, 2021, p. 2), DMOs have faced great challenges and have adapted quickly to the current conditions. Today, destinations are focusing on how to stimulate demand through various strategies due to the severe impact of the recent pandemic on tourism destinations. According to the Statista Dossier on worldwide business travel (López, 2022), business travel spending has reached US$504 billion despite the decline of 61% in business travel spending worldwide in 2020. Despite the downturn, business travel is expected to regain its position more slowly than leisure travel (ETC, 2020, p. 23). A study by Global Business Travel Association (2021) on business trips reveals that 56% of respondents are equally likely to blend business travel with a vacation, whereas 19% of respondents are much more likely to have a bleisure experience than before the pandemic. According to Martínez-Garcia, Ferrer-Rosell, and Coenders (2012, p. 13), for business travellers, there are substantial differences in terms of hotel category (higher), length of stay (shorter), and activities performed at the destination (less). Therefore, one of the strategies is to attract business travellers with bleisure offerings in order to create greater revenue. The significance of the bleisure market lies in the shorter travel distances and less frequent trips taken during the COVID-19 pandemic (Abdullah, Dias, Muley, & Shahin, 2020). In this sense, the concept of bleisure travel, encapsulating the notion of "work hard, play hard" in real life, is becoming more important for the travel industry.

Although there has been a strong link between leisure tourism and business tourism throughout history (Swarbrooke & Horner, 2007, p. 31), the term 'bleisure' has recently emerged as a term that stands for the blend of professional travel with personal experiences at the destination. Hence, studies on the evolution of business tourism into bleisure tourism have gained impetus over just the last decade (Chung, Choi, Yoo & Kim, 2020; Lichy & McLeay, 2017; Walia et al., 2021). This research covers the proliferation of bleisure offerings among destinations that aim to encourage business travellers with leisure activities in order to revitalise their destination experience. Until recently, business travellers were only targeted by hotels to maximise their revenue due to the increased number of overnight stays. The bleisure market, whether undertaken by an individual businessperson or a group of delegates, represents a great potential for tourism destinations and tourism companies. This lucrative segment generates incremental revenue with regard to greater tax, and increased employment; it can lead to an enhancement of a destination's reputation (Davidson, 2003, p. 31), and a flattening of the effects of seasonality. Tourism businesses, such as attractions, restaurants, hotels, travel agencies, souvenir shops, and sightseeing companies, build an overall destination experience and benefit from the revenue that bleisure travellers generate.

Literature review

Thanks to digitalisation, there is a blurring of the boundaries between work and social life (Kachinewska, 2016: 517), which has given rise to privacy concerns. In the tourism context, the distinction between business and leisure is also blurred. Nevertheless, achieving the right balance between work and leisure is vital to a person's wellbeing (Kachinewska, 2016, p. 518). Bleisure is a hybrid concept and a recent trend that goes beyond bringing a partner to the conference as work–life boundaries blur (BBC, n.d.). Although the phenomenon is not a new one, the marketing practices of destinations aimed at business people and their acquaintances for leisure activities are relatively recent. Combining business and leisure into one trip may boost the traveller's morale, develop a positive relationship with the family members when they travel together and raise the performance of the businesspeople at work.

Business travel consists of trip preparations, passenger experiences, destination experiences, and homecoming (Unger, Uriely, and Fuchs, 2016, p. 153). The findings of Unger et al. (2016, p. 148) also reveal that the destination experience phase is considered a work-related activity rather than a recreational activity. Business travel typically possesses an opportunity for travellers to participate in leisure activities during their stays or to extend the duration of their trips to enrich personal experiences. Bleisure travel is on the rise with or without extended stays. Travellers may spend their time off at a local restaurant for dinner, in a live concert, or at an evening visit to a museum in an attempt to have a glimpse of the destination's authenticity and also to relax and enjoy a bit when the workday is over. Business trips happen all year round, but business travellers have mostly limited time at the destination. Therefore, they appreciate every moment that is off the beaten track.

This lucrative market segment represents business travellers who have the potential to spend more or stay longer other than the primary business and professional purposes. Business travellers do not take bleisure trips unless they have time (58%), want to explore the destination (17%), or afford it (14%) (The GBTA Foundation, 2017, p. 5). A recent bleisure travel study by Expedia (2016) pinpoints that 66% of bleisure travellers tend to spend more on leisure activities as they save on travel expenses. Furthermore, the report points out that the decision to transform a business trip into a bleisure trip is based on the attractiveness of destinations such as New York, Seattle, Los Angeles, Chicago, and Washington, D.C.

Bleisure marketing strategies aim to motivate business travellers to have a better experience at the destination beyond business events (Chung et al., 2020, p. 300). The benefits targeting the bleisure segment are of great appeal for destinations whereas this type of travel also brings various advantages to the business travellers such as saving on international travel costs and efforts while enjoying the destination attributes. Combining business and pleasure on one trip can also be a major incentive for business travellers, as corporate businesses often pay for ticket and visa application costs. The research conducted by Expedia (2016) reveals that 43% of all business trips across domestic and international destinations are bleisure trips. Bleisure has increased to 52% of international business travel, confirming that overseas travel is likely to positively influence bookings (Expedia, 2016). These numbers show how leisure activities are increasingly being included in business travel. They also illustrate that the destination where the business event takes place is a determining factor for business travelers to combine business and leisure (The GBTA Foundation, 2017, p. 3).

Bleisure is mainly associated with the new generations as they are far more tech-savvy than any other generation based on the technology's occupational benefits. Research concerning Millennials (Glover, 2010, pp. 157–158) pinpoints that there is a positive attitude towards overseas travel and also frequent short breaks which are likely to continue in the future. The findings of Li, Li, & Hudson (2013, p. 161) also support that Millennials (Generation Y – 1981 to 1990) seek to expand their travel horizons and explore new destinations. Similarly, Pendergast (2010) stated that Millennials attempt to get much out of their travel as they are considered to be experience-hungry. According to Pinho & Marques (2021, p. 359), tourism suppliers should adapt their offerings to the changing nature of the Millennials for bleisure tourism as this phenomenon has never been more significant. The GBTA Foundation's (2017, p. 8) research results imply that Millennials (48%) participated in bleisure travel at a higher rate than either Gen X travellers (33%) or Baby Boomers (23%).

However, the motivation behind having a bleisure travel trip varies. Bleisure travellers are motivated by the tangible, intangible, push-and-pull factors that motivate each typology seeking new skills, adventure, novelty, knowledge transfer, and research/funding partnership opportunities (Lichy & Mcleay, 2017, p. 525). Thus, a leisure activity takes its basic form with food, which is considered a vital component of the hospitality industry (Cleave, 2020, p. 476). Food is not only a crucial element in business trips but also a social element. In addition to the venues, providing leisure activities based on natural and cultural resources is of great importance for destinations to be valued for bleisure trips (Marques & Santos, 2017, p. 448). Chen (2019, p. 252) indicates that destination activities are one of the three main elements of the strategies business travellers employ to alleviate their stress and exhaustion during trips. For instance, it would be a great relief to explore the city and establish a positive change in mood, particularly for frequent business travellers. Numerous studies refer to the bleisure-related behaviour of conference attendees (Tretyakevich & Maggi, 2012; Yoo, Mcintosh, & Cockburn-Wootten, 2016). Yet the findings of Yoo et al. (2016, p. 449) highlight that accompanying partners enjoy the conference travel during both their own free time and couple time. Besides, attending a conference renders a great opportunity to strengthen spousal bonds through leisure activities (Yoo et al., 2016, p. 456). In the case in which a business traveller travels to the same few destinations, attending events as short-term attractions would be an outstanding appeal. Whether or not to be a bleisure traveller also depends on the characteristics of the traveller like being a sponsored, single, familiar with the destination, and accompanied by a friend (Davidson, 2003, p. 33).

Most bleisure travellers have busier schedules than traditional leisure travellers (Lichy & Mcleay, 2017, p. 526). As a result, 90% of business travellers extend their business trips for leisure for more than one day while only 23% extend for more than three days (The GBTA Foundation, 2017, p. 23). Therefore, existing products have to be tailored and new products have to be developed to suit the needs of the bleisure traveller. Instead of assuming that business travellers will adjust their work schedules while travelling, personalised leisure activities or tour programs might be developed. To entice business travellers, DMOs and stakeholders should collaborate (Pinho & Marques, 2021, p. 349) since travellers who take a break from business travel and spend their free time exploring the area might generate revenue for the local businesses and contribute to the local economy (Chung et al., 2020, p. 305). Considering the potential impact of bleisure travel on the local economy, partnerships between local businesses and the meeting planners should be improved for bleisure marketing (Chung et al., 2020, p. 306). According to Pinho and Marques (2021, p. 359), bleisure in cities could be increased with the valuation of specific services, local tourist resources, accessibility and connection to the world, hospitality, and the promotion and marketing strategies of the destination. In addition, guided tours may be of interest to conference delegates, despite notable differences in leisure behaviour depending on the nationalities of business travellers (Tretyakevich & Maggi, 2012, p. 395).

Methodology

This chapter examined the content of official websites to reveal the focus of DMOs on bleisure travel. The qualitative research method was preferred as the research methodology. According to Creswell and Creswell (2017), a qualitative research method can be chosen when it is not possible to use quantitative research methods. In this direction, the research process began with determining destination websites for data collection. Members of Destinations International (which was previously known as Destination Marketing Association International – DMAI) were selected as a sample for this chapter in order to gather appropriate data. Destinations International is considered the world's largest and most reliable resource for DMOs. Thus, the primary data were collected by the researchers by visiting each website of 541 DMOs that are members of Destinations International. Afterward, the qualitative content analysis method was employed as it is one of the most commonly used techniques for analysing and categorising qualitative data (Serafini & Reid, 2019; Lindgren et al., 2020). This method, as in this research, primarily plays a vital role in categorising large amounts of data efficiently (Schreier, 2019).

The data collection process for content analysis consisted of three stages. In the first stage, the authors created a detailed control chart for each destination comprising of six different indicators: (1) name of the city, (2) name of the country, (3) name of the destination marketing organisation, (3) bleisure offerings, (4) types of bleisure offerings, and (6) detailed explanation. In the second stage, the researchers visited each website of 541 destinations respectively, through the home page, menu sidebars, and additional links. When a bleisure offering was available on the destination website, the content of the product was analysed and the information about the offering with its details was recorded in the control chart. Finally, in the third stage, whenever there was no visible bleisure offering, the researchers thoroughly explored each website to pinpoint a destination's bleisure offerings. In this sense, researchers used the 'search' tools to find any information to identify the bleisure-like traits. The content analysis of the websites was employed by the researchers between the period December 2021 and January 2022. Thereby, the contents of the websites were examined, categorised, and interpreted using a unit of analysis created from the results of the control charts. The inter-coder reliability of this study was calculated and found to be 87%, which represents a perfect fit between the two coders according to Cohen's Kappa Formula (Mikkonen & Kyngäs, 2020).

Findings

Within the scope of this study, 541 official websites were examined in detail to find clues about the 'bleisure travel'. The study findings illustrate that 362 destinations directly or indirectly target bleisure travellers as a tourism market segment. To target business people for leisure activities, only London's official tourism website uses the term "bleisure" among such destinations. In addition, the study findings reveal that the concept of bleisure is not used by the remaining 179 destination websites as a strategy to target business travellers. The findings indicate that destinations, targeting business travellers as potential members of the bleisure market and displaying relevant products on their websites, lack attractiveness.

Moreover, those destinations' websites are not bleisure traveler-friendly and are time as well as effort-consuming. With the exception of https://www.iamsterdam.com the information at the destination websites provided for bleisure travellers does not offer customised offerings and is not beyond what is available to regular travellers. Nevertheless, the bleisure offers of 191 destinations are positioned directly on the homepage, while the remaining 171 destinations indirectly offer bleisure products through internal links, which refer to another page on the same website. The results of the study also showed that bleisure offers are mostly found under the main sections of "about us", "meet", "conferences", "meetings", "meetings & conferences", "convention", "professionals", "plan a leisure event", "plan your conference", "incentives", "business trips", and "extend your trip". In line with the qualitative content analysis, bleisure offers of the destinations were categorised and five distinctive elements were generated. As indicated in Figure 32.1, these elements are respectively; "food and beverage", "recreational activities", "itineraries", "attractions", and "events".

The study findings revealed that "food & beverage" is the first element of bleisure offerings created by all destinations to attract business travellers for leisure purposes. Within the context of this category, it was observed that bleisure offerings of destinations are blended by local cuisines, local tastes, local products, local restaurants, and local pubs and bars. In addition, study findings indicated that tasting activities, tasting trails, gastronomic workshops, gastronomic routes, and foodie maps are used effectively by destinations as a customised bleisure product to increase the personal experiences of the professionals.

In addition, "recreational activities" were found to be the second-highest category of bleisure offerings designed by destination marketers to enrich the business meetings with leisure activities or to extend the duration of a business trip. Within this category, it has been observed that destinations offer various recreational activities to businesspeople such as sports facilities (e.g., water sports, golf, cycling, and thematic walks), relaxing activities (e.g., rest, relaxation, spa, wellness, relax, and restore-based offerings), outdoor activities, group activities, and shopping facilities. Moreover, "itineraries" were indicated as the third

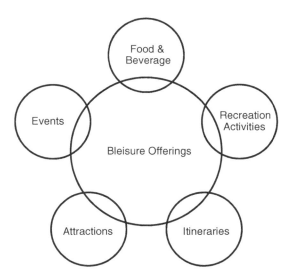

Figure 32.1 Bleisure offerings of destinations.

Source: Generated by the authors.

category of bleisure offerings. Based on the content analysis, it has been found that some destinations create customised products for bleisure travellers while others offer customised and non-customised itineraries or standard (non-customised) itinerary types. In addition, some destinations offer customised itineraries (e.g., incentive trips, guided tours, come early-stay late programs, and special packages) to attract the bleisure market, as well as non-tailored itineraries (e.g., walking tours, bike tours, thematic tours, wine tasting tours, and city tours) on their websites. Few destinations demonstrate a standard of itineraries such as historical tours, religious tours, excursions, short city tours, long city tours, shopping tours, sightseeing tours, or basic recreational tours specifically designed for bleisure travellers.

"Attractions" as another category showed itself in the sections of "list of top attractions", "top group attractions", or "list of places to go". According to the research results, managers of the destination websites aim to establish a strong bond with the bleisure travellers by highlighting attractions, leisure activities, and programs aimed at creating an appeal. For instance, the findings illustrate that attractions like museums, monuments, heritage, nature, rural retreats, sightseeing locations, beaches, casinos, stadiums, and nightlife were listed as major attractions of destinations to attract bleisure travellers and provide outstanding experiences. The fifth category of bleisure-based offerings of a destination has been identified as "events". It was observed that destinations offer numerous events on their websites, such as cultural events, live concerts, performances, festivals, sporting events, and local events, on their official websites to enhance and diversify their personal bleisure experiences during their stay.

Findings reveal what DMOs' current marketing practices are and how they are communicated to bleisure travellers through their official websites. It has been observed that many destination authorities are striving hard to grab the attention of business travellers, despite other DMOs that neglect this profitable segment. Research findings also prove that there is little focus on developing bleisure offerings if a DMO targets international bleisure travellers. A bleisure traveller is attracted to a destination depending on its image, proximity to the place of residence, accessibility, and provided tourism information (Davidson, 2003, p. 36). Therefore, the information provided by the DMOs through several communication channels including destination websites is likely to assist the business travellers in their decision-making process. Furthermore, when destinations implement effective strategies for meeting planners or individual business visitors, travellers are more likely to address the leisure travel opportunities that arise from business trips.

The research of Expedia (2016) also supports the significance of websites in generating bleisure travel demand. According to the study, regardless of the business component of travel, most bleisure travellers individually collect information or book leisure components, such as hotels (70%), airfare (52%), and restaurants (50%). Thus, destinations should create specific offerings that suit the needs of bleisure travellers and highlight them on their websites, preferably providing an internal link on the main page. In addition, our findings provide insight into the marketing strategies of DMOs as employed on the websites regarding bleisure travel. The results show that five major bleisure offerings come to the stage and act as a vital role on destination websites. These bleisure offerings can be categorised as food and beverage, recreational activities, itineraries, attractions, and events. Another noteworthy finding of the report by Expedia (2016) is that major events, such as festivals, cultural events, sporting events, and music concerts, are also a significant factor in motivating bleisure travellers. In parallel with this, our research findings show that destination websites contain various information about events that have the potential to attract bleisure travellers.

Discussion and conclusion

COVID-19 forced the tourism industry to reconsider the existing systems because of the sudden and intense decline in tourism arrivals. In this sense, COVID-19 is an opportunity and a threat for bleisure travellers. However, fear of exposure to COVID-19 while travelling and other travellers' non-compliance with safety regulations and protocols are two major hurdles for bleisure travelers (Walia et al., 2021, p. 7). Despite the hurdles during the pandemic, the bleisure market has gained more significance and DMOs have highly valued this segment by focusing on innovative marketing strategies, as exemplified in the chapter's findings.

As stated by Chung et al. (2020, p. 305), DMOs undertake several bleisure marketing programs to increase the quality of business travellers' experiences and to stimulate extra spending. Chung et al. (2020, p. 308) also quote that bleisure marketing programmes are more likely to fail when a customer-centric approach that enriches the business traveller's experience is neglected by destination marketers. Business travellers should, therefore, be inspired by customised offerings like odd hours or condensed versions of tours that they can experience while at the destination. Targeting this group and encouraging them to leave their hotels and conference rooms and discover the exciting city features is a logical and feasible strategy. Thus, to receive greater economic contributions from business travellers, DMOs' concentration on the bleisure market should be for the MICE delegates (Davidson, 2003) and for the individual business travellers (Lichy & McLeay, 2017). Regarding existing literature, one of the MICE travel motivations is found to be travel opportunities (Chiang, King, & Nguyen, 2012, p. 27). Since MICE trips are typically longer than business trips, this market is the most appropriate target for bleisure travel. Specifically, international travellers attempt to make the most of their visits while in foreign destinations. Working hard and being away from home can be awarded by some fun, enjoyment, relaxation, or wellness. This award may to a great extent boost the performance and increase the efficiency of the businessperson.

Among the international destinations that represent the best examples for bleisure; London, Paris, Barcelona, and Amsterdam come to the fore, respectively. The financial capital of Europe, London attracts many businesspersons and conference delegates from all over the world (Statista, 2022). The study's findings reveal that London's destination website reflects its success in bleisure travel by dedicating a special section for this category of tourist. Numerous sizable collaborations, seminars, and meetings are held in Paris, another renowned economic hub (Statista, 2021). In this regard, Paris, as the commercial hub of France, functions as a full-fledged bleisure destination with tailored options, as demonstrated on the Paris destination website. Yet Amsterdam represents a variety of customised tour packages for bleisure travellers, like 'Amsterdam in 3 Hours', 'Amsterdam in 1 Day', and 'Amsterdam in Two- or Three-Day Trip' depending on how much time they have at the destination (a few days, even a few hours).

Another well-known destination bursting with culture, history, cuisine, and art is Barcelona. Due to her abundance of resources and venues, Barcelona draws many business travellers from throughout the world, especially in recent years (Rico et al., 2019; Ramos & Mundet, 2021). Other well-known MICE destinations include Berlin, Orlando, Rome, Singapore, Las Vegas, Bangkok, Nassau, and Dubai (Global Meetings and Events Forecast, 2020). Although they provide suitable bleisure products with high performance and quality, they fail in using their websites as a direct marketing channel to promote their bleisure services. Additionally, to destination websites, effective social media channels help in increasing destination visibility. In other words, having social media accounts and integrating them effectively and seamlessly with the main website play a critical part in gaining a competitive edge and maximising revenue.

In light of the sustainability of destinations in 2032, 2042, and 2052, bleisure travel represents a promising offering. Contrary to mass tourism, bleisure travel supports Sustainable Development Goals No: 11 of UNWTO by reducing the carbon footprint due to dual-purpose single travel and accelerating the decrease of air pollution. Given that resources become more scarce throughout time, effective use of resources will become more crucial. In this sense, bleisure travel will be viewed as an alternative product for environmentally conscious and responsible tourists in the future. In the next few decades, the tourism sector will continue to undergo significant transformation as a result of demographic shifts. With the emergence of Generation Z, we are witnessing incremental changes in tourist choices and experiences, and destinations and tourism businesses are changing their services accordingly. It is anticipated that new generations with particular characteristics would challenge the current bleisure travel structure. Moreover, thanks to digital advances, current bleisure offerings will be more visible and accessible with easier and faster data flow and effective social media integration. Technology, however, may present threats as well as opportunities, potentially replacing actual bleisure travel with an experience in the Metaverse universe.

From a scholarly point of view, this chapter is most significant in identifying bleisure marketing strategies of DMOs that want to appeal to the lucrative bleisure market segment. From a practical standpoint, the study concludes that, as demonstrated on official websites, destinations do not have adequate bleisure travel practices. In addition, destinations have been found to lack clarity and visibility in communicating with the audience and fail to drive the attention of potential bleisure travellers. Therefore, DMOs should foster collaboration and coordination among stakeholders to assist the growth of the bleisure travel and to offer such services as an umbrella concept for destinations. It should be kept in mind that meeting planners typically provide recommendations to a conference organiser or the executive committee of an association (Crouch & Louviere, 2004). Given that, DMOs should encourage destination management companies, meeting planners, and travel agencies to arrange tailor-made offerings for the business travel market. In the case of individual business travellers seeking leisure experiences on their own, DMOs should be able to provide information about such services on their websites. From a social perspective, bleisure travel that includes enjoyment and relaxation can be rewarding and can make up for hard work and being away from home. In this regard, the content of bleisure products should be designed to allow business travellers to get away from their work as well as to maximise revenue. As with other studies, the chapter is not without its limitations as it only covered DMOs that are members of Destinations International Foundation, excluding destinations that are not members.

References

2020 Global Meetings and Events Forecast. (2020). American Express Meetings & Events. https://www.amexglobalbusinesstravel.com/content/uploads/2019/09/2020-Global-Meetings-Forecast-Final-US.pdf

Abdullah, M., Dias, C., Muley, D., & Shahin, M. (2020). Exploring the impacts of COVID-19 on travel behavior and mode preferences. *Transportation Research Interdisciplinary Perspectives*, 8, 100255. https://doi.org/10.1016/j.trip.2020.100255

BBC. (n.d.). *The Rise of the Bleisure Traveller*. BBC Capital. Retrieved January 2, 2022, from https://www.bbc.com/storyworks/capital/bleisure-bound/bleisure-travel-trend

Chen, H. (2019). A pilot study of business travelers' stress-coping strategies. *Tourism and Hospitality Research*, 19(2), 252–258. https://doi.org/10.1177/1467358417740747

Chiang, C.-C., King, B., & Nguyen, T.-H. (2012). Taiwan's MICE visitors: Business, leisure, and education dimensions. *International Journal of Culture, Tourism and Hospitality Research*, 6(1), 21–33. https://doi.org/10.1108/17506181211206225

Chung, J. Y., Choi, Y. K., Yoo, B. K., & Kim, S. H. (2020). Bleisure tourism experience chain: Implications for destination marketing. *Asia Pacific Journal of Tourism Research*, 25(3), 300–310. https://doi.org/10.1080/10941665.2019.1708760

Cleave, P. (2020). Food as a leisure pursuit, a United Kingdom perspective. *Annals of Leisure Research*, 23(4), 474–491. https://doi.org/10.1080/11745398.2019.1613669/FORMAT/EPUB

Creswell, J. W., & Creswell, J. D. (2017). *Research Design: Qualitative, quantitative, and mixed methods approaches*. Sage publications.

Crouch, G. I., & Louviere, J. J. (2004). The determinants of convention site selection: A logistic choice model from experimental data. *Journal of Travel Research*, 43, 118–130. https://doi.org/10.1177/0047287504268233

Davidson, R. (2003). Adding Pleasure to business: Conventions and tourism. *Journal of Convention & Exhibition Management*, 5(1), 29–39. https://doi.org/10.1300/J143v05n01_03

European Travel Commission (ETC). (2020, November). *European Travel Commission – European Tourism: Trends & Prospects Quarterly Report (Q3/2020)*. Retrieved December 23, 2021, from https://etc-corporate.org/uploads/2020/11/ETC-Quarterly-Report-Q3-2020-Final-Public.pdf

Expedia. (2016). *Unpacking Bleisure Traveler Trends*. Retrieved January 1, 2022, from https://advertising.expedia.com/about/press-releases/more-than-40-percent-of-business-trips-are-extended-for-leisure-purposes/

Global Business Travel Association. (2021, May). *Coronavirus Poll Results*. Retrieved January 15, 2022, from https://www.gbta.org/DesktopModules/DnnSharp/SearchBoost/FileDownload.ashx?file=18860&sb-bhvr=1

Glover, P. (2010). Generation Y's future tourism demand: Some opportunities and challenges. In Benckendorff, P., Moscardo, G. and Pendergast, D. (Eds), *Tourism and Generation Y*, (pp.155–163). Wallingford: CABI.

Kachinewska, M. (2016). Bleisure: Business and leisure equilibrium. In Ivanova, M., Ivanov, S., & Magnini, V. P. (Eds.). *The Routledge Handbook of Hotel Chain Management* (pp.542–554). London: Routledge.

Li, X., Li, X. (Robert), & Hudson, S. (2013). The application of generational theory to tourism consumer behavior: An American perspective. *Tourism Management*, 37, 147–164. https://doi.org/10.1016/j.tourman.2013.01.015

Lichy, J., & Mcleay, F. (2017). Bleisure: Motivations and typologies. *Journal of Travel & Tourism Marketing*, 35(4), 517–530. https://doi.org/10.1080/10548408.2017.1364206

Lindgren, B. M., Lundman, B., & Graneheim, U. H. (2020). Abstraction and interpretation during the qualitative content analysis process. *International Journal of Nursing Studies*, 108, 103632. https://doi.org/10.1016/j.ijnurstu.2020.103632

López, A. M. (2022, February 1). *Global business travel industry – statistics & facts*. Statista. Retrieved January 21, 2022, from https://www.statista.com/topics/2439/global-business-travel-industry/#dossierKeyfigures

Marques, J., & Santos, N. (2017). Tourism development strategies for business tourism destinations: Case study in the central region of Portugal. *Tourism*, 65(4), 437–449.

Martínez-Garcia, E., Ferrer-Rosell, B., & Coenders, G. (2012). Profile of business and leisure travelers on low-cost carriers in Europe. *Journal of Air Transport Management*, 20, 12–14. https://doi.org/10.1016/j.jairtraman.2011.09.002

Mikkonen, K., & Kyngäs, H. (2020). Content analysis in mixed methods research. In Kyngäs, H., Mikkonen, K., Kääriäinen, M. (Eds.), T*he Application of Content Analysis in Nursing Science Research* (pp. 31–40). Cham: Springer. https://doi.org/10.1007/978-3-030-30199-6_4

Pendergast, D. (2010). Connecting with Millennials: Using tag clouds to build a folksonomy from key home economics documents. *Family & Consumer Sciences*, *38*(3), 289–302.

Pinho, M., & Marques, J. (2021). The bleisure tourism trend and the potential for this business-leisure symbiosis in Porto. *Journal of Convention and Event Tourism*, *22*(4), 346–362. https://doi.org/10.1080/15470148.2021.1905575/FORMAT/EPUB

Ramos, S. P., & Mundet, L. (2021). Tourism-phobia in Barcelona: Dismantling discursive strategies and power games in the construction of a sustainable tourist city. *Journal of Tourism and Cultural Change*, *19*(1), 113–131.

Rico, A., Martínez-Blanco, J., Montlleó, M., Rodríguez, G., Tavares, N., Arias, A., & Oliver-Solà, J. (2019). Carbon footprint of tourism in Barcelona. *Tourism Management*, *70*, 491–504.

Schreier, M. (2019). Content analysis, qualitative. In P. Atkinson, S. Delamont, A. Cernat, J.W. Sakshaug, & R.A. Williams (Eds.), *SAGE Research Methods Foundations*. https://dx.doi.org/10.4135/9781526421036753373

Serafini, F., & Reid, S. F. (2019). Multimodal content analysis: Expanding analytical approaches to content analysis. *Visual Communication*. https://doi.org/10.1177/1470357219864133

Statista. (2021, October 1). Travel and tourism in France – Statistics & Facts. https://www.statista.com/topics/3768/travel-and-tourism-in-france/#dossierKeyfigures

Statista. (2022, May 19). International business visits to London 2009–2019. https://www.statista.com/statistics/473732/business-visits-london-uk/#statisticContainer

Swarbrooke, J., & Horner, S. (2007). *Consumer behaviour in tourism*. London: Routledge.

The GBTA Foundation. (2017). Extending Business Travel into Leisure Time – Bleisure Study, (June), 1–24.

Tretyakevich, N., & Maggi, R. (2012). Not just for business: Some evidence on leisure motivations of conference attendees. *Current Issues in Tourism*, *15*(4), 391–395. https://doi.org/10.1080/13683500.2011.592180

Unger, O., Uriely, N., & Fuchs, G. (2016). The business travel experience. *Annals of Tourism Research*, *61*, 142–156. https://doi.org/10.1016/J.ANNALS.2016.10.003

Walia, S., Kour, P., Choudhary, P., & Jasrotia, A. (2021). COVID-19 and the bleisure travellers: An investigation on the aftermaths and future implications. *Tourism Recreation Research*, 1–11. https://doi.org/10.1080/02508281.2021.1946653

Yoo, H., Mcintosh, A., & Cockburn-Wootten, C. (2016). Time for me and time for us: Conference travel as alternative family leisure. *Annals of Leisure Research*, *19*(4), 444–460. https://doi.org/10.1080/11745398.2016.1147361

33 "Glamping"

Camping in its "Green" and luxurious version

Spyridoula Dimitra Souki

"Glamping": Camping in its "green" and luxurious version
"Glamping is defined as a form of camping involving accommodation and facilities more luxurious than those associated with traditional camping".

(Cambridge Dictionary, 2017)

Introduction

Glamping represents a global trend, which has been widely acknowledged in recent years. As is suggested by the term itself (from the abbreviation of the words glamourous and camping), the philosophy of glamping refers to the experience of a luxurious stay in nature, under the conditions which are posed for mild touristic development of the destinations and an assurance of environmental sustainability. It is about the upgrading of camping in a more luxurious version. Glamping philosophy is of interest to the economic units, as with a relatively small-scale investment, businesses can look forward to a multiple short-term amortisation, while the specific place where the investment takes place can be reused in the future for a different activity. Destinations can expect multiple benefits. The most basic is the turning of the model of "sunlust" into a more environmentally friendly model, known as "4E" (Environment and clean nature; Educational tourism, culture and history; Event and mega event; and Entertainment and fun).

If in the above venture we take into account the demand for it, which, in global terms, for the most part, refers to the generations of Millennials and Zers – leaders in search of luxurious camping holidays – somebody can easily perceive the potential of development for the glamping trend, principally if one takes into account the fact that the specific age groups not only constitute the most rapidly developing demographic groups regarding new campers, but also simultaneously constitute the greatest percentage of consumers and potential consumers.

Beyond these groups, the practice of glamping can be implemented to incorporate other target groups too – people residing in urban areas, young couples, families with children and mainly people who intend to spend just to live the experience. It outlines a responsible way of holidays, which is in absolute accordance with the selection criteria and affects the decision of tourists for the choice of the accommodation, as well as for the choice of the destination and the trip.

An overview of glamping

Camping tourism has been a familiar type for many years; during the last century it has developed into a well-established industry (Timothy and Teye, 2009; Brooker and Joppe, 2013; MacLeod, 2017). Centuries before becoming our favourite pastime, camping was literally, a way of life. The term camping was first coined in 1508 when it was designed "a place usually away from urban areas where tents or simple buildings (such as cabins) are erected for shelter or for temporary residence (as for labourers, prisoners, or vacationers)".

Although the term glamping is a relatively recent phenomenon in tourism and outdoor hospitality, in the true sense of the word, glamping has been documented for centuries. In most cases, it refers to a great variety of tents and canvas-covered wagons. Most of these tent constructions were constantly moved in the progression of wars or colonisation, and some designs are still used today by nomadic societies in regions such as the Middle East, Asia and Africa. They use a wide variety of materials, including goat hair, wool felt and animal hides. Over the centuries tent frames and coverings have used a wide variety of materials, from tusk, bone and stick frames with animal hide and/or vegetation coverings, to cotton canvas, which emerged as the predominant and most practical covering. In recent decades, tent frames have also evolved to steel, turned wooden poles, bamboo, and other newer more sophisticated materials.

Early tent dwelling with luxuries was present before the Roman era. It was a prominent feature of Hannibal's historic crossing of the Alps into Italy with his herd of legendary African elephants in the second of the three Punic Wars. The Ottomans also used tents to such an extent that their camps were widely known as tent cities, while Native American tribes used their well-known and distinct conical teepees, structures which dated back to the 15th century (Barebones, 2013). The Mongolians were famous for their yurts, while Eskimos with their Igloo designs foreshadowed the evolution of dome and bubble tents (Kilburn, 2020).

Modern-day glamping, as we now know it, started in Africa around the mid-1950s, but the tents at this time were relatively small. In the 1970s and 1980s glamping took on a more serious role when tent designs became somewhat more creative, and their quality improved with new canvas fabrics that were more durable and 100% waterproof. Interiors became more comfortable, creating a cosier atmosphere for the guests. Many of these were hunting camps and safari lodges where the tents included ensuite bathrooms that catered directly for wealthier guests.

Camping continued to rise in the 1950s, with tent holidays allowing poorer families to experience a holiday for the first time. With the mass development of camping in the middle of the last century, camping began to shift away from the early posh idea of camping as a luxurious activity in nature towards camping as a simple tourism accommodation. As such, it became popular and available to all the people and not just the rich.

The transformation of camping began in the last decade of the 20th century. The development of caravans, motorhomes and mobile homes spurred the transformation of simple campsites with modest facilities into high-quality holiday parks and resorts. Although glamping contradicts the original idea of camping, the opinion is that it is also able to attract a new camping market among the current guests of hotels and apartments who long for glamour and comfort, thus bringing together the best of camping and the best of the hotel industry (Cvelić and Milohnić, 2014).

Gradually, the trend of camping has evolved and has been fully integrated into the tourist map under the term glamping, gaining a large share of loyal travellers. Of course, it became popular with some differences, which are necessary for the adaptation to modern reality and the needs of today. In this sense "Glamping is defined as a form of camping that involves accommodation and facilities more luxurious than those associated with traditional camping" (Cambridge Dictionary, 2017).

The term was first added to the Oxford Dictionary in the early 2000s. It marks the noble marriage of luxury with nature, which, as the term glamping itself (from the abbreviation glamourous and camping) implies, refers to the experience of luxury living in nature, under the conditions set for mild tourism development of destinations and certainly to ensure sustainability. Glamping is camping plus glamour, or glamourous camping. It has also been called five-star camping (Latza, 2011).

Major trends and issues for glamping up to today

How does glamping introduce a new philosophy to tourism?

Glamping seems to have gained ground as it is a highly profitable investment for hoteliers, while the growing need to seek more authentic experiences on the part of consumers has also favoured its development. For business stakeholders or for destinations this new trend is the basis for strategic planning of future investments and for guests it is a new and exciting way of holidaymaking.

For travellers or camping guests in the 21st century, the experience of glamping has become a new, unique combination of spacious and comfortable living in the outdoors and in nature, combined with outdoor activities and a 'close to nature' experience. Economic uncertainty has caused many to abandon expensive vacations and choose glamping, which is more affordable but still offers good amenities. It is evident that comfort, convenience, hassle-free, luxury, privacy, relaxing, discovering and peace of mind are common reasons for glamping being preferred over camping (Adamovich et al., 2021).

We are talking about a huge opportunity for tourism and hotel units, with many possibilities and infinite extensions. It is not just about staying in one tent; it is much more. We are talking about upgrading camping, to a more luxurious version. This is what, after all, many travellers are searching for – especially in the post-COVID era. This is a new philosophy in tourism. In the broadest sense of the word, glamping refers to the pursuit of a sense of freedom, in conditions of comfort and at a relaxed pace, which is by no means a luxury and which, without exaggeration, offers the traveler an affordable extravagance (Souki, 2021). To match the guests' concept of glamourous camping, eco-tangibles are also of utmost importance (Fhado and Pereira, 2017).

Glamping is all about the experience. It is about immersing yourself in your surroundings, taking great gulps of air, feeling the earth under your feet, and allowing your daily stress to dissipate. It is about getting back to nature without getting back to basics. You will not be living out of a rucksack and sleeping on the floor. Glamping, while fulfilling the condition of distance, does not create distances, in the sense that the customer does not feel isolated or cut off from activities or other social groups, unless this is what they desire, in which case the concept of autonomy and the personalised provision of experiences and services, as well as the concept of belonging to a group, are feasible when desired (Souki, 2021).

The stakeholder and their interest and involvement for glamping

This innovative form of accommodation in campsites is driving a new strategic shift towards the enhancement of quality and competitiveness. Glamping has established itself as a response to numerous factors of new demand: the need for escapism, rest, relaxation and personal wellness, curiosity about new types of accommodation, and the desire for adventure and for developing new social relationships (Milohnić et al., 2019).

The growth of such offerings is fueled by customers' demand for comfort and luxury and resulting in the evolvement of new sub-sectors in camping and outdoor hospitality (Brooker and Joppe, 2013). New guests, who were not previously campers, discovered these holiday parks as novel, attractive locations for holidays, where they could be in the outdoors while enjoying luxurious indoor living.

Glamping's popularity has motivated investors to create their own glamping space and become hosts, transforming almost any structure into a glamping getaway – from treehouses to wagons to airplanes. Glamping has encompassed any kind of travel accommodation deemed unique or unusual, such as geodesic domes, treehouses, Airstream caravans, yurts (Figure 33.1), windmills, caravans, train cars, capsules, bubbles, safari tents, bell tents, pods, and even in specially designed caves, with or without electricity, with air conditioning, bathroom, kitchen, in general with all the facilities and amenities that one would have in a luxury hotel and which, of course, with small differences can be adjusted to each customer's needs (Souki, 2021).

Figure 33.1 Glamping in yurts in Sweden.

Photo: Unsplash.com

For entrepreneurs, the benefits are many. Due to its lower investment costs and quicker return on investment compared to other hospitality ventures, glamping makes sense financially. It is definitely a very good investment in tourism, with relatively little risk while the investor can expect amortisation in a relatively short period of time. The structure of the glamp site is free-standing and self-contained. In theory, it could be disassembled and moved easily, in contrast to a traditional bricks-and-mortar dwelling such as a hotel. That is, the space itself can be reinvested and reused for different uses.

Concerning the certification, licencing, and operation of companies in the field of glamping it is necessary to meet certain specifications. For example, campsites are typically assumed to have a lower environmental impact per guest-night than hotels or other tourist accommodation. This is primarily because facilities such as catering, laundry services and swimming pools are not as widely available. In addition, as part of a greener philosophy, campsites are seen as having to implement practices to reduce energy, water use and waste accumulation. As campsites are usually located in rural areas, the main environmental impacts arise from transport to and from the site and from the impact of visitors on local biodiversity (Styles et al., 2013).

Glamping units, as the extension of the campsites to their most luxurious version, must not only applaud green policies, but also ensure and promote sustainability, which is summarised in the following definition: "Development aiming to serve its needs present, utilizing the available resources in such a way that the prospects for the development of future generations are viable" (Brundtland Report, 1987).

The above project presupposes ethical, responsible and sustainable practices, such as respect for the environment, biodiversity conservation, and rational use of resources, but beyond that it requires the active participation and involvement of the tourist in alternative activities and local actions.

Businesses, as well as glamping-oriented destinations, should therefore take care of:

- Information/provision of alternative activities to guests: provide a variety of proposed alternative activities that do not burden the environment, in order to inform tourists about the actions of local communities and their involvement/participation in them.
- Environmental education of guests: provide guests with interactive on-site education with regard to environmental issues, including courses, nature trails, or equipment such as low-carbon transport (bicycles, electric bicycles), biodiversity and conservation, renewable energy (RE), rational use of water, recycling, and waste prevention.
- Environmental management of outdoor areas: maximise on-site biodiversity through planting of native species, minimise water consumption for irrigation and use grey water or rainwater, minimise light pollution arising from outdoor lighting (e.g., through use of correctly angled low-pressure sodium lamps).
- Energy efficiency and renewable energy installation: minimise energy consumption for water-heating, lighting by installing low-flow fittings, good building insulation, and fluorescent or LED lighting, and to install on-site renewable energy generating capacity (e.g., solar water heating), heat may be recovered from washroom grey water using a heat pump.
- Water efficiency: minimise water consumption through the installation of low-flow taps and showers, shower-timer controls.

- Waste minimisation: minimise residual waste by implementing waste prevention, by providing convenient on-site waste sorting facilities, and by contracting waste recycling services.
- Minimising the use of chemicals: laundry, dishwashers, de-icing, disinfectants, pools

Glamping is a very beneficial trend for destinations which implies a form of mild tourism activity, on the business side and on the consumer side.

The potential scenarios for the next decades

What should be the plan for the next 10, 20 or 30 years for glamping? To answer the previous question, which inevitably sets the framework for what should be the attitude of stakeholders, investors, and tourism policy makers of countries or DMOs, we must investigate what the needs of consumers are for the product. First, we need to explore what the target group of glamping is and secondly what is the perceived utility for consumers of the value of glamping, in terms of their needs, desires, interests and ability to pay for it.

The answer lies in the model of consumer behaviour "What, where, how many and how often". Consumers are finally willing to sacrifice a small number of overnight stays for the benefit of upgrading their experience and staying in luxury organised camps – glamping, and, if so, how often can they do it? Will they invest in target existing customers or in new ones? Can the glamping trend attract a share of buyers who used to spend on other holiday products?

The popularity of glamping, particularly among the younger generations, is driving the overall transformation of classical camping into glamping, with numerous implications for the general competitiveness of the sector (Milohnić et al., 2019). Millennials (born between 1980 and 1995) are the leaders in the demand for luxury camping holidays and represent the fastest-growing demographic in the world in terms of young campers, followed by the representatives of Gen Z (born between 1996 and 2010), whose population reached the 2.56 billion people mark in 2020 which is the largest that this group has ever been (Georgiev, 2021).

If one considers that the above age group constitutes the largest consumer (which spends directly or indirectly, through the members of the family it supports) or potential consumers, especially with the gradual integration of the Zers in the labour market, the need arises on the part of companies to adapt to the needs of these parts of consumers and to meet their expectations. This group is travelling more than ever before in history, while a large percentage of Zers' representatives will soon have their own money to organise and make their own tourist trips (Georgiev, 2021).

These age groups have tremendous opportunities for economic and social progress, resulting in a youth dividend for countries that embrace this demographic and their youthful vitality. Concerning the features of the above age groups, these persons are excellent technologically trained and dependent people. The youngest of the representatives of the Z generation, have not experienced life outside of the digital age, also known as the "Tap & Go" or the "5 Screens" generation. These consumers are willing to pay more for better travel experiences, and the accommodations they seek. They like to be even more outdoor, and nature plays a major role in the way they spot the luxury in glamping. Add fishing, the gathering of berries and mushrooms and even hunting with a bow and arrow and you have the picture of a young generation taking glamping further into nature (Jensen, 2018). However, they are not willing to part with their digital devices. A trend that has recently developed in the Z Generation is that of flashpacking, used to define the affluent backpacker, whose backpack contains several digital devices (Urban Dictionary, 2019, Flashpack, 2020).

The coming Generation A (born after 2010) or the next generations will be digitally more advanced. They are an optimistic, eco-friendly cohort that cares about the planet.

The big question is: Detoxification from technology or interconnected glamping? If we consider that our main consumers are young people, who are technologically dependent, is it finally feasible? It seems somewhat oxymoronic, Glamping's philosophy, which refers to more relaxed rhythms and contact with nature, at the same time presupposes technological dependence. If we assume this, is the purpose of escaping from routine finally achieved? This is an issue for further study.

Beyond the above target groups, the glamping trend, as it is a mild action, could be addressed to many other target groups of consumers. Employees who need a short break from their office duties, people who live in urban centres and want an escape in nature, young couples, families with children, solo travellers, and even older people, as there are no longer any barriers or restrictions on their living conditions, tourists from foreign countries, which has been a trend for many years – all are potential customers of this accommodation type.

A trend that seems to have a perspective in the coming decades and is related to the evolution of glamping is that of extreme glamping. Extreme sport is becoming particularly fashionable. These might include climbing the highest mountains without air supply, diving with sharks or running around the world for six months. One of the more extreme versions of glamping already exists north of the Polar Circle, in the northern part of Norway. The destination has all the components of a comfortable, yet adventurous Arctic adventure: a dogsledding trail, sauna, hot tub, and an overnight stay in a glamping tent overlooking a snow-capped landscape (Jensen, 2018).

The percentage of people who are interested in extreme sports is rising, and most of these people belong to the age groups of Millennials and Zers, who already seek out glamping. So, they constitute already consumers that could easily buy glamping products in their most extreme version.

Another issue that will be of concern in the coming decades is that of the product life cycle. The glamping trend is in the introductory stage into the market and only in a smaller percentage of destinations is in the growth stage. This means that the glamping product is expected to be more profitable in the future, meaning that it is in the interest of businesses to invest in it. What should concern us in the coming decades is what actions should be taken simultaneously in conjunction with glamping, i.e., what other products could strengthen and enrich this trend in order to face the upcoming competition, either from the product itself or from similar products, Finally, businesses will have to face and delay the maturity stage of the product.

Opportunities and challenges: How to build the experience

The very nature of glamping means there is an accommodation type for everyone, while the comfort levels and price also range wildly, meaning that there is really something for everyone and for every budget. The concept is based on differentiation and individualised provision of services, in combination with nature rules and harmonisation with the environment and nature-based activities (Brochado and Pereira, 2017).

As the future of business depends on the consumers it targets and in order to be considered to maintain its sustainability, it may have to limit the volume of segments shown to cause the greatest damage by their chosen activities. As mentioned above, the current consumer is willing to pay more in order to live the experience. Businesses should therefore invest in the promotion of the consumer experience, as defined by the "4 Realms of Experience", well known as the "4Es" model. The "4Es" consist of adding educational, esthetic, escapist, and entertainment experiences to the business (Pine and Gilmore, 1999).

The four experiences vary depending on the customer's active or passive participation and on absorption or immersion in the experience. Active-passive participation entails the level of customer involvement in creation of the experience. Absorption is "occupying customers' attention by bringing the experience into the mind" and immersion is "becoming physically or virtually a part of the experience itself" (Pine and Gilmore, 1999).

The customer typically absorbs entertainment and educational experiences and immerses in esthetic and escapist experiences. Therefore, it is important to have the opportunity to buy a vacation that is stylish and which, simultaneously, gives the feeling of escaping from the daily routine. However, research has shown that there is a correlation between

> environmental stimuli and arousal levels. Arousal is a state of individual vigilance whether or not the person is ready to react to a psychological and physiological stimulus. When the environment is calm, it is less stimulating, and people are in a relaxed rather in an than alert state. People do not readily respond, and so they are not arousable. As a result, a calm environment is pleasant but not arousable.
>
> (Wang et al., 2020)

In this sense alternative actions, such as bicycles, hiking trails, wine tasting, in general whatever the green philosophy suggests, could be of potential interest to the above consumer groups. These proposed actions are mild and have little impact on the environment.

Does glamping contribute to SDGs? If so, how? Opportunities and challenges

Glamping took centre stage when academics revealed just how robust it had been in the face of worldwide challenges, allowing it to thrive while other areas of tourism failed. Despite the global economic crisis of recent years, political instability, the refugee phenomenon, the impact of the COVID pandemic, the environmental impact, the glamping trend, not only was unaffected, but it seemed to be gaining ground.

This is mainly because there is a growing trend for alternative forms of tourism or forms of tourism with a mild environmental footprint. Environmental concerns generally have risen rapidly up the political agenda in most countries in the first years of the new century. As an antithesis to the logic of mass tourism, the alternative forms of tourism began to grow in order to satisfy specific needs which were in demand; hence they are aimed at specific market segments and include products which differ from the dominant model of mass tourism, in terms of the resources utilised, the degree of spatial concentration, and the choice of activities on the part of the visitors.

Glamping describes such a trend, and trends are known to affect things for long periods of time, possibly shifting the focus or direction of industry and society in a completely different direction. The growing awareness of tourism impacts seems to be a long-term trend, which has led to a greater focus on developing sustainable experiences, products, and services for the mindful traveller.

From the perspective of communities, glamping has found its place into many strategic development fields. The environmental impact of buildings has become a key subject in the new millennium and has turned glamping accommodation into sustainable and desirable accommodation for many communities. Even in cases where glamping units are not holistic and green, they promote a greener holiday model, compared to other traditional accommodations. For this reason, in developed countries there is an increasing interest in the environmental contribution of glamping to the protection of the sustainability and in the preservation of the tourist resources of the host communities.

Effectively managed, glamping can play an important role in more sustainable developments at visited destinations. Because of its sustainability and mobility, glamping accommodation is being recommended for locations that were previously out of bounds, such as protected nature areas or forests. For communities with protected nature areas, glamping is a new chance to develop tourism.

The question is: how can we achieve societal change through promotion of the glamping trend? Does the glamping trend promote ethical, responsible, and sustainable practices and, if so, how can this help achieve the SDGs? The 2030 Agenda for Sustainable Development, adopted by all United Nations Member States in 2015, provides a shared blueprint for peace and prosperity for people, the planet and for partners (known as the 5Ps), now and in the future. At its heart are the 17 Sustainable Development Goals (SDGs), which are an urgent call for action by all countries – developed and developing – in a global partnership. Specifically, in the 2030 Agenda for Sustainable Development SDG target 8.9, has the aims of, "by 2030, devising and implementing policies to promote sustainable tourism that creates jobs and promotes local culture and products". The importance of sustainable tourism is also highlighted in SDG target 12.b. which aims at "developing and implementing tools to monitor sustainable development impacts for sustainable tourism that creates jobs and promotes local culture and products" (United Nations, 2022a).

These integrated and indivisible goals seek to balance the three dimensions of sustainable development: the economic, social, and environmental, seeking the transition from the anthropocentric to a more ecological and green consumption, and to a more pro-environmental behaviour on holidays, transportation, and accommodation. In addition, considering that the SDGs are interrelated, the pursuit of one goal would, to a large extent, ensure that other similar or complementary goals are met. Environmental goals act as a catalyst for achieving all other objectives.

We can consider that glamping has a positive impact on sustainability goals, as they are defined by UNWTO as "tourism that takes full account of its current and future economic, social and environmental impacts, addressing the needs of visitors, the industry, the environment and host communities", as it promotes a more sustainable lifestyle and a more sustainable tourism behaviour, helping to save resources, which is a major issue today (Cultural heritage, society, and/ethics, 2022).

The operation of glamping-type accommodation requires specifications regarding the consumption of water and energy (pursuit of SDG6: Clean Water and Sanitation and SDG7: Affordable and Clean Energy), which indirectly have a positive impact on climate change, biodiversity and the marine environment (pursuit of SDG13: Climate Action, SDG15: Life on Land and SDG14: Life Below Water) and which overall create the conditions for sustainable production and consumption patterns (pursuit of SDG12: Responsible Consumption), as well as for a "Sustainable Cities or Communities" (pursuit of SDG11: Sustainable Cities and Communities).

The set of the above goals, in relation to the 5Ps, focuses on a P: Planet, but since the goals are interconnected, it indirectly achieves the pursuit of other goals, related to the P: People (SDG1 and SDG5), to the P: Prosperity (SDG8 and SDG10) and to the P: Partnership (SDG17). As mentioned above, the tourism activity of the glamping type of business presupposes a mild form of development. As a result, local communities, which were not previously developed, are being strengthened (pursuit of SDG1: No Poverty). In this way, social and regional inequalities are reduced (pursuit of SDG10: Reduce Inequalities), jobs are created (pursuit of SDG8: Decent Work and Economic Growth) which, to a large extent, ensure employment for women (pursuit of SDG5: Gender Equality) while achieving a balanced tourist development and decongesting areas where they were located overtourism phenomena (pursuit of SDG17: Partnerships for the Goals).

Each of the goals also affects the 5Ps: People, Planet, Prosperity, Peace, and Partnership (United Nations, 2022b).

Conclusions

More urgent efforts have been made to shift from the "sunlust" model to a more environmentally friendly model, known as "4E" (environment and clean nature; educational tourism, culture and history; event and mega event; entertainment and fun).

Undertaking business practices, such as glamping, implies responsibility and respect for the environment and sustainability, which in no way goes unnoticed by the newly-sought traveller, as the responsible way of vacation, which now affects, to a large extent, their decision for the reservations, and for the choice of a destination.

This chapter is intended to fulfil identified gaps in tourism research and offers a contribution by exploring the possible prospects for the trend, based on the interactions developed and the correlation between the behaviour of entrepreneurs, stakeholders, destinations, and consumers regarding the trend of glamping. How are consumers reacting? What do they expect? Do they intend to spend more to live the experience? What should be the tourism policies of the destinations to maintain sustainability?

Special emphasis is given on approaching the new generations (mainly Millennials and Zers) and familiarising them with the concept of sustainability of tourism, mainly because these generations, in addition to the most important public consumer of tourism products, simultaneously constitute the shapers of the course of tourism.

Figure 33.2 is a visual abstract of this chapter.

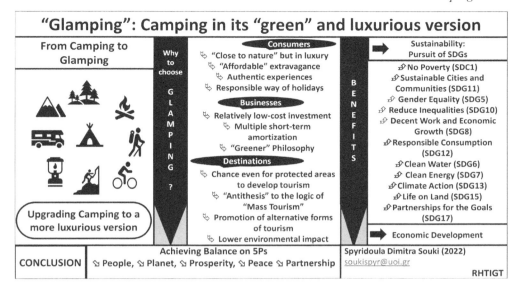

Figure 33.2 Visual abstract glamping.

References

Adamovich, V., Nadda, V., Kot, M., & Haque, A. (2021). Camping Vs. Glamping Tourism: Providers' Perspective. *Journal of Environmental Management and Tourism*, 6(54), 1431–1441.
Barebones, O. I. (2013). History of the glamping movement. https://blog.glamping.com/history-of-the-glamping-movement [accessed on 04.03.2022].
Brochado, A., & Pereira, C. (2017). Comfortable experiences in nature accommodation: Perceived service quality in Glamping. *Journal of Outdoor Recreation and Tourism*, 17, 77–83.
Brooker, E., & Joppe, M. (2013). Trends in camping and outdoor hospitality – An international review, *Journal of Outdoor Recreation and Tourism*, 3, 1–6.
Brundtland Report. (1987). Report of the World Commission on Environment and Development. Our Common Future. New York: United Nations.
Cambridge Dictionary. (2017). Cambridge University Press. http://dictionary.cambridge.org/dictionary/english/glamping [accessed on 04.03.2022].
Cvelić, B. J., & Milohnić, I. (2014). Change management in camping tourism. In: *Suvremeni trendovi u turizmu*, pp. 154–173.
Flashpack.com. (2020). Flash Pack. https://www.flashpack.com/about-us/ [accessed on 04.03.2022].
Georgiev, D. (2021). Gen Z Statistics – What we know about the new Generation. https://review42.com/resources/gen-z-statistics/ [accessed on 04.03.2022].
Jensen, J. (2018). Glamping – A global trend: How did it become a major trend and how will it evolve in the future? Nordisk GO magazine. https://nordisk.eu/inspiration-to-great-outdoor-experiences/glamping-a-global-trend. [accessed on 04.03.2022].
Kilburn, H. (2020). The real definition of "glamping" in hotel design. https://hoteldesigns.net/industry-news/the-real-definition-of-glamping-in-hotel-design/ [accessed on 04.03.2022].
Latza, B. N. (2011). Camping on the Ritz. *Newsweek*, 57(23), 60.

MacLeod, N. (2017). Camping tourism. In Linda L. L. (ed.). *The SAGE International Encyclopedia of Travel and Tourism*. University of Massachusetts, Amherst: SAGE Publications, pp. 219–225.

Milohnić, I., Bonifačić, J. C., & Licul, I. (2019). Transformation of camping into Glamping Trends and Perspectives. *ToSEE – Tourism in Southern and Eastern Europe*, 5, 457–473.

Pine, B., & Gilmore, J. H. (1999). *The experience economy*. Boston, MA: Harvard Business School Press.

Souki, S. D. (2021). Glamping: The new luxury travel trend and how to make the most out of it https://www.hotelieracademy.org/author/soukispyrgmail-com/ [accessed on 04.03.2022].

Styles, D., Schönberger, H., & Galvez Martos, J. L. (2013). JRC IPTS. Scientific and Policy Report on Best Environmental Management Practice in the Tourism Sector. http://susproc.jrc.ec.europa.eu/activities/emas/documents/TourismBEMP.pdf [accessed on 04.03.2022].

Timothy, D. J., & Teye, V. B. (2009). Camping. In: Timothy, D. J., Teye, V.B. (eds) *Tourism and the Lodging Sector*. London: Butterworth-Heinemann, pp. 227–237.

United Nations. (2022a). Sustainable Development. The 17 Goals. https://sdgs.un.org/goals. [accessed on 04.03.2022].

United Nations. (2022b). The 5Ps of the SDGs: People, Planet, Prosperity, Peace, and Partnership https://unsdg.un.org/latest/videos/5ps-sdgs-people-planet-prosperity-peace-and-partnership. [accessed on 17.03.2022].

Urban Dictionary. (2019). Flashpacker. https://www.urbandictionary.com/define.php?term=Flashpacker. [accessed on 04.03.2022].

Wang, J., Xie, C., Huang, Q., & Morrison, A. M. (2020). Smart tourism destination experiences: The mediating impact of arousal levels. *Tourism Management Perspectives*, 35, pp. https://doi.org/10.1016/j.tmp.2020.100707.

34 VFR travel

Opportunities, trends, and issues

Elisa Zentveld

Introduction

When considering trends and issues in global tourism, it is beneficial to consider the area of visiting friends and relatives (VFR) travel. Too often, VFR travel is overlooked in strategic discussions about tourism, perhaps because VFR travel is regarded as a segment of tourism that cannot be influenced, or perhaps because it is seen as being of negligible benefit to the core tourism industries in a destination. VFR travel is an area of tourism that is often taken for granted. This chapter aims to explain why VFR travel should not be taken for granted, and in what ways it is critically important concerning tourism issues and trends.

VFR travel is a major component of tourism around the world (Backer et al., 2020) and has shown itself to be resilient in economic downturns and crises (Backer & Ritchie, 2017). VFR travel can also be regarded as a sustainable form of tourism. VFR travel involves connecting with people. In regional communities that do not have typical tourism drawcards (e.g., significant natural or human-made tourism attractions), VFR travel may represent more than half of the visitor market. Thus, VFR travel tends to benefit a wide set of regions economically and socially. VFR travel can also be considered to support cultural heritage because VFR travellers rely on advice from the local resident they have travelled to see for advice on activities in the region. Locals often tend to be aware and respectful of local cultural heritage; therefore, VFR travel is less likely to disrupt the culture. Despite this, VFR travel remains "one of the most underexplored tourism contexts in the literature" (Lin et al., 2022, p. 18). Research in the area is surprisingly relatively new, commencing in 1990 (Zentveld, Labas, et al., 2022a).

This chapter addresses four key matters. Firstly, this chapter will outline the definition of VFR travel and how misunderstanding of the definition in scholarly circles and tourism industries has limited the development and adoption of VFR travel. Secondly, this chapter will explain how VFR travel data are tracked and interpreted has practical and theoretical implications. Thirdly, this chapter will outline in what ways VFR travel is highly relevant; especially in the years moving forward from the COVID-19 pandemic that consumed the world. Fourthly, this chapter will highlight the major trends and issues and outline what this may mean for scholarship and tourism industries.

Defining VFR travel

Defining VFR travel is an important aspect of understanding the field. In terms of general conversations, it is less important if one person's understanding is different to another person's understanding. However, one of the key aspects of this book is about tracking and interpreting global trends and issues in tourism. It is not possible to do this reliably unless the basis for the discussion is firstly clear and specified. It is not possible to follow trends if the trend points are not consistent and/or do not follow a correct and comprehensive definition. Defining VFR travel is not as simple as merely providing a brief statement to set the boundaries of what is regarded as VFR travel. VFR travel is more complex than it appears at first blush.

To explain this, some scenario questions will be set. Must VFR travel involve an overnight stay, or can it include day trips? Does VFR travel need to involve staying with the people who the travel party have travelled to see? Do all people who stay with friends or relatives state that VFR is their travel purpose? These few questions can provide a brief and basic starting point for where different understandings, and different data, can arrive from.

Categorising and defining VFR travel can vary between disciplines because of the different lenses of analysis. For example, in medicine, VFR travel tends to be focused on different boundaries, because travel movement of people visiting friends or family can be associated with higher risks of carrying diseases.

The difficulties and complexities of defining VFR travel and why that is significant are important to establish. For example, in medical studies, the definition impacts the resultant medical risk identified from the study. The different ways in which VFR travel is defined make "it difficult to assess and compare clinical and research findings" (Barnett et al., 2010, p. 163). Since VFR travellers "are a group identified with an increased risk of travel-related illness" (Barnett et al., 2010, p. 163), having an appropriate definition is extremely important.

The need to revisit the definition of VFR travel for travel medicine studies was highlighted in an editorial in the *Journal of Travel Medicine* where it was noted that previous definitions of VFR travellers "usually included variations on the theme that the travellers involved were recent immigrants who were returning to their country of origin to visit friends and relatives" (Arguin, 2010, p. 147). The article explores the importance of including immigrant/ethnicity status in a definition, identifying that "it does not seem to matter what part of the world VFR travellers come from. All groups, including Asians returning to Asia and Africans returning to Africa, appear to be at increased risk of certain travel-related conditions compared to non-VFR travellers" (Arguin, 2010, p. 147). The article explains that "there appears to be something inherent in this paradigm of returning to one's country of origin that is independent of genetic factors or specific cultural background" (Arguin, 2010, p. 147) and further argues for the removal of the word "friends" in VFR travel and to focus exclusively on "visiting relatives".

This example from medicine reveals the importance of having an accurate definition for VFR travel. Through capturing different datasets, entirely different results will be obtained, and the revealed risk indicators could be misleading. Similarly, different datasets of VFR travel in tourism will capture different volumes and identify different results.

In the tourism literature, some research defines VFR travel based on the purpose of the visit. Seaton and Palmer's (1997) research utilised U.K. Tourism Survey (UKTS) statistics. As a result, this led to the adoption of the UKTS statistical parameter of defining a VFR traveller as someone whose primary purpose is to visit friends or relatives. Similarly, Yuan et al. (1995) stated that a "VFR traveller is one who reported visiting friends and relatives as the major purpose for the trip" (p. 19). McKercher (1995) stated "that the primary purpose of most participants in this type of travel is to visit with their friends and relatives is axiomatic" (p. 246).

VFR travel might instead be assessed based on the type of accommodation. King (1994) stated that VFR travel is categorising visitors by the type of accommodation that they used. Boyne et al. (2002) proposed that

> a VFR tourism trip is a trip to stay temporarily with a friend or relative away from the guest's normal place of residence, that is, in another settlement or, for travel within a continuous settlement, over 15 km one-way from the guests' home.
>
> (p. 246)

Boyne et al. (2002), however, admitted that their definition "largely avoids rather than confronts some of the key conceptual issues" (pp. 246–27). Kotler et al. (2006) stated that "VFR, as the name suggests, are people that stay in the homes of friends and relatives" (p. 748). Kotler et al.'s (2006) definition would seem to suggest that VFR travellers do not stay in commercial accommodation. In fact, according to Navarro and Turco (2004), the perception that VFR travellers make little use of commercial accommodation and do not tend to frequent restaurants, cafés, pubs and clubs is the reason why VFR travel had not been clearly defined at that time.

Definitions for VFR travel based on the type of accommodation or purpose of the visit are not comprehensive. Table 34.1 outlines the percentages of domestic visitors in Australia who were staying with friends/relatives versus those who stated that VFR was their main purpose of visit. The reported percentage of VFR travellers differs, depending on whether they are classified by the purpose of visit or by accommodation type. This highlights the importance of a definition that is comprehensive as different definitions will provide different results and accordingly, assessing trends and issues can vary.

An important aspect of the data that are presented in Table 34.1 is that they were collected during COVID times when movement was thwarted by various lockdowns. When comparing these data to those from Backer (2012a) as presented in Table 34.2, it is evident that some of these percentages are different to usual. In particular, some of the states that are a long-haul destination (e.g., Western Australia) show very different results in Table 34.1 to those presented in Table 34.2. Notably, Backer (2015), who analysed data across several years, noted the consistency of the percentages across the years.

One aspect to consider is that for family/friends living within close proximity, it is possible that VFR travel was a more likely segment for some people compared to other forms of

Table 34.1 Relationship between VFR typologies for domestic travel by Australians in 2021

	VFR by accommodation (%)	*VFR by the purpose of visit (%)*
New South Wales	40	35.7
Victoria	38.9	35.5
Queensland	32.1	32.4
South Australia	30.8	27.5
Western Australia	24.1	25.2
Tasmania	27.4	np
Northern Territory	16.5	13.4
Australian Capital Territory	49.9	45

np = non publishable as sample size was too low.
Source: adapted from Tourism Research Australia, 2022.

Table 34.2 Relationship between VFR typologies for domestic travel by Australians in 2008–2009

	VFR by accommodation (%)	VFR by the purpose of visit (%)
New South Wales	39	34
Victoria	38	34
Queensland	37	31
South Australia	39	39
Western Australia	40	31
Tasmania	34	27
Northern Territory	37	11
Australian Capital Territory	38	33

Source: Backer (2012a).

travel. This may be because the motivation was high and possibly regarded as essential for some VFR events (e.g., travel to care for a sick family member or funeral) and it may be seen as less risky, especially when staying with friends or relatives. That is, if the state/territory went into lockdown, and someone was planning to travel to stay with a friend or family member, then there was no risk of losing the accommodation booking deposit. Long-haul destinations (e.g., Western Australia) would be seen to carry a higher risk for those outside of the state, than small areas, such as the Australian Capital Territory.

Another anomaly to consider in these recent data is that, potentially, people were travelling to escape family violence. Among the few allowed reasons for leaving the home in Australia, fleeing family violence was one of those. The COVID-19 pandemic resulted in lockdowns that then led to an increase in the prevalence of family violence around the world (Carrington et al., 2021).

Differences between VFR by purpose of visit and accommodation is not unique to Australia. Seaton and Palmer (1997) believe that there are around 40% more people staying with friends and relatives than people categorising themselves as VFR travellers by the purpose of visit. Such differences result in different measurements being used, which may result in misunderstandings by tourism operators. Therefore, defining VFR by the purpose of visit or by accommodation is not fully representative of a definition of VFR travel. Whilst these measurements can be used as a categorising tool for separating VFR data, these fail as definitions. Similarly, there are problems with the idea that VFR travellers are defined solely in terms of their trip purpose. This seems to be assuming that people who cite their major purpose of visit as being VFR are also staying with friends and relatives. It is easy to identify that not all visitors that are staying with friends or relatives cite VFR as their main purpose for their visit.

The underestimation of VFR travel based on classification problems was a central point made by Jackson (1990), who showed that, in 1986, 23% of visitors travelling from Hong Kong to Australia stated VFR as their main purpose and yet 61% of visitors in that same period were staying with friends or relatives. This example is indicative of the problems leading to the underestimation of VFR travel because people on holidays are unlikely to classify themselves as VFR travellers, but VFR travellers could self-classify themselves quite reasonably as being on a holiday (Jackson, 1990). It is easy to see how these datasets can cause an underestimation of VFR travel. VFR travellers may see themselves as holidaymakers since, in many instances, they are indeed going on a holiday. In addition, visiting friends and relatives may be a major reason for travelling to a particular destination, yet not be the primary purpose (Morrison et al., 1995).

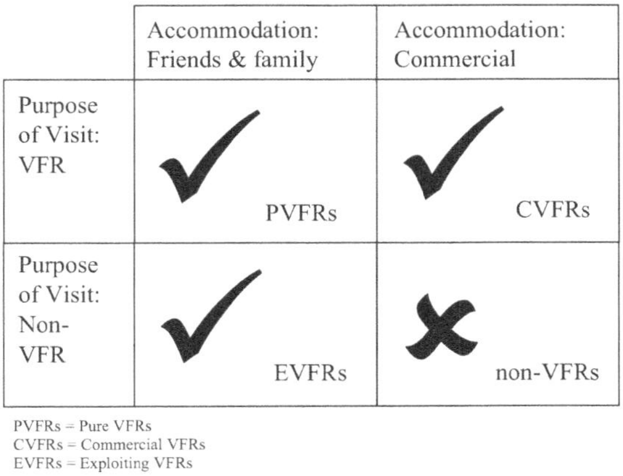

	Accommodation: Friends & family	Accommodation: Commercial
Purpose of Visit: VFR	✓ PVFRs	✓ CVFRs
Purpose of Visit: Non-VFR	✓ EVFRs	✗ non-VFRs

PVFRs = Pure VFRs
CVFRs = Commercial VFRs
EVFRs = Exploiting VFRs

Figure 34.1 VFR travel definitional model.
Source: Backer (2012a).

A definition was put forward by Backer (2012a) that "VFR travel is a form of travel involving a visit whereby either (or both) the purpose of the trip or the type of accommodation involves visiting friends and/or relatives" (p. 75). The definition was also presented visually as a matrix (Figure 34.1). It highlights that some VFR travellers can be staying with friends and relatives and also state that VFR is their main purpose of visit (PVFRs). VFRs can also state that VFR is their main purpose of visit, but that they select commercial accommodation (CVFRs). VFRs can be staying with friends and relatives, but may not state that this is their main purpose of visit (EVFRs).

The implications to practice and theory of VFR travel data collection

The previous section has highlighted how there can be different definitions of VFR travel and that the different definitions result in different calculations and outcomes. The differences in Table 34.1 were observable, although such differences were recorded in COVID-19 times amongst lockdowns impacting travel in the country. In a study undertaken by Backer (2012a), using data from 2008 to 2009, she estimated that the size of VFR travel was underestimated by 20% if using VFR by accommodation data. A follow-up study using national raw data across several years revealed the same finding (Backer, 2015). This highlights the problems of using the wrong definition. Similarly, as outlined in the medical studies discussed in the previous section, inaccurate conclusions regarding medical risk can be arrived at by using a definition that is not inclusive or well-thought through.

A particular problem for VFR travel is that official data collect overall visitor data and present reports based on the type of accommodation or purpose of visit. These are not designed to measure a segment, such as VFR travel, as it is not within scope. It makes it difficult for tourism practitioners to ascertain the size of the segment and trends and issues. Collecting raw data is time-consuming, but through collecting raw data (based on the data for the three VFR types as presented in the VFR definitional model (Figure 34.1)) the size of VFR travel is possible. This then allows for practitioners to properly assess issues and trends. The other option is for tourism practitioners to refer to official data for the type of accommodation and add 20%. This is a reasonable estimate, at least in Australia, as was presented by Backer (2012a). Her theory was undertaken based on analysing official data and comparing it to data across the VFR definitional model from three contrasting regions. In 2015, she re-tested her theory after being given access to the official national data from the National Visitor Survey data from Tourism Research Australia over several years. She coded the data and analysed it based on the VFR definitional model and the figures she arrived at (Backer, 2015) indicated that there was no significant difference between those analysed longitudinal data and the estimated model she had done previously.

Tourism in 2023 and beyond: the relevance of VFR travel

The motivation to travel can be understood to be "that set of needs and attitudes which predisposes a person to act in a specific touristic goal-directed way" (Pizam et al., 1979, p. 195). The motivations to travel and the objectives for travel may not be the same. For example, a person "may be motivated to travel to attend a family function to satisfy any of his needs of belonging, status, or recognition, though his stated objective for such travel may be to visit friends and relatives" (Pizam et al., 1979, p. 195). What can add to the complexity of motivation is that, for family tourism, there may be different motivations for each member within the family unit. One member may be wanting to travel for a particular purpose. Other members may not be interested to travel. One member of the travel party may consider the trip's purpose to be VFR, whilst another member may consider that same trip to be a holiday.

In terms of travel motivations from 2023, it is entirely plausible that people are especially motivated to see friends and relatives. After the COVID years, in which international borders were closed, state and territory borders were closed, and many businesses were closed; social connections were also closed. Restrictions included physical distancing in social settings, closed schools, stay at home orders, the closure of leisure facilities and personal hygiene protocols (McCracken et al., 2020). Such closures of workplaces and the closure of international and state borders resulted in economic impacts, loss of jobs, and reduced income. This also resulted in various social impacts that included a reduction in social support as well as isolation and loneliness. Various studies highlighted the ensuing psychological effects, including early research in first-affected countries such as China (Wang et al., 2020), Italy (Mazza et al., 2020), the U.K. (Groarke et al., 2020), and the U.S. (Tull et al., 2020), as well as Sweden (McCracken et al., 2020). Those studies highlighted increased rates of loneliness and increased mental health problems such as insomnia and anxiety, as well as depression. Specifically, the point-prevalence rates were twice the usual 12-month prevalence for anxiety and depression and were similar in magnitude to the lifetime prevalence rates usually found in developed nations (Kessler et al., 2007).

In addition, people with higher income and those with anxiety and depressive symptoms also started to turn to alcohol with increased alcohol consumption reports in Australia, Belgium, France, the U.K., and the U.S. (OECD, 2021). There was also an increase in family violence, and high alcohol intake can add to the risk aspects of family violence, and emergency calls from family violence increased by 60% in EU countries (OECD, 2021). Whilst the social isolation was considered necessary for managing the health risks of COVID-19 spread, it also resulted in "significant social, economic, and psychological consequences, which can be the catalyst for stress that can lead to violence" (Usher et al., 2020, p. 2).

The impact of social isolation on loneliness and mental health, especially among those who would usually travel to visit friends and relatives as their central point of connection, is hard to categorise (Groarke et al., 2020; O'Connor et al., 2021). The impact that COVID-19 had on VFR travel has been described as "profound" given that connecting with friends and family has always been taken for granted (Kelly, 2022, p. 364) More than just taken for granted, "in times of need and crisis, a core human response is to turn inwards, to family, for support" (Kelly, 2022, p. 635). Whilst it is not entirely clear to what extent restrictions from COVID-19 had on the general population, the importance of connecting as a human being has been long known, with even Aristotle highlighting that man was a social creature (Aristotle, 350 B.C., n.d.). Specifically, VFR travel has been identified as adding to the quality of life (Backer, 2019) and reducing the impact of loneliness on the elderly (Backer, 2020).

Looking further ahead, into the 2040s and 2050s, VFR travel will always be important. Reconnecting with people who are important in our lives will be unlikely to diminish. The pandemic has highlighted how important VFR is, because people took it for granted and then then realised how vital those connections were. However, what society may see in the future, are some changes in some previously long-standing cultural aspects. For example, kissing the hand of the elderly has been a long-standing sign of cultural respect in Turkey, but had to be discontinued in COVID times and, accordingly, some of those types of aspects might diminish into the future (Zentveld, Erol, et al., 2022a).

Trends and issues: VFR travel as a first-mover market

Looking at issues for VFR travel, it is easy to recognise the deficiencies of observing trends due to the problems with data deficiencies, as identified earlier in this chapter. A key highlight was revealed earlier in this chapter by examining official national data in Australia based on the only forms available – the purpose of visit or type of accommodation. Neither is a measurement tool, and each will hold limitations. Trying to examine trends and make forecasts based on incomplete data is problematic.

Despite not being able to put forward any forecasts in light of examining existing data, it is possible to make some general statements about VFR travel in terms of its potential as a first-mover market in these present economic and social connections. As outlined earlier in this chapter, people could no longer catch up with friends and relatives even if they had the motivation to do so. There were many times in various countries when people could not even catch up with a neighbour. There were, in some countries at various times, very harsh lockdown conditions where someone could only leave home for a limited set of reasons and where even grocery shopping was restricted to one member of the household. Weddings and funerals were restricted to extremely small numbers. Accordingly, those years highly restricted all forms of travel, including VFR travel, and VFR travel therefore "presents as a first-mover market in a recovery period" (Zentveld & Yousuf, 2022, p. 602).

Such restrictions and lack of opportunities to reconnect and celebrate special events such as weddings, christenings, graduations, milestone birthdays, and anniversaries created a sense of loss and loneliness for some. In some cultures, these impacts were profound. For example, in Turkey, where circumcision is an important cultural event, and a sign of respect is to kiss the hand of an older person, the COVID restrictions caused conflict due to the banning of these components (Zentveld et al., 2022a). That presents an opportunity for many to celebrate perhaps the milestone birthday, albeit a year or two later. Or to celebrate other missed events. This could create a buoyant time for VFR travel, with reconnecting or celebrated missed events being a key driver.

In fact, according to Zentveld et al. (2022a), the various factors from COVID-19 in combination "create an environment that is ripe for targeting" for VFR travel. Further,

VFR travel may be considered to be a priority for people globally, in the next few years after times when there had been risks, uncertainty, and disconnection. In particular, VFR travel may be especially appropriate for destination management organisations (DMOs) to pursue as it provides four key benefits (Zentveld et al., 2022a):

1 VFR travel can add to the quality of life for VFR travellers and hosts.
2 VFR travel might allow staff to be retained in tourism firms during times where other customers might be present due to downturns.
3 Images and the reports' perceptions of destinations and destination attractions can be enhanced in showing VFR guest activity through photography as well as the related stories.
4 DMOs can urge residents to encourage and also invite friends and family members to visit to boost local economies.

Such aspects can be regarded as key aspects for regional communities looking to encourage tourism and revitalise. Specifically, VFR travel has not only been viewed as a first-mover market in post-COVID times but it has been seen as an appropriate market to target after tourism crises and as a form of recovery after disasters (Backer & Ritchie, 2017).

Conclusions

VFR travel is a significant form of tourism around the world. VFR is acknowledged as being a substantial percentage of domestic overnight visitors – that is, around half of the total volume (Backer, 2012a; Braunlich & Nadkarni, 1995; Hu & Morrison, 2002). Whilst acknowledging that VFR travel has had inadequate research attention despite being the oldest form of tourism (Backer, 2012b), it is well known in academic and industry circles, substantial in size (by volume of visitor movement), and significant in terms of its importance socially, economically, and fundamentally.

During two years of substantial loss of social connections and travel movement as a result of restrictions from COVID-19 across the globe, "many people increasingly understood the importance of family and friends and felt the impact of loneliness and isolation. Those aspects resulted in negative impacts of wellbeing and a loss of quality of life" (Zentveld et al., 2022a, p. 1). Understanding how important social connections are for people, and that after two years of experiencing isolation, loneliness, social disconnection, and a lack of ability to celebrate family events, VFR travel is likely to rate higher for people than previously. Whilst in the past, marketing to VFR travel may not have been regarded as "sexy" (Backer, 2007), it is argued that, in a post-COVID world, the importance of connections with friends and relatives has been raised, the loss felt, and, accordingly, VFR travel is expected to be a higher-order priority and motivation for people as society moves through the post-COVID world towards the 2030s and beyond.

As populations grow, VFR travel will continue to grow with it. As populations become dispersed, VFR travel will move with the population flow. An ageing population will see suburbs designed with the older person in mind, who might take longer to cross the road and need the pedestrian crossing timer to be longer. Commercial accommodation may also become more dispersed with longer-term apartment-style accommodation to enable VFRs to have their own commercial accommodation when visiting older friends and family who may not have homes that can suitably accommodate visitors (Backer, 2020). DMOs are especially well placed to grow VFR travel given that VFR travel has been identified as a first-mover market in a post-pandemic period (McKinsey & Company, 2020).

References

Arguin, P. M. (2010). Editorial: A definition that includes first and second generation immigrants returning to their countries of origin to visit friends and relatives still makes sense to me. *Journal of Travel Medicine*, *17*(3), 147–149. https://doi.org/10.1111/j.1708-8305.2010.00412.x

Aristotle. (350 B.C.E.) n.d.. *Politics*. Indoeuropeanpublishing.com.

Backer, E. (2007). VFR Travel – An examination of the expenditures of VFR travellers and their hosts. *Current Issues in Tourism*, *10*(4), 366–377.

Backer, E. (2012a). VFR travel: It is underestimated. *Tourism Management*, *33*(1). https://doi.org/10.1016/j.tourman.2011.01.027

Backer, E. (2012b). VFR Travel: Why marketing to Aunt Betty matters. In H. Schänzel, I. Yeoman, & E. Backer (Eds.), *Family Tourism: Multidisciplinary Perspectives* (pp. 81–92). Bristol, UK: Channel View Publications.

Backer, E. (2015). VFR Travel: Its true dimensions. In E. Backer & B. King (Eds.), *Visiting Friends and Relatives: Exploring the VFR Phenomenon*. Channel View Publications.

Backer, E. (2019). VFR Travel: Do visits improve or reduce our quality of life. *Journal of Hospitality and Tourism Management*, *38*, 161–167.

Backer, E. (2020). Visiting older friends and relatives. In A. M. Morrison & J. A. Coca-Stefaniak (Eds.), *Routledge Handbook of Tourism Cities* (pp. 242–251). Routledge.

Backer, E., Erol, G., & Düşmezkalender, E. (2020). VFR travel interactions through the lens of the host. *Journal of Vacation Marketing*, *26*(4), 397–411. https://doi.org/10.1177/1356766720927753

Backer, E., & Ritchie, B. W. (2017). VFR travel: A viable market for tourism crisis and disaster recovery? *International Journal of Tourism Research*, *19*(4), 400–411. https://doi.org/10.1002/jtr.2102

Barnett, E. D., MacPherson, D. W., Stauffer, W. M., Loutan, L., Hatz, C. F., Matteelli, A., & Behrens, R. H. (2010). The visiting friends or relatives traveler in the 21st century: Time for a new definition. *Travel Med*, *17*(3), 163–170.

Boyne, S., Carswell, F., & Hall, D. (2002). Tourism and Migration: New relationships between production and consumption. In C. H. A. M. Williams (Ed.), *Tourism and Migration: New relationships between production and consumption* (pp. 241–256). Kluwer.

Braunlich, C., & Nadkarni, N. (1995). The importance of the VFR market to the hotel industry. *The Journal of Tourism Studies*, *6*(1), 38–47.

Carrington, K., Morley, C., Warren, S., Ryan, V., Ball, M., Clarke, J., & Vitis, L. (2021). The impact of COVID-19 pandemic on Australian domestic and family violence services and their clients. *Australian Journal of Social Issues*, *56*(4), 539–558. https://doi.org/10.1002/ajs4.183

Groarke, J. M., Berry, E., Graham-Wisener, L., McKenna-Plumley, P. E., McGlinchey, E., & Armour, C. (2020). Loneliness in the UK during the COVID-19 pandemic: Cross-sectional results from the COVID-19 Psychological Wellbeing Study. *PLoS ONE*, *15*(9 September), 1–18. https://doi.org/10.1371/journal.pone.0239698

Hu, B., & Morrison, A. M. (2002). Tripography: Can destination use patterns enhance understanding of the VFR market? *Journal of Vacation Marketing*, *8*(3), 201–220.

Jackson, R. (1990). VFR Tourism: Is It Underestimated? *The Journal of Tourism Studies*, *1*(2), 10–17.

Kelly, C. (2022). 'I Just Want to Go Home': Emotional Wellbeing Impacts of COVID-19 Restrictions on VFR Travel. *Tourism and Hospitality*, *3*, 634–650.

Kessler, R., Angermeyer, M., Anthony, M., Graaf, D., Demyttenaere, K., Gasquet, I., Girolamo, G., Gluzman, S., Gureje, O., Haro, J., Kawakami, N., Karam, A., Levinson, D., Medina Mora, M., Oakley Browne, M., Posada-Villa, J., Stein, D., Adley Tsang, C., Aguilar-Gaxiola, S., … Ustun, T. (2007). Lifetime prevalence and age-of-onset distributions of mental disorders in the World Health Organization's World Mental Health Survey Initiative. *World Psychiatry*, *6*(October), 168–176.

King, B. (1994). What is ethnic tourism? An Australian perspective. *Tourism Management*, *15*(3), 173–176. https://doi.org/10.1016/0261-5177(94)90101-5

Kotler, P., Bowen, J., & Makens, J. (2006). *Marketing for Hospitality and Tourism* (4th ed.). New York: Pearson Education.

Lin, P. M., Peng, K.-L., & Au, W.-C. (2022). To return or not to return? Identifying VFR travel constraints during the pandemic. *Journal of Travel & Tourism Marketing, 39*(1), 18–30. https://doi.org/10.1080/10548408.2022.2045246

Mazza, C., Ricci, E., Biondi, S., Colasanti, M., Ferracuti, S., Napoli, C., & Roma, P. (2020). A nationwide survey of psychological distress among italian people during the COVID-19 pandemic: Immediate psychological responses and associated factors. *International Journal of Environmental Research and Public Health* [revista en Internet] 2020 [acceso. *International Journal of Environmental Research and Public Health, 17*(3165), 1–14. https://www.ncbi.nlm.nih.gov/pmc/articles/PMC7246819/pdf/ijerph-17-03165.pdf

McCracken, L. M., Badinlou, F., Buhrman, M., & Brocki, K. C. (2020). Psychological impact of COVID-19 in the Swedish population: Depression, anxiety, and insomnia and their associations to risk and vulnerability factors. *European Psychiatry, 63*(1), 1–9.

McKercher, B. (1995). The destination-market matrix: A tourism market portfolio analysis model. *Journal of Travel & Tourism Marketing, 4*(2), 23–40.

McKinsey & Company. (2020). The travel industry turned upside down: Insights, analysis, and actions for travel executives. In *McKinsey Global Institute*.

Morrison, A. M., Hsieh, S., & O'Leary, J. (1995). Segmenting the visiting friends and relatives market by holiday activity participation. *The Journal of Tourism Studies, 6*(1), 48–63.

Navarro, R., & Turco, D. (2004). Segmentation of the visiting friends and relatives travel market. *Visions in Leisure and Business, 13*(1), 4–16.

O'Connor, R. C., Wetherall, K., Cleare, S., McClelland, H., Melson, A. J., Niedzwiedz, C. L., O'Carroll, R. E., O'Connor, D. B., Platt, S., Scowcroft, E., Watson, B., Zortea, T., Ferguson, E., & Robb, K. A. (2021). Mental health and well-being during the COVID-19 pandemic: Longitudinal analyses of adults in the UK COVID-19 Mental Health & Wellbeing study. *British Journal of Psychiatry, 218*(6), 326–333. https://doi.org/10.1192/bjp.2020.212

OECD. (2021). *The effect of COVID-19 on alcohol consumption, and policy responses to prevent harmful alcohol consumption*. Paris: OECD.

Pizam, A., Neumann, Y., & Reichel, A. (1979). Tourist Satisfaction: Uses and misuses. *Annals of Tourism Research, 6*(2), 195–197.

Seaton, A., & Palmer, C. (1997). Understanding VFR tourism behaviour: The first five years of the United Kingdom tourism survey. *Tourism Management, 18*(6), 345–355.

Tourism Research Australia. (2022). *National Visitor Survey results year ending December 2021*. https://www.tra.gov.au/data-and-research/reports/national-visitor-survey-results-december-2021/national-visitor-survey-results-december-2021

Tull, M. T., Edmonds, K. A., Scamaldo, K. M., Richmond, J. R., Rose, J. P., & Gratz, K. L. (2020). Psychological Outcomes Associated with Stay-at-Home Orders and the Perceived Impact of COVID-19 on Daily Life. *Psychiatry Research, 289*(May), 113098. https://doi.org/10.1016/j.psychres.2020.113098

Usher, K., Bhullar, N., Durkin, J., Gyamfi, N., & Jackson, D. (2020). Family violence and COVID-19: Increased vulnerability and reduced options for support. *International Journal of Mental Health Nursing, 29*(4), 549–552. https://doi.org/10.1111/inm.12735

Wang, S., Zhang, Y., Ding, W., Meng, Y., Hu, H., Liu, Z., Zeng, X., & Wang, M. (2020). Psychological distress and sleep problems when people are under interpersonal isolation during an epidemic: A nationwide multicenter cross-sectional study. *European Psychiatry, 63*(1). https://doi.org/10.1192/j.eurpsy.2020.78

Yuan, T., Fridgen, J., Hsieh, S., & O'Leary, J. (1995). Visiting Friends and Relatives Travel Market: The Dutch Case. *The Journal of Tourism Studies, 6*(1), 19–26.

Zentveld, E., Erol, G., & Düsmezkalender, E. (2022a). VFR Travel in Turkey during and Post-COVID-19. *Tourism and Hospitality, 3*, 651–665.

Zentveld, E., & Yousuf, M. (2022). Does Destination, Relationship Type, or Migration Status of the Host Impact VFR Travel? *Tourism and Hospitality, 3*, 589–605.

35 Transformational tourism

A visionary approach to sustainable tourism?

G. L. W. Roshini N. Nandasena, Alastair M. Morrison, Wenjie Cai and J. Andres Coca-Stefaniak

Introduction

Transformational tourism has the potential to generate meaningful tourism through memorable tourism experiences (Kim, 2010). The transformative potential effect of travel has been compared to therapy (Kottler, 1998) and education (Reisinger, 2013), as people engage in experiences that involve culture, nature and social encounters (Morgan, 2010). Similarly, transformational tourism experiences have been associated with various tourism typologies, including ecotourism, voluntourism, religious and pilgrimage tourism, backpacker and adventure tourism, cultural and heritage tourism, wellness and yoga tourism, and dark tourism (Nandasena et al., 2022). The outcomes of these experiences include critical self-reflection, a greater understanding of society and the world, improved tourist–host relationships and a better appreciation of local culture. This chapter explores tourists' transformational process through their experiences in Sri Lanka. Based on an empirical study, two themes were identified: (1) The healing and inspiration of Sri Lanka; and (2) self-reflective actions towards encountering poverty. Additionally, this chapter outlines a number of future potential avenues for research and practice in this field and provides a better grounding for transformational tourism studies in sustainable development.

Kirillova et al. (2017) emphasised that transformations are highly personal, contextual and strongly influenced by motivations as well as experiences. However, and in spite of over three decades of research in this field, there is no consensus on a single accepted definition of transformational tourism experiences (TTE), possibly partly as a result of the myriad of disciplines of knowledge that have contributed to this field of research. For instance, focusing on the more psychological aspects of TTE, Reisinger (2013) argued that inner transformation is deeply situated and entangled with tourism destinations. From a mobilities perspective, Lean (2012) labelled TTEs as a "complex social phenomenon" (p. 169) and called for studies to investigate their impact beyond the individual. Kirillova et al. (2017) and Coghlan and Weiler (2018) suggested that emotional responses to extraordinary events tend to lead to critical self-awareness and reflections, resulting in personal change and a re-definition of the self. In turn, Sheldon (2020) described four tourism transformation scenarios – deep human connectivity, deep environmental connectivity, self-inquiry and engaged contribution – which provide opportunities for inner transformation. Additionally, the concept of the "transformational moment" (p. 8) was posited by the same author, which is rooted in consciousness. Building on this growing body of knowledge, this chapter aims to investigate transformational tourism through the lens of memorable experiences, which are seen as precursors to transformational ones. Similarly, it is argued that the exact time or place where a transformation may occur cannot be predicted, chiefly given that the passing of time plays a key role in processes of self-reflection, which may, in turn, last hours, days, months or even decades. Sterchele (2020) showed that after visiting a tourism destination, a memorable tourism experience (MTE), can be a catalyst for deeper and more lasting transformational processes. Duerden et al. (2018) asserted that some tourism experiences may evolve further over a period of time to become extraordinary as people continue to reflect on their experiences to integrate them further into their lives, regardless of whether those experiences were positive or negative. Similarly, tourism experiences in unfamiliar (Kottler, 1998; Morgan, 2010; Reisinger, 2013) and unexpected (Coughlan and Connolly, 2001) situations may also become memorable and emotionally charged (Jefferies and Lepp, 2012), and potentially life-changing. Thus, transformational tourism is defined here as the outcome of self-reflective processes among tourists as a result of memorable experiences, leading to changes in their view of the world around them, changes in their everyday behaviours and/or thinking, physical changes and changes in how they relate to others. This has been captured visually through an artistic rendering shown in Figure 35.1. Research by Yang et al. (2015), for instance, has shown how healing experiences arising from wellness tourism are key in the way that people transform mentally as well as physically. Phillips (2019) and Pung et al. (2020) suggested that travel offers unique contexts for individuals to learn new skills under differing conditions, and as a result, reflecting, challenging their worldviews, and enhancing their existential authenticity.

Since 2020, the global COVID-19 pandemic greatly impacted the tourism industry and seemed to spur a new wave of transformational tourism studies (Ateljevic, 2020), positioning transformational tourism as a turning point for back to normal or the new normal in the re-built conception of a tourism sector that should re-assess its relationship with local communities. In spite of this, the majority of research to date in this field has tended to focus primarily on individual transformation, whilst local communities and the tourist–host perspective have been largely overlooked. The next section of this chapter

Figure 35.1 Artistic rendering of transformational tourism conceptual model (authors).

analyses how perceptions and different dimensions of TTEs are dealt with in scholarly studies. Although, this chapter acknowledges that transformative learning theory (TLT) (Mezirow, 1978) has provided the foundation for a great deal of research in this field, the dominance of this theoretical underpinning is challenged critically. Similarly, and based on an extensive literature review of TTE research, this chapter posits a new conceptual model for transformational tourism. Thereafter, aspects of this conceptual model are investigated through field research carried out in the form of semi-structured interviews with individuals who had visited Sri Lanka. This chapter ends with an analysis of future trends and research directions for transformational tourism.

Transformational tourism experiences (TTE)

In the early days of research on TTE, academics tended to focus deliberately on tourists' perspectives, behaviours and transformation with Mezirow's (1978) TLT as the dominant theoretical framework for this research. This prevalence of Mezirow's theory is somewhat surprising, particularly given that it was initially developed for adult education and transformative processes that were arguably linked to education alone. In terms of focus on tourism typologies, a recent systematic literature review covering 42 years of research in transformational tourism (Nandasena et al., 2022) showed that the fastest growth in scholarly activity in this field corresponds to the last 10 years. Tourism typologies, such as pilgrimage, spiritual and religious tourism, have attracted much attention from scholars for their transformative potential, followed by other typologies such as culture and heritage tourism and voluntourism, which were investigated in this context, especially between 2013 and 2017. Other typologies, such as ecotourism, wellness, wellbeing and yoga tourism, are attracting much scholarly enquiry in this respect.

All in all, there is a large variety of factors involved in the development of a transformative experiences anchored in tourism. These include the full spectrum of the tourism system. In other words, developments, experiences and circumstances before, during and after the visit. Similarly, TTE outcomes, such as risk taking, facing challenges, gaining confidence and personal development, are often found in tourists who engage in adventure and backpacker tourism. Freedom, controlling negative emotions such as fear, anger and anxiety are discussed more in religious and spiritual tourism types. For example, Song and Yan (2020) discussed three types of inner experiences, feelings, enlightenment or transformation and sensory awareness being in a Buddhist religious site. Ross (2013) investigated tourists' ability to extract meaning and personal wellbeing from their experiences, leading to enhanced levels of empathy and justice that resulted in changing views on the meaning of life as a result of religious and spiritual tourism. Similarly, Wearing and McGehee (2013) argued the case for voluntourism as an agent of change and a force for "personal growth and a change in worldview" (p. 126). In the context of adventure tourism, Folmer (2019) found that adventure tourists tend to find their inspiration in nature and that social relationships and personal achievements (e.g., improvements in self-control, resilience, joy and fulfilment) can be key ingredients for their transformative experiences.

From the host perspective, transformational tourism can be perceived as a sustainable ambassador (Lean, 2012) in a destination. It can empower local communities as well as help hosts and guests to reflect on their respective responsibilities. TT might be an advantageous supplement for sustainable tourism development. Sustainability in TT is an emerging topic. Kim et al. (2019), for example, illustrated the two-way link between community-based ecotourism and a sustainable transformative economy. Butcher (2011) suggested that ecotourism has the capability to tackle poverty and address the Millennium Development Goals (MDGs). Massingham et al. (2019) described personal aspects of experiences such as positive and negative emotions, connections, reflections, and elements of experience (e.g., animal encounters, educational shows) associated with ecotourism that supported different forms of conservation. Lyons and Wearing (2008) noted transformative experiences from volunteering and highlighted its privileges. Moreover, the benefits from TT can be further deepened through social inclusiveness, poverty reduction, and resource efficiency. Knollenberg et al. (2014) depicted volunteer tourist transformation through Taylor's (2008) three elements of self-reflection, engaging in dialogue, and intercultural experience that facilitate more sustainable outcomes. Transformative volunteering can lead towards the maximisation of positive impacts and the minimisation of negative effects. However, these transformative experiences are yet to be fully linked with destination sustainability and its contribution to achieving the SDGs.

Academic studies on TTE thus far have a focus on theoretical debates about the concept, while personal and internal transformations are predominating the theoretical based on the foundation of TLT. The impact of TT on destinations and local communities has started to attract academic attention, including within destination management and marketing. Less research attention is being paid to hosts and local communities. Also, host–guest relationships and the future trajectories of transformed individuals have not been sufficiently investigated. Another priority is to connect TTE with sustainable and responsible tourism in achieving the SDGs (UNWTO, 2018). These current priorities and future needs will be greatly facilitated by a sound conceptual model for transformational tourism and that is the next topic for this chapter.

Conceptual model of transformational tourism

An artistic rendering of the proposed conceptual model is provided in Figure 35.1. Derived from a comprehensive review of the research literature on transformational tourism, the model envisages three types of experiences as non-memorable, non-transformational experiences (NMNTTEs), memorable tourism experiences (MTEs), and transformational tourism experiences (TTEs). The motivations for NMNTTEs include relaxation, leisure, and entertainment, and these trips do not necessarily become MTEs. MTEs can be the triggers for TTEs and tend to result from social interaction, knowledge acquisition, local hospitality, authenticity, and novelty. MTEs result in revisits, recommendations, and positive word-of-mouth (WoM). TTEs are definitely memorable and are from interactions with nature, local people, local culture, and from unity with others. Their outcomes are self-reflection, better understanding of others, knowledge gain, new and closer relationships, and a clearer understanding and vision of the world.

Transformational experiences in Sri Lanka

To further examine the conceptual model, an empirical study was conducted from September to December 2021. The U.K. is the one of the top source markets of visitors to Sri Lanka (SLTDA, 2020). In line with this, British tourists who visited Sri Lanka were selected for data collection. Nine in-depth semi-structured interviews were conducted, each lasting between 40 and 60 minutes. In addition, three YouTube travel vlogs published by British tourists after their visits to Sri Lanka were analysed. A total of 12 participants were recruited (Table 35.1). After thematic analysis, two themes emerged.

Transformational tourism 447

Table 35.1 Participant information

Participant	Age	Gender	Education level	Job	Travel behaviour				Reason of visited Sri Lanka	Most memorable experiences got during the trip in Sri Lanka
					Length of stay	Travel Frequency	Most interest destination/s to visit			
P1	44	Male	Diploma	n/a	Most 3-10 days	Any time	Anywhere in the world; Domestic		Explore Buddhism	Visit Buddhist temples and places, engage with Buddhism related cultural events, communicate with the local community
P2	25	Female	Undergraduate	Management consultant	5 days-2weeks	3 times a year	Europe		Volunteer	Local people; Local culture; food
P3	25	Female	Masters	Content Manager in a small business	Depends on the purpose	Anytime	Europe		Volunteer	New relationship; local people; local culture
P4	68	Male	Masters	Retired Teacher	10-14 days	Several times a year	Europe		Leisure	Meet local people, local culture, food
P5	56	Male	Masters	Operational support manager	10-14 days	5-6 times a year	All over the world		Exploring culture; visiting friends	Local culture; Food
P6	64	Male	Diploma	Retired Dental Surgeon	1-3 weeks	At least 3 times a year	UK, Dubai, Singapore, France		Revisit	Build new relationships; local people; local culture
P7	28	Male	Undergraduate	Company Director	4-10 days	3-4 times per year	Europe		Leisure	Food, need more time for experience
P8	26	Female	Diploma	Animal carer	Long-time stay (6 months)	Once a year	Anywhere		Working	Beaches, local people, local culture
P9	28	Female	Undergraduate	n/a	Depends	Depends	Anywhere		Solo traveller/ backpacker	Friendly people, nature, sceneries
P10 (YouTuber)	28	Female	n/a	n/a	Long stay	-	Asia		Working	New relationships, local people, beaches
P11 (YouTuber)	-	Male	n/a	-	-	-	Travel all around the world		Exploring my love for language, culture, spirituality	Explore the Vedda Tribe
P12 (YouTuber)	-	Male	-	quit my job	-	-	-		Meet friends	Local people, local culture, sceneries, train trips, food

The healing and inspiration of Sri Lanka

The participants found trips to Sri Lanka helped them to heal from unexpected major life events and inspire them to make changes. Respondent P6 decided to revisit Sri Lanka after his wife passed away. For P6, Sri Lanka is the place where they shared many cherished memories as a couple. Revisiting Sri Lanka is considered his own way to mourn for his late wife:

I was terribly struggling my life after her death. I wanted to go to Sri Lanka and see the places again where I spent with her last time… I used to walk on the beach every morning and evening, remembering our old things.

(P6, M)

While mourning for his late wife, he also took his time in Sri Lanka as an opportunity to reflect and figure out the future. The short trip turned into long-term healing in Sri Lanka.

I understand the reality of life, I understand I really need a change… I decided to stay in Sri Lanka, I did not think forever, but nice people were there. They smiled at me, said good morning, hello. Neighbours sent food sometimes [...] you know unknowingly I started to talk to them [...] Sometimes they did not understand what I said. I did not fully understand what they told me (laughing).

(P6, M)

The genuine hospitality of the locals and the healing power of Sri Lanka played a significant role in navigating P6 through troubling times. Now, after 15 years, he has permanently settled in Sri Lanka with a relationship that ended up in a marriage and two children.

P10 also found healing and inspiration in Sri Lanka. After an unexpected life event, she found herself somewhat lost:

"It wasn't really me. I feel lost in different ways." The trip in Sri Lanka helped him to take back control of his life: "(from) the journey I find empowerment, confidence and stay away from control, take back control of my life and next steps that I should take."

Participants explained the healing and inspirational power of Sri Lanka was attributable to its beautiful nature and spirituality. Participants indicated that the unexpected beauty and serene nature helped them to be calmer, and present. The engagement with nature made them feel genuinely relaxed and happy:

I felt like you know I fly over the mountains, just feel free… (deep breath) you know I don't know how to explain it, but I feel happy in myself.

(P9, F)

Complementing the beautiful nature, participants also explored the meaning of spiritual happiness from Buddhism. Sri Lanka is an open society and extends religious freedom, whether to Sinhala Buddhists, Tamil, Muslims, or Christians, Sri Lanka has inclusivity in its religious prospects. P1, with the aim of exploring the path of Buddhism, highlighted his experience in Sri Lanka as a country practising Theravadin Buddhism, and recognised the devotion and the amicability of the Sri Lankan Buddhist community:

The massive Stupa in Anuradhapura, no words to explain it, the relief I got from being in that place and spending time meditating was immense.

(P1, M)

As a transformative result, P1 developed knowledge of new lifestyles such as calm kindness and hospitality by engaging with Buddhism and cultural events.

Self-reflections and actions when encountering poverty

The lived experience of poverty when travelling in Sri Lanka left an impression on participants coming from the U.K., a developed economy. P5 recalled the interactions with local children, and was shocked and saddened by the poverty in Sri Lanka:

> *You know I saw barefoot children, people in dirty clothes [...] its poverty [...] they don't have even basic things [...] food [...] clothes. Their living condition is so bad, I feel I need to help them. I gave them some money several times, just very small, 500 rupees [...] just less than two pounds. Once a small boy, he gave me a big smile. I still remember how his eyes twinkled... [low voice]*

Despite the struggle, locals still provided the most genuine hospitality beyond the barrier of communication that really touched the participants:

> *Sitting down with the local people was a different experience. I couldn't talk with them, I didn't know the language, but they smiled with me in friendly ways and offered me food and snacks.*
>
> (P6, M)

Also experiencing poverty in his travel, P4 saw the segregation of rich and poor and how the poor suffer because of unfairness even within the rule of law:

> *I heard that ... (He told the story about a truck accident, that it caused the death of a couple who were driving on a tuk tuk) it's upsetting [...] for the people in the road because he was a very nice man and there's no justice, well everyone just seems to accept it, but it doesn't sit with well Westerners because it's unethical and goes ignored, nothing is done about it.*

With his experience, P4 saw through the society, the parity between powerful and powerless people and unfair treatment of the general public because of politics in countries like Sri Lanka. Such experiences helped P4 to form a more embodied and comprehensive understanding of poverty and social classes in Sri Lanka. It also challenged his taking-for-granted view of justice and law and led to a more critical and reflexive worldview.

After returning from her trip, P3 compared her life in the U.K. with people's living conditions in Sri Lanka:

> *I offered them (locals) two big Nescafe (instant coffee and milk powder). It was like five pounds, but it wasn't cheap for them, you realised how much more it values for them. This comparing to me when I'm back here, I heard my sister talking about an apartment that she wants to rent, my brother wants this watch and already had one for Christmas, this and that [...] Like it made you question why she wanted to talk about her apartment? Do you really need this watch while you have one? It made me realise how people consume their basic needs.*
>
> (P3, F)

Figure 35.2 Volunteers working alongside local teachers to deliver basic and interactive English lessons at pre-schools in the Hikkaduwa area of Sri Lanka (https://travelteer.co.uk/programmes/english-development).

The embodied experience of poverty, and interactions with locals, made P3 question the capitalist lifestyle in her social circle and reshaped her perceptions towards material things.

Some participants determined to help locals by engaging in voluntourism (Figure 35.2). P2 found joy by teaching children:

One of my powerful emotional and memorable things is working with children. They were very happy to see me, you know […] you feel that you can make a difference to that, that was very rewarding to be helping and supporting people who might not otherwise have that help, you know they are really enjoying meeting me, I feel they need my help, it's something you get joy out from that too […], I want to continue doing that where I can.

Such overwhelming and powerful emotions that P2 experienced through helping local children were a transformational and meaningful experience not only for herself, but also for the local community. For P2, the experience has inspired her to help more disadvantaged people in the future; whilst children in the local community are equipped with the knowledge, which is the first step of getting out of poverty.

The findings suggest that the calming nature, spirituality, and genuine hospitality of Sri Lanka serve as a destination to heal from unexpected life events, and to reflect on personal purposes, take control of one's life, and make changes. Whilst some transformations are internal, some resulted in staying in Sri Lanka for the long term. In addition, the poverty in Sri Lanka was a shock for participants travelling from the U.K. It offered them an opportunity to reflect on their lifestyles, understand the fairness (or unfairness) of justice, and engage in real change within local communities through giving and teaching. Such embodied experience of poverty could potentially make a real difference in participants, such as actions for justice and fairness for the Global South, co-transformations with locals, and re-examining the capitalist lifestyle and the real meaning of happiness.

Figure 35.3 is a depiction of images from Sri Lanka and how they fit with the three types of experiences in the conceptual model. These are accompanied with descriptions of the photos and, in some cases, with quotes from the British tourists interviewed in the pilot study.

Transformational tourism 451

Figure 35.3 Depiction of tourism experiences and quotes about travel in Sri Lanka.

With a recognition that transformational tourism is an emerging construct, the next topic in this chapter is a discussion of future trends and research directions for transformation tourism.

Future trends and research directions

Five future trends and research directions are proposed (Figure 35.4). First, studies on transformational tourism so far mostly focus on the individual tourist perspective, with

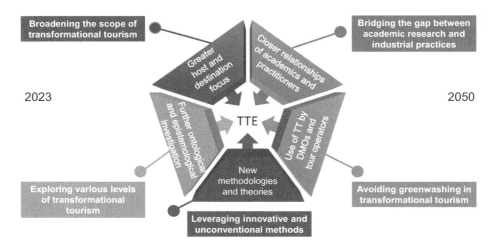

Figure 35.4 Future trends and research directions for transformational tourism.

limited studies investigating the host and destination perspectives (Isaac, 2017; Wanitchakorn and Muangasame, 2021). Future research should contribute to broadening the scope of transformational tourism with discussions on the forms of tourism, and the ways they can transform quality of life in the host communities. In this case, pro-poor tourism, voluntourism, and community-based tourism can be considered as forms of transformational tourism. However, how do the transformational experiences of these tourism typologies differ? Even within the same tourism typology, transformational experiences may be influenced considerably by the value system and cultural background of each individual. For instance, how would the transformational experience of an adventure tourist on the path to Santiago de Compostela (Spain) differ from that of a religious pilgrim and what implications should this have for the management and marketing of other long-distance pilgrimage paths around the world walked by secular and religious travellers? Future conceptualisation and synthesis are required to understand the transformative elements in these forms of tourism. In addition, responding to Teoh et al.'s (2021) co-created perspective of conceptualising transformative tourism experiences, future studies are encouraged to focus on the transformative experiences from the host–guest perspective. Researchers can explore how meaningful interactions between hosts and guests facilitate two-way transformational experiences for both parties. Future studies focusing on tourist transformations should also consider the contextual aspects of destinations, particularly, how unique destination offerings can afford certain types of transformative experiences. Furthermore, this broadened scope of transformational tourism should be studied within the framework of SDGs, particularly focusing on the wellbeing of tourists, long-term social and economic impacts on local communities and destinations through a long-lasting, transformative lens. Such discussion will also contribute to the fusing of transformational tourism and meaningful tourism.

Second, the gap between how transformational tourism is studied in academia and how it is leveraged in tour packaging and destination promotions should be further explored. Questions such as how practitioners understand and use the term of transformational tourism, and how they develop a transformative experience is worth further investigation, especially from the perspective of meaningful tourism experiences (Sterchele, 2020). Building on Sheldon (2020) and Soulard et al. (2019), questions such as if the transformative outcomes are measured and monitored by these operators and destinations, and if they are engaged in the process of transforming tourists and the host communities should be asked. Tour operators and DMOs can play crucial roles in facilitating the development of transformative experiences. Therefore, there is a need to bridge the gap between academic research and industrial practices by encouraging knowledge exchange and delivering genuine transformative experiences that benefit tourists and host communities.

Third, future research should investigate how the terms 'transformational' and 'transformative' have been used by DMOs and tour operators. In recent years, transformation has become a buzzword for tourism marketing as tourists are looking for more meaningful and in-depth experiences with long-term impacts. As a result, the TT concept has been adopted in many promotional materials. With the current trends of greenwashing in marketing and public relations, it is worth exploring if 'transformation' is also used for such purposes without much engagement with experience design for the transformative activities. Future research can investigate how DMOs and tour operators are using transformation as the key marketing focus and how they are delivering TTEs. It is also interesting to see how the various stakeholders perceive and understand TTEs. Indeed, it is important that tour operators avoid the use of the term "transformational" to describe visitor experiences and services where transformative outcomes *per se* have not been purposefully embedded in the design of the visitor experience. Transformational tourism should not be allowed to turn into a fad – perhaps in an analogous way to greenwashing claims by some organisations – and this is an issue that some tourism practitioners have already raised (see, for instance, Baginski, 2020). Conversely, scholarly research also has a responsibility to investigate this phenomenon in a similar way to how greenwashing practices have been not only denounced by scholars but also researched extensively as regards their impact on consumer perceptions and actual behaviours.

Fourth, new methodological approaches and new theories are called for to investigate the process of transformation. Most studies reviewed are qualitative by nature and predominantly use transformative learning theory (Reisinger, 2013). Innovative and unconventional methods need to be leveraged such as combining physiological measurements (including emerging technologies in this respect such as neurological sensors, smart clothing or the Internet of the Senses, to mention but a few) and subjective narratives to unpack the triggers and effects of the transformational process. Furthermore, and adopting a tourism futures perspective, what will be the impact of the Metaverse on memorable or even transformational tourism experiences? Will the Metaverse merely create an alternative reality or will it develop to a stage where it could become altogether transformational? If that is an option, how should immersive experience design in the Metaverse differ from the more familiar paradigms currently adopted in the physical world, given the known differences in neurological processes involved (Bratu and Sabău, 2022)? One of the challenges to exploring transformational experiences is the nature of the complex, individual, and internal processes (Coghlan and Weiler, 2018), which sometimes can be challenging to articulate and recall. Future research should focus more on embodied and situated experiences and use methods such as autoethnography and interpretative phenomenological analysis to understand the sense-making and self-change in the experiences. It is also suggested that the theoretical contributions of transformational tourism should go beyond transformative learning theory from the adult education discipline, and engage theories from sociology, psychology, and anthropology to enrich the knowledge production. Similarly, although our understanding of the neurological processes involved in learning are relatively well understood, our understanding of the neurological triggers of transformative experiences remains in its infancy. Research to bridge this gap could have major implications for experience design in tourism. Fifth, the term "transformational tourism" requires further ontological and epistemological investigation given the inconsistent and even conflicting interpretations in various studies. Any life event, regardless of being big or small, can be considered transformational. In the words of Heraclitus: "no man ever steps in the same river twice, for it's not the same river and he's not the same man"; most existing transformational tourism studies are related to life-changing outcomes (Noy, 2004) or explicit perceptual changes through learning (Robledo and Batle, 2015; Sin, 2009). Therefore, if all tourism experience is understood as transformational, various levels of transformation should be explored (e.g., physical, cognitive, and life transformations). In addition, different types of tourism (e.g., backpacking, volunteering, and spiritual tourism) can link to various levels of transformation. Future conceptual and empirical research should push the scope of transformational tourism studies and develop a system linking various forms of tourism and levels of transformations for future investigations. Moreover, should transformational tourism be limited to physical experiences? Indeed, in a wider arena, transformational tourism may have a major role to play in the development, management and marketing of the emerging concept of wise destinations (Coca-Stefaniak, 2020), which bridges slow tourism and smart tourism to deliver personalised visitor experiences at an individual level. Similarly, it could be argued that transformational tourism remains to be researched from the perspective of medical, health and wellness tourism, where this element of the experience remains somewhat sidelined (see, for instance, a recently published literature review on this by Zhong et al., 2021).

Stakeholder actions, initiatives, and the SDGs

Table 35.2 provides recommendations for actions and initiatives to be undertaken by these stakeholders in the future.

Table 35.2 Recommended stakeholder actions and initiatives

Stakeholders	Required actions and initiatives
Tourists	• Co-create transformational tourism experiences • Engage in responsible travel • Interact more with local people and cultures
Tourism operators and organisations	• Add to knowledge on transformation tourism experiences • Provide transformational tourism experiences
Community	• Co-create memorable and transformational tourism experiences • Engage more with tourists
Government	• Develop policies in support of transformational tourism • Provide industry training on transformational tourism
Environment	• Encourage pro-environmental behaviour • Prepare guidelines for protection and conservation of natural areas

Earlier in the chapter, it was stated that research linking the UN Sustainable Development Goals (SDGs) and transformational tourism is scarce and that transformative experiences are yet to be fully linked with destination sustainability and its contribution to achieving the SDGs (Buhalis et al., 2023). It was recommended that a broadened scope of transformational tourism should be placed within the framework of the SDGs, with a focus on the wellbeing of tourists, long-term social and economic impacts on local communities and destinations through a long-lasting, transformative lens. Table 35.3 takes this recommendation one step further by outlining the potential contributions of transformational tourism to the 17 SDGs.

Table 35.3 SDGs and potential contributions of transformational tourism

SDG numbers and titles	SD goal explanations	TT potential contributions
SDG 1. **No poverty**	End poverty in all its forms everywhere	Creating greater awareness and understanding of poverty
SDG 2. **Zero hunger**	End hunger, achieve food security and improved nutrition and promote sustainable agriculture	Promoting food safety and security
SDG 3. **Good health and well-being**	Ensure healthy lives and promote well-being for all at all ages	Encouraging local people and communities to improve lifestyles and well-being
SDG 4. **Quality education**	Ensure inclusive and equitable quality education and promote lifelong learning opportunities for all	Volunteering to teach children and others in communities in need
SDG 5. **Gender equality**	Achieve gender equality and empower all women and girls	Supporting women-owned and managed tourism enterprises
SDG 6. **Clean water and sanitation**	Ensure availability and sustainable management of water and sanitation for all	Reducing use of water
SDG 7. **Affordable and clean energy**	Ensure access to affordable, reliable, sustainable and modern energy for all	Using alternative and clean energy sources
SDG 8. **Decent work and economic growth**	Promote sustained, inclusive and sustainable economic growth, full and productive employment and decent work for all	Supporting community-based and pro-poor tourism businesses and projects
SDG 9. **Industry, innovation and infrastructure**	Build resilient infrastructure, promote inclusive and sustainable industrialisation and foster innovation	Using infrastructure wisely and in a sustainable manner
SDG 10. **Reduced inequalities**	Reduce inequality within and among countries	Discouraging all forms of discrimination
SDG 11. **Sustainable cities and communities**	Make cities and human settlements inclusive, safe, resilient and sustainable	Encouraging sustainable actions and initiatives within cities
SDG 12. **Responsible consumption and production**	Ensure sustainable consumption and production patterns	Purchasing and consuming responsibly
SDG 13. **Climate action**	Take urgent action to combat climate change and its impacts	Reducing carbon footprints
SDG 14. **Life below water**	Conserve and sustainably use the oceans, seas and marine resources for sustainable development	Following environmental guidelines and protocols in water

(*Continued*)

Table 35.3 (Continued)

SDG numbers and titles	SD goal explanations	TT potential contributions
SDG 15. **Life on land**	Protect, restore and promote sustainable use of terrestrial ecosystems, sustainably manage forests, combat desertification, and halt and reverse land degradation and halt biodiversity loss	Following environmental guidelines and protocols on land
SDG 16. **Peace, justice and strong institutions**	Promote peaceful and inclusive societies for sustainable development, provide access to justice for all and build effective, accountable and inclusive institutions at all levels	Advocating peace and harmony Supporting effectively governed organisations
SDG 17. **Partnerships for the goals**	Strengthen the means of implementation and revitalise the global partnership for sustainable development	Co-creating innovations and projects that support achievement of the SDGs

Conclusion

The transformative lens has major implications for every element of the tourism system (Morrison et al., 2018) – from the development of destinations to their management, marketing, strategic positioning and future-proofing. Furthermore, it could be argued that the recent COVID-19 pandemic has effectively resulted in an inflexion point or catalyst for transformational tourism (Buhalis, 2022; Soulard et al., 2020). The development of transformational tourism experiences should be embraced by key decision-makers at tourism destinations not as a convenient – and somewhat manipulative – marketing ploy, as posited earlier, but as a genuine strategic positioning to develop positive impacts for tourism, which has often been much maligned as a sector of the economy for contributing little in exchange for substantial negative impacts on local communities and the environment. The role of local communities in the tourism system could be reinvented, as communities play a key active role in transformational processes by providing meaning, purpose, reflection, interconnection and, ultimately, much needed face-to-face relationships in a world where people have never been more connected (technologically) and yet feel lonelier than ever before. Furthermore, transformational tourism could and should become a key channel for countries to deliver on the SDGs. The emerging results from this ongoing research have shown that it was exactly some of the key challenges of SDGs such as the reduction of poverty, zero hunger, good health and wellbeing, quality education, and gender equality, to mention but a few, that were often the triggers for transformational experiences among tourists. Overall, and if transformational tourism should evolve from a niche or add-on element of the service offer of destinations to a more strategic positioning paradigm, would the tourism sector and destination managers be ready for this fundamental long-term shift? Given the intricacies of experience design and the fact that experiences are highly personal, would it be realistic to suggest that all tourism experiences and all destinations offering them should aim for some level of transformation among their customers as one of their success criteria? Realistically, that may not always be possible. However, it is important to reassess how tourism destinations should rise to the challenge of changing people in a meaningful, lasting and inspirational way, one at a time.

References

Ateljevic, I. (2020). Transforming the (tourism) world for good and (re)generating the potential 'new normal'. *Tourism Geographies*, 22(3), 467–475.

Baginski, M. (2020). Transformational tourism: VisitScotland touts latest trend. *Travel Industry Today*, 8 April 2020, https://travelindustrytoday.com/transformational-tourism-visitscotland-touts-latest-trend/

Bratu, S., & Sabău, R.I. (2022). Digital commerce in the immersive metaverse environment: Cognitive analytics management, real-time purchasing data, and seamless connected shopping experiences. *Linguistic and Philosophical Investigations*, 21, 170–186.

Buhalis, D. (2022). Tourism management and marketing in transformation. In D. Buhalis, (Ed.), *Encyclopedia of Tourism Management and Marketing*. Cheltenham, UK: Edward Edgar Publishing, https://www.elgaronline.com/view/nlm-book/9781800377479/9781800377479.xml?v=toc

Buhalis, D., Leung, X. Y., Fan, D., Darcy, S., Chen, G., Xu, F., Wei-Han Tan, G., Nunkoo, R., & Farmaki, A. (2023). Tourism 2030 and the contribution to the sustainable development goals: The tourism review viewpoint. *Editorial, Tourism Review*, 78(2), 293–313. https://doi.org/10.1108/TR-04-2023-620

Butcher, J. (2011). Can ecotourism contribute to tackling poverty? The importance of 'symbiosis'. *Current Issues in Tourism*, 14(3), 295–307.

Coca-Stefaniak, J. A. (2020). Beyond smart tourism cities–towards a new generation of "wise" tourism destinations. *Journal of Tourism Futures*. https://doi.org/10.1108/JTF-11-2019-0130

Coughlan, R., & Connolly, T. (2001). Predicting affective responses to unexpected outcome. *Organizational Behavior and Human Decision Processes*, 85(2), 211–225.

Coghlan, A., & Weiler, B. (2018). Examining transformative processes in volunteer tourism. *Current Issues in Tourism*, 21(5), 567–582.

Duerden, M.D., Lundberg, N.R., Ward, P., Taniguchi, S.T., Hill, B., Widmer, M. A., & Zabriskie, R. (2018). From ordinary to extraordinary: A framework of experience types. *Journal of Leisure Research*, 49(3–5), 196–216.

Folmer, A., Tengxiage, A., Kadijk, H., & Wright, A. J. (2019). Exploring Chinese millennials' experiential and transformative travel: A case study of mountain bikers in Tibet. *Journal of Tourism Futures*, 5(2), 142–156.

Isaac, R. (2017). Transformational host communities: Justice tourism and the water regime in Palestine. *Tourism Culture & Communication*, 17(2), 139–158.

Jefferies, K., & Lepp, A. (2012). An investigation of extraordinary experiences. *Journal of Parks and Recreation Administration*, 30, 37–51.

Kim, J. H. (2010). Determining the factors affecting the memorable nature of travel experiences. *Journal of Travel & Tourism Marketing*, 27(8), 780–796.

Kim, M., Xie, Y., & Cirella, G. (2019). Sustainable transformative economy: Community-based ecotourism. *Sustainability*, 11, 1–15.

Kirillova, K., Lehto, X. Y., & Cai, L. (2017). What triggers transformative tourism experiences? *Tourism Recreation Research*, 42(4), 498–511.

Knollenberg, W., McGehee, N., Boley, B., & Clemmons, D. (2014). Motivation-based transformative learning and potential volunteer tourists: Facilitating more sustainable outcomes. *Journal of Sustainable Tourism*, 22(6), 922–941.

Kottler, J.A. (1998). Transformative travel. *The Futurist*, 32(3), 24–29.

Lean, G. (2012). Transformative travel: A mobilities perspective. *Tourist Studies*, 12(2), 151–172.

Lyons, K., & Wearing, S. (2008). Absences in the volunteer tourism phenomenon: The right to travel, solidarity tours and transformation beyond the one-way. In D. Higgins & R. Mundine (eds.), *Journeys of discovery in volunteer tourism: International case study perspectives*. (1st ed., pp. 182–194). CABI.

Massingham, E., Fuller, R. A., & Dean, A. J. (2019). Pathways between contrasting ecotourism experiences and conservation engagement. *Biodiversity and Conservation*, 28, 827–845.

Mezirow, J. (1978). Perspective transformation. *Adult Education*, 28(2), 100–110.

Morgan, A. (2010). Journeys into transformation: Travel to an 'other' place as a vehicle for transformative learning. *Journal of Transformative Education*, 8(4), 246–268.

Morrison, A. M., Lehto, X. Y., & Day, J. (2018). *The tourism system*. Dubuque, IA: Kendall Hunt Publishing.

Nandasena, G.L.W.R.N., Morrison, A.M., & Coca-Stefaniak, J.A. (2022). Transformational tourism – A systematic literature review and research agenda. *Journal of Tourism Futures*.

Noy, C. (2004). This trip really changed me: Backpackers' narratives of self-change. *Annals of Tourism Research*, 31(1), 78–102.

Phillips, B. (2019). *Learning by going: Transformative learning through long-term independent travel*. Springer Vieweg. in Springer Fachmedien Wiesbaden GmbH.

Pung, J., Gnoth, J., & Del Chiappa, G. (2020). Tourist transformation: Towards a conceptual model. *Annals of Tourism Research*, 81, 1–12.

Reisinger, Y. (2013). *Transformational tourism: Tourist perspectives*. Wallingford, UK: CABI.

Robledo, M., & Batle, J. (2015). Transformational tourism as a hero's journey. *Current Issues In Tourism*, 20(16), 1736–1748.

Ross, G. (2013). Meaning making, life transitional experiences and personal well-being within the contexts of religious and spiritual travel. In S. Filep & P. Pearce (Eds.), *Tourist experience and fulfilment: Insights from positive psychology* (pp. 105–123). Abingdon: Routledge.

Sheldon, P. (2020). Designing tourism experiences for inner transformation. *Annals of Tourism Research*, 83, 102935.

Sin, H. L. (2009). Volunteer tourism – "Involve me and I will learn?" *Annals of Tourism Research*, 36(3), 480–501.

Song, Y., & Yan, L. (2020). Who is Buddha? I am Buddha: The motivations and experiences of Chinese young adults attending a Zen meditation camp in Taiwan. *Journal of Convention & Event Tourism*, 21(4), 263–282.

Soulard, J., McGehee, N., & Knollenberg, W. (2020). Developing and testing the transformative travel experience scale (TTES). *Journal of Travel Research*, 60(5), 923–946.

Soulard, J., McGehee, N. G., & Stern, M. (2019). Transformative tourism organizations and glocalization. *Annals of Tourism Research*, 76, 91–104.

Sterchele, D. (2020). Memorable tourism experiences and their consequences: An interaction ritual (IR) theory approach. *Annals of Tourism Research*, 81, 311–322.

Sri Lanka Tourism development authority (SLTDA) (2020). "Annual statistical report 2019", Available at: https://sltda.gov.lk/en/annual-statistical-report (Accessed: 17th July 2022).

Taylor, E. (2008). Transformative learning theory. *New Directions for Adult and Continuing Education*, 119, 5–15.

Teoh, M.W., Wang, Y., & Kwek, A. (2021). Conceptualising co-created transformative tourism experiences: A systematic narrative review. *Journal of Hospitality and Tourism Management*, 47, 176–189.

Wanitchakorn, T., & Muangasame, K. (2021). The identity change of rural–urban transformational tourism development in Chiang Mai heritage city: Local residents' perspectives. *International Journal of Tourism Cities*, 7(4), 1008–1028.

Wearing, S., & McGehee, G. (2013). Volunteer tourism: A review. *Tourism Management*, 38, 120–130.

Yang, J. Y., Paek, S., Kim, T., & Lee, T. H. (2015). Health tourism: Needs for healing experience and intentions for transformation in wellness resorts in Korea. *International Journal of Contemporary Hospitality Management*, 27(8), 1881–1904.

Zhong, L., Deng, B., Morrison, A. M., Coca-Stefaniak, J. A. and Yang, L. (2021). Medical, health and wellness tourism research: A review of the literature (1970–2020) and research agenda. *International Journal of Environmental Research and Public Health*, 18, 10875, https://doi.org/10.3390/ijerph

36 Sport tourism in times of the VUCA world

Ekaterina Glebova, Fateme Zare, Robert Book, Michel Desbordes and Gabor Geczi

Introduction

VUCA is an acronym constructed to embrace together four phenomena: volatility, uncertainty, complexity, and ambiguity (Heritage & Center, 2018). The world remains driven by the VUCA conditions, affecting many industries, including sport and tourism. Today sport tourism is facing numerous changes, challenges, and, consequently, opportunities (Glebova, 2022). However, in a complex environment, without relevant skills and experiences, often it is difficult to identify and use these opportunities.

As a result of this chapter, the readers will:

- Understand the role of the global context in the sport tourism industry
- Disclose how social and economic issues may affect sport tourism and how technological development fosters entertainment and mobility
- Comprehend the nature, features, and dimensions of sport tourism
- Distinguish different types of sport tourism and their nature and purposes
- Be aware of developing issues and trends in sport tourism
- Recognise the importance of new technologies wide dissemination and its effect on the sports industry, entertainment, and mobility
- Consider sport tourism as a marketing tool influencing city and country brand image
- Foresee the obstacles and opportunities for sports infrastructure deployment and define future research directions

Defining sport tourism

Sport tourism is a term that has currently been bandied about a great deal. Sport, whether it be recreational, amateur, or elite, involves a significant amount of travel to compete and play in different areas. Sport tourism does not have a standard definition yet, even though many people have different definitions. Sport tourism can be defined broadly as tourists travelling to destinations primarily to engage in sport activities or events (Standeven & Knop, 1998). Several scholars define sport tourism as participating in passive and active sport holidays and claim that the dominant activity or purpose of travel can either be sport or tourism (e.g., Ritchie & Adair, 2004; Standeven & Knop, 1998). The concept of sport tourism is defined by Standeven and Knop (1998, p. 12) as "all forms of active and passive involvement in sporting activity, participating casually or in an organised way for non-commercial or business/commercial reasons that necessitate travel away from home and work locality". In this manner, it can be said that tourism and sport are interconnected.

According to Van Rheenen et al. (2017), sport tourism was first classified as a new profession rather than a topic of study. An example of this is the definition of sport tourism by Kurtzman (1993, p. 6), which defined sport tourism as "the use of sport as a touristic endeavor". Later, in 1998, Gibson (1998, p. 10) defined sport tourism as "leisure-based travel that takes individuals temporarily outside of their home communities to play, watch physical activities or venerate attractions associated with these activities".

There has been a debate over whether sport tourism can be classified into two types (active and passive) (Standeven & Knop, 1998) or three types (event, nostalgia, and active) (Gibson, 1998). Currently, there are three basic types of behaviour associated with sport tourism (Uvinha et al., 2018). Gibson (2003, p. 207) categorises and defines three types of sport tourism: "active sport tourism is one where participants travel to compete in sports, sport tourism event is one in which participants travel to attend a sport event and nostalgia sport tourism where participants visit sports-related attractions such as halls of fame, famous stadia, or sports-themed cruises". In active sport tourism, tourists actively participate in a form of non-event-based or disorganised sport activity, such as club holidays for land-based activities like golf or tennis, or water-based activities such as swimming, sailing, windsurfing (De Knop, 1990).

Sport event tourism is the second category, in which visitors attend sporting events, such as the Olympic Games, the FIFA World Cup, national sports championships, and regional or local competitions. Based on Uvinha et al. (2018), the "being there" experience is the essence of this subgroup of sport tourism, which varies from watching an event on television or on the Internet. Finally, nostalgia sport tourism is a form of sport tourism that turns mega-event venues into tourist attractions.

History

Sport has always compelled people to travel, whether as a motive, a desire, or a concern. There has been an increase in participation across a wide range of sporting activities over the past decade or two. Visitors, whether participants or spectators, travel to a sporting event to indulge and satiate themselves (Zauhar, 2004).

In terms of sports tourism, especially major-event tourism, sport watching or participation, has a long history. Consider, for example, the Greek Olympic Games; gladiatorial events during the Roman period; medieval and Renaissance jousting, shooting, and archery competitions; major horse races beginning in the eighteenth century; and the appeal of inter-urban, national, and international team and individual sport competitions from the late 1800s to the present (Huggins, 2013).

The coverage spans four key periods in the history of sports tourism: Ancient Greece, the Early Modern, and the nineteenth and twentieth centuries. García Romero (2013), regarding Ancient Greece, mentioned that people travelled to Olympia for various reasons. Competitions and spectators attended sporting festivals for a variety of reasons, including sport as well as religion and culture. Therefore, the early Olympic Games should be recognised as significant tourist destinations. However, travelling to Olympia, housing circumstances, and staying in Olympia, which turned into a congested campsite during the Games, were other significant issues in Ancient Greece for visitors. For instance, travellers struggled with difficulties in terms of travelling, delay, and weather considerations, as well as piracy and robbery (García Romero, 2013). The Greek experience has shaped the history of sport tourism. The great Greeks were satisfied with the enjoyment of the sport environment. Furthermore, the athletes enjoyed their success. Many enthusiastic spectators and eager participants travelled to various sporting destinations because of their strong interest in competitive investments (Zauhar, 2004).

Another critical historical period was the early modern period. It is commonly known that early modern sporting events drew big crowds, but, as a result of to poor transportation, the majority of spectators were locals (McClelland, 2013). Sport tourism was relatively limited during the middle ages and early modern periods. However, it gradually expanded to include sporting events, adventures, training, attractions, resorts, tours, and even the sporting cruises that are now popular in the U.S. (Kurtzman, 2005).

There is little research on sport tourism in the middle ages and early modern times. During the middle ages, Medieval tournaments and jousts, which originated in France and quickly spread across Europe, had a sporting character. They drew participants who travelled long distances and also proved popular with spectators (Powicke, 1988).

The 19th century was another key historical period in terms of sport tourism. In this century, the sport evolved into more modern forms and formations. There was a huge increase in the number of sport associations, federations, clubs, and leagues throughout the world during this century. Sports formations, such as team affiliations and league affiliations, increased active and passive participation (Zauhar, 2004). Some 19th-century events that helped the growth of sport tourism include horse racing (1823), the first yacht race in North America (1835), skating races in North America (1868), the first automobile race in Chicago (1885), basketball making its debut in front of 200 spectators (1892), football's first professional match (1895), and the organisation of ten American bowling leagues (1895).

Historically, leisure travel and mobility were generally a luxury available to a wealthy elite. However, cost reduction, event management, access to information, and middle-class development boosted a surge in mass tourism in recent decades, including sport tourism.

Concurrently, the development of various challenging sports increased and intensified spectator interest. According to Zauhar (2004), in those days when travelling was more convenient and available, more people attended sporting events, contests, destinations, and environments – either as participants or as spectators. The advancement of media technology has helped fans in their appreciation of athletes, their skills, and their capabilities.

Modern view on sport tourism

Sport tourism is a difficult concept to define clearly since a multifaceted relationship exists between sport and tourism. According to Gibson (2017), there have been growing efforts in sport tourism recently. Sport tourism has been the subject of debate over the past two decades, relating to topics such as whether it should be regarded as active or passive (Standeven & Knop, 1998) or divided into categories such as active, event, and nostalgia (Gibson, 1998); whether it should be considered sports or just sport (Weed & Bull, 2012); and also whether nostalgia should be treated as remembrance (Pigeassou, 2004) or heritage tourism (Ramshaw & Gammon, 2005).

Over the last decade, scholars have integrated sport tourism with other concepts like anthropology (Chalip, 2006), geography (Higham & Hinch, 2006), social psychology (Kaplanidou & Vogt, 2007), marketing (Ziakas, 2010), and feminist theory, and sociology (Mansfield, 2007). According to Van Rheenen et al. (2017), the five fundamental conceptual aspects that have impacted sport tourism definitions over the last two decades – sport as a motivator for travel, time, space, participation experience, and linkage to an economic market – still require more examination and clarity.

Weed (2008) distinguished five different types of sport tourism: (1) tourism with sports content, (2) sports participation tourism, (3) sports training, (4) sports event, and (5) luxury sport tourism. According to him, tourism with sports content is the kind of tourism where the sport itself is not the first reason for the trip.

Glebova (2022) proposes that sport tourism refers to travel or mobility with a purpose related to sports, specifically, participating or spectating sport events or activities. It addresses the satisfaction of sports consumer needs with sports products and services (Erb & Hautbois, 2018; Schut & Glebova, 2022). Overall, there are three main groups of consumers in the sports industry: performers, trainers, and spectators. Accordingly, we think of all of them as sport tourists, following various purposes: training, work, education, and leisure. Thus, the role of digital technologies in sport tourism is crucial for all stakeholders regardless of their purposes.

VUCA context

The VUCA concept is mentioned in this chapter to emphasise the turbulence of the present-day economic and social situation for many industries, including sport tourism. It can be explained by many overlapping factors, particularly, globalisation, the capitalism crisis, technological transformation, and the COVID-19 pandemic, among others. Through the emerging technologies, the digitalisation of the economy, new consumption patterns, and the spread of modern transportation, modern sport tourism has rapidly evolved.

Smart cities' sport infrastructure encompasses facilities, systems, goods, and services that enable the sports and healthy lifestyle leisure, using data and technology to engage people to do sports, promote sports culture and physical activity, organise sports events of various scales, create efficiencies, optimise resources, improve sustainability, create economic development, and enhance the quality of life for people in the city.

We live in times of total digitalisation of all fields of life, meaning that technological development and consumer habits (Glebova & Desfontaine, 2020) can be seen as the main drivers of changes in delivering customer experiences. The dissemination and use of technologies are widespread across the world by all sports fans, athletes, coaches, and managers: smartphones, mobile applications, the Internet of Things, immersive technologies (extended reality: virtual, augmented, mixed), and others. All existing technologies are developing and evolving, first of all, in terms of consumer (user) experiences. However, new immersive technologies can offer conceptually new ways, forms, and courses of human–computer interaction. Notably, the Metaverse can adversely affect the way people watch sports. It enables fans to experience the game in a kind of virtual reality with a feeling of real presence in the stadium. Overall, immersive environments, like the Metaverse, gradually change the way consumers perceive reality concerning the digital world.

Global trends in sport tourism

Fields of tourism and sport have been upended by new business models (e.g., Uberisation) and the diffused use of digital platforms, rapidly distributing everything from streamed matches to social communications. It has a crucial impact on cultures and societies. Furthermore, the COVID-19 pandemic (and its aftermath) accelerates technological and social trends.

Innovativeness

Typically, innovations appear in sport tourism in the form of new products, services, tools, or methods. It is a trend used by sport marketing professionals. For example, the Staples Center has undergone a name change, becoming Crypto.com Arena. It follows a current trend of technology innovations, implementing it in rebranding and philosophy.

Safety and sanitary measures

In times of pandemic, sanitary measures apply, including social distancing, quarantine, tourism bans, facial masks, testing (vaccination) obligations, and cross-border regulations. It makes mobility less comfortable for consumers, and, sometimes even impossible (Ruiz Estrada, 2022). An example of this would be the case of Novak Djokovic at the Australian Open 2022. According to the Australian immigration minister, unvaccinated players could fuel opposition to the COVID-19 vaccination. Accordingly, the decision by the Minister of Immigration to revoke Djokovic's visa for reasons of public interest was upheld by three judges of the Federal Court (Alva, 2022). The courts rejected the challenge brought by the unvaccinated tennis star whose visa had been revoked for "health and good order." Djokovic said he was "extremely disappointed" but accepted the ruling (BBC, 2022).

Cybersecurity

Service providers (transport, information, sports media, event organisers) receive and operate consumer data. As an industry that focuses on protecting its customers from physical attacks, it would appear that cybersecurity has been neglected by sport and tourism fields. Since the amount of sensitive data is collected by companies and institutions, sport tourism field stakeholders should adopt cybersecurity measures and stay regularly updated. Bazazo et al. (2019) find the importance of cybersecurity, along with physical security in tourism, which is the most important key in the process of development, marketing, and management of tourist sites at the time being, including all forms of sport tourism and sporting facilities.

Comfortable travel and stadium access

With the development of technologies and service fields, travelling and attending to the stadium becomes more comfortable and easier in terms of access to information, ticketing, stadium access, and security.

Sustainability

Sports tourism plays a crucial role in the development of tourism destination image, and it may be beneficial for the host community. Thus, sports tourism is considered to be an economic activity with an enormous influence on place marketing and development management. However, it can also generate negative social and environmental impacts on tourism destinations and this fact attracts our attention to the construct of sustainability at an intersection with sport and tourism (Jiménez-García et al., 2020) and related issues (Schwark, 2004). For example, Air France is working on reducing its CO_2 emissions. It is announced to customers: "Between 2005 and 2019, Air France cut its CO_2 emissions by 6%, despite an increase in traffic. We must continue on this path and step up our actions. The next step is to achieve a 15% reduction in CO_2 emissions by 2030 compared with 2005.

We have also set ourselves the goal of achieving zero net emissions by 2050, an ambitious but necessary goal to keep global warming below 2°C by the end of the century." Air France finds that investment in a modern, more fuel-efficient fleet as the main tool for reducing carbon footprint.

Sport tourism contemporary issues

Constantly evolving, sport tourism is facing different difficulties and challenges, particularly the quality of information, privacy, ethics, mobility, and environment and climate risks.

In sports tourism, it is essential to assign accountability for the accuracy of media content, especially online. Social media is an essential part of sports entertainment and tourism cultures and one of the main sources of fan visual content, functioning for all the stakeholders. Unfortunately, misinformation and "informational pollutions" are frequently transmitted along with valid information on social media platforms. The use of social media channels and networks is widespread across the world by all sport tourists and fans, and the adoption of related tools may give a competitive advantage to sports managers and other stakeholders. Technological companies, social activists, business leaders, and researchers express concern over the ways that communication technology has enabled bad actors to weaponise information. This can be considered as a threat inherent to digitalisation and has the potential to devaluate the voices of public and private institutions and experts.

The construct of misinformation combines information with the prefix mis-, meaning "wrong", for example, mistake, misspelling, and misunderstanding are common words besides misinformation that use mis- to mean "wrong." Furthermore, disinformation is knowingly spreading misinformation. It means a kind of false information in form of manipulated narrative or facts or misleading or biased information.

Digital technologies' impact on the sport (and also on sport tourism) has been amplified by the pandemic. The live sport spectacle was overwhelmed because of COVID-19 restrictions, and numerous sports events of all scales have been cancelled, postponed, or were organised behind closed doors. However, the pandemic also boosted demand for Internet-based alternatives and mediatory watching.

Personal data protection

Modern technologies can allow for improving media quality and personalisation of sports content and services. It raises privacy issues and the responsibility to protect privacy in both ways: by law and by technologies.

Mobility

First, digital technologies provide a full range of sports entertainment through mediatory watching. Emerging immersive technologies (for example, Metaverse) have been announced with the intention of giving opportunities to feel a kind of physical presence in a stadium, without actually being there. However, the social and psychological impact (short and long term) of these technologies is as yet unknown.

Second, sport tourism cannot exist without human mobility. Mass travel and tourism may seem encumbered by multiple factors, including sanitary measures and the postponement of sport events. Sport tourists are facing this reality, often being discouraged to travel and choosing mediatory sports watching.

Environmental and climate risks

Tourism is considered to be responsible for a certain part of greenhouse gas emissions in the world, meaning that environmental problems arise locally. Today sport tourism managers' mission is to integrate digitisation so that sporting events and related mobility can be developed, managed, and maintained sustainably. The Olympic and Para-Olympic Games, due to be held in Paris in 2024, officially promise to be "spectacular and sustainable", becoming "the first major sporting event to positively impact the climate", and prioritising frugality and utility. The Olympic movement has increasingly taken account of climate and environmental considerations in a commitment that was formalised in the IOC's Olympic Agenda 2020.

Local and international conflicts, politics, sanctions

Russia and Russian athletes have been dropped from many international sports leagues and organisations since its invasion of Ukraine in February 2022. After the breach of the Olympic Truce by the Russian government and supporting this breach by the Belarusian government in February 2022, the Executive Board (EB) of the International Olympic Committee (IOC) discussed the dilemma now faced by the Olympic Movement. They stated that Russian and Belarusian athletes and officials are not recommended to participate in international competitions. The IOC's concerns with regard to the Olympic Movement were two things: peace and fairness. Therefore, the IOC issued some resolutions, including asking international sports federations and sports event organisers not to invite or allow the participation of Russian and Belarusian athletes and officials in international competitions. It is only acceptable for Russian and Belarusian nationals to compete as neutral athletes and on neutral teams. There should be no display of their national symbols, colours, flags, or anthems. As of 25 February 2022, the IOC Executive Board still recommends no sports events be held in Russia or Belarus.

Figure 36.1 Sport tourism in 2022: Trends, problems, solutions, predictions for future.

466 *Ekaterina Glebova et al.*

More and more sports have banned Russian athletes from competing. A number of international sports, including ice skating, skiing, basketball, track, and some tennis competitions, soccer and hockey, rowing, badminton, canoeing, and triathlon, have all prevented Russian nationals from competing. As a result of the IOC's request to international sports federations, Russian athletes will not be allowed to participate in these events. However, Russians have not been banned from other sports, such as swimming, cycling, and auto racing, as recommended by the IOC. According to the International Swimming Federation (FINA), swimmers from Russia and Belarus could compete neutrally under the FINA flag and sing the FINA anthem.

Another international sporting federation, the International Basketball Federation, has also suspended Russia. Besides, according to the International Volleyball Federation, Russia will not host the men's world championship in August. Teams and clubs from Russia have also been suspended from international competitions.

The future of sport tourism

Today we cannot know exactly how long the world and society will stay in a state of VUCA. To this end, contemporary sport tourism managers should attempt to navigate this fast-changing and unpredictable environment. In the age of media, digital transformation, and technological innovations the future of sports tourism will depend on a response to future environmental, ethical and socio-economic challenges (Figure 36.2). Within this context, immersive technologies have a hugely disruptive potential for the field. The Metaverse will be serving users across the globe in the foreseeable future. Virtual and augmented spaces and environments are a powerful opportunity for the entire sports tourism ecosystem. With mass adoption, a big part of the sport tourism economy can be shifted to the Metaverse. Many leading sport and entertainment brands (Nike, Disney, the NFL

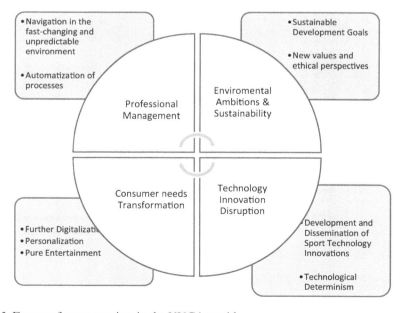

Figure 36.2 Future of sport tourism in the VUCA world.

among others) are actively working on the integration and development of their business activities in the Metaverse.

Furthermore, a real-world setting can be reflected and re-created digitally. A digital venue twin can be defined as a virtual interactive representation of an entire venue system. It is supposed to be hyper-realistic and uses real-time data and simulations for a user. The Paris Olympic Games 2024 project is the first-ever digital venue twin, provided by OnePlan (Oneplanevents, 2022), the official supporter of GIS mapping and software for the Olympic and Paralympic Games Paris 2024. In the framework of this partnership, a digital interactive copy of the event will be constructed. This technology reduces the need for physical presence and visits for stakeholders, including sport tourists, eliminating CO_2 emissions associated with this mobility. Potentially, events' digital twins bring numerous benefits for all stakeholders: (1) lower maintenance costs, (2) reduced health, safety, and environmental risks, and (3) an enhanced strategy to improve system performance, among others. Digital twin software technology is capable to create an accurate virtual replica of a physical sporting event as a holistic system to boost productivity, streamline operations, increase benefits for many stakeholders.

Environmental enthusiasm and care are the key trends for the coming years. It is affecting all industries, especially tourism and transportation. Leading global companies and institutions are concerned about climate, and they aim to significantly restrict the carbon footprint, and ensure the industry's long-term sustainability.

References

Alva, S. (2022). *Australian Immigration Minister Welcomes Djokovic's Deportation Verdict; Read Statement* https://www.republicworld.com/sports-news/tennis-news/australian-immigration-minister-welcomes-djokovics-deportation-verdict-read-statement-articleshow.html

BBC. (2022). *Novak Djokovic: Tennis star deported after losing Australia visa battle* https://au.news.yahoo.com/novak-djokovic-loses-australian-visa-070001524.html

Bazazo, I.K., Al-Orainat, L.M., Abuizhery, F., & Al-Dhoun, R.A. (2019). Cyber Security Applications in the Modern Tourism Industry. *Journal of Tourism, Hospitality and Sports*, 43.

Chalip, L. (2006). Towards Social Leverage of Sport Events. *Journal of Sport & Tourism*, *11*(2), 109–127. https://doi.org/10.1080/14775080601155126

De Knop, P. (1990). Sport for All and Active Tourism. *World Leisure & Recreation*, *32*(3), 30–36. https://doi.org/10.1080/10261133.1990.10559120

Erb, G., & Hautbois, C. (2018). Sport marketing management and communication In David Hassan (ed.), *Managing sport business.* (pp. 269–318). London: Routledge.

García Romero, F. (2013). Sports tourism in Ancient Greece. *Journal of Tourism History*, *5*(2), 146–160. https://doi.org/10.1080/1755182X.2013.828784

Gibson, H. (2017). Sport tourism and theory and other developments: Some reflections. *Journal of Sport & Tourism*, *21*(2), 153–158. https://doi.org/10.1080/14775085.2017.1319514

Gibson, H. J. (1998). Sport tourism: A critical analysis of research. *Sport Management Review*, *1*(1), 45–76. https://doi.org/10.1016/S1441-3523(98)70099-3

Gibson, H. J. (2003). Sport Tourism: An Introduction to the Special Issue. *Journal of Sport Management*, *17*(3), 205–213. https://doi.org/10.1123/jsm.17.3.205

Glebova, E. (2022). Sport Tourism Digital Marketing (*Encyclopedia of Tourism Management and Marketing*) (pp. 1–4). Cheltenham, UK: Edward Elgar Publishing.

Glebova, E., & Desfontaine, P. (2020). Sport et technologies numériques: vers de nouvelles expériences spectateur. *Economica*.

Heritage, U. A., & Center, E. (2018). Who first originated the term VUCA (Volatility, Uncertainty, Complexity and Ambiguity). *USAHEC Ask Us a Question. The United States Army War College*.

Higham, J., & Hinch, T. (2006). Sport and tourism research: A geographic approach. *Journal of Sport & Tourism*, *11*(1), 31–49. https://doi.org/10.1080/14775080600985267

Huggins, M. (2013). Sport, tourism and history: Current historiography and future prospects. *Journal of Tourism History*, *5*(2), 107–130. https://doi.org/10.1080/1755182X.2013.828782

Jiménez-García, M., Ruiz-Chico, J., Peña-Sánchez, A. R., & López-Sánchez, J. A. (2020). A Bibliometric Analysis of Sports Tourism and Sustainability (2002–2019). *Sustainability*, *12*(7), 2840. https://www.mdpi.com/2071-1050/12/7/2840

Kaplanidou, K., & Vogt, C. (2007). The Interrelationship between Sport Event and Destination Image and Sport Tourists' Behaviours. *Journal of Sport & Tourism*, *12*(3-4), 183–206. https://doi.org/10.1080/14775080701736932

Kurtzman, J. (1993). Inaugural address – sports tourism international council. *Journal of Sport & Tourism*, *1*(1), 5–17. https://doi.org/10.1080/10295398608718526

Kurtzman, J. (2005). Sports tourism categories. *Journal of Sport & Tourism*, *10*(1), 15–20. https://doi.org/10.1080/14775080500101502

Mansfield, L. (2007). Involved-detachment: A balance of passion and reason in feminisms and gender-related research in sport, tourism and sports tourism. *Journal of Sport & Tourism*, *12*(2), 115–141. https://doi.org/10.1080/14775080701654762

McClelland, J. (2013). The accidental sports tourist: travelling and spectating in Medieval and Renaissance Europe. *Journal of Tourism History*, *5*(2), 161–171. https://doi.org/10.1080/1755182X.2013.828785

Pigeassou, C. (2004). Contribution to the definition of sport tourism. *Journal of Sport & Tourism*, *9*(3), 287–289. https://doi.org/10.1080/1477508042000320205

Powicke, M. R. (1988). *Juliet RV Barker. The Tournament in England 1100–1400*. Wolfeboro, NH: Boydell & Brewer, Ltd. 1986. Pp. 206. $40.00. *Albion*, *20*(2), 295–296.

Ramshaw, G., & Gammon, S. (2005). More than just Nostalgia? Exploring the heritage/sport tourism Nexus. *Journal of Sport & Tourism*, *10*(4), 229–241. https://doi.org/10.1080/14775080600805416

Ritchie, B. W., & Adair, D. (2004). *Sport tourism: Interrelationships, impacts and issues* (Vol. 14). Bristol, UK: Channel View Publications.

Ruiz Estrada, M. (2022). The Worldwide Holocaust of the XXI Century: The COVID-19. 10.13140/RG.2.2.35083.82728/1.

Schut, P.O., & Glebova, E. (2022). Sports Spectating in connected stadiums: Mobile Application Roland Garros 2018. *Frontiers in Sports and Active Living 4*, 802852. doi:10.3389/fspor.2022.802852

Schwark, J. (2004). Future trends in sport tourism–a question of the development by social protagonists. *Journal of Sport Tourism*, *9*(4), 315–315.

Standeven, J., & Knop, P.D. (1998). *Sport tourism*. Champaign, Illinois: Human Kinetics Publishers.

Oneplanevents (2022) Map and Plan your event site together. https://www.oneplanevents.com/ [last access: 30/04/2022]

Uvinha, R. R., Chan, C.-S., Man, C. K., & Marafa, L. M. (2018). Sport tourism: a comparative analysis of residents from Brazil and Hong Kong. *Revista Brasileira de Pesquisa em Turismo*, *12*, 180–206.

Van Rheenen, D., Cernaianu, S., & Sobry, C. (2017). Defining sport tourism: a content analysis of an evolving epistemology. *Journal of Sport & Tourism*, *21*(2), 75–93. https://doi.org/10.1080/14775085.2016.1229212

Weed, M. (2008). *Olympic tourism/Mike Weed*. Oxford: Butterworth-HeinemannA.

Weed, M., & Bull, C. (2012). *Sports tourism: Participants, policy and providers*. Routledge.

Zauhar, J. (2004). Historical perspectives of sports tourism. *Journal of Sport & Tourism*, *9*(1), 5–101. https://doi.org/10.1080/1477508042000179348

Ziakas, V. (2010). Understanding an event portfolio: the uncovering of interrelationships, synergies, and leveraging opportunities. *Journal of Policy Research in Tourism, Leisure and Events*, *2*(2), 144–164. https://doi.org/10.1080/19407963.2010.482274

37 German holiday travel demand trends

Dirk Schmücker, Anne Köchling and Martin Lohmann

Introduction

The future developments in the tourism demand of Germany as an international source market are of particular interest to the global tourism industry. In pre-COVID times, more than 55 million Germans took at least one holiday trip of five days or more per year. Usually, Germans account for more than 70 million holiday trips per year. Three-quarters of those longer holiday trips are international ones. Additionally, there are almost 60 million German short-haul travellers per year (Lohmann et al., 2020). In terms of international tourism expenditure, Germany is ranked third, after China and the U.S. (UNWTO, 2020). Against this background, this chapter examines the expected developments in holiday demand from the source market of Germany. The trends reported here represent a summary of the findings of a larger trend study conducted by the authors in 2020 (Lohmann et al., 2020), which was updated in 2021 (Schmücker et al., 2021). A particular challenge in this context was the COVID-19 pandemic and the subsequent reactions in policies and societies that led to an unprecedented disruption in global tourism.

The focus of this analysis is on the development of travel behaviour in holiday trips of five days or more. Holiday tourism constitutes a major part of all overnight trips to a destination outside travellers' usual environments for a duration of less than one year (definition of tourism in the International Recommendations for Tourism Statistics, cf. UNSD & UNWTO, 2010).

The authors consider a trend to be a reliably observable development in the past that also informs a justified assumption on how it will continue in the future (Lohmann et al., 2020, p. 1; for other meanings of the concept cf. Altehenger et al., 2011, or Powers, 2019, pp. 7–11). Thus, with respect to the coming years, trends are understood to be the probable medium- and long-term developments of the future based on what is known today. The present paper focuses on measurable trends in holiday travel demand in the German population.

The empirical basis for the analysis is provided by the *Reiseanalyse* (RA; 'Travel Analysis'), which is an annual survey on the holiday travel behaviour of the German-speaking population in Germany and their holiday-related attitudes and motives (FUR, 2021; Lohmann et al., 2020, pp. 132–133). The RA is a non-commercial project supported by the *Forschungsgemeinschaft Urlaub und Reisen e.V.* (FUR; 'Research Association for Holidays and Travel'). The study differentiates between holiday trips of five days or more, and shorter holiday trips (of two to four days). Since 1970, the RA data have been collected every year from a random sample that is representative of the German-speaking resident population aged 14 and older in Germany, with a minimum of 6,000 personal interviews (face-to-face)

DOI: 10.4324/9781003260790-46

being conducted per year. Since 2010, additional information has been collected annually with the help of online surveys that are conducted in several rounds. The 50-year time series provides a reliable overall picture of the development of holiday demand in Germany over the past decades, and it also provides indications of the future demand.

In terms of the trend assessment, regular developments in the past have been identified, analysed, and extrapolated into the future. Thereafter, the quantitative findings describing future travel behaviour in many facets have been adjusted based on an extensive literature review and the subsequent discussion on the identified drivers and attenuators and their interactions that are able to change these trends (Figure 37.1). One may characterise this approach as 'data-based-considering.' Drivers and attenuators may arise from: the environment, such as social, political, economic, technological or natural influencing factors, including climate change issues (IPCC, 2021); developments within the tourism industry; and changes in personal prerequisites of the demand, including the ability and motivation to travel (Lohmann & Beer, 2013). For example, the development of the demographic structure, in which there is a rising share of elderly people from Germany holidaying (Statistisches Bundesamt, 2019), was considered, leading to a change in the tourism demand structure.

As in many other source markets, the COVID-19-induced collapse in tourism in 2020 was evident in the German demand for holiday travel, and it is identified as a disruption in the time series. Accordingly, when assessing the future trend developments, pandemic-induced factors that influenced demand were considered in addition to the usual influencing factors. To gain a better understanding of the consumers' reactions to the pandemic and the development of basic travel needs, several additional surveys were conducted from May 2020 to November 2021. In addition, the pandemic became a focus of the literature review and reflection in terms of its potential long-term impact on the German holiday demand. Since the beginning of the pandemic, many researchers have analysed the possible effects of the crisis on tourism (for an overview, see Utkarsh & Sigala, 2021; Zopiatis et al., 2021).

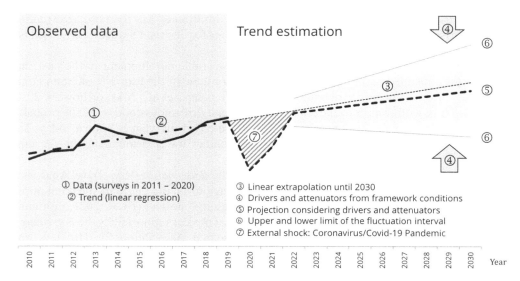

Figure 37.1 Trend estimation for the future: Schematic illustration of the approach.
Source: Authors

Based on the literature review, COVID-19-induced influencing factors that might be relevant to and/or having an effect on the German market have been discussed in terms of transformation, which is the prospect for a long-term change, and recurrence, which is the prospect for getting back on track. With regard to potential transformations beyond the pandemic, various aspects have been identified in the literature. Some scholars expect the pandemic to bring about a change in values that could lead to more mindful travel behaviour and a stronger demand for sustainable travel (Chen et al., 2021; Li et al., 2021; O'Connor & Assaker, 2021). These studies were preceded by calls from the scientific community to focus on the need for a shift towards more sustainable travel behaviour (Haywood, 2020; Higgins-Desbiolles, 2020). Another research focus centred around pandemic-related fears, the risk perception of travel, and related influences on travel behaviour (Çakar, 2021; Kim et al., 2021; Köchling et al., 2022; Kock et al., 2020; Neuburger & Egger, 2020). Moreover, the potential for a change in travel images to a negative assessment of travel in general resulting from negative media coverage of holidays during the pandemic was examined (Mayer et al., 2021). Another aspect that might promote long-term change in travel behaviour is a habituation effect to destinations or types of travel that have proven successful during the pandemic (e.g., more domestic travel) since reverting to what is known reduces the perceived risk (Duan et al., 2022; Rasoolimanesh et al., 2021). Furthermore, supply-side changes, such as business closures or capacity constraints, could also contribute to a long-term transformation (Strasdas et al., 2020).

This chapter offers an overview of the key factors driving the German holiday demand and concludes with an outlook on its expected future development.

Key factors driving the German holiday travel demand

Key factors driving the future development of the German holiday travel demand can mainly be found in three domains:

1 Stabilising factors based on the high appreciation of holiday travel in the German society, materialising in a number of key figures such as high participation rates, a stable market size and growing travel distances coming mostly from air travel
2 Disruption of stability through the effects of the COVID-19 pandemic
3 Dynamic factors leading to change in demand, among them the high and growing positive attitudes towards a more sustainable tourism development on the consumer side.

The following data underline the importance of these factors.

Stabilising factors and disruption: Key figures

The German holiday travel demand in the last few decades was quite stable, but this changed in 2019 (Lohmann et al., 2020). Participation rates (i.e., the share of the population aged 14 years and above who took at least one holiday trip of five days or longer within the year) were hovering at around 75%, with a minimum of 73.6% in 2005 and a maximum of 78.2% in 2019. The number of Germans taking holiday trips of five days and longer increased slowly, from around 63 million at the beginning of the decade to 71 million in 2019. However, this increase occurred between 2009 (64.8 million) and 2010 (69.5 million) because, in 2010, German-speaking foreigners living in Germany were included in the definition of the population for the first time (when only Germans were included in the sample before this). The same pattern can be seen when analysing the number of days spent during holiday trips: The number increased from 853 million in 2002 to 880 million in 2019, with a large increase from 2009 (788 million) to 2010 (886 million) due to the change in the definition of the population.

As opposed to the stability in the total number of trips since 2011, the number of trips to a destination abroad increased from 43.8 million in 2002 to 52.1 million in 2019. Another real increase can be seen in the distances travelled for holiday reasons: While holidaymakers travelled 91 billion kilometres in 2010 (a one-way distance), they covered an aggregated distance of 123 billion kilometres in 2019. On closer examination, it becomes evident that this change results from an increase in air travel only, while most other modes have stable performance levels. Because the number of days spent during a holiday was stable or has even declined, it can be inferred that German holidaymakers covered more kilometres (which is potentially detrimental to the climate and environment) to spend a day at a destination (which is potentially beneficial for the destinations visited).

These four main indicators showed massive decreases in 2020, when COVID-19 first made an appearance. The participation number dropped to 63.1 million (index 84; 2002 = 100), the number of trips decreased to 50.5 million (index 80), the days spent lowered to 590.3 million (index 69), and distances travelled fell to 60.6 billion (index 67). The number of trips to destinations abroad even dropped, to an index of 63. Figure 37.2 shows the key figures for the demand for holiday trips of five days and longer in the German market.

Attitudes towards sustainability

In terms of their attitudes towards sustainability, the German population is, compared to that of most other European countries, considerably more enthusiastic when adopting policies and programmes centred around the environment, climate change, and public welfare (Otto & Gugushvili, 2020). When it comes to sustainability in holiday travel, there are growing positive attitudes about sustainability, which are coupled with a large gap between attitude and behaviour (Passafaro, 2020; Schmücker et al., 2018; Ulker-Demirel & Ciftci, 2020). In January 2019, 56% of the German population claimed that they had a positive attitude about more sustainable holiday trips, but only 4% reported that sustainability was a deciding factor for their trips, while another 23% considered sustainability as one of many factors (Schmücker et al., 2019, 9).

The positive attitude towards sustainability in holiday travel has slowly grown but this growth has been constant since January 2013, where 51% of the population had a positive attitude, to the 67% who had a positive attitude in January 2021. Thus, there is an increasing openness to engage in more sustainable holiday alternatives.

Future trends in German holiday demand

As developments over time, the trends reported here comprise a part in the past up to the year 2019, which we describe on the basis of the RA data, and a part which indicates the probable future direction. As outlined earlier, in the process of the data-based-considering approach used in this study, various sources were used to estimate the future trends: the existing RA data series; general tendencies and correlations resulting from an analysis of the time series; the future preferences expressed by respondents in the surveys; and the potentially influential factors from the economic, societal, and natural frameworks as well as the activities of tourism providers. All of this is based on the literature review.

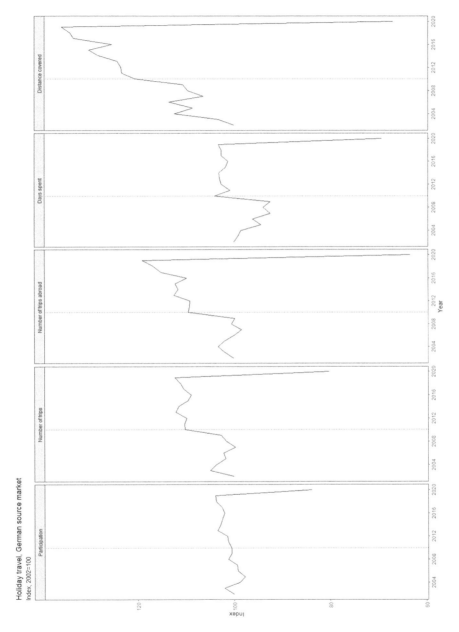

Figure 37.2 Key figures for the demand for holiday trips of five days and longer in the German market.

Speculative elements cannot be ruled out when assessing the impact of these factors but considerations are backed by data where possible. The resulting value for 2030 was extended by a range of further plausible values in order to adequately account for uncertainties in the estimation of future trends (Lohmann et al., 2020, 5). Table 37.1 shows key indicators of tourism demand for 2019 and 2020, as well as the projected target values of the trends until 2030 (Schmücker et al., 2021).

Interestingly, the key indicators expected for 2030 are very similar to the values for 2019 and previous years. Despite some dynamics, such as the share of online booking of travel services, the general picture is characterised by stability of the tourism demand volume and structure. With the COVID-19 pandemic and the political and societal reactions to it, in the years 2020 to 2022 (at least), an unprecedented disruption in the tourism sector was experienced. But with the assumption that societies will adapt in several ways to SARS-CoV-2 or other viruses, the trends for the coming years point to a stable situation.

In terms of the volume of trips, in the period up to 2030, there is an initial decline early in the decade as a result of the coronavirus crisis. But soon, probably around 2024, holiday travel participation and the number of holiday trips will almost return to pre-pandemic levels while the number of short breaks will continue to grow. Both of these indicators will primarily depend on holidaymakers' own assessments of their personal finances. The amount spent per trip in real terms is set to remain at approximately the same level as today.

With respect to holiday trip destinations, the share of destinations abroad is set to increase back to approximately 75% by 2030. Nevertheless, Germany will be the number

Table 37.1 Structure of holiday tourism demand in Germany in 2019 and 2020, and expected structure for 2030

Year	2019	2020	2030 trends towards…		
Characteristics:			Lower limit	Mean	Upper limit
Participation rate (% of pop.)	**78**	**63**	76	78	80
Volume of holiday trips (million)	**70.8**	**50.5**	65,5	69.5	72,5
Destination (% of trips)					
Domestic	26	45	23	26	29
Abroad	74	55	71	74	77
Mediterranean	38	26		36	
Rest of Europe	28	25		30	
Long-haul	8	4		6	
Mode of transport (% of trips)					
Car, Camper	43	61	39	43	47
Rail, Bus	12	10	9	12	15
Air	42	26	39	43	47
Accommodation (% of trips)					
Hotel or similar	54	43	48	51	54
Holiday home/flat	24	30	23	26	29
Cruise ship	3	1	3	3	4
Organisation (% of trips)					
Package tour	45	32	42	45	48
Online booking involved (% of pre-booked trips)	44	49	63	67	71

Data source: RA 2020 and 2021; 2030 authors' estimations (Schmücker et al., 2021).

one destination, in addition to a strong demand for short breaks. Within Germany, the coastal regions in the North and the mountains in the South are the preferred holiday areas.

The most important area of outbound holiday tourism from Germany is the Mediterranean. The trend for the Mediterranean as a whole is set to remain stable, with the ratio of holidays in the European part of the Mediterranean to those in the non-European part remaining similar. Spain is set to prevail as the unrivalled leader with similar market shares as today, followed by Italy and Turkey. Austria and Greece are set to rank in fourth and fifth place.

Based on the interest expressed, there is growth potential for long-haul destinations, particularly outside the summer months. However, the effects of the coronavirus crisis are expected to be particularly marked in this sector and exacerbated by its impact on the airline industry. A return to the volume recorded in 2019 may only be expected in the long-term: after 2030, if at all.

With regard to the mode of transport, car and air transport currently dominate with a market share of just over 40% each. If the trends of the past ten years were to continue, air travel would gain further market share at the expense of the car in the period up to 2030. However, trends in terms of the choice of holiday destination and general conditions are likely to dampen this dynamic trend. Therefore, it is expected that the distribution among modes of transport in 2030 will be similar to that in 2019.

In terms of holiday accommodation, no more than minor variations in the market shares of different holiday accommodation types are expected in the future. Hotels are set to dominate the market, ahead of holiday apartments and cottages or villas. There is some growth potential for holiday homes and the camping sector (particularly motorhomes). Cruises at sea represent one of the market sectors hardest hit by the coronavirus crisis and will barely be able to regain pre-pandemic levels.

In terms of travel preparations, which are the activities before leaving for a holiday including information gathering, decision-making, planning and booking, the key driver of change is the sharp increase in Internet use over the last twenty years. Foreseeable developments in the period up to 2030 represent a continuation of the associated trends.

Inspiration regarding a holiday destination or type of holiday very often continues to come from recommendations by family and friends or ideas and experiences. In marketing communications, offline channels (e.g., brochures and posters) retain some importance, although online options are increasingly being used. With regard to specific information, online sources will become the standard, along with tips from friends and family. Mobile devices are being used in increasing amount, before and during a trip.

Package tours will remain an important sector in the German market, especially in terms of trips to the Mediterranean and long-haul destinations. Tour operators will offer more individualised trips. Thus, in formal terms, it is an organised trip, but the travellers will feel more independent.

All of these trends are probable developments, from today's perspective, based on the information from the time series on German tourism demand that have been collected since 1970 and accounting for the framework conditions. Changes in these framework conditions, such as a new virus, political developments or natural disasters in destinations or in Germany, will affect the development of the tourism demand in Germany. Such changes are possible, but it is not possible to foresee these changes in detail. From what is known today, the demand trends point towards continuity.

This stability is not new. Since 2000, the past development of German holiday travel behaviour and the expected trends for the coming decades have been tracked in several studies (Lohmann et al., 2020, 7). A basic stability and some moderate developments without big cracks in single aspects have been regularly identified. The stability is mainly based on two factors: the high-value-position holiday travel has in German society as an integral part of ensuring good quality of life; and a reliable personal economic situation for the majority of the travellers.

Nevertheless, many researchers, industry experts, and members of the public seem to be surprised that there have not been, and nor will there be, major changes, given that there are so many striking events in the framework for tourism, such as natural catastrophes, wars, terrorist attacks, accidents, and the like. All these events grab attention for the specific area of influence and, at the same time, reduce sensitivity to other aspects of influence. One may call this a variant of *inattentional blindness* (Simons & Chabris, 1999): With the focus on what is holding people's attention presently, people tend to underestimate all the other factors influencing tourism demand in the long run.

The COVID-19 pandemic and the political and societal reactions to it are an example of this. Compared to former crises, this one seems to be even more impactful due to its global spread, and a long-lasting reaction in consumer behaviour in tourism should have been expected as a consequence. In fact, in 2020 and in 2021, Germans' tourist behaviour has changed in terms of volume (i.e., there are less trips) and structure (e.g., destinations; cf. Table 37.1). Thus, consumers adapt to the given circumstances (restrictions in the case of COVID-19) in their attitudes, comprising their cognitive and emotional components, and in their actual behaviour. However, they are maintaining their high levels of appreciation for holiday travel and their touristic preferences throughout the pandemic.

Conclusion and outlook

It can be concluded that the German holiday travel demand prior to the COVID-19 crisis was very stable. For the travel industry, the German holidaymakers were a reliable source of income but there was little possibility of growth. This was a reassuring message not only for the outgoing tourism industry in Germany (travel agencies, tour operators, and transport companies) but also for destinations worldwide. In addition, individual sectors had clear growth opportunities, including air and cruise travel.

The restrictions arising from the COVID-19 situation have obviously disrupted this stability. Regarding future prospects, this study examined the potentially influential factors. The forces pulling the trend lines back to the paths foreseeable before COVID-19 and the forces bringing the trend lines more permanently away from what could be seen before the crisis in particular were discussed. It was found that, for most sectors and for the market as a whole, recurrence is the more likely path. The main reasons for this assessment are the drivers of stability found in the market, specifically the high value people place on holiday travel. In most cases, the restrictions accompanying COVID-19 are exactly that: temporary barriers that prevent people from taking the type of holiday they would like to take.

There are, however, exceptions to this rule. Notably, air travel and possibly cruise travel will not return quickly to the growth paths seen before the crisis. This is partly due to the observable shift in German attitudes towards more sustainable travel and a greater demand for climate action, as outlined in SDGs 12 and 13 (i.e., responsible consumption and production and climate action; UN, 2015).

What will bring German tourism demand back to pre-pandemic levels (recurrence) is essentially the strong motivation to engage in holiday tourism, together with the well-established habit of travelling. Surveys during the pandemic in Germany showed an increased motivation for holidays (Schmücker et al., 2021): Taking holiday trips is at the top of the list of consumer priorities in Germany, and holiday-travel-related motivations and attitudes indicate steady tourist demand in quantitative and qualitative terms.

Of course, not all tourists are the same; they are highly diverse individuals and will continue to be so in the future. Nevertheless, there are certain aspects in which they will differ from today's consumers. These include general trends (e.g., demographic changes) on the one hand and more individual trends on the other, which is a result of accumulated travel experience and quality demands and the higher number of choices that are perceived to be satisfactory (multi-optional approach). To conclude, German tourists of the future can be described as experienced, proficient, demanding, multi-optional, and flexible (Schmücker et al., 2021). The tourism industry should react to this with target group-oriented offers.

Dynamics in tourism demand from Germany may originate from different areas. A particularly important driver here is the perception of climate change issues in society (with the impact being no increase in air travel). Additional factors are the labour market for tourism companies (e.g., for hotels, with the impact being higher prices that lead to higher market share of holiday apartments) and new developments in communication technology (with the impact being the increased use of mobile devices for information en route).

With respect to the behavioural changes resulting from the measures enacted to fight COVID-19, recurrence is what is expected for tourism demand in Germany. Instead of a transformation process, it is rather a process of returning to continuity. Thus, in holiday travel, German consumers show true resilience, including in their adequate response to changing framework conditions during the pandemic and in their return to their previous standards after the impact of the pandemic will have diminished.

References

Altehenger, J. E., Abu-Er-Rub, L., & Gehrig, S. (2011). The transcultural travels of trends. An introductory essay. *Transcultural Studies*, *2*(2), 140–163. https://doi.org/10.11588/TS.2011.2.9073

Çakar, K. (2021). Tourophobia: fear of travel resulting from man-made or natural disasters. *Tourism Review*, *76*(1), 103–124. https://doi.org/10.1108/TR-06-2019-0231

Chen, Y., Dai, Y., Liu, A., Liu, W., & Jia, L. (2021). Can the COVID-19 risk perception affect tourists' responsible behavior intention: an application of the structural equation model. *Journal of Sustainable Tourism*, 1–20. https://doi.org/10.1080/09669582.2021.1977938

Duan, J., Xie, C., & Morrison, A. M. (2022). Tourism crises and impacts on destinations: A systematic review of the tourism and hospitality literature. *Journal of Hospitality & Tourism Research*, *46*(4), 667–695. https://doi.org/10.1177/1096348021994194

European Commission (2020). *Report on the impact of demographic change*. https://ec.europa.eu/info/sites/default/files/demography_report_2020_n.pdf

FUR Forschungsgemeinschaft Urlaub und Reisen (Ed.). (2021). *What is the Reiseanalyse?* Retrieved November 22, 2021. https://reiseanalyse.de/what-is-the-reiseanalyse/

Haywood, K. M. (2020). A post COVID-19 future – tourism re-imagined and re-enabled. *Tourism Geographies*, *22*(3), 599–609. https://doi.org/10.1080/14616688.2020.1762120

Higgins-Desbiolles, F. (2020). Socialising tourism for social and ecological justice after COVID-19. *Tourism Geographies*, *22*(3), 610–623. https://doi.org/10.1080/14616688.2020.1757748

IPCC (2021). Climate change 2021: The physical science basis. Contribution of working group I to the sixth assessment report of the intergovernmental panel on climate change [Masson-Delmotte, V., P. Zhai, A. Pirani, S.L. Connors, C. Péan, S. Berger, N. Caud, Y. Chen, L. Goldfarb, M.I. Gomis, M. Huang, K. Leitzell, E. Lonnoy, J.B.R. Matthews, T.K. Maycock, T. Waterfield, O. Yelekçi, R. Yu, and B. Zhou (eds.)]. Cambridge University Press. In Press.

Kim, J., Park, J., Lee, J., Kim, S., Gonzalez-Jimenez, H., Lee, J., Choi, Y. K., Lee, J. C., Jang, S., Franklin, D., Spence, M. T., & Marshall, R. (2021). COVID-19 and extremeness aversion: The role of safety seeking in travel decision making. *Journal of Travel Research*. https://doi.org/10.1177/00472875211008252

Kock, F., Nørfelt, A., Josiassen, A., Assaf, A. G., & Tsionas, M. G. (2020). Understanding the COVID-19 tourist psyche: The evolutionary tourism paradigm. *Annals of Tourism Research*, *85*, 103053. https://doi.org/10.1016/j.annals.2020.103053

Köchling, A., Gundersen Engeset, M., Reif, J., Yarar, N., Ritalahti, J., Holmberg, E., & Velvin, J. (2022). Between fearful homebodies and carefree travel lovers: identifying tourist segments during the COVID-19 pandemic in Finland, Germany, and Norway. *Current Issues in Tourism*. https://doi.org/10.1080/13683500.2022.2026304

Li, M., Im, J., Fu, X., Kim, H., & Zhang, Y. E. (2021). Proximal and distal post-COVID travel behavior. *Annals of Tourism Research*, *88*(9), 103159. https://doi.org/10.1016/j.annals.2021.103159

Lohmann, M., & Beer, H. (2013). Fundamentals of tourism: What makes a person a potential tourist and a region a potential tourism destination? *POZNAŃ UNIVERSITY of ECONOMICS REVIEW*, *13*(4), 83–97.

Lohmann, M., Yarar, N., Sonntag, U., & Schmücker, D. (2020). *Reiseanalyse trend study 2030*. Forschungsgemeinschaft Urlaub und Reisen e.V.

Mayer, M., Bichler, B. F., Pikkemaat, B., & Peters, M. (2021). Media discourses about a superspreader destination: How mismanagement of COVID-19 triggers debates about sustainability and geopolitics. *Annals of Tourism Research*, *91*, 103278. https://doi.org/10.1016/j.annals.2021.103278

Neuburger, L., & Egger, R. (2020). Travel risk perception and travel behaviour during the COVID-19 pandemic 2020: A case study of the DACH region. *Current Issues in Tourism*, *24*(7), 1003–1016. https://doi.org/10.1080/13683500.2020.1803807

O'Connor, P., & Assaker, G. (2021). COVID-19's effects on future pro-environmental traveler behavior: An empirical examination using norm activation, economic sacrifices, and risk perception theories. *Journal of Sustainable Tourism*, *30*(1), 89–107. https://doi.org/10.1080/09669582.2021.1879821

Otto, A., & Gugushvili, D. (2020). Eco-social divides in Europe: Public attitudes towards welfare and climate change policies. *Sustainability*, *12*(1), 404. https://doi.org/10.3390/su12010404

Passafaro, P. (2020). Attitudes and tourists' sustainable behavior: An overview of the literature and discussion of some theoretical and methodological issues. *Journal of Travel Research*, *59*(4), 579–601. https://doi.org/10.1177/0047287519851171

Powers, D. (2019). *On trend: The business of forecasting the future*. Champaign-Urbana, IL: University of Illinois Press.

Rasoolimanesh, S., Seyfi, S., Rastegar, R., & Hall, C. (2021). Destination image during the COVID-19 pandemic and future travel behavior: The moderating role of past experience. *Journal of Destination Marketing & Management*, *21*(1), 100620. https://doi.org/10.1016/j.jdmm.2021.100620

Schmücker, D., Lohmann, M., Köchling, A., & Sonntag, U. (2021). *Reiseanalyse Trendstudie 2030 – UPDATE 2021: Urlaubsnachfrage im Quellmarkt Deutschland [Reiseanalyse trend study 2030 – UPDATE 2021]*. Forschungsgemeinschaft Urlaub und Reisen e.V.

Schmücker, D., Sonntag, U., & Günther, W. (2019). *Nachhaltige Urlaubsreisen: Bewusstseins- und Nachfrageentwicklung: Grundlagenstudie auf Basis von Daten der Reiseanalyse 2019* (FKZ UM18165020; p. 81). BMU.

Schmücker, D., Günther, W., Kuhn, F., Weiß, B., & Horster, E. (2018). *FINDUS: Finding sustainability information for holiday travel*. (BfN Skripten 505). Bundesamt für Naturschutz. https://doi.org/10.19217/skr505

Simons, D. J., & Chabris, C. F. (1999). Gorillas in our midst: Sustained inattentional blindness for dynamic events. *Perception*, *28*, 1059–1074.

Statistisches Bundesamt (Ed.). (2019). *A changing population: Assumptions and results of the 14th coordinated population projection*. https://www.destatis.de/EN/Themes/Society-Environment/Population/Population-Projection/Publications/Downloads-Population-Projection/germany-population-2060-5124206199004.pdf

Strasdas, W., Lund-Durlacher, D., Giraldo, M., Kück, F., & Lehners, S. (2020). *Die Corona-Krise und ihre Implikationen für die nachhaltige Entwicklung des Tourismus [The Corona crisis and its implications for sustainable tourism development]*. Hochschule für Nachhaltige Entwicklung. https://www.hogapage.de/wp-content/uploads/sites/16/2020/07/Ergebnisbericht_Befragung_Corona-Krise_Nachhaltigkeit.pdf

United Nations. (2015). *Transforming our world: 2030 agenda for sustainable development*. https://sustainabledevelopment.un.org/content/documents/21252030%20Agenda%20for%20Sustainable%20Development%20web.pdf

UNSD United Nations Statistics Division & UNWTO United Nations World Tourism Organization. (2010). International Recommendations for Tourism Statistics 2008 (IRTS 2008). https://unstats.un.org/unsd/publication/seriesm/seriesm_83rev1e.pdf

UNWTO World Tourism Organization (Ed.). (2020). *World Tourism Barometer: January 2020* (Issue 1). https://www.e-unwto.org/doi/epdf/10.18111/wtobarometereng.2020.18.1.1

Wagner, P., Grimm, B., & Koch, A. (2020). *Summary of the Reiseanalyse 2020*. Forschungsgemeinschaft Urlaub und Reisen (FUR) e.V.

Utkarsh, & Sigala, M. (2021). A bibliometric review of research on COVID-19 and tourism: Reflections for moving forward. *Tourism Management Perspectives*, *40*, 100912. https://doi.org/10.1016/j.tmp.2021.100912

Ulker-Demirel, E., & Ciftci, G. (2020). A systematic literature review of the theory of planned behavior in tourism, leisure and hospitality management research. *Journal of Hospitality and Tourism Management*, *43*, 209–219. https://doi.org/10.1016/j.jhtm.2020.04.003

Zopiatis, A., Pericleous, K., & Theofanous, Y. (2021). COVID-19 and hospitality and tourism research: An integrative review. *Journal of Hospitality and Tourism Management*, *48*, 275–279. https://doi.org/10.1016/j.jhtm.2021.07.002

38 New trends in wellness tourism
Restoration and regeneration

Melanie Kay Smith

Introduction

The aim of this chapter is to analyse new trends in wellness tourism following the post-COVID era, where the focus shifted from hedonic to more restorative forms of tourism. Some authors predicted an increasing interest in health and wellness tourism post-COVID (Jiang and Wen, 2020). Pocinho, Garcês and Neves de Jesus (2022:7) stated that "Wellbeing and wellness can be attractive factors for new tourists and thus open doors to developing new products and activities in destinations". This, they argued, can make it possible to 'refresh' tourism, to change tourists' behaviour and to help solve pre-COVID problems like overtourism. Discussions about the future of tourism include the concept of resilience which applies not only to destinations but to residents and tourists as well. Pocinho et al. (2022) argue that resilience is a concept that is intimately related to wellbeing and helps to deal effectively with adversity. This is a broad subject that naturally lends itself to essential discussions about the impacts of tourism, resident wellbeing and sustainable destination development. One of the Sustainable Development Goals focuses specifically on Good Health and Wellbeing (SDG3), with several others emphasising especially resident wellbeing (e.g., SDG 11 Sustainable Cities and Communities). In the future, it is predicted that wellbeing will become more central to government and stakeholder policy. Sustainable destination management will prioritise resident wellbeing and tourism businesses and industry will offer more wellness programmes for tourists. This chapter focuses more on the latter than on the wellbeing of local residents, but it is recognised that the two should be inextricably connected in a more resilient and regenerative future.

Health, wellbeing and the impacts of COVID-19

The COVID-19 pandemic clearly engendered an unprecedented mental as well as physical health crisis (Rokni, 2021; Bhalla, Chowdhary and Ranjan, 2021; Yang and Wong, 2021). Anxiety abounded with regards to catching the disease and not recovering, not to mention the economic losses suffered by businesses, the lack of social contact and the curtailment of cultural, leisure and tourism opportunities. Although it could be argued that the latter activities are marginal compared to the greater concerns about physical health and lack of income, previous studies are a testament to the fact that wellbeing is greatly enhanced by leisure and travel. Governments tend to afford citizens paid holidays because they provide escapism and respite from the monotony and rigours of everyday life. Travel arguably provides an antidote to an exhausting environment and allows people to seek restoration (Lehto and Lehto, 2019). Along with leisure, tourism also provides opportunities for people to socialise and meet up with friends and relatives. For this reason, social tourism is offered to those citizens who otherwise cannot afford to take a holiday, a subject that has become a major focus of research in recent years (McCabe and Qiao, 2020).

Notwithstanding the argument that tourism is a privilege for many people, it could also be viewed as a necessary path to recuperation and good physical and mental health. Although many potential tourists might be wrestling with their conscience about the environmental impacts of tourism and the future of the planet, it is also important to consider the livelihoods of those people in destinations which are dependent on tourism. As always, the balance between the environmental impacts and social and economic benefits of tourism development needs to be taken into account. It is for this reason that the UNWTO established the co-creative Travel for Sustainable Development Goals (T4SDG) platform to share good practice on the journey to 2030 and beyond.

Even before COVID came along, studies had highlighted the importance of travel for health and wellbeing, especially in quality of life and life satisfaction research (Neal, Uysal and Sirgy, 2007; Sirgy, Kruger, Lee and Yu, 2011; Dolnicar, Yanamandram and Cliff, 2012; Chen and Petrick, 2013). Tourism is especially important for the enhancement of subjective wellbeing or happiness (McCabe and Johnson, 2013; Chen, Lehto and Cai, 2013; Nawijn and Filep, 2016; de Bloom et al., 2017; Pyke, Hartwell, Blake and Hemingway, 2016; Kwon and Lee, 2020). Several studies measured the short- and long-term impacts of holidays on wellbeing (Chen, Lehto and Cai, 2013; Nawijn, De Bloom and Geurts, 2013; Kirillova, Lehto and Cai, 2017; Mitas, Nawijn and Jongsma, 2016). Switching off from one's devices and gadgets is also becoming an important aspect of psychological wellbeing while on vacation (Ayeh, 2018; Egger et al., 2020; Floros, Cai, McKenna and Ajeeb, 2021).

Debates have ensued about how far tourism affords hedonic or eudaimonic experiences. Purely hedonic experiences might be pleasure-orientated and short-term, such as beach holidays, party tourism or wellness spa visits, whereas more eudaimonic experiences are connected to learning, physical challenge, spiritual enrichment or self-development of some kind (Smith and Diekmann, 2017). It has been argued that the ideal form of tourism should conform to Seligman's (2002) authentic happiness model which incorporates a pleasant life (hedonism and fun), a good life (ethics, altruism, sustainable behaviour) and a meaningful life (self-development, transformation, transcendence). Several authors have indicated the transformational potential of tourism (Reisinger, 2013; Fu, Tanyatanaboon and Lehto, 2015; Knobloch, Robertson and Aitken, 2016; Sheldon, 2020). It has been argued that transformational tourism goes beyond wellness travel and includes many of those activities that have been defined as eudaimonic previously, including educational tourism, volunteering, ethical and community-based tourism. Such forms of tourism may change lives as well as whole societies and destinations through a shift in consciousness (Sheldon, 2020). Transcendence has also been referred to as an essential state for wellbeing (Wong, 2016), including in the context of tourism (Sheldon, 2020). This is arguably especially true in the case of spiritual or nature-based tourism. This chapter will focus predominantly on wellness tourism while acknowledging the transformative potential of other forms of tourism. One of the most important of these in the next few decades should be nature-based tourism that advocates stewardship of the environment as well as encouraging people to reconnect with the natural world within a living systems framework (Bellato et al., 2022).

Previous studies had tried to prove whether the impacts of wellbeing (especially the hedonic ones) were different during a weekend away compared to a weekend at home (De Bloom et al., 2017). Later studies were inconclusive about the impacts of staycations and whether excursions close to home were as beneficial as longer trips (Lin et al., 2021). Packer (2022) concluded that short breaks relatively close to home could actually afford as many benefits as long distance or international travel. This could have important implications for sustainability; however, it was also suggested that tourists would benefit more from multiple short breaks throughout the year rather than one long trip once a year. The most important characteristic of a holiday is that it enables people to detach from work and relax in an environment that is conducive to this purpose. Even in the COVID era, some tourists were willing to take the risk of travelling because of the mental and social benefits that it brings, including relaxation, social connectedness and personal growth (Aebli et al., 2021). In the future, there may be some reluctance to travel because of concerns about environmental impacts of transport or rising costs, but there is arguably no replacement for cultural experiences, not to mention the economic benefits for destinations and their citizens.

From COVID to wellness

It has been argued that there is a strong connection between resilience and wellbeing to help deal with crises and adversity (Pocinho et al., 2022). Wellbeing and wellness can also become attractive products for destinations and tourists (Wen and Wu, 2020; Pocinho et al., 2022). Choudhary and Qadir (2021) provided a summary of some of the public media sources and studies that highlighted the increasing interest in wellness after the COVID pandemic arrived. They highlighted, in particular, people's desires to strengthen their immune systems, to eat more healthily, to escape daily stress and to rejuvenate. The therapeutic benefits of tourism have been categorised according to different activities and settings, for example, medical tourism, nature and adventure tourism, outdoor recreation and therapeutic landscapes or wellbeing tourism in spas (Buckley and Westaway, 2020). Other authors have suggested a healing tourism concept (Ma et al., 2021), which increases social wellbeing and a sense of eudaimonia. Healing tourism should ideally take place in natural environments and should focus on lifelong wellness. In addition to medical, nature-based and spa treatments, complementary and alternative medicine (CAM) was proposed as a means of mitigating the indirect effects of COVID on mental health (Bhalla, Chowdhary and Ranjan, 2021). The latter authors also proposed nature-based, spiritual and transformational tourism, especially non-religious spiritual travel to natural landscapes that can engender transformation. Indeed, wellness tourism has often been defined as a form of tourism that can contribute to multiple domains of life by visiting, for example, spas, retreat centres, spiritual landscapes or wellness hotels and resorts. However, it is important to differentiate what is meant by wellness as opposed to health, wellbeing, healing and the plethora of other terms that are used to describe the benefits of tourism.

Wellness tourism

Defining wellness tourism is the subject of ongoing academic interest but it has been given less attention than other forms of health tourism (Zhong et al., 2021) and studies thus far have failed to tap into the deeper meaning of wellness as a concept (Stará and Peterson, 2017). It is especially important to define wellness tourism clearly given that previous studies about the role and benefits of tourism tended to focus more on wellbeing, happiness, life satisfaction or quality of life (Sirgy et al., 2011; Dolnicar, Yanamandram and 2012; Chen, Lehto and Cai, 2013; McCabe and Johnson, 2013; Nawijn and Filep, 2016;

Pyke et al., 2016; de Bloom et al., 2017; Kwon and Lee, 2020). Oliver, Baldwin and Datta (2018) state that quality of life represents the general wellbeing of individuals and society and that wellness is the process of improving those aspects of life that contribute to quality of life and wellbeing. They also suggest that wellness signifies the relationship between health and quality of life. Having reviewed numerous wellness models, they conclude that a pivotal notion is that "wellness is a holistic concept comprised of various interrelated components of everyday life that are utilised to predict overall health" (ibid., p. 49).

Wellness can be defined as being more personal and individual than wellbeing or quality of life which contain multiple objective as well as subjective dimensions (Smith and Diekmann, 2017). Wellness has been described as the path to wellbeing (Nahrstedt, 2004) with all of the choices and decisions that entails. Oliver, Baldwin and Datta (2018) argue that all wellness models are holistic and multi-dimensional focusing on lifestyle behaviours, actions and processes. They list physical fitness, emotional stability and spiritual growth as well as wider quality of life issues like financial security and social connectedness. Damijanić (2019) identifies factors connected to a wellness-related lifestyle as health awareness, fitness, diet, social interactions, cultural diversity and personal development. Stoewen (2017) argues that wellness is about self-care and self-stewardship, including the cultivation of healthy habits. She defines it as "a lifestyle, a personalised approach to living life in a way that allows you to become the best kind of person that your potential, circumstances, and fate will allow" (ibid., p. 862). Wellness is often defined in terms of numerous domains of life which need to be balanced or harmonised. Smith et al. (2022) demonstrates some of the tourism products, services and experiences that can form part of these domains:

- Physical (e.g., beauty treatments in spas; relaxation in thermal waters; fitness activities)
- Emotional (e.g., retreat programmes based on counselling or mindfulness)
- Spiritual (e.g., yoga and meditation retreats; temple stays; nature-based therapies)
- Social (e.g., couple and family spas; group activities in retreats)
- Occupational (e.g., stress relief in spas; work–life balance retreat programmes)
- Intellectual (e.g., creative activities in retreats; psychological workshops)

However, Stoewen (2017) argues that although all of these domains are important, they do not have to be equally balanced at all times. Instead, individuals should strive towards 'personal harmony' that feels authentic to them. Dini and Pencarelli (2021) identify the main elements of what they call the wellness tourism offer system as follows:

- Hot springs
- Spas
- Care of body and mind (e.g., fitness, beauty)
- Medical tourism
- Natural environment
- Spirituality
- Culture (e.g., different traditions and approaches to wellness)
- Enogastronomy (i.e., healthy nutrition, local food)
- Sports
- Events (arguably a subsidiary attraction although there are sauna festivals in Estonia or yoga festivals in India)

A recent netnographic study emphasises the importance of the physical body in wellness tourism including exercise, but most notably culinary experiences. The same study also highlighted the importance of mental wellness activities leading to growth and transformation (e.g., Dillette, Douglas and Andrzejewski, 2021). In summary, Smith and Puczkó, in the UNWTO/ETC report (2018, p. 53), define wellness tourism as:

> Forms of tourism which aim to improve and balance all of the main domains of human life including physical, mental, emotional, occupational, intellectual and spiritual. The primary motivation for wellness tourists is to engage in preventative, proactive, lifestyle-enhancing activities such as fitness, healthy eating, relaxation, pampering and healing treatments.

Motivations for and benefits of wellness tourism

In their systematic review, Kemppainen et al. (2021) identify a consensus in the literature that medical tourism is more concerned with curing and treating illness, whereas wellness tourism is more focused on preventative and holistic wellbeing promotion. The health condition of medical and wellness tourists is very different: "The wellness service users are generally defined as relatively healthy people who are not in need of curative treatments but look for physical and mental improvements, self-pampering and a better state of being" (ibid., p. 8). Some studies have suggested scales that could be used to demonstrate the benefits of wellness tourism. These can include relaxation, stress relief and escapism, as discussed earlier, but could also refer to more specific physical objectives relating to fitness or body appearance, psychological needs relating to self-image or self-esteem as well as transcendence in the form of reflection, contemplation and meaning (Voigt, 2010). In addition to these benefits, motivational factors might also include indulgence, which connects closely to hedonism and is one of the benefits of a spa environment, for example (Voigt et al., 2011). More recent studies of wellness tourists suggest that relaxation is the most important motivation followed by self-pampering, but health improvement is not necessarily a major consideration (Árpási, 2018). This could change in the post-COVID era, especially for those tourists suffering from a form of 'long COVID'. A recent scale for wellness tourism was developed which also included a question about COVID (Kessler, Lee and Whittingham, 2020). The authors identified several factors as important motivators for wellness tourists. These include relaxation, which was reflected in statements like "To return to life feeling rejuvenated" and "To escape the demands of everyday life" and nature and disconnect, which was reflected in statements like "To experience activities outdoors" and "To connect with nature". A self-care category included "recovery from a major life event" alongside stress reduction and a question was also asked about COVID in which respondents emphasised hygiene and safety, as well as the desire to meet like-minded people who were concerned about their health and wellness.

Table 38.1 summarises types of wellness tourism according to motivation and benefits sought. Hedonic types of wellness tourism are usually wellness-spa based and include beauty treatments or pampering, but they can also include more unusual experiences like culinary or gastro-spas, beer spas or spa parties (especially popular with young people). Healing types of wellness tourism have a medical foundation and are recognised by the World Health Organisation as evidence-based therapies, even though they are not practiced in all countries' medical systems. This includes balneology (healing water and mud treatments) or thalassotherapy (seawater-based treatments and therapies). Restorative or

Table 38.1 Types of wellness tourism (author)

Hedonic	Healing	Restorative	Eudaimonic
Beauty, pampering, entertainment	**Climate therapy**	**Natural landscapes**	**Self-development, transformation**
• Wellness spas • Culinary or gastro-spas • Spa parties	• Balneotherapy • Thalassotherapy	• Views of landscapes • Outdoor recreation • Eco-therapy	• Holistic retreats • Spiritual practices

regenerative benefits are increasingly being derived from nature and landscape-based wellness practices, which can be passive (i.e., enjoying fresh air and views) or active (e.g., nature-based recreation or eco-therapies). The fourth category is for those tourists who are looking for deeper and more psychological or emotional experiences through mental wellness practices, like yoga, meditation and other holistic or complementary therapies.

Spas tend to be based on more hedonic relaxing and pampering activities than other forms of wellness facilities (e.g., retreats). Within the balneology tradition (e.g., in Central and Eastern Europe) waters are used for physical healing too. They are usually combined with other forms of climate therapy like mud treatments, heliotherapy (sunshine cures), thalassotherapy (seawater-based treatments), alpine therapy (mountain environments), as well as physiotherapy. Some authors emphasised the importance of medical spas in post-COVID recovery therapies (Aluculesei et al., 2021), especially those that use natural resources to heal respiratory disorders as well as strengthening immune systems.

Nature-based restoration and regeneration

Following on from the concept of climate therapy and natural resource-based healing, it is important to briefly mention the growing emphasis on reconnecting to nature and landscape in the context of wellness. The term restorative is derived from previous academic studies that refer to 'Attention Restoration Theory', which connects to the positive contribution of tourism to health and wellbeing (Lehto and Lehto, 2019; Packer, 2022), mainly in natural landscapes (Qiu, Sha and Scott, 2021). During COVID, studies demonstrated the benefits for mental health of being in green areas or having green views, even when people were forced to stay at home and not travel. Indeed, the importance of nature-based and outdoor experiences for tourism has been highlighted by several authors (Santos et al., 2020; Buckley and Westaway, 2020).

Numerous researchers have highlighted the health and wellbeing benefits of landscapes, for example, Abraham et al. (2010) summarised the wellbeing benefits of landscapes or outdoor environments in their scoping study as follows:

- Mental wellbeing: nature as restorative
- Physical wellbeing: walkable landscape
- Social wellbeing: landscape as bonding structure

Maller et al. (2008) included the following:

- Physical: settings for recreation, sport and other leisure activities
- Mental: restoration from fatigue, peace and solitude, artistic inspiration and education

- Spiritual: reflection and contemplation, feeling a sense of place, connecting to something greater than oneself
- Social: including couples, families, networks and associations' recreational activities and events
- Environmental: preservations and conservation of ecosystems

In their research on national parks, Wolf et al. (2017) list many of the possible benefits which include physical fitness, re-engagement with nature and mental restoration. Smith and Csurgó's (2018) study of the wellbeing benefits of natural landscapes suggested that the most important domains include physical dimensions such as recreation and leisure activities in nature; mental dimensions including peace, tranquillity and relaxation; spiritual dimensions relating mainly to sense of place; and a social dimension which is inherent in the connection between local residents and tourists. Different types of landscape might afford different kinds of benefits, for example, mountains might offer the most transcendental experiences (Sharpley and Jepson, 2011), while deserts offer a deeply spiritual experience (Moufakkir and Selmi, 2018). The overall health benefits of blue spaces have been noted by numerous authors, including Gascon, Zijlema, Vert, White and Nieuwenhuijsen (2017). In their study of different types of landscapes, Ram and Smith (2019) confirmed that seaside landscapes afford the most benefits to visitors overall and that desert landscapes are the most spiritual. Discussions about regenerative tourism have defined regeneration as the development of more respectful and caring relations between humans and nature (Dredge, 2022). This means that tourists should become more aware of the benefits that are afforded by nature-based experiences and in return, provide greater care for natural landscapes.

The following section focuses in more depth on the final category of wellness tourism, which includes retreat centres that are usually located in beautiful and peaceful natural landscapes.

Towards eudaimonia: Retreat-based wellness tourism

Retreats have traditionally afforded visitors a sanctuary to which they could escape from the monotony, stress and busyness of their everyday lives. Although their purpose is firstly rest and relaxation (Kelly, 2012), retreats ideally also provide some elements of hedonism or fun, combined with deeper eudaimonic practices which encourage self-development and transformation (Glouberman and Cloutier, 2017; Kelly and Smith, 2017). Some healing or health-enhancing complementary therapies are usually offered (Cohen et al., 2017) but the main focus is on emotional wellbeing or mental wellness. Typical activities include yoga, meditation, fitness, nutritional programmes, creative practices, digital detox (technology-free stays), and, more latterly, post-COVID recovery. The length of stay varies but is usually several days with the most common length of time being six to ten days (Norman and Pokorny, 2017). Retreats attract more women than men and tend to be mainly for middle-class, educated professional people (Kelly and Smith, 2017). Many guests are suffering from the negative effects of urban living and work-related burnout, thus they benefit from being in a quiet, peaceful, natural setting. Most retreats provide healing holidays in natural environments which correspond to the post-COVID recommendations of recent studies (Ma et al., 2021; Qiu, Sha and Scott, 2021; Soga et al., 2021). Indeed, some authors have suggested that the natural environment or landscape around the retreat can be as important to the experience as the activities (Ashton, 2018; Jiang, Ryan and Zhang, 2018). The Retreat

Company portal includes the category of 'Rural Hideaway', which includes retreats offering the chance to be healed by 'primordial sounds' in nature, 'desert bliss', 'moon- or star-gazing' and so forth. One day programmes were also offered during COVID which were focused specifically on the therapeutic benefits of nature using 'ecotherapy':

> We will use this day to make a break with the worst of lockdown and get our bodies and minds to relax preparing us for a return to normality. We'll spend some time understanding the importance of relaxing both physically and mentally and how both are necessary.

The retreat sector is quite closely connected to spiritual travel, which Kato and Progano (2017, p. 245) describe as "subjective and individual travel for spiritual betterment and self-discovery". Research among Millennials indicated that spirituality represents firstly 'a strong connection to the self' followed by 'being connected to nature and the natural world' (Smith, Kiss and Chan, 2022). Natural landscapes can be important to spiritual travellers (Sharpley and Jepson, 2011; Bone, 2013; Gezon, 2017; Jiang, Ryan, & Zhang, 2018), including some elements of adventure or challenge (Cheer, Belhassen & Kujawa, 2017), for example, pilgrimage (Kato & Progano, 2017). Spiritual tourists typically stay in temples, monasteries, ashrams, yoga and meditation centres or retreats and often focus on personal healing (Norman and Pokorny, 2017).

The connection to eudaimonic wellness tourism comes from the process of wanting to connect with the true or authentic self (Kelly and Smith, 2017) and to become a better person or transform (Reisinger, 2013; Sheldon, 2020). Retreats arguably function in a similar way to the self-help movement and could even be considered to be a part of it, as the participant is encouraged to self-diagnose their needs or problems, to choose a relevant topic or programme and to undertake the activities recommended. In the immediate post-COVID period, it was recognised that rather than intensive self-development, guests rather required rest and recuperation, as well as building their physical immune systems and mental resilience. One example of this is Euphoria retreat in Greece, which offered healing programmes with the aim to "release the negative emotions, stress, tension and anxiety that have built up, perhaps even subconsciously, during the time of the pandemic" and nurture participants back to feeling like themselves again – "renewed, restored and re-energised".

Some retreat centres even offered home-based programs during lockdown, such as the Home Detox and Healing Retreats which delivered boxes of organic juices and supplements in addition to supplying online support and guidance from experts (e.g., nutritionists, coaches) in the form of live workshops, group interaction opportunities and individual counselling on a range of topics such as coping with trauma, stress or anxiety, as well as relationships and life purpose. Online yoga and meditation classes were also offered. A Wellbeing Coach training programme offered a

> nourishing and therapeutic journey of inner discovery and growth without leaving the comfort of your own home... [it]... explores your current challenges, gaining clarity around your levels of emotional, physical and spiritual wellbeing, along with developing a vision of your 'preferred future self'.

Smith et al. (2022) provided a discourse analysis of the retreat portal 'The Retreat Company' which has existed since the mid-1990s and includes around 500 retreat companies in more than 17 countries. Retreats are categorised according to around 100 different topic headings,

Table 38.2 Examples of types of retreats and their purported benefits

Restore and revitalise retreat: activities and therapies	Promised benefits	Discourse analysis
• A peaceful, comfortable and nurturing environment • Delicious and nutritious food that helps to strengthen your immune system and detox your body • A relaxing, revitalising and inspiring programme of classes, complementary treatments and talks	"You will leave feeling relaxed, in better health, and strengthened so that you can continue with renewed energy and vitality, step back into your normal life with a feeling of wholeness and direction and have a clear sense of your priorities".	The text emphasises the peaceful and comfortable environment, as well as the 'support' and 'nurturing' that takes place. In modern living, many people (especially those who are carers themselves) often look for caring when they go to retreats. The talks aim to 'inspire' and 'revitalise' and the physical health programs mention 'strengthening the immune system' (this became especially important during COVID too) and 'detox' (popular in numerous retreats to remove the toxins of modern living). Participants are also encouraged to express themselves, which is another common feature of retreats. Here, to 'explore and express your emotions'. Retreats often promise to 'replenish' and restore 'vitality' and 'energy' which is depleted by diseases like cancer, COVID or stress. This retreat also emphasises a return to 'wholeness' (which is why retreats are often described as 'holistic'). Like many retreats, it also claims to offer 'direction' and 'a clear sense of your priorities'.

Anxiety and depression recovery retreat: activities and therapies	Promised benefits	Discourse analysis
• Psychotherapy • Positive Psychology • Cognitive Behaviour Therapy CBT • Emotional Freedom Technique • Hypnotherapy • Neuro-linguistic programming • Yoga • Mindfulness and 'mindful self-compassion' • Massage	"We will help you to understand depression and anxiety as well as address it so you can get back to normal life……you will learn how to manage and unload negative thoughts to live a happy and more positive life. You will be able to put down negative thoughts and emotions such as guilt and stress, feel more comfortable and come away feeling emotionally balanced and joyful with excitement for life ahead".	This retreat focuses on reducing guilt and stress, 'unloading negative thoughts', and making participants feel 'emotionally balanced and joyful with excitement for life ahead'. One of the aims is also to teach people to understand depression and anxiety so that they can address it, which emphasises the 'take home' and long term benefits of retreat programs. Participants can develop the physical, emotional and psychological techniques "to become the person you were meant to be'. This suggests a return to the true self or a self that is better or more balanced than the current one.

New trends in wellness tourism   489

Jubenescence wellness and wellbeing retreat: activities and therapies	Promised benefits	Discourse analysis
• Holistic and natural health • Weight loss and management • Stress management • Recovery • Recuperation • Digital detox • Personal development • Life coaching	"We all work or serve others and sometimes need quality time out to recharge. If you feel highly stressed or lost after a relationship, career or health upheaval; are suffering burnout, depression or want to restructure the way you operate, it could be time to rethink and understand more the 'Why'."	The promotion of this retreat revolves around the concepts of energy restoration and regeneration, which includes the verbs to 'reboot' and 'recharge'. Participants are encouraged to take time out for themselves and to consider how their lives could be improved during the process of relaxation and recuperation. Health upheavals could well include COVID as well as feelings of burnout following an intense period of lockdown. It is suggested that participants will be more resilient and able to tackle their everyday lives on return from the retreat.

Typical vocabulary used to promote retreats

- Supportive and motivating verbs from the retreat organisers, for example, 'to help', 'to guide', 'to teach', 'to coach', 'to encourage', 'to enable'.
- Verbs that encourage self-development and life-changes, for example, 'to heal', 'to cleanse', 'to re-balance', 'to re-connect', 'to grow', 'to renew'.
- Verbs relating to eudaimonic personal growth and transformation, for example, 'to become', 'to improve', 'to enhance', 'to cultivate', 'to learn'.
- References to the future self and long term wellbeing, e.g., 'the person you were meant to be', 'your purpose', 'a clear sense of your priorities', 'the future wellbeing journey of You', 'for life ahead', 'a new path' and 'lasting change'.

Examples:

The Place Retreat

"You will have total care in a safe space, while healing and recovering from your negative blocks or past trauma. We will guide you to overcoming your fears and becoming the person that you want to be, living the life you want to have, resulting in a feeling of being reborn."

Mankind360 Health and Wellbeing Retreat

"We offer real support, coaching and guidance personally designed with you. Our unique and bespoke 360 review covers the past, present and future wellbeing journey of You."

Visitor testimonials of experiences and benefits

(Continued)

Table 38.2 (Continued)

Escapism and recuperation

"It was excellent for me to retreat from 'civilisation' […]. It has been awakening, energising, restful, interesting and freeing…" (The Barn, Scotland)

"The week that brought me back to life!!! When I first arrived at NaturalZest, I truly had forgotten what the word 'zest' meant. I was very low – in fact, I was depressed" (Natural Zest, Zakynthos, Greece)

Connection to nature and landscape

"A place I love to visit to reconnect with nature and touch peace: with its virgin forests, wild horses, spectacular cliff walks, and long sandy beaches" (Ayurveda Retreats, UK)

"I learnt how to stop battling with myself and understood the healing powers of nature" (Yes Your Entire Self, Scotland)

"To be surrounded by mountains was utterly breath-taking, every day was a joy and as each morning dawned another experience would commence" (Lauvitel, France)

Self-development and transformation

"It has been an adventure in self-discovery and personal development." (The Barn, Scotland)

"This is a place of gentle, natural transformations, a space away from the madness of everyday life where I find peace, inspiration, hope, love & most importantly a sense of who we are.". (The Barn, Scotland)

"This has been a transformative experience for me… I never anticipated just how quick and profound a change I would experience" (Living Harmony, UK)

Life changes and new beginnings

"I have just returned home from a 10 day stay at Natural Zest, Zante and it has been a life changing and totally spiritual journey for me…" (Natural Zest, Zakynthos, Greece)

"We came to The Place looking for connection and a new beginning and we found so much more" (The Place, Bali, Indonesia)

"I kind of feel like a butterfly not yet emerged" (Living Harmony, UK)

"The valuable things learned and the people I shared it with are unforgettable - the hints and tips are still embedded into my new routine and improved way of life…..I've taken away lots from the weekend that I know has added to my journey in life." (Yes Your Entire Self, Scotland)

(Adapted from Smith, 2022b).

ranging from anxiety to detox to stress management to yoga. Emphasis is firstly placed on rest, recuperation and escapism but 'transformation vacations' are also referred to. The vocabulary tends to be soothing, supportive and nurturing as well as encouraging and enabling. This can motivate participants to become more resilient in the face of change and crisis, at the same time as recuperating in a restorative environment. Table 38.2 provides a summary of some of the promotional language used, the promised benefits, as well as some experience-based comments from visitor testimonials.

Conclusion

It has been argued that resilience is closely connected to wellbeing as it strengthens the individual's capacity to deal with adversity (Pocinho et al., 2022). In addition to restoration as an antidote to exhaustion (Lehto and Lehto, 2019), wellness tourism can also provide spaces and activities for building future resilience as well as regeneration. Wellness has been defined as a holistic, personal path that is based on lifestyle choices and healthy habits (Stoewen, 2017; Oliver, Baldwin and Datta, 2018) requiring the balance of various dimensions of health, including the physical, mental, social and spiritual (Smith, 2022a). Numerous activities can be incorporated, such as fitness, diet, social interaction and personal development (Damijanić, 2019). Following on from this, wellness tourism becomes a form of tourism in which the individual makes positive choices, ranging from healing in thermal water to relaxing in spas to self-development programs in retreats (Dini and Pencarelli, 2021). Increasingly, health nutrition and culinary experiences are playing a role as well as a growing emphasis on mental wellness (Dillette, Douglas and Andrzejewski, 2021).

Research on wellness tourists suggests that relaxation is still an important motivating factor but with elements of escapism, self-care and rejuvenation (Kessler, Lee and Whittingham, 2020). Wellness spas were often described as hedonic (Voigt et al., 2011), but post-COVID, even non-medical spas offered physical and mental recovery packages which used climate and nature-based as well as complementary therapies (Bhalla, Chowdhary and Ranjan, 2021). The most restorative forms of tourism appear to be taking place in natural landscapes, while the most eudaimonic take place in holistic retreats. Research about length of stay is inconclusive, as also is whether or not the benefits of staying closer to home are just as great. Most forms of health tourism are available in shorter or longer forms, ranging from a long weekend in a pampering wellness spa to a week in a retreat centre to a three-week stay in a curative, climate therapy resort.

Escapism can also be offered in the form of hedonic or fun activities, as well as more eudaimonic programs for those seeking transformation or even transcendence through self-development or spiritual practices. Ideally, all of these activities need to take place in a resident-friendly and sustainable environment to be truly regenerative.

It could be suggested that wellness tourism journeys in the future will follow a process that is represented in Figure 38.1. The tourist begins with the most important activity within wellness, which is rest or relaxation. She or he recuperates from physical illness or mental stress and then restores lost energy or health. The immune system is strengthened and the tourist develops a greater capacity for dealing with crisis or stress, leading to greater resilience in the future. Much is now being written about regenerative tourism, which also includes the sustainability of the destination and quality of life of its inhabitants. Within this process, the wellbeing of the tourist is also central and he or she emerges regenerated and ready to contribute to society, provide stewardship for nature and potentially change the world.

Figure 38.1 The five Rs of wellness tourism.

Future trajectories

In addition to creating a focus on tourists' personal wellness, it is necessary to consider the wider context for sustainable and transformative tourism and future trajectories for development. Studies are emerging that call for transformative travel and tourism within the regenerative economic paradigm (Ateljevic, 2020). Many of these proposals are closely connected to the priority SDGs in tourism, especially to SDG12 Responsible Consumption and Production as well as to SDG8 Decent Work and Economic Growth. Employers need to play a key role in looking after not only the economic wellbeing of their workers, but also their physical and psychological wellness. The retreat sector data shows far too many incidences of work-related burnout which leaves human beings very little energy to address other important personal, social and environmental issues. The transformation of personal mindsets might actually be an important path to greater planetary wellbeing in the future. There is clearly a need for a shift in consciousness away from 'me' towards 'we' in order to develop greater empathy, compassion and collaboration (Dredge, 2022). Stakeholders should ideally learn to take a living systems approach to tourism development, which means that humans are seen as part of nature rather than the anthropocentric view that humans are separate and dominating the rest of nature (Bellato et al., 2022). Arguably, the retreat sector provides many of the personal experiences and collaborative environments that are conducive to engendering social change. Even though wellness tends to be a personal journey, the shared pathways in increasingly sustainable and eco-friendly retreats pave the way to a better future. If we were to predict what this might mean for wellness tourism, the future could look something like this:

- 2032: greater provision of personal wellness journeys (e.g., in retreats, resort spas and wellness hotels) leading to more eco-friendly and socially compassionate and empathetic mindsets.
- 2042: an increased number of communal living environments with circular economies and regenerative agriculture (e.g., transition towns, slow cities, eco-villages) which become wellness tourist attractions and provide inspiration for more sustainable living.
- 2052: a decrease in urban living and greater opportunities for employment in rural landscapes within communal environments. Stakeholders take a living systems approach. Sustainable transport takes people to alternative settings for holidays to learn about different cultural and smart processes. Personal wellness and communal wellbeing are the major focus of life and at the forefront of government policy, business and tourism practices.

References

Abraham, A., Sommerhalder, K. and Abel, T. (2010). Landscape and well-being: a scoping study on the health-promoting impact of outdoor environments. *Int J Public Health*, 55, 59–69. https://doi:10.1007/s00038-009-0069-z

Aebli, A., Volgger, M. and Taplin, R. (2021). A two-dimensional approach to travel motivation in the context of the COVID-19 pandemic. *Current Issues in Tourism*, 29, 1–6. https://doi.org/10.1080/13683500.2021.1906631

Aluculesei, A.-C., Nistoreanu, P., Avram, D. and Nistoreanu, B.G. (2021). Past and Future Trends in Medical Spas: A Co-Word Analysis. *Sustainability*, 13, 9646. https://doi.org/10.3390/su13179646

Árpási, Z. (2018). Wellness Tourism: What Motivates the Consumer. *Valahian Journal of Economic Studies*, 9 (23), Issue 1. https://doi.org/10.2478/vjes-2018-0009

Ashton, A. S. (2018). Spiritual retreat tourism development in the Asia Pacific region: investigating the impact of tourist satisfaction and intention to revisit: A Chiang Mai, Thailand case study. *Asia Pacific Journal of Tourism Research*, 23 (11), 1098–1114. https://doi.org/10.1080/10941665.2018.1526198

Ateljevic, I. (2020). Transforming the (tourism) world for good and (re)generating the potential 'new normal', *Tourism Geographies*, 22(3), 467–475. https://doi.org/10.1080/14616688.2020.1759134

Ayeh, J. K. (2018). Distracted gaze: Problematic use of mobile technologies in vacation contexts. *Tourism Management Perspectives*, 26, 31–38. https://doi.org/10.1016/j.tmp.2018.01.002

Bellato, L., Frantzeskaki, N., Briceño Fiebig, C., Pollock, A., Dens, E. and Reed, B. (2022). Transformative roles in tourism: adopting living systems' thinking for regenerative futures. *Journal of Tourism Futures*. https://doi.org/10.1108/JTF-11-2021-0256

Bhalla, R., Chowdhary, N. and Ranjan, A. (2021). Spiritual tourism for psychotherapeutic healing post COVID-19. *Journal of Travel & Tourism Marketing*, 38(8), 769–781. https://doi.org/10.1080/10548408.2021.1930630

de Bloom, J., Nawijn, J., Geurts, S., Kinnunen, U. and Korpela, K. (2017). Holiday travel, staycations, and subjective well-being. *Journal of Sustainable Tourism*, 25(4), 573–588. https://doi.org/10.1080/09669582.2016.122 9323

Bone, K. (2013). Spiritual retreat tourism in New Zealand. *Tourism Recreation Research* 38(3), 295–309. https://doi.org/10.1080/02508281.2013.11081755

Buckley R. and Westaway D. (2020). Mental health rescue effects of women's outdoor tourism: A role in COVID-19 recovery. *Annals of Tourism Research*, 85, 103041. https://doi.org/10.1016/j.annals.2020.103041

Cheer, J. M., Belhassen, Y. and Kujawa, J. (2017). The search for spirituality in tourism: Toward a conceptual framework for spiritual tourism. *Tourism Management Perspectives* 24, 252–256. https://doi.org/10.1016/j.tmp.2017.07.018

Chen, C. C. and Petrick, J.F. (2013). Health and Wellness Benefits of Travel Experiences: A literature review. *Journal of Travel Research* 52(6), 709–719. https://doi.org/10.1177/0047287513496477

Chen, Y., Lehto, Y. and Cai, L. (2013). Vacation and well-being: A study of Chinese tourists. *Annals of Tourism Research* 42, 284–310. https://doi.org/10.1016/j.annals.2013.02.003

Choudhary, C. and Qadir, A. (2021). Impact of COVID-19 on wellness and spa industry, *International Journal of Spa and Wellness*, 4(2–3), 193–203, https://doi.org/10.1080/24721735.2021.1986970

Cohen, M. M., Elliott, F., Oates, L., Schembri, A. and Mantri, N. (2017). Do Wellness Tourists Get Well? An Observational Study of Multiple Dimensions of Health and Well-Being After a Week-Long Retreat. *The Journal of Alternative and Complementary Medicine* 23(2), 140–148. https://doi.org/10.1089/acm.2016.0268

Damijanić, A.T. (2019). Wellness and healthy lifestyle in tourism settings. *Tourism Review*, 74(4), 978–989. https://doi.org/10.1108/TR-02-2019-0046

Dillette, A. K., Douglas, A. C. and Andrzejewski, C. (2021). Dimensions of holistic wellness as a result of international wellness tourism experiences. *Current Issues in Tourism*, 24(6), 794–810. https://doi.org/10.1080/13683500.2020.1746247

Dini, M. and Pencarelli, T. (2021). Wellness tourism and the components of its offer system: A holistic perspective. *Tourism Review*, 77 (2), 394–412. https://doi.org/10.1108/TR-08-2020-0373

Dolnicar, S., Yanamandram, V. and Cliff, K. (2012). The contribution of vacations to quality of life. *Annals of Tourism Research*, 39(1), 59–83. https://doi.org/10.1016/j.annals.2011.04.015

Dredge, D. (2022). Regenerative tourism: transforming mindsets, systems and practices. *Journal of Tourism Futures*. https://doi.org/10.1108/JTF-01-2022-0015

Egger, I., Lei, S. I., & Wassler, P. (2020). Digital free tourism–An exploratory study of tourist motivations. *Tourism Management*, 79, Article 104098. https://doi.org/10.1016/j.tourman.2020.104098

Floros, C., Cai, W., McKenna, B. and Ajeeb, D. (2021). Imagine being off-the-grid: millennials' perceptions of digital-free travel. *Journal of Sustainable Tourism*, 29(5), 751–766. https://doi.org/10.1080/09669582.2019.1675676

Fu, X., Tanyatanaboon, M. and Lehto, X. Y. (2015). Conceptualizing transformative guest experience at retreat centres. *International Journal of Hospitality Management* 49, 83–92. https://doi.org/10.1016/j.ijhm.2015.06.004

Gascon, M.; Zijlema, W.; Vert, C.; White, M.P. and Nieuwenhuijsen, M.J. (2017). Outdoor blue spaces, human health and well-being: A systematic review of quantitative studies. *International Journal of Hygiene and Environmental Health* 220(8), 1207–1221. https://doi.org/10.1016/j.ijheh.2017.08.004

Gezon, L. (2017). Global scouts: youth engagement with spirituality and wellness through travel, Lake Atitlán, Guatemala. *Journal of Tourism and Cultural Change*. 16, 1–14. 10.1080/14766825.2017.1310217.

Glouberman, D. and Cloutier, J. (2017). Community as Holistic Healer on Health Holiday Retreats: The Case of Skyros. In M. K. Smith and L. Puczkó (eds.) *The Routledge Handbook of Health Tourism* (pp. 152–167) London: Routledge.

Jiang, T., Ryan, C. and Zhang, C. (2018). The spiritual or secular tourist? The experience of Zen meditation in Chinese temples. *Tourism Management*, 65, 187–199. https://doi.org/10.1016/j.tourman.2017.10.008

Jiang, Y. and Wen, J. (2020). Effects of COVID-19 on Hotel Marketing and Management: A Perspective Article. *IJCHM*, 32, 2563–2573. https://doi.org/10.1108/IJCHM-03-2020-0237

Kato, K. and Progano, R.N. (2017). Spiritual (walking) tourism as a foundation for sustainable destination development: Kumano-kodo pilgrimage, Wakayama, Japan. *Tourism Management Perspectives*, 24, 243–251. https://doi.org/10.1016/j.tmp.2017.07.017

Kelly, C. (2012). Wellness Tourism: Retreat Visitor Motivations and Experience. *Tourism Recreation Research*, 37(3), 205–213. https://doi.org/10.1080/02508281.2012.11081709

Kelly, C. and Smith, M. K. (2017). Journeys of the self: the need to retreat. In M. K. Smith and L. Puczkó (eds.) *Routledge Handbook of Health Tourism* (pp. 138–151). London: Routledge.

Kemppainen, L., Koskinen, V., Bergroth, H., Marttila, E. and Kemppainen, T. (2021). Health and Wellness–Related Travel: A Scoping Study of the Literature in 2010-2018. *Sage Open*, 11(2). https://doi.org/10.1177/21582440211013792

Kessler, D., Lee, J.-H. and Whittingham, N. (2020). The wellness tourist motivation scale: a new statistical tool for measuring wellness tourist motivation. *International Journal of Spa and Wellness*, 3(1), 24–39. https://doi.org/10.1080/24721735.2020.1849930

Kirillova, K., Lehto, X. and Cai, L. (2017). Tourism and Existential Transformation: An Empirical Investigation. *Journal of Travel Research*. 56(5), 638–650. https://doi.org/10.1177/0047287516650277

Knobloch, U., Robertson, K. and Aitken, R. (2016). Experience, Emotion and Eudaimonia: A consideration of tourist experiences and Well-being. *Journal of Travel Research*, https://doi.org/10.1177/0047287516650937

Kwon, J. and Lee, H. (2020). Why travel prolongs happiness: Longitudinal analysis using a latent growth model. *Tourism Management*, 76, 103944. https://doi.org/10.1016/j.tourman.2019.06.019

Lehto, X. Y. and Lehto, M.R. (2019). Vacation as a public health resource: Toward a wellness-centered tourism design approach. *Journal of Hospitality and Tourism Research*, 43(7), 935–960. https://doi.org/10.1177/1096348019849684

Lin, Z., Wong, I. A., Kou, I. E. and Zhen, X. (2021). Inducing wellbeing through staycation programs in the midst of the COVID-19 crisis. *Tourism Management Perspectives*, 40. https://doi.org/10.1016/j.tmp.2021.100907

Ma, S., Zhao, X., Gong, Y. and Wengel, Y. (2021). Proposing "healing tourism" as a post-COVID-19 tourism product. *Anatolia*, 32(1), 136–139. https://doi.org/10.1080/13032917.2020.1808490

Maller, C., Townsend, M., St. Ledger, L., Henderson-Wilson, C., Pryor, A. and Prosser, L. (2008). Healthy parks healthy people: The health benefits of contact with nature in a park context: a review of current literature, *Social and Mental Health Priority Area*, Occasional Paper Series. Melbourne, Australia: Faculty of Health and Behavioural Sciences.

McCabe, S. and Johnson, S. (2013). The happiness factor in tourism: Subjective well-being and social tourism. *Annals of Tourism Research*, 41, 42–65. https://doi.org/10.1016/j.annals.2012.12.001

McCabe, S. and Qiao, G. (2020). A review of research into social tourism: Launching the Annals of Tourism Research Curated Collection on Social Tourism. *Annals of Tourism Research*, 85, 103103, https://doi.org/10.1016/j.annals.2020.103103.

Mitas, O., Nawijn, J. and Jongsma, B. (2016). Between tourists: tourism and happiness. In M. K. Smith and L. Puczkó (eds.) *Routledge Handbook of Health Tourism* (pp. 47–64). London: Routledge.

Moufakkir, O. and Selmi, N. (2018). Examining the spirituality of spiritual tourists: A Sahara desert experience. *Annals of Tourism Research* 70, 108–119. https://doi.org/10.1016/j.annals.2017.09.003

Nahrstedt, W. (2004). Wellness im Kurort: Neue Qualität für den Gesundheitstourismus in Europa. *Spektrum Freizeit*, 26(2), 37–52.

Nawijn, J., De Bloom, J. and Geurts, S. (2013). Pre-vacation time: Blessing or burden? *Leisure Sciences*, 35, 1, 33–44. https://doi.org/10.1080/01490400.2013.739875

Nawijn, J. and Filep, S. (2016). Two directions for future tourism well-being research. *Annals of Tourism Research* 61, 221–223. https://doi.org/10.1016/j.annals.2016.07.007

Neal, J. D., Uysal, M. and Sirgy, M. J. (2007). The effect of tourism services on travelers' quality of life. *Journal of Travel Research*, 46(2), 154–163. https://doi.org/10.1177/0047287507303977.

Norman, A. and Pokorny, J. J. (2017). Meditation retreats: Spiritual tourism and well-being interventions. *Tourism Management Perspectives* 24, 201–207. https://doi.org/10.1016/j.tmp.2017.07.012

Oliver, M. D., Baldwin, D. R. and Datta, S. (2018). Health to wellness: A review of wellness models and transitioning back to health. *The International Journal of Health, Wellness and Society*, 9(1), pp. 41–56. https://doi.org/10.18848/2156-8960/CGP/v09i01/41-56

Packer, J. (2022). Taking a break: Exploring the restorative benefits of short breaks and vacations. *Annals of Tourism Research Empirical Insights*, 2(1), 100032. https://doi.org/10.1016/j.annale.2020.100006

Pocinho, M., Garcês, S. and Neves de Jesus, S. (2022). Wellbeing and Resilience in Tourism: A Systematic Literature Review during COVID-19, *Frontiers in Psychology*. https://doi.org/10.3389/fpsyg.2021.748947

Pyke, S., Hartwell, H., Blake, A. and Hemingway, A. (2016). Exploring well-being as a tourism product resource. *Tourism Management* 55, 94–105. https://doi.org/10.1016/j.tourman.2016.02.004

Qiu, M., Sha, J. and Scott, N. (2021). Restoration of Visitors through Nature-Based Tourism: A Systematic Review, Conceptual Framework, and Future Research Directions. *International Journal of Environmental Research and Public Health* 18, 2299. https://doi.org/10.3390/ijerph18052299

Ram, Y. and Smith, M. K. (2019). An assessment of visited landscapes using a Cultural Ecosystem Services framework. *Tourism Geographies*, https://doi.org/10.1080/14616688.2018.1522545

Reisinger, Y. (2013). *Transformational Tourism: Tourist Perspectives*. Wallingford: CABI.

Rokni, L. (2021). The Psychological Consequences of COVID-19 Pandemic in Tourism Sector: A Systematic Review. *Iranian Journal of Public Health*, 50(9), 1743–1756. https://doi.org/10.18502/ijph.v50i9.7045.

Santos, A., Gonzalez, C., Haegeman, K., and Rainoldi, A. (2020). *Behavioural Changes in Tourism in Times of COVID-19*. Luxembourg: Publications Office of the European Union.

Seligman, M. E. P. (2002). *Authentic Happiness*. New York: Free Press.

Sharpley, R. and Jepson, D. (2011). Rural tourism: A spiritual experience? *Annals of Tourism Research*, 38(1), 52–71. https://doi.org/10.1016/j.annals.2010.05.002

Sheldon, P. J. (2020). Designing tourism experiences for inner transformation. *Annals of Tourism Research*, 83, 102935. https://doi.org/10.1016/j.annals.2020.102935

Sirgy, M. J., Kruger, S., Lee, D. and Yu, G. B. (2011). How does a travel trip affect tourists' life satisfaction? *Journal of Travel Research* 50(3), 261–275. https://doi.org/10.1177/0047287510362784

Smith, M. K. (2022a). Wellness Tourism. In D. Buhalis (ed.) *Encyclopedia of Tourism Management and Marketing*. Cheltenham: Edward Elgar. https://doi.org/10.4337/9781800377486.wellness.tourism

Smith, M. K. (2022b). Retreating Towards Subjective Wellbeing. In D. A. Fennell and R. W. Butler (eds.) *Tourism Hope, Happiness & the Good Life*. Bristol: Channel View.

Smith, M. K. and Csurgó, B. (2018). Tourism, Wellbeing and Cultural Ecosystem Services. A Case Study of Őrség National Park, Hungary. In I. Azara, E. Michopoulou, F. Niccolini, and A. Clarke (eds.) *Tourism, Health, Wellbeing and Protected Areas* (pp. 26–38). Wallingford: CABI.

Smith, M. K. and Diekmann, A. (2017). Tourism and wellbeing. *Annals of Tourism Research*, 66, 1–13. https://doi.org/10.1016/j.annals.2017.05.006

Smith, M. K., Kiss, R. and Chan, I.Y.F. (2022). Millennials' perceptions of spirituality, wellness and travel. In S. K. Walia and A. Jasrotia (eds.) *Millennials, Spirituality and Tourism* (Chapter 6). London: Routledge.

Smith, M. K. and Puczkó, L. (2018). *Exploring Health Tourism*. Report for UNWTO/ETC, https://www.unwto.org/global/publication/exploring-health-tourism (accessed 25 March 2022).

Soga, M., Evans, M. J., Tsuchiya, K. and Fukano, Y. (2021). A room with a green view: the importance of nearby nature for mental health during the COVID-19 pandemic. *Ecological Applications*, 31(2), 1–10. https://doi.org/10.1002/eap.2248

Stará, J. and Peterson, C. (2017). Understanding the concept of wellness for the future of the tourism industry: A literature review. *Journal of Tourism and Services*, 8, 18–29. ISSN 1804-5650

Stoewen, D. L. (2017). Dimensions of wellness: Change your habits, change your life. *Canadian Veterinary Journal*, 58(8), 861–862. https://www.ncbi.nlm.nih.gov/pmc/articles/PMC5508938

Voigt, C. (2010). Understanding wellness tourism: An analysis of benefits sought, health-promoting behaviours and positive psychological well-being [Doctoral dissertation]. University of Southern Australia.

Voigt, C., Brown, G. and Howat, G. (2011). Wellness tourists: In search of transformation. *Tourism Review*, 66(1/2), 16–30. https://doi.org/10.1108/16605371111127206

Wen, J. and Wu, M.-Y. (2020). How special is special interest tourism – and how special are special interest tourists? A perspective article in a Chinese context. *Current Issues in Tourism*, 23(16), 1968–1972.

Wolf, I. D., Ainsworth, G. B., and Crowley, J. (2017). Transformative travel as a sustainable market niche for protected areas: a new development, marketing and conservation model. *Journal of Sustainable Tourism*, 25(4), 1–24.

Wong, P. T. P. (2016). Meaning-seeking, self-transcendence, and well-being. In A. Batthyany (ed.) *Logotherapy and existential analysis: Proceedings of the Viktor Frankl Institute* (Vol. 1; pp. 311–322). Cham: Springer.

Yang, F. X. and Wong, I-K.A., (2021). The social crisis aftermath: tourist well-being during the COVID-19 outbreak. *Journal of Sustainable Tourism*, 29(6), 859–878. https://doi.org/10.1080/09669582.2020.1843047

Zhong, L., Deng, B., Morrison, A.M., Coca-Stefaniak, J.A. and Yang, L. (2021) Medical, Health and Wellness Tourism Research—A Review of the Literature (1970–2020) and Research Agenda. *International Journal of Environmental Research and Public Health*, 18, 10875. https://doi.org/10.3390/ijerph182010875

39 Accelerated trends in tourism marketing and tourist behaviour

Metin Kozak

Introduction

Despite its much longer historical background, particularly since the 1980s, the world of marketing has entered a new era, becoming increasingly consumer-oriented. Thus, consumers have begun to be at the centre of all production and marketing activities in the business world. In the first wave, commencing from the early 2000s, mass consumption has gained more emphasis with technology development. The tourism and hospitality industry have also been directly affected by such developments, and we have seen new ways of marketing methods and new types of tourism activities/products. As a second wave, one more feature of the 21st century is that it has mainly been dominated by either regional or global incidents such as terrorism and pandemics.

Given the changes in the structure of the consumer society, the emergence of a tourist/consumer who has new expectations, acts more with emotions, thinks hedonic, can be described as active, digital and experiential, has led to the transition from market/product logic to a more consumer/tourist-centred/based approach (Batat & Frochot, 2014). It is crucial to create these experiences with co-creation (Tussyadiah & Zach, 2014) or service-dominant logic (Vargo & Lusch, 2004). Technology is also included in this process. Tourism marketing has been transformed in the last decade with the evolution of social culture and the development of digital marketing tools (Kim & Wang, 2021; Kotler et al., 2017). The sharing economy and the digital evolution have transformed the marketing channels in the tourism industry (Gretzel, 2016; Berné et al., 2012, 2015a). With the emergence of online social networks and online review sites, new tourism marketing channels have emerged (Zaman et al., 2016).

Together with disseminating the latest pandemic worldwide, marketing methods and consumer behaviour have undergone another dramatic transformation once again. Its initial outcomes have been in practice now, e.g. more individualised lifestyles, more personalised marketing and consumerism, more concerns with regard to safety and security, more awareness of fashion, and more engagement on social media. Consequently, this chapter aims to examine the new trends that are likely to be encountered in tourism marketing based on the possible changes in consumer behaviour in the light of the developments of the last two decades and two waves.

Trends in tourism marketing

Information and communication technologies have developed rapidly, and, as a result, marketing processes in the tourism industry have been affected and changed respectively

Table 39.1 Major trends in tourism marketing

Types of orientation	Period	Focus	Means	End
Production orientation				
Innovative and robust products and services	1960–1970	Satisfying high demand	New technology generating mass production at low prices	Profit through mass sales and stable market conditions
Sales orientation				
Existing products and services	1970–1980	Maintain and improve existing products and services	Improvements and adaptations of the existing marketing mix	Profit through sales volume
Marketing orientation				
Business and leisure markets	1980–2000	Business and leisure-oriented customers' needs and wants	Integrated marketing, including marketing research	Profit through customer satisfaction
Social marketing-orientation				
Business and leisure markets AND the needs and wants of communities and the environment	2000-now	Socially concerned business activities	Integrated marketing considers the needs and wants of both customers and society.	Profit through enhanced (brand) image and customer satisfaction

Source: Adopted from Bowie & Buttle, 2004, p. 12.

(Berné et al., 2015b). Technological developments have revolutionised the shortening of lead times in marketing services and changed the relationships within tourism value chains (Gretzel, 2016; Romero & Tejada, 2020). Technology and digitalisation, which are the two main forces for innovation in tourism, are not sufficient because a successful innovation starts with a good understanding of the customer's wishes and needs by thinking in a customer-oriented fashion (Bigné & Decrop, 2019) and because tourists are becoming more demanding, sophisticated and knowledgeable (Cooper, 2016; McCabe, 2014). As with the form of pure marketing, it is also possible to summarise the critical stages of the evolution of tourism marketing orientation in terms of four periods: production, sales, marketing and social marketing (Bowie & Buttle, 2004; Cooper, 2016; Kotler et al., 2017) (Table 39.1).

Production orientation: In the 1960s and 1970s, there was a prevailing idea that as many products as possible (beds and aeroplane seats) should be made available to meet demand. Organisations/companies should devote their energies to continuous product improvements. Traditional marketing (Schmitt, 1999), which includes rational consumers interested in the functional characteristics of products and services, does not consider the psychological dimensions of experiences (Batat & Frochot, 2014). Since the 1960s, tourism has been understood as a consumer activity phenomenon, and thus the marketing approach has started to take hold. In order to enable the development of more informed marketing strategies, the primary sources of current data on travel markets have been tried to be determined (McCabe, 2014).

Sales orientation: It is the concept that large tour operators developed computer reservation systems to increase sales in the 1970s and 1980s. The focus here is on understanding the decision-making process and convincing consumers to buy rather than building a longer-term relationship. There is a prevailing idea that consumers will not buy enough products/goods/services unless they make an extensive sales and promotion effort. In the 1970s, tourism marketing focused on the importance of the tourism product (Jeffries, 1971). By the end of the 1970s, place image has become necessary for destination marketing as it can affect people's perceptions, choices and behaviours (Ashworth & Goodall, 1990; Bigné et al., 2001; Britton, 1979; Crompton, 1979a; Dilley, 1986; Echtner & Ritchie, 1993; Goodall, 1990; Goodall & Ashworth, 1988; Mansfeld, 1992). In the 1980s, service marketing emerged as a subdiscipline of marketing and became remarkable (Vargo & Lusch, 2004). Thus, marketing has become an accepted discipline in the tourism industry and academics (e.g., Kaynak et al., 1986; Meidan, 1984; Shafi, 1985; Stynes, 1983). Travel and tourism advertising techniques have begun to be discussed (Reilly, 1980; Uzzell, 1984). Effective strategy development plans in tourism marketing have been studied (Gilbert, 1990; Papadopoulos, 1987, 1989a, 1989b). Again, tourist motivations and behaviours were sought to be understood (Crompton, 1979b; Dann, 1981; Gilbert, 1989; Pearce, 1982).

Marketing orientation: Marketing orientation is a concept that requires the production of consumer-oriented products and the design of marketing processes to focus on consumer needs and meet the needs of tourists. The idea is that determining the needs and desires of target markets and providing the desired satisfaction levels more effectively and efficiently than the competitors are dominant. In tourism marketing, it has become a matter of using information instead of intuition and habit (Burke, 1986). Incorporating information into their marketing decisions meant that the information was presented clearly and easily accessible. Thus, it would save time and money and ensure customer satisfaction. This could result in positive word-of-mouth marketing to potential customers. Therefore, marketing information could reduce marketing costs, increase profitability and make business success more likely.

Social marketing orientation: With realising the harmful effects of tourism and issues such as climate change, marketing has begun to adopt the concepts of social responsibility and ethical behaviour. Not only being consumer-oriented, it also takes into account the needs of the society. In line with the needs, wishes and expectations of the target markets, the idea of being more effective and efficient than the competitors by protecting or improving the welfare of the consumer and society is dominant. It is envisaged that ecologically-minded tourism marketing will become more environmentally oriented and socially responsible by 1990 and in the 21st century (Krippendorf, 1987). As a result, from a macro marketing perspective, concerns about the sustainability of a destination have begun to increase (Belk & Costa, 1995; Middleton & Hawkins, 1998; Peattie, 1999). Voase (1999) presents an exciting marketing perspective, noting that tourists create their dramas about places through symbolic interaction at the destination and states that tourism destinations are primarily psychological and symbolic.

From the mid-1980s to the mid-1990s, green and sustainable marketing theories and practices emerged (Jamrozy, 2007). Haywood (1990) pioneered the critical analysis of the concept of marketing in tourism, enabling the consideration of holistic approaches to tourism and the development of destination marketing practices. In the 1990s, textbooks appeared (e.g., Middleton, 1994). Tourism researchers have begun to focus on the need for market orientation, recognising that marketing must develop meaningful relationships that seek to understand customer needs and increase loyalty (Bramwell & Rawding, 1996; Gartner, 1994; Haywood, 1990).

In addition, marketing ethics, whose ideas and practices were not associated with the tourism industry in the 1990s (Chonko & Hunt, 1985; Davis, 1992), were applied to the tourism industry (Wheeler, 1991, 1993, 1995). Based on the natural harmony between tourism and social marketing, social marketing emerged to convey the multifaceted benefits of recreation and tourism activities (Bright, 2000). Later, Beeton (2001) introduced the concept of demarketing, focusing on the behaviour of tourists, which requires them to be temporarily or permanently discouraged. Social marketing has become an increasingly important theme in the tourism literature as it promotes environmentally friendly consumer behaviour (Gössling et al., 2009; Peeters et al., 2009; Scott et al., 2012; Truong & Hall, 2013). With the increasing interest in ecology, new tourism market niches, such as ecotourism, have emerged (Eagles, 1992; Herbig & O'Hara, 1997).

In the following twenty years, from the theoretical point of view, as in generic tourism research, tourism marketing has become more affluent in terms of carrying out more in-depth empirical studies and has been contributed to by a larger group of researchers representing a more significant geographical mindset (Correia & Kozak, 2022). As a result, more specific journals central to the study of tourism marketing have appeared, e.g., *Journal of Travel & Tourism Marketing*, *Journal of Vacation Marketing*, and *Journal of Destination Marketing & Management*. This follows almost three decades after the launch the first generic marketing journals dating back to the 1960s. In addition, there has been numerous amounts of books on tourism marketing and tourist behaviour published over the past four decades.

Trends in tourist (consumer) behaviour

Marketing has developed towards a service-centred logic in recent years (Lusch & Vargo, 2006; Vargo & Lusch, 2004). Service-dominant logic is essential for marketers and marketing research (Li, 2014). With service-dominated logic, tourism authorities direct tourists to participate in product design and innovation (Lee et al., 2010). For this reason, a more service-oriented logic-based marketing approach can be adopted (Li, 2014). By operating in terms of co-creation, customers and service providers share their knowledge and skills, thereby increasing the value of the experience. With a better understanding of the tourist's values and needs, a tourism destination or service provider can provide solutions and resources that will meet the tourist's expectations through the process of co-creation, thereby gaining a competitive advantage (Li, 2014; Tussyadiah & Zach, 2014) and thus increasing the perceived value of the service (Bitner et al., 2000; Pugh, 2001). Co-production and co-creation are integrated concepts, as service production and consumption activities are linked (Lusch & Vargo, 2006). In the value creation process, tourist motivation, participation and knowledge are essential (Prebensen et al., 2013). As value is created jointly by companies and consumers in the co-creation process (Payne et al., 2008; Prahalad & Ramaswamy, 2002, 2004a), more knowledge-intensive tourism operations and smart tourism destinations should be developed (Gretzel, 2011; Wang et al., 2013).

Dramatic/gamified interactions for tourist experience value: Tourists create experience value in tourism by interacting with people and natural or manufactured elements (Prebensen, 2014). Countless little experiences that influence future intentions add to an overall experience. The experience can be compared to a theatre or a play where tourists are involved in drama (Goffman, 1959).

Experience economy and experiential marketing: The concept of the experience economy has evolved as consumers are empowered to co-create their experiences (Prahalad &

Ramaswamy, 2004b). As a result of the developments in technology, with the tourism experiences created together with empowered consumers adopting developing technologies (Tussyadiah & Fesenmaier, 2009), the traditional roles and processes of creating experience have also changed (Neuhofer & Buhalis, 2014). Tourism destinations, authorities and businesses should establish relationships with tourists, offer attractive and quality experiences to tourists, and facilitate the tourist to create brand experiences together through social media (Foley et al., 2014). Since the tourist experience is at the centre of value creation, it can be helpful to understand tourist behaviour with experiential marketing (Batat & Frochot, 2014).

Consumer-centred marketing: consumer-centred marketing provides an understanding of the motivations, habits, attitudes and values that guide consumers' opinions about the brands offered. In addition, tourists play an active role in designing their holidays by personalising their holiday packages. With consumer-centred marketing, organisations can have detailed information about their customers, and thus a profound understanding of customers can be developed (Niininen et al., 2006).

Customer value, satisfaction and loyalty: Value is the difference a customer perceives from other alternatives due to an evaluation of all of the benefits and costs of an offer. Customer satisfaction is the performance of the products and services that are directly related to the extent to which they meet customer expectations (Dasgupta, 2011). Tourists are considered rational consumers who make post-consumption evaluations (Foster, 2014). Destinations should keep visitors satisfied and happy. Thus, it makes them revisit that destination and encourages them to recommend others to visit that destination (Kozak & Rimmington, 2000, 2001a, 2001b). As a result, loyal tourists are created (Dasgupta, 2011).

Cross-cultural marketing: In cross-cultural marketing, the product or service must be adapted for each market, taking into account the cultural characteristics of the host country (Chen & Pizam, 2006). Culture has a significant impact on consumers' tastes, preferences, and behaviours of tourism products and services and outcomes may differ based on the cultural background (Kozak, 2001a, 2001b, 2002). Therefore, marketing managers should design strategies per the values and norms of their target markets.

Travellers' stories and archetypal re-enactments: To support brand building from a marketing perspective, archetypes and stories are bridges that connect consumers and places, not only from the point of view of marketing managers but also from the point of view of consumers. By experiencing the stories of travellers, tourists can interact with destinations and revive archetypal themes (Woodside et al., 2014).

The role of emotions: The reason for the increasing interest in the emotional dimensions of tourists' experiences (Ekinci & Hosany, 2006; Gnoth, 1997; Goossens, 2000; Hosany et al., 2016) is because tourists' emotional reactions have become the main determinants of satisfaction, behavioural intentions and attitudes (Bigné et al., 2005; del Bosque & Martín, 2008). Emotions affect tourism and leisure service purchasing decisions and choosing attractions, facilities and destinations (Goossens, 2000; Kwortnik & Ross, 2007).

Harmonisation of tourism marketing and tourist behaviour

Whether online marketing methods or traditional marketing methods are more useful depends on whether the applied marketing campaign leads potential tourists to visit and spend at the destination (Pratt, 2014). Considering that applicants for online information usually examine the first three pages of search results, the ranking and position of the destination management organisations' websites in popular search engines become essential for the effectiveness of online marketing (Xiang & Fesenmaier, 2005). Online reviews are influential and vital for travel information search and decision-making (Vermeulen & Seegers, 2009). For this reason, tourism marketers should listen to the consumer's voice by thinking customer-oriented since the tourist, who is empowered by digital technologies such as online sites, smartphones and social media, is digitally connected and well-informed (Pratt, 2014).

The Internet offers the ability to instantly communicate with every customer. It also allows for customer feedback, making it possible for companies to customise offers and services. Through the Internet, companies/organisations provide a 24/7 response service. This is the main reason consumers adopt the Internet so much. It allows them to shop at home 24/7 without worrying about the time zone (Hudson, 2014). By integrating social and mobile media into their marketing mix, marketers build brand websites that present information and promote the product/service. Many of these sites also serve as online brand communities where customers can come together and share brand-related information (Kotler et al., 2017).

In tourism marketing, social media are essential when researching travel information (Jauhari, 2017; Kotler et al., 2017; Xiang & Gretzel, 2010). Social media data are valuable because users create it (Horster & Gottschalk, 2012) and are vital for knowledge discovery and the co-creation of value with a data-mining approach (Brejla & Gilbert, 2014). Because visitors share their experiences and personal comments through social media, which shows the importance of social media for destination image (Gretzel & Yoo, 2014; Stickdorn, 2014; Tham et al., 2013).

Search engines provide tourism destinations and businesses opportunities to interact with their potential visitors (Xiang et al., 2014). Search engine marketing is a form of marketing in the digital environment where businesses and organisations try to gain visibility on search engine results pages, either paid or free (Moran & Hunt, 2015). The importance and dominance of search engines have increased as the focus of online marketing has shifted from the usability of the developed website to attracting and influencing online travellers (Xiang et al., 2014).

Blogs are widely used in tourism to read and write reviews about accommodation and travel services (Munar, 2009). Travel blogs, also known as the virtual travel community, are platforms where travellers share their experiences and are easily accessible and can affect the decisions and behaviours of consumers who read the posts made here (Bosangit, 2014). Information/experiences shared on blogs can provide marketers with important information on how to market the destination. This can also help improve the destination image (Bosangit, 2014).

Affordable handheld devices that offer wireless connectivity, especially mobile phones, are now no longer a luxury but a necessity (Niininen et al., 2006). Accessing location-based applications and services via smartphone is an attribute consumers value in their tourism experience (McCabe et al., 2014). Mobile commerce, which includes smartphones and tablets, is an effective channel to reach many users. When users leave the places they visit, the products or services they view on the Internet will be shown to them again later. Leveraging this Internet history, many companies collect massive consumer behaviour data. Thus, it becomes possible for them to customise their offers (Camilleri, 2018). Big data means a massive amount of data continuously and in real time from different data sources, and it is also of interest to tourism marketing (Inanç-Demir & Kozak, 2019). Because the platform that creates the big data allows experimental studies to be done. Thus, information production through big data will be moved to a new level in terms of speed and quantity (Dolnicar & Ring, 2014). Big data can create a competitive advantage in the tourism industry (Vinod, 2013).

Future of tourism marketing and tourist behaviour

The future of tourism marketing is still driven by changes and developments in social (e.g., demographic characteristics), political (e.g. regionalism, globalisation), economic, environmental (e.g., climate change, biodiversity, resource use) and technological (e.g., social media, blogs) fields (Cooper, 2016). While the rapid change caused the strategies that offered the opportunity to win in the past to become outdated today, customer-oriented marketing has become the critical factor on the road to success (Kotler et al., 2017). In the future, tourism authorities need to better plan and manage, and all stakeholders involved in tourism should act more consciously and responsibly on social and environmental issues. With new smart management systems and techniques, tourism will continue to focus on destinations other than individual facilities and visitor experiences and values (Cooper, 2016; Kozak & Baloglu, 2011). Due to the effects of the pandemic, not only the advancements in technology but also its collaboration with public health appear to be more dominant in the design of future tourist behaviour and tourism marketing (Wen et al., 2021, 2022).

It will be possible for different types of consumer behaviour to emerge in the coming years due to the global factors such as the pandemic, migration and technology on the one hand and the more educated and experienced consumer segments on the other hand. The tourism industry, which is likely to become more competitive due to the increasing demand, will also seek different methods of reaching potential consumers directly. Understanding cultural differences may gain even more criticality as consumers could live in a different place from where they were born. It is possible that different tourist behaviours may emerge due to the ageing population and the increase in single populations. With a more experience with certain products or brands, consumers may benefit more from one-to-one personal products and one-to-one personalised marketing methods while having a shorter but more holiday experience. The "tourist" label may have little value, and tourists may lead a quieter lifestyle of holiday experience like the citizens of the destinations visited. The impact of external factors such as health and climate change on tourist behaviour will be among those sensitive or even fragile issues that need to be studied for many years. Parallel to such changes on the global and the consumer sides, tourism marketing will be forced directly in adapting to the change while understanding tourist behaviour may position itself in the centre of future studies.

References

Ashworth, G. J., & Goodall, B. (1990). *Marketing tourism places.* London, UK: Routledge.
Batat, W., & Frochot, I. (2014). Towards an experiential approach in tourism studies. In S. McCabe (Ed.), *The Routledge handbook of tourism marketing* (pp. 109–123). Oxon, UK: Routledge.
Beeton, S. (2001). Cyclops and Sirens – Demarketing as a proactive response to negative consequences of one-eyed competitive marketing. *Travel and Tourism Research Association 32nd Annual Conference Proceedings* (pp. 125–136).
Belk, R. W., & Costa, J. A. (1995). International tourism: An assessment and overview. *Journal of Macromarketing, 15*(2), 33–49. doi:10.1177/027614679501500204
Berné, C., Garcia-Gonzalez, M., & Mugica, J. (2012). How ICT shifts the power balance of tourism distribution channels. *Tourism Management, 33*(1), 205–214. doi:10.1016/j.tourman.2011.02.004

Berné, C., García-González, M., García-Uceda, M. E., & Múgica, J. M. (2015a). The effect of ICT on relationship enhancement and performance in tourism channels. *Tourism Management*, *48*, 188–198. doi:10.1016/j.tourman.2014.04.012

Berné, C., Gómez-Campillo, M., & Orive, V. (2015b). Tourism distribution system and information and communication technologies (ICT) development: Comparing data of 2008 and 2012. *Modern Economy*, *6*(2), 145–152. doi:10.4236/me.2015.62012

Bigné, J. E., & Decrop, A. (2019). Paradoxes of postmodern tourists and innovation in tourism marketing. In E. Fayos-Solà & C. Cooper (Eds.), *The future of tourism: Innovation and sustainability* (pp. 131–154). Cham: Springer.

Bigné, J. E., Andreu, L., & Gnoth, J. (2005). The theme park experience: An analysis of pleasure, arousal and satisfaction. *Tourism Management*, *26*(6), 833–844. doi:10.1016/j.tourman.2004.05.006

Bigné, J. E., Sánchez, M. I., & Sánchez, J. (2001). Tourism image, evaluation variables and after purchase behaviour: inter-relationship. *Tourism Management*, *22*(6), 607–616. doi:10.1016/s0261-5177(01)00035-8

Bitner, M. J., Brown, S. W., & Meuter, M. L. (2000). Technology infusion in service encounters. *Journal of the Academy of Marketing Science*, *28*(1), 138–149. doi:10.1177/0092070300281013

Bosangit, C. (2014). Virtual communities: Online blogs as a marketing tool. In S. McCabe (Ed.), *The Routledge handbook of tourism marketing* (pp. 520–533). Oxon, UK: Routledge.

Bowie, D., & Buttle, F. (2004). *Tourism marketing: An introduction.* Oxford, UK: Butterworth-Heinemann.

Bramwell, B., & Rawding, L. (1996). Tourism marketing images of industrial cities. *Annals of Tourism Research*, *23*(1), 201–221. doi:10.1016/0160-7383(95)00061-5

Brejla, P., & Gilbert, D. (2014). Exploratory use of web content analysis to understand cruise tourism services. *International Journal of Tourism Research*, *16*(2), 157–168. doi:10.1002/jtr.1910

Bright, A. D. (2000). The role of social marketing in leisure and recreation management. *Journal of Leisure Research*, *32*(1), 12–17. doi:10.1080/00222216.2000.11949878

Britton, R. A. (1979). The image of the Third World in tourism marketing. *Annals of Tourism Research*, *6*(3), 318–329. doi:10.1016/0160-7383(79)90106-3

Burke, J. F. (1986). Computerised management of tourism marketing information. *Tourism Management*, *7*(4), 279–289. doi:10.1016/0261-5177(86)90037-3

Camilleri, M. A. (2018). *Travel marketing, tourism economics and the airline product: An introduction to theory and practice.* Cham: Springer International Publishing.

Chen, P.-J., & Pizam, A. (2006). Cross-cultural tourism marketing. In D. Buhalis & C. Costa (Eds.), *Tourism management dynamics: Trends, management and tools* (pp. 187–195). Oxford, UK: Elsevier Butterworth-Heinemann.

Chonko, L. B., & Hunt, S. D. (1985). Ethics and marketing management: An empirical examination. *Journal of Business Research*, *13*(4), 339–359. doi:10.1016/0148-2963(85)90006-2

Cooper, C. (2016). *Essentials of tourism.* Harlow, UK: Pearson Education Limited.

Correia, A., & Kozak, M. (2022). Past, present and future: Trends in tourism research. *Current Issues in Tourism*, 1–16. doi:10.1080/13683500.2021.1918069

Crompton, J. L. (1979a). An assessment of the image of Mexico as a vacation destination and the influence of geographical location upon that image. *Journal of Travel Research*, *17*(4), 18–23. doi:10.1177/004728757901700404

Crompton, J. L. (1979b). Motivations for pleasure vacation. *Annals of Tourism Research*, *6*(4), 408–424. doi:10.1016/0160-7383(79)90004-5

Dann, G. M. S. (1981). Tourist motivation an appraisal. *Annals of Tourism Research*, *8*(2), 187–219. doi:10.1016/0160-7383(81)90082-7

Dasgupta, D. (2011). *Tourism marketing.* Noida, India: Dorling Kindersley.

del Bosque, I. R., & Martín, H. S. (2008). Tourist satisfaction a cognitive-affective model. *Annals of Tourism Research*, *35*(2), 551–573. doi:10.1016/j.annals.2008.02.006

Dilley, R. S. (1986). Tourist brochures and tourist images. *The Canadian Geographer/Le Géographe Canadien*, *30*(1), 59–65. doi:10.1111/j.1541-0064.1986.tb01026.x

Dolnicar, S., & Ring, A. (2014). Tourism marketing research: Past, present and future. *Annals of Tourism Research*, *47*, 31–47. doi:10.1016/j.annals.2014.03.008

Eagles, P. F. J. (1992). The travel motivations of Canadian ecotourists. *Journal of Travel Research*, *31*(2), 3–7. doi:10.1177/004728759203100201

Echtner, C. M., & Ritchie, J. R. B. (1993). The measurement of destination image: An empirical assessment. *Journal of Travel Research*, *31*(4), 3–13. doi:10.1177/004728759303100402

Ekinci, Y., & Hosany, S. (2006). Destination personality: An application of brand personality to tourism destinations. *Journal of Travel Research*, *45*(2), 127–139. doi:10.1177/0047287506291603

Foley, A., Fahy, J., & Ivers, A.-M. (2014). Brand experience in tourism in the Internet age. In S. McCabe (Ed.), *The Routledge handbook of tourism marketing* (pp. 140–150). Oxon, UK: Routledge.

Foster, C. (2014). Customer satisfaction in tourism The search for the Holy Grail. In S. McCabe (Ed.), *The Routledge handbook of tourism marketing* (pp. 165–177). Oxon, UK: Routledge.

Gartner, W. C. (1994). Image formation process. *Journal of Travel & Tourism Marketing*, *2*(2–3), 191–216. doi:10.1300/j073v02n02_12

Gilbert, D. (1990). Strategic marketing planning for national tourism. *The Tourist Review*, *45*(1), 18–27. doi:10.1108/eb058038

Gilbert, D. C. (1989). Tourism marketing-its emergence and establishment. *Progress in tourism, recreation and hospitality management*, *1*, 77–90.

Gnoth, J. (1997). Motivation and expectation formation. *Annals of Tourism Research*, *24*(2), 283–304. doi:10.1016/S0160-7383(97)80002-3

Goffman, E. (1959). *The presentation of self in everyday life*. New York, US: Doubleday.

Goodall, B. (1990). The dynamics of tourism place marketing. In G. Ashworth & B. Goodall (Eds.), *Marketing tourism places* (pp. 259–279). London, UK: Routledge.

Goodall, B., & Ashworth, G. (1988). *Marketing in the tourism industry (RLE Tourism): The promotion of destination regions*. London, UK: Routledge.

Goossens, C. (2000). Tourism information and pleasure motivation. *Annals of Tourism Research*, *27*(2), 301–321. doi:10.1016/S0160-7383(99)00067-5

Gössling, S., Haglund, L., Kallgren, H., Revahl, M., & Hultman, J. (2009). Swedish air travellers and voluntary carbon offsets: Towards the co-creation of environmental value? *Current Issues in Tourism*, *12*(1), 1–19. doi:10.1080/13683500802220687

Gretzel, U. (2011). Intelligent systems in tourism: A social science perspective. *Annals of Tourism Research*, *38*(3), 757–779. doi:10.1016/j.annals.2011.04.014

Gretzel, U. (2016). The new technologies tsunami in the hotel industry. In M. Ivanova, S. Ivanov, & V. Magnini (Eds.), *Routledge handbook of hotel chain management* (pp. 490–497). London, UK: Routledge.

Gretzel, U., & Yoo, K.-H. (2014). Premises and promises of social media marketing in tourism. In S. McCabe (Ed.), *The Routledge handbook of tourism marketing* (pp. 491–504). Oxon, UK: Routledge.

Haywood, K. M. (1990). Revising and implementing the marketing concept as it applies to tourism. *Tourism Management*, *11*(3), 195–205. doi:10.1016/0261-5177(90)90042-8

Herbig, P., & O'Hara, B. (1997). Eco-tourism: A guide for marketers. *European Business Review*, *97*(5), 231–236. doi:10.1108/09555349710179843

Horster, E., & Gottschalk, C. (2012). Computer-assisted webnography. *Journal of Vacation Marketing*, *18*(3), 229–238. doi:10.1177/1356766712449369

Hudson, S. (2014). Challenges of tourism marketing in the digital, global economy. In S. McCabe (Ed.), *The Routledge handbook of tourism marketing* (pp. 475–490). Oxon, UK: Routledge.

Inanç-Demir, M., & Kozak, M. (2019). Big data and its supporting elements: Implications for tourism and hospitality marketing. In M. Sigala, R. Rahimi, & M. Thelwall (Eds.), *Big data and innovation in tourism, travel, and hospitality: Managerial approaches, techniques, and applications* (pp. 213–223). Cham: Springer.

Jamrozy, U. (2007). Marketing of tourism: A paradigm shift toward sustainability. *International Journal of Culture, Tourism and Hospitality Research, 1*(2), 117–130. doi:10.1108/17506180710751669

Jauhari, V. (2017). *Hospitality marketing and consumer behavior: Creating Memorable Experiences*. Oakville, Canada: Apple Academic Press.

Jeffries, D. J. (1971). Defining the tourist product—and its importance in tourism marketing. *The Tourist Review, 26*(1), 2–5. doi:10.1108/eb057631

Kaynak, E., Odabasi, Y., & Kavas, A. (1986). Tourism marketing in a developing economy: Frequent and infrequent visitors contrasted. *The Service Industries Journal, 6*(1), 42–60. doi:10.1080/02642068600000004

Kim, S., & Wang, D. (2021). *Future of Tourism Marketing*. Oxon, UK: Routledge.

Kotler, P., Bowen, J. T., Makens, J. C., & Baloglu, S. (2017). *Marketing for hospitality and tourism*. Essex, UK: Pearson Education Limited.

Kozak, M. (2001a). Comparative assessment of tourist satisfaction with destinations across two nationalities. *Tourism Management, 22*(4), 391–401. doi:10.1016/s0261-5177(00)00064-9

Kozak, M. (2001b). Repeaters' behavior at two distinct destinations. *Annals of Tourism Research, 28*(3), 784–807. doi:10.1016/s0160-7383(00)00078-5

Kozak, M. (2002). Comparative analysis of tourist motivations by nationality and destinations. *Tourism Management, 23*(3), 221–232. doi:10.1016/s0261-5177(01)00090-5

Kozak, M., & Baloglu, S. (2011, eds.). *Managing and marketing tourist destinations strategies to gain competitive edge*. New York: Taylor & Francis.

Kozak, M., & Rimmington, M. (2000). Tourist satisfaction with Mallorca, Spain, as an off-season holiday destination. *Journal of Travel Research, 38*(3), 260–269. doi:10.1177/004728750003800308

Krippendorf, J. (1987). Ecological approach to tourism marketing. *Tourism Management, 8*(2), 174–176. doi:10.1016/0261-5177(87)90029-x

Kwortnik, R. J., & Ross, W. T. (2007). The role of positive emotions in experiential decisions. *International Journal of Research in Marketing, 24*(4), 324–335. doi:10.1016/j.ijresmar.2007.09.002

Lee, G., Tussyadiah, I. P., & Zach, F. (2010). A visitor-focused assessment of new product launch: The case of Quilt Gardens Tour^{SM} in Northern Indiana's Amish Country. *Journal of Travel & Tourism Marketing, 27*(7), 723–735. doi:10.1080/10548408.2010.519677

Li, X. (2014). Linking service-dominant logic to destination marketing. In S. McCabe (Ed.), *The Routledge handbook of tourism marketing* (pp. 15–26). Oxon, UK: Routledge.

Lusch, R. F., & Vargo, S. L. (2006). Service-dominant logic: Reactions, reflections and refinements. *Marketing Theory, 6*(3), 281–288. doi:10.1177/1470593106066781

Mansfeld, Y. (1992). From motivation to actual travel. *Annals of Tourism Research, 19*(3), 399–419. doi:10.1016/0160-7383(92)90127-b

McCabe, S. (2014). Introduction. In S. McCabe (Ed.), *The Routledge handbook of tourism marketing* (pp. 1–12). Oxon, UK: Routledge.

McCabe, S., Foster, C., Li, C., & Nanda, B. (2014). Tourism marketing goes mobile: Smartphones and the consequences for tourist experiences. In S. McCabe (Ed.), *The Routledge handbook of tourism marketing* (pp. 534–546). Oxon, UK: Routledge.

Meidan, A. (1984). The marketing of tourism. *The Service Industries Journal, 4*(3), 166–186. doi:10.1080/02642068400000069

Middleton, V. T. C. (1994). *Marketing in travel and tourism*. Oxford, UK: Butterworth-Heinemann.

Middleton, V. T. C., & Hawkins, R. (1998). *Sustainable tourism: A marketing perspective*. Oxford, UK: Butterworth-Heinemann.

Moran, M., & Hunt, B. (2015). *Search Engine Marketing, Inc.: Driving search traffic to your company's web site*. New Jersey, US: International Business Machines Press.

Munar, A. M. (2009). Challenging the brand. *Bridging Tourism Theory and Practice*, 17–35. doi:10.1108/s2042-1443(2009)0000001004

Neuhofer, B., & Buhalis, D. (2014). Experience, co-creation and technology: Issues, challenges and trends for technology enhanced tourism experiences. In S. McCabe (Ed.), *The Routledge handbook of tourism marketing* (pp. 124–139). Oxon, UK: Routledge.

Niininen, O., March, R., & Buhalis, D. (2006). Consumer centric tourism marketing. In D. Buhalis & C. Costa (Eds.), *Tourism management dynamics: Trends, management and tools* (pp. 175–186). Oxford, UK: Elsevier Butterworth-Heinemann.

Papadopoulos, S. I. (1987). Strategic marketing techniques in international tourism. *International Marketing Review*, *4*(2), 71–84. doi:10.1108/eb008331

Papadopoulos, S. I. (1989a). A conceptual tourism marketing planning model: Part 1. *European Journal of Marketing*, *23*(1), 31–40. doi:10.1108/eum0000000000539

Papadopoulos, S. I. (1989b). Strategy development and implementation of tourism marketing plans: Part 2. *European Journal of Marketing*, *23*(3), 37–47. doi:10.1108/eum0000000000559

Pearce, P. L. (1982). *The social psychology of tourist behaviour*. Oxford, UK: Pergamon Press.

Peattie, K. (1999). Trappings versus substance in the greening of marketing planning. *Journal of Strategic Marketing*, *7*(2), 131–148. doi:10.1080/096525499346486

Peeters, P., Gössling, S., & Lane, B. (2009). Moving towards low-carbon tourism: New opportunities for destinations and tour operators. In S. Gössling, C. M. Hall, & D. Weaver (Eds.), *Sustainable tourism futures: Perspectives on systems, restructuring and innovations* (pp. 240–257). New York, US: Routledge.

Prahalad, C. K., & Ramaswamy, V. (2002). The co-creation connection. *Strategy & Business*, *27*, 51–60. https://www.strategy-business.com/article/18458

Prahalad, C. K., & Ramaswamy, V. (2004a). Co-creating unique value with customers. *Strategy & Leadership*, *32*(3), 4–9. doi:10.1108/10878570410699249

Prahalad, C. K., & Ramaswamy, V. (2004b). Co-creation experiences: The next practice in value creation. *Journal of Interactive Marketing*, *18*(3), 5–14. doi:10.1002/dir.20015

Pratt, S. (2014). Determining what works, what doesn't and why: Evaluating tourism marketing campaigns. In S. McCabe (Ed.), *The Routledge handbook of tourism marketing* (pp. 209–220). Oxon, UK: Routledge.

Prebensen, N. K. (2014). A framework for dramatising interactions for enhanced tourist experience value. In S. McCabe (Ed.), The Routledge handbook of tourism marketing (pp. 27–37). Oxon, UK: Routledge.

Prebensen, N. K., Vitterso, J., & Dahl, T. I. (2013). Value co-creation significance of tourist resources. *Annals of Tourism Research*, *42*, 240–261. doi:10.1016/j.annals.2013.01.012

Pugh, S. D. (2001). Service with a smile: Emotional contagion in the service encounter. *Academy of Management Journal*, *44*(5), 1018–1027. doi:10.2307/3069445

Reilly, R. T. (1980). *Travel and tourism marketing techniques*. Illinois, US: Merton House Publishing.

Romero, I., & Tejada, P. (2020). Tourism intermediaries and innovation in the hotel industry. *Current Issues in Tourism*, *23*(5), 641–653. doi:10.1080/13683500.2019.1572717

Schmitt, B. H. (1999). *Experiential marketing: How to get customers to sense, feel, think, act, and relate to your company and brands*. New York, US: Free Press.

Scott, D., Gössling, S., & Hall, C. M. (2012). International tourism and climate change. *Wiley Interdisciplinary Reviews: Climate Change*, *3*(3), 213–232. doi:10.1002/wcc.165

Shafi, M. (1985). Tourism Marketing: Pros and Cons. *Tourism Recreation Research*, *10*(1), 39–40. doi:10.1080/02508281.1985.11014359

Stickdorn, M. (2014). Service design: Co-creating meaningful experiences with customers. In S. McCabe (Ed.), *The Routledge handbook of tourism marketing* (pp. 330–344). Oxon, UK: Routledge.

Stynes, D. J. (1983). Marketing tourism. *Journal of Physical Education, Recreation & Dance*, *54*(4), 43–46. doi:10.1080/07303084.1983.10629565

Tham, A., Croy, G., & Mair, J. (2013). Social media in destination choice: Distinctive electronic word-of-mouth dimensions. *Journal of Travel & Tourism Marketing*, *30*(1–2), 144–155. doi:10.1080/10548408.2013.751272

Truong, V. D., & Hall, C. M. (2013). Social marketing and tourism: What is the evidence? *Social Marketing Quarterly*, *19*(2), 110–135. doi:10.1177/1524500413484452

Tussyadiah, I. P., & Fesenmaier, D. R. (2009). Mediating tourist experiences. *Annals of Tourism Research*, *36*(1), 24–40. doi:10.1016/j.annals.2008.10.001

Tussyadiah, I. P., & Zach, F. (2014). Capacity for co-creation among destination marketing organisations. In S. McCabe (Ed.), *The Routledge handbook of tourism marketing* (pp. 425–434). Oxon, UK: Routledge.

Uzzell, D. (1984). An alternative structuralist approach to the psychology of tourism marketing. *Annals of Tourism Research*, *11*(1), 79–99. doi:10.1016/0160-7383(84)90097-5

Vargo, S. L., & Lusch, R. F. (2004). Evolving to a new dominant logic for marketing. *Journal of Marketing*, *68*(1), 1–17. doi:10.1509/jmkg.68.1.1.24036

Vermeulen, I. E., & Seegers, D. (2009). Tried and tested: The impact of online hotel reviews on consumer consideration. *Tourism Management*, *30*(1), 123–127. doi:10.1016/j.tourman.2008.04.008

Vinod, B. (2013). Leveraging big data for competitive advantage in travel. *Journal of Revenue and Pricing Management*, *12*(1), 96–100. doi:10.1057/rpm.2012.46

Voase, R. (1999). "Consuming" tourist sites/sights: A note on York. *Leisure Studies*, *18*(4), 289–296. doi:10.1080/026143699374862

Wang, D., Li, X. (Robert), & Li, Y. (2013). China's "smart tourism destination" initiative: A taste of the service-dominant logic. *Journal of Destination Marketing & Management*, *2*(2), 59–61. doi:10.1016/j.jdmm.2013.05.004

Wen, J., Hou, H., Kozak, M., Meng, F., Yu, C.-E., & Wang, W. (2021). The missing link between medical science knowledge and public awareness: Implications for tourism and hospitality recovery after COVID-19. *European Journal of Management and Business Economics*, *30*(2), 230–242. doi:10.1108/EJMBE-11-2020-0329

Wen, J., Kozak, M., Yang, S., & Liu, F. (2022). COVID-19: Potential effects on Chinese citizens' lifestyle and travel. *Tourism Review*, *76*(1), 74–87. doi:10.1108/tr-03-2020-0110

Wheeler, M. (1991). *Tourism marketers in local government: Critical issues and ethical components* [Unpublished doctoral dissertation]. University of Surrey, Guildford.

Wheeler, M. (1993). Tourism marketers in local government. *Annals of Tourism Research*, *20*(2), 354–356. doi:10.1016/0160-7383(93)90060-g

Wheeler, M. (1995). Tourism marketing ethics: an introduction. *International Marketing Review*, *12*(4), 38–49. doi:10.1108/02651339510097720

Woodside, A. G., Muniz, K., & Sood, S. (2014). Archetype enactments in travellers' stories about places: Theory and advances in positivistic and qualitative methods. In S. McCabe (Ed.), *The Routledge handbook of tourism marketing* (pp. 221–230). Oxon, UK: Routledge.

Xiang, Z., & Fesenmaier, D. R. (2005). An analysis of two search engine interface metaphors for trip planning. *Information Technology and Tourism*, *7*(2), 103–117. doi:10.3727/1098305054517291

Xiang, Z., & Gretzel, U. (2010). Role of social media in online travel information search. *Tourism Management*, *31*(2), 179–188. doi:10.1016/j.tourman.2009.02.016

Xiang, Z., Pan, B., & Fesenmaier, D. R. (2014). Foundations of search engine marketing for tourist destinations. In S. McCabe (Ed.), *The Routledge handbook of tourism marketing* (pp. 505–519). Oxon, UK: Routledge.

Zaman, M., Botti, L., & Vo-Thanh, T. (2016). Weight of criteria in hotel selection: An empirical illustration based on TripAdvisor criteria. *European Journal of Tourism Research*, *13*, 132–138. doi:10.54055/ejtr.v13i.236

Davis, J. J. (1992). Ethics and environmental marketing. *Journal of Business Ethics*, *11*, 81–87.

Payne, A., Stoubacka, K., Frow, P. and Knox, S. (2008). Managing the co-creation of value. *Journal of the Academy Marketing Science*, *36*, 83–96.

Hosany, S., Ekinci, Y. and Uysal, M. (2016). Destination image and destination personality: An application of branding theories to tourism places. *Journal of Business Research* *59*(5), 638–642.

40 Re-enacting dark histories

Brianna Wyatt

Introduction

Dark tourism is recognised as a travel activity to places of, or associated with, historic death, tragedy and the seemingly macabre (Stone, 2006). As a growing and popular form of tourism, dark tourism comprises attractions and events encouraged by a growing public interest in the consumption of places of historic death and suffering (Qian et al., 2022). Because dark tourism attractions are the physical manifestations of death and tragedy, they are traditionally observed as places for reflection, commemoration, and learning, but can also cause negative feelings of, for example, fear, anxiety, or rage (Biran et al., 2011). Places like Auschwitz and Chernobyl are perhaps two of the more iconic representations of dark tourism in this regard. However, the growing temporal distance from death-related events and increased presence of death and tragedy in media has influenced society to become desensitised to the image and presentation of death (Bowman & Pezzullo, 2010). In fact, studies have shown society has become more curious about death, resulting in an increased desire to learn about past pain and suffering (Sharma & Nayak, 2019). This, coupled with advancements in technology, have further influenced visitors to seek out more unique, memorable experiences that are engaging, personal, and even immersive (Alabau-Montoya & Ruiz-Molina, 2020; Light & Ivanova, 2021). In response, there has been an increasing development of *lighter* dark visitor attractions – places considered lighter with respect to Stone's (2006) Darkness Spectrum on the basis of their higher commercial and tourism infrastructure and use of edutainment interpretation (Chapter 11), which, as a strategic effort that blurs education with entertainment, helps to create the more memorable and engaging experiences that visitors seek (Wyatt et al., 2021). To create engaging and immersive experiences, these lighter attractions generally rely on edutainment methods, which include guided tours, sensory stimulating technologies, amusement or thrill rides, staged scenes of period-inspired props and mannequins, and/or re-enactments – a growing cultural phenomenon, propelled by society's fascination with reliving the past (Agnew, 2004; Skipalis, 2012; Wyatt et al., 2021).

Within dark tourism, the re-enactment of dark histories has become salient on a global scale, blurring the boundaries of education and entertainment with popular culture and high art (Perry, 2020). Spectacles of war, death, and suffering have been long observed at historic battlefields (e.g., Battle of Gettysburg, U.S.), historic sites (e.g., Laura Plantation, U.S.), and in public spaces (e.g., Feria de la Brujería de Trasmoz, Spain). However over the past two decades, re-enactments have become even more prominent at lighter dark visitor attractions. For example, they may be elaborate performances to provide a greater sense of authenticity, often observed with battlefield re-enactment events (see e.g., Figure 40.1 – Hale Farm & Village Civil War Re-enactment, U.S.). They may also be guided tours

Figure 40.1 Hale Farm & Village Civil War re-enactment.
From [Union Calvary], by Chris Chow, 2021, Unsplash (https://unsplash.com/photos/cvM6BHn2cAE).

through in-situ locations where groups of visitors are led by a costumed guide who tells them about the history and location (e.g., The Real Mary King's Close, U.K.), or they may be interactive, co-created accounts in which visitors actively participate in the re-enactment performance (e.g., *Follow the North Star*, Conner Prairie living history museum, USA).

Demonstrating the growing trend of re-enactment in dark tourism, many studies have shed light on their scope by exploring a range of topics. These include the morality and appropriateness of re-enacting dark histories and its impact on public memory (e.g., Agnew, 2020; Florence, 2022), the role and authority of re-enactors (e.g., Potter, 2016), the visitor experience and narrative development (e.g., Tschida, 2022), their overall design and management (e.g., Wyatt et al., 2021), and visitor engagement and preferences for such experiences (e.g., Light & Ivanova, 2021). Underpinning much of the literature surrounding the re-enactment of dark histories, and extending existing dark tourism discourse concerning the morality of packaging death for tourism consumption, are debates on whether such activities are voyeuristic and exacerbate ongoing social issues (Wiedenhoft Murphy, 2010), or whether they produce opportunities for deeper learning and understanding (de Groot, 2016) with a potential to resolve issues of stereotypes and/or public memory (Tschida, 2022). Exploring these contexts, this chapter discusses the growing trend of re-enactment in dark tourism. It highlights current trends and ongoing challenges and issues before offering a discussion of future possibilities, including how technology can create more immersive experiences, as well as the ability re-enactment has to make purposeful and meaningful change now and in the future.

Re-enacting dark histories – A growing trend within dark tourism

The re-enactment of dark histories exists within a range of diverse spaces, including film, television, theatre, museums, events, and visitor attractions (Agnew, 2004). In the context of dark tourism, re-enactment is a method used to enhance interpretation – a purposeful strategy designed to create informative and engaging visitor experiences by using a range of static and interactive methods (Smith, 2016). The aim of re-enactment is to bring history to life. Most re-enactments within lighter dark tourism experiences create sensory stimulation using, for example, smell pods, which can be used to make a room smell damp or musty, thereby helping to create a unique simulated experience. They also use costuming and props, as well as lighting, sound effects, and graphic imagery to further enhance the experience's atmosphere (Kidd, 2011). Re-enactors also manipulate their physical attributes (e.g., vocal tone, speech, behaviour, posture, gait, hair colour or style) to embody the characters they are portraying (Jablon-Roberts & Sanders, 2019; Ward & Wilkinson, 2006).

To create effective simulated accounts of the past, re-enactments must be carefully and strategically designed, with all sets, staging, and costuming looking correct for the respective time period (Kidd, 2011; Jablon-Roberts & Sanders, 2019). However, within dark tourism, some argue that no amount of authenticity or likeness in sets, costumes, and props could begin to define the horrors of, for example, slavery (Synnott, 1995), and any attempt to do so would most certainly exploit and trivialise the suffering of those who once existed (Alderman et al., 2016). Criticisms of re-enactment within dark tourism have become even stronger within the last two decades as lighter dark visitor attractions have become more popular. These attractions have been marked as inauthentic and inconsequential (Powell & Iankova, 2016) as a consequence of their high commercial infrastructure and satirical re-enactments of historical suffering, tragedy, murder, punishment, and death. Yet Light and Ivanova (2021) have shown that many visitors find these forms of re-enactment not only educational, but that they allow them an opportunity to consider their own mortality in a safe and reassuring way.

More attractions are now using co-created re-enactment by inviting visitors to act and actively participate in creating their experience in order to enhance their engagement and the experiences' memorability. For example, most of Merlin Entertainment's Dungeon Experiences call upon visitors to re-enact scenes of torture, court judgement, and execution (simulated hanging via a free-fall drop ride). At Tallinn Legends in Estonia, visitors must help an Alchemist to create the Philosopher's Stone to escape the plague and the Danse Macabre. *Follow the North Star* at Conner Prairie (USA) requires visitors to assume the role of runaway slaves seeking freedom in the North along the Underground Railroad. Their goal is to escape capture from bounty hunters and they are helped along the way by Quakers all enacted by staff. This particular experience is so immersive that staff will sometimes need to break character to reassure visitors the experience is only a re-enactment and that they are not actually in danger (Magelssen, 2006). This experience is not to trivialise this horrific time. Rather, it is to educate visitors of the realities of this horrific time, to provoke a visceral response, and to generate greater appreciation and understanding. Completing this experience, visitors participate in a debrief where they discuss their experience and what they have learned from it (Magelssen, 2006). The Battle of Bannockburn Memorial and Museum in the U.K. also allows visitors to co-create their experience as they assume the role of an English or Scottish soldier and are tasked with re-enacting the battle in a 3D immersive gaming experience. It is only in this experience that the choices visitors make on the virtual battlefield can change the outcome and course of history.

The abovementioned re-enactment experiences are not anomalies. Rather, they exist within a wider scope of dark tourism re-enactment experiences. Drawing on Stone's (2006) Darkness Spectrum, re-enactments could be understood by their level of darkness, or, rather, their seriousness. Re-enactments that have a higher educational focus and lower entertainment value are generally more serious, and, thus, would be considered darker in nature. These re-enactments are generally set within in-situ locations underpinned with higher ideological framings and thus, generally, require the consultation of the local community to ensure historical accuracy and a stronger sense of authenticity. For example, *The Proud and the Punished* at the Cascades Female Factory in Australia. In contrast, re-enactments that focus less on education and have a higher entertainment value are generally less serious and instead use humour or satire. For example, the York Dungeons in the U.K. While most strive to maintain historical accuracy in the information told to visitors, their overt commercialism and sense of fun places these re-enactments at the centre of critical debate. There are some re-enactments that blur the divergent characteristics depending on the story, the purpose and agenda, and/or audience reactions, which are generally reliant on being historically accurate, but may not necessarily have a strong sense of authenticity or seriousness (e.g. Sick to Death Museum, U.K.).

Re-enactment in dark tourism – Current issues and challenges

While some see the performed space as a means for visitors to verify and engage with the past, and even internalise their own values or develop a sense of identity (de Groot, 2016, Tschida, 2022), there is a continuing fear and discussion over whether re-enactments within dark tourism, being as they are of contested and tragic histories, are appropriate and/or harmful to the education of audiences (Mittermeier, 2016). Stemming from criticisms concerned with trivialisation (e.g., Powell & Iankova, 2016), re-enactment within dark tourism is an activity underpinned with ongoing controversy relating to the performative elements and sense of enjoyment and/or entertainment, as well as matters of authority. While few scholars have explored the imbalance of power between re-enactors and visitor attraction management (e.g., Potter, 2016), there are concerns and questions of historical ownership, who has the right to interpret and then re-enact history, and how history ought to be interpreted and portrayed.

Voiced participation

As a growing trend within dark tourism, the re-enactment of dark histories is saturated with concerns relating to including the local community and voiced participation, which directly relates to historical ownership. Voiced participation may be considered the practice of consulting communities for whom the interpreted culture, heritage, and/or histories are about (Tschida, 2022). It requires their inclusion in and ownership of decision-making practices for interpretation, particularly the re-enactment of their culture, heritage, or history (Tschida, 2022). Although voiced participation exists within larger discussions of community involvement or the involvement of marginalised communities in tourism development-related decisions, it is an issue that has long permeated the heritage and the dark tourism industries. The main issue is that interpretation decisions, particularly those of re-enactments, are typically made by power-holders with commercial interests who omit or ignore the voices of those for whom the history is about (Florence, 2022). Wielde Heidelberg (2015) suggests the reason behind such omissions are typically due to personal or organisational preferences or needs to evade certain topics or issues to avoid confrontation on polarising issues. However, this can have a devastating effect on the accurate portrayal of re-enactments and on visitor learning and public memory. As Tschida (2022) explains, voiced participation within the context of re-enactments can help to challenge existing historical narratives and stereotypes, outmoded and colonialism practices, and can ultimately lead to the questioning of previous understandings of, and relationships to, often marginalised people.

Historically, minorities and marginalised groups have been removed from interpretation discussions of their culture and history, which has resulted in colonialised and inaccurate representations within heritage tourism (Tschida, 2022). However, concerns of social equity and representativeness, particularly in re-enactments, has led to a rise in active and voiced participation in interpretation developments to ensure re-enactments are not planned in isolation from the people who own the history (Fallon & Kriwoken, 2003). Because voiced participation provides space and ownership over the re-telling and contextualisation of one's heritage and past, a fully voiced re-enactment will not reflect inaccuracies or reinforce negative stereotypes or frames created by dominant groups (Tschida, 2022). Honest interpretations may be uncomfortable for some, which, for example, was made evident by the public outcry over the 1994 slave auction re-enactment at Colonial Williamsburg. However, in order to address enslavement history honestly, the living history museum, under the direction of Dr. Robert C. Watson, Professor of African American history, involved members of the African American community to not only establish a greater understanding of African and African American experiences, but also an opportunity for voiced participation (Carson, 1998). It could be argued that such interpretations had been long overdue, particularly since over 2,000 visitors came to witness the performance; and by providing space and ownership for voiced participation, Colonial Williamsburg established the notion that re-enactment, as a form of storytelling, was a radical, but popular medium for mass education (Carson, 1998). Since this initial performance, Colonial Williamsburg has continued to be more racially inclusive by interpreting the enslaved experience through re-enactment. *What holds the future?* is their more recent interpretation, which ends with a debrief for the audience and re-enactors to co-create a thought-provoking discussion concerning social inequalities, racism, slavery, and gender issues (Krstović, 2018). Similar re-enactments have been observed in, for example, *My story – My voice* at Colonial Williamsburg, and *Follow the North Star* at the Conner Prairie living history museum (U.S.), all with the intent to foster greater learning and understanding.

While concerns for the re-enactment of dark histories is not resolved, the effectiveness of a re-enactment is dependent on the commitment of the site or attraction to portray history honestly, as well as on the power and space for decision-making given to those who own the history. Additionally, the effectiveness of re-enactments is influenced by the re-enactors themselves and their ability to judge, in real time, visitors' reception of their portrayals (Potter, 2016). If designed and performed carefully, and with voiced participation, re-enactments can convey the gravity and significance of past events to foster greater visitor understanding, engagement, and empathy (Tschida, 2022). As Perry (2020) suggests, re-enactments have many uses, they are not just for kitsch entertainment and nostalgic indulgence, but also provide therapeutic functions and education. They are transformational and allow the present to recollect and remember the past in order to improve for the future (Perry, 2020).

Dealing with temporal distance

While including voiced participation is an effective way to help ensure historical accurateness and sensitivity is given, temporal distance creates another challenge for re-enactments within the scope of dark tourism. Deciding when enough time has lapsed between death and suffering and the interpretation of it for dark tourism purposes is an impossible question. Although some argue 100 years is a safe timeframe (Wright, 2018), there is no hard-and-fast rule as to when dark histories can be re-enacted. In fact, Perry (2020) reminds us that post-war (World War II) demonstrative re-enactments were immediately performed and recorded photographically for archival documentation, which included survivors re-enacting their experiences of torture, execution, and ignominies while imprisoned in concentration camps. While there is a clear difference between archival documentation practices and tourism experiences, Perry (2020) notes re-enactment, in all its forms, helps to bring the past to life in the present so that it may be safeguarded for the future. Such thinking was observed by the Kazet theatre group in 1945–1947, in which displaced persons and survivors of the Holocaust performed in Bergen-Belsen dramatic scenes of their experiences as a therapeutic function to re-establish social bonds, create a sense of community, and to engage with traumatic recovery (Warren, 2017). Similar scenes were observed in displaced persons camps across Europe, where survivors re-enacted their experiences in ghettos and concentration camps, and musicians, orchestras, and poets created recitals while wearing prisoner clothing (Perry, 2020). These re-enactments of the immediate past were argued to provide survivors with a new coping strategy and a way to validate their experience as one of heroic resistance (Perry, 2020).

These post-war re-enactments were heavily criticised, raising moral and ethical questions concerning appropriateness and the limitations of authenticity and accuracy in re-enactment practice (Perry, 2020). Such questions persist today and is one reason why most re-enactments in dark tourism focus on events that occurred before the mid-20th century. For example, 16th-century public executions (e.g., *The Last Days of Anne Boleyn*, Tower of London, London, U.K.); 17th-century witch trials and persecution (e.g., *Cry Innocent: The People vs. Bridget Bishop*, Salem, U.S.); 18th-century crime and punishments (e.g., National Justice Museum, Nottingham, U.K.); 19th-century famine (e.g., The Perseverance: Fleeing the Famine Bus Tour, Ireland); civil and religious unrest of the early 20th century (e.g., 1914 Rise of the Rebel Bus Tour, Ireland). Yet, as time continues to pass, re-enactments of events from the mid-20th and early-21st centuries have started to emerge. For example, re-enactments of the Normandy beach assault (e.g., Saunton D-Day, Devon, U.K.) and Gulag experiences (e.g., *Night at the Museum*, Karlag Museum, Kazakhstan). Although these examples seek to educate audiences and memorialise the events, their theatricality fuels existing discourse of temporal distance and appropriateness.

The future of re-enactment within dark tourism

As we move forward into the future, dark tourism experiences will continue to adapt alongside societal changes and demand. This will include engaging with principles of inclusivity, transparency, sustainability, and innovation, which are also essential for enhancing organisational operations and business management (Cranmer et al., 2021). Such engagements will not only enhance visitor experiences and learning, but also foster better business practices.

Technological influences

Given the growing interest in experiences that offer immersion, simulation, and co-creation, the future of re-enactments within dark tourism will likely incorporate greater immersion and simulation using virtual and augmented reality technologies, particularly to

Re-enacting dark histories 515

enhance visitors' physical experience of history (Agnew et al., 2020). The future (e.g., 2025–2035) might allow for more co-created re-enactment experiences, such as *Follow the North Star* at Conner Prairie (U.S.), but at the same time utilise advanced technologies like those at the Battle of Bannockburn Memorial and Museum (U.K.) to make the physical environment even more immersive. Such re-enactment experiences could draw on, for example, the Star Wars: Galactic Starcruiser experience at Walt Disney World (U.S.) – a two-night live action role-playing experience that integrates live re-enactment and advanced simulation technologies. Wearable technologies, such as glasses, headgear or gloves, are also a possibility for future dark tourism experiences (Wright, 2021), as well as simulation rides or experiences (e.g., Figure 40.2) which can further immerse visitors in a more personal experience. In fact, Wright (2021) provides an example of how this might occur, describing how future visitors to Auschwitz-Birkenau might one day wear smart-glasses with AR technology to overlay images onto the visitors' reality, allowing them to interact with prisoners and guards.

Inclusivity and transparency influences

As society continues to move forwards into the future, questions about injustices and inequalities, new and historically grounded, will likely challenge the traditional high-brow thinking of how history ought to be remembered and interpreted. Within dark tourism, there will likely be a shift with explorations of alternative endings or 'what if?' possibilities had those events never occurred (Agnew, 2020; Lamb, 2020). Such experiences will encourage deeper considerations of dark histories and critical self-reflection. Scholarly focus will move away from how re-enactments are delivered to how audiences engage with the past and encourage audiences to question their understanding of the past in order to develop a

Figure 40.2 Zero Latency VR experience.

From [Réalité Virtuelle Zero Latency Montréal, Rue Jean Talon Est, Montréal, QC, Canada], by Maxime Doré, 2021, Unsplash (https://unsplash.com/photos/4WYdpGych4c).

stronger sense of identity and better understand their role and impact in society (de Groot, 2016). Future re-enactments will begin to address dark histories more honestly – not whitewashing truths, thereby fostering moral courage among people to transform those histories into learned lessons that bring an end to hostile emotions like rage, anger, and fear to foster reconciliation and recovery (Močnik, 2020).

Sustainability influences

Future dark tourism re-enactments that address dark histories honestly will support the United Nation's Sustainable Development Goals (SDG), specifically SDG10 (Reduced Inequalities) and SDG16 (Peace, Justice and Strong Institutions). Sotto-Santiago et al., (2020) demonstrated how re-enactments may be used to address racial inequalities and structural racism, as they create safe spaces for open, vulnerable discussions of difficult topics. Similarly, in her discussions with Dred Scott, Ater (2022) demonstrated re-enactment's ability to flip the script and unpack the complexities of dark histories that are often omitted from narratives. To omit the truth because it is uncomfortable for some is to forget the existence of those who suffered, and, thus, re-enactment allows for narrative liberation and an opportunity for society to face the realities from which it developed (Ater, 2022). By addressing dark histories honestly and fully, future re-enactments will not only challenge the dominant narratives that claim to be historically accurate, but they will also support the UN's (and society's) ongoing discussions and actions concerning social inequalities, which can in turn support the efforts towards greater inclusivity and accountability for peace and human rights.

Conclusions

Over the past few decades, re-enacting dark histories has increasingly become part of mainstream culture, and society's uncanny desire for reliving the past may reside in the fact that their experience of the world is becoming almost exclusively dependent on media (Perry, 2020). Although there has been a growing desire for real, experiential experiences within dark tourism that offer affective and visceral responses, this desire is not new and has existed since the first century BC (e.g., Munoz-Santos, 2017).

If we reflect on society's fascination with the re-enactment of dark histories, we can see, as demonstrated in Figure 40.3, a constant seeking for episodes of entertainment value. However, in the first few decades of the 20th century, what may follow the end of World War I, society was forced to grapple with tragedy in a very different way, and as a result there was a strong desire for more commemorative and educational interpretations of the

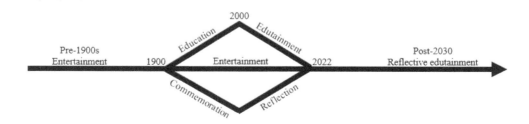

Figure 40.3 A timeline of re-enacting dark histories.

past. It was not until the 21st century with advancements in technology, which this chapter has earlier highlighted, that society began to seek experiences that were interactive and engaging through edutainment interpretation that specifically relies on forms of re-enactment, as well as experiences that offer spaces for critical reflection of how the past is understood. As we move into the future, it is likely that the need for edutainment and critical reflection will merge, offering immersive and simulated experiences that rely heavily on co-creation and visitors' re-enacting the past to establish a deeper understanding to improve the future.

This chapter has shown that although criticisms persist, re-enactments of dark histories generally create unique and memorable experiences that contemporary visitors seek, whilst, at the same time, opportunities for them to engage in deeper discussions about the past, society, and public memory. Advancements in technology and actions for societal changes will certainly change the future landscape of re-enacting dark histories, offering possibilities for more honest and inclusive retellings of the past. As such, these future trends will certainly reinforce the value of re-enactments in dark tourism. Thus, this chapter concludes in arguing scholars and practitioners can no longer deny the very present public preference for re-enactments, nor their potential benefits in improving the present for the future.

References

Agnew, V. (2004). Introduction: What is reenactment? *Criticism, 46*(3), 327–339. https://www.jstor.org/stable/23127321

Agnew, V. (2020). Dark tourism. In V. Agnew, J. Lamb & J. Tomann (Eds.) *The Routledge handbook of reenactment studies* (pp. 44–48). London: Routledge.

Agnew, V., Lamb, J., & Tomann, J. (2020). Introduction: What is re-enactment studies? In V. Agnew, J. Lamb & J. Tomann (Eds.) *The Routledge handbook of reenactment studies* (pp. 1–10). London: Routledge.

Alabau-Montoya J., & Ruiz-Molina, M. E. (2020). Enhancing visitor experience with war heritage tourism through information and communication technologies: Evidence from Spanish Civil War museums and sites. *Journal of Heritage Tourism, 15*(5), 500–510. https://doi.org/10.1080/1743873X.2019.1692853

Alderman, D., Butler, D., & Hanna, S. (2016). Memory, slavery, and plantation museums: The river road project. *Journal of Heritage Tourism, 11*(3), 209–218. https://doi.org/10.1080/1743873X.2015.1100629

Ater, R. (2022). Examining the cauldron of what is America: An interview with Dred Scott. *Public Art Dialogue, 11*(2), 120–140. https://doi.org/10.1080/21502552.2021.1997431

Biran, A., Poria, Y., & Oren, G. (2011), Sought experiences at (dark) heritage sites. *Annals of Tourism Research, 38*(3), 820–841. https://doi.org/10.1016/j.annals.2010.12.001

Bowman, M., & Pezzullo, P. (2010). What's so dark about dark tourism? Death, tours, and performance. *Tourist Studies, 9*(3), 187–202. https://doi.org/10.1177%2F1468797610382699

Carson, C. (1998). Colonial Williamsburg and the Practice of interpretive planning in American history museums. *The Public Historian, 20*(3), 11–51. https://doi.org/10.2307/3379773

Cranmer, E. E., Urquhart, C., tom Dieck, M. C., & Jung, T. (2021). Developing augmented reality business models for SMEs in tourism. *Information & Management, 58*(8), 103551. https://doi.org/10.1016/j.im.2021.103551

de Groot, J. (2016). *Consuming history: Historians and heritage in contemporary popular culture.* London: Routledge.

Fallon, L. D., & Kriwoken, L. K. (2003). Community involvement in tourism infrastructure - The case of the Strahan Visitor Centre, Tasmania. *Tourism Management. 24*(3), 289–308. https://doi.org/10.1016/S0261-5177(02)00072-9

Florence, K. (2022). At the table or on the menu at Indiana's Feast of the Hunters' Moon. In C. Rex & S. E. Watson (Eds.), *Public memory, race, and heritage tourism of early America* (pp. 68–85). London: Routledge.

Jablon-Roberts, S., & Sanders, E. A. (2019). The underlying definition of historical accuracy, Dress, *The Journal of the Costume Society of America*, *45*(2), 107–125. https://doi.org/10.1080/03612112.2018.1537647

Kidd, J. (2011). Performing the knowing archive: Heritage performance and authenticity. *International Journal of Heritage Studies*, *17*(1), 22–35. https://doi.org/10.1080/13527258.2011.524003

Krstović, N. (2018 June 22) The Colonial Williamsburg Living History Museum, in Williamsburg, Virginia, USA [Paper presentation], *Places to think: Museums, libraries, theatres* (pp. 186–191). Paris. Available from: https://www.researchgate.net/profile/Rossila-Goussanou/publication/326366179_Le_Memorial_de_l'abolition_de_l'esclavage_de_Nantes_une_invitation_a_la_reflexion_a_travers_l'experience_immersive/links/5b7a986192851c1e1221fe7b/Le-Memorial-de-labolition-de-lesclavage-de-Nantes-une-invitation-a-la-reflexion-a-travers-lexperience-immersive.pdf#page=188

Lamb, J. (2020). Conjecture. In V. Agnew, J. Lamb & J. Tomann (Eds.) *The Routledge handbook of reenactment studies* (pp. 34–38). London: Routledge.

Light, D., & Ivanova, P. (2021). Thanatopsis and mortality mediation within "lightest" dark tourism. *Tourism Review*, *77*(2), 622–635. https://doi.org/10.1108/TR-03-2021-0106

Magelssen, S. (2006). "This is drama. You are characters": The tourist as fugitive slave in Conner Prairie's "Follow the North Star". *Theatre Topics*, *16*(1), 19–34. https://doi.org/10.1353/tt.2006.0011

Mittermeier, S. (2016). Windows to the past: Disney's America, the culture wars, and the question of Edutainment. *Polish Journal for American Studies*, *10*, 127–146. https://paas.org.pl/wp-content/uploads/2013/10/PJAS_vol10.pdf

Močnik, N. (2020). Trauma. In V. Agnew, J. Lamb & J. Tomann (Eds.) *The Routledge handbook of reenactment studies* (pp. 219–223). London: Routledge.

Munoz-Santos, M. (2017). 'Why Ancient Rome Staged Epic, Violent Sea Battles', *National Geographic History Magazine*, 26 September 2017. Available from: https://www.nationalgeographic.com/history/magazine/2017/09-10/roman-mock-naval-sea-battles-naumachia/

Perry, R. E. (2020). The Holocaust is present: Reenacting the Holocaust, then and now. *Holocaust Studies: A Journal of Culture and History – Special Issue: Performative Holocaust Commemoration in the 21st Century*, *26*(2), 152–180, https://doi.org/10.1080/17504902.2019.1578460

Potter, A. (2016). She goes into character as the lady of the house: Tour guides, performance, and the Southern plantation. *Journal of Heritage Tourism*, *11*(3), 250–261. https://doi.org/10.1080/1743873X.2015.1100626

Powell, R., & Iankova, K. (2016). Dark London: Dimensions and characteristics of dark tourism supply in the UK capital. *Anatolia*, *27*(3), 339–351, https://doi.org/10.1080/13032917.2016.1191764

Qian, L., Zheng, C., Wang, J., de los Angeles Perez Sanchez, M., Parra Lopez, E., & Hanliang, L. (2022). Dark tourism destinations: The relationships between tourists' on-site experience, destination image and behavioural intention. *Tourism Review 77*(2), 607–621. http://dx.doi.org/10.1108/TR-08-2020-0360

Sharma, P., & Nayak, J. K. (2019). Dark tourism: Tourism value and loyalty intentions. *Tourism Review 74*(4), 915–929. http://dx.doi.org/10.1108/TR-11-2018-0156

Skipalis, B. (2012). Construction of heritage and identity in the plague village: Examining the intersections of local identity, heritage tourism and local heritage museum in Eyam. University of Manchester. Retrieved from https://www.research.manchester.ac.uk/portal/files/60988331/FULL_TEXT.PDF

Smith, M. (2016). *Issues in cultural tourism studies* (3rd ed). London: Routledge.

Sotto-Santiago, S., Mac, J., Duncan, F., Smith, J. (2020) "I didn't know what to say": Responding to racism, discrimination, and microaggressions with the OWTFD approach. *MedEdPORTAL*, *16*, 10971. https://doi.org/10.15766/mep_2374-8265.10971

Stone, P. (2006). A Dark Tourism Spectrum: Towards a typology of death and macabre related tourist sites, attractions and exhibitions. *TOURISM: An Interdisciplinary International Journal*, *54*(2), 145–160.

Synnott, M. G. (1995) Disney's America: Whose patrimony, whose profits, whose past? *The Public Historian*, *17*(4). https://doi.org/3378384

Tschida, D. A. (2022) Rendezvous with history: Grand Portage National Monument and Minnesota's North Shore. In C. Rex & S. E. Watson (Eds.), *Public memory, race, and heritage tourism of early America* (pp. 136–152). London: Routledge.

Ward, C., & Wilkinson, A. (2006). *Conducting meaningful interpretation: A field guide for success.* Wheat Ridge, CO: Fulcrum Publishing.

Warren, L. M. (2017). *The Kazet Theatre: A bridge from death to life*. [Doctoral dissertation, Drew University]. https://walter.drew.edu/ETD/CSGS/DLitt/2017/Warren/

Wiedenhoft Murphy, W. A. (2010). Touring the troubles in West Belfast: Building peace or reproducing conflict? *Peace & Conflict*, *35*(4), 537–560. https://doi.org/10.1111/j.1468-0130.2010.00655.x

Wielde Heidelberg, B. A. (2015). Managing ghosts: Exploring local government involvement in dark tourism, *Journal of Heritage Tourism*, *10*(1), 74–90, https://doi.org/10.1080/1743873X.2014.953538

Wright, D. W. M. (2018) Terror park: A future theme park in 2100. *Futures*, *96*, 1–22. https://doi.org/10.1016/j.futures.2017.11.002

Wright, D. W. M. (2021) Immersive dark tourism experiences: Storytelling at dark tourism attractions in the age of 'the immersive death'. In M. H. Jacobsen (Ed.) *The age of spectacular death* (pp. 89–109). London: Routledge.

Wyatt, B., Leask, A., & Barron, P. (2021). Designing dark tourism experiences: An exploration of edutainment interpretation at lighter dark visitor attractions. *Journal of Heritage Tourism*, *16*(4), 433–449. https://doi.org/10.1080/1743873X.2020.1858087

Index

Pages in *italics* refer figures and pages in **bold** refer tables.

adaptive cycle (Holling Loop) 345–346
Airbnb 103, 182, 249, 318, 383–392, **387**
aircraft 22, 24–27, 30
airlines 22–27, *24*, 30, 180, 195, 235, 248–250, 261, 265, 293
airports 15, 22–23, 26–30, *28*, **325**, 326, **329**, 334
ambiguity *see* VUCA
augmented reality 27, 64, 132, 139, 140, 144, 193, 202, 211, 242, 295, 514
Australia 11, 17, 35, 63, 73, 74, 76, *81*, 106, 113, 142, 151, 152, 252, 352, 397, *398*, 399, **435**, **436**, 437, 438, 439, 463, 512
authenticity 75, 80, 84, 88, 90, 97, 118, 119–120, 123–124, 128, 129, 139, 148–149, 154, 155, 159–160, 167, 204, 291, **304**, 444, 446, 511, 512, 514

Baby Boomers 131, 292, 353, 355, 413
biodiversity 45, 47, 49, 50, 263, 294, **312**, 394, 397, **402**, 425, 430, 456, 503
bleisure 158, 202, 411–420, *415*
business travel 22, 195, 240, 261, 296, **304**, 411–420

camping **327**, **402**, 421–432, 475
Canada 35, 46, 106, 151, 127–137
carbon emissions 14, 25, 29, 30, 53, 249, 465
carbon footprint 25, 30, 48, **312**, 418, 455, 464, 467
Caribbean 34, 151, 153, 259
China 9–12, 16, 17, 35, 41, 71, 72, 74, 77–80, 94, 182, 184, 193, 194–195, 197, 294, 310, 314, 438, 469
climate change 13, 14, 15, 39, 45, 47–49, 51, 52, 96, 144, 154, 238, 242, 243, 249, **257**, 262–263, 267, 268, 271, 289, **312**, 347, 348, 363, 369, 394, 396, 397, 399, **402**, 430, 455, 470, 472, 477, 499, 503
(the) Clink 373–382, **376**, *376*, **378**

co-creation 73, 128, 132, 138, 163, 164, 165, 167, 170, 172, 192, 199, 241, 291, 310, 497, 500, 502, 514, 517
complexity *see* VUCA
consumer behaviour 73, 202, **257**, 262, 267, 335, 426, 476, 497, 500–501, 503
corporate social responsibility (CSR) 314, 360, 378, 380
creative tourism 163–175, *164*, *171*
Creativity 132, 163–174, 201, 236, 289, 310
crisis/crises 27, 63, 64, 65, 67, *259*, 321–337, 338–351, **340**, **344**, **349**
cruise lines/cruise tourism 34–44, *35*, **36**, 45–54, **47**, *52*, 154, 240, 250, **257**, 261–262, 265, 476
culinary tourism 84–102, 373, 377, 379
cultural management 123, 127–137
cultural tourism 62, **75**, 93, 94, 97, 108, 119, 127–137, *130*, *131*, *135*, 157, 163, 164, 165, 168, 170, 268

dark tourism 138–147, *139*, *140*, 375, 443, 509–519, *510*, *515*, *516*
declining nature 394–406, 398, **401–402**
degrowth 250
destination management 275, 277–278, 301–316, **302**, **304**, 305, **307–308**, 446, 480
destination management organisation (DMO) 13, 180, 240, 251, 279, 301–316, **311**, **312–313**, 334, 339, 418, 440, 502
destination marketing 156, 266, 279, 301, 303, 308, **498**, 499
digital detox 199–208, *204*, 291, 486, **489**
digital natives 203, 205, 213–214, 295, 322, 354, 357
digital wellbeing 201, 203–205
digital-free tourism (DFT) 199–208, *204*
disconnect 199–201, 484
disintermediation 181–182
Disney 10, 40, 141

Disneyfication 141
Diversity 121, 124, 131, 134, 150, 353, 355, 358–360, 366, 483

edutainment 138–147, 509, *516*, 517
Egypt 278, 339, 341, 342–344, 348, 349
environmental impacts 29, 45–54, 273, 292, 360, 394–406, 425, 429, 463, 481
ethics 117–126, 134, 151, 154, 156, 158, 159, 291, 356, 400–**402**, 464, 465, 466, 481, 499, 500
experience design 202–205, 453, 454, 456

fine-dining restaurants 379
first-mover market 439, 440
food culture 84–102, *88*, *91*, *92*
food economy 92, 96

gastronomy 16, 84–102, 106, 108, 128, 379, 483
Generation X **353**
Generation Y; *see also* Millennials
Generation Z 35, 131, 205, 213–216, 290–292, 295, 352–362, **353**, *357*, *358*, 421, 427
German holiday demand 469–479, *470*, *473*, **474**
Germany 35, 139, 143, 322, 365, 387, 469–479, *470*, *473*, **474**
glamping 421–432, *424*, *431*
global warming 238, **257**, 262, 263, 464
governance 76, 95, 152, 166, 170, 236, 274, 275, 278, 293, 303, 305, 306, 309, 338, 399
greenhouse gas (GHG) emissions 11, 15, 40, 47, 48, 51, 52, 238, 262, 292, 465

health tourism 482, 491
heritage justice 148–162, *159*
heritage tourism 90, 117–126, *118*, *120*, 149, 150, 151, 153–155, 158–160, 236, 443, 445, 461, 513
high-speed rail (HSR) 9–21, *18*, 247
Himalayan region 103–116
Holling Loop 345–346
Homestay 103–116, *105*, *109*, *110*, *111*
human resource management (HRM) 64, 224, 225, 357, 358, 359

identity 84–86, 89, 90, 93–95, 108, 112, 118, 121–124, 128, 131, 148, 149, 151, 152, 155, 156, 157, 159, 160, 163, 168, 237, 295, 321, 355, 365, 379, 512, 516
impact assessment 133
inclusive research 370
inclusivity 94, 160, 279, 280, 359, 448, 514, 515–516
India 11, 17, 103–116, *105*, *109*, *110*, *111*, 272, 280, 294, 483
influencer 185, 209, 214, 216–217, *217*, 248, 291, 380

information and communication technologies (ICTs) 179–232, 240, 241, 243
interior design 224, 226, **228**
intermediation 179–188, *183*
interpretation 120–124, 138–147, 398, 400, 509, 511–514, 516, 517
interviews 105, 445, 446, 469

Japan 12, 96, 194, 217, 229

leadership 68, 237, **257**, 264, 265, 268, 305
leisure travel 182, *183*, 185, 411–420, 461
lifelogging 210, 211–212, 213
lighter dark visitor attractions 509, 511

meaningful work 156, 355–356, 360
medical tourism 482, 483, 484
Mediterranean 34, 84, 90, 92–94, 96, 260, 474, 475
memorable tourism experiences (MTEs) 443, 444, 446, 451
Metaverse 193, 195, *196*, 199, 202, 209–220, *211*, *215*, *217*, **213**, 315, 418, 453, 462, 466, 467
Millennials 35, 68, 131, 200, 203–205, 290, 291, 294, 321–337, 353, 355, 356, 413, 421, 426, 427, 430, 487
mirror worlds 210–214
morals 400, 401
Multi-Crisis Destination Index (MCDI) 338–339, 341, **340**, **344**, 348, **349**
multi-crisis destinations 338–351, *341*, *342*, *343*, *346*
mystery box 194–195

natural and human-induced disasters **257**
New Zealand 63, 151, 249, 252, 367, 373, 374

online travel agencies (OTAs) 16, 179–188, 192, 389
overtourism 38, 66, 96, 128, 129, 132, 205, 236, 238, 240, 242, 243, 246–255, *247*, 291, 306, 309–310, 387, 391, 395, 396, 401, 430, 480

peace 73, 119, 123, 124, 144, 150, 168, 247, 264, 267, 271, 313, 322, **340**, 342, **344**, 348, 373, 429, 430, 456, 465, 516
peer-to-peer 182, 191, 383–393
policy/policies 235–285, *276*
prisons 373–382, **376**, *376*, **378**

refugee crisis 363–372, **364**, *364*, *366*
regeneration 118, 119, 128, 158, 159, 480–496
regional development 71, 72, 74, 169, 170
regulation 39, 40, 45, 50–52, 106, 157, *239*, 383–393

rehabilitation 374, 375, 377, 379, 380
reintermediation 182, 185–186
reiseanalyse (travel analysis) 469
resilience 72, 169, 242, 273, 274, 276, 278, 280, 345–349, 360, 368, **402**, 445, 477, 480, 482, 487, 491, 492
restoration 118, 156, **401**, 480–496
ride-hail 383–393
risk management 253, **304**
risk perception 279, 323, 324–325, 328, 332, 334, 471
robots/robotics 22, 23, 27, 30, 194, 199, 202, 221–232, **227–228**

safety and security 61–70, *66*, *67*, 321–337, 338–351, 363–372
Saudi Arabia *295*
service automation 221–232
sharing economy 383–393, *385*, **387**
short-term rental 383–393
smart device 192
smart tourism 199, 236, 240–241, 243, 252, 291, 310, 454, 500
social change 321, 373–382
social justice 130, *135*, 150, 154, 158, 289, 365, 370
South Africa 272, 279, 375
South Korea 139, 214, 215, 216
spas 62, 482, 483, 484, 485, 491, 492
sport tourism 459–468, *465*, *466*
Sri Lanka 347, 443–458
Sustainability *see* SDGs
sustainable development *see* SDGs
Sustainable Development Goals (SDGs) (United Nations) 14, 15, 38, 47, 53, 73, 76, 77, 80, *81*, 84, 93–97, 119, 133, 144, 155, 160, 164, 167, 168, 197, 201, 238, 242, 271, 290, 292, 293, 311–313, **312–313**, 314, 322, 348, 349, 369, 373, 380, 394, 397, 408, 428, 429, 431, 446, 452, 455, **455–456**, 476, 480, 481, 492, 516
sustainable tourism 12, 59, 94, 96, 118, 150, 165, 204, 205, 236, 237, *239*, 246, 253, **257**, 263, 266–267, 269, 274, 278, 279, 280, 293, 310, **312**, 314, 379, 394–406, **401–402**, 429, 443–458, 471

terrorism 61, 63, 65, 119, 218, 240, 263, 264, 275, 321–337, 326–**333**, 338, **340**, 341, 344, 497
training restaurants 373, 375, 376, 377, 379
transformational tourism 443–458, *444*, **447**, *450*, *451*, *452*, **455**
transformative learning theory (TLT) 445, 453
transportation 9–21, 22–33, 34–54
trend study 469
trip planning 189–198, *196*

Uber 213, 383–393, *385*, **387**, 462
Ukraine 117, 314, 321, 346–348, 363, 364, 368, 370, 465
Uncertainty *see* VUCA
UNESCO 107, 117–126, 154, 212
United Kingdom (U.K.) 139, 142, 200, 322, 324, 373–382, 434
United States (U.S.) 139, 140, 144, **302**, 307, 510, 511
unmanned aerial vehicles (UAV) or drones 26, 27, 30, 222, 400
unplugged 199–201, 203, 204
urban tourism 235–245
urbanisation 152, 235–245, *239*, *243*, **241**, 399

(virtual) influencers 209, 214, 216–217, 248, 291, 380
virtual worlds 210–215, *515*
visiting friends and relatives travel (VFR) 433–442, **435–436**, *437*
volatility *see* VUCA
VUCA (volatility, uncertainty, complexity, ambiguity) 459–468

Wellbeing 93, 94, 134, 148–150, 152, 155, 157, 159, 160, 165, 199–206, 240, 242, 268, 272, 279, 280, 291, 294, 295, **304**, **312**, 348, 412, 440, 445, 452, 455, 456, 480–496, **485**, **488–490**
wellness tourism 444, 454, 480–496, 485–487, 491, *492*
wine consumption 71, 72, 76–80
wine tourism 71–83, *73*, *76*, *81*, 198, 199
workforce 68, 205, 225, 230, 235, 257, 266, 311, 321, 352–362, 377
world tourism cities 235–245